NICHIBEI YAKYU: US TOURS OF JAPAN,

VOLUME I: 1907-1958

EDITED BY ROBERT K. FITTS, BILL NOWLIN, AND JAMES FORR

ASSOCIATE EDITORS LEN LEVIN AND CARL RIECHERS

Society for American Baseball Research, Inc.
Phoenix, AZ

Nichibei Yakyu: US Tours of Japan, Volume I: 1907-1958
Edited by Robert K. Fitts, Bill Nowlin, and James Forr
Associate editors Len Levin and Carl Riechers

ISBN 978-1-970159-89-9 ebook
ISBN 978-1-970159-90-5 paperback
Library of Congress Control Number: 2022920934

Cover Design: Rachael Sullivan
Cover photographs from top to bottom, left to right: Cover of the January 1929 issue of Yakyukai, ca. 1911
postcard of Kazuma Sugase, 1955 Yankees tour program, 1931 All-American tour program, San Francisco Seals
1949 tour of Japan program
All images in the book are from the collection of Robert Fitts unless otherwise indicated.

Cronkite School at ASU
555 N. Central Ave. #416
Phoenix, AZ 85004
Phone: (602) 496-1460
Web: www.sabr.org
Facebook: Society for American Baseball Research
Twitter: @SABR

CONTENTS

FOREWORD

NICHIBEI YAKYU: US TOURS OF JAPAN 1907-2018

By Allan H. "Bud" Selig

Throughout my tenure as Commissioner of Baseball, I often said that baseball was a social institution with important social responsibilities. In that context, I would mention Jackie Robinson's entry into major-league baseball on April 15, 1947, which forever ended the game's racial barrier, as, perhaps, baseball's proudest and most defining moment. But baseball, as a social institution, is not limited only to national interests. I have always believed it also is in the game's best interest to serve the sport and expand its fan interest throughout the world.

Baseball's long and rich history in Japan dates back more than 150 years – to the 1870s – when American visitors played the first game there. In 1872 an American educator, Horace Wilson, introduced baseball to his Japanese students in Tokyo, which led to the founding of the first Japanese baseball team, the Shinbashi Athletic Club in 1878. By the early part of the twentieth century, baseball was being played in schools throughout the country and had become Japan's most popular sport. Baseball had become a pastime enjoyed by the people of two completely different cultures.

Early in the twentieth century there were numerous goodwill tours featuring American teams from all levels — college, professional, semi-pro, Negro Leagues and Japanese American — against Japanese players that took place in both countries. But the most famous tour surely was the one that US major leaguers made to Japan after the 1934 World Series. The All-American team included Babe Ruth, Lou Gehrig, Jimmie Foxx, Charlie Gehringer, and others. They played 18 games in 12 cities against Japanese competition over four weeks. It was a huge success even though at the start there was skepticism among some people in both countries because of the conflicts that were brewing in the 1930s.

But Babe Ruth and company were a sensation. News reports in Japan estimate that a half-million Japanese cheered the players as they rode through Tokyo in a motorcade upon entering the city. The Japanese fans warmly welcomed all the American players, but Ruth was the big hero. They chanted "Banzai Babe Ruth!" whenever he appeared on the field or anywhere in public. The tour produced competitive games and the performances of their own players produced great national pride. It also led to the formation of the Japanese professional baseball league two years later. However, whatever goodwill the 1934 All-Americans tour generated between the two countries would come to an end several years later.

After World War II baseball resumed in Japan and once again the sport became wildly popular. There were a few US tours along the way, including one by the Brooklyn Dodgers in the 1950s. But it wasn't until 1986 that the National and American Leagues began their all-star tours of Japan, sending a delegation to play against their Japanese counterparts every other year.

During my commissionership, I envisioned a greater global opportunity to expand the game and its influence in Japan as well as in other foreign destinations by playing regular-season games and even opening the season overseas. At first we stayed close to home. At the urging of the San Diego Padres, we held a three-game series between the New York Mets and San Diego Padres in Monterrey, Mexico, in August 1993 and we opened the 1999 season – again in Monterrey – with a game between the Padres and Colorado Rockies. While these events were certainly successful, they did not draw the kinds of crowds we did in Tokyo for four season openers during my term as Baseball Commissioner in 2000, 2004, 2008, and 2012.

The 2000 series was especially memorable. On March 29 and 30, at the Tokyo Dome in Japan, two teams – the New York Mets and Chicago Cubs – for the first time in major-league baseball history played regular-season games overseas. Each team won a game before massive crowds of 55,000 fans for each game.

The next season opener in Japan, in 2004, was equally memorable but for a different reason. This two-game series, between Tampa Bay and the New York Yankees, featured Japanese star Hideki Matsui, who had played in the Tokyo Dome for the Yomiuri Giants of the Nippon Professional Baseball League and, at this time, played in the Yankees outfield. The fans, of course, went crazy over Matsui and he rewarded them with a two-run home run in the second game, which was won by New York. The teams split the series. Each game drew a sold-out crowd of 55,000.

Matsui wasn't the only Japanese star to return home and play an opening series for a US major-league team. Four years later, in late March of 2008, Daisuke Matsuzaka, who had played for the Seibu Lions of the NPB two years before, started for the Boston Red Sox in the first game against the Oakland A's. Matsuzaka pitched five strong innings. The Red Sox won the game in extra innings and Hideki Okajima, who also had joined the Red Sox from Japan's Nippon Professional Baseball league, picked up the win in relief.

And then, another four years later, in 2012, Seattle opened the season at the Tokyo Dome against Oakland along with its All-Star outfielder and Japanese legend Ichiro Suzuki, who was beginning his 12th season with the Mariners. Ichiro had been a great player in Japan with the Orix Blue Wave in the NPB and continued his greatness with the Mariners. He had four hits and an RBI in the first game, while Oakland won the second game.

The other Opening Games played overseas during my tenure took place in San Juan, Puerto Rico, in 2001 and in Sydney, Australia, in 2014.

Another global adventure MLB launched was the World Baseball Classic in partnership with the Major League Baseball Players Association. The agreement, which was to allow the participation of major leaguers, set the stage for an international baseball tournament to be played every four years. MLB players could play for a foreign team as well as for the US team. Japanese baseball played a key role in the Classic. Not only did

Japan host games in each of the four tournaments but it won the first two tournament titles. Ichiro Suzuki and Daisuke Matsuzaka both played for Japan during those two tournaments and both times Matsuzaka was named the World Baseball Classic Most Valuable Player.

Suzuki, Matsuzaka, and Matsui were not the only Japanese players to make an impact. More than 60 Japanese-born players have played in US major-league baseball over the years, beginning with Masanori Murakami, who pitched for the San Francisco Giants toward the end of the 1964 season and through the next season. But it took another 30 years before Hideo Nomo signed with the Los Angeles Dodgers and became the second Japanese player. Nomo was the National League Rookie of the Year in 1995 and threw two no-hitters during his 12-year US career.

Ichiro Suzuki, of course, had a stellar 19-year career and, I believe, will surely make the Hall of Fame. Besides accumulating a lifetime .311 batting average and accumulating more than 3,000 hits after transitioning from nine years in the Japan Pacific League, he too was a Rookie of the Year in addition to being named the 2001 American League Most Valuable Player during his first season.

And at present there is Shohei Ohtani who entered the major leagues with the Los Angeles Angels in 2018 as the first bona fide hitter/pitcher since Babe Ruth. He was the American League's Rookie of the Year and in 2021 was the unanimous choice for the AL Most Valuable Player Award. In 2021 he was the first player in baseball history to play in the All-Star Game as both a hitter and pitcher.

Baseball in Japan has come a long way over the last 150 years and much of its success, if not all of it, can be attributed to "Baseball's Bridge Across the Pacific," beginning with that first game played in Yokohama between American residents and visiting crew members on board the *USS Colorado* as well as American teacher Horace Wilson, who introduced the game to his students, all the way to the present, when Angels outfielder-pitcher Shohei Ohtani, a native of Japan, is on the top tier of American baseball.

INTRODUCTION

By Robert K. Fitts

The year 2022 marks the official 150th anniversary of Japanese baseball. Tradition states that Horace Wilson, a baseball fanatic from Gorham, Maine, introduced the game in 1872 to his students at Daiichi Daigaku (renamed Kaisei Gakko the following year). Since that time, the United States and Japan's shared love of baseball has spawned thousands of individual friendships and helped bring the nations together during times of peace, conflict, and reconciliation.

Beginning in 1907, more than 100 North American and Hawaiian ballclubs have crossed the Pacific to promote the game and further international goodwill (Table 1). These series are known in Japan as Nichibei Yakyu. Nichibei means "Japan and the US" derived from the first kanji used to write Japan (日本) and the United States of America (米国). 日 is read as nichi, 米 as bei. Yakyu is the Japanese name for baseball. Despite their importance to baseball history and international diplomacy, there is no comprehensive book that focuses on tours of Japan. *Nichibei Yakyu: US Tours of Japan* volumes I and II fill that gap.

Nichibei Yakyu: US Tours of Japan, Volume I: 1907-1958 contains chapters on all 14 of the professional teams plus selected college, amateur, and semipro squads that played in Japan during this period. Each chapter is accompanied by game results and, when available, player statistics. Volume II covers the 29 major-league teams that played in Japan between 1960 and 2018. Game results and player statistics are included for each of these tours.

Each tour is far more complicated than can be explored in the short space allowed in this volume. So these chapters are just summaries. We hope that readers will use these essays as starting points for further research. Furthermore, as most of the authors do not read Japanese, the majority of chapters rely only on English-language sources. We encourage future researchers to delve into sources available in Japan to get a fuller picture of these tours and understand the Japanese perspective.

Throughout these volumes, Japanese names are written in Western style – given name followed by family name – as opposed to Japanese style, in which the family name comes first. Readers should also be aware that, especially before 1950, Japanese sometimes changed the way their given names are pronounced. Kanji can usually be read and pronounced in at least two ways: *kun'yomi* (Japanese reading) and *on'yomi* (Chinese reading). Prior to World War II, many Japanese would use both pronunciations of their first name, the choice depending on the social situation. Usually players settled on one name when on the diamond but sometimes a player would decide to change his first name. To aid readers, we have used the same first name for each person throughout these volumes, even when a person has changed his name between seasons. For example, Waseda University player and manager Chujun Tobita is always called Chujun (his *on'yomi* pronunciation, which he used as a college player) rather than Tadayori (his *kun'yomi* pronunciation, which he used later in life). We have made one exception to this rule. In the endnotes, we use the first name the author used at the time of publication. So, in the endnotes, Chujun Tobita is often listed as Suishu Tobita (his usual pen name).

In the first half of the twentieth century, Japan's public educational system differed from the system used in the United States. After compulsory primary school for all children, selected students between the ages of 12 and 17 attended middle schools. The top middle-school graduates often went on to one of the elite higher schools for three years before attending college. Touring American amateur baseball clubs regularly played Japanese middle-school teams. For the ease of North American readers, in these volumes we refer to Japanese middle schools as high schools, since the student players were about the same age as American high schoolers.

Readers should also note that until recently American newspapers used language and terms now recognized as derogatory and demeaning. An effort has been made not to perpetuate the use of this language except when these terms' use in a direct quote is unavoidable or provides insight to the speaker's mindset.

Many people have helped make this project possible. We would like to thank Bill Staples Jr., who first suggested that a book on the tours of Japan would make a good SABR project. Yoichi Nagata and Yusuke Suzumura helped with Japanese-language sources and provided many of the first names of Japanese college players not listed in English-language sources. Carl Riechers and James Forr did outstanding jobs fact-checking the articles. Carter Cromwell, Robert Garratt, Andy McCue, Keith Robbins, Robert Shadlow, Dennis Snelling, Steve Treder, and Dave Wilkie proofread chapters. Finally, Len Levin painstakingly copyedited each chapter.

TABLE 1:

List of all known tours of Japan by North American and Hawaiian teams before 1945 and all teams from Organized Baseball after 1945

1907 St. Louis Hawaii

1908 Reach All-Americans

1908 University of Washington

1909 University of Wisconsin

1910 University of Chicago

1913 Giants-White Sox

1913 Stanford University

1913 Hawaii Japanese School (Hawaii Chugaku)

1913 University of Washington

1914 Seattle Asahi

1914 Seattle Nippon

1915 Honolulu Asahis

1915 University of Chicago

1916 St. Louis Hawaii

1918 Seattle Asahi

1920 Honolulu Asahis

1920 Seattle Mikado

1920 Doyle's All-Stars

1920 University of Chicago

1921 Suquamish Indians

1921 Canadian Stars

1921 Hawaii All-Stars

1921 Seattle Asahi

1921 Vancouver Asahi

1921 Sherman Indians

1921 University of California, Berkeley

1921 University of Washington

1921 Hawaiian Nippon

1921 Hawaiian Hilo

1922 Herb Hunter's All-Americans

1922 Indiana University

1922 San Francisco Collegians

1923 Seattle Asahi / Mikados

1924 Fresno Athletic Club

1925 Philadelphia Bobbies

1925 San Jose Asahi

1925 University of Chicago

1925 Sacramento Nippon

1926 Honolulu Asahis

1926 Stanford University

1926 University of Washington

1927 Fresno Athletic Club

1927 Philadelphia Royal Giants

1927 University of California, Berkeley

1928 Ty Cobb

1928 Aratani Guadalupe

1928 Stockton Yamato

1928 University of Illinois

1928 University of Southern California

1928 McKinley High School of Honolulu

1929 University of Michigan

1929 University of California, Berkeley

1930 Seattle Taiyo Athletic Club

1930 University of Chicago

1931 Kono Alameda All-Stars

1931 Los Angeles Nippons

1931 Major League All-Stars

1932 Hunter, O'Doul, Lyons & Berg

1932 Philadelphia Royal Giants

1932 University of Michigan

1932 University of Hawaii

1932 Athens (California) Athletic Club

1932 Honolulu Braves

VOLUME I: 1907-1958

1933 Honolulu Asahis	1974 New York Mets
1934 Harvard University	1978 Cincinnati Reds
1934 All-Americans	1979 AL & NL All-Stars
1935 Wheaties All Americans	1981 Kansas City Royals
1935 Yale University	1984 Baltimore Orioles
1936 Honolulu Braves	1986 Major League All-Stars
1937 Kono Alameda All-Stars	1988 Major League All-Stars
1940 Honolulu Asahis	1990 Major League All-Stars
1949 San Francisco Seals	1992 Major League All-Stars
1950 DiMaggio & O'Doul	1993 Los Angeles Dodgers
1951 Lefty O'Doul All-Stars	1996 Major League All-Stars
1953 Eddie Lopat All-Stars	1998 Major League All-Stars
1953 New York Giants	2000 Mets & Cubs
1955 New York Yankees	2000 Major League All-Stars
1956 Brooklyn Dodgers	2002 Major League All-Stars
1958 St. Louis Cardinals	2004 Yankees & Rays
1960 San Francisco Giants	2004 Major League All-Stars
1962 Detroit Tigers	2006 Major League All-Stars
1966 Los Angeles Dodgers	2008 Athletics & Red Sox
1968 St. Louis Cardinals	2012 Mariners & A's
1970 San Francisco Giants	2014 Major League All-Stars
1971 Baltimore Orioles	2018 Major League All-Stars

1907 ST. LOUIS BASEBALL TEAM FROM HAWAII

By Yoichi Nagata

Located on the pathway between the US mainland and Japan, Hawaii was important in the history of US-Japan baseball exchanges. The baseball ties between the two islands began in 1907, triggered by a rivalry between two Tokyo universities.

In June 1907, Suejiro Ito was dispatched to Hawaii by the Toyo Migration Company to survey the labor situation of the 50,000 Japanese immigrants working in the sugar and pineapple fields. There, he came across a rumor that Waseda University was negotiating with Stanford University for a baseball team tour of Japan. Ito, a graduate of Keio University, thought, "I wanted my alma mater to be the first to invite a foreign team to Japan. Before Waseda."[1]

For many years the college teams were the pinnacle of baseball in Japan. Right after the turn of the twentieth century, a group of teams in the Tokyo area,

Waseda, Keio, Gakushuin University, First Higher School, and the Yokohama Cricket and Athletic Club (YC&AC: a sports club of foreign residents), battled to be the top team in Japan. The two universities, Waseda and Keio, developed a fierce rivalry. The Waseda-Keio match was called the Sokei-sen (the abbreviation for Waseda-Keio game), and it was watched with great interest by baseball fans across the country.

The history of the Sokei-sen began as follows. Keio University founded its official university baseball club in 1892. Waseda, on the other hand, had to wait for nine years, until 1901, for its baseball club to be born. In 1903 the latecomer Waseda University sent a written challenge to Keio University. Following proper etiquette, Waseda asked in a humble manner for the more experienced Keio team to teach them baseball. The letter read, "Our team is still underperforming, and

The Champions of the Baseball of St. Louis 手撰球野スイルトンセ

The 1907 St. Louis of Hawaii team.

our players are still immature. We would be honored to have a lesson from you in the near future."[2] The first game of the Sokei-sen was played on November 21, 1903, with Keio beating Waseda, 11-9.

However, things changed in 1905. Waseda upset Keio, not on the field but in the international scene. Waseda carried out a monumental tour of North America, becoming the first Japanese team to visit the United States. The Waseda team, led by baseball director Isoo Abe, swung around the US West Coast, winning seven games and losing 19 against colleges, high schools, and semipros. Although the results were not encouraging, Waseda brought back to Japan the latest in baseball techniques and strategies, known as "scientific baseball," including the hit-and-run, second-shortstop cooperative play, and pregame warmup, as well as equipment such as baseball shoes and gloves.[3] Waseda willingly shared the new knowledge with other teams. With this, Waseda became the leaders of Japanese baseball.

After the US tour, the Waseda-Keio rivalry flared up even more. In the fall of 1906, the two teams planned a three-game series. After Keio won the first game, the school's cheering group congregated outside the home of Waseda's founder, Count Shigenobu Okuma, and shouted, "Banzai Keio!" The Waseda students viewed this as an extreme insult. At the second game, Waseda packed the stands with 1,200 cheerers, in clear violation of the agreement that limited the cheering groups to 250. The horde celebrated Waseda's victory by marching to the former home of the late Keio founder Yukichi Fukuzawa (who had died in 1901) and yelling, "Banzai Waseda!" Fearing a riot at the third game, Keio president Eikichi Kamata and Isoo Abe of Waseda agreed to cancel the final match. The Sokei-sen would not be played for years to come.

The void left by the extinction of the Sokei-sen caused a sense of crisis in Japan's top baseball world. A number of attempts were made to revive the Sokei-sen, but all failed. For example, at the end of 1906, the Tokyo Sports Press Club made a vain effort to mediate between the two schools. Another attempt was made in the summer of 1907 when Leroy E. McChesney, baseball captain of the YC&AC, proposed a formation of Japan's first baseball league "Keihin Yakyu Domei," but Keio refused to join. Waseda won the first and last championship, as the league lasted only one fall season.[4]

Ito was annoyed that Waseda had been the first Japanese team to travel abroad so he wanted to make sure that Keio would be the first to invite a foreign team to Japan. Luckily enough for Ito's plan, Kakugoro Inoue, a graduate of Keio University and member of Japan's House of Representatives, stopped in Honolulu on the way back from a four-month tour of Europe and the United States. On August 22, Ito met with Inoue to ask for his cooperation for Keio to bring over a baseball team from Hawaii. Inoue gave his word ("I will give my all for our alma mater") and left for Japan.[5]

Ito selected the St. Louis College alumni team for the Japan tour, because it had recently won the 1907 championship of the Honolulu Baseball League.[6] The *Pacific Commercial Advertiser* thought highly of the team: "The makeup of this team is nearly as strong as any aggregation which could be picked up in the Territory [of Hawaii]."[7] The *Hawaiian Star* noted that a Japanese student who had seen St. Louis play believed that the team would be a very attractive drawing card if it came to Japan.[8]

The captain of the St. Louis team, Pat Gleason, brimmed with confidence and excitement: "We will certainly show those Japs something that they do not know about baseball, and the chances are we will come back with another championship tacked on our pennant."[9] It was a once-in-a-lifetime chance for many of the St. Louis players who had never been away from the islands.

The passenger ship *Siberia*, with the 10-man squad on board, departed Honolulu harbor in the midst of the singing of "Aloha Oe" on October 16, and arrived at Yokohama port on October 27. Ito accompanied the team as manager. At the port, they were welcomed by several thousand fans, including Keio students, YC&AC players, and members of the Tokyo Sports Press Club. A 1½-hour train ride took the Hawaii team from Yokohama to Shinbashi Station in the center of Tokyo, where another big crowd greeted them. The team's accommodations were two guest rooms converted from reading rooms in a hall on the Keio University campus. Captain Gleason and his wife, separated from the players, stayed at the Imperial Hotel.

The visitors were thrilled with the great welcome, and so was the Japanese side with the unprecedented achievement. "After a year of great desolation, baseball fans were overjoyed when a word got out that a Hawaii team was coming."[10] Until then, the only opportunity for Japanese to play Americans was against the YC&AC or sailor teams from US battleships calling at Yokohama port. Tokyo newspapers were filled with praise for the hosting Keio and high hopes for the US-Japan baseball games. Keio decided to cover the cost of the St. Louis tour by collecting admission fees.

No sooner had the Hawaiian players changed clothes than they came out for practice at Keio's Mita Tsunamachi Grounds. The curious Tokyo crowd was impressed with their workout. "The Hawaii players have outstanding ability, more than expected," a newspaper commented.[11]

At this point, the lack of prior communication was exposed. The Japanese had been informed that a college team would come; however, it was revealed that the visitors were all semipro-caliber graduates of the school, except one student player, Lo On. The Japanese baseball circles were upset. This issue would hang on for a long time in Japanese baseball history. Chujun Tobita, Waseda's center fielder and later coach, still claimed, even 47 years later, "We were cheated."[12]

The practice was followed by a welcoming party.

On their first day in Tokyo, it suddenly got cold with a low temperature of 42 degrees Fahrenheit and it dropped further on the following day.[13] The Hawaiian players brought their heaviest clothes for the seasonal Japanese weather, but still they were chilled to the bone. They needed six or seven layers of blankets and a fire in the fireplace to sleep.[14]

Game 1: On October 31, a "Welcome St. Louis" drapery was hung over Keio Grounds as 10,000 packed the ballpark. The St. Louis and Keio teams came out to the field to the music of a military band.

The St. Louis team starting lineup for Game 1 was:

1. En Sue, CF

2. Eddie Fernandez, LF

3. Henry Bushnell, 3B

4. Johnny Evers, SS

5. Lo On, RF

6. George Bruns, 2B

7. Pat Gleason, 1B

8. Bob Leslie, P

9. Luis Soares, C

St. Louis scored its first run in Japan in the bottom of the third. With one out, Leslie hit a hard grounder to shortstop Katsumaro Sasaki, who couldn't handle it. It was followed by a base hit to center by Soares to put runners on first and third. En Sue then flied out to left to score Leslie.

In the top of the fifth, Keio came back with three runs on a hit-by-pitch, two bunt singles, two sacrifice bunts, and an error by third baseman Bushnell.

In the sixth, fleet-footed En Sue, a Chinese Hawaiian, got on with a bunt single, stole second, and advanced to third on a passed ball. Bushnell then singled to score him. En Sue's baserunning amazed Japanese baseball fans. A high-school student who was dying to see the St. Louis games wrote his impressions on the swift player later: "En Sue was as short as Keio's Katsumaro Sasaki, however, his running speed was marvelous. I had never imagined that a human being could run as fast as he did."[15]

The 1905 Waseda tour brought back many new baseball techniques, and one of them was how to bunt. But the Japanese just used it to advance a runner. En Sue demonstrated how to bunt for a hit with no runners on.

In the eighth, St. Louis tied the game at 3-3. With two outs, runners on first and third, and Bruns at bat, Evers, the runner on first, jumped for second. Keio pitcher Yasuichi Aoki threw to second. At that moment, Fernandez, the runner on third, dashed home to tie the game.

The game went into extra innings. In the top of the 13th, with no outs, Eizo Kanki on first, and Tokuichi Takahama on third, Keio shortstop Sasaki laid down a beautiful bunt. Catcher Soares picked up the ball and tagged out Takahama in a rundown play. Then Soares saw Sasaki running to second, and made a wild throw to second. The ball went into the outfield, and Kanki and Sasaki scored to win the game.

It was a mutual surprise when the St. Louis team lost after 13 hard-fought innings, 5-3. "The semipro St. Louis team showed its competence in hitting but didn't play well in defense. Especially the blunder in the final scene startled the crowd," wrote the newspaper *Miyako Shimbun*.[16]

Keio backstop Nenosuke Fukuda, a cool analyst, spoke to reporters about the win: "The biggest reason why St. Louis lost was that they slighted us and played lousily. In fact, it was not that Keio was strong, but just that luck favored Keio in this game."[17]

The St. Louis team's sluggish play seemed to be caused by sea legs. But manager Ito knew why. "I am unwilling to admit, but shortstop [Evers] and second baseman [Bruns] pushed themselves to play despite they were not feeling well. The shortstop had caught a cold and had a high fever this morning. And the second baseman's hemorrhoids started hurting last night and he felt terrible during the game. It was the first game so they pushed themselves to play. Ha, Ha, Ha, I am a sore loser."[18]

The 10-man Hawaiian team was a real nine without able substitutes, because captain Gleason played only game 1. Instead, in game 2 and after, Oliver Jones played.

Game 2: On November 7 more fans turned out at Keio Grounds for the first St. Louis-Waseda game. It started raining in the sixth inning. The weather was bad, and Waseda suffered a bad defeat. Pitcher Leslie shut out Waseda, allowing one hit. In the sixth, Chujun Tobita hit a bloop single to right. Kinichiro Shishiuchi bunted to try to advance Tobita to second, but instead popped out to pitcher, and Tobita was doubled off first. So Leslie faced only 27 batters, striking out 10 with no one left on base. The *Yomiuri Shimbun* reported: "There are almost no Japanese hitters who can hit Leslie's fastball."[19]

St. Louis won, 2-0, on nine hits including three triples. During the game Shigeo Morimoto, the Waseda first baseman, was accidentally kicked in the face by a runner, leading the *Kokumin Shimbun* to joke, "That was a real stomping and kicking. Waseda was defeated as if it had been trampled."[20]

Game 3: November 9 was blessed with rare fine weather for the season. The Saturday ballgame brought many baseball fans to Keio Grounds. For this game Bushnell started on the mound and Leslie played first base. They were the team's only pitchers, and had to alternate positions every other game.

Bushnell's short interval between pitches annoyed Keio batsmen. Still Keio tied the score at 2-2 in the top of the seventh on a triple by second baseman Yaichiro Sakurai and a bunt by left fielder Kiyoshi Yoshikawa. In the bottom of the inning, St. Louis threatened with runners on first and third with no outs. Soares hit a fly ball to center to allow Jones, the runner on third, to cross the plate. Evers hit a groundball to third, and third baseman Kanki seemed to field it well, but he slipped, allowing another run and making the score 4-2.

Keio had a good game at the plate with five hits, including two triples off Bushnell, but fielding blunders cost it the game.

Off the diamond, the Hawaiians had a great time in Japan, and were impressed with Japanese hospitality. For some players it was their first time to see snow, and they asked what the white thing on the top of Mt. Fuji was.[21] Captain Pat Gleason exclaimed, "Totally unexpected!" when he saw Tokyo's modern infrastructure, including its advanced railroad system.[22] Pitcher Leslie wrote to his father back in Hawaii: "We are being treated splendidly here by the Japanese. They

are the most polite people that you could find anywhere. The food is simply grand, and for fruits it beats Honolulu all to pieces."[23]

Game 4: On Sunday, November 10, the St. Louis players went out to enjoy sightseeing in Yokohama, and got to the ball field just five minutes before game time. *Tokyo Asahi Shimbun* thought the team's tardiness "was because they took Waseda lightly."[24] Without warming up, the Hawaiians had an easy victory over Waseda, 4-0, behind Leslie's second consecutive one-hit shutout. Leslie cruised through nine innings, fanning 13 batters, at least one in every inning, and allowing two walks and a hit-by-pitch besides a single. High-school second-grader Kanji Kunieda, who was in the stands, remembered the superb pitching: "Leslie was a big man. His arm was as big as my thigh. He used his whole body to throw fire balls. They were blindingly fast."[25]

After four games, it was obvious that St. Louis was superior to the Japanese collegians in pitching and batting. The *Japan Times* said: "The only thing that puts Keio and Waseda on the same level as St. Louis is their fielding," and predicted, "From now on who would win is obvious."[26]

Game 5: St. Louis blanked Keio, 4-0, despite Keio's enthusiastic play.

Game 6: St. Louis beat Keio by a large margin, 10-1. "It was not a baseball game, but it was rather a teaching session," reported the *Chuo Shimbun*.[27]

It was cloudy and chilly, but a good day for baseball. However, the number of spectators was not even half of that at the previous games. "Those who already knew what the Hawaii team was capable of must have felt uncomfortable watching their country men beaten, as Keio is no longer a match for the Hawaii team," the *Tokyo Asahi Shimbun* commented.[28]

Game 7: On November 16, St. Louis played its third and last game against Waseda. Waseda put up a good fight compared with its previous two games. Future Japanese Hall of Famer Atsushi Kono pitched well, and Waseda had seven hits off Bushnell. Still Waseda fielding errors resulted in a crushing defeat, 9-2.

As Waseda and Keio were no match for the Hawaiian team, the Japanese not surprisingly theorized that the results were due to the obvious difference between collegians and semipros.[29]

On November 17, the fifth and final game against the Keio team was rained out and was rescheduled for the next day. In the evening Keio University held a farewell party for the Hawaii players.

Game 8: Keio shuffled its starting lineup for the first time with Mango Koyama pitching and three new players in the outfield. On the surface, the changes seemed to have worked, because Keio won the close contest over St. Louis, 5-4.

Keio led the game, 5-0, in the top of the fifth. In the bottom of the inning, St. Louis scored three runs on Jones's triple and third baseman Kanki's error. "It was the first and last time the St. Louis players were taking the game seriously," noted the *Miyako Shimbun*.[30]

The smallest crowd in the St. Louis series in occasional rain saw a number of lackluster performances by the Hawaiian players. Good defensive fielders Evers and Lo On made a few errors, catcher Soares allowed a passed ball, and the whole team suffered a slump in hitting.

Tokyo newspapers pointed out St. Louis' fishy plays:[31]

- In the first inning, center fielder En Sue misplayed a routine fly ball. The error resulted in two runs for Keio.

- In the second, left fielder Manpei Kameyama hit a grounder to second. Second sacker Lo On fielded and threw to first. But first baseman Leslie failed to catch it. The error led to two runs.

- In the fifth with two outs, Evers muffed an easy grounder, resulting in two runs for Keio.

- Leslie was on third with one out in the ninth. Jones hit a fly ball to left, enough for a sacrifice, but Leslie did not tag up.

The *Miyako Shimbun* took a step forward to use the expression of "sluggish plays like throwing the game," and criticized St. Louis, saying, "It was a disgrace to Keio and an insult to Japanese baseball."[32] Another newspaper inferred the reason: "As expected from a [semi-] professional baseball team, they let Keio carry the flowers in the last game and paid their respect to their host before leaving for home."[33] Of course Captain Gleason denied the charge on their two losses: "I give you my word that we lost it by their playing better on those days."[34]

Manager Ito, who was blamed for throwing the game for his alma mater's honor, disclosed the inside story. "Seventy people from Keio and Waseda Universities gathered at the party the previous night. Leslie and Soares loved to drink. They toasted with every one of the attendees there. Around two o'clock in the morning, I got a phone call from a policeman, saying two foreigners were stuck in the ditch in Shiba Park. I rushed to the scene and fetched the two awfully drunken men. However the battery of Leslie and Soares appealed to us to start the final game against Keio University, because with Leslie pitching and Soares catching, the Hawaii team had lost Game 1 to Keio. We had some anxiety, but we let them start. As feared, the game went like we expected."[35]

After the eight-game series in Tokyo, on November 19 the St. Louis team moved on to Yokohama for a doubleheader.

Game 9: In the opener, the Hawaiian team pounded McChesney's YC&AC team, 18-0. Bushnell struck out 11 batters, allowing only three hits to the Yokohama Americans. The YC&AC team, a good competitor with Waseda and Keio, was beaten by a large margin. It showed that the Tokyo teams had not had an opportunity to play against faster clubs before St. Louis. The second game of the day, between the Hawaiian team and the local Yokohama Commercial School team, could not continue after four innings due to darkness.

The next day, a party of 250 people from Keio and Waseda Universities and baseball circles gathered to see the St. Louis players off at Yokohama port. The team left on the *America Maru* for Honolulu with a record of seven wins and two losses.

The St. Louis aggregation, as the first foreign baseball team to invade Japan, elevated Japanese baseball to a new stage. Their splendid hitting, fast fielding, and inside plays were all revelations to Japanese players.

Isoo Abe, later dubbed the Dean of Scholastic Baseball, confessed after the series, "It will take another decade for Japanese baseball to catch up with the St. Louis team. The team was too strong for us to play against."[36] However, he said it was an invaluable opportunity for Japanese baseball: "The fact that we were able to put up a good fight against such a strong opponent was not a failure but a success, I believe."[37]

Abe never failed to show rivals the utmost courtesy, saying, "I would like to express my deepest gratitude to Keio University for making the baseball world more exciting this fall."[38] Keio seemed to have made it even with Waseda in the hierarchy of Japanese baseball; however, the St. Louis series didn't promote reconciliation between the two schools. It would take 18 more years for the Sokei-sen to resume on the field.

1907 ST. LOUIS GAMES IN JAPAN

Date	Place	Opponent	Score	Winner	Loser
October 31	Tokyo	Keio University	3-5	Aoki	Leslie
November 7	Tokyo	Waseda University	2-0	Leslie	Kono
November 9	Tokyo	Keio University	4-2	Bushnell	Aoki
November 10	Tokyo	Waseda University	4-0	Leslie	Kono
November 12	Tokyo	Keio University	4-0	Bushnell	Aoki
November 14	Tokyo	Keio University	10-1	Leslie	Aoki
November 16	Tokyo	Waseda University	9-2	Bushnell	Kono
November 18	Tokyo	Keio University	4-5	Koyama	Leslie
November 19	Yokohama	YC&AC	18-0	Bushnell	Frey
November 19	Yokohama	Yokohama Commercial	cancelled after four innings		

NOTES

1   Suejiro Ito, "Memories of My Baseball Life Part 2," *Shin Aichi Shimbun*, February 15, 1936: 4.

2   "Waseda University Baseball Club to the Keio University Baseball Club," Letter dated November 5, 1903. Baseball Hall of Fame and Museum, Tokyo.

3   Suishu (Chujun) Tobita, ed., *Waseda Daigaku Yakyubushi* (Tokyo: Tomon Club, 1925), 59-60.

4   Yoichi Nagata, *Why Wasn't Babe Ruth Able to Hit a Home Run at Koshien Stadium?* (Osaka: Toho Shuppan, 2019), 7-24.

5   Ito.

6   Honolulu newspapers called the team the St. Louis baseball team, the St. Louis College team, the St. Louis alumni baseball team, or the St. Louis Saints.

7   "Baseball Team May Go Today," *Pacific Commercial Advertiser*, October 16, 1907: 3.

8   "St. Louis Team May Go to Japan," *Hawaiian Star*, August 22, 1907: 6.

9   "Ball Team Trip to Japan Settled," *Hawaiian Star*, August 22, 1907: 5.

10   "Big Game Between Hawaii and Keio," *Yokohama Boeki Shimpo*, November 1, 1907: 3.

11   "Rare Baseball Team Comes to Tokyo," *Mainichi Dempo*, October 28, 1907: 3.

12   Suishu (Chujun) Tobita, "Memoir of Baseball: Visits of Foreign Teams," *Baseball Magazine* 9, no. 6 (June 1954): 114.

13   "Historical Weather Data," Japan Meteorological Agency of the Ministry of Land, Infrastructure and Transport, http//www.data.jma.go.jp/obd/stats/etrn/view/daily, accessed November 7, 2021.

14   "Detailed Report of the Visiting Team," *Yamato Shimbun*, October 29, 1907: 3.

15   Kanji Kunieda, "Baseball Memories: Invasion of the Hawaii Team," *Shukan Shokugyo Yakyu*, June 4, 1949: 4.

16   "Fierce Battle Between Keio and Hawaii," *Miyako Shimbun*, November 1, 1907: 5.

17   "Keio Players View of Hawaiian Players," *Mainichi Dempo*, November 1, 1907: 3.

18   "Manager Ito Talks Big," *Mainichi Dempo*, November 1, 1907: 6.

19   "Miscellaneous Impressions of the First Game Between Hawaii and Waseda," *Yomiuri Shimbun*, November 9, 1907: 3.

20   "Waseda Beaten," *Kokumin Shimbun*, November 9, 1907: 4.

21   "Rare Baseball Team Comes to Tokyo."

22   Ito.

23   "Japanese Are Good Hosts," *Pacific Commercial Advertiser*, November 20, 1907: 5.

24   "Hawaii Players and Our Baseball," *Tokyo Asahi Shimbun*, November 12, 1907: 4.

25   Kunieda.

26   "International Baseball: Keio's Second Defeat," *Japan Times*, November 13, 1907: 3.

27   "World of Sports," *Chuo Shimbun*, November 15, 1907: 3.

28   "Baseball Competition Between St. Louis and Keio," *Tokyo Asahi Shimbun*, November 15, 1907: 4.

29   "Review of Keio-Hawaii Game," *Tokyo Mainichi Shimbun*, November 16, 1907: 5.

30   "Keio vs. St. Louis: Final Game," *Miyako Shimbun*, November 19, 1907: 5.

31   "St. Louis Loses to Keio by a Run," *Tokyo Nichinichi Shimbun*, November 19, 1907: 4; "Keio vs. St. Louis: Final Game," 5; "Keio Wins the Final Game," *Chuo Shimbun*, November 19, 1907: 3.

32   "Keio vs. St. Louis: Final Game."

33   "Surprising Victory," *Kokumin Shimbun*, November 19, 1907: 5.

34   "Saint Louis Team Will Play: Dividing Ball Game Receipts," *Hawaiian Star*, November 30, 1907: 1.

35   Suejiro Ito, "Memories of My Baseball Life Part 2," *Shin Aichi Shimbun*, February 17, 1936: 6.

36   Isoo Abe, "Review of the Hawaii Baseball Team," *Undo no Tomo* 2, no. 11 (November 1907): 3.

37   Abe.

38   Abe.

1908 UNIVERSITY OF WASHINGTON TOUR OF JAPAN

By Carter Cromwell

Links between Japan and the Seattle area are nothing new. They were first forged in the late nineteenth century when Japanese began immigrating to the Pacific Northwest, and they've strengthened over the years. One of the consequential connections has been baseball.

In 1905 a team from Japan's Waseda University toured the American West Coast and played against various US teams. That led to a trip to Japan three years later by a group of a dozen University of Washington players, and those two journeys set the stage for frequent travels by Japanese and Seattle teams. The 1914 Seattle Nippon was the first Japanese American club to go to Japan, and the 1921 Suquamish Tribe became the first Native American team to do so. Teams from the University of Washington also made trips to Japan in 1913, 1921, and 1926 (and then

returned 55 years later, in 1981). Before World War II, 13 clubs from the Pacific Northwest traveled to Japan, and about a dozen Japanese university teams made the reverse trip.[1] The 1908 University of Washington tour was the first US collegiate tour of Japan and the first by a mainland US team. It was made possible by arrangements completed by Professor Isoo Abe, a Japanese college athletic instructor who had been the driver behind Waseda's trip to the United States in 1905.[2] Professor Abe – known in Japan as the "Father of University Baseball" – had been impressed by the hospitality shown by the University of Washington and the Seattle residents during the 1905 visit. In addition, the University of Washington had accepted the largest number of Japanese students in the United States at the time and was familiar to the Japanese people.[3]

1908 University of Washington and Waseda teams

Abe had persuaded his university to subsidize the 1905 tour, despite the fact that Japan was fighting a war with Russia at the time.[4] Baseball historian Kerry Yo Nakagawa said, "From a baseball standpoint, [Waseda was] the best team in Japan, and they wanted to test the water of American baseball at the university level. They wanted to dissect the American game, use it as a laboratory to learn."[5]

Three years later, that still held true, and Waseda invited the University of Washington to come to Japan. Washington did not send its official team, but all 11 players making the trip had played for the Huskies and were from the state of Washington. They included first baseman Webster Hoover of Everett, pitcher Huber Grimm of Centralia, right fielder Byron Reser of Walla Walla, second baseman Arthur Hammerlund of Spokane, catcher Roy Brown and pitcher Earle Brown of Bellingham, third baseman Ralph Teats and center fielder Leo Teats of Tacoma, and shortstop Walter Meagher, pitcher Ed Hughes, and left fielder Percy Logerlof of Seattle. Howard Gillette managed the team.[6]

The team had been scheduled to leave Seattle on September 1. Instead, it left on the vessel *Tosa Maru* on August 18, and docked in Yokohama on September 3, much earlier than expected and 16 days prior to the first scheduled game, so there were few Japanese there to greet the team. One of the Washington players said they had come earlier to visit attractions that their fellow Japanese students had told them about, and they also wanted to have time to prepare since they knew that the Keio team had played well during a recent tour of Hawaii.[7]

Game 1 was scheduled for September 19, and the buildup began immediately.

The *Jiji Shinpo* newspaper wrote, "We usually think that most American baseball teams are professional teams. However, they are college students and do not play baseball for money. Probably because of that, those twelve men are very graceful youngsters with high spirits. They wore fine suits and a golden ring with a diamond and looked very handsome." The newspaper also rated the University of Washington as the third-best college team in the United States behind Yale and Harvard, though the source of that rating is unknown.[8]

Some 2,000 spectators watched Washington's first practice. The *Tokyo Asahi Shinbun* wrote that the practice "drew more spectators than some official games," adding that "since [the Washington players] have been training hard in baseball's mother country,

their movements in fielding practice were very steady and also dynamic."[9]

Writing in the 1910 university yearbook, the *Tyee*, shortstop Walter Meagher said the players were surprised to see so many people at the initial practice. "We were so stage-struck that we didn't practice as long as we intended. Soon, however, we got so used to the crowds that we were disappointed if they did not come."[10]

Ticket prices ranged from 20 sen to 50 sen (a currency demonetized at the end of 1953) and were sold at seven locations in Tokyo.[11] A sen was worth one one-hundredth of a yen. Between 1897 and December 1931, the yen's value was frozen at 50 US cents. Therefore, the most expensive tickets cost a half-yen, or 25 US cents. Though the *Japan Times* called the 50-sen cost "a large sum" in one article,[12] it also said that "those interested in the sport would not afford to miss such a fine treat, and we hope that the days will be favoured with beautiful weather."[13]

The *Japan Times* also reported that "[u]ncommon interest is aroused by the baseball match to be played on the Waseda ground between Waseda and [the] Washington University team. Tickets for spectators have been issued to the number of 15,000 for that day; still the number is considered inadequate to meet the demand."[14] Even "the Americans resident in Yokohama will come up to town by a special train to Mejiro to see the baseball game at Waseda. They will root for the Washington team."[15]

Poor weather unfortunately kept many fans away when the series got under way on September 19, but many people – variously reported as 6,000 or 7,000 – showed up despite clouds and drizzling rain. They saw Washington rally with three runs in the eighth inning to overcome a 2-1 deficit and win 4-2.

Washington got a run-scoring triple by center fielder Leo Teats, an RBI single by Reser, and an error by Waseda left fielder Moriichi Nishio. The visitors' other run had come in the third inning when Webster Hoover scored on a passed ball by Masaharu Yamawaki. Takeshi Iseda's third-inning sacrifice bunt and Yamawaki's single in the sixth that scored Iseda accounted for Waseda's two runs.[16]

According to the *Seattle Daily Times*, "Captain Edward F. Hughes, of the U of W team" wrote that "Washington won ... but had to keep moving all the time. The University only obtained three hits off the Waseda pitcher and these came in a bunch in the same inning, netting three runs. The Nipponese were lightning fast on their feet and are accurate fielders."[17]

A reporter for the *Jiji Shinpo* overheard two students talking after the first game. One said that Washington had lost badly to the University of Santa Clara, which had easily defeated Keio in an exhibition game. "Now I understand why they didn't play as well as we expected. ... They are not as good as St. Louis [the Hawaiian semipro team that had toured Japan in 1907], for sure. The Waseda team will win the next game."[18]

He was right.

Game 2 was scheduled for the next day, but heavy rain forced its postponement to September 23. When the game finally commenced, Washington scored single runs in the third and fifth innings, while Waseda got one in the fourth, so the Huskies carried a 2-1 advantage into the last half of the eighth inning. Then Waseda broke through with five runs en route to a 6-3 victory. The hosts scored once on a bases-loaded error by UW first baseman Hoover, a two-run single by Kinichiro Shishiuchi, and two more on a throwing error by shortstop Meagher.

The *Japan Times* observed, "One fault of the American boys is that they become easily confused when the game is unfavorable to them. But they have many strong points. They talk boisterously when in the field, while Waseda boys are very silent. Keio boys are said to imitate the American players in this noisy talking, but we rather think the Japanese method is more becoming to the Japanese."[19]

Game 3 of the series matched Washington against Keio on September 26 and was "an interesting game" before "a large assembly of spectators," according to the *Japan Times*. Each team scored a run in the first inning. Eizo Kanki's fly out for Keio scored Katsumaro Sasaki, and the Huskies countered with Grimm's double that drove home Hoover. Keio went ahead 2-1 in the fourth inning when Kanki stole home – or, as the *Japan Times* story put it, "Kanki made an adventure and got home." The article further revealed that "Washington made strenuous efforts to recover arrears, but their efforts were frustrated by the excellent fielding of Keio. ... The game closed with 2 to 1 in favour of Keio."[20]

Game 4 the following day again matched Washington and Keio, and it was the polar opposite of the previous day's low-scoring affair. This time, Keio took a 6-1 lead after four innings and then scored five more runs in the fifth inning en route to a 14-3 victory. Nenosuke Fukuda, Yokote, Katsu, Sasaki, and Tokuichi Takahama all scored in Keio's decisive fifth-inning outburst.[21]

The *Japan Times* reported, however, that the "Washington boys ... endured the defeat with good grace and admirable fortitude. Pitcher Grimm when deposed to center went thither with quite amiable good humour. The sympathy of all spectators were with the vanquished and they often cheered for them."[22]

By then standing 1-3 on its tour, the Washington team had a four-day break before playing its next game, against the Yokohama Cricket & Athletic Club, a team made up of Americans, on October 1. Each team scored twice in the first inning, but Washington took control with a three-run third inning, as Leo Teats, Grimm, and Meagher crossed the plate. Yokohama got a run in the sixth inning, and UW scored once in the seventh to account for the final 6-3 score. The *Japan Times* wrote that the "game was perhaps the best ever played in Yokohama."[23]

Two days later came a rematch between Washington and Waseda, with the Huskies taking a 4-1 victory to even their record on the trip at 3-3. Hoover, Leo Teats, and Meagher scored in the fourth inning for Washington, and Hammerlund crossed the plate in the seventh. Yamawaki scored Waseda's only run in the fourth inning. In contrast to its coverage of previous games, the *Japan Times* printed only a one-paragraph story about this game and reported that "Waseda batters were remarkably idle."[24]

The next day Washington again played Keio and again lost, this time by 3-2, making the Huskies 0-3 against Keio on the tour. Kanki, Denji Murakami, and Ryokichi Sawahara scored for Keio in the first, fourth, and seventh innings, respectively. Hoover singled and later scored for UW in the sixth inning. In the ninth, he tripled and later came across to pull his team to within one run, but the Huskies could get no closer.

The *Seattle Post-Intelligencer* noted that Keio was a "stumbling block" for the "tourists. ... The Keio players had returned home from a ballplaying tour of the Hawaiian Islands and were in perfect training. The Washington players entered the games stale and out of shape from climactic conditions." Team manager Gillette was quoted as saying, "Our pitchers were considerably distressed by bad arms throughout all our stay in Japan, but ... there was not a game in which we did not get more hits than our opponents." (Keio actually outhit Washington twice.)[25]

A day later, UW took a 4-1 victory over the Yokohama Commercial School, as Hoover and Grimm scored first-inning runs, Ralph Teats crossed the plate in the fourth, and Meagher came across in the fifth.

On October 7 Washington and Waseda again played, with UW winning 5-3 in 15 innings. Washington opened with a run in the first inning. Waseda scored twice in the second inning to take a 2-1 lead, but UW tied the game in the fourth inning. The score remained tied, 2-2, until each team scored a run in the 12th. Washington finally got the game-winning runs when Ralph Teats and Hoover crossed the plate in the 15th inning. According to the 1910 University of Washington yearbook, the *Tyee*, "Meagher described the victory as the best game ever played in Japan."[26]

The Washington team concluded its 10-game tour on October 9 with a 14-5 victory over the Yokohama Cricket & Athletic Club. Yokohama scored four runs in the first inning to take a 4-0 lead, but UW scored three times in the second inning, once each in the third, fifth, and sixth, and then twice in the seventh for an 8-4 advantage. Then came a six-run rally in the eighth inning that put the game out of Yokohama's reach. Ralph Teats, Hoover, Leo Teats, Meagher, Reser, and Roy Brown all scored for Washington in the decisive inning.

The Washington team began its 15-day trip home on October 10. As reported by the *Japan Times*, "The baseball team from the University of Washington ... who has given such a splendid series of baseball games in Tokyo and Yokohama[,] left Yokohama for home by the ... steamer *Tosa Maru* yesterday. ... Teams from Waseda and Keio Universities ... and others saw the party off. The Washington boys looked very brilliant and happy in their school uniform. When the ship was to weigh anchor, Waseda and Keio college yells were given, and [the] Washington team replied with their college yell. The ship sailed amid hearty wishes of bon voyage of the home teams."[27]

In his master's thesis, "Seattle and the Japanese-United States Baseball Connection, 1905-1926," Ryoichi Shibazaki writes that "when Ichiko defeated the Yokohama Athletic Club in 1896, the Japanese people took it as the victory of the Japanese over Americans, rather than a simple win in baseball. In so doing, the Americans were treated like the enemy by the Japanese media. However, the Japanese people and media treated the Washington team fairly and warmly. ... [I]t suggests that the Japanese people had adjusted to the Western culture fairly well by that time and could abandon the hostile feeling toward the American people who were often treated as 'invaders' a decade before."[28]

Indeed, between their arrival and their first game, the Washington players were squired around Tokyo and visited temple sites, attended a theater performance, and met politicians. "We were royally entertained by Count Okuma, the great Japanese diplomat [and founder of Waseda University], who showed us about his garden and magnificent mansion," Meagher wrote in the school's yearbook.[29]

The trip was considered a rousing success. It was said that the total attendance for the 10 games was 70,000, and the attendance for the first game – variously reported as either 6,000 or 7,000 – came despite the drizzling rain much of the time.[30] Reportedly, crowds of 9,000 people showed up for two of the games with Waseda.[31]

"We arrived home Oct. 25, all in good health and feeling we had one of the greatest trips that any college team had ever taken," Meagher concluded.[32]

Gillette, the Washington manager, said, "The Japanese boys played better ball than we thought they would, and our work was hardly up to standard. The Japanese players proved the shiftiest men on their feet I have ever seen on a baseball diamond, and their fielding was probably superior to that of the average American amateurs."[33]

In the same article, the *Seattle Evening Star* fully acknowledged the Japanese baseball prowess, though in a manner that indicated Americans' prevailing attitude at the time toward Asians and Japanese in particular – "It is an indication of the Jap's adaptability that he defeated the Americans four times out of ten. He simply beat the Americans at their own game."

Gillette added, "Our reception by the Japanese from the hour we left Seattle could not have been more cordial. Every detail and arrangement was carried out harmoniously and the cordiality provided makes us all feel that Japan's ball players and their loyal fans constitute sportsmen to emulate."[34]

An article in the *Seattle Post-Intelligencer* reported that "the entire press of Japan treated the visit of the American ballplayers as the one big athletic incident of the year." There was "intense interest ... and every detail of the game was studied with care." The story added that "the spirit of fairness ... was the subject for favorable remark by each of the returning players," and it also said that "from the standpoint of closer athletic relations with Japan, the trip is reported as peculiarly successful."[35]

Okuma, the Japanese diplomat, "gave a dinner at which he delivered an address highly commending the spirit of athletics and expressing a wish for an extension of the tests of skill between his people and Americans."[36]

Meagher, the team's shortstop, wrote that "We ... took a short trip to Nikko, the great temple site of Japan. ... This was one of the finest visits we had while in Japan. ... We attended a Japanese theatre a few nights afterwards. ... Ushers conducted us to chairs in the first balcony, prepared especially for us. We could not understand much about the play, but the acting and scenery interested us a great deal."[37]

Shibazaki wrote that while the impact of the UW tour "on Japanese baseball, culture, and politics was almost invisible," it did "set a precedent for other American colleges such as the University of Wisconsin, University of Chicago and Stanford University." Teams from those schools, as well as the University of Washington, visited Japan in later years "and became main figures in the Japanese-United States baseball connection during this decade."[38]

Additionally, since the 1908 tour, bonds between UW and the Waseda and Keio universities have steadily grown. There are currently four programmatic relationships between Washington and Waseda.[39] As well, Washington and Keio have "inclusive exchange programs at the undergraduate and graduate levels. For many years, comprehensive agreements between the Universities' Schools of Pharmacy, Nursing, and Law have enabled the institutions to work together in teaching and research."[40]

1908 UNIVERSITY OF WASHINGTON GAMES IN JAPAN

Date	Place	Opponent	Score	Winner	Loser
September 19	Tokyo	Waseda University	4-2	Hughes	Oi
September 23	Tokyo	Waseda University	3-6	Oi	Grimm
September 26	Tokyo	Keio University	1-2	Koyama	Brown
September 27	Tokyo	Keio University	3-14	Fukuda	Hughes
October 1	Yokohama	YC&AC	6-3	Hughes	Nicholl
October 3	Tokyo	Waseda University	4-1	Brown	Oi
October 4	Tokyo	Keio University	2-3	Hughes	Murakami
October 5	Yokohama	Yokohama Commercial	4-1	Hughes	Suzuki
October 7	Tokyo	Waseda University	5-3	Grimm	Oi
October 9	Yokohama	YC&AC	14-5	Hughes	Lo On

NOTES

1   John Rosapepe, "A Pastime with a Past," *Seattle Times*, March 20, 2003. https://archive.seattletimes.com/archive/?date=20030320&slug=japan20; Columns Staff, "Husky Baseball Is No Stranger to Globetrotting," *University of Washington Magazine*, March 1, 2019. https://magazine.washington.edu/husky-baseball-is-no-stranger-to-globetrotting/.

2   "University Boys Tell of Japan's Baseball Spirit," *Seattle Post-Intelligencer*, October 26, 1908: 1.

3   Ryoichi Shibazaki, "Seattle and the Japanese-United States Baseball Connection, 1905-1926," Master of Science Thesis, University of Washington, 1981, 40-41.

4   Robert K. Fitts, "Baseball and the Yellow Peril: Waseda University's 1905 American Tour," *Baseball 10* (2018): 141-159.

5   Rosapepe.

6   Walter Meagher, "The Japan Trip," *The 1910 Tyee of the University of Washington* (Seattle: University of Washington, 1910), 148.

7   Shibazaki, 41.

8   Shibazaki, 42.

9   Shibazaki, 42.

10   Meagher, 146.

11   Shibazaki, 43.

12   "Baseball at Waseda: Initial Victory for Washington," *Japan Times*, September 20, 1908: 2.

13   "Baseball Match Between Washington and Waseda Teams," *Japan Times*, September 16, 1908: 3.

14   "Waseda Baseball Display," *Japan Times*, September 18, 1908: 6.

15   "Baseball," *Japan Times*, September 19, 1908: 3.

16   "Baseball at Waseda: Initial Victory for Washington."

17   "Washington Takes First Game," *Seattle Daily Times*, October 12, 1908: 11.

18   Shibazaki, 44.

19   "Waseda Baseball: Collapse of Visitors," *Japan Times*, September 25, 1908: 6.

20   "Baseball at Waseda: Keio Defeats Washington," *Japan Times*, September 27, 1908: 2.

21   Yokote's and Katsu's first names are unknown.

22   "Keio-Washington Baseball: Washington's Disasters," *Japan Times*, September 29, 1908: 6.

23   "Baseball at Yokohama," *Japan Times*, October 2, 1908: 2.

24   "Waseda Baseball," *Japan Times*, October 4, 1908: 6.

25   "University Boys Tell of Japan's Baseball Spirit," *Seattle Post-Intelligencer*, October 26, 1908: 1.

26   Columns Staff.

27   "Washington Baseball Team: Departure from Yokohama," *Japan Times*, October 11, 1908: 2.

28   Shibazaki, 44-45.

29   Meagher, 148.

30   "Japanese Teams Defeat Americans," *Seattle Evening Star*, November 2, 1908: 13.

31   "University Boys Tell of Japan's Baseball Spirit."

32   Rosapepe.

33   "Japanese Teams Defeat Americans."

34   "Japanese Teams Defeat Americans."

35   "University Boys Tell of Japan's Baseball Spirit."

36   "University Boys Tell of Japan's Baseball Spirit."

37   Meagher, 146.

38   Shibazaki, 45.

39   "Connections between the UW and Waseda University" Japan Studies Program, University of Washington, February 17, 2017: https://jsis.washington.edu/japan/news/connections-uw-waseda-university/.

40   "Japan's Keio University and the University of Washington Launch a Dual Masters Law Program," *Asia Matters for America*, June 13, 2017: https://medium.com/asia-matters-for-america/japans-keio-university-and-the-university-of-washington-launch-a-dual-masters-law-program-a0a71c339d9.

1908 REACH ALL-AMERICAN TOUR

By Robert K. Fitts

The "King of Baseball" was on the prowl for a new opportunity. Mike Fisher, known by everybody as Mique, was a born promoter and born self-promoter. He was a risk taker, tackling daunting projects with enthusiasm and usually succeeding. He was the quintessential late-nineteenth-century American man; through hard work and gumption this son of a poor Jewish immigrant transformed himself into a West Coast baseball magnate.

Born in New York City in 1862, Fisher grew up in San Francisco. Renowned for his speed, he played baseball in the California League during the 1880s before an industrial accident in March 1889 damaged his left hand and sidelined his career. Fisher soon became a policeman in Sacramento, rising to the rank of detective. During his time away from the game, he

put on weight and by 1903 was a repeat champion in the fat men's races held at local fairs.

In February 1902, a new opportunity presented itself when the California League offered Fisher the Sacramento franchise. Fisher pounced on it. In December 1902, the league transformed into the Pacific Coast League, but within a year Fisher relocated his franchise to Tacoma, Washington. Hampered by poor attendance, despite winning the 1904 championship, Fisher sold his share in the team but stayed on as manager as the franchise moved to Fresno in 1906. But his stay in Fresno was short as he left the team after the 1906 season. Without a franchise, Fisher turned to promoting and, in the fall of 1907, took a squad of PCL all-stars to Hawaii.[1]

"So pleased is Mike Fisher with the reception that his team has met with here," reported the *Hawaiian*

1908 Reach All-Americans with Mike Fisher

Gazette, "that he is already planning for more worlds to conquer. He is now laying his lines for a trip to be made … next year, which will extend farther yet from home. ... The plan, as outlined by Fisher, will include a start from San Francisco, with a team composed exclusively of players from the National and American leagues," and a stop in Hawaii before continuing on to Japan, China, and the Philippines.[2] It was the first time an American professional squad headed to the Far East.

By early December 1907, Fisher had teamed up with Honolulu athlete and sports promoter Jesse Woods to organize the trip.[3] Woods sent a flurry of letters to Asian clubs to gauge their interest. In February, John Sebree, the president of the Manila Baseball League, responded "that Manila would meet any reasonable expense in order to see some good fast baseball by professional players."[4] In early March, Woods received a letter from the Keio University Baseball Club stating that they would help arrange games in Japan for the American team. The *Hawaiian Gazette* noted, "This was good news for Woods, who has been in doubt as how such a trip would be received by the Japanese. There has been so much war talk that Woods was afraid that Japanese might refuse to play baseball with us."[5] A letter in early April from T. Matsumura, the captain of the Yokohama Commercial School team, confirmed the enthusiasm for the tour in Japan: "When you visit our country, you would certainly receive a most hearty welcome from our baseball circles."[6] Isoo Abe, the manager of the Waseda University team, added, "We are preparing to give you a grand ovation. We are going to make you feel at home, and we will strive to make your visit to Japan to be one that will linger long in your memories."[7]

In late June, Woods sailed for Asia to finalize the details for the tour. The touring team was now known as the Reach All-Americans. With the name change, it is likely that the A.J. Reach Company sponsored the team but despite extensive research, the nature of the sponsorship is unknown.[8] Woods's reports from the Far East were encouraging. "I have all the arrangements made. Forfeit money is up everywhere, and everything is on paper. The team will take in Japanese and Chinese ports and Manila."[9]

While Woods was working out the itinerary, Fisher built his roster. As usual, he thought big. It would be "a galaxy of the best players in the country."[10] He began by engaging Jiggs Donahue, the Chicago White Sox' slick-fielding first baseman, to manage and help recruit the team. "I do not know why Mike Fisher came to me

to ask me to get up the team, for I did not know him," Donahue told a reporter. "I will willingly undertake the work, however, for I believe it will prove to be a grand trip and a success."[11] Donahue quickly recruited fellow Chicagoans Frank Chance, Orval Overall, and Ed Walsh and began working on the leagues' two biggest stars, Honus Wagner and Napoleon Lajoie. "Both Wagner and Lajoie are said to be enthusiastic over the plan," reported the *Inter Ocean* of Chicago, "but cannot decide whether or not they will be able to arrange their affairs in such a way as to make the trip, which will last two or three months."[12] By June, Fisher had added New York Highlanders star Hal Chase, Chicago's Doc White, and Bill Burns of the Senators. Although Wagner and Lajoie declined the invitation, Fisher's team received a boost on August 23 when Ty Cobb announced that he would join the tour. The recently married star planned to take his bride on the trip as a honeymoon.

At the last minute, things began to unravel. First, Frank Chance and Ed Walsh decided not to go, then near the end of the major-league season Orval Overall, Doc White, and Jiggs Donahue dropped off the roster. In early September, Hal Chase deserted the Highlanders after a dispute with management and returned to his home in California. With Chase suspended from Organized Baseball, Fisher cut him from the team. The news only got worse.

On October 17, just two weeks before the team's scheduled departure for the Far East, Ty Cobb announced that his wife was in poor health and that he might not make the trip. A week later Cobb was still undecided. After an appearance at the Georgia State Fair, he told reporters that he might winter in Georgia as "the hunting is a lot better around Royston than in Japan." On October 27 Cobb officially announced that he would remain home with his ailing wife.[13] The true reason for Cobb's cancellation soon emerged. In mid-October, Cobb had demanded that Fisher pay travel expenses for his wife. Fisher refused. He would pay the players' travel expenses as agreed but not for their guests. Not happy with the decision, Cobb pulled out of the tour.[14]

In place of the advertised "galaxy of the best players in the country," the Reach All-Americans now consisted of four marginal big-leaguers (Jack Bliss, Bill Burns, Jim Delahanty, and Patsy Flaherty) and eight Pacific Coast League players (Joe Curtis, Babe Danzig, Bill Devereaux, Jack Graney, Heinie Heitmuller, George Hildebrand, Harry McArdle, and Nick Williams). On November 3 a large crowd gathered at the Pacific Mail Dock in San Francisco to wish the team luck as they boarded the *S.S. China*. After a brief stop in Honolulu, where the team played no games, the All-Americans continued to Japan.

The All-Americans were the third US team to play in the Land of the Rising Sun that fall. In September, the University of Washington varsity became the first American college squad to visit the country. The team stayed for five weeks, playing 10 games against Japanese university clubs. A week after the Washington team left Japan, the American Great White Fleet, an armada of 16 battleships designed to display the country's formidable power but painted white to symbolize peace, arrived in Yokohama. To emphasize shared values, the sailors played a series of nine baseball games against Keio and Waseda Universities. The visitors were no match for the college squads as Keio won all five of its games and Waseda won three of its four games.

The *China* arrived in Yokohama on Sunday morning, November 22, three days behind schedule. Although a launch packed with dignitaries met the ship before it docked, the elaborate welcoming ceremony was curtailed as the team needed to get to Tokyo for an afternoon game. An 11 A.M. train took the All-Americans to the capital, where they checked into the Imperial Hotel and changed into their gaudy uniforms.

Produced by the A.J. Reach Sporting Company, the uniforms consisted of scarlet blazers with blue bindings and a star on the left sleeve; white pants; white jerseys trimmed in blue with "Reach All Americans" in block letters across the front; and "a shield bearing the stars and stripes on the left arm." Both the undershirt sleeves and "the stockings were startling productions resembling barbers poles with a series of parallel bands of red, white and blue."[15]

The team traveled across town to open their tour against Waseda University, whose team had visited the United States in 1905, playing 26 games against collegiate, amateur, and California State League teams. Eight thousand spectators thronged the small ballpark, which contained no grandstands and only a handful of crude bleachers. Most fans sat on earthen embankments either on elevated platforms where they squatted on cushions or on seats terraced into the little hills.[16] Reporter H.L. Baggerly, who accompanied the team on the tour, noticed, "In Japan, baseball is a man's game exclusively, for as yet I have to see my first native woman in attendance. ... We have found the spectators quite as enthusiastic as the Americans. Clever plays are liberally applauded, especially when

made by the home club, and the [Japanese] start to root just as soon as they get men on base.[17] To the Americans' surprise, "the Japanese fans divided themselves into equal rooting sections, one side with the Stars and Stripes flying, yelling for the Yankees, and the other, Waseda enthusiasts, with the university pennants waving supreme."[18]

As Count Shigenobu Okuma, the university's founder and a former prime minister, prepared to throw out the ceremonial first pitch, the American pitcher Jack Graney "took his sporting cap and put it on the count's head, replacing the latter's silk hat. The count with a smile accepted this and holding the ball in his right hand cast it and it was caught by the catcher. The ceremony being duly ended amidst deafening cheers the game was opened."[19]

Graney dazzled the Waseda batters.[20] His "swerve and drop were produced in such variety and with such perfection that the batters might well be excused for fanning the air in fruitless efforts to strike the elusive ball." As a result, "very little hitting was done by the home team. A few 'flies' rose into the air and fell into

（ンテブヤキ）手投學大應慶
君馬一瀬菅
部通普應慶（學中身出）市戸神（地生出）

Keio's ace Kazuma Sugase

sure and steady hands, and only twice did a Waseda player get onto first base, whilst none of them ever got to second."[21] Although Hiroshi Oi pitched well, limiting the Americans to seven hits, the visitors' timely hitting led to a comfortable 5-0 victory. The highlight was Heinie Heitmuller's drive over the center-field fence, believed to be the longest hit made in Japan to that date.[22] The friendly game was marred by an argument between an unidentified All-American player and the umpire. Although arguing with umpires had a long and colorful history in the United States, it was nearly unheard of in Japan and was a major breach of etiquette. "This incident, however, smoothed itself out."[23] Despite the loss, the visitors and the press praised the Waseda players for their "grit and ginger."[24]

To make up the games missed by their tardy arrival, the All-Americans played a doubleheader on November 23 at the Mita grounds in Tokyo despite frigid temperatures and strong chilling winds. In the morning, they faced the Tokyo Club, an aggregation of graduated stars from Waseda and Keio universities. Several of the players, including pitcher Atsushi Kono, catcher Masaharu Yamawaki, and outfielder Kiyoshi Oshikawa, had played in the United States with the 1905 Waseda team. But the game turned into a mere warm-up as the visiting professionals pounded the former stars, 19-1. Aided by "a hurricane of wind which blew in the batters' faces," Babe Danzig "pitched so fast that the batters could do nothing with his shoots. … During this time the American players, through a combination of fourteen hits and eleven errors, ran up [the] score."[25]

The main event was the afternoon match against Keio University, Japan's top squad. During the recent games against Washington University and the Great White Fleet, Keio had swept all eight games. "In spite of the wind and dust," reported the *Japan Times*, "the ground was crowded by spectators who numbered over 10,000."[26] "Seldom have I seen such interest in a baseball game in the States," added Mike Fisher. The fans "had a sneaking idea that their crack team would whip us, and they wanted to see it done."[27]

Fisher started his best pitcher, Bill Burns, who 11 years later would be one of the conspirators in the Black Sox Scandal, while Keio countered with Nenosuke Fukuda. The crowd witnessed a thrilling pitching duel. "There was no international courtesy about the game," wrote B.W. Fleisher in *Collier's Weekly*. "The Americans played ball for all they knew how. … Keio managed to hold down the All Americans to 1 to 0 until the eighth inning, neither side making a safe hit until the third."[28] The Americans tacked on two more runs to win 3-0. "They gave us a good fight as the score would indicate," noted Fisher, "but we won and hope to win every game we play while we are away on this long trip."[29]

After this tight game with Keio, the All-Americans were rarely challenged again during their stay in Japan. The next day, November 24, saw a rematch with the Tokyo Club. To make the game more competitive, the two teams swapped batteries. Graney and Nick Williams started for Tokyo while pitcher Denji Murakami and catcher (first name unknown) Yokote played for the Americans. But the swap did not go as planned. Murakami "walked three men in succession, and the Japanese [fans] thought it was intentional," recalled Fisher. "It looked as if a riot would eventuate for a while. The rooters were calling us all sorts of names – fortunately, we did not understand [what] the crowd was yelling – so we pulled our pitcher out of the box."[30] With the pitchers back on their usual teams, the Americans won comfortably, 11-4.

After three days in Tokyo, the All-Americans moved to Yokohama. Founded in 1858 as a settlement for foreign traders, Yokohama soon grew into a major city with Western institutions including an English-language newspaper, brewery, racetrack, racquet club, and cricket club. By 1871, American residents had formed a baseball team and began playing at the Yokohama Cricket and Athletic Club. After visiting Japan, tour organizer Jesse Woods recalled, "My first stop was at Yokohama, Japan and I was taken to the Yokohama [Cricket] and Athletic grounds shortly after my arrival. It was a treat for me to find such a beautiful field almost in the center of the city. It is the finest I have ever seen, as far as turf is considered, and can only be compared to a billiard table. This field is surrounded by 1/2-mile bicycle and running track, inside are the cricket, baseball and tennis courts. … Conveniently located is the handsome clubhouse, with every facility that an athlete could desire. Refreshments are always served."[31] The club's baseball team, consisting solely of foreigners, played a pivotal role in the development of Japanese baseball, when it lost three straight games to the all-Japanese First Higher School (known as Ichiko) in 1896. The victorious schoolboys became national heroes and spurred the spread of the game across Japan.

On November 25 the Yokohama Cricket and Athletic Club hosted the All-Americans. Nobutaka Mitsuhashi, the mayor of Yokohama, gave a short speech before throwing out the first ball. Although the club's weekend warriors fought bravely, they "were outplayed from the start" by the visiting professionals and lost 17-1.[32]

The highlight of the series was the November 26 rematch against Keio University. A large enthusiastic crowd packed the stands at the cricket club. The All-Americans offered Keio a three-run handicap, which the collegians refused. "In consequence," noted the *Japan Times*, it "was a spirited game." Mango Koyama started for Keio and after setting down the Americans in the first, gave up three runs in the second. The All-Americans tacked on three more runs, finishing the game with six. Meanwhile, Bill Burns dominated the Keio hitters, allowing no hits into the eighth inning when Nenosuke Fukuda's groundball somehow "flew over [the] pitcher and he got [on] first." Burns walked the next batter before pinch-runner Eizo Kanki was thrown out trying to steal third to end the inning. That would be all for Keio as the Americans cruised to a 6-0 victory in just 1 hour and 15 minutes.[33]

The next day the All-Americans defeated the city's other club, the Yokohama Commercial School, 11-0. In Tokyo, on November 28, Patsy Flaherty, starting his first game on the tour, bettered Burns's performance by throwing a perfect game against Waseda University as the Americans won, 3-0. Strangely, the game was not covered in the English-language newspapers in Japan.

The All-Americans spent the next week in the Tokyo area, splitting their time between the capital and Yokohama, as they continued the series against Keio, Waseda, and the Tokyo Club with a pair of games against each. The Americans won each game comfortably, finishing off Keio 6-0 and 15-2, Waseda 13-2 and 10-0, and Tokyo 8-5 and 3-0.

As the team traveled around Tokyo, the players were stuck by the popularity of America's national pastime. Bill Devereaux noted, "The first game we played was at Tokyo. It was on a Sunday. To reach the grounds from our hotel we had to drive fully two miles, and on our way we passed several parks and, believe me, there were baseball games between small boys and big in every one of them."[34] "Every college, every high school, every middle school in Japan has its baseball team, and judging by the number of apparently infantile youngsters who sport baseball uniforms in the parks, the primary and kindergarten schools are similarly equipped," explained reporter Joseph Ohl. Even "Japanese girls take great interest in baseball. They are not much in evidence at the college contests, for these are held within the college enclosers: but

there are always many of them watching the games in the parks. They flock by themselves, understand the game and show understanding by discriminate applause. They go to see the game, not to flirt, and they devote their whole attention to what is going on in the field; which may be hard to believe but is nevertheless true."[35]

On December 4, the All-Americans left Tokyo by train for Kobe. According to the *Morning Union*, "Fisher secured a special car for his men, who traveled in all the luxury possible in this country. Everything went along smoothly until lunch. ... A Japanese dining car, like the other cars here, is about the size of a chicken coop and the provisions are in proportion to the size of the cars. The players gave the dining car an awful storming at lunch, and after dinner there wasn't enough food left to feed a sick canary. It was the conductor's first experience with a bunch of hungry ballplayers, who can eat as no other set of men. As an illustration, Bill Devereaux devoured three orders of ham and eggs and one steak."[36]

Their first game in the new city was on December 5 against the Kobe Country Club, a team consisting of Americans living in the city. Like their rivals in Yokohama, the recreational ballplayers were no match for the visiting professionals. "The Americans simply toyed with the Kobe boys, winning by the one-sided score of 14 to 2. Flaherty, who pitched, didn't half extend himself and besides holding Kobe down to a few hits slammed out a couple of home runs."[37]

The All-Americans closed out their official games with a doubleheader on December 6. In the opening, the professionals faced the Kobe Club, an aggregation of the local squad and the top players from Keio University. On the mound for the Japanese was the tall, bespectacled 18-year-old Kazuma Sugase, the son of a German father and Japanese mother. He would become the best pitcher of his generation and was singled out by John McGraw as "one of the greatest all-around athletes in Japan," but he could not hold the Americans, who won 6-1. In the second game, the All-Americans embarrassed the local Kobe Federation, 14-1.[38] The Kobe games were so popular that local fans persuaded the All-Americans to play two informal games the next day. In the first match, the city's top high-school players, reinforced by some members of the Kobe Club, had a chance to play against the professionals. Not surprisingly, the All-Americans won easily, 10-0. The second match was a pickup game with combined-roster teams, played just for fun.

Neither of these last two games was included in the official tour results.[39]

During their two-week stay in Japan, the All-Americans won all of their 17 games by a combined score of 164 to 19. One reporter noted that "if the boys had tried awfully hard, they could have blanked them in nearly every contest."[40] "We are insects compared with the giants," a Keio player supposedly concluded.[41] Observers noted, "the weak point of the Japanese team is their batting. … [but] considering that they are novices at the game, they are simply marvelous at all the other points. They are quick, active, and heady."[42] "They put up a mighty nice fielding game," noted Bill Devereaux. "The infield work of the Keio club was as snappy and fast as any I've seen this season. … They don't bat the ball as hard as we do, but they are going to improve."[43] "They watch the playing of our men with the keenest attention," explained Fisher. "They are anxious to pick up the fine points and become expert at playing our national game."[44]

H.L. Baggerly noted, "While the attendance of the games of the All-Americans has exceeded expectations, the receipts are only fair. Ten, 20 and 30 cents are the maximum prices a manager can charge right now and get the money. There are hard times in Japan as well as America. … Wages are very low. ... Hence if a [Japanese] gives up 30 cents at the box office to see a baseball game he is parting with a large chunk of his salary."[45] The exchange rate also hurt Fisher's bottom line. While 30 cents was dear to a Japanese worker, it barely covered Fisher's expenses. "Mike Fisher … almost fainted on the diamond when he saw the huge crowd that came out for the first game," wrote columnist Bob Ray in 1934. "Mike's team's share of the receipts was so big he had to hire a truck to haul the huge pile of coin down to the bank. 'I had visions of retiring and becoming one of the filthy rich,' says Fisher 'But when we got to the bank and exchanged it for American money, that big truck-load of coin amounted to only $18.75.'"[46]

On December 7 the All-Americans sailed for Shanghai, where they played a doubleheader against the local club, before moving on to Hong Kong and Canton.[47] In the British colony, they played a mixed doubleheader – a baseball game and a cricket match. Not surprisingly, the Americans won at baseball, but cricket was another matter. "The Hongkongers kept slugging away and we hadn't got them out by teatime," recalled Devereaux. "They had scored, if I remember rightly, 678 runs for six men out. Oh, but it was a painful experience alright!"[48] The team arrived in Manila on Christmas. Although baseball had only been introduced to the Philippines 10 years earlier, US troops stationed on the islands gave the All-Americans their first stiff competition during the tour. The professionals played six games against military teams and four against squads of expatriates aided by Filipino schoolboys enrolled in missionary schools. Army teams beat the professionals twice and lost another by a run in 11 innings. After a brief stop in Japan, the All-Americans finished their tour in Hawaii, where they won three games comfortably against the All-Hawaii team before losing the last game, which featured Bill Burns on the mound and Jack Bliss behind the plate for the All-Hawaiians.

As the All-Americans returned to San Francisco on February 15, Fisher was pleased with the team's accomplishments. "Our trip through Japan should go down in history, as it was one of the greatest baseball invasions ever made. We won [over] the people every place we went, and we sent all of Japan baseball mad."[49] H.L. Baggerley summed up the tour perfectly: "I can say without fear of contradiction that the trip has been an unqualified success and promoters Fisher and Woods are entitled to all the glory. From a financial point of view, it has been successful. Money has been made – not a mint of money, but enough to remunerate the enterprising promoters for their labor and loss of time. … The All-Americans have done some noble missionary work. They have made scores of converts to our national game. It would be a great thing if a team could tour the Orient annually. Interest in baseball would intensify with every visit. Japan has caught the spirit and will welcome with open arms any and all ambassadors of our national game."[50]

REACH ALL-AMERICAN GAMES IN JAPAN

Date	Place	Opponent	Score	Winner	Loser
November 22	Tokyo	Waseda	5-0	Graney	Oii
November 23	Tokyo	Tokyo Club	19-1	Danzig	Kono
November 23	Tokyo	Keio	3-0	Burns	Fukuda
November 24	Tokyo	Tokyo Club	11-4	Graney	Murakami
November 25	Yokohama	YC&AC	17-1	Flaherty	Nicholl
November 26*	Yokohama	Keio	6-0	Burns	Koyama
November 27*	Yokohama	Yokohama Commercial	11-0	Graney	Suzuki
November 28	Tokyo	Waseda	3-0	Flaherty	Oii
November 29	Tokyo	Keio	6-0	Graney	Fukuda
November 30	Tokyo	Tokyo Club	8-5	Devereaux	Aoki
December 1	Yokohama	Waseda	13-2	Burns	Oii
December 2	Yokohama	Keio	15-2	Flaherty	Fukuda
December 3	Yokohama	Waseda	10-0	Burns	Oii
December 3	Yokohama	Tokyo Club	3-0	Graney	Masuda
December 5	Kobe	Kobe Country Club	14-2	Flaherty	Fry
December 6	Kobe	Kobe Club	6-1	Burns	Sugase
December 6	Kobe	Kobe Federation	14-1	Unknown	

Secondary sources often interchange the dates of these two games

1908 REACH ALL-AMERICAN TOUR BATTING STATISTICS

Americans Batting Statistics	BA	G	AB	R	H	SB
Heinie Heitmuller	.259	14	58	13	15	6
Jim Delahanty	.250	13	56	12	14	10
Bill Devereaux	.291	14	55	16	16	10
Babe Danzig	.146	14	55	15	8	11
Harry McArdle	.327	14	52	18	17	7
Jack Bliss	.130	14	46	13	6	10
Joe Curtis	.216	11	37	19	8	11
Patsy Flaherty	.313	10	32	7	10	3
Nick Williams	.286	7	21	5	6	7
Jack Graney	.050	9	20	5	1	3
Bill Burns	.118	5	17	2	2	1
George Hildebrand	.364	3	11	4	4	3

JAPANESE BATTING STATISTICS

Japanese Batting Statistics	BA	G	AB	R	H	SB
Yamawaki (Waseda)	.269	7	26	4	7	0
Sasaki (Keio)	.167	5	18	0	3	1
Kanki (Keio)	.188	5	16	2	3	2
Koyama (Keio)	.125	5	16	0	2	2
Iseda (Waseda)	.062	5	16	0	1	0
Fukabori (Waseda)	.188	5	16	0	3	0
Tobita (Waseda)	.077	4	13	0	1	0
Abe (Keio)	.083	4	12	0	1	0
Fukuda (Keio)	.083	4	12	0	1	0
Higo (Keio)	.083	4	12	0	1	0
Ogawa (Waseda)	.000	4	12	0	0	0
Nishio (Waseda)	.000	4	12	0	0	0
Nomura (Waseda)	.000	4	12	0	0	0
Kameyama (Keio)	.000	4	11	0	0	0
Oi (Waseda)	.091	4	11	0	1	0
Murakami (Keio)	.000	3	10	0	0	0
Ohashi (Keio)	.200	2	5	0	1	0

NOTES

1 Thom Karmik, "Mique Fisher and the PCL," Baseball History Daily, May 6, 2013. https://baseballhistorydaily.com/2013/05/06/mike-fisher-and-the-pacific-coast-league/.

2 "Fisher Plans Trip to Orient," *Hawaiian Gazette*, November 29, 1907: 5.

3 "Fisher's Stars Love That Dear Honolulu," *Grass Valley* (California) *Morning Union*, December 10, 1907: 7.

4 "Manila See Good Ball," *Honolulu Advertiser*, February 18, 1908: 3.

5 "Baseball Tour to Orient," *Honolulu Hawaiian Gazette*, March 3, 1908: 5.

6 Frank B. Hutchinson Jr., "Local Players to Invade the Orient," *Chicago Inter Ocean*, May 10, 1908: 18.

7 "Ball Team for Japan. Mike Fisher Will Take a Strong Nine to the Land of the Mikado." *Brooklyn Daily Eagle*, June 4, 1908: 8.

8 Keith Robbins, "The 1908 Reach All American Tour," unpublished manuscript in author's collection.

9 "Jess Woods Has Trip of Star Team to Orient All Fixed," *Honolulu Evening Bulletin*, September 21, 1908: 7.

10 "Woods Will Take Team," *Honolulu Advertiser*, March 24, 1908: 3.

11 "Jiggs Donahue Going to Japan," *Pittsburgh Press*, March 19, 1908: 8.

12 Hutchinson.

13 "Cobb's Trip to Japan Doubtful," *Detroit Times*, October 17, 1908: 2; "Cobb May Cut Out Jap Trip and Spend Winter in Georgia," *Atlanta Georgian and News*, October 23, 1908: 36; "Cobb Abandons Trip to Japan," *Topeka State Journal*, October 27, 1908: 2.

14 "Cobb Will Be Left at Home," *Butte Daily Post*, October 31, 1908: 6.

15 "Reach-Alls Far Too Good for Orient," *Hawaiian Star*, December 7, 1908: 6.

16 H.L. Baggerly, "Japs Eager to Become Expert in Baseball," *St. Louis Post Dispatch*, December 20, 1908: 28.

17 Baggerly, "Japs Eager to Become Expert in Baseball."

18 "American Nine Defeats Waseda," *Oakland Tribune*, November 23, 1908: 11.

19 "The Reach All Team," *Japan Times*, November 25, 1908: 6.

20 Despite the attention given to the tour, accurate box scores do not survive for all games. Some published box scores are incomplete and contain errors. There are also discrepancies between articles published in Japanese and English, making it difficult in some cases to verify the starting pitchers. For example, some articles state that Bill Burns started this first game. Furthermore, the first names of the Japanese players were rarely published so these are sometimes lost to time.

21 Joseph Ohl, "Japan Coming Along with Baseball Game," *Duluth News Tribune*, November 8, 1908: 2; "Reach-Alls Far Too Good for Orient."

22 "Japs Give Champs a Royal Time," *Grass Valley Morning Union*, December 16, 1908: 7.

23 "Reach All Stars Far Too Good for Orient."

24 "American Nine Defeats Waseda."

25 "Japs Give Champs a Royal Time."

26 "The Reach All Team."

27 "Mique Fisher Is Heard From," *Pacific Commercial Advertiser*, December 5, 1908: 3.

28 B.W. Fleisher, "Baseball in Japan," *Collier's Weekly* 42, no. 15: 29.

29 "Mique Fisher Is Heard From."

30 "Michel Fisher's Impressions," *Honolulu Evening Bulletin*, February 10, 1909: 7.

31   Jesse Woods, "All the East Has Baseball Fever," *Grass Valley Morning Union*, October 8, 1908: 7.

32   "Baseball," *Japan Weekly Mail*, November 28, 1908: 654.

33   "Reach and Keio Baseball," *Japan Times*, November 27, 1908: 2.

34   Bill Devereaux, "Baseball Nippon's National Game," *Honolulu Evening Bulletin*, February 2, 1909: 6.

35   Ohl.

36   "All Americans Are Champion Eaters," *Grass Valley Morning Union*, December 29, 1908: 7.

37   All Americans Are Champion Eaters."

38   Conflicting sources exist for the final games in Kobe. Yoshikazu Matsubayashi lists a doubleheader on December 6 while Shinsuke Tanaka notes a single game on the 6th and a doubleheader on December 7. Yoshikazu Matsubayashi, *Baseball Game History: Japan vs. U.S.A.* (Tokyo: Baseball Magazine, 2001); Shinsuke Tanaka, *Kobe no Yakyushi: Reimeiki* (Kobe: Rokko Shuppan, 1980), 644-656.

39   Tanaka, 654-656.

40   "Jack Graney Pitches Great Ball in Japan," *Oregon Daily Journal* (Portland), December 29, 1908: 9.

41   Fleisher.

42   Fleisher.

43   Devereaux.

44   "Mique Fisher Is Heard From."

45   Baggerly, "Japs Eager to Become Expert in Baseball."

46   Bob Ray, "The Sports X-Ray," *Los Angeles Times*, November 9, 1934: Part II, 14.

47   "Baseball Team in China," *Lincoln* (Nebraska) *Evening News,* January 29, 1909: 8.

48   "Mike Fisher's Players Arrive," *Hawaiian Star*, January 30, 1909: 3.

49   Mike Fisher, "Baseball Tour of Americans a Success," *San Francisco Call*, February 16, 1909: 8.

50   H.L. Baggerly, "Baggerly Writes of Travels of Baseball Champions," *Honolulu Evening Bulletin*, January 30, 1909: 1, 3.

VOYAGE TO THE LAND OF THE RISING SUN: THE WISCONSIN BADGER NINE'S 1909 TRIP TO JAPAN[1]

By Joe Niese

In 1905, President Theodore Roosevelt sent his eldest daughter, Alice, and Secretary of War William Howard Taft on a tour of the Far East, making stops in China, Japan, Korea, and the Philippines. The trip was part of Roosevelt's plan to act as mediator in the Russo-Japanese War, in the process solidifying the United States' place in the hierarchy of trading in the Orient. While the visit was successful on both accounts, by the end of the decade the relationship between Japan and the United States was growing contentious over actions being taken in South Manchuria (China). In essence, the United States was on the brink of being blocked out of Oriental trading by Japan's South Manchurian train line. Taft, who became president in 1909, saw an opportunity to work toward an agreement of some kind, where both countries could continue to utilize the area. Hoping that a resolution could be made, Taft saw a prospect for bonding in one of the two nations' few common grounds—the baseball diamond. The University of Wisconsin-Madison had a series of games planned for the fall in Japan, and Taft wanted to capitalize on the game's international appeal.

Baseball was one of the University of Wisconsin's first athletic teams. The first recorded game was played on April 30, 1870, when the university's team, the Mendotas, thumped the Capital City Club, 53-18. In 1877 a baseball association was formed. By the first

University of Wisconsin and Keio University, September 22, 1909

decade of the 1900s, the school's baseball program had become a victim of the game's nationwide success. Seemingly every club and fraternity on campus was fielding a team. In January 1909, when financial constraints arose, university officials proposed that the intercollegiate team be dropped in favor of skating and intramural baseball. Ultimately, the plan never came to fruition, but the baseball team, under coach Tom Barry, did little to prove its worth, ending with a 4-8 record and a fifth-place finish in the Big Ten Conference.

During the tepid 1909 season, Genkwan Shibata, a native of Toyama, Japan, and an honor student in the university's commerce program, had been negotiating a series of games between the school team and ballclubs in Japan.[2] "Shibby" worked with Professor Masao Matsuoka of Tokyo's Keio University (a 1907 alumnus of Wisconsin) to bring the plan to fruition. Just before commencement, it was announced that the university would send a baseball team to Japan in the fall for a series of games. To offset some of the cost, Keio helped sponsor the trip, guaranteeing up to $4,000 toward Wisconsin's finances. This was the second time in as many years that an American university had traveled to Japan to play an exhibition series. The previous fall, Waseda University sponsored a trip for the University of Washington.

Due to Barry's commitments as the head football coach, a replacement baseball coach was sought out. The university didn't have to look far, turning to part-time political science faculty member Charles McCarthy. The timing couldn't have been any better for McCarthy, who had recently suffered a self-described "nervous breakdown."[3] A renaissance man, he had been steeped in work for the past decade. After obtaining his doctorate in American history from Wisconsin-Madison in 1901, McCarthy helped set up the Wisconsin Legislative Library.[4] His knowledge of economics made him a frequent sounding board for President Roosevelt. He remained at the university as a part-time political science lecturer and assistant football coach. He was also heavily involved in the state's progressive movement and the political movement's quintessential work, the "Wisconsin Idea."

As much as McCarthy was involved in politics, he was an athlete at heart. Despite his slight frame, McCarthy had been an All-American fullback and standout punter at Brown University. While attending law school at the University of Georgia, he took over the football coaching duties from Glenn Scobey "Pop" Warner. He coached for two years (1897-98),

leading the team to a 6–3 record. When he came to Wisconsin as a doctoral student, he immediately immersed himself in the athletic program, focusing on football. In the years leading up to the trip to Japan (1907-09), he "played an extremely important part in the athletic situation" at the university.[5]

In addition to McCarthy acting as coach and university representative, Shibata was named business manager and interpreter. Ned Jones was the press correspondent.[6] Everyone on the Badgers' 13-man roster was a Wisconsinite: catchers Elmer Barlow and Arthur Kleinpell; pitchers Douglas Knight and Charles Nash; first baseman Mike Timbers; second basemen John Messmer and Kenneth Fellows; third baseman Arthur Pergande; shortstops J. Allen Simpson and Oswald Lupinski; and outfielders David Flanagan, Harlan Rogers, and R. Waldo Mucklestone.

The Badgers didn't have any future major leaguers, but they were a talented group. Knight pitched for former big leaguer Emerson "Pink" Hawley's Oshkosh Indians of the Wisconsin-Illinois League while waiting for the trip. Barlow and Messmer attracted interest from professional ball teams.[7] Messmer, the team's best all-around athlete, was the university's first nine-letter winner, collecting three each in football, baseball, and track.[8] He also captained the swim team, dabbled in water polo, and was a "prime candidate for the crew team," perhaps the school's most popular and competitive athletic team.[9] Rogers was a three-sport star (football, basketball, and baseball).

In July, University president Charles R. Van Hise received a letter from President Taft, an ardent baseball fan, for McCarthy to pass along to Thomas J. O'Brien, the ambassador to Japan. It read:

My dear Ambassador: I am advised that the faculty of the University of Wisconsin has accepted the invitation of the Keio University of Japan to play a series of ten games of baseball with the Japanese university in the month of September.

I am glad such a trip is to be undertaken, as it can not but be of advantage to the universities in the encouragement of manly sports and athletics, and will lead to a better understanding between the universities of the two countries.

I shall greatly appreciate any courtesies of consideration within your power which you may be able to extend to the team while in Japan which may add to the usefulness and pleasure of their visit there.[10]

University of Wisconsin professors also praised the trip as a great educational experience for the students. McCarthy assured faculty that though the excursion would cause the student-athletes to miss the beginning of the fall semester, he would make sure that they were keeping up with their academic pursuits while in Japan.

Shibata, though an academic achiever, was strictly thinking about the games. In a letter to the players, he expressed this sentiment: "We cannot come back to the university with defeats; the Japanese men never love unworthy opponents. I desire to show them that Wisconsin can raise men too."[11] Shibata guaranteed that it would be an experience they would never forget, commenting, "Please take care of your health and I can promise to show you the time of your life in Japan."[12]

On August 22, 1909, the group boarded the Great Northern Railway's Oriental Limited in Minneapolis. Two days were spent traveling through Minnesota, North Dakota, Montana, Idaho, and into Washington where they were given a scenic tour of the state as they made their way to Seattle. When they pulled into King Street Station on August 24, nearly 2,000 miles from Madison, they were greeted by a cheer of "U Rah Rah Wisconsin!" by Western alumnus of the university.

For several days the team made trips to Tacoma and Port Ludlow, Washington, for exhibition games. Finally, on the morning of August 31, the group enthusiastically boarded the *Aki Maru* of the Nippon Yusen Kaisha Line. Over the next two weeks, the Midwestern boys endured sea sickness and suspect food, while taking in the sights (including humpback whales). Finally, on September 16 they arrived in Japan, docking at the Yokohama pier. A large banner greeted them that read "Wisconsin Cead Mille Tfailte," Gaelic for "A Hundred Thousand Welcomes to Wisconsin."

The Badgers were met by hundreds of Keio students who greeted them with the university's "U Rah Rah Wisconsin!" cheer. Professor Matsuoka had prepared a group to act as Badger backers, writing Shibata "for the words of the Wisconsin yell, the words and music of the college song, and 500 cardinal-colored armbands, to be used by Japanese students who were to represent Wisconsin fans at the games."[13]

When the Badgers came to Japan, Keio was considered to be the top team in the country, and they were given great support in their training. Supposedly, "as soon as the Wisconsin faculty sanctioned the trip the Keio boys were hurried off to a cool, quiet place in Northern Japan to spend the summer in practice. Each day they spent six hours in practice, and when it came time for the first game they were in the best of physical condition."[14] This was apparent when the two teams held a joint practice the first day the Wisconsin boys arrived. As one member of Badgers recalled, "That afternoon we had our first practice. After we were done the Keio team came on the field. They proved to us that we could not play ball at all. That first practice of theirs was one of the 'classiest' affairs that we had ever seen."[15]

Keio's serious approach to the series may have been a response to the thorough beating they took the year before. Although they had success during the University of Washington's 1908 visit, a group of professionals visited the island that November and December. The Reach All-Americans, made up of Pacific Coast Leaguers and a few second-string major leaguers, traveled to the Orient on a barnstorming tour, leaving with a record of 17-0, including four decisive defeats of Keio.

On September 22, 1909, the Badgers traveled to the ballpark by rickshaw to play Keio in the first game. They were told that a large crowd was expected, but as they made their way to the park, the streets were eerily silent. Even when they arrived, there was no one outside the ballpark. They were shocked by what they saw when they entered the gates. David Flanagan recalled the scene, "Sitting there before us, grave and silent as a multitude in a church, was a crowd of twenty-five thousand Japanese fans."[16]

Silence was an essential part of the Japanese game plan, for both players and fans. When the Wisconsin players started their chatter, or "line of talk," they were hissed by the crowd. The Japanese felt that the "encouraging of a player by another on his own team was intended to rattle the opposition."[17] Unfazed, the Badger nine continued their talk, and, according to Oswald Lupinski, "before the close of the international series our opponents were making just as much, and perhaps more noise than we were."[18]

The first two games went into extra innings, both Wisconsin losses. The first was a 3-2, 11-inning affair that saw the Badgers outhit Keio, 7 to 3. The second lasted 19 innings, ending in a 2-1 loss. More importantly, Doug Knight, who had pitched all 11 innings in the first game and the first 16 of the second, injured his arm and wasn't able to pitch for the next few games. In both games, Japanese pitcher Kazuma Sugase stifled the Americans. A few years later, when John McGraw led a group of major leaguers on a world tour, he described Sugase as "one of the greatest all-around athletes in Japan" in "the same position here that Jim Thorpe occupied in the United States after the last Olympic games."[19]

Sugase wasn't the only Keio player whose skills caught the attention of the American players. Three others impressed, including Nenosuke Fukuda, the university's catcher, who had a throwing arm that "kept base runners glued to the bases."[20] A Badger described shortstop Katsumaro Sasaki as "one of the fastest fielding players that we had ever seen and his fielding would possibly win for him a place in our major leagues." The other standout was center fielder Manpei Kameyama, the "best runner in Japan."[21]

As a whole, the Japanese team's approach to the game reflected the Deadball Era in which they played: midline pitching backed by superb defense, and weak hitting supplemented with keen baserunning, bunting, and squeezing. "The Japs are a bit weak with the bat, but play a fielding game which can hardly be improved upon," recalled Lupinski. "They are dangerous men on bases, and when a runner reaches first he generally goes all the way around to home. They use the squeeze play and the bunting game extensively. Often a base runner goes from first to third on a bunt."[22]

In the first two contests, Wisconsin felt that differences in rules interpretations by umpire Takeji Nakano cost them the game. A former player and coach for Ichiko, Nakano umpired games between Keio and Waseda for years and was known for his fairness. He was inducted into the Japanese Baseball Hall of Fame in 1972.

The Badgers gracefully accepted the umpire's decisions, which "won for the Americans the general approbation of the Japanese public and all foreigners who witnessed the games."[23] According to Genkwan Shibata, after the game, Nakano, true to his nature, approached the Wisconsin team and "excused himself for his mistakes."[24]

Scoring information for the entire series of games was sparse, because the Japanese box scores included only runs, hits, and errors. For a few games, putouts were recorded. The summary under the box score included only extra-base hits and the pitchers' records.

After starting 0-2, the Badgers rebounded to win the next three, with Charles Nash taking over the pitching duties from the injured Knight. The first game saw Wisconsin shut out a group of Americans living in Tokyo, 10-0. In the next contest, the Badgers

edged the Tokyo Club, 8-7. The game wasn't as close as the score indicated, with the Japanese team scoring six unearned runs in the eighth inning. Knight, now playing in the outfield, hit a solo home run. Messmer hit a two-run home run in the next game, helping the Badgers defeat Waseda University, 7-4.

The Badgers' power surge continued into the next game when they looked to defeat Keio on October 4. Wisconsin finally solved Sugase, the Japanese ace, delivering two triples and two doubles. The offensive outburst still wasn't enough as Keio was victorious for the third consecutive game, 5-4. Errors had plagued the Badgers throughout the trip, but according to the *Japan Advertiser*, "The fortunate hitting of the Keio team when a hit was most needed won the game for them."[25]

Away from the diamond, the Badgers were allowed to experience Japanese culture, reveling in the colleges, shops, temples, theaters, and museums. They traveled by rickshaw, ate with chopsticks, and occasionally indulged in sake. Excursions to the cultural sites of Kamakura and Enoshima greatly enhanced the foreign experience. Additionally, they frequented Keio students' homes, where they talked and dined with their families. The Wisconsin boys became celebrities, drawing a crowd as they walked through the streets. American culture was also of great interest. Several of the players conducted classes in English at the university. Coach McCarthy took on a much more ambitious schedule, delivering a lecture series on American law and making presentations to the transportation department.

One of the most memorable social affairs took place on the evening of October 6 at the Chitose Ro, the premier teahouse in Yokohama. After a lavish meal, entertainment was provided by "the most beautiful geisha girls."[26] Several speeches were given; the most notable was by Mayor Nobukata Mitsuhashi of Yokohama, who lauded the Badgers on their sportsmanship. He ended by saying, "You have come, and by your example taught us that this is not only possible, but that it really forms the highest, best kind of sport, for a man to be as keen as mustard at the game, and yet have such excellent control over his own feelings as to submit without question to the decision of the umpire."[27]

The next day, October 7, Nash shut out Waseda, 5-0, four times escaping jams that saw the Japanese university put men on second and third with no one out. Two days later, Waseda's pitcher, Takayuki Omura, threw his own shutout, 3-0. Waseda scored runs on a hit, an error, and a passed ball in the first inning, and a similar combination of miscues accounted for two more in the sixth. Wisconsin had an opportunity to tie the game in the seventh, but a few close calls by umpire Nakano "took considerable ginger out of the Badgers."[28] This time, Wisconsin wasn't as courteous in their treatment of Nakano, openly berating him, for which the Japanese press "complained in letters" to the *Washington Post*.[29]

After a two-day excursion to Nikko, a tourist site in the mountains, roughly 90 miles north of Tokyo, the Badgers returned to the capital city for a final game against Keio. It was a wet, rainy day, and the Wisconsin boys "seemed to be more at home in the slippery going."[30] They roughed up Sugase for 10 hits. In the fifth inning alone, they had five singles, a double, and a triple, resulting in six earned runs. Nash was at his best, shutting out the university, 8-0. It was the Badgers' first victory over Keio and put their

final record for the tour at 5-4. After the game, a large farewell banquet was held for the Badgers at one of Tokyo's largest social clubs, the Kojunsha Club. It was attended by the Keio and Waseda teams, prominent businessmen, and members of the media.

When the team departed from Yokohama the next morning, they were shown off by the Keio and Waseda teams, who showered them with remembrances, flowers, and fruit. Sixteen days later, on October 29, they arrived in Seattle. When they returned to Wisconsin on November 3, a large rally was held and mementos of the trip were displayed for several weeks. An unidentified member of the Badgers summed up the feelings of his teammates: "All of us hope some day to meet again as friends, the best true sportsmen we have ever met."[31] On a larger scale, Wisconsin Secretary of State William A. Frear gushed that "Wisconsin unlocked[ed] the door of social fraternity with Japan in a manner never before equaled."[32]

1909 UNIVERSITY OF WISCONSIN GAMES IN JAPAN

Date	Place	Opponent	Score	Winner	Loser
September 22	Tokyo	Keio University	2-3	Sugase	Knight
September 26	Tokyo	Keio University	1-2	Sugase	Nash
September 28	Tokyo	Tokyo Americans	10-0	Unknown	Unknown
September 29	Tokyo	Tokyo Club	8-7	Rogers	Fukuda
October 2	Tokyo	Waseda University	7-4	Nash	Matsuda
October 4	Tokyo	Keio University	4-5	Koyama	Knight
October 7	Tokyo	Waseda University	5-0	Nash	Matsuda
October 9	Tokyo	Waseda University	0-3	Omura	Knight
October 12	Tokyo	Keio University	8-0	Nash	Sugase

NOTES

1   Adapted from *NINE: A Journal of Baseball History and Culture* Volume 22, No. 1 (Fall 2013) by permission of the University of Nebraska Press. Copyright 2014 by the University of Nebraska Press.

2   Shibata was the university's first Japanese student to be elected to Phi Beta Kappa, the academic honor society.

3   Marion Casey, *Charles McCarthy: Librarianship and Reform* (Chicago: American Library Association, 1981), 62.

4   The first of its kind in the United States, the Legislative Library became the model for the Congressional Reference Service of the Library of Congress.

5   Irma Hochstein, "College Spirits and Patriotism," *Wisconsin Alumni Magazine* 23, no. 1 (November 1921): 12.

6   After the trip, Jones stayed in Tokyo, writing for the *Japan Advertiser*.

7   Barlow, who was finishing up law school, turned down offers from professional teams to pursue a career in law.

8   Messmer qualified for the 1908 Olympic track team in discus but withdrew because one of his brothers was severely ill.

9   "Wisconsin Athletic Hall of Fame," Wisconsin Sports Development Corporation, https://www.wihalloffame.com/john-messmer.

10   "Taft Speaks Kind Words," *Daily Northwestern* (Northwestern University), July 28, 1909.

11   "Badgers Ready for Japan," *Racine* (Wisconsin) *Daily Journal*, August 12, 1909: 3.

12   "Badgers Ready for Japan."

13   Harold Seymour and Dorothy Seymour-Mills, *Baseball: The People's Game* (New York: Oxford University Press, 1990), 171.

14   David Flanagan, "Wisconsin vs. Japan in Baseball," *Independent* 67 (December 1909): 1493.

15   Walter Buchner, "A Member of the Wisconsin Team: Our Opponents," *Wisconsin Magazine* 7, no. 2 (November 1909): 29.

16 Flanagan: 1495.

17 "Wisconsin's Ball Players Find Japs Hard to Beat," *Washington Post*, November 21, 1909: Sports 3.

18 Oswald Lupinski, "To Japan with the Ball Team," *Wisconsin Engineer* 14, no. 2 (February 1910): 137.

19 John McGraw, "Americans Defeat Great Jap Pitcher," *New York Times*, December 8, 1913: 9.

20 Fukuda, who later changed his name to Zensuke Shimada, was inducted into the Japanese Baseball Hall of Fame in 1991.

21 Buchner: 29-30.

22 Lupinski: 136.

23 "University of Wisconsin vs. Japan," *Spalding's Official Base Ball Guide*, vol. 34 (New York: American Sports Publishing, 1910), 305.

24 Genkwan Shibata, "The Japanese Trip," *Wisconsin Magazine* 7, no. 2 (November 1909): 26.

25 "Wisconsin's Ball Players Find Japs Hard to Beat," *Washington Post*, November 21, 1909: Sports 3.

26 Lupinski: 138.

27 Lupinski: 138.

28 "Wisconsin's Ball Players Find Japs Hard to Beat."

29 "Wisconsin's Ball Players Find Japs Hard to Beat."

30 "Wisconsin's Ball Players Find Japs Hard to Beat."

31 Buchner: 30.

32 Seymour and Seymour-Mills, 171.

RESTART OF LEGEND:
THE WASEDA-CHICAGO RIVALRY 1910-2008

By Christopher Frey

On the fourth day of spring in the 20th year of the Imperial Heisei era, just as the cherry blossoms were starting to bloom, another chapter in one of the most significant stories in US-Japan sports history was about to be written. It was Saturday, March 22, 2008, and while the Boston Red Sox held off the Hanshin Tigers and the Oakland Athletics rallied to beat the Yomiuri Giants in an exhibition double bill at Tokyo Dome, what really mattered that day was the long-awaited return of another American baseball team: the University of Chicago Maroons.[1]

The Chicago squad was coming for its sixth Japan tour, once again at the invitation of Waseda University, as part of that prestigious Tokyo-based institution's 125th-anniversary celebrations.[2] Given that the first time the Maroons came was in 1910 while the last had been in 1930 – not to mention Waseda's five return tours between 1911 and 1936 – Chicago's arrival was touted as renewing a nearly 100-year-old rivalry, with promotional posters and merchandise declaring it to be the "Restart of Legend."[3]

The matchups between Waseda and Chicago in the late-Meiji, Taisho, and early-Showa eras were truly epic battles fought on both sides of the Pacific, yet they sprang from the labors of an idealistic Japanese professor with support of two Maroons turned missionaries, so these baseball exchanges were always imbued with goodwill. As the 10 series were contested

1930 University of Chicago team in Japan

over the course of three decades, American dominance slowly gave way to spirited Japanese play inspired by the unlikely pairing of a manager who derided putting too much importance on results and his team's former captain turned coach who became hellbent on winning. And although the two teams were torn apart by war, the baseball ties between Chicago and Waseda would fully heal when at long last their legendary rivalry was restarted in 2008.

The bond between Waseda and Chicago began forming in 1904, shortly after Fred Merrifield – former standout third baseman and Maroons captain – was sent to Tokyo as a missionary by the American Baptist Union.[4] By the time Merrifield arrived, Waseda had just won Japan's college baseball crown quite impressively, doing so only a few years after Professor Isoo Abe – one-time pastor and graduate of Doshisha and Hartford Theological Seminary – established their first full-fledged team in 1901.[5] Abe had inspired his men to the title by promising that if they won he would arrange a trip across the Pacific to play against other university nines. Upon learning that a former Chicago ballplayer was teaching Sunday school nearby, Abe begged the American to become their part-time coach.[6] Merrifield was happy to help and spent several days a week with the club. Although he wasn't able to accompany Waseda to the United States due to his missionary obligations, he suggested they take a token of his baseball pedigree with them by adopting the same type and color of lettering he had worn while playing for his alma mater. So Abe's team embarked on the first-ever foreign trip by a Japanese sports team donning jerseys with "Waseda" emblazoned in the same shade of maroon worn by Chicago.[7] Merrifield then said in a letter published by the *Chicago Tribune*: "Give the Japanese player a little more training in the fine points of the game and I prophesy he will hit your curves, field and slide with the zest, and make his share of the fun. And then, after bowing politely to the umpire, he will go home and teach his younger brother to do still better at the great game of baseball."[8]

After Waseda returned with a decent record of 7-19, Merrifield resumed coaching the team. By early 1907 he and Abe were trying to arrange a tour all the way to Chicago; but before a plan could be set, an illness forced his resignation from the Baptist Union. Yet it still seemed providence was at play, for another former Maroon standout was soon on his way.

Alfred Place, who hit a club-best .357 playing alongside Merrifield in 1900, was being sent over by the Foreign Christian Ministry.[9] It was reported that "[h]e will work among the students of the Imperial and Waseda universities … and while he is teaching them athletics, he will also endeavor to win them over to Christianity."[10] After arriving in Tokyo in January of 1908, Place helped Waseda secure wins over the University of Washington later that year and the University of Wisconsin during its Japan tour in 1909.[11] Now with some success against American teams on both sides of the Pacific, on April 18, 1910, Abe wrote to University of Chicago Director of Athletics Alonzo Amos Stagg, issuing a formal invitation:

> It is a great pleasure for me to ask you if it is possible for the University of Chicago baseball team to come over to Japan. … If you come here next fall, all the baseball fans will surely welcome you with open arms. … You know Fred Merrifield and Alfred Place have done a great deal in coaching our teams, and we believe we can give you tolerably good games if you would come here.[12]

It was agreed that Chicago would tour Japan that October and play five games against both Waseda and Keio University.[13] Although Stagg regretted to inform Abe he couldn't "visit Japan with the boys" due to football-coaching duties, he would do everything he could to ensure that his team was ready.[14] After receiving Place's scouting reports as well as insights from Merrifield, who was now living in Michigan, captain J.J. Pegues later recalled, "[W]e determined to go prepared to play our best game," while noting that they spent the summer practicing and playing against local semipro teams.[15] Pegues added, "As a result, we were really in better shape for a hard series in the fall than during the regular spring college season. … The teams of Waseda and Keio also spent the summer months in practice; so that all three teams were in the pink of condition."[16]

The Chicago team even took lessons on Japanese language and culture, then were honored with letters of introduction to the Imperial Japanese government from President William Howard Taft and Secretary of State Philander C. Knox.[17] Shortstop Robert Baird recounted in 1976 that their trip was deemed "an opportunity for each member of the team to consider himself as an American ambassador of goodwill to improve relations between the two countries." Baird added, "Even today, sixty-six years later, I am sure that every one of us accepted this responsibility to a high degree."[18] All of this preparation served them well, for upon arriving at Yokohama aboard the *Kamakura*

Maru on September 26, 1910, they were surrounded by reporters.[19] As Pegues later detailed in an article for *The Independent*:

> Thruout [sic] our stay we were considered not only as guests of Waseda University, but also as guests of the Japanese nation, and while objects of constant curiosity, we were at the same time subject to every form of Japanese politeness. Also I may say that while the Japanese stared at us constantly and questioned us continually, we returned both stares and questions with interest, as they seemed far stranger to us than we can have seemed to them. … When we were hauled thru the streets of Yokohama in "rickshaws," on our way to the train for Tokio [sic], we insisted on leaving the tops of our man-drawn carriages down in spite of the steady rain; so that we might have an unobstructed view of the strange sights … and it was only thru stern necessity that we forewent sightseeing during our first few days in Tokio [sic], and devoted our time to practising [sic] for the games now close at hand.[20]

Pegues noted how they were "requested to practice in secret as far as possible, and without previous announcement, as it was feared students would desert their class-room work to watch us in action." Yet large crowds still came to see the Maroons train, leading him to declare, "Only a 'world's series' could excite such interest at home, and we looked forward with much curiosity to the first game."[21] In the meantime, the players stayed at the Imperial Hotel and were guests of honor at a banquet held at a Western-style restaurant fit for dignitaries, with Abe presiding while the American team's chaperone, Professor Gilbert Bliss, said the University of Chicago hoped to return the favor the following year.[22]

Stagg had appointed his ace, Harlan Orville "Pat" Page, as the team's player-manager, who, in addition to his baseball duties, served as a "Special Correspondent" for the *Chicago Tribune*. In Page's report about that evening, he described how, "Following the twenty courses of both American and Japanese variety the two teams sang their alma mater, and the old Chicago yell drowned out the Waseda battle cry, although the new dress suits of the Maroons interfered with the vocal efforts."[23] The US ambassador to Japan, Thomas O'Brien, also hosted Chicago along with players from both the Japanese universities, as well as "a number of the Japanese nobility," including Waseda's founder and former Prime Minister Shigenobu Ōkuma.[24] "After a musical concert the guests adjourned to the garden, where American dainties were served," Page recalled, and then added that "Mr. O'Brien promised to be with the Maroons at the games."[25]

When the day finally arrived for the opener, "The fences were draped with red and white bunting and the entrance festooned with American and Japanese flags," Pegues recalled and then noted, "Practically all of the spectators had entered the field when we arrived, an hour and a half before the game was to commence, and as we passed in we were greeted with a great outburst of handclapping."[26] Despite lopsided support for Waseda, Pegues acknowledged how "[e]veryone rose to salute us and then settled down once more and waited for the game to start."[27] Before getting underway, Waseda's cheer captain Nobuyoshi "Shinkei" Yoshioka – infamously known as the "Heckling Tiger Beard Shogun" – led a parade of the team's most hard-core supporters down behind the third-base line.[28] Yoshioka had been recruited a few years earlier to lead the cheering squad after Abe observed that students in America would chant their "college yell to take away the enemy's spirit."[29]

Afforded the courtesy of whether or not to bat first, Chicago elected to start off in the field, with Page on the mound and Fred Steinbrecher behind the plate, William Sunderland at first, Orno Roberts at second, John Boyle at third, and Baird at shortstop, with an outfield consisting of Mansfield Cleary in left, Frank Collings in center, and Pegues in right, while on the bench were pitcher Glen Roberts, catcher Frank Paul, and outfielder Herman Ehrhorn.[30] So aligned, Page threw out the first pitch at 10 minutes past three o'clock on October 4.[31]

The leadoff hitter for Waseda was second baseman Keito Hara, who to the delight of Shogun Yoshioka and the Japanese fans "drove a clean hit to the outfield," and as Pegues recalled, "to our amazement, as we had expected absolute quiet, the whole crowd rose as one man and yelled till they were hoarse."[32] Yet instead of becoming rattled by the chorus of cheers, Pegues said, "Once the noise commenced we felt natural. The odd surroundings faded out of our minds and we were playing baseball, not some queer Japanese game."[33] Chujun Tobita flied out to Collings in center and third baseman Takeshi Iseda's fly to Pegues advanced Hara to second, but Page then induced a grounder from Hitoshi Oi to end the threat.[34] In the bottom of the first, with Oi on the mound, Collings grounded out but

Pegues tripled and came home on a passed ball. Then Boyle walked and scored when Steinbrecker hit one over Jukichi Ogawa in center.[35] Chicago tallied three more in the second, one each in the fourth and sixth, and two more in the eighth.[36] The Japanese scored once in the sixth as catcher Sutekichi Matsuda hit a triple and scored on a fly out to center, and Ogawa scored an unearned run in the seventh, but as Iseda tried to score in the ninth, he was thrown out at home to end the game as a 9-2 Chicago victory.[37] Yoshioka was disappointed that the team hadn't done better and Tobita felt largely responsible after going 0-for-4, but they must have felt even worse upon seeing Keio lose to Chicago by only two runs.[38]

In the second game against Waseda, Tobita tried to make amends by going 3-for-4 with a steal and showed his determination by knocking Glen Roberts to the ground when they collided at first base, but his team's only other hits were a triple by left fielder Goro Mikami and a single by pitcher Takayuki Omura, as Roberts fanned 11 in the 5-0 shutout.[39] Chicago then crushed Waseda 15-4 in their third game and went on to rout the school's alumni, 11-2, while it twice took them 10 innings to beat Keio in their next two matchups.[40]

Waseda and Chicago then traveled to Osaka, where, as Page wrote, "The teams were greeted at the Imperial station with many flowers and escorted through the city by a Japanese lantern parade."[41] With everything organized and promoted by the *Mainichi Shimbun*, there were more than 12,000 in attendance at the first game, and Page heard "that a number camped on the ball grounds all night so as to see the Maroons in action."[42] Osaka's mayor threw out the first pitch and it seemed the tides had turned in favor of Waseda, which took an early lead against Roberts, but Chicago's hitting proved too much: The team rallied and cruised to an 8-4 win.[43] "Before the largest crowd of the international series," Chicago then crushed Waseda, 20-0, as Page declared, "Never before was such a swatfest witnessed in Japan."[44] In the finale, Waseda took an early lead but ultimately lost yet again by another lopsided score, 12-2.[45]

As the players returned from Japan unbeaten, several hundred students gathered to "welcome home the University of Chicago baseball team, from its triumphal invasion of the Orient."[46] A few days later the players were "formally welcomed at a spirited and joyous baseball mass meeting," and a theater troupe put on an "American-Japanese Night performance."[47] The team was praised by Stagg, who along with

Japanese Consul Keiichi Yamasaki then jointly proclaimed, "[I]f Japan and America ever were to have a war, it would be in the form of a baseball contest."[48]

In Tokyo, Abe tried to remain optimistic by telling the press that Chicago was a top team on par with Harvard and Yale, but critics were still harsh about the team's embarrassing losses.[49] Tobita claimed responsibility and quit.[50] Losing so badly devastated Tobita, who described his initial encounter with the sport while in elementary school at the age of 10, saying, "From the first day I saw the leather ball, it was as if my heart had completely taken up residence inside it." Yet it wasn't his first time being crushed by defeat. When Tobita was 16 and playing competitively for his school in Mito, it became clear how much the sport meant to him. After his previously undefeated team lost a game to Ibaraki prefectural rivals Shimotsuma, he "cried tears of regret" as the opposing "troops" were "wrapped in honor." At that time, Tobita would later recall, "What I vowed secretly in my heart was the great desire to avenge Shimotsuma." Starting that following day, Tobita set to work with his teammates, who were desperate to "erase the only stain they had left," but a rematch was never secured and so they had to settle for vicarious vengeance by defeating the Ikubunkan team from Tokyo after hearing that they had beaten Shimotsuma. Tobita suffered another humiliation when he was held hitless in a 15-0 drubbing by Keio University's feeder school, after which he admitted, "We were ashamed to go home in broad daylight, so we waited for dusk and snuck home through the back gate." This time, he and his teammates would eventually exact revenge directly, but Tobita's animosity apparently stayed with him as he decided to enroll at Keio's archrival in 1907. Yet when Tobita joined Waseda's baseball team that spring, the notoriously explosive "Sōkei-sen" series of baseball "battles" with Keio were still on hiatus due to concerns from administrators that emotions on and off the field had been getting way out of hand. Now, just three years later, feeling horrible that he had let Chicago stain the reputation of both his team and that of Abe, he essentially committed baseball *harakiri* by walking away from the game.[51]

Abe's reputation took a serious hit, too, and his tenure as manager was even in doubt when he reportedly resigned ahead of Waseda's upcoming 1911 tour of America. Yet it was later clarified that Abe "was unable to come, occupied as he is with his faculty work and the worries involved as president of the baseball association."[52] Whatever the case, Abe then made a managerial change that, although only temporary, surely had an impact on his players both on and off the field.

Although the ballclub was chaperoned by Professor Takizo Takasugi, the man whom Abe asked to take charge of Waseda's team was their former foe and recent graduate, Pat Page.[53] This wasn't simply aimed at trying to improve the skills of his squad, for these exchanges weren't just about wins and losses to Abe, as he first made clear on their 1905 tour when he told an audience at Stanford:

We are not here to win games, but to learn to play baseball as it is played in America. And it is not in baseball only that this trip should be a help to our men. It will broaden their views and help them to a better understanding of the world, and I expect they will gain from it far more than they put into it.[54]

After returning from that trip, he and his captain, Shin Hashido, shared the latest techniques they learned in America, which Abe then combined with his own spiritual and moral views to create a new form of Japanese baseball philosophy.[55] In Abe's lecture, entitled "Three Primary Virtues of Baseball," he spoke of "wisdom, humanity, and courage," while he "communicated to the team the importance of cultivating and strengthening the spirit." He insisted that his team adhere to two key principles: "The first is to fight with the same passion throughout the entire match. … The second is to avoid placing all importance on winning or losing."[56] Abe shared similar sentiments with Page before his team's departure for America, writing that "international friendship was more important than any other consideration in making the trip."[57] Page clearly valued the friendship too, for he gave up a chance to pitch an exhibition game against the Cubs so he could be in San Francisco when Waseda arrived on April 13, 1911, and even though the team went on to lose all three of its matches against Chicago and ended the tour with a record of 17-35-1, Page was encouraged by their performance.[58] Waseda may have fared even better if Page hadn't prematurely relinquished his management duties to get married in mid-June, at which point the entire squad saw him off as guests at his wedding.[59]

After his honeymoon, Page went to work at his alma mater as a coach under Stagg, so four years later when the Maroons returned to Japan in 1915, he was once again managing Chicago against the Japanese.[60]

Waseda now had Atsushi Kōno as its part-time coach, the hurler mentored by Merrifield who earned the nickname "Iron Man" while pitching 24 out of 26 games during its 1905 tour. Fans hoped that his coaching would help his pitchers tame Chicago's bats. Although Waseda's pitchers fared better than in 1910, Chicago won the opener 5-3 in front of a crowd of 20,000. Then the Maroons swept the Tokyo series by winning the next three games 2-0, 1-0, and 5-0, with the latter a masterpiece by Page, who abandoned his role as manager to take the mound and faced only one over the minimum while striking out nine.[61]

As with the 1910 tour, three additional games were then played in Osaka. The Maroons shut out Waseda 3-0 in the opener behind the pitching of Paul "Shorty" Des Jardien, a 6-foot-4 ace who reportedly agreed to join the Cubs upon graduating but instead stayed with the Maroons to go to Japan. But in the second game, Rowland George spotted Waseda a three-run lead. Fearing Chicago's unbeaten streak in Japan was in jeopardy, Page lifted George and took over on the mound, pitching in relief and holding Waseda scoreless the rest of the way as the Americans rallied and won 5-3. The Maroons then completed their sweep with a 9-1 victory in the finale, which, combined with three wins over Keio in Tokyo, gave Page and the university another perfect Japan tour record.[62]

Backup first baseman Dave Wiedemann saw little on-field action during that tour, yet in 1973 at the age of 78 he recounted the trip fondly: "We were royally entertained because at the time Japan was one of the Western Allies and Prime Minister Okuma also was honorary president of Waseda."[63] Okuma had taken time to entertain the Maroons in the garden of his private villa, where he told them, "Chicago's visit in 1910 did much for younger Japan," and declared that baseball "has practically become the National sport of Japan."[64] Okuma added, "Exchange visits by athletic organizations form a real means of promoting better understanding and peaceful sentiment," before concluding his remarks by expressing his "hope that the relation of the University of Chicago and Waseda University would always be cordial."[65] Relations at that time were clearly cordial, for no one objected to Page playing even though he was technically ineligible, with everyone instead simply marveling at his pitching prowess. This served as another example of Abe's insistence that his players not place too much importance on winning or losing.

In 1916 Waseda went on a return tour to the United States and once again lost all three of its games in

Chicago, this time not even coming close, falling 7-1, 9-2, and 8-4.[66] They would have to wait another four years for a chance to beat their American rivals, but for the next series in Japan, Waseda was to have its first full-time coach. Abe previously discussed the idea of dedicating someone to the job, but the problem was securing funds for a salary. After he consulted with the alumni club, it was decided membership fees would be charged to raise money for that purpose.[67] Hearing of the plan, Tobita was instantly intrigued, for over the past 10 years every time he watched baseball he was tormented by the losses suffered to Chicago in 1910. He nearly gave up his ideas of vengeance as he wondered if his children might one day repair his legacy, yet knew that such an idea was ridiculous to expect of his own boys. But now Tobita realized, "Maybe I could get revenge on Chicago with my own hands."[68]

Despite his wife's apprehensions, given that the position paid two-thirds less than what he earned as a reporter for the *Yomiuri Shimbun*, Tobita thought, "I couldn't afford to throw away a once-in-a-lifetime opportunity to avenge Chicago," so he took the job.[69] Coach Tobita then became a man possessed – described as looking like a demon on the diamond – as he prepared his team for its next battle with Chicago.[70] Practices were so arduous that they became known as "Death Training," yet Tobita simultaneously embraced some aspects of Abe's baseball philosophy.[71] "The purpose of training is not health but the forging of the soul, and a strong soul is only born from strong practice," Tobita explained, while stressing, "In many cases it must be a baseball of pain and a baseball practice of savage treatment."[72] Although many were unsure of his methods, Tobita proudly said that his players "truly enjoyed baseball and practiced hard with a cheerful spirit."[73] Most important to Tobita was that his players were now also eager for their chance at vengeance against Chicago.[74]

When the Maroons returned to Japan in 1920 for their third tour, they too had a new coach. Page had moved on to Butler University and handed the reins over to Fred Merrifield, who had returned to Chicago as a professor.[75] After a 13-year absence, Merrifield arrived in Yokohama with his team on May 4, and as he would recall, "Professor Abe, 'Father of Baseball in Japan' went to great expense of time and money to give us a perfect time for the five weeks we were there."[76] The players were then treated to "tiffin with Marquis Okuma and came thru with out [sic] a social error in their first meeting with nobility."[77] As for baseball, the Maroons had a strong squad with seven seniors

on their roster, so they looked forward to the best-of-seven series against Waseda along with a four-game series with Keio, and for the first time, games against Tokyo Imperial University and Hosei University, as well as a match against Kwansei Gakuin, located in the heart of western Japan.[78]

On May 11 Tobita's long-awaited rematch against Chicago finally got underway.[79] After both teams scored a run in the first, the second inning saw the Maroons add two while Waseda added three to take a 4-3 lead. The Japanese stretched the advantage to 6-4 in the sixth inning; however, the visitors came back with two in the seventh and the game ended in a 6-6 tie when play was halted in the 12th by darkness.[80] This was the closest Waseda had ever come to beating Chicago, yet the momentum didn't carry over as the Maroons never trailed in the next game against their hosts, which they won 4-2.[81] After giving up 10 combined runs in the two games, Tobita had

Paul Hinkle and Juro Ito, starting pitchers of the May 19, 1920 Chicago – Waseda game

lost confidence in his pitchers' ability to contain the Americans and began to despair, but then Shukichi Matsumoto literally came out of left field and surprised his coach by saying, "Please let me pitch."[82]

Matsumoto was a highly regarded pitcher while growing up in Osaka who suffered a shoulder injury that forced him off the hill before joining Waseda. Yet after studying Chicago's batters for two games he told his coach he was confident he could get the job done. Knowing Matsumoto was never one to brag, Tobita agreed to let him take the mound, then watched him use superb control to allow only three hits in a shutout, while Herbert "Fritz" Crisler gave up two runs and took the loss.[83] Tobita described it as an "extraordinary performance" that led to Waseda's first-ever win over the Maroons, but the jubilation was short-lived as the Americans bounced back to beat Waseda in Osaka by a score of 3-1.[84] The next day Tobita called upon Matsumoto again, and although he gave up two runs in the sixth and the tying run in the eighth, he kept the score tied for another four innings until Tokuyoshi Tominaga made a clever bunt to outsmart Chicago captain and catcher Clarence Vollmer and squeeze in the run that made it 4-3. Matsumoto then closed out Chicago in the bottom of the 14th, "achieving his second great victory."[85]

In Kyoto on June 1, however, Chicago held off Tobita's men to win, 4-3, then reasserted their dominance with an 8-1 blowout in Nagoya, so although Waseda's long winless streak against the Maroons finally ended, they still lost the series.[86] Meanwhile, Chicago barely squeaked by Keio 1-0 in 10 innings, was held to a 3-3 draw in another 10-inning affair halted by rain, and then was beaten in its two other meetings with Keio, 2-1 and 1-0, marking the first time the team lost a series to a Japanese opponent.[87] In its other two Tokyo matchups, Chicago had little trouble beating Imperial University, 5-0, and defeated Hosei University 4-1, while in Kobe the Maroons outlasted Kwansei, 6-4.[88] For Tobita, all this meant that Waseda still had a ways to go in relation to its two biggest rivals,[89] while Merrifield in a tour recap acknowledged the progress Japanese baseball had made:

Needless to say, we did not play as well as Chicago teams of other years, and all the Japanese teams had apparently improved in the mastery of our game. We were fortunate indeed to win eight games, tie two, and lose only four. Several other games were nip and tuck, and a breath would have turned them the other way.

With the full Spring and Summer practice we would doubtless have cleaned up the entire series, as our predecessors had done; but we had to make the best of a serious handicap against teams that played practically the year round. If they, in turn, play as well in their return game of 1921, they will give our American teams a bad time. ... This exchange of international courtesies, this cultivation of wholesome and friendly athletic rivalry is good seed sown for a great future harvest of good will.[90]

For Waseda's return tour in 1921, Abe accompanied Tobita and the team, which played in Hawaii and on the mainland en route to Chicago.[91] The pitching staff became depleted due to injury and illness, so Tobita relied heavily on Goro "Iron Arm" Taniguchi, who lost, 4-2, in the first game vs. Chicago, but rebounded with wins over Northwestern and Page's team at Butler, before tossing three innings of relief against Indiana.[92] Iron Arm was sent out again for the rematch against Chicago, but after giving up four runs in six innings he pleaded to be relieved. Tobita wanted to send him back to the slab but was rebuked by Abe, who recognized that Taniguchi's arm was wrecked.[93]

Clearly desperate, Tobita declared that he would suit up and take second base so that the ailing Matsumoto could move to the mound, but even though Page played during the Japan tour the previous year, Abe emphatically rejected this idea too. Tobita then reluctantly accepted a brave offer from shortstop Tadashi Kubota to step up to the mound, and although he gave up a run in the eighth, the first-time pitcher threw a scoreless ninth to keep Waseda close, allowing his team to respond with an amazing three-run rally to tie the game.[94] Although Chicago retook the lead with two runs in the 10th, Waseda never gave up and fought back again for an incredible 8-7 win.[95] Tobita later reflected, "The fierce battle turned out to be a bizarre victory for Waseda yet as Stagg Field was filled with cheers, Americans came down from the stands one after another to shake hands with us."[96]

Four years later, with Merrifield now retired from coaching, Chicago was skippered by Nels Norgren, a former Maroon who as a freshman missed out playing against Waseda in 1911, but then coached the University of Utah in an 8-4 loss to the 1916 Kono-led team.[97] Since returning, Norgren had "topped off his career to date with the restoring of Chicago to Conference honors on the diamond in the Spring of

1925," and now he had his own chance for redemption against Waseda.[98]

Far from deterred, Tobita's mindset was fixed: no matter how elite the Maroons were, he couldn't let them get away with the series this time.[99] With the opener taking place on a national holiday and Waseda's ace Yoshikazu Takeuchi on the mound, it had all the makings of a Japanese fairy tale.[100] It was a pitchers' duel, and in the bottom of the ninth with one out, the bases loaded and down, 2-0, Tobita sent up a right-handed pinch-hitter, Sadayoshi Fujimoto.[101] Lefty Joe Gubbins called for a towel to dry his sweaty hands, then proceeded to throw three strikes to sit Fujimoto down without a swing.[102] Tobita then sent up right-handed pinch-hitter Eijiro Mizuno, who worked the count full, setting up a dramatic finish:

> Joey started a wide hook that looked like it was headed about two inches wide of the plate. That would have been ball four and would have forced in a run, leaving the bases still full. But just before the ball reached the plate it hooked in and darted across a corner of the rubber. The umpire yelled "strike three," and the dazed Mizuno, who had been all ready to start for first base had to chart his course along another tack. Nobody cared very much, however, just where Mizuno went, for a crowd of more than 20,000 was giving vociferous tribute to the courage and skill of Joey Gubbins. Joey, only 21 and modest, was looking for the quickest and most obscure route to the club house.[103]

Tobita had let the chance slip away, but he was determined not to lose to Chicago again. The rest of the Japanese teams also put up fierce competition against the Americans, as the next four games all ended in scoreless draws: a rain-shortened five-inning tie with Keio, two extra-inning games with Meiji halted by darkness, and a nine-inning rainout against Waseda.[104] Norgren would later point out, "In order to keep their heads above water, both teams had to make perfect plays at the plate, double plays, brilliant catches and stops in the field."[105] The "jinx" was finally broken when in the second game against Keio, with the score tied, 2-2, in the ninth, shortstop Albert McConnell pulled off a daring squeeze play to send Bob Howell home for the winning run.[106] Chicago and Waseda then played to a 1-1 tie in 10 innings, but Tobita's men finally seized their first win of the series in the next game when Fujimoto shut out the Maroons, 1-0.[107]

The Americans then battled two professional teams, defeating Takarazuka twice but losing, 2-1, to Daimai in 10 innings, then traveled to Korea, where they easily notched five straight victories.[108] While Chicago played in Seoul, Waseda and Keio faced off for the first time in nearly 20 years with a double-header kicking off the new Tokyo Big Six Baseball League.[109] In the opener, Waseda's Yoshikazu Takeuchi had a perfect game broken up in the ninth en route to an 11-0 win. Fujimoto followed that performance by allowing only one run in a 7-1 decision to complete the two-game sweep of Keio.[110]

Abe was surely proud of his team for capturing the first real Japanese baseball championship since 1906, but for Tobita it didn't really matter, for in his mind Waseda's biggest foe was still Chicago.[111] While "in Korea the team seemed to find its batting eye," and when Chicago returned to Japan they continued their hot hitting, beating Montetsu 14-0 and the Fukuoka All-Stars 12-3.[112] Norgren's pitchers had taken their play to the next level, too, as Gubbins threw a no-hitter in Kyoto backed by 14 runs to turn the tables against Daimai. William Macklind followed that with a one-hitter in a 6-0 win against a team from Nagoya in Chicago's last game outside of Tokyo.[113]

The Maroons thus returned to the capital for their final game of the tour, which as fate would have it was also to be the decisive match of the Waseda series, now deadlocked at 1-1-2.[114] Norgren selected Gubbins, who was well rested after his no-hitter, while the obvious choice for Tobita was Takeuchi, who after his near-perfect game against Keio went on to beat Hosei and shut out the powerful Meiji team.[115]

The winner-take-all matchup between Waseda and the University of Chicago had all the makings of a pitchers' duel; however, when the game got underway in front of a capacity crowd packed into the newly built stands at Totsuka Stadium, "The Maroon team started with a rush and scored four runs."[116] It was clear Takeuchi didn't have it that day, meanwhile Gubbins' fastball was so good that it seemed Waseda was surely doomed.[117] If they lost the series yet again, Tobita knew it would mean another long wait for a chance at redemption, and he doubted if "in the fever of a broken heart, it would be possible to endure another five years."[118] So Tobita pulled Takeuchi and replaced him with Fujimoto, then stared at the ground frozen with grief.[119]

But in the bottom of the fifth Waseda's luck started to change, as the number-seven hitter, Toshinobu Yasuda, swung at the first pitch he saw from Gubbins and hit a blooper into right field.[120] When Fujimoto followed this with a single past second, Norgren figured Waseda's number-nine hitter was going to bunt so he adjusted his infield accordingly.[121] Tobita recognized the trap, so he called Yukisato Nemoto over before he entered the box and told the left-hander to look for an inside pitch to pull.[122] Nemoto stepped to the plate and prayed for a changeup but got a fastball instead, yet somehow he still managed to turn on it and sent the ball "like a meteor through space" until it skimmed the outfield fence, scoring Yasuda and putting Fujimoto on third while Nemoto made it into second with a double.[123] Takehiko Yamazaki then belted a triple to right that pulled Waseda within one, but Gubbins finally settled down and got out of the inning.[124]

Entering the seventh, Norgren lifted his southpaw in favor of Macklind. The righty gave up a double to Shinjiro Iguchi and issued a walk to Kimitsugu Kawai.[125] With the right-handed Fujimoto due up, Tobita was faced with a tough decision: let his pitcher bat, or bring in a left-handed pinch-hitter. Although Fujimoto blew his chance by taking three straight strikes from Gubbins in the first game of the series, Tobita elected not to make a change, and what a decision this turned out to be, as Fujimoto took Macklind deep with a three-run homer over the center-field fence.[126] Waseda added to its lead in the eighth with Yamazaki sending one over the right-field wall, clouted its way to a 10-4 victory, and in the process won a series against the Maroons for the first time.[127]

It was a historic season in which Waseda swept Keio in the first Sōkei-sen fought in nearly two decades, then beat Hosei, Meiji, Rikkyu, and Imperial to secure the first Tokyo Big Six Baseball League championship. But looking back, Tobita would say that despite all this, "beating Chicago had a different flavor."[128] His players weren't as thrilled as they had been when they defeated Keio and Meiji, and the fans didn't seem as happy either, but Tobita went home in a dreamy state, and as he held his two children in his arms, tears rolled down his cheeks.[129] He thought to himself, "I had done what I had to do," believing his steep debt to the Waseda team and to his mentor, Abe, was at least partly repaid.[130] So the next day, without telling his wife his intentions, Tobita met with Abe and tendered his resignation.[131] His manager stared at him for a while, and then said, "I'll discuss it with my seniors."[132] But as much as Tobita respected Abe, he knew his decision could not be reversed, no matter what the circumstances, so he gathered his players on the first-base bench to say goodbye:

I was so full of gratitude that hot tears fell harshly on the players as I shook hands with each of them. They all hung their heads except one, Takeuchi, who said, "It's still good, don't you want to do more?" He sounded as if he was giving me an order in a ridiculous voice full of Kyoto dialect. Then as soon as I crossed the threshold at home, I said, "Hey, I quit coaching today." As expected, my wife looked a little surprised, but [my children] Tadahiro and Chuei suddenly shouted 'Banzai.'"[133]

The Maroons, despite losing their series to Waseda, returned home with a record of 19 wins, 8 losses, and 5 ties. Norgren would have to wait longer than expected for a rematch since Waseda decided to postpone its return tour until 1927. By then Waseda had a new coach, Tadao Ichioka, who was a catcher when Waseda hosted Chicago in 1915.[134] After the teams split two games, Norgren was redeemed as the Maroons clinched the 1927 series with a 9-3 win in the finale.[135]

Three years later, Norgren prepped his team for its 1930 Japan tour by playing 13 games while en route to Seattle, from where they set sail on August 20.[136] The coach later recalled, "Without exception, the boys played a class of ball that was encouraging when one contemplated the approaching contests in Japan."[137] By the time the Maroons arrived at Yokohama, Abe had retired from Waseda and was elected to the Diet in 1928, literally and figuratively getting off the sidelines in an attempt to stem the tide of militarism and advance a social democratic agenda.[138] Yet there were still two familiar faces to greet Norgren at the port, as both coach Ichioka and manager Takasugi were still with the team.[139] After taking the electric tram to Tokyo, Norgren and his squad of a dozen players were greeted with a rousing welcome from the Waseda students and then spent a half-hour posing for pictures and being filmed alongside the Japanese team.[140]

Chicago was to play two games apiece against Waseda, Keio, and Meiji at Jingu Stadium, with a capacity of 50,000, as well additional games vs. Waseda and other teams outside Tokyo.[141] In the opener, Chicago and Waseda both scored three runs in the first three frames, after which the Japanese scored five more runs and held on to win 8-5.[142] Then, as Norgren later recalled, "The going was hard! We were defeated in the next four games, by Waseda, 8 to 3, Keio, 4 to 2, and Meiji, 10 to 5, and 6 to 1."[143] Chicago finally won its first game of the tour when it bettered Keio, 2-1, but fell again to Waseda 7-6 in Yokohama.[144] Everything began to change, however, once the Maroons reached Takarazuka, where they outlasted Waseda, 6-4, in 10 innings, then beat them again the next day, 4-1.[145] Chicago went on to beat Kwansei, 6-4, and twice defeated Waseda's alumni, 3-1, and 4-1, before tying the Tokyo Club, composed of all-star collegiate graduates, 1-1, in 12 innings.[146]

One last game was to be played against Waseda in front of a large crowd in Maebashi, about four hours north of Tokyo, where Chicago completed its turnaround by beating its hosts, 4-1, and in the process clinched a series split with Waseda.[147] This was followed by a finale against the Waseda alumni who up to this point had never beaten Chicago, but this time the "old boys" finally broke through, scoring a run in the ninth to win 5-4.[148] Norgren later shared his reflections on the tour:

After being completely snowed under in the first five games of the series, the boys fought their way out from underneath and finished with a record of seven victories, seven defeats, and one tie. We broke even with Waseda and Keio, but Meiji holds two victories over us.

Five years ago I thought the popularity and the development of baseball in Japan had reached its peak. I found that in five years there was considerable growth in the popularity of baseball as well as in the proficiency of the teams. The keen rivalry which results in close games between the six teams of the University League in Tokyo has taken the fancy of fans, and their interest is greater in this series than it is in any series with a foreign team. While games with American college teams sometimes bring out crowds of about 25,000 spectators, the crucial games between the Tokyo universities has [sic] been known to attract a throng of 40,000 to 50,000 people. In the case of the championship series in the fall of 1929 between Waseda and Keio, they had a sell-out for both games which meant between 50,000 and 60,000 people. Naturally, such interest is due to the keen rivalry developed through the proficient performance of the members of the league. There is no doubt in my mind that only a champion college team can hope to win more than half of its games against Waseda, Keio, and Meiji Universities, as they are playing ball today. The day is past when a college team can make a clean sweep of the

series in Tokyo, unless it is a team of unusual calibre.[149]

For reasons not entirely clear, there was no return tour in 1931 and although Chicago had been traveling to Japan every five years since 1910, there was no tour in 1935, but Chicago once again welcomed Waseda back to the Midway in May 1936.[150] Now coached by Kyle Anderson, who was the leadoff hitter on Norgren's 1927 squad, Chicago rocked Shozo Wakahara and withstood a late rally to win 18-16.[151] The Japanese ace bounced back, striking out 17 in a 10-5 victory, then followed that with a no-hitter against Yale, but he failed to repeat his heroics in the rubber match with Chicago, as the Maroons routed Waseda and took the series with a 13-3 win.[152] That was the last time the two teams met for more than 70 years, so when Chicago finally returned, it truly marked the restart of a legendary rivalry.

Before taking the field on Easter Sunday in 2008, the Maroons donned suits while Waseda wore their student uniforms to attended Mass at Noboricho Cathedral, and then both teams paid their respects at Hiroshima's Peace Memorial Park.[153] Some of the Chicago players were familiar with their university's role in the development of the atomic bomb. (Manhattan Project scientists created the world's first nuclear reactor inside a makeshift laboratory built beneath the stands at old Stagg Field.)[154] Ahead of the trip, Maroon southpaw Nathan Ginsberg discussed the Chicago-Hiroshima connection with a reporter, yet noted, "As important as that is and as tough as it may be to concentrate, we want to go out and win a few games."[155] Indeed, most of the media attention focused on the history of the baseball rivalry itself, with pitcher Payton Leonhardt saying, "It has hit home with us that this is a tradition that has dated back far more than we can comprehend. That is what is driving us." Co-captain and outfielder Mike Serio added, "Every decision made, and every play we have, in the back of everyone's head is that we have to win in Japan," while co-captain and first baseman, Dominik Meyer admitted, "We will try to do our best and not embarrass ourselves."[156]

In the opener at Hiroshima Municipal Stadium, the Maroons were, in fact, embarrassed, losing 15-0 in front of some 14,000 fans. After Waseda's lopsided victory, a reception was held at which dignitaries praised the visitors, not for their performance that day, but for the historic role their school played both in the evolution of Waseda's team as well as baseball throughout Japan.[157] In the next game, played under the lights in the Osaka Dome, Serio scored his team's first run of the series, but Chicago was held scoreless the rest of the way while Waseda's up-and-coming batters scored six runs in the final three innings for an 8-1 win.[158]

Ahead of the finale at Seibu Dome, just outside Tokyo, Wasaburo Yawata, son of right fielder Kyosuke Yawata, who played against Chicago during Waseda's 1911 tour, presented flowers to Waseda coach Atsuyoshi Otake, while Junko Kuwano and her daughter Kiyoko presented a bouquet to Chicago coach Brian Baldea.[159] Junko's father was Goro Mikami, left fielder on Waseda's 1910-1911 tours, who after graduating from Waseda played in the United States for Knox College and then professionally for the barnstorming All Nations club.[160] A reporter noted at the time, "If this news is flashed around among the ball playing universities it ought to do more to cement peace and promote international good feeling than the tracts which are being scattered by many of the Japanese-American organizations."[161]

So as Junko watched along with Kiyoko and Wasaburo at her side, the Waseda team looked to secure its first ever series sweep of the Maroons on either side of the Pacific.[162] Then just as Merrifield prophesied over a hundred years before, the Japanese players proceeded to hit the American curves and made their share of the fun while on their way to a 10-0 victory, after which they bowed politely to the umpire.[163]

1910 UNIVERSITY OF CHICAGO GAMES IN JAPAN

Date	Place	Opponent	Score
October 4	Tokyo	Waseda University	9-2
October 6	Tokyo	Keio University	3-1
October 8	Tokyo	Waseda University	5-0
October 14	Tokyo	Keio University	2-1
October 18	Tokyo	Waseda University	15-4
October 19	Tokyo	Keio University	5-2
October 20	Tokyo	Tomon Club	11-2
October 25	Osaka	Waseda University	8-4
October 26	Osaka	Waseda University	20-0
October 27	Osaka	Waseda University	12-2

1915 UNIVERSITY OF CHICAGO GAMES IN JAPAN

Date	Place	Opponent	Score
September 24	Tokyo	Waseda University	5-3
September 26	Tokyo	Keio University	4-1
October 8	Tokyo	Tokyo Americans	20-0
October 9	Tokyo	Waseda University	2-0
October 11	Tokyo	Keio University	6-1
October 13	Tokyo	Waseda University	1-0
October 15	Tokyo	Keio University	3-0
October 16	Tokyo	Waseda University	5-0
October 19	Osaka	Waseda University	5-3
October 20	Osaka	Waseda Univesrity	5-3

1920 UNIVERSITY OF CHICAGO GAMES IN JAPAN

Date	Place	Opponent	Score
May 11	Tokyo	Waseda University	6-6
May 13	Tokyo	Keio University	1-0
May 15	Tokyo	Imperial University	5-0
May 17	Tokyo	Hosei University	4-1
May 19	Tokyo	Waseda University	4-2
May 21	Tokyo	Keio University	3-3
May 22	Tokyo	Keio University	1-2
May 25	Tokyo	Waseda University	0-2
May 28	Osaka	Waseda University	3-1
May 29	Osaka	Waseda University	3-4
June 1	Kyoto	Waseda University	4-3
June 2	Kobe	Kwansei Gakuin	6-4
June 7	Nagoya	Waseda University	8-1
June 10	Tokyo	Keio University	0-1

1925 UNIVERSITY OF CHICAGO GAMES IN JAPAN

Date	Place	Opponent	Score
September 23	Tokyo	Waseda University	2-0
September 26	Tokyo	Keio University	0-0
September 28	Tokyo	Meiji University	0-0
October 3	Tokyo	Meiji University	0-0
October 5	Tokyo	Waseda University	0-0
October 6	Tokyo	Keio University	3-2
October 12	Takarazuka	Waseda University	1-1
October 13	Takarazuka	Waseda University	0-1
October 15	Takarazuka	Takarazuka Club	7-6
October 17	Takarazuka	Daimai Club	1-2
October 18	Takarazuka	Takarazuka Club	8-5
October 30	Kokura	Montetsu	14-0
October 31	Fukuoka	Fukuoka All-Stars	12-3
November 4	Kyoto	Daimai Club	14-1
November 7	Nagoya	Nagoya Club	6-0
November 9	Tokyo	Waseda University	4-10

1930 UNIVERSITY OF CHICAGO GAMES IN JAPAN

Date	Place	Opponent	Score
September 5	Tokyo	Waseda University	5-8
September 6	Tokyo	Waseda University	3-8
September 9	Tokyo	Keio University	2-4
September 10	Tokyo	Meiji University	5-10
September 12	Tokyo	Meiji University	1-6
September 13	Tokyo	Keio University	2-1
September 15	Yokohama	Waseda University	6-7
September 19	Takarazuka	Waseda University	6-4
September 20	Takarazuka	Waseda University	4-1
September 22	Takarazuka	Kwansei Gakuin	6-4
September 24	Takarazuka	Tomon Club	3-1
September 25	Takarazuka	Tomon Club	4-3
September 27	Shizuoka	Tokyo Club	1-1
October 1	Maebashi	Waseda University	4-1
October 4	Sendai	Tomon Club	4-5

NOTES

(Article titles originally in Japanese have been translated into English)

1   "Opening Series Japan 2008," mlb.com/mlb/events/ opening_series/y2008/; Jodi S. Cohen, "Honoring Old Rivalry a World Away," *Chicago Tribune*, March 15, 2008: 1-2.

2   David Hilbert, "Chicago Baseball to Tour Japan," Uchicago.edu, February 15, 2008. http://athletics.uchicago.edu/news0708/bb-waseda-021408.htm.

3   Waseda Alumni Club, "Restart of Legend: Waseda University vs. the University of Chicago," Tokyo, NTT Quaris, 2008: 3.

4   Ernest Wilson Clement, "Duncan Baptist Academy," *American Baptist Missionary Union Ninety-First Annual Report* (Boston: Missionary Rooms, 1905), 276-277.

5   Suishū Tobita, *Fifty-Year History of the Waseda University Baseball Club* (Tokyo: Waseda University Baseball Club, 1950), 74-91.

6   Waseda University, *Centennial History of Waseda University: Volume II* (Tokyo: Waseda University Press, 1990), 146.

7   Waseda University, 149.

8   Fred Merrifield, "Love Baseball in Japan," *Chicago Tribune*, April 23, 1905: 9.

9   "Base Ball Team: 1900," *Cap and Gown: Volume VI* (Chicago: University of Chicago, 1901), 218-221; *They Went to Japan: Biographies of Missionaries of the Disciples of Christ* (Indianapolis: United Christian Missionary Society, 1949), 29-30; "Religious and Charitable," *Pittsburgh Press*, October 26, 1907: 5.

10   "Athlete as Missionary: Rev Alfred W. Place to Introduce Baseball and Football to Students of Japanese Universities," *Boston Globe*, October 28, 1907: 5.

11   Tobita, *Fifty-Year History*, 107, 113; "Certified Copy of the Registration of an American Citizen at the American Consulate-General, Yokohama, Japan," Deputy Consul General of the United States of America, January 20, 1911.

12   David E. Sumner, *Amos Alonzo Stagg: College Football's Greatest Pioneer* (Jefferson, North Carolina: McFarland, 2021), 149.

13   "Maroon Nine to Visit Japan," *Chicago Tribune*, June 19, 1910: 23.

14   Sumner, 149; "Maroons May Learn Tricks," *Chicago Tribune*, June 21, 1910: 10.

15   J.J. Pegues, "International Baseball," *Independent*, January 19, 1911: 70; Gerald R. Gems, *The Athletic Crusade: Sport and American Cultural Imperialism* (Lincoln: University of Nebraska Press, 2006), 36; "Miss Anna H. Marshall Becomes Wife of Fred Merrifield at Home Wedding," *Rock Island Argus*, September 5, 1907: 5.

16   Pegues, 70-71.

17   H. Orville Page, "Maroons on Trip of 19,000 Miles," *Chicago Tribune*, August 28, 1910: 25; "Undergraduate Life: The Japanese Trip," *University of Chicago Magazine* 3 no. 1, (1910): 50; Pegues: 70.

18   Robert W Baird, "The Longest and Most Successful Baseball Trip of All Time," *University of Chicago Magazine*, Autumn 1976: 56-59.

19   Pegues: 71-72.

20   Pegues: 71-72.

21   Pegues: 72.

22   H. Orville "Pat" Page, "Maroon Team Guests of Japs," *Chicago Tribune*, October 30, 1910: Sec. III, 4; Gilbert A. Bliss, "Bliss Writes Story of Arrival In Japan," *Daily Maroon*, October 28, 1910: 1-3; Katarzyna Joanna Cwiertka, *Modern Japanese Cuisine: Food, Power and National Identity* (London: Reaction Books, 2006), 14-15.

23   Page, "Maroon Team Guests."

24   Page, "Maroon Team Guests."

25   Page, "Maroon Team Guests."

26   Pegues: 72.

27   Pegues: 72.

28 "International Base-Ball Match at Waseda University, Ushigome, Tokyo," *Gurahikku (The Graphic)* 4, 1910: 233.

29 Waseda University, 575.

30 "International Baseball Match at Waseda," *Japan Times*, October 5, 1910: 6.

31 "International Baseball Match at Waseda;" "Invasion of the East," *Cap and Gown: Volume 16* (Chicago: University of Chicago, 1911), 12.

32 Pegues: 72.

33 Pegues: 73.

34 "International Baseball Match at Waseda," *Japan Times*, October 5, 1910: 6.

35 "International Baseball Match at Waseda," *Japan Times*, October 5, 1910: 6.

36 "International Baseball Match at Waseda," *Japan Times*, October 5, 1910: 6.

37 "International Baseball Match at Waseda"; Pegues, 73.

38 "The Supporters of Waseda," *Gurahikku (The Graphic)* 4, 1910: 217; "International Base-Ball Match at Waseda University: 251; Yujiro Koike and Yuko Kusaka, "The Theory of Human Building of Tobita Suishu in Baseball," 74. https://rose-ibadai.repo.nii. ac.jp/?action=pages_view_main&active_action=repository_view_main_ item_detail&item_id=17522&item_no=1&page_id=13&block_id=21; Suishu Tobita, *Thirty Years of Hot Ball: History of Japanese Baseball in the Early Days* (Tokyo: Chuo Koron Shinsha, 2005), 353-354.

39 "International Baseball Match at Waseda," *Japan Times*, October 9, 1910: 2; H. Orville "Pat" Page, "Page Writes of Conquests," *Chicago Tribune*, November 2, 1910: 11.

40 "International Baseball Match at Waseda," *Japan Times*, October 7, 1910: 6; "Invasion of the East," 12-13; Tobita, *Fifty-Year History*, 119; H. Orville "Pat" Page, "Clean Sweep for U. Of C. Ball Team," *Chicago Tribune*, November 16, 1910: 10.

41 H. Orville "Pat" Page, "Page Tells of Japan Trip," *Chicago Tribune*, December 28, 1910: 8; "Invasion of the East," 12.

42 Page, "Page Tells of Japan Trip."

43 Page, "Page Tells of Japan Trip."

44 H. Orville "Pat" Page, "Japs Treated to Real 'Thrillers,'" *Chicago Tribune*, November 22, 1910: 14; "Page Tells of Japan Trip."

45 "Maroon Nine Continues Victories Over Japs," *Chicago Tribune*, October 28, 1910: 11; Page, "Japs Treated to Real 'Thrillers'."

46 "Return from Japan," *University of Chicago Magazine* 3, Number 3, January 1911: 167.

47 "Return from Japan."

48 "Return from Japan."

49 "International Base-Ball Match at Waseda University: 233.

50 Tobita, *Fifty-Year History*, 118; Waseda University, 577; Koike and Kusaka, 74.

51 Koike and Kusaka, 72-74; Tobita, *Fifty-Year History*, 96; Tobita, *Thirty Years of Hot Ball*, 353-354.

52 "Abe Resigns as Waseda Manager," *Honolulu Advertiser*, April 1, 1911: 3; "Waseda Baseball Team Will Tour the United States," *Japan Times*, March 9, 1911: 6.

53 "Japanese Team Tour Schedule Given Out," *Washington Times*, April 8, 1911: 11.

54 "Professor Abe Lectures," *Daily Palo Alto*, May 1, 1905: 6; Robert K. Fitts, *Issei Baseball* (Lincoln: University of Nebraska Press, 2020), 57.

55 Shin Hashido, *Recent Baseball Techniques* (Tokyo: Hakubunkan, 1905), 199-208; Sheng-Lung Lin, "The Development of the New Bushido Yakyu Culture," *Journal of Physical Culture* 16, December 2014: 49-104.

56 Hashido, 199-208; Lin.

57 "Baseball and Peace," *Chicago Tribune*, March 29, 1911: 6.

58 "Jap Ball Team Arrives Today," *San Francisco Call*, April 13, 1911: 13; "American Tour of Waseda University (Japan) Team," *Official College Base Ball Annual for 1912* (New York: American Sports Publishing, 1912), 23-27.

59 "'Pat' Page Gains Bride in Athletic Romance," *Chicago Examiner*, June 15, 1911: 2; Tobita, *Fifty-Year History*, 122-123.

60 "Chicago Team Coming, Some Lively Games Expected by Local Nines," *Japan Times*, August 14, 1915: 5.

61 Waseda University, 1070; "20,000 Japs See Ball Game," *New York Times*, September 25, 1915: 13; H. Orville "Pat" Page, "Maroons Score Two Shutouts; Win Seven Straight in Japan," *Chicago Tribune*, November 13, 1915: 11; H. Orville "Pat" Page, Baseball Tour of the Far East, *Cap and Gown: Volume 21* (Chicago: University of Chicago, 1916), 273-275; Tobita, *Fifty-Year History*, 139-140.

62 H. Orville "Pat" Page, "Maroon Nine Sweeps Series; Wins Ten Straight in Japan," *Chicago Tribune*, November 16, 1915: 11.

63 John Husar, "Baseball in 1915: Have Yen, Will Travel," *Chicago Tribune*, April 20, 1973: Sec 3, 1.

64 "20,000 Japanese Fans Saw Chicago Varsity Team Win," *Boston Evening Globe*, September 24, 1915: 7; Tobita, *Fifty-Year History*, 14-23.

65 H. Orville "Pat" Page, "Japan Greets Maroon Team with Spirit," *Chicago Tribune*, October 24, 1915: 23; "20,000 Japanese Fans Saw Chicago Varsity Team Win."

66 *Cap and Gown: Volume 22* (Chicago: University of Chicago, 1917), 276-278.

67 Waseda University: Volume III: 517.

68 Tobita, *Thirty Years of Hot Ball*, 352-355.

69 Tobita, *Thirty Years of Hot Ball*, 355-360

70 Koike and Kusaka, 74.

71 Lin, 49-50.

72 Robert Whiting, *You Gotta Have Wa* (New York: Collier Macmillan, 1989), 38-39.

73 Tobita, *Thirty Years of Hot Ball*, 375.

74 Koike and Kusaka, 74.

75 "Pat Page Quits as Maroon Coach," *Quad City Times*, February 11, 1920: 21; "Dozen Maroons Named for Ball Tour of Orient," *Chicago Tribune*, April 2, 1920: 13.

76 Fred Merrifield, "1920 Baseball Team in Japan," *Cap and Gown: Volume 26* (Chicago: University of Chicago, 1921), 411.

77 Ted Curtiss, "High Spots on the Japan Trip," *Cap and Gown: Volume 26* (Chicago: University of Chicago, 1921), 413.

78 "The Baseball Schedule and Scores of the Games Played in Japan, 1920," *Cap and Gown: Volume 26* (Chicago: University of Chicago, 1921), 410.

79 Tobita, *Fifty-Year History*, 167.

80 "U. of Chicago Plays 6-6 Tie with Waseda College," *Chicago Tribune*, May 14, 1920: 12; Tobita, *Fifty-Year History*, 167.

81 Tobita, *Fifty-Year History*, 168.

82 Tobita, *Thirty Years of Hot Ball*, 290.

83 Tobita, *Thirty Years of Hot Ball*, 290-291.

84 "The Baseball Schedule and Scores of the Games Played in Japan, 1920."

85 Tobita, *Thirty Years of Hot Ball*, 291.

86 "Chicago University Baseball Nine Defeated Waseda at Kyoto," *Japan Times and Mail*, June 3, 1920: 8; "The Baseball Schedule and Scores of the Games Played in Japan, 1920."

87 "Chicago Wins Fast Ten Innings Game," *Japan Times and Mail*, May 15, 1920: 1; "Keio Nine Holds Chicago to Tie," *Japan Times and Mail*, May 22, 1920: 8; "The Baseball Schedule and Scores of the Games Played in Japan, 1920."

88 "The Baseball Schedule and Scores of the Games Played in Japan, 1920."

89 Tobita, *Thirty Years of Hot Ball*, 292-293.

90 Merrifield, "1920 Baseball Team in Japan," 411.

91 Tobita, *Fifty-Year History*, 176-182.

92 James Crusinberry, "Japs Play Well, But Bat in a Whisper, So Maroons Win, 4-2," *Chicago Tribune*, May 11, 1921: 18; "Maroons Win from Japanese Ball Team," *Decatur* (Illinois) *Herald and Review*, May 11, 1921: 4; "Japanese Win By 17 to 1," *New York Times*, May 12, 1921: 14; "Japs Nose Out Butler, 2 to 1," *Indianapolis Star*, May 15, 1921: 25, 35; Tobita, *Thirty Years of Hot Ball*, 61; Tobita, *Fifty-Year History*, 182.

93 "Japs Nose Out Maroons," *Quad City Times*, May 19, 1921: 7; Tobita, *Thirty Years of Hot Ball*, 61-62.

94 Tobita, *Thirty Years of Hot Ball*, 63-65; "Japs Nose Out Maroons": 7.

95 "The Waseda Series," *Cap and Gown: Volume 27* (Chicago: University of Chicago, 1922), 377; Tobita, *Thirty Years*, 65-66; "Japs Nose Out Maroons," 7.

96 Tobita, *Thirty Years of Hot Ball*, 66.

97 "Japanese Team Displays Real Diamond Class," *Salt Lake Herald-Republican*, May 13, 1916: 15; "Cal's Comments," *Green Bay Press Gazette*, September 10, 1921: 5.

98 "The Baseball Coach," *Cap and Gown*, Volume 31 (Chicago: University of Chicago, 1926), 409.

99 Tobita, *Thirty Years of Hot Ball*, 386-387.

100 "The Japanese Trip," *Cap and Gown:* Volume 27 (Chicago: University of Chicago, 1926), 415.

101 "Maroons Beat Waseda, 2-0," *Chicago Tribune*, September 24, 1925: 21; Luther A. Huston, "20,000 Tokyo Fans Cheer as Chicago Boy Fans Man with Bases Full in Ninth," *Tampa Tribune*, November 2, 1925: 11; "Japanese Trip," *Cap and Gown: Volume 31* (Chicago: University of Chicago, 1926), 415.

102 Tobita, *Thirty Years of Hot Ball*, 386-387; "Maroons Beat Waseda, 2-0," 21; "Huston.

103 Huston.

104 "Fourth Called Game for Chicago Maroons," *Honolulu Star-Bulletin*, October 6, 1925. Sec. II, 9; "Maroons and Waseda U. Nines Play Scoreless Tie," *Chicago Tribune*, October 6, 1925: 26; Tobita, *Thirty Years of Hot Ball*, 386-387; "The Japanese Trip," 415.

105 Nels Norgren, "The Japan Trip, The Seventh International Baseball Series," The University of Chicago Magazine, VOL. XVIII NO. 3, January 1926: 114.

106 "The Japanese Trip," 416.

107 "U. Of C. Nine Like Grid Team; Plays to a Tie," *Chicago Tribune*, October 13, 1925: 30; "The Japanese Trip," 416; "Maroons Lose to Waseda," *Chicago Tribune*, October 14, 1925: 32; Tobita, *Fifty-Year History*, 250;

108 "The Japanese Trip," 416-417.

109 Waseda, Centennial History, V. III: 517-525.

110 "Keio Loses First Tilt of Japan's Big Series," *Honolulu Advertiser*, October 20, 1925: 6; Waseda, Centennial History, V. III: 517-525.

111 Tobita, *Thirty Years of Hot Ball*, 386.

112 "The Japanese Trip," 417.

113 "The Japanese Trip," 417.

114 "The Japanese Trip," 417.

115 Tobita, *Thirty Years*, 116.

116 "The Japanese Trip," 417.

117 Tobita, *Thirty Years of Hot Ball*, 116.

118 Tobita, *Thirty Years of Hot Ball*, 387.

119 Tobita, *Thirty Years of Hot Ball*, 117.

120 Tobita, *Thirty Years of Hot Ball*, 326.

121 Tobita, *Thirty Years of Hot Ball*, 327.

122 Tobita, *Thirty Years of Hot Ball*, 327.

123 Tobita, *Thirty Years of Hot Ball*, 327.

124 Tobita, *Thirty Years of Hot Ball*, 328.

125 Tobita, *Thirty Years of Hot Ball*, 328.

126 Tobita, *Thirty Years of Hot Ball*, 327-328.

127 "The Japanese Trip," 417; Tobita, *Thirty Years of Hot Ball*, 328.

128 Tobita, *Thirty Years of Hot Ball*, 328.

129 Tobita, *Thirty Years of Hot Ball*, 388.

130 Tobita, *Thirty Years of Hot Ball*, 388.

131 Tobita, *Thirty Years of Hot Ball*, 388.

132 Tobita, *Thirty Years of Hot Ball*, 388.

133 Tobita, *Thirty Years of Hot Ball*, 388.

134 "Japanese Team Displays Real Diamond Class": 15; Tobita, *Fifty-Year History*, 266.

135 "Chicago Nine Scores Win Over Waseda Team," *Wisconsin State Journal* (Madison), June 2, 1927; "Waseda Evens Series; Beats Maroons," *Chicago Tribune*, June 3, 1927; "Maroons Beat Waseda," *Chicago Tribune*, June 8, 1927: 23; Tobita, *Fifty-Year History*: 266-267.

136 Nelson H. Norgren, "Japan Trip," *Cap and Gown: Volume 36* (Chicago: University of Chicago, 1931), 182.

137 Norgren, "Japan Trip," 182.

138 "Politics as Practiced in Orient Will Be Detailed by Speaker at Men's Meeting," *Mansfield* (Ohio) *News-Journal*, January 15, 1928: 5.

139 Tobita, *Fifty-Year History*, 298-304; Abe Resigns as Waseda Manager," *Honolulu Advertiser*, April 1, 1911: 3.

140 Nelson H. Norgren, "Ninth International Baseball Series," *University of Chicago Magazine*, December 1930: 71.

141 Norgren, "Ninth International Baseball Series": 72.

142 Norgren, "Japan Trip," 183.

143 Norgren, "Ninth International Baseball Series": 73.

144 "Maroon Ball Nine Loses to Waseda University, 7-6," *Chicago Tribune*, September 16, 1930: 24; Norgren, "Ninth International Baseball Series": 74; Tobita, *Fifty-Year History*, 304.

145 "Chicago Beats Waseda," *New York Times*, September 21, 1930: S6; Norgren, "Ninth International Baseball Series": 74; Tobita, *Fifty-Year History*, 304.

146 Norgren, "Ninth International Baseball Series,": 74; Tobita, *Fifty-Year History*, 304.

147 Norgren, "Ninth International Baseball Series": 74; Tobita, *Fifty-Year History*, 304.

148 Norgren, "Ninth International Baseball Series": 74.

149   Norgren, "Japan Trip," 185.

150   "Maroon Diamond Squad Faces Waseda University in Three Game Series Opening Friday," *Daily Maroon*, May 27, 1936: 4; "Waseda Is Due Tomorrow for Maroon Series," *Chicago Tribune*, May 27, 1936: 22.

151   "Maroon, Waseda Teams Split Two Weekend Games," *Daily Maroon*, June 2, 1936: 4.

152   "Maroons Defeat Waseda 13 to 3 to Win Series," *Chicago Tribune*, June 18, 1936: 24; Tobita, *Fifty-Year History*: 383-384; "Maroons, Waseda to Play Deciding Game Tomorrow," *Chicago Tribune*, June 16, 1936: 24; "Japanese Pitcher Hurls No-Hitter Against Yale," *Scranton Tribune*, June 9, 1936: 15.

153   "Baseball: Japan 2008 Blog," University of Chicago. edu, March 25, 2008. https://athletics.uchicago.edu/about/ history/travel_blogs/baseball_japan_2008_blog.

154   David N. Schwartz, "What It Was Like to Witness the World's First Self-Sustained Nuclear Chain Reaction," *Time* magazine, December 1, 2017.

155   Joe Lombardi, "Have Bat, Will Travel (Japan) Ex-Dobbs Ferry Standout Also Pitches for Chicago Squad," *White Plains* (New York) *Journal News*, March 18, 2008: 23.

156   Cohen, "Honoring Old Rivalry a World Away": 1-2.

157   "Baseball: Japan 2008 Blog."

158   Jodi S. Cohen, "U. of C. Team Wins Fans, but No Games, in Japan," *Chicago Tribune*, April 4, 2008: 2-8; "Baseball: Japan 2008 Blog."

159   Junko Kuwano, daughter of Goro Mikami, email correspondence, February 2022; "Baseball: Japan 2008 Blog."

160   "Japanese Baseball Player Captain of College Team," *Chicago Tribune*, April 11, 1915: 23; Kuwano; "Japan Tour 2008."

161   "Jap Will Lead Knox College Team," *Buffalo Commercial*, April 17, 1915: 8.

162   Kuwano.

163   "Waseda University 125th Anniversary Exchange Game March 25 at Seibu Dome," *Waseda Sports*, March 25, 2008; Kuwano; "Baseball: Japan 2008 Blog."

DECLARATION OF VICTORY: THE MEANING AND ACHIEVEMENTS OF THE STANFORD UNIVERSITY BASEBALL TEAM'S 1913 JAPAN TOUR

By Yusuke Suzumura

The Stanford University Baseball Team is closely connected to the development of baseball in Japan. This stems from 1904-05, when Waseda University was planning an expedition to the United States and negotiated with different universities there, and Stanford University was the first to respond. One of the reasons Stanford accepted Waseda's request was that Zentaro Morikubo was a student at Stanford and facilitated negotiations between the two universities.[1] Zentaro was the son of Sakuzo Morikubo, a member of the House of Representatives in Japan's Imperial Diet; Zentaro later became a member of the Japan Amateur Athletic Association and was appointed a member of the Japan Baseball Umpires' Association (an organization founded in 1916 with the intent of spearheading the establishment of baseball rules in Japan). As such, Zentaro Morikubo was a prominent figure in the baseball world at the time.[2]

The Waseda team traveled to the United States in 1905, played against the Stanford Cardinals twice, and lost both games. They lost because the Waseda team's play did not extend much beyond the rudimentary stages of throwing and hitting the ball, whereas the Stanford team approached the sport in an organized and systematic manner.[3]

Stanford and Keio players discuss the controversial ninth-inning call on May 29, 1913

53

On March 31, 1913, Keio University announced an invitation to the Stanford University baseball team to visit Japan later that spring.[4] At the time, St. Mary's College and Santa Clara University were the two best college baseball teams on the West Coast, and Stanford was second to these universities, alongside the University of California and the University of Washington. Stanford had won games against all of these universities before they visited Japan, and therefore Keio was "expected to probably lose."[5]

An 11-man contingent boarded the passenger ship *Nippon Maru* and departed San Francisco on May 10, 1913.[6] Graduate student R.W. Wilcox was the manager.[7] The players were Ray Maple, pitcher; Al Gragg, pitcher; Leslie Dent, catcher; Tom Workman, first base; Louis Cass, second base; Pete McCloskey, third base; Zeb Terry, shortstop; Arthur Halm, left field; Walter Argabrite, center field; and Heinie Beeger, right field.[8]

The trip was scheduled for 10 weeks, longer than any previous trip by a Stanford team. They planned to play at least 12 games, starting with Keio in Japan, with a two-week visit to Hawaii on the way home. Keio provided 7,000 yen ($3,500) to cover the trip expenses. In 1913, 7,000 yen was equivalent to approximately 28 million yen (approximately $240,000) in 2022.[9] In addition, the Stanford baseball team raised $200 from a match against the Santa Cruz Colored Giants; the university donated $250; and the Quadrangle Club donated $50, making for a total of $500.[10] With the funds provided from the Japanese side and the donations from Stanford, the large amount of money they were able to raise suggests high expectations for the trip in both countries.

The Stanford group arrived at Yokohama around 8 A.M. on May 27.[11] The *Japan Times* reported, "Immediately after the health inspection, the six-foot huskies were swarmed by a gang of newspaper reporters, and the Keio ball players and students who went out in a launch to meet them. 'Banzai' and college cheers were exchanged on the deck."[12] The team held a press conference at the request of the Japanese press, in which they described how they spent their time training during the 17-day voyage on the *Nippon Maru*. "Thankfully, the seas were calm, so we were able to practice every day. We still ended up dropping 15 of the four-dozen balls into the sea. However, perhaps because of the daily practice, everyone gained weight, with some of us gaining as much as 12 kg [about 26 pounds]."[13]

Obviously, the team had indulged in a comfortable lifestyle during the voyage. However, when the Stanford players arrived at Yokohama, despite their massive weight gain, their physiques drew little attention from the Japanese, who remarked only that their physiques were "imposing."[14]

By way of example, the *Yomiuri Shimbun* favorably introduced the players in the following terms: "They are all elegant young gentlemen, dressed in winter suits and caps. Their physiques seem particularly imposing when one looks at the All-Philippines Baseball Team. Based on this alone, they would seem to have the power to overwhelm the Japanese baseball world."[15]

The All-Philippines Baseball Team had come to Japan on May 10, and had planned to stay until June 1 and play a total of 10 games with Waseda, Keio, Meiji University, and Yokohama Commercial School.[16] Some of the games were canceled due to rain, and the Philippines team ended up playing eight games, of which it won only one, against Waseda, losing the other seven.[17]

The All-Philippines Baseball Team was said to have "selected the very best of Philippine baseball," with a total of 16 members, of which 13 were players, and one was a substitute. The players were generally of medium build and height, and while three had excellent physiques, another three were of smaller stature.[18] While the results of the games are not necessarily always decided on the basis of physique, when one considers that the Philippines team had won only one out of the eight games, it is perhaps unsurprising that people thought that physique played a part in the team's poor performance. The comment that "[t]heir physiques seem particularly imposing when one looks at the All-Philippines Baseball Team" can be taken not only as a comparison of the physiques of the All-Philippines players and the Stanford University players but also as an indication that there were high expectations for the latter based on the superiority of their physiques.

It should be noted that an article in the *Tokyo Asahi Shimbun* reported that "the players bore no signs of fatigue and were very comfortable during their 17-day voyage, with each gaining about 750 g [about 1.5 pounds]."[19] Compared with the *Yomiuri Shimbun* article, none of the players seems to have gained a large amount of weight. While it is difficult to judge which description is accurate, we can nevertheless deduce that the players did indeed gain weight during the voyage.

The Stanford team was evaluated favorably by the Japanese during their time in Japan, as illustrated by the *Tokyo Asahi Shimbun*: "They are all the very best of young gentlemen morally influenced by Dr. Jordan, who resembled a messenger of the god of peace, and they seem to be very pleasant and friendly upon first meeting in the American style."[20]

"Dr. Jordan" was David Starr Jordan, who became the first president of Stanford University in 1891 and also became the first chancellor of the university in June 1913. Jordan visited Japan frequently from 1900 to investigate his academic specialty of ichthyology, the study of fish.[21] Moreover, Jordan was a researcher, university administrator, anti-imperialist, and antiwar activist. Rather than his role as an ichthyologist and educator, the assessment of Jordan in Japan related to his opposition to the anti-Japanese-immigration movement in the United States, which was the most significant concern between the two countries at the time; he was on the side of the Japanese, arguing that "no parliament should pass the Japanese Exclusion Act."[22] In addition, he was described as "a great player for peace" who "loved peace and was convinced that peace was a global truth."[23]

Thus, the baseball players were depicted as gentlemen inspired by Jordan precisely because they were at Stanford University. In addition, the more distinctive players in the group were thus described:

> Pigeon-toed and with a liking for beans, Cass is the odd man out in the group – so pigeon-toed in fact that his fellows tease him every which way. He made everyone laugh by saying that he was going to advertise himself in the papers as a pigeon-toed rickshaw man when he arrived in Tokyo. Argabrite's family runs a bean shop, and he also has a great liking for beans, hence the nickname "Bean." Workman is extremely timid and never left his lifeboat during the voyage.[24]

While matters such as physique and family business have nothing to do with baseball itself, these topics were a good source of information to better know the players. The fact that such articles seeking to convey the personalities of the players were published, even if they were primarily intended to amuse the readers and satisfy their curiosity, demonstrates that people had a high level of interest in the Stanford University baseball team.

Having thus attracted people's attention, how did the Stanford players adjust once they were in Japan?

They started practicing at 1 P.M. on May 28 at Keio University's Tsunamachi Grounds, with the practice lasting for 1 hour and 30 minutes. Second baseman Cass hit a succession of home runs to left field and left fielder Halm hit "a fire-breathing home run like a powerful cannon" with a long shot to right field.[25] In defensive practice, the players threw the ball with machine-like accuracy, catching even difficult throws. Although they had not yet shown their full potential, the Stanford players were praised as "the epitome of the American national sport."[26]

The players' track records were good as well, and as a team they were the strongest since the Stanford University baseball team was founded. They were said to be among the best teams on the West Coast, having won four times and lost once against Santa Clara University, which had previously defeated the Waseda University baseball club, 10-2. The cleanup hitter was Louis Cass, and the ace pitcher was Ray Maple, a side-arm thrower. Maple, first baseman Tom Workman, and shortstop Zeb Terry had such a high level of skill that they had been invited to join professional clubs. Maple turned down an offer to join the Philadelphia Athletics, Walkman received an offer from the Boston Red Sox, and Terry was invited to join the Portland Beavers of the Pacific Coast League and later had a seven-year major league career.[27]

Given this context, it was thought that Keio, Meiji, and the Tomon Club, which consisted of graduates of the Waseda University baseball club, would not be able to compete with the Stanford team.[28] In fact, the Stanford team did not perform as well as its track record would have suggested.

The Americans played eight games in Tokyo: a five-game series against Keio, two games against Meiji University, and a game against Tomon. Then Stanford and Keio traveled together and played in Nagoya and Osaka. They did not play against Waseda because their schedules were incompatible.

The series with Keio began at the university's Tsunamachi Grounds in the Mita section of Tokyo on May 29. Maple took the mound for Stanford but Keio elected to start Shinryo Ishikawa, their second-string pitcher, to measure the visitors' ability. The Cardinals jumped out to a 2-0 lead in the second inning, but Ishikawa remained steadfast and shut out the Americans for the remainder of the afternoon. Meanwhile, Maple limited Keio to just three hits and a single run as Stanford held a 2-1 lead going into the ninth inning.

Maples began the ninth by walking first baseman Shoji Goto, who was lifted for pinch-runner Daisuke Miyake. After a strikeout, Shigeru Takahama singled to right field, where Heinie Beeger bobbled the ball, allowing the runners to advance to second and third. With the tying and winning runs in scoring position, Shungo Abe strode to the plate. On the next pitch, Miyake broke toward the plate as Abe swung and missed. Caught in a rundown between third and home, Miyake scampered back to third, beating the throw, but his momentum carried him over the base. With Miyake's feet off the bag, McCloskey applied the tag and then threw to shortstop Terry and he tagged out Takahama, who had strayed off second. Sure of the inning-ending double play, Terry dropped the ball near the mound and the Cardinals walked off the field. Seconds later, Miyake trotted home and stepped on the plate. After a brief conference, the umpire ruled that Miyake had been safe at third and his run counted. Without a loud protest, the Stanford players returned to their positions and recorded the final out. The 2-2 deadlock continued until the top of the 12th inning when a hit batsman, a force out, a stolen base, and a single gave Keio a run and the 3-2 victory.[29]

After the game, reporters and fans condemned both the umpires and the Keio players for taking advantage of the obvious missed call.[30] The Stanford team's attitude was praised thusly, "It is a mark of their generosity that, by the grace of the American gentlemanly temperament, Miyake was allowed to carry on without their contesting the decision."[31]

On the last day of May Stanford sent Al Gragg to the mound against Shunichi Nakamura and his Meiji University teammates. The two pitchers were nearly untouchable: Gragg surrendered just three hits and a walk while Nakamura held the Cardinals to a single hit and a base on balls. The score was 0-0 when Argabrite led off the top of the ninth with a bunt single. As Argabrite broke for second, Workman laid down a bunt between first base and the mound. Nakamura fielded it but his throw glanced off Workman, and as first baseman Takase retrieved the ball, Argabrite raced around the bases to score the winning run.[32]

After opening game, Keio pounded Stanford in their second meeting. "The American nine was so completely smashed," wrote the *Japan Times*, "that it was a painful task to find and gather up the fragments that lay scattered round … [the diamond]." Keio batters managed only four walks and six hits off Maple, but four of the hits were doubles and the porous Stanford defense committed seven errors as the Japanese scored eight runs. Kazuma Sugase, the tall, bespectacled Keio captain, "shone brighter than the aurora borealis on the mound and with the ash" as he held the Cardinals to three runs on five hits and went 2 for 3 with two doubles and two runs scored at the plate.[33] The magazine *Yakyukai* praised the outcome as "a superb victory for the Mita army."[34]

The rout continued in the second game against Meiji. "Meiji Slaughters Stanford," the *Japan Times* headlined its report. A hard rain left the diamond in poor condition and the "muddy and slippery ground made it difficult for the infielders, and incidental fun was provided more than once. When a runner slid into a base, he generally got up with a thick coating [of] mud."[35] Gragg took the mound for Stanford but Meiji found him "an easy proposition and got to him fast and furious," as it cruised to a 5-2 victory.[36]

After consecutive blowouts, the reporter for the *Japan Times* wrote, "With his heart down in his boots and with a trembling hand, the scribe pens his obituary on the passing of the Cardinals."[37] But the writer had dismissed the visiting Americans too quickly. On June 8 they stormed back in the third game against Keio. Perhaps overconfident, Keio put Ishikawa instead of Sugase on the mound and "like a wounded and frenzied tiger, the Cardinals turned on the Keio gladiators with a snarl and deadly ferocity, and chewed them up."[38] As Maple was no-hitting Keio through the first eight innings, Stanford scored single runs in the third and fifth before breaking the game open with six runs in the seventh. In the bottom of the ninth, Miyake and then Goto singled to foil Maple's no-hit game, but neither scored as Stanford won 8-0.

Keio's boisterous fans took their frustrations out on the umpire, Lieutenant Burnett of the American Embassy. According to the *Japan Times*:

Many of his decisions on balls and strikes were strongly protested from the bleachers and grandstand. In addition, he made a few close decisions on bases and at the plate. ... The howls of protest from the bleachers developed into a united uproarious denunciation of the arbiter. Jeering cheers and ovations were given him every now and again. Immediately after the game, the Keio players went and shook hands with Lieutenant Burnett one by one. …

While Lieutenant Burnett was shaking hands, a large crowd of unthankful and enraged fans rushed about him from all directions to mob him. A policeman, Keio professors, and

Keio and Stanford players with baseball bats straightaway stood guard round Mr. Burnett. The threatening mob rapidly gained in size every second. The mob was highly worked up and would have struck at nothing. "Kill him! – Eat him up!" Hysterical outbursts of indignation were uttered repeatedly to stir the mob. Nothing could have stopped the excited mob, but for the appeasing, even appealing, efforts of Keio professors and students.[39]

As expected, Stanford had little trouble with the Waseda alumni team, the Tomon Club, on June 12.[40] The Tomon Club's lineup included future Japanese Hall of Famers Shin Hashido, Kiyoshi Oshikawa, and Chujun Tobita as well as Goro Mikami, who a few months later left for the United States to play for Knox College in Illinois and later for the professional All Nations barnstorming team. But with the exception of Mikami, these great players were past their prime. The former stars played a sloppy game, committing 11 errors and walking six batters, as Stanford won 6-1.[41]

On June 14 Maple once again took the mound for the Cardinals, but this time Keio countered with its ace, Sugase. According to the *Japan Times*, the two "fought for all they were worth. … Where Maple had speed, Sugase had curves; where one had mystifying floaters; the other had nasty underhand smokers; where one had the name of the best pitcher Stanford ever had, the other was cracked up to be the most clever and heady slabster that ever honored the Japanese diamond."[42] For seven innings the aces matched each other. Maple allowed just one hit, Sugase just two. Neither walked a batter nor allowed a run. But in the top of the eighth, Sugase hit Arthur Halm with an inside curve. Weak-hitting Pete McCloskey then slashed a single between third and short, moving Halm to third. A fly ball by Maple scored Halm and won the game, 1-0. The Stanford victory evened the series at two wins apiece and set up a game 5 showdown on the following afternoon.

Despite pitching a complete game the day before, Sugase took the mound again for Keio in the final matchup. Stanford rested Maple and countered with Gragg. Once again, the Japanese hit Gragg hard. Keio began the game with back-to-back doubles by Kenichi Kakeyama and Miyake, followed by an RBI single by Goto and another double by Akira Kusaka. Goto and Kusaka were left on base but Keio added two more runs in the fourth and another in the fifth to build a 5-0 lead. Meanwhile, Sugase "stood on the mound as firmly as Fuji-yama and showed himself as formidable and impregnable as a Dreadnought. His delivery was the goods of smoky, fast breaking, and hypnotic brand."[43] The Cardinals scored a lone run in the ninth as Sugase cruised to a 5-1 victory to capture the series.

The two teams next traveled west for a three-game series with a match in Nagoya and two in Osaka. Away from Tokyo, Stanford dominated Keio, winning 4-0 on June 17 in Nagoya, romping, 10-0, on June 21 in Osaka, and finishing the sweep with a 5-4 victory the following day as 25,000 watched in Osaka. On June 28 the Stanford Cardinals boarded the ocean liner *Nippon* and after a rousing sendoff by the Keio ballplayers, headed for Hawaii.[44] Stanford stayed in Honolulu for about three weeks, winning six of the nine games against the U.S. All-Service team, the Punahou School, alumni from the St. Louis School and the Portuguese Athletic Club.[45]

Although the Cardinals ended their tour of Japan with a 6-4 record, their losses disappointed their hosts. We may ask why the Stanford team did not live up to expectations in Japan. As we have already seen, one of the major reasons may have been poor management of the team's physical condition during their long voyage to Japan. Other reasons may have included poor field conditions and being insufficiently prepared for the environment – games were postponed by rain, indicating that the ground was still muddy when the games were played. Their performance may have been impacted by the fact that Maple, their ace pitcher, did not pitch as well as expected by someone who was being invited into the world of professional baseball.[46] Furthermore, their second pitcher, Gragg, was not effective, losing twice.

Overall Stanford outhit and outscored Keio. Stanford recorded 58 hits and 34 runs in eight games against Keio, 24 more hits and 14 more runs than Keio (Table 1). Stanford won five games; Keio won three. Therefore, although Stanford had the upper hand over Keio in terms of batting power, they appear to have been close in terms of overall strength including pitching and defensive ability.

TABLE 1: THE RESULTS OF THE GAMES BETWEEN STANFORD UNIVERSITY AND KEIO UNIVERSITY.

Teams	Wins	Game #	1	2	3	4	5	6	7	8	Total
Stanford University	5	Runs Scored	2	3	8	1	1	4	10	5	34
		Hits	9	4	14	4	5	5	10	7	58
Keio University	3	Runs Scored	3	8	0	0	5	0	0	4	20
		Hits	5	6	3	1	6	4	2	7	34

Although the Stanford team drew significant attention upon its arrival in Japan, the newspaper coverage dwindled as the team moved through the games with each university, with articles reporting their return to the United States appearing only in the bottom corner of the paper.[47]

The situation was the same back at Stanford University. Certainly, the *Stanford Daily* printed a group photo of the Stanford and Keio players with the caption "In the Land of the Chrysanthemum," and an explanation that the team had gone to a place 6,000 miles away from their homeland, played baseball with Japanese universities, and enjoyed Japanese culture including visiting the ancient city of Kyoto. However, compared with the detail provided when the team set off on its trip, there was little coverage after it returned from a tour in which it was victorious but not overwhelmingly so.[48]

In Japan, the Stanford team was criticized. "At first we had high expectations for them and were greatly disappointed," alluding to the Japanese proverb, "When I actually see Mt. Fuji, it is lower than I had heard." Stanford's points to be commended were only two: Terry's defense, baserunning, and captaincy, and Maple's control of the slow ball.[49] The evaluations – "they were not too bad" and "the Stanford team had better hitting, so Keio, which had a better battery but inferior hitting, was defeated finally" – also suggest the disappointment in Japan with the large difference between the visitors' prior reputation and the actual results of the games.[50]

Does this mean that Stanford University's trip to Japan in 1913 was a fruitless endeavor? If we focus solely on games won and lost, the Stanford team failed to achieve its intended purpose in the sense that it did not win a resounding victory against the developing Japanese student baseball teams. However, from the perspective of promoting friendship and goodwill between Japan and the United States through baseball, the trip was of great value. Zeb Terry, who began his seven-year major-league career with the Chicago White Sox in 1916 and is considered "one of the greatest baseball players in Stanford history," considered the trip to Japan a "treasured" memory.[51] Terry and the Stanford players were overwhelmed by the VIP treatment by the Japanese.[52]

The Stanford team visited various places around Tokyo between games. On June 5 they saw a performance of *Kanadehon Chushingura* at the Kabuki-za Theater and paid a courtesy visit to the legendary kabuki actor Onoe Kikugoro VI, who was known to be a baseball enthusiast. In addition, on June 6, at the invitation of the Imperial Theater, the team accompanied the Keio players to performances of Mozart's opera *The Magic Flute*, Puccini's opera *Tosca*, as well as a performance of the kabuki play *Terutora Haizen* by Chikamatsu Monzaemon starring Matsumoto Koshiro VII. On the day of the performance, Sada Yacco, who had starred in *Tosca,* presented handheld fans as souvenirs to the players of both universities, and the Stanford team presented her with a bouquet in return. These events can be seen as a sign of goodwill between Japan and the United States outside the stadium.[53]

Thereafter, at a reception held at the Kojunsha Club on June 2 for the Stanford and Keio players, manager Wilcox said on behalf of the American team: "We are delighted that our visit to Japan on this occasion has given us the opportunity to truly learn about Japanese customs and culture, and we hope that gathering together players from both universities will contribute to the friendship between Japan and the United States both today and in the future."[54] These words indicate that, from the perspective of US-Japan relations, the Stanford team's visit to Japan went beyond baseball games, also serving as a platform for exchange for the young representatives of both Japan and the United States.

1913 STANFORD UNIVERSITY GAMES IN JAPAN

Date	Place	Opponent	Score	Winner	Loser
May 29	Tokyo	Keio University	2-3	Ishikawa	Maple
May 31	Tokyo	Meiji University	1-0	Gragg	Nakamura
June 1	Tokyo	Keio University	3-8	Sugase	Maple
June 4	Tokyo	Meiji University	2-5	Nakamura	Gragg
June 8	Tokyo	Keio University	8-0	Maple	Ishikawa
June 12	Tokyo	Tomon Club	6-1	Halm	Oi
June 14	Tokyo	Keio University	1-0	Maple	Sugase
June 15	Tokyo	Keio University	1-5*	Gragg	Sugase
June 17	Nagoya	Keio University	4-0	Maple	Sugase
June 21	Osaka	Keio University	10-0	Unknown	Unknown
June 22	Osaka	Keio University	5-4	Maple	Sugase

* *According to the* Stanford Daily, *the final score of this game was 6-1, not 5-1. See "On the Trip,"* Stanford Daily, *September 2, 1913: 9.*

NOTES

1 Gantetsu Hashido, "A Team Which Has a Close Relationship with Japan," *Yakyukai*, 3(8), 1913: 2-3.

2 Sheng-Lung Lin, *Samurai Baseball Culture in Taiwan During the Period of Japan's Colonization*, Waseda University, Doctoral Dissertation, 2012, 102-103.

3 Hashido.

4 "Keio University Invites Stanford University," *Tokyo Asahi Shimbun*, April 1, 1913: 5.

5 Hashido.

6 Masao Shimakura, "A Study of the Pacific Line as the Stage of Ship's Band: A History of the Development from Meiji to Early Showa Eras," *Abstracts of the 2017 Annual Meeting, The Human Geographical Society of Japan*, 108-10; "Stanford Has Come," *Yomiuri Shimbun*, May 27, 1913: 3.

7 "Cardinal Ball Players Sail for Land of Mikado," *Stanford Daily*, May 19, 1913: 16.

8 "Cardinal Ball Players Sail for Land of Mikado."

9 Yuichi Yoshino, "How Much Is Old 'One Yen' Today?" Mitsubishi UFJ Trust and Banking Cooperation, October 7, 2020, https://magazine.tr.mufg.jp/90326 (accessed on February 6, 2022).

10 "Eleven Men Sail for Japan Saturday Noon," *Stanford Daily*, May 7, 1913: 4.

11 "Declaration of Victory," *Yomiuri Shimbun*, May 28, 1913: 3.

12 "Stanford Sends a Hummer," *Japan Times*, May 28, 1913: 1.

13 "The Arrival of the Players of Stanford University," *Tokyo Asahi Shimbun*, May 28, 1913: 5.

14 "Declaration of Victory."

15 "Declaration of Victory."

16 "The Schedule of Games Against the All Philippines Baseball Team," *Yomiuri Shimbun*, May 5, 1913: 3.

17 "Final Score: Yokohama Commercial School 6, All Philippines Baseball Team 4," *Tokyo Asahi Shimbun*, June 1, 1913: 5.

18 "The Arrival of the Players of the All Philippines Baseball Team," *Tokyo Asahi Shimbun*, May 12, 1913: 5.

19 "The Arrival of the Players of the All Philippines Baseball Team."

20 "The Arrival of the Players of Stanford University."

21 Koichi Shibukawa, "The Fishes of Shizuoka: A History of Fish-Fauna Research and Some Future Perspectives," in Yoshinori Yasuda and Mark J. Hudson, eds., *Multidisciplinary Studies of the Environment and Civilization: Japanese Perspectives* (New York: Routledge, 2017), 17-18.

22 "Dr. Jordan's View Against the Issue Concerning with Japanese People," *Yomiuri Shimbun*, February 8, 1907: 2.

23 "The Great Ambassador of the Peace Has Come," *Tokyo Asahi Shimbun, August* 27, 1911: 5.

24 "Declaration of Victory."

25 "How Did the Players of Stanford University Practice?" *Tokyo Asahi Shimbun*, May 29, 1913: 5.

26 "How Did the Players of Stanford University Practice?"

27 "Declaration of Victory," "Stanford Sends a Hummer."

28 Hashido.

29 "Keio Beats Stanford Boys," *Japan Times*, May 30, 1913: 1.

30 "The First Game Against Keio University," *Yakyukai* 3, no. 8 (1913): 28-29.

31 "The Baseball Games between Japan and the USA (The First Day)," *Tokyo Asahi Shimbun*, May 30, 1913: 5.

32 "Stanford Wins Close Game," *Japan Times*, June 1, 1913: 1.

33 "Keio Klouts Kalifornia," *Japan Times*, June 3, 1913: 1.

34 "The Second Game Against Keio University," *Yakyukai* 3, no. 8 (1913): 35-36.

35 "Meiji Slaughters Stanford," *Japan Times*, June 5, 1913: 1.

36 "Meiji Slaughters Stanford."

37 "Meiji Slaughters Stanford."

38 "Stanford Defeats Keio," *Japan Times*, June 10, 1913: 1.

39 "Stanford Defeats Keio."

40 "The Game Against the Tomon Club," *Yakyukai* 3, no. 8 (1913): 45.

41 "California Beats Tomon," *Japan Times*, June 13, 1913: 1.

42 "Stanford Defeats Keio," *Japan Times*, June 15, 1913: 1.

43 "'Assimilate' B.B. All Right," *Japan Times*, June 17, 1913: 1.

44 "Stanford B.B. Boys Happy," *Japan Times*, June 29, 1913: 8.

45 "On the Trip," *Stanford Daily*, September 2, 1913: 9.

46 "Review of the Games against Stanford University," *Yakyukai* 3, no. 8 (1913): 88-89.

47 "The Last Win of the Stanford University Team," *Tokyo Asahi Shimbun*, June 28, 1913: 5.

48 "Stanford Ball Team Wins Majority of Games in Orient," *Stanford Daily*, September 1, 1913: 1.

49 Taguchi Oson, "We Overestimated Them a Little," *Yakyukai* 3, no. 8 (1913): 8.

50 Koyama Mango, "They Were Not Too Bad," *Yakyukai* 3, no. 8 (1913): 7-8.

51 Don Liebendorfer, *The Color of Life Is Red: A History of Stanford Athletics, 1892-1972* (Palo Alto: National Press, 1972), 230; Niall Adler, "Zeb Terry," Society for American Baseball Research, BioProject, https://sabr.org/bioproj/person/zeb-terry/ (accessed on April 10, 2022).

52 Adler.

53 "Visit to the Imperial Theater," *Yakyukai* 3, no. 8 (1913): 95.

54 "The Stanford University Baseball Team's Movements," *Yakyukai* 3, no. 8 (1913): 93-94.

THE 1913-14 CHICAGO WHITE SOX-
NEW YORK GIANTS WORLD TOUR

By Stephen D. Boren and James E. Elfers

INTRODUCTION
BY STEPHEN D. BOREN

On January 27, 1913, John McGraw of the National League champion New York Giants and Charles Comiskey, owner of the American League Chicago White Sox, announced their plans for a world tour to be held after the 1913 World Series.[1] The tour would be modeled after the 1888-1889 "Great Baseball Trip Around the World" when A.G. Spalding's Chicago National League Club, led by captain Adrian "Cap" Anson, and a team selected from the National League and American Association by John M. Ward traveled the globe playing in New Zealand, Australia, Ceylon, (Egypt, and Europe.[2] When Comiskey heard of the Spalding world trip he supposedly stated, "Someday I will take a team of my own around the world."[3]

The tour would begin in Cincinnati and the teams would barnstorm across the country until they reached Vancouver, British Columbia, on November 19. From there, they would sail to Japan, China, the Philippines, Australia, Ceylon, Egypt, Italy, France, and the United Kingdom, before returning to New York on March 6, 1914. Comiskey's close friend Ted Sullivan, a former manager and minor league executive, was named the advance scout to organize the tour, and sailed from

Keio University with the New York Giants and Chicago White Sox December 7, 1913
(Library of Congress, Prints & Photographs Division, LC-DIG-ggbain-16209)

San Francisco to Honolulu, Japan, and Australia. While Spalding's tour had supposedly broken even, Sullivan felt that this one would make money. A few months later, Comiskey's advance agent, Dick Bunnell, sailed for Europe to complete the arrangements on that continent.[4]

In June 1913, after White Sox manager James Callahan "called on President Woodrow Wilson to explain the proposed world tour … Wilson expressed his approval not only because he said he considered himself a base ball fan, but because he thought the movement might result in the creation of an international league."[5] Wilson also thought the tour might help advance international peace and amity.[6]

Many New York players were not enthusiastic about the proposed tour. The original plan required each person to personally put up $1,500 for expenses and for all to share equally in the profits. The players thought it would be a great trip but too expensive.[7] The sponsors understood the players' reluctance to make the financial commitment. McGraw initially refused to discuss the trip until the Giants were sure of winning the pennant and thus a share of the World Series money, until on July 29 he held a team meeting and for the first time officially informed his players of the world tour. He showed them the financial arrangements and received a large number of positive commitments, from Christy Mathewson and Chief Meyers among others. Meanwhile, Comiskey and Callahan began contacting players from other American League teams in case their players refused to go under the proposed conditions.[8]

On September 24 Charles Comiskey announced that 75 people would go on the World Tour. Each player would be required to post $300 to guarantee his appearance on the ship but once on board, the money would be refunded. For such an unprecedented tour with so many passengers, great logistic and fiscal planning was needed, and both Comiskey and McGraw were prepared to write checks of $100,000 to defray additional expenses.[9]

On October 7 Harry M. Grabiner, Comiskey's personal representative, announced that he was finalizing the plans for the massive around-the-world trip. He said he expected the tour to be the largest sporting event ever. Preliminary reports from foreign countries suggested that baseball would be a worldwide topic before the players returned home. Grabiner said he had multiple requests for exhibition games from American Western cities. The tour was advertised like a circus with long billboard posters. Arrangements were made to film the games in foreign cities, as well as life on the ship and receptions with foreign monarchs and ambassadors.[10]

The tour left Chicago on the night of October 19 on a special train of five all-steel cars including an observation car and a combination baggage and buffet car. This traveling hotel was the party's home as they barnstormed across the Midwest and West Coast, playing 31 games in 27 cities, before sailing for Japan from Vancouver a month later.[11]

By the time the teams reached Vancouver, their rosters had shrunk. Christy Mathewson and Chief Meyers decided not to accompany the teams across the Pacific. To even the squads, the White Sox loaned Urban "Red" Faber to the Giants.[12] The final Giants roster consisted of pitchers Bunny Hearn (Giants), George Wiltse (Giants), and Faber (White Sox); catcher Ivey Wingo (Cardinals); first baseman Fred Merkle (Giants); second baseman Larry Doyle (Giants); third baseman Hans Lobert (Phillies); shortstop Mickey Doolin (Phillies); and outfielders Lee Magee (Cardinals), Jim Thorpe (Giants), and Mike Donlin (Giants).[13]

Of the 11 "New York" players, there were only three pitchers. There were no backup infielders, outfielders, or catchers. Counting Mike Donlin, who did not play in the major leagues in 1913 (he did return to the Giants in 1914), there were only six actual members of the New York Giants, and of those six, only Merkle and Doyle were regulars. Hearn had been in only two games (1-1 record) and Wiltse had not won a single game.

In the end, few of the White Sox players were willing to go. Of the 13 players on the roster, only six were White Sox and one was manager Callahan, who had played in only six games all season. There were three pitchers but no backup infielders. The official "White Sox" roster consisted of pitchers Jim Scott (White Sox), Joe Benz (White Sox), and Walter Leverenz (St. Louis Browns); catchers Andy Slight (Des Moines, Western League) and Jack Bliss (Cardinals); first baseman Tom Daly (White Sox); second baseman Germany Schaefer (Washington Senators); shortstop Buck Weaver (White Sox); third baseman Dick Egan (Brooklyn Robins); and outfielders Tris Speaker (Red Sox), Sam Crawford (Tigers), and Steve Evans (Cardinals). Jack Bliss had previously been to Japan as a member of the 1908 Reach All-Americans.

Besides the 24 players, the party included McGraw; Comiskey; umpires Bill Klem and Jack Sheridan;

Chicago secretary N.L. O'Neil; A.P. Anderson (manager of the tour); Dick Bunnell (manager and director of the tour); Ted Sullivan (author and lecturer); and Chicago newspaper writers Gus Axelson (*Record-Herald*) and Joseph Farrell (*Tribune*). There were also wives, McGraw's personal physician, Dr. Frank Finley, several children, and other friends.[14]

On November 19, 1913, the tourists boarded the RMS *Empress of Japan* in Vancouver and began their journey across the Pacific. For 17 days, the passengers endured tossing seas, driving rains, and even a typhoon. Most of the players suffered from seasickness and some, like Tris Speaker and Red Faber, could barely eat.[15] On December 6 they finally arrived in Yokohama, three days behind schedule. Prior to their arrival, only three American college squads and one professional team had traveled to Japan. The lone professional team, the Reach All-Americans, consisted mostly of minor-league players with a smattering of undistinguished major leaguers. McGraw and Comiskey's clubs would showcase major-league stars to the Japanese fans for the first time.

THE LAND OF THE RISING SUN[16]
BY JAMES E. ELFERS

Nothing, absolutely nothing, prepared the tourists for the reception they received in Japan. More like a homecoming than greetings from a foreign nation, the docks were a riot of color, teeming with droves of fans and sportswriters. Japan was every bit as mad about baseball as was the United States. Under gray, raw skies, amid the crowd of rabid baseball fans, US consul general Thomas Sammons ferried out in a tug to be the first to greet the tourists. Accompanying Sammons were several Japanese officials and sportswriters who served as the welcoming committee. While the Japanese needed interpreters to converse with the players, many of them knew at least one American phrase, greeting the players with a big "Howdy!"[17]

The ballplayers found the local press corps every bit as savvy as their US counterparts. In an impromptu press conference, they asked penetrating questions and made pithy observations. "The great manager McGraw's pin made of diamond on his necktie was shining with the rising sun," wrote a reporter for *Jiji Shimpo*, a Tokyo daily.[18] A reporter for the *Keihin Press* asked about game strategy: "What strategy would the managers employ against each other and against Keio University?"[19]

The Americans were more candid with the Japanese press corps than they had been with their own. When disappointed reporters asked why Mathewson had not come, the tourists replied, "He was a bad sailor and also he didn't like the ship. We tried to bring him but he declined."[20]

The Japanese press was also disappointed not to find Jeff Tesreau and Fred Snodgrass among the players disembarking from the *Empress of Japan*. Nonetheless, they dutifully listed the names of every player and other tourists in the party. The Japanese media were particularly taken with Comiskey. Witness this quote from the *Keihin Press*: "Callahan, the manager of the Chicago team, and Comiskey were in high spirits. He is a dauntless looking man who also looked the gentleman."[21]

After making their way through the crush of well-wishers and reporters, some of whom had even boarded the ship to get interviews, the party made its way to customs and examinations by doctors. Some members of the party, especially the women, were a bit apprehensive at what to expect, but everyone sailed through. The processing completed; the tourists boarded rickshas to take them to the consul general's residence. Germany Schaefer immediately dubbed them "gin rickeys" (a pun based on the then-current pronunciation of the word for the vehicles, "jinrickshas").[22]

Comiskey, Callahan, and McGraw chose a different mode of transport. Accompanied by their families, they rode in automobiles to the consulate. Just as in the United States, every luxury materialized for the tourists' use. The only tourist not enjoying himself was Red Faber, still languishing on board the *Empress*. The ship's surgeons would not allow the former Iowa farm boy out of the sickbay until he was strong enough to rejoin his teammates.

After a brief meeting with consul general Sammons at his residence, it was back into rickshas and cars for the trip to the Grand Hotel. Throngs of Japanese tagged along behind the cars and rickshas to the consul's residence. This same throng shadowed the tourists to the Grand Hotel. Rest was not on the agenda, however. About all the players had time for was to check in and change; a game was scheduled for that afternoon at the baseball grounds at Keio University. The players were forced to play even before they had lost their sea legs.[23]

Owing to the lateness of the arrival of the *Empress*, the tourists' schedule in Japan had to be trimmed by two games. Cut were the games scheduled for Kobe and Osaka. Three contests remained, all of them in Tokyo.

For the players, just being in Japan was an accomplishment in itself. Joe Farrell noted, "The fans can now understand why base ball world tours are 25 years apart. It takes that long to forget the initiation on the Pacific."[24]

Arrival at the Grand Hotel precipitated a flurry of activity. Joe Farrell sets the scene: "Arriving at the Grand, the lobby bore a resemblance to a Chicago department store in a bargain rush. The main floor was thronged with vendors of kimonos and mandarin coats. All the ladies were busy bargainers at once. The male members rushed to the nearest silk shirt stores to select material and get measured for the lightest kind of stuff, for it is only a week before the party will be sweltering near the equator."[25]

After a very hasty lunch, the tourists dashed back to the rickshas and were delivered to the train station. Arriving a little after noon, the tourists were once again ferried by the human-powered craft to the ballpark at Keio University. Along the way, a wheel came off the ricksha carrying the Thorpes, tumbling the newlyweds into a Tokyo street, but uninjured. After dusting themselves off, the adventurous Iva and Jim climbed into another ricksha and continued their trek.[26]

Keio University was the most prestigious collegiate baseball power in Japan. In 1911 Keio sent its team to barnstorm against college teams in the United States. Now, two years later, they got a chance to play host. Keio was at first embarrassed about the condition of its field. Thinking that it did not compare to the fields they had seen in the States, either in size or amenities, T. Kimishima of the Keio Base Ball Association offered these words, "I hereby wish to make an apology to you, the greatest of all exponents of the game. It is in an embarrassed state of mind that the Association invites teams to have the use of this midget field, but at all events your welcome is not belittled."[27]

After reassuring Kimishima that the field was better than 30 percent of the fields in the United States, the game began. The proceedings were so rushed that the ballplayers didn't even get to work out beforehand. McGraw did treat the crowd to a game of shadow ball, which put the crowd into hysterics. This was the very first game of shadow ball the Japanese had ever seen, and it was the perfect icebreaker. The tourists found one element of conforming to local custom most amusing. The Japanese tradition of removing one's shoes when entering a house meant that before and after the game, each player had to doff his spikes before entering the clubhouse. Wooden cloglike slippers were provided for navigating the clubhouse.[28]

The game was intensely covered by the Japanese media. Every Tokyo paper had at least one reporter there, and some papers sent as many as five. To everyone's delight, the sun chose this moment to break through the clouds. The early December day became almost springlike and far more tolerable for both fans and players. After lots of picture-taking by the assembled news outlets, umpires Klem and Sheridan were introduced, and the ceremonial first pitch was thrown from the mound by President Eikichi Kamata of Keio University to consul general Sammons half crouching at home plate.

Five thousand citizens wedged themselves into Keio's baseball grounds and cheered themselves hoarse. Space was at such a premium that many of the fans sat on bamboo mats crammed into any open plot of land. To the Americans, it was all very heady and overpowering. The intensity of the Japanese fans and their knowledge of the game impressed the Americans. Veteran sportswriter Gus Axelson claimed that they were every bit as loud as any group of Giants fans under Coogan's Bluff.[29]

The Giants and White Sox played fair baseball considering how seasick everyone had been for so long, with the White Sox winning 9-4. The seasick Texan Tris Speaker had a great game, two home runs, and a couple of hard liners. The very short right- and left-field fences and the exotic atmosphere probably made everyone play much better than they felt.

Just as he had done in the States, Bill Klem, in his most windows-rattling bass voice, elaborately introduced each player as he strode up to the batter's box. Klem's mammoth vocal power, elaborate style, and pugnacious attitude were unlike anything the Japanese had encountered before in an umpire. Klem quickly became a favorite of both the crowd and the sports reporters. Just how much of an impact he made could be seen in the next day's *Jiji Shimpo*. The paper had sent a caricaturist to the game to capture the day's activities. Klem's caricature was rendered larger than anyone else's.

For Japanese fandom, the tour was nirvana. Although their nation had adopted baseball as its national pastime, no games of major-league caliber had ever been played there. A.G. Spalding had completely bypassed Japan 25 years earlier during his tour. Preferring to journey to nations under British or American rule, Spalding made his trail considerably more southern. From Hawaii, Spalding's All-Stars sailed to New Zealand and Australia before dodging north to Ceylon, Egypt, Italy, France, and Great Britain. Only in Italy and France had Spalding been out of the British sphere of influence.

In 1908 Japan had been visited by the Reach All-Americans, but the tourists consisted of only one team, none of whom could even remotely be considered star players. They specialized in steamrolling local nines. The Reach All-Americans drubbed their Japanese opponents, sweeping all 17 games. The only positive aspect of the 1908 tour as far as the Japanese were concerned was that the humiliation fueled their desire to excel at the sport and to one day beat the Americans at their own game.

The tour by Comiskey and McGraw promised to bode far more goodwill for everyone. In the intervening years, players who had visited Japan on their own had smoothed over some of the hard feelings remaining from the Reach All-Americans. During the winter of 1910, Giants Arthur "Tillie" Shafer, a utility outfielder and second baseman, and Tommy Thompson, a pitcher, visited Japan and dispensed a great deal of good coaching on the finer points of the game to this very same Keio University. (Curiously, although Shafer was still on the Giants roster in 1913, he expressed no interest in going on the tour.)

The abilities of the American major leaguers, even after enduring the strength-sapping Pacific Ocean, were far above what everyone in Japan was familiar with. It was like knowing a few dance steps and then having Vernon and Irene Castle show up to give you a tutorial. They watched each play carefully, studying and learning. Of the various baseball skills, the art of pitching was the area where the Japanese lagged furthest behind the Americans. To the American sportswriters present, it seemed as if the Giants and White Sox had left their arms on the *Empress*, yet their pitchers still packed more heat than the locals had ever seen. The Japanese were also impressed with the prodigious home-run power of the tourists. Though the year 1913 is considered a part of the Deadball Era in the United States, it was a far livelier version of the game than the one in Japan.

After this game the tourists returned to the Grand Hotel for some hurried sightseeing and a feast that they could finally keep down. The banquet entertainment included geishas. Iva Thorpe was awed by their grace. Like all the banquets of the tour, this one included speeches and toasts and lasted until late in the evening.[30]

The next morning, Sunday, December 7, 1913, was the date for what was perhaps the most eagerly anticipated baseball game in Japan's history. A team composed of White Sox and Giants was scheduled to challenge the Keio University team. For this event, 7,000 people crammed into Keio's ball ground. This was to be the first game of a doubleheader. The White Sox and Giants were to play each other again in the afternoon, the last contest in Japan. The morning game marked the first time that the teams would challenge a local nine on their global sojourn. For the first time the two teams would play as one. The starting lineup of American big-leaguers that day consisted of Lee Magee, Larry Doyle, Fred Merkle, Hans Lobert, Mickey Doolan, and Ivey Wingo of the Giants, Tris Speaker, and Sam Crawford, of the White Sox. Death Valley Jim Scott of the White Sox pitched, and the Giants' Mike Donlin replaced Crawford in right field after six innings. The early-morning hour of play meant that right field would be bathed in glare, leading Sam Crawford to remark, "And to think I came 7,000 miles to play the sun field."[31] Klem and Sheridan umpired the game, as they had all the others. Klem crouched behind the squatting catchers while Sheridan worked the bases. Klem's booming voice and mannerisms were soon being imitated by the crowd.

Keio University's baseball team was the best collegiate team and therefore the best team in all of Japan. There was no question that much Japanese pride rested on this contest. Keio batted first and played full bore. Shigeki Mori, Keio's center fielder, tripled and a play later scored on Daisuke Miyake's single. The crowd exploded with joy. By good fortune, Frank McGlynn and Victor Miller had the movie camera rolling. As Mori crossed the plate, Miller used the panoramic lens to get a wide shot of the 7,000 screaming fans in full ecstasy.

Moments later the Japanese were retired without further scoring. The Americans now got a chance to silence the crowd. Lee Magee, playing left field, matched Shigeki Mori by leading off with a triple. He scored immediately on Larry Doyle's single. After the Americans were shut down in the second inning, the floodgates opened. The White Sox-Giants plated 16 runs, scoring in every inning. Keio scored only two more runs, for a final score of 16-3.[32]

The game was not such a blowout as the score might indicate. The Americans found the Japanese to be very good ballplayers. Gus Axelson said of their playing that it was a "revelation to the major leaguers."[33] While their fielding, work on the bases, and ability to think on their feet were nearly as adept as the pros, the Japanese had one glaring weakness: pitching. Keio could not hit much American pitching, and their pitcher could not serve up much that the Americans could not hit.

The Japanese pitcher, Kazuma Sugase, also served as team captain. Nearly as tall as Jim Scott, he looked quite professorial in his owlish glasses. His arm, while mastering Japanese players, was no match for the White Sox and Giants. Every member of the team except Doolin and the still sea-woozy Weaver touched home at least once. Sugase did go the distance, however, and did not surrender any home runs. He walked fewer than did Scott, and he recorded three strikeouts. On the negative side, Magee tripled twice, Merkle was hit by a pitch, and Sugase had to endure three passed balls by his stone-gloved catcher, Tokuichi Takahama. The defensive highlight of the game for the Japanese had to be turning an exotic (third to first to third) double play that sent an awed Tris Speaker back to the bench.

Jim Scott started poorly but kept getting better as the game progressed. After he shook off the cobwebs of idleness and seasickness, his pitching completely mastered the university students. Scott surrendered single runs in the first, third, and fifth innings, then shut Keio down. In the ninth inning Scott was humming along so well that he struck out the side, ending the game with an awesome flourish. The game took a brisk 1 hour and 48 minutes from start to finish. What had started as a sporting event became a delightful encounter between cultures. Politeness ruled the day. The Americans were applauded by their hosts every time they made a good play. McGraw and the American pros were sincerely impressed with the Japanese's abilities. Had a major-league-quality pitcher been on the mound for the Japanese, the results of the game could easily have been very different.

Great shouts of appreciation from the 7,000 fans erupted at the conclusion of the game, with lengthy ovations that poured over the Americans like a wall of sound. After the game there was just enough time for a quick lunch while the field was prepared for the afternoon contest. For the second time, the tourists played a morning-afternoon doubleheader. The first one had been on November 16 in Oakland and San Francisco, when everyone, even after a month of nonstop touring, had been in better shape.

The afternoon show, the last game played by the tourists in Japan, saw 6,000 fans retain their seats from the first game. The Japanese continued to revel in the tourists' skillful ballplaying. The Giants and White Sox used their regular lineups against each other, with most of those who had played in the morning back in action in the afternoon. The White Sox swept the "series" in Japan, winning the second game, 12–9.

This game ended with one of the most thrilling plays of the entire tour. Tris Speaker threw Mike Donlin out at the plate from the deepest part of center with an absolutely perfect throw to Ivey Wingo. An amazed John McGraw called it one of the greatest plays he had ever seen. The awed Japanese fans cheered the play in a riotous cacophony of sound. No dramatist could have come up with a more appropriate ending to the game or the series in Japan.[34]

The women of the party were not in attendance for either of the day's games. Rather than sit through more baseball, all of the wives were on the *Empress*, sailing ahead of their mates to Osaka. The men joined them many hours later; after the second game the athletes caught the first train out of Tokyo for Osaka.

The Japanese press ran out of superlatives and hyperbole in describing what they had witnessed. The *Yokohama Gazette* stated: "The games played have been a revelation to those who had not witnessed anything of the sort before."[35] The *Japan Advertiser* of Tokyo said: "The teams seem to move like clockwork. Each signal is exactly followed and the umpire's decision is obeyed silently. It is this system of arbitration that the ball player of this country must note and develop so that further friction in international base ball games may be averted. The speed and alacrity of the base stealing, too, was a revelation to the Japanese."[36] The *Tokyo Times* reported:

> Like a cyclone the big men of America came
> and went, creating a whirlwind of sensation.
> What did they do? Well ask the fans; they
> know it. And also ask those people living
> down in the Mita Road, and they will give
> complete statistics of windows smashed,
> houses damaged, and dogs in the street hit
> by flying balls. They worked more wonders
> and showed more true ball playing than the
> Japanese fans could see. The cyclonic visit of
> the American stars has left its memory in the
> sporting history of Japan – besides those me-
> mentos on some houses in the neighborhood
> of the Keio grounds. And fortunate was the

Keio team, which was able to get practical suggestions and advice from such base ball brains as John McGraw and Jim Callahan.[37]

After the game some of the party returned to the Grand Hotel. Most of the players, however, checked into the Imperial Hotel in Tokyo, which was much closer to the ballpark. Everyone tried to squeeze in some sightseeing and banqueting before reporting to the train station for a journey by rail to Osaka.[38]

Upon boarding the 7:00 P.M. train at the station for the nearly 13-hour train ride, the players had one more culture shock. The size of the train's berths was a most depressing discovery. Built for the smaller stature of the Japanese, the berths measured only five feet eight inches long and two feet wide. Ivey Wingo in particular was especially perturbed. Wingo caught both ends of the doubleheader and wanted nothing more than to lie down and rest his aching bones. That was, however, impossible for the 5-foot-10-inch, 160-pound catcher to do comfortably. Wingo whined that he would probably be crippled for life if he got into his berth. Sleep is a powerful force, though, and before long all of the men, including 6-foot Tris Speaker, were crammed into their berths speeding through the night-shrouded Japanese landscape, the only sound, snores mixed with the steady hum of steel upon steel.[39]

The ballplayers' train pulled into the Osaka terminal at 7:30 A.M. on December 9. Awaiting the train was the city's large, loud, and enthusiastic welcoming committee. Cheers went up, along with calls for McGraw, Callahan, and Doyle. All of the players emerged stiff-limbed and bleary-eyed to a thunderous ovation. McGraw and Callahan were presented with two elaborate floral wreaths, each carried by young Japanese girls. Elsewhere, men hoisted banners with welcoming messages in English high above the milling crowd.

The committee and the citizens of Osaka were greatly disappointed that the game scheduled for their city had been canceled. The chairman of the welcoming committee, an English-speaking editor of the *Osaka Daily News*, while understanding the reason for the cancellation, could not hide his sadness. Callahan and McGraw made brief speeches. Then it was on to Kobe to the thunderous shouts and cheers of the Japanese.

The players arrived in Kobe at 9:00 A.M. The wives had already spent a most enjoyable day in Kobe shopping, sightseeing, and socializing. For the next three hours the men went on a buying spree. Kimonos, silk, summer clothing, souvenirs, jewelry, gifts for spouses and girlfriends – in short, everything that could be bought. At 12:30 in the afternoon everyone returned to the *Empress*. At 2:00 P.M. the ship sailed out of the harbor, making for Nagasaki at full speed. Nagasaki was like no other city in Japan. The fastest coaling station on the planet, the city moved at a quicker pace than the rest of the country. Unlike elsewhere in Japan, where women played a subservient role, in Nagasaki they were an essential part of the coaling operations, the city's prime source of revenue.

Women dressed in white performed most of the work. As soon as a ship dropped anchor in the harbor, coal barges surrounded it, and coaling operations commenced. Men threw ropes woven out of rice plants over the side of the vessel. These were then lashed to the deck, a process that took only a matter of seconds. Once the ladders were in place, an army of women, each standing above the other on the rungs of the rice ladder, passed a 28-pound basket of coal up from the barge to the ship's bunkers. Once emptied, the basket was tossed back to the coaling barge to be refilled for another journey up the ladder. There were about 25 crews working on each side of the *Empress* from noon until 10:30 P.M. The women toiled like ants moving earth. When they were finished, 1,500 tons of coal had been transported into the ship's cavernous bunkers. For their labors, the women received the equivalent of 20 US cents.[40]

Witnessing this toil was too much for some tourists. As Frank McGlynn put it, "[T]he liberal hearted members of the world touring party threw coins to the patient laborers, and no doubt a great majority of them were happier at their day's pay than on many a similar occasion."[41]

Unlike Kobe and Osaka, no game had been planned for Nagasaki; December 9 had been a scheduled treat for the players, an open date. To the players' delight, Nagasaki offered more diversions and attractions than did even Tokyo. For the first time since they had sailed out of Seattle, the players got a chance to relax and enjoy themselves.

The Thorpes did some Christmas shopping, toured around town in rickshas, then, like most visitors to Nagasaki, ascended the thousands of steps to the top of the temple. Here as well they got to see how the ordinary Japanese citizen lived. Iva took note of the local custom of attaching a piece of rice paper to the door to ward off evil spirits. Away from the more urban and industrial centers of Kobe and Tokyo, the tourists encountered a Japan more ancient, mysterious, and delightful than they imagined.[42]

But like just about everywhere the tourists appeared, trouble followed. Fred Merkle, Mike Donlin, Germany Schaefer, and a few other of the tour's bachelors went out for drinks with the officers from an American liner whom they had befriended. In some dive near the waterfront, the sailors and the ballplayers stumbled across a pool table. Like delighted children encountering a favorite toy or delinquents finding their favorite vice, the group proceeded to play round after round.

Billiard balls and alcohol shots chased each other for hours. Finally, close to 10:30 P.M., the players realized that the launch for the *Empress* would soon be leaving and that if they didn't catch it, there was a chance all of them might get left in Nagasaki. If nothing else, they had to get back on time to avoid a tongue-lashing from McGraw. One of the hard-partying athletes chose to take one last shot for the road and, in his drunken state, sent the cue ball careening off the table and onto the floor before it disappeared under a couch. Too

drunk to bend over, the players left the ball where it was and beat a hasty return to the *Empress*.[43]

The players' actions, however, did not escape the notice of the harbor police. Unable to find his valuable cue ball, which, after all, was made out of solid ivory, the owner of the bar reported it stolen and named the American ballplayers as the prime suspects. To the athletes' chagrin and the steamship line's supreme displeasure, Nagasaki's harbor police boarded the *Empress*, demanding the missing cue ball and an explanation from the plastered Americans.

Germany Schaefer approached the police, turned on the charm, and confessed to his misadventure. While Schaefer was trying to charm his way out of arrest, word came to the police that the location of the "missing" cue ball had been discovered, and the *Empress* was now free to sail.

Immediately inflated by the American press, the cue-ball story became fodder for US tabloids and scandal sheets. Axelson and Farrell, the writers on the tour, protected the athletes they covered; they did their best to sweep the story under the rug. After all, it just would not do to have reports of drunken ballplayers in the newspaper.

Under the cold light of a waning moon, hours past the scheduled departure time of midnight, the *Empress* slipped out of Nagasaki for Shanghai.

1913 CHICAGO WHITE SOX AND NY GIANTS GAMES IN JAPAN

Date	Place	Opponent	Score	Winner	Loser
December 6	Tokyo	White Sox vs. Giants	9-4	Benz	Witlse
December 7	Tokyo	Keio University	16-3	Scott	Sugase
December 7	Tokyo	White Sox vs. Giants	12-9	Leverenz	Hearn

NOTES

1 "A Joint Tour," *Sporting Life*, February 1, 1913: 1.

2 *Spalding's Base Ball Guide and Official League Book for 1889* (Chicago and New York: A.G. Spalding & Bros, 1889), 83-99.

3 Harvey T. Woodruff, "The Tour of the World," *Sporting Life*, October 11, 1913: 5.

4 "Latest News by Telegraph Briefly Told," *Sporting Life*, May 17, 1913: 7.

5 "Wilson Will Help," *Sporting Life*, June 21, 1913: 6.

6 "Fine Plans for the World Tour," *Sporting Life*, June 28, 1913: 2.

7 Joseph Vila, "World Tour Cost Deters," *Sporting Life*, July 19, 1913: 8.

8 "The World Tour Assured," *Sporting Life*, August 2, 1913: 2; Joseph Vila, "World Tour Cost Deters," *Sporting Life*, July 19, 1913: 8.

9 "Cost of World Tour," *Sporting Life*, September 27, 1913: 1.

10 Woodruff.

11 "Start of World Tour," *Sporting Life*, October 25, 1913: 1; James E. Elfers, *The Tour to End All Tours* (Lincoln: University of Nebraska, 2003), 94.

12 "The Tour of the World," *Sporting Life*, November 22, 1913: 4.

13 "The Tour of the World," *Sporting Life*, November 29, 1913: 5, 9.

14 "The Tour of the World," *Sporting Life*, November 29, 1913: 9; Anon., *World Tour 1913-1914* (Chicago: S. Blake Willsden, 1914).

15   Elfers, 98-107.

16   Adapted from *The Tour to End All Tours: The Story of Major League Baseball's 1913-1914 World Tour* by James E. Elfers by permission of the University of Nebraska Press. Copyright 2003 by the University of Nebraska Press.

17   Gus Axelson, "Sox Take First in Orient Play: Romp at Tokio," *Chicago Sunday Record Herald*, December 7, 1913: Sports section, 1.

18   *Jiji Shimpo*, December 7, 1913.

19   *Jiji Shimpo*, December 7, 1913.

20   *Jiji Shimpo*, December 7, 1913.

21   *Jiji Shimpo*, December 7, 1913.

22   Joe Farrell, "World Tourists' Rough Voyage Across Pacific Ocean," *The Sporting News*, January 1, 1914: 5.

23   Frank McGlynn, "Striking Scenes from Around the World: Part I," *Base Ball Magazine* September 1914: 67.

24   Farrell.

25   Farrell.

26   Iva Thorpe, Personal Diary. Private Collection.

27   Farrell.

28   Farrell; Frank McGlynn, "Striking Scenes from Around the World: Part II," *Base Ball Magazine*, October 1914: 69.

29   Axelson.

30   Thorpe; Farrell.

31   Gus W. Axelson, "Japanese Quick to Adopt Big League Ways," *Chicago Record-Herald*, December 28, 1913.

32   McGlynn, "Striking Scenes from Around the World Part I": 68.

33   Axelson, "Japanese Quick to Adopt Big League Ways."

34   Gus W. Axelson, *Commy: The Life Story of Charles A. Comiskey* (Chicago: Riley & Lea, 1919), 251.

35   "How Press of Japan Viewed Invasion of World Tourists," *The Sporting News*, January 8, 1914: 3.

36   "How Press of Japan Viewed Invasion of World Tourists."

37   "How Press of Japan Viewed Invasion of World Tourists."

38   McGlynn, "Striking Scenes from Around the World Part II": 69.

39   McGlynn, "Striking Scenes from Around the World Part II": 70.

40   McGlynn, "Striking Scenes from Around the World Part II": 71.

41   McGlynn, "Striking Scenes from Around the World Part I": 71.

42   Thorpe.

43   McGlynn, "Striking Scenes from Around the World Part II": 71-72.

RETURNING HOME: THE 1914 SEATTLE NIPPON AND ASAHI JAPANESE AMERICAN TOURS

By Robert K. Fitts

INTRODUCTION

Between 1890 and 1910, over 100,000 Japanese immigrated to the West Coast of the United States. Many settled in the urban centers of San Francisco, Los Angeles, and Seattle. Within a few years, each of these immigrant communities had thriving baseball clubs. The first known Japanese American team was the Fuji Athletic Club, founded in San Francisco around 1903. A second Bay Area team, the Kanagawa Doshi Club, was created the following year. That same year, newsmen at the *Rafu Shimpo* organized Los Angeles's first Issei (Japanese immigrant) team. Other clubs followed in the wake of Waseda University's 1905 baseball tour of the West Coast. Many players learned the game while still in Japan at their high schools or colleges. Others picked up the sport in the United States. The first Japanese professional club was created the following year by Guy Green of Lincoln, Nebraska. His Green's Japanese Base Ball Team, consisting of Japanese immigrants from Los Angeles, barnstormed throughout the Midwest in the spring and summer of 1906.

Seattle's first Japanese American club, called the Nippon, was also organized in 1906. Shigeru Ozawa, one of the founding players, recalled that the team was not very good at first and was able to play only the second-tier White amateur nines. By 1907 the team had a large local following. In its first appearance in the city's mainstream newspapers, the *Seattle Star* noted that "before one of the largest crowds seen at Woodlands park the D.S. Johnstons defeated the Nippons, the fast local Jap team, by a score of 11 to 5."[1] In May 1908, before a game against the crew of the USS *Milwaukee*, the *Seattle Daily Times* reported that the Nippon "have picked up the fine points of the great national game rapidly from playing the amateur teams around here every Sunday."[2]

Two months later, the *Daily Times* featured the team when it took on the all-female Merry Widows. Mistakenly referring to the Nippons as "the only Japanese baseball club in America," the newspaper reported, "when these sons of Nippon went up against the daughters of Columbia, viz., the Merry Widow Baseball Club, it is a safe assumption that the game played at Athletic Park yesterday afternoon was the

Seattle Nippon and Keio University in 1914

most unique affair in the annals of the national game."[3] Over a thousand fans, including many Japanese, watched the Nippons win, 14-8.

Soon after the game with the Merry Widows, second baseman Tokichi "Frank" Fukuda and several other players left the Nippon and created a team called the Mikado. The Mikado soon rivaled the Nippons as the city's top Japanese team, with the *Seattle Star* calling them "one of the fastest amateur teams in the city."[4] In both 1910 and 1911, the Mikado topped the Nippon and Tacoma's Columbians to win the Northwest Coast's Nippon Baseball Championship.[5]

As Fukuda's love for baseball grew, he realized the game's importance for Seattle's Japanese. The games brought the immigrants together physically and provided a shared interest to help strengthen community ties. It also acted as a bridge between the city's Japanese and non-Japanese population, showing a common bond that he hoped would undermine the anti-Japanese bigotry in the city.

In 1909 Fukuda created a youth baseball team called the Cherry – the West Coast's first Nisei (Japanese born outside of Japan) squad. Under Fukuda's guidance, the club was more than just a baseball team. Katsuji Nakamura, one of the early members, explained in 1918, "The purpose of this club was to contact American people and understand each other through various activities. We think it is indispensable for us. Because there are still a lot of Japanese people who cannot understand English in spite of the fact that they live in an English-speaking country. That often causes various troubles between Japanese and Americans because of simple misunderstandings. To solve that issue, it has become necessary that we, American-born Japanese who were educated in English, have to lead Japanese people in the right direction in the future. We have been working the last ten years, according to this doctrine."[6]

As the boys matured, the team became stronger on the diamond and in 1912 the top players joined with Fukuda and his Mikado teammates Katsuji Nakamura, Shuji "John" Ikeda, and Yoshiaki Marumo to form a new team known as the Asahi. Like the Cherry, the Asahi was also a social club designed to create the future leaders of Seattle's Japanese community, and forge ties with non-Japanese through various activities, including baseball.[7] Once again the new club soon rivaled the Nippon as Seattle's top Japanese American team.

THE NIPPON TOUR

During the winter of 1913-14, Mitomi "Frank" Miyasaka, the captain of the Nippon, announced that he was going to take his team to Japan, thereby becoming the first Japanese American ballclub to tour their homeland. To build the best possible squad, Miyasaka recruited some of the West Coast's top Issei players. From San Francisco, he recruited second baseman Masashi "Taki" Takimoto. From Los Angeles, Miyasaka brought over 30-year-old Kiichi "Onitei" Suzuki. Suzuki had played for Waseda University's reserve team before immigrating to California in 1906. A year later, he joined Los Angeles's Japanese American team, the Nanka. He also founded the Hollywood Sakura in 1908. In 1911 Suzuki joined the professional Japanese Base Ball Association and spent the season barnstorming across the Midwest. Miyasaka's big coup, however, was Suzuki's barnstorming teammate Ken Kitsuse. Recognized as the best Issei ballplayer on the West Coast, in 1906 Kitsuse had played shortstop for Guy Green's Japanese Base Ball Team, the first professional Japanese club on either side of the Pacific. He was the star of the Nanka before playing shortstop for the Japanese Base Ball Association barnstorming team in 1911. Throughout his career, Kitsuse drew accolades for his slick fielding, blinding speed, and heady play.

To train the Nippons in the finer points of the game, Miyasaka hired 38-year-old George Engel (a.k.a. Engle) as a manager-coach. Although Engel had never made the majors, he had spent 14 seasons in the minor leagues, mostly in the Western and Northwest Leagues, as a pitcher and utility player. Miyasaka also created a challenging schedule to ready his team for the tour. They began their season with games against the area's two professional teams from the Northwest League. On Sunday, March 22, they lost, 5-1, to the Tacoma Tigers, led by player-manager and future Hall of Famer Joe "Iron Man" McGinnity. The following Sunday the Seattle Giants, which boasted seven past or future major leaguers on the roster, beat them 5-1. Despite the one-sided loss, the *Seattle Daily Times* noted, "the Nippons … walked off Dugdale Field yesterday afternoon feeling well satisfied with themselves for they had tackled a professional team and had made a run."[8]

In April 1914, Keio University returned for its second tour of North America. After dropping two games in Vancouver, British Columbia and a third to the University of Washington, Keio met the Nippons on April 9 at Dugdale Park in what the *Seattle Daily Times* called "the world's series for the baseball championship of Japan."[9] On the mound for Keio was the great Kazuma Sugase, the half-German "Christy Mathewson of Japan," who had starred during the school's 1911 tour. The team also included future Japanese Hall of Famers Daisuke Miyake, who would manage the All-Nippon team against Babe Ruth's All-Americans in 1934, and Hisashi Koshimoto, a Hawaiian-born Nisei who would later manage Keio.

Nippons manager George Engel was in a quandary. His usual ace Sadaye Takano was not available and as Keio would host his team during its coming tour of Japan, he needed the Nippons to prove they could challenge the top Japanese college squad. Engel reached out to William "Chief" Cadreau, a Native American who had pitched for Spokane and Vancouver in the Northwestern League, one game for the 1910 Chicago White Sox, and would later pitch a season for the African American Chicago Union Giants.[10] Pretending that he was a Japanese named Kato, Cadreau started the game. According to the *Seattle Star*, "Engel was very careful to let the Keio boys know that Kato, his pitcher, was deaf and dumb. But later in the game Kato became enthused, as ball players will, and the jig was up when he began to root in good English."[11] Nonetheless, Cadreau handled Keio relatively easily, striking out 13 en route to a 6-3 victory.[12]

Throughout the spring and summer, the Nippons continued to face the area's top teams, including the African American Keystone Giants, to prepare for the trip to Japan. Yet in their minds, the most important matchup was the three-game series against the Asahi for the Japanese championship. The Nippons took the first game, 4-2, on July 12 at Dugdale Park but there is no evidence that they finished the series.[13] Not to be outdone by their rivals, the Asahi also announced that they would tour Japan later that year. Sponsored by the *Nichi-nichi* and *Mainichi* newspapers, the Asahi would begin their trip about a month after the Nippons left for Japan.

The Nippon left Seattle aboard the *Shidzuoka Maru* on August 25.[14] Their departure went unreported by the city's newspapers as international news took precedence. Germany had invaded Belgium on August 4, opening the Western Front theater of World War I. Throughout the month, Belgian, French, and British troops battled the advancing Germans. Just days before the ballclub left for Japan, the armies clashed at Charleroi, Mons, and Namur with tens of thousands

of casualties. On August 23, Japan declared war on Germany and two days later declared war on Austria.

After two weeks at sea, the Nippon arrived at Yokohama on September 10.[15] The squad contained 11 players: George Engel, Frank Miyasaka, Yukichi Annoki, Kyuye Kamijyo, Masataro Kimura, Ken Kitsuse, Mitsugi Koyama, Yohizo Shimada, Kiichi Suzuki, Sadaye Takano, and Masashi Takimoto. Accompanying the ballplayers was the team's cheering group, consisting of 21 members and led by Yasukazu Kato. The group planned to attend the games to cheer on the Nippon and spend the rest of their time sightseeing.

As the *Shidzuoka Maru* docked, a group of reporters, Ryozo Hiranuma of Keio University, Tajima of Meiji University, and a few university players came on board to welcome the visiting team. The group then took a train to Shinbashi Station in Tokyo, where they were met by the Keio University ballplayers at 2:33 P.M. The Nippon checked in at the Kasuga Ryokan in Kayabacho while the large cheering group, which needed two inns to accommodate them, settled down at the Taisei-ya and Sanuki-ya.[16]

Only two hours later, the Nippon arrived at Hibiya Park for practice. Not surprisingly, after the voyage they were not in top form. The *Tokyo Asahi* noted, "Even though the Seattle team is composed of Japanese, their ball-handling skills are as good as American players, and … their agile movements are very encouraging. … They hit the ball with a very free form, but yesterday, they did not place their hits very accurately, most likely due to fatigue. … The Seattle team did not have a full-fledged defensive practice with each player in position, so we did not know how skilled they were in defensive coordination, but we heard that the individual skills of each player were as good as those of Waseda and Keio. In short, the Seattle team has beaten Keio University before, so even though they are Japanese, they should not be underestimated. On top of that, they have good pitching, so games against Waseda University and Keio University are expected to arouse more than a few people's interest, just like the games against foreign teams in the past."[17]

The Nippon would stay in Japan for almost four months, but the baseball tour itself consisted of just eight games – all played during September against Waseda and Keio Universities. The players spent the rest of the time traveling through their homeland and visiting family and friends.

The Nippon opened their tour on September 12 against Waseda at the university's Totsuka Grounds. "It was a clear, crisp autumn day and a perfect day for baseball, and the crowd was very happy to see them. At 1:30 P.M. the Waseda University team entered, and at the same time the Seattle team entered in their vertical striped uniforms. [Tokyo] mayor [Yoshiro] Sakatani appeared in a dashing suit with a smile on his face, climbed up to the mound and threw the first pitch."[18]

Engel decided not to let Sadaye Takano, his usual starting pitcher, face the Japanese colleges. Instead, Engel took the mound himself, although he had not pitched professionally for two years. In his final season with Vancouver of the Northwestern League, he went 7-4 in 87 innings. Now, at 39 years old, he faced a tough Waseda lineup.

The enthusiastic crowd was treated to a tight game of small ball. In the top of the first, Seattle's "Taki" Takimoto eked out a two-out walk but was thrown out trying to steal second. In the bottom half of the inning, leadoff batter Kichibei Kato walked. Engel bore down and struck out Kazuyoshi Yokoyama. As the umpire called strike three, catcher Yohizo Shimada fired the ball to first, trying to catch a napping Kato off the bag. But the throw got away, and Kato circled the bases for the first run as the Nippon players chased down the rolling ball.

Over the next three innings, both Engel and Waseda starter Tamizo Kawashima no-hit their opponents. In the bottom of the fifth, Waseda scored twice on a walk, a single, an error, and a squeeze play to lead, 3-0. Seattle struck back in the sixth as Miyasaka tripled and scored on a single by Yukichi Annoki. In the seventh, Seattle scored three more to take a 4-3 lead. Waseda seemed "stunned and helpless" as the Nippon "desperately tried to control the remaining two innings."[19] But they could not. In the bottom of the eighth, Kawashima reached base on an error, stole second, and scored on consecutive hits by Kato and Yokoyama to knot the score.

Ken Kitsuse led off the ninth inning with a walk, moved to second on a sacrifice, and streaked to third on a fly out to center field. With two outs and the go-ahead run at third, Kawashima battled with Nippon center fielder Annoki. Kawashima prevailed, striking out Annoki, but Waseda catcher Tadao Ichioka dropped the third strike and threw wildly to first as Kitsuse scampered home. Engel pitched a scoreless ninth to preserve the 5-4 victory.

The three-game series against Keio University began on September 15 at the Mita grounds. Engel started on the mound for Seattle against their ace, Kazuma Sugase. After their loss to the Nippon in Seattle, the collegians were looking for revenge and they played aggressive ball from the first pitch.[20] Keio center fielder Jinkichi Kaji began the game with a bunt hit down the third-base line. Shigeki Mori then singled, and Daisuke Miyake beat out a bunt to load the bases with no outs. Engel then got cleanup hitter Akira Kusaka to hit a weak grounder back to the mound. Engel threw home for the first out but the catcher's throw to first base was dropped and Mori scored. The next batter, Shigeru Takahama, also grounded back to the pitcher. Engel threw to second for the out, and Takimoto threw to first to complete the double play, but first baseman Frank Miyasaka once again dropped the ball as Miyake scored. A single by Shungo Abe knocked in another to give Keio a 3-0 lead. "It looked like the game was already decided."[21] Keio went on to score four more times as Sugase shut out the Nippon on just four hits and did not allow a runner to get to second base in the 7-0 win. An observer noted, "The Seattle team looked really listless, completely lackluster, as if they had been debilitated by the bad plays in the first and second innings."[22]

Four days later, on September 19, Nippon had a chance to redeem themselves in the second game against Keio. Engel pitched again for Seattle but Keio started Hisao Numata. This time Seattle jumped out to an early lead, scoring once in the second and three in the fourth as they knocked out Numata. Engel, meanwhile, pitched brilliantly, allowing just three hits through seven innings.

In the eighth inning, however, Seattle's defense nearly betrayed them again. With one out, Unosuke Hirai hit a routine fly ball to left field. Kiichi Suzuki, playing shallow, misjudged it and it flew over his head for a double. Sugase (who came in to relieve Numata) then tripled to score Hirai. After Kaji grounded out to the pitcher, Mori hit a fly ball to left that should have ended the inning, but the ball popped out of Suzuki's glove and Sugase scored. The Nippon immediately appealed, arguing that Suzuki had successfully made the catch before the ball came loose. The umpire, however, disagreed and allowed the run to count. In disgust, Takimoto marched off the field. Unused to such poor sportsmanship, the fans were "very critical" of Takimoto's behavior.[23] A subsequent error by shortstop Kimura allowed Mori to score and reduce Seattle's lead to one run, before Engel struck out

Takahama to end Keio's last threat of the game.[24] After the 4-3 Nippon victory, the press praised Engel. The "39-year-old veteran pitcher showed off his strong arm again and fought hard for the Seattle team, his energy was unmatched by any of the younger players on the Seattle team. Keio's hitters were tormented."[25]

On September 20 at 2:30 P.M. the Nippon faced Waseda for the second time. Having pitched a complete game the day before, Engle decided to start Sadaye Takano. It did not go well. Waseda tagged Takano for three runs in the second inning. Engel quickly pulled Takano and brought in second baseman Takimoto to pitch. He did worse – surrendering another three before getting the third out and then giving up seven runs in the third inning. By the end of the game, Waseda had pounded out 23 runs on 16 hits with 10 walks against four pitchers as the porous Seattle defense committed 10 errors. Meanwhile, Waseda starter Tamizo Kawashima stifled the Nippon by allowing just four hits and two runs.[26]

Two days later Seattle took on the Waseda alumni Tomon Club. An article in the annual *Yakyu-Nenpoh* noted that "the Tomon players, although aging, are all fierce fighters who once enjoyed fame." The starting lineup included future Japanese Baseball Hall of Fame members Shin Hashido, Kiyoshi Oshikawa, and Chujun Tobita. Engel, once again, took the day off and started Yohizo Shimada on the mound. The game began ominously for Seattle. After a leadoff walk to Kimura, followed by an infield hit by Koyama, third batter Takimoto hit the ball back to the pitcher. The pitcher caught the ball on the fly, and immediately threw to first to catch Koyama straying off first. Then the first baseman quickly threw to second to nab

Kimura before he could return to the base: triple play. The "stunned" Nippon's concentration and defense fell apart.[27] Seattle made seven errors, nearly all at key moments, as Tomon coasted to an easy 15-3 victory.

Engel returned to the mound for the third and deciding game against Waseda on September 26. The Nippon started well as two-out hits by Kimura, Miyasaka, and Shimada loaded the bases with Takimoto up. With two balls on Takimoto, Waseda pitcher Kawashima threw ball three. Kimura, having lost count of the balls and thinking Takimoto had walked, ambled home, only to be tagged out to end the inning. The rest of the game was tight. Waseda moved ahead with a run in the first and two in the third, only to see its lead evaporate with a three-run Seattle fourth. The collegians retaliated with two runs in the bottom of the fifth to lead 5-3. In the seventh the Nippon tied the game again, with two runs on a triple, a groundout, and a single, followed by two Waseda errors. But once again, the visitors' comeback was short-lived. In the bottom of the seventh, Waseda scored three on two triples, a hit batsman, and a squeeze bunt. Kawashima pitched no-hit ball in the final two innings to preserve the Waseda 8-5 victory.[28]

The deciding game against Keio on September 27 was the highlight of the tour. To the delight of the fans at Mita Tsunamachi Field, both teams battled in a "fierce game."[29] Despite having pitched a complete game the previous day against Waseda, Engel took the mound. Once again, their ace Kazuma Sugase started for Keio. Umpiring the game were two future Hall of Famers Nenosuke Fukuda and Chujun Tobita. Both men later changed U.S.-Japan baseball relations

Seattle Asahi and Keio University in 1914

by playing important roles in the two greatest upsets during the pre-World War II tours.

Engel and Sugase both pitched brilliantly. At the end of nine innings, each pitcher had surrendered just two hits and held the opposition scoreless. The pitchers' duel and shutouts continued into the 12th inning as the teams "battled desperately."[30] In the bottom half of the inning, Sugase reached first with one out on a fielder's choice. Akira Kusaka then slashed a grounder that "slipped passed [sic] [second baseman] Takimoto's right hand, allowing Sugase to advance to third and Kusaka to second." The next batter, Yoichi Togashi, hit a hard line drive at right fielder Frank Miyasaka. Miyasaka, who usually played first base, "panicked" and fumbled the ball, allowing Sugase to score the winning run.[31]

After losing both of the three-game series against Waseda and Keio, Nippon finished out their tour on September 28 with a game against the Mita Club — Keio's alumni team. Having pitched 21 innings in the past two days, Engel allowed Takano to start the game. For five innings Takano pitched well, shutting out Mita on just two hits as his teammates scored six runs off Mita starter Nenosuke Fukuda (the umpire from the previous day's game). In the sixth inning, the game fell apart for Seattle. With four hits and a Nippon error, Mita scored four times, knocking out Takano. Annoki took over the mound, quelled Mita's rally, and shut down the opposition for two more innings. But in the bottom of the ninth, Mita scored twice to tie the game and send it into extra innings. Neither team scored in the 10th as a haze settled over the ballpark, darkening the sky. After the inning, the teams agreed that it was too difficult to see, and the game ended in a 6-6 tie.[32]

Engel left for Seattle soon after the Mita game but most of his teammates stayed in Japan until February. For Ken Kitsuse the trip was highly productive. He left Japan with a bride, marrying 16-year-old Suye Hoshiyama on November 30 in Tokyo.[33]

Back home, Engel explained away the Nippon's disappointing 2-5-1 record. "George has many tales to tell about the 'Land of the Rising Sun,' some of which are on the hard luck order," reported the *Seattle Daily Times*, noting that "some of their losses were by small scores." Nevertheless, Engel praised his Japanese hosts. He "speaks very highly of the treatment received by the local lads in Japan. The Keio and Waseda baseball nines, both of which visited the United States last year, have shown marked improvement in their play. ... Engle [sic] has in his possession a whole truckload of autographed bats and balls

and the usual amount of Oriental souvenirs. The best story told by George on his return, however, is that his trusty right wing, which used to mow down the Northwestern League batters in order, has once more its former strength, and he proudly announces that more will be heard from the rejuvenated wing in the future. George's 'comeback' stock is accompanied by the announcement that he will personally conduct a tour of the Orient with the Northwestern League champions next year, if arrangements can possibly be made."[34] This tour, however, never materialized.

THE ASAHI TOUR

As the Seattle Nippon were finishing up their games, Frank Fukuda and his Asahi team arrived in Yokohama on the afternoon of September 24, 1914. Led by Fukuda and manager Katsuji Nakamura, the team consisted of nine additional players between 17 and 29 years old: Junji Aisawa, Shinji "John" Ikeda, Hidekichi Kobayashi, Sukehiko "James" Kondo, Shirajiro Kouchi, Yoshiaki Marumo, Tako Osawa, Fukuo Sano, and Masao Yasuda.[35] Fukuda played second base for the squad.

For Frank Fukuda, the trip to the home country was about more than baseball. He "thought that seeing and understanding their old country was indispensable for his Nisei players to become better citizens and to establish a better Japanese community in Seattle."[36] Following the concept of *kekehashi* (literally "bridge" but in this case a bridge of understanding), Fukuda felt that an understanding of both Japanese and American values could prepare his players to become civic leaders capable of bridging the cultural gaps between Issei and Nisei as well as Japanese Americans and greater American society. Ideally this cultural bridge would reduce misunderstandings and bigotry, ultimately allowing Japanese to assimilate into American society while still maintaining their distinctive traditions.[37] Speaking at Keio University several years later, manager Nakamura explained:

"All members here have really wanted to visit Japan. We have dreamed of meeting the people who have the same blood as ours. Now our dreams came true. It is impossible to express how delighted we are. One of the reasons for our tour is to observe Japanese society and economy, but the most important objective is to learn *Yamato damashii* [Japanese spirit] in order to become a Japanized American — born Japanese, rather than become an Americanized Japanese. And if we do something in American style with the Japanese way of thinking, we believe we can produce a superior combination of those two cultures."[38]

The day before the Asahi arrived, the *Yokohama Boeki Shimpo* ran an article entitled, "Welcome Asahi Players!" noting that "they are called the Seattle Asahi Study Group" and "they came for sightseeing, discovering their mother country, and to study." "Because they were born in the United States," the article continued, "they have heard about Japan and imagined it, but this is the first time they will take steps on the mother country. We should imagine their excitement and joy [and] we should welcome them with courtesy."[39]

A welcoming committee led by Ryozo Hiranuma and the staff of the *Yokohama Boeki Shimpo* met the players at the dock. The next day as the players acclimated to their new surroundings, the Yokohama Elementary School welcomed them to Japan with a speech in English.[40]

The baseball tour opened against Yokohama Commercial High School at Yokohama Park Field on September 26. The high school had one of the top teams in the Tokyo area, routinely playing against Waseda and Keio Universities as well as visiting American teams. After Yokohama Commercial's principal, Susumu Misawa, threw the first ball at 3:30, James Kondo took the mound for Asahi. The game was a thrilling but ugly affair, marred by 12 errors and 10 walks. Both pitchers wormed out of trouble several times as the clubs entered the eighth inning tied, 2-2. By then dusk had fallen. The players struggled through the inning before declaring the game a tie in the top of the ninth due to darkness.

The teams met again the next day. It was another tight game as the Asahi surged ahead in the first inning with two runs, but Yokohama tied the score with runs in the third and fourth before going ahead, 3-2, in the seventh without a hit as a muffed grounder followed by a wild pickoff attempt brought in a run. In the bottom of the eighth, Asahi evened the score to set up an exciting final inning. Yokohama thrilled its fans by erupting for three runs in the top of the inning before holding off a bottom-of-the-ninth Asahi rally to win, 6-4.

Immediately after the game, the Asahi players left for Osaka, where they would play the Kansai champion, Osaka Shogyo, the following day.[41] Once again, a close game was ended early due to darkness. Asahi led 7-5 in the eighth inning when the teams agreed to end play. The following afternoon, September 29, Asahi took on Kobe High School (home to future alumnus, writer Haruki Murakami). In another hard-fought

game, Asahi lost, 6-5. The travelers next went to the neighboring city of Nishinomiya, where they played Kwansei Gakuin, a private nondenominational Christian university founded in 1889 by the American missionary Walter Russell Lambuth. The collegians had little trouble with the visiting amateurs, holding the Asahi to just two hits as they won comfortably, 5-3.

The Asahi then traveled northeast to the ancient capital of Kyoto, where they spent several days touring cultural sites. They visited the famed Golden Pavilion and Kiyomizu Temple as photographers for *Yakyukai* magazine clicked away.[42] On the morning of October 4, Asahi overwhelmed Kyoto Dai-ni Chugaku (Kyoto Second High School) in a sloppy display of small-ball tactics. Kyoto held Seattle to just one hit, but the Asahi took advantage of six walks and four errors to steal 10 bases and score seven runs. Asahi's defense was also porous; they committed six errors and surrendered four walks. But nonetheless, they held the high schoolers to just two runs to gain the victory. The following summer, the Kyoto high schoolers went on to win the inaugural national high-school championship tournament at Koshien.

Later that afternoon, the Asahi played their final game in Kyoto, against the Third Higher High School, commonly known as Sanko. Usually a strong team, Sanko had just finalized its roster for the coming season and many local fans came to the ball grounds to see the new players in action. The spectators were treated to a tight pitchers' duel. Asahi starter Kondo held his opponents to just three hits and a single unearned run, but Sanko's starter Yokochi did even better, striking out nine and not allowing a hit for the first seven innings. The high schoolers entered the eighth inning with a 1-0 lead when Asahi outfielder Junji Aisawa reached second on an error and then scored on Seattle's first and only hit of the afternoon. The game ended as a 1-1 draw.

Fukuda and his team were probably pleased with the results so far. They had played well against five top high schools and one college, winning two, losing three, and tying two. As they returned to Tokyo, they stopped in Nagoya and lost two games to Aichi Prefectural High School (Aichi Dai-Ichi Chugaku), 7-3 and 9-4, but their greatest challenge loomed ahead – Waseda and Keio Universities.[43]

At 3 P.M. on Saturday, October 10, a beautiful warm fall afternoon with clear blue skies and the temperature just shy of 71 degrees, James Kondo took the mound against the Waseda nine.[44] Although the university always fielded a top squad, the 1914 club was not one of Waseda's strongest. The team contained two future members of the Japanese Hall of Fame, Tadao Ichioka and Tatsuo Saeki. Both were good players, but both were inducted for their later off-field accomplishments – Ichioka became the general manager of the 1934 All-Nippon team and the Yomiuri Giants, while Saeki became an umpire and organizer of high-school baseball.

Kondo held Waseda scoreless until the fourth inning, when Shirin Cho smacked a triple and Yoshio Asanuma, who later also became a general manager for the Yomiuri Giants, drove him in with a single. The collegians tacked on another three runs in the fifth as Cho singled in Kichibei Kato and then came home on a triple by Asanuma, who subsequently scored on a balk. In the eighth, Waseda scored two more runs on a bases-loaded infield hit by Kazuyoshi Yokohama to push their lead to 6-0. Meanwhile, Waseda hurler Tamizo Kawashima dominated the Asahi batters, striking out five and surrendering a lone hit to Yoshiaki Marumo. Asahi had a chance in the eighth when third baseman John Ikeda drove the ball to deep center field, over Cho's head. Cho, however, sprinted back and to the fans' delight made a diving catch to preserve the 6-0 shutout.

The next afternoon, the Asahi ended their tour against Keio University at the Mita grounds. For the second consecutive day, Kondo took the mound for Asahi. Keio hit him hard in the first inning, jumping out to a quick 3-0 lead. Most observers felt that this was the start of a one-sided rout, but Kondo regained control and shut down the Keio batters for the next seven innings. To nearly everybody's surprise, Asahi scored one in the third and then surged ahead in the seventh on three-run homer by Ikeda. "Hugely confused," Keio went to the bench in the eighth inning and brought in Kazuma Sugase and Akira Kusaka as pinch-hitters.[45] The tactic worked as Keio rallied for four runs to win, 7-4.

With their fourth consecutive loss, the Asahi ended the baseball tour with a 2-7-2 record. They had lost all three contests against the collegians but had played evenly with some of Japan's top high-school teams. Yet, as a cultural exchange the Asahis' trip was a resounding success. The players learned about their parents' homeland, attended receptions, and created ties with Japanese ballplayers. Frank Fukuda and the Asahi returned to Japan twice more – in 1918 and 1921 – each time strengthening cultural and economic bridges between Japan and Seattle.

Other Japanese American teams followed the Nippon's and Asahi's lead. Between 1915 and 1940, 14 North American and six Hawaiian Nisei clubs visited Japan. Some went just to play baseball but many followed the philosophy of *kekehashi* and went to learn about their parents' land and build bridges between the two cultures.

1914 SEATTLE NIPPON GAMES IN JAPAN

Date	Place	Opponent	Score	Winner	Loser
September 12	Totsuka Grounds, Tokyo	Waseda University	5-4	Engel	Kawashima
September 15	Mita Grounds, Tokyo	Keio University	0-7	Sugase	Engel
September 19	Mita Grounds, Tokyo	Keio University	4-3	Engel	Numata
September 20	Totsuka Grounds, Tokyo	Waseda University	2-23	Kawashima	Takano
September 22	Totsuka Grounds, Tokyo	Tomon Club	3-15	Shirai	Shimada
September 26	Totsuka Grounds, Tokyo	Waseda University	5-8	Kawashima	Engel
September 27	Mita Grounds, Tokyo	Keio University	0-1	Sugase	Engel
September 28	Mita Grounds, Tokyo	Mita Club	6-6	None	None

1914 SEATTLE ASAHI GAMES IN JAPAN

Date	Place	Opponent	Score	Winner	Loser
September 26	Yokohama Park	Yokohama Commercial	2-2	None	None
September 27	Yokohama Park	Yokohama Commercial	4-6	Masuda	Ikeda
September 28	Osaka	Osaka Shogyo	7-5	Marumo	Yatani
September 29	Kobe	Kobe High School	5-6	Kubota	Kondo
September 30	Nishinomiya	Kwansei Gakuin	3-5	Miki	Marumo
October 4	Kyoto	Kyoto Dai-ni	7-2	Marumo	Matsuda
October 4	Kyoto	Third Higher School	1-1	None	None
October 6	Nagoya	Aichi-Itchu	3-7	Unknown	Kondo
October 7	Nagoya	Aichi-Itchu	4-9	Unknown	Marumo
October 10	Tokyo	Waseda University	0-6	Kawashima	Kondo
October 11	Tokyo	Keio University	4-7	Ishigawa	Kondo

ACKNOWLEDGMENT

I would like to thank Yoichi Nagata for providing me with Japanese-language newspaper accounts of the games and helping me with Japanese names; Tomohiko Oda for translating the chapter covering the Nippon's tour in *Yakyu-Nenpoh* and the newspaper article welcoming the Nippon in *Tokyo Asahi*; Emi Kikuchi for translating the "Welcome Asahi Players!" article in *Yokohama Boeki Shimpo*, and Carla Grace for translating the chapter covering the Asahi's tour in *Yakyu-Nenpoh*.

NOTES

1 "Johnstons Win Again," *Seattle Star*, July 22, 1907: 2.

2 "Gossip About the Players," *Seattle Daily Times*, May 24, 1908: 16.

3 "Unique Ball Game Played Here," *Seattle Daily Times*, July 10, 1908: 16.

4 "Fast Mikado Baseball Team," *Seattle Star*, July 9, 1910: 2.

5 "Jap Teams Get into the Game," *Tacoma Times*, May 6, 1910: 2; Mikado baseball team with Northwest Japanese Baseball Tournament trophy, Seattle, 1911, Frank Fukuda Photograph and Ephemera Collection, University of Washington Libraries Special Collections.

6 Ryoichi Shibazaki, *Seattle and the Japanese-United States Baseball Connection, 1905-1926* (Seattle: University of Washington Master's Thesis, 1981), 87-88.

7 "Amateur Baseball," *Seattle Daily Times*, July 6, 1912: 11; Shibazaki, 79.

8 "Tigers Beat Nippons," *Seattle Daily Times*, March 23, 1914: 12; "Seattle Takes Game from Jap Team," *Seattle Star*, March 30, 1914: 7; "Nippons Lose Well-Played Game," *Seattle Daily Times*, March 30, 1914: 14.

9 "Nippons Defeat Fast Keio Team," *Seattle Daily Times*, April 10, 1914: 21.

10 Cadreau is often called Bill Chouneau in baseball records.

11 "Redskin Is a Good Jap; Wins a Game," *Seattle Star*, April 10, 1914: 13.

12 "Nippons Defeat Fast Keio Team."

13 "Nippons Beat Asahis in Close Game," *Seattle Daily Times*, July 13, 1914: 10.

14 "An Advance of 25 to 100 Per Cent on Grain and Flour Rates to Points in Orient," *Lewiston Fergus County Democrat*, August 27, 1914: 9.

15 "Shipping and Mail Notices," *Japan Times*, September 11, 1914: 6.

16 "Seattle Baseball Team Arrives," *Tokyo Asahi*, September 11, 1914: 5.

17 "Seattle Baseball Team Arrives."

18 Takuo Ito, ed., *Yakyu-Nenpoh* (Tokyo: Mimatsu Shouten, 1915), 25.

19 Ito, 26.

20 Ito, 28.

21 Ito, 28.

22 Ito, 29.

23 Ito, 32.

24 Ito, 30-32; "Seattle vs. Keio," *Tokyo Nichi Nichi*, September 20, 1914: 7; "Keio Defeated," *Tokyo Asahi*, September 20, 1914: 5.

25 Ito, 32.

26 Ito, 34-35.

27 Ito, 37.

28 Ito, 39-41.

29 Ito, 41.

30 Ito, 42.

31 Ito, 42.

32 Ito, 44-46; "Seattle and Mita Tie," *Tokyo Asahi*, September 29, 1914: 5.

33 Robert K. Fitts, *Issei Baseball* (Lincoln: University of Nebraska Press, 2020), 215.

34 "George Engle Back from Japan," *Seattle Daily Times*, October 23, 1914: 21.

35 As Japanese sources rarely list players' full names, the first names have been gleaned from various newspaper articles, census reports, and ships' passenger lists. Japanese names are often misspelled in English documents so their actual names may differ from those listed in the chapter. The identification of Kondo as Sukehiko (born July 14, 1892, in Hawaii) is not definite but fits all available facts.

36 Shibazaki, 80.

37 Shibazaki, 80; see also Samuel O. Regalado, "Baseball's *Kakehashi*: A Bridge of Understanding and the Nikkei Experience," in Mark Dyreson, J.A. Mangam, and Roberta J. Park, eds., *Mapping an Empire of American Sport: Expansion, Assimilation, Adaptation and Resistance* (New York: Routledge, 2013), 60-75.

38 "Watashitachi no Kokorogake – Bokuku no Tameni," *Mita Shimbun*, September 19, 1918; translated and quoted in Shibazaki, 87.

39 "Welcome Asahi Players!" *Yokohama Boeki Shimpo*, September 23, 1914: 1.

40 "Welcome Asahi Players!"

41 The Kansai area is the second most populated region of Japan, consisting of Osaka, Kyoto, Nara, Wakayama, Hyogo, and Shiga Prefectures.

42 "Kansai ni okeru Shiatoru Asahi Yakyudan," *Yakyukai*, Vol 4, No 12, inside cover, 8.

43 *Nagoya Shimbun*, October 7, 1914: 5; October 8, 1914: 5.

44 "Weather Report," *Japan Times*, October 11, 1914: 4.

45 Ito, 57.

ALL-STARS, AMATEURS AND ACRIMONY: GENE DOYLE'S 1920 TOUR

By John J. Harney

It began with big dreams and ended in chaos and farce. The 1920 tour was a lot of things all at once: a high profile, all-star tour that served as a diplomatic mission to engender positive relationships between two rising global powers, the United States and the Empire of Japan; a largely successful business enterprise planned and carried out by experienced entrepreneurs; and a debacle that saw a baseball tour with high hopes collapse in acrimony and accusations of skullduggery. Certainly, it was not boring.

The first mentions of the tour in the American press started to show up in the late spring and early summer of 1920. California-based sports promoter Gene Doyle was promising big things. Specifically, Doyle sought to take an all-star team to Japan to play in exhibition games against local teams. Boasting the cream of the American professional ranks, the tour would feature teams representing each of the major leagues.[1] Doyle had successfully persuaded Buck Weaver, star third baseman of an impressive Chicago White Sox team that had rather surprisingly lost to the Cincinnati Reds in the World Series the season before, to lead the group to Japan.

It was not solely an American enterprise. Doyle was in partnership with two Japanese businessmen, Yumindo Kushibiki and Tommy Tominaga. Kushibiki was by this time a well-known figure in the United States, known as the "Japanese Exhibition King"

米國職業野球團一行

Doyle's 1920 All-Americans

for his work in introducing the American public to Japanese cultural artifacts at the Columbian Exposition at Chicago in 1893 and, closer in proximity to the 1920 tour, the Panama-Pacific International Exposition of 1915 in San Francisco. Tominaga was more of an obscure figure, an "Americanized Japanese" who had attended high school in Los Angeles but graduated from Waseda University, a bright star in both Japan's academic and baseball worlds.[2] In truth, he was a fairly minor player who succeeded in establishing himself as a go-between for Kushibiki and Doyle, but his involvement helped give credence to the feasibility of a tour to Japan and lent the endeavor an air of cultural exchange as an act of American generosity.

The advantages of the tour seemed clear enough, at least to Doyle, who utilized a network of contacts in the California press to hype up interest. The visit of John McGraw and Charles Comiskey's World Tour to Japan in 1913 gave sufficient precedent, and Doyle and his fellow organizers sang all the right notes. This tour would deepen friendship between the two countries, and also allow the Americans to assist their fellow baseball people in Japan to kick-start professional baseball in that country. The commercial advantages also appeared to be evident and the American papers, long since used to the reality of barnstorming and off-season financial opportunities for baseball players, naturally went along in those assumptions.

From the start, then, Doyle's tour – and in the months to come and in the years since it would come to be associated primarily with its central organizer and promoter more than any of the players – was a hybrid of naked commercial interest and a somewhat ambivalent commitment to deepening cultural ties across the Pacific and facilitating a natural leadership position for the United States in the growth of the game across the world. Doyle had big plans; but it wasn't to be.

For one thing, Weaver did not join them. Embroiled in the growing Black Sox scandal of the fall of 1920, he dropped out of the tour. He had been the big draw, the biggest name attached to the tour on the day of its announcement. Doyle had intended for Weaver to serve as captain of the AL team and de facto head of the playing squad as a whole.[3] Initially, this had seemingly been successful: By July, Doyle was able to claim that Weaver had helped in signing a host of major leaguers, including St. Louis Browns first baseman George Sisler, Detroit Tigers catcher Eddie Ainsmith, and Weaver's White Sox teammate Happy Felsch.[4] Tominaga and others talked a big game

indeed, happily comparing the coming tour to the around-the-world Giants-White Sox Tour of 1913.[5] It was not to be. Ainsmith, however, stuck with Doyle, and along with Sam Bohne, a Seattle Indian about to begin a career with the Cincinnati Reds in 1921, formed the core leadership of the team. The other big names evaporated.

The rest of the purportedly all-star group was made up of players from the Pacific Coast League, many of whom had a veneer of legitimacy by having had a cup of coffee in the majors. Outfielder Herbert Harrison Hunter had played a handful of games over the years with the New York Giants, the Chicago Cubs, and most recently the Boston Red Sox. Jack Sheehan had appeared briefly for the Brooklyn Robins. One player, catcher Everett Gomes, was so unknown, even to the press on the West Coast, that in reports on the tour they would refer to him simply as "Catcher Gomes." Still Doyle persevered. Early plans of a tour around California were scrapped, and they moved to head directly to East Asia with a brief stopover in Honolulu.

The Hawaiian reception to the tour was enthusiastic. The local lodge of Elks served as hosts and sponsors of the team, and, expecting a dawn arrival, planned to treat the visitors to a sightseeing trip by automobile around Honolulu, followed by a formal lunch and a game later in the afternoon.[6] The Hawaiian hosts got their game – Ainsmith led the AL team to victory over the NL players – but in the end the tourists stopped by the islands for only a few hours. The players returned to the *S.S. Korea* shortly after and were soon on their way. Doyle was on a high. "So far the trip has been a success," he wrote to the *Los Angeles Express*'s Harry Grayson, painting a pretty picture. The players were all in good spirits: Ainsmith was living up to his role of tour captain well, "[f]ull of pepper and keeps the [players] hustling."[7] Bohne was growing a mustache, and another PCL veteran, Portland Beaver Sammy Ross, was doing a bang-up job running the Filipino band on the entertainment committee. Doyle wanted to be very clear: All was well. So united were the boys, in fact, that to a man they were livid with Minneapolis Millers infielder Carl Sawyer, the latest player to drop out. "[W]hat the gang thinks of him isn't fit for print," Doyle told Grayson.[8]

This merry band arrived in Japan ready for anything and everything. The Japanese baseball world gave it to them. The visit, coming in late November and December in the offseason between fall and spring collegiate seasons, was primed for the attention of an enthusiastic and knowledgeable baseball-loving public. Baseball in Japan by 1920 was continuing to grow, with increasingly sophisticated youth and collegiate baseball infrastructures but a still-nascent professional scene. Excitement for the visit of the Americans was high. The *Osaka Mainichi Shimbun* reported on the anticipated arrival of the team on November 22, scheduled at 3:30 P.M. on the *S.S. Korea*. The article showcased large photographic inserts featuring a number of the players, including the aforementioned Carl Sawyer. News of Sawyer's "treachery" had not yet reached the Japanese editors. The Americans themselves were ready for Japan, the paper said that they had been "swinging bats and leaping about the deck" of the ship in anticipation of landfall near Tokyo.[9]

The opening game in Japan, a competition between teams representing the AL and the NL to fit the tour's billing as an all-star tour from the major leagues, took place on November 25. The occasion had actually been delayed two days by rain, despite Doyle and Kushibiki's original intention for the players to get to work almost as soon as they made landing in Japan, perhaps taking to the field on the day of arrival. Nevertheless, the opening exhibition was a success. The NL came out 2-1 winners, but Ainsmith was heralded as the big star, blasting the only home run of the game.[10]

The Americans played their first game against Japanese collegiate opposition the next day. Waseda University was home to arguably the most prestigious baseball program in Japan. Waseda had played the first intercollegiate varsity baseball game in the country, a 1903 contest vs. Keio University. By 1920, Waseda was one of six major college teams. In 1924, these teams would formally come together to compete annually in the "Big Six League"; but already the universities played each other in a de facto annual championship with fall and spring seasons. The All-American team faced four collegiate teams in total: Waseda, Keio, Meiji University, and Hosei University. This represented the top tier of Japanese baseball talent, the best-drilled, and – despite their youth – the most competitively seasoned.

The Americans won 19-2 in the most lopsided game of the tour. If the Japanese baseball public felt any humiliation at the result, they hid it well. If anything, the astounding score only verified further the visitors' bona fides. Here surely was a great American side, the best possible baseball team visiting to play on Japanese fields.[11] The visitors struck out only three times, with 13 hits to Waseda's three and six stolen bases with no answer from their hosts. Waseda right

fielder Tsunekichi Oshita had a day in keeping with the students' exuberance and inexperience: His three errors had proved crucial, but he had also gone 2-for-4, including a triple. On the American side, Ainsmith was emerging as the star of the tour, going 3-for-6 (including two triples), participating in turning a double play, and stealing two bases.

Ray French, an established veteran from the Western League and PCL who had by virtue of two games for New York in the 1920 season made it possible to bill him as a New York Yankee, celebrated the win by climbing atop the scoreboard and howling to a crowded stand of Japanese fans below. The tour had begun in earnest.[12] French's antics fit the Japanese press's presentation of the visit neatly, as a fusion of advancing diplomatic and cultural relations between the two countries and as a wild celebration of the fun in baseball. Newspapers ran pictures of the large crowd entering the stadium, holding American and Japanese flags aloft together, and of Gene Doyle with his captains Ainsmith and Bohne, all relaxed or outright beaming with pleasure. "Wild fun!" ran the editor's caption.[13]

The visitors continued to roll against Keio University. An 11-0 win featured 10 hits for the Americans to the students' three, with a home run from one of the tour's few bona fide major leaguers: two-way player (and Detroit Tiger) George Cunningham, playing center field. Still, the Keio players had put up some meaningful resistance; the American victory relied on big performances from Cunningham, Wally Hood, and the once-upon-a-time Tiger Carl Zamloch at first base. The rest of the lineup, including Japanese media darling Ainsmith, had a rough day at the plate with only three hits among them. Meanwhile the Japanese press was still reflecting on French's antics atop the scoreboard against Waseda, with a short bylined feature beside another photograph of the infielder smiling and waving a little pennant from his perch.[14]

Only a few days in Tokyo remained; the Osaka press was already hyping a packed schedule for the American team once they arrived farther west, with six games in three days in early December. The Americans got into the spirit of things with an exhibition game between the AL and NL players in the morning of November 28 before their second game against Keio. The NL came out ahead, 12-6, with plenty of hits – 24 in all – but, perhaps disappointingly for the Japanese crowd, no home runs.

Things took a more positive turn for the local fans that afternoon. The Keio team, led by their pitcher Mori Iida, held the visitors to one run in the closest game of the tour. The students actually outhit their opponents too, by seven to four. The hits by Doyle's team were spread among only three players, including one by pitcher George Ross to go with his shutout, while all but two of the Keio players got on base during the contest. The Americans stole only one base, an area where they had dominated their opponents since arriving in the country, and the young Japanese players committed fewer errors, with only two to the tourists' three. Still, the result did not follow. Keio's resistance broke in the sixth inning, when Ainsmith scored the winning run after reaching base on a triple. But Japanese pride received a bit of a fillip when Herb Hunter, who had umpired the game, expressed his astonishment to the Japanese reporters present at the delightful skill of the Keio players.[15]

Keio had proved that Japanese ballplayers deserved to share the field with seasoned American professionals; after the tight 1-0 game on November 28, everyone could relax a little and enjoy the fun. Doyle's men played their part. Their second game against Waseda ended with another resounding win, 10-2, before the Americans moved on to Kobe.[16]

The Kansai region, home to the cities of Kobe and nearby Osaka, was ready for them. The failure of the White Sox and Giants in 1913 to play any games in Kansai was a bit of a sore point; Osaka saw itself as just as much a major city as the capital, Tokyo, and its vast and growing economic and industrial output was home to a vigorous baseball community. The *Mainichi Shimbun* welcomed the tour with a brief article in English on its front page. "Of all the good things brought to this country from America, perhaps the most Japanized is Base Ball," it read. Kansai was home not only to many high-school and collegiate teams but to "many Base Ball teams organized not by students but by businessmen."[17]

The tourists' days in Osaka and Kobe saw them six games in a hectic three days, during which the Americans played exhibition games between NL and AL sides in the morning and faced Japanese opposition in the afternoon. The first team, scheduled for December 3, was more collegiate opposition: Meiji University, one of the baseball programs soon to form the "Big Six League." On the two days immediately following they faced the Star and Diamond ballclubs, teams composed of players from across the college sides they had already faced on the tour.

The interest around the games, and the *Mainichi Shimbun*'s promotion of them, was tremendous. The newspaper for days framed the three-day schedule in the very center of its front page, and on December 3, the day of the opening games, showcased a letter in English from a Mr. M. Tamagawa of Hiroshima in which he gushed about the American game but also stressed its universal appeal and its value to the Japanese: "I am *for* the Base Ball – manly, beautiful, healthy game, and believe that it should be encouraged in all schools and should be nationalized as in America."[18]

The manliness of the game seemed confirmed a few pages later, with a large photograph of a large, somewhat abused-looking hand reaching out through the middle of the page. "Ainsmith's knotty hand" ran the headline, as the article reminded Japanese readers of Ainsmith's work as batterymate to the legendary Walter Johnson – no small part, either, of Ainsmith's fame back in America.[19] He was very much put forward to the Kansai public as the star of the tour. "Fan focus will be on manly Ainsmith," the paper stated confidently, under a photograph of a large and enthusiastic crowd greeting the visiting players at Umeda railway station in Osaka.[20]

Manliness aside, Ainsmith and his teammates delivered. On the morning of December 3, they played a tight game, which the NL won 2-0.[21] They then dispatched Meiji University, 6-0, that afternoon, a result that confirmed the Americans' superiority without unduly humiliating their hosts. Ainsmith gave his Japanese fans plenty to cheer about, with a putout at home that earned acclaim in the newspaper report and a large action photograph to honor the moment. Below Ainsmith's heroics lay photographs of French – apparently now fully inhabiting the role of the barnstorming team cheerleader – dancing and leaping in frenzied joy, and of Doyle with his two captains, carrying gifted floral arrangements large enough to hide the athletes from their knees to their necks. The mood overall was a friendly one. Ainsmith spoke to reporters after the game and was sure to stress that although the Meiji boys had lost, they had shown courage, and that the pitchers' fastballs and skillful curveballs had given the American pros plenty to worry about.[22]

Next came the Japanese teams drawn from the combined collegiate rosters. The Star club went down to the tourists 8-1, with a Wally Hood home run to excite the crowd.[23] The next day the Americans defeated the Diamond club, 16-2, in their biggest win on the tour since the opening day against Waseda University. By this point, the exhibition all-star games between AL and NL teams had become the prime draw. Large photographic spreads in the papers of crowds for the all-star games, AL and NL captains greeting each other, and a group photograph of Japanese and American men in suits smiling and holding aloft flags from both countries dominated Japanese readers' attention.[24] In contrast to the one-sided victories over the local teams, the Americans put on a great show when playing the intrasquad games. The NL half of the touring team came out as winners of the three-game series with close 2-0 and 4-3 wins on either side of a 5-4 win for the AL. Despite another game later in the month, a 6-1 win over Hosei University on December 26, the Japanese leg of the tour felt as though it had come to a grand conclusion.

It was here that everything went wrong. Though there was little hint of it to the Japanese public, the touring players had not been getting on as well as it seemed. In particular, they had fought over money. Many felt that Doyle was holding out on them. Things came to a head and the team disbanded. Doyle took the loyalists with him to the Japanese colony of Taiwan off the southeastern coast of China, where they played seven games against local teams.[25] Trips to China itself and to the American colony of the Philippines, which Doyle had advertised somewhat off the cuff while offering little in the way of detail, were either called off or never arranged.

By mid-January, half of Doyle's squad was on the way home, with some using the layover in Honolulu to complain about what had happened. Players claimed Kushibiki shared at an open meeting in Japan that he had furnished $20,000 for expenses. It was the first many of the players had heard of it. They told stories of paltry sums – with players receiving only 42 yen (just over $20) each, in front of packed houses where each fan paid between 3 and 10 yen – and of Doyle hiding from the players, barricading himself into a room by putting trunks against the door.[26] By late January the news was breaking in California newspapers. Frank Gay, Carl Zamloch, Sammy Bohne, Hunkey Schorr, Bill Pertica, Everett Gomes, Don Rader, Johnny Butler, and Jack Killilay had all abandoned Doyle in Asia.[27]

For his own part, Doyle was quick to hit back. Writing while still in Japan, he complained bitterly of a clique led by Bohne causing trouble from the start.[28] A few weeks later, in a generous piece written by his friends at the *Los Angeles Evening Express,* Doyle repeated his charge that Bohne was a troublemaker who riled up many of the players. Disagreements over money and how to calculate it lay at the heart of the dispute. Doyle denied the charge that he had refused to monitor the take at the gates by stating clearly that he never planned to do so, and claimed that the failure of the players to take up the job showed they "either figured they were getting a square deal or they hated work."[29] Doyle also shared some more unsavory tales from the trip, of players throwing biscuits at distinguished Japanese hosts at dinner and of one player wandering hotel corridors in a state that left Lady Godiva "well dressed in comparison."[30] The tour, initially proposed as an all-star expedition featuring the best players from the major leagues, had ultimately imploded amid acrimony and harsh accusations.

As a result, Doyle's tour tends not to feature highly among the many baseball tours between the United States and Japan. Even in Japanese histories, the 1920 visit has earned relatively scant attention, especially when compared with the tours that followed.[31] But there's no question that Doyle's team was well received at the time, that it drew big crowds and put smiles on a lot of baseball fans' faces. For Japanese fans, the story of the tour was straightforward: a team made of major-league players had traveled to Japan to play a series of exhibition games. True, there was no Babe Ruth or any of the now scandalized Chicago White Sox, but for many who attended the games, it seemed that the early dreams shared by Doyle and Kushibiki of a combined major-league tour of Japan had been mostly realized. Despite the one-sided nature of most of the contests, the tight game against Keio University gave Japanese fans some reason to believe their players could compete with professionals from the sport's homeland. American and Japanese flags had flown together above large crowds clamoring to see the visiting teams.

In the United States the tour was a different story altogether. American readers had little detail of the tour's events until weeks after the players had left Japan, and then the discussion was dominated by accusations of scandal on one side and sabotage on the other. The grander ambitions of the tour had clearly failed. Yet for all his problems and his mistakes, Gene Doyle had proved it possible that American teams, even if somewhat haphazardly organized, could tour Japan. At least one of Doyle's party took the lesson to heart and would return: Herb Hunter.

1920 DOYLE'S ALL-AMERICAN GAMES IN JAPAN AGAINST JAPANESE OPPONENTS

Date	Place	Opponent	Score	Winner	Loser
November 26	Tokyo	Waseda University	19-2	Pertica	Taniguchi
November 27	Tokyo	Keio University	11-0	Robertson	Ono
November 28	Tokyo	Keio University	1-0	Ross	Nitta
November 29	Tokyo	Waseda University	10-2	Zamloch	Matsumoto
December 3	Nishinomiya	Meiji University	6-0	Pertica	Watanabe
December 4	Nishinomiya	Star Club	8-1	Killilay	Sawa
December 5	Osaka	Diamond Club	16-2	Ross	Ishikawa
December 26	Nishinomiya	Hosei University	6-1	Cunningham	Sanagawa

NOTES

1 "Plans for Baseball Tour of the Orient," *The Sporting News*, July 22, 1920: 1.

2 Harry M. Grayson, "Big League Stars Sail Direct for Japan," *Los Angeles Evening Express*, July 7, 1920: 25.

3 "Gene Doyle Will Take All-Stars to Japan," *Los Angeles Evening Express*, April 16, 1920: 31.

4 Grayson, "Big League Stars Sail Direct for Japan."

5 "All Major Ball Clubs Will Tour West and Orient," *Anaconda* (Montana) *Standard*, August 8, 1920: 33.

6 "Elks to Welcome Ball Players of Big League and Show 'Em Around," *Honolulu Advertiser*, November 9, 1920: 14.

7 Harry M. Grayson, "Doyle's Players Enjoying Trip the Orient," *Los Angeles Evening Express*, December 11, 1920: 10.

8 Grayson, "Doyle's Players Enjoying Trip the Orient."

9 "Dai yakyudan kitaru" (Major League Baseball Team Arriving), *Osaka Mainichi Shimbun*, November 23, 1920: 6.

10 "Honba senshu no shosen" (The First Battle of the Authentic Warriors), *Tokyo Nichinichi Shimbun*, November 26, 1920: 7.

11 "Waseda Players Made Game Fight," *Japan Times & Mail*, November 27, 1920: 8.

12 "Sasuga wa purofeshonaru" (Naturally the Professionals), *Tokyo Nichinichi Shimbun*, November 27, 1920: 8.

13 "Waseda tai beigun daiyakyudan hekitosen" (The Opening Contest Between Waseda and the American Major Leagues Team), *Osaka Mainichi Shimbun*, November 27, 1920: 7.

14 "Keio tai beigun daiyakyudan daiikkaisen" (First game Between Keio and American Major Leagues Team), *Osaka Mainichi Shimbun*, November 28, 1920: 11.

15 "Keiogun no kaiwagi ni shinpan Hantashi odoruku" (Umpire Hunter Astonished at Delightful Skill of the Keio Team), *Osaka Mainichi Shimbun*, November 29, 1920: 7.

16 "Teito no saishusen" (Capital's Final Contest), *Tokyo Nichinichi Shimbun*, November 30, 1920: 7.

17 "Welcome! The American Base Ball Teams," *Osaka Mainichi Shimbun*, December 2, 1920: 1.

18 M. Tamagawa, "On Base Ball," *Osaka Mainichi Shimbun*, December 3, 1920: 1.

19 "Einsumisukun no fushikuredatta te" (Ainsmith's Knotty Hands), *Osaka Mainichi Shimbun*, December 3, 1920: 7.

20 "Fan no nekkyo ni mukaerarete beiyakyudan no chakuhan" (Boisterous Fun Greets the American Team in Osaka), *Osaka Mainichi Shimbun*, December 3, 1920: 2.

21 "Nashonarugun katsu" (National Team Wins), *Osaka Mainichi Shimbun*, December 4, 1920: 2.

22 "Honruida wa kyo tobasu" (Home Runs Sent Flying Today), *Osaka Mainichi Shimbun*, December 4, 1920: 7.

23 "Beigun teppeki no shubi o kugutta Sutagun no surudoi kogekiburi." (American Squad's Iron Wall Defence Untroubled), *Osaka Mainichi Shimbun*, December 5, 1920: 11.

24 "Beigun ryochiimu no sessen" (American Teams' Close Game), *Osaka Mainichi Shimbun*, December 6, 1920: 7.

25 "General and Local," *Japan Times & Mail*, December 27, 1920: 4.

26 "Big League Players Back in Honolulu with Criticism of Doyle's Management of Tour," *Honolulu Advertiser*, January 19, 1921: 14.

27 "Double-crossed? Doyle Club Breaks," *Los Angeles Record*, January 28, 1921: 30.

28 Harry M. Grayson, "Killefer Heads Angel Band to Elsinore," *Los Angeles Evening Express*, March 7, 1921: 25.

29 "L.A. Promoter Gives His Side of Japan Row with Faithless Nine," *Los Angeles Evening Express*, March 10, 1921: 30.

30 E.I. Moriarty, "Ball Player Threw Biscuit at Japanese Banquet Declares Gene Doyle," *Los Angeles Record*, March 10, 1921: 14.

31 Kenzo Hirose, *Nihon no yakyushi* (Tokyo: Nihon Yakyusi Kankokai, 1964), 33.

THE 1921 NATIVE AMERICAN TOURS OF JAPAN

By Yoichi Nagata, Robert K. Fitts, and Mark Brunke

In the late nineteenth century as the American frontier closed, the myth of the Wild West began. Buffalo Bill's Wild West show, dime novels, and, later, Western movies created a fictious past dominated by stereotypes of cowboys, gunslingers, and Indians. In most of these genres, Native Americans were depicted as exotic, almost non-human, wild and cruel savages. This stereotype proliferated throughout the United States, Europe, and even Japan. Nonetheless, Wild West entertainment became popular throughout the United States and Europe. In 1921 two baseball promoters tried separately to capitalize on this international fad by bringing Native American baseball teams to Japan. But neither tour turned out as planned.

The genesis for these tours took place on the Nebraska plains in 1895 when Guy Wilder Green, a law student at the University of Nebraska and player-manager of the Stromsburg town baseball club, organized a game against the Genoa Indian Industrial School. To his surprise, "Even in Nebraska, where an Indian is not at all a novelty … when the Indians came to Stromsburg, business houses were closed and men, women and children turned out en masse. … I reasoned that if an Indian base ball team was a good drawing card in Nebraska, it ought to do wonders further east if properly managed."[1] After graduating from law school in 1897, Green created the All-Nebraska Indian Base Ball Team (soon shortened to the Nebraska Indians) which became one of the nation's most popular barnstorming baseball clubs. From 1897 to 1906 the Nebraska Indians played 1,637 games in 17 states and Canada.

In 1906 much of the United States was enthralled by all things Japanese. Japan had just emerged as the improbable victor in the Russo-Japanese War, and the Waseda University baseball club had recently toured the West Coast. Green decided to capitalize on the fad by creating an all-Japanese baseball club to barnstorm across the Midwest. It became the first Japanese professional team on either side of the Pacific, as pro ball would not come to Japan until 1921.

Although Green would advertise that he had "scour[ed] the [Japanese] empire for the best men obtainable," he did nothing of the sort.[2] In early 1906 Green instructed Dan Tobey, the Caucasian captain of the Nebraska Indians, to form a team from Japanese immigrants living in California. Led by player-manager Tobey, Green's Japanese Base Ball Team embarked on a 25-week tour that covered over 2,500 miles through nine Midwestern states as they played about

Harry Saisho, promoter of the 1921 Sherman Indians tour
Courtesy of Jesse Loving, Ars Longa Art Cards

170 games against town teams and independent clubs. Despite success on the diamond, Green disbanded the club at the end of the season. Two members of the squad, Tozan Masuko and Atsuyoshi "Harry" Saisho, went on to organize their own Japanese barnstorming teams and eventually the Native American tours of Japan.

TOZAN MASUKO AND THE 1921 SUQUAMISH TOUR

Born in 1881 in the village of Niida in Fukushima Prefecture, Tozan Masuko spent most of his childhood in Tokyo, where he became enamored with the newspaper industry.[3] To further his education, he came to the United States on his own at the age of 14 in 1896. He attended an American high school, where he fell in love with baseball. After graduation, he became a reporter for *Shin Sekai* in San Francisco before moving to Los Angeles to work for the *Rafu Shimpo* in 1904. There, he joined the newspaper's baseball team and accompanied Guy Green's Japanese Base Ball team during its 1906 barnstorming tour, occasionally filling in as a utility player or umpire.

In 1907 the *Rafu Shimpo* transferred Masuko to Denver, where he decided to create his own professional Japanese barnstorming team. The Mikado's Japanese Base Ball Team played 22 games in the summer of 1908 in Colorado, Kansas, and Missouri before rain cut its season short. The following year, he teamed with Harry Saisho to organize another barnstorming team called the Japanese Base Ball Association, which planned to tour the Midwest. That tour also failed after just a few games. During both tours, Masuko tried to promote the teams with exaggerations and outright lies, claiming his squads of local immigrants were "composed of the best nine players from the Japanese Empire ... picked from the colleges of Japan ... straight from the Orient."[4] Tozan remained in Denver as editor of the *Denver Shimpo* for nine more years before moving to Salt Lake City to become editor of the *Utah Nippo* in 1917. By 1920, however, Masuko had moved to Yokohama, Japan. Drawing on his past experience promoting the Mikado's and JBBA baseball teams, Tozan decided to become a sports promoter. The endeavor did not go well: A tendency to exaggerate and a lack of scruples got in the way.

Masuko began his new career by bringing Ad Santel and Henry Weber to Japan to "test the relative merits of American wrestling with Japanese jujitsu." Santel, who is still considered one of the greatest "catch wrestlers" of all time, was the reigning world light-heavyweight champion. Since 1914 he had been wrestling Japan's top judo champions – often defeating them easily. As a result, he was well-known in Japan. Weber, a 6-foot, 200-pound blond who "looked like a Greek god," was not Santel's equal on the mat but was nonetheless a renowned wrestler and Santel's manager.[5]

A large crowd met Santel and Weber on the pier as they arrived in Yokohama on February 26, 1921. Beneath banners bearing the wrestlers' names in both English and Japanese, kimono-clad girls presented the visitors with wreaths of flowers and bouquets as the crowd cheered "Banzai!" Tozan accompanied the wrestlers to Tokyo, where they would spend the next week preparing for a match against Japan's experts from the Kodokan Judo Institute – the school created by the sport's founder, Jigoro Kano.[6]

Although Masuko had arranged for a prominent judo expert to provide opponents for Santel and Weber, he had never contacted the Kodokan itself. Members of the school were outraged when they heard of Masuko's plans. Kodokan representatives decreed that any student who took part in the match would be expelled, as "the spirit of Bushido prevents ... taking part in any professional show of judo."[7]

Despite the edict, several judo experts accepted the challenge and wrestled Santel and Weber on March 5 and 6 at Yasukuni Shrine. Sellout crowds of 6,000 to 8,000 attended each day, bringing in an estimated 24,000 yen. After the matches, the wrestlers asked for their 35 percent cut of the gate receipts plus reimbursement for their travel expenses. Masuko, however, claimed that the matches had produced a profit of only 196 yen and promised to pay when cash became available. They next went to Nagoya, where Tozan had arranged two more matches. Despite strong attendance, the wrestlers still did not receive their money. A few days later in Osaka, Santel and Weber refused to enter the ring unless they were paid upfront. Masuko coughed up 300 yen and the matches took place. Noting the large crowds, the wrestlers demanded 1,000 yen prior to the third match. After much wrangling, they eventually accepted a check from a local promoter.[8]

The next morning, when Santel presented the check at the bank, he was told that the promoter had no account, making the check worthless. Returning to the Osaka promoter's office, Santel learned that Masuko and the local promoter "had drawn on the money due to them until there was nothing left." The American wrestlers searched in vain for Tozan, who had left Osaka and gone into hiding.[9]

A sympathetic judo expert stepped forward and arranged bouts to raise enough money for Santel and Weber to return to the United States. As he left, Santel told reporters, "Our stay in Japan has been very pleasant in some ways, and we will not carry away the impression that everyone here is bad. ... There are swindlers everywhere and we just happen to become connected with two in Japan." Santel and Weber declined to bring charges against Masuko as legal fees and further time in Japan would have been prohibitively expensive.[10]

A few months later, Tozan once again brought athletes to Japan. This time he returned to the sport he loved and planned to bring the first Native American baseball club to Japan. On July 2, 1921, he arrived in Seattle on board the *Fushimi Maru*.[11] By the first week of August, Masuko was making arrangements for a team of Suquamish Indians, a group of Native Americans from the western shores of Puget Sound, who had been playing baseball since the late nineteenth century, to accompany him back to Japan. How Masuko learned of the Suquamish team is unknown, but the *Bremerton Searchlight* reported, "In their efforts to secure an all-Indian ball team for the trip, the promoters have tried out practically every Indian ball team on the coast and the fact that the Suquamish team was finally chosen is a considerable boost for the local players."[12]

Masuko, who said he was a representative of the Sennichitochi Real Estate and Building Corporation of Osaka, claimed the Suquamish were being invited by Meiji University.[13]

Howard Myrick, who ran the Seattle branch of the A.G. Spalding & Brothers sporting-goods company, was responsible for assembling the squad but the exact relationship between Masuko and Spalding is unknown.[14] The Suquamish players believed their contracts were with Spalding, but, to their chagrin, that would not be the case.[15]

On the morning of August 6, 1921, at 10 A.M., Masuko and the Suquamish ballclub boarded the *Alabama Maru* at Pier 6 in Seattle and sailed for Yokohama.[16] The squad was an amalgamation of teenage outfielders, semipro veterans, and a legendary pitcher who was called "the Chief Bender of the Northwest."[17] He threw a fastball, a curve, and a signature pitch called the "clam ball" that would rise as it approached the hitter.[18] Accompanying the Suquamish was a semipro team from Ballard, Washington, that had been renamed the Canadian Stars for the Japanese visit.[19] The teams planned to stay in Japan for about two months.[20]

The Canadian Stars and the Suquamish teams were familiar with each other. They met two weeks earlier on July 24, with the Canadian Stars, at that time called the Ballard Merchants, winning, 11-3. The game was started by the main pitchers for both teams. The purveyor of the "clam ball," 31-year-old Louie George, started for Suquamish, and a future major-league pitcher, 24-year-old Rube Walberg, in a breakout semipro season that would catapult him into professional baseball, started for Ballard. The Suquamish had Arthur Sackman pitching relief and Lawrence Webster was at catcher.[21] The game was previewed in the *Seattle Daily Times* on July 22, giving us an idea of the perception of the Suquamish style of play: "The Ballard Merchants are going to Suquamish, looking for an easy game, but you never can tell about Indian ball players, as they do not do what is expected of them. In some cases, they break up all kinds of defensive plays by hitting pitch-outs for home runs and making their opponents very uncomfortable."[22] The Suquamish team was referred to in the same newspaper as being "made up of the best Indian ball players in the Northwest."[23]

The regular Suquamish team that competed in Seattle area semipro games formed the core of the team that traveled to Japan. Many of their regular players, however, could not travel for two months because of work and stayed home. Enough players stayed behind that the Suquamish had a separate team that continued playing to the end of the semipro season in October.[24]

Seven players on the touring team were members of the Suquamish Tribe: Lawrence "Web" Webster, 22 years old, catcher and outfielder; Charles Thompson, 28, third base and shortstop; Harold "Monte" Belmont, 18, outfield; Roy Loughrey, 20, outfield; Woody Loughrey, 17, outfield; Richard Temple, 18, center field and utility; and Arthur Sackman, 17, outfield and pitcher. The five younger players had experience playing baseball at Indian boarding schools.[25]

Needing to supplement the core of the Suquamish club, the team brought along Louie George and four nonnative players – known as "boomers." The 31-year-old George was a member of the Port Gamble S'Klallam Tribe and, according to the *Seattle Daily Times,* "is the star of the team. This pitcher is a veteran of many tight pitching duels with Seattle hurlers, having played with Indian teams for years. He also is a heavy slugger and a good outfielder."[26] Having lost the end of his thumb in a motorcycle accident, George threw an unusual pitch he called a "clam ball." His nephew Ted George remembered, "It was a pitch that rolled off a shortened thumb at a unique angle ... rising as it approached the batter. ... It befuddled hitters ... and when mixed with a blazing fastball and killer curve became stuff of legend."[27]

The nonnative "boomers" were 31-year-old Lee "Bill" Rose, first base, catcher, and utility, who became the team's captain; 27-year-old Roy "Cannon Ball" Woolsey, pitcher, outfield, and coach; 27-year-old James C. Smith, second base; and 23-year-old John Lukanovic, outfield, first base, and pitcher. All four were longtime Northwest Coast semipro players.[28]

Woody Loughrey recalled that during the 16-day trip to Japan, the squad "worked out on the ship, out on the open deck. See it got pretty rough all right" and on "the better days, why, we worked out up there playing catch and running up and down the deck."[29] Lawrence Webster added, "[T]hat continued rise and fall of those boats itself was awful monotonous, so we started playing catch on the boat. And we started out with about three dozen baseballs so we could keep our arms in shape. By the time we got over there, we had two, just two, not two dozen. That's all we had [the rest went overboard]. So we hung on to those two and we got over, and we got some new ones that was made over in that country. And there was quite a bit of difference in the baseball. While the size was practically the same, theirs was dead, you'd hit it and it wouldn't go very far."[30]

The two clubs arrived in Yokohama on the steamer *Alabama* at noon on August 22, 1921. The Suquamish immediately went to their inn to change into uniforms and then to the Yokohama Park Grounds to practice. "A big gathering of Japanese fans" waited at the park "to give the invading teams an enthusiastic welcome ... and to watch their every movement with bat and glove." The clubs were expected to stay in Japan for two months, playing collegiate teams in Tokyo and touring the country.[31]

Promoter Tozan Masuko bragged to reporters that he had a big tour planned and that his powerful Native American squad would battle against the top Japanese teams. "The tour would start in Tokyo against Meiji University, and then the Indians will play Waseda, Keio, Hosei and Rikkyo Universities, Mita and Tomon Clubs and others. After the Tokyo series, they will go to the Tohoku region with Meiji University, playing in Fukushima, Morioka, Hokkaido, Niigata, and Nagaoka before heading to Kansai for games against Daimai and Star Clubs and other teams. Though depending on circumstances, they are eager to barnstorm even in Shikoku, Kyushu, Manchuria and Korea."[32]

But none of this was true. Meiji University had neither committed to sponsor the tour nor travel with the visitors to Tohoku. In fact, Masuko had not arranged any games and would put together the schedule on the fly.

The next day the Indians and Stars worked out at Yokohama Park. The *Japan Times* commented, "The boys, who seem to be generally excellent as ball-players, have shaken off the effects of their trans-oceanic voyage, and cavorted around yesterday in true 'big league' style."[33] After the practice, the teams headed back to their respective hotels – the Canadian Stars staying at the decent seaside hotel, Joshuya, in Honmachi-dori while the Suquamish were housed at the inexpensive merchant inn Daiichi Tsuruya Ryokan in Isezaki-cho. An article in *Tokyo Asahi Shimbun* headlined "Miserable Baseball Team" reported:

> They stroll around the streets at night wearing check-patterned yukata [light cotton kimonos worn in the summer or used as bathrobes]. Nobody will notice that they are baseball players who will press hard on the university teams. They are not accustomed to tatami and futon, however, since the first night in Japan, they seem to be sleeping well, probably because of fatigue from practice. Because they don't speak Japanese, there is no way for them to complain. So, the twelve men just meekly spend their days wearing what they were given by the ryokan, and sleeping on futon at night, even if they don't feel comfortable with the way they are treated. ... As for meals, they go out three times a day and eat something very simple at the dirty bars nearby. They get only ice and tobacco at the ryokan and are enduring their circumstances. The Indians say they love Japan, and the fans can't help but feel sorry that the Indians are being subjected to such miserable treatment.[34]

The Suquamish team's tour opened on Sunday, August 28, with a game against Meiji University at Keio University's Mita Tsunamachi Grounds. It was the first baseball game of the fall season, so despite a light rain, about 10,000 fans came out to see the first

Native American squad to visit Japan. After a local band entertained the crowd, the spectators burst into applause as the two teams marched onto the diamond for the opening ceremonies. Koichi Sugimura, the former ambassador to Germany who had strong ties to the school, threw out the first pitch, and the game got underway with Louie George on the mound for the Indians and Tairiku Watanabe for Meiji.

The game, however, did not live up to expectations; Meiji won 10-0, limiting the visitors to just two hits. "The American pitchers were sadly off in the matter of control, apparently having no idea where the plate was located," said a report in the *Japan Times*. "At times they seemed to be aiming in the general direction of Seattle or San Francisco and had the Japanese batsmen in the state of palsy, wondering who would get hit next. Altogether the two Indian mounds men issued a total of 14 free passes to first, in addition to which they hit three men, one of whom (Watanabe) was carried to the hospital suffering from a slight concussion of the brain."[35]

The beaning occurred when Watanabe came to the plate in the bottom half of the second inning. Sixty-one years later, Lawrence Webster remembered:

Louie George was pitching that game for us, and he hit this one guy in the head with one of his fast balls. I never could understand why the guy didn't duck. He just stood there. The only thing I could figure was Louie had thrown him a curve and, you know, generally start one of those pretty well toward the batter and then it will curve away. Well, he jumped way back from that and then it went right over the plate. So, when he got the next one, just a straight fast ball, I guess, he thought it would do the same thing. He just stood there and took it. Well, he had a concussion all right. ... It was pretty bad.[36]

Watanabe was rushed to nearby Heimin Hospital and needed to recuperate for some time at the Yugawara hot spring before he returned to the mound later that fall. But the Suquamish team were not told of Watanabe's recovery. In fact, they believed the opposite. "I heard," continued Webster, "oh, it must have been almost a year later, that he had died from it. So, I was kind of glad we didn't hear that while we were still in Japan."[37]

Leonard Forsman, the Suquamish Tribal Council chairman, wrote in 2021, "The Suquamish players forever lived with the memory of their best pitcher, Louie

George, striking Watanabe with a lethal beanball. Louie felt long-term remorse for the tragic accident. ... However, in 2019, Yoichi Nagata, a Japanese baseball researcher and author, contacted the Suquamish Museum about a book chapter he was writing about the Suquamish team's 1921 visit to Japan. His review of newspapers and other accounts revealed ... [the true fate of] Tairiku Watanabe. ... So, the story of the deceased Japanese baseball player, passed down for nearly 100 years, finally was corrected by Mr. Nagata bringing some relief to the descendants of Suquamish ball players and hopefully some peace to the spirits of the original team members."[38]

The day after the game, the newspaper columnists were harsh. "The Indian team was weaker than expected," concluded the *Yamato Shimbun*. "There was a huge difference of the abilities of the teams, and [the Suquamish] are probably like a high school team." [39] "I was surprised watching the game," wrote a reporter for the *Chuo Shimbun*. "First of all, as a team, it was worthless. My view is that with that kind of skills, to play the top four universities is making a mockery of our baseball. ... I am truly sorry for Watanabe who got injured in such a ridiculous game." [40]

The second game, held on August 31 against the Canadian Stars, went no better for the Suquamish. In fact, it went worse. "With the aid of a bewildering assortment of plays, long drives and excellent pitching, the Canadian Stars baseball team defeated the Suquamish Indian (U.S.) team at the Keio Grounds yesterday afternoon, before some 7,000 fans," summed up the *Japan Times*. "Inability to hit, coupled with poor fielding at critical moments and a lack of pep, caused the defeat of the Indians in their second shutout game in Japan, by a score of 20 to 0." Perhaps worse than surrendering 20 runs, the Suquamish struck out 18 times as they were no-hit by Stars pitchers Rube Walberg and Vietor Pigg. "If ever there was a sodden, cheerless, disheartened afternoon for those youngsters, yesterday was the one," concluded the newspaper. "All the pep they had proposed faded away before the game began. The sympathy of the fans, however, was showered on the Indians for their spunk in playing steadily despite the odds."[41]

Three days later, on September 3, the Suquamish club lost again as "throughout the game Keio slammed the ball almost at will," during a 16-0 blowout. Keio rookie pitchers Shuhei Aoki and Kazuo Shimada held the Indians to just three hits as they struck out 12.[42]

In a 1982 interview about the tour, Suquamish catcher Lawrence Webster said, "[T]hose first three games we played, we just got skunked. Especially that first one. We hadn't lost our sea legs yet."[43] The three blowouts would affect the entire tour, preventing the Suquamish from playing in large venues and attracting opponents who could draw big crowds. As a result, ticket sales brought in little money with dire consequences.

The team stayed in Yokohama for a few more days but was unable to find an opponent.

On September 7 Louie George was returning to his hotel from Tokyo late in the evening (11:30 P.M.) when he was struck by a trolley car while attempting to cross tracks. The *Japan Times* noted, "It was storming at the time and it is believed that he was not able to see the car coming."[44] Luckily, the pitcher suffered only heavy bruising on his face and left shoulder. The *Tokyo Asahi Shimbun* reported that George had been intoxicated at the time of the accident.[45]

It was at this point that the team began to barnstorm across Japan. As the Canadian Stars headed south, the Suquamish began a trek north with their promoter Masuko and his assistant Aoki. Lawrence Webster described the nature of the barnstorming approach: "We'd play their college team or high school team whatever it is one day. And most of the games were set up for two days, consecutive days. If we beat them, then we had to play their town team, which would – may be the college team plus some more players. And

Tozan Masuko, promoter of the 1921 Suquamish tour

every night after the first game, whether we won it or – well, we won all of those we made on a tour – they set up a banquet. I sometimes think they were trying to get us too drunk to play the next day. Of course, they'd – outside of the meal, they'd have beer, whiskey, and sake lined up in front of you. And some other wine, I couldn't read the name on it. There was one thing I did learn on that trip was not to drink sake. Of course, they like to serve that warm. ... It didn't agree with me at all."[46]

The Indians' first known stop was the city of Ryugasaki in Ibaraki Prefecture, about 50 miles north of Tokyo. On September 12 the Suquamish played a doubleheader at the Ryugasaki High School Grounds.[47] As this was the first visit of a foreign baseball team to the prefecture, a throng came to witness the spectacle. The opening game ended in a 2-2 tie with the strong Ryugasaki High School, which was in the process of winning five consecutive Kanto Baseball Tournaments (1918-22). But this would be the last setback on the diamond for the Indians. Their 12-2 victory over the All-Ryugasaki team in the second game began a monthlong winning streak.[48]

Three days later, the Suquamish were in Mito, the capital of Ibaraki, for a doubleheader on Thursday, September 15, at the Mito High School Grounds. There, they beat an All-Mito squad, 7-0, in the opener (a seven-inning game) and blew out the Mito Commercial School, 10-1, in the second game (a five-inning game).[49] From Mito, the team traveled 45 miles to the northwest to Utsunomiya, capital of Tochigi Prefecture. On Saturday, September 17, the team continued to roll with a 19-2 win over the Utsunomiya Baseball Club at the city's Municipal South School Ground that was ended after the eighth inning by darkness.[50]

Woody Loughrey remembered the Japanese players "were pretty short ... [so] they are hard to pitch to and they are tricky on the base running. They steal on you. They will do anything to get you ... off beam. ... [T]hey are pretty tricky. They are good ball players. Fast. ... But the only thing we had advantage on them, we could hit. We could hit better than they did. And our pitcher was better."[51]

The Suquamish left Utsunomiya by train after the game, arrived at Fukushima City at 1 A.M., and settled in at a ryokan (the name of the ryokan is unknown) in front of the station. Once again they were the first foreign ballclub to visit the city. The *Fukushima Minpo* printed a large picture of the team with an accompanying article and the locals came out to welcomed them as celebrities.[52]

The game against the All-Fukushima club was scheduled for 2:30 P.M. at the high-school grounds but fans began arriving by midmorning to get the best seats. A small riot broke out by the entrance when spectators found out that they would be charged admission for the event, but they soon settled down and filed into the park. Many had brought *bento* and ate lunch while they waited. By 1:30 a tightly-packed crowd ringed the field and even the surrounding trees were covered with spectators.

Just before game time, the Suquamish team, led by Masuko, entered the diamond wearing uniforms emblazoned with a logo of a Native American warrior with a deep red face. The 3,000 spectators swelled up with "cheers that could have shaken Mount Shinobu" (located north of the city).[53] Their adoring fans were not disappointed.

The game began slowly with neither team scoring in the first three innings but in the fourth Fukushima gained a run without a hit on two errors and some "exquisite bunting." The Indians struck back with three in the sixth, five in the eighth, and one in the ninth. When there was a hit or a stolen base, to the delight of the fans one of the Suquamish players would turn to the spectators and bow or turn his hat sideways and clap his hands while he jumped up and down. The crowd, loving the antics, cheered gustily. Meanwhile, Roy Woolsey held the Japanese hitless during the 9-1 victory. At 11 that night, the team boarded a train for Niigata.[54]

The team arrived at Niigata Station on September 19 at 9:30 A.M. where they were greeted by officers of the Niigata Baseball Association. The Suquamish players spent the morning in the city's streets distributing flyers to advertise the afternoon's game at the Niigata Baseball Association Grounds against the Niigata Commercial Club, the champion of Niigata baseball. The *Niigata Shimbun* held the Indian team in high esteem. "The team has a reputation for being solid because it is from the home of baseball. Besides that, all the players are well educated and do everything gentlemanly."[55]

The game started with two runs for the Indians on hits by George and Belmont. They added three more in the top of the second, but in the bottom of the inning, the Commercial Club scored three runs on three doubles. The Indians seemed to secure a victory with another run in the fifth and two in the seventh to make the score 8-3. In the bottom of the seventh, however,

the few thousand spectators watched an exciting rally by the local team. Starter John Lukanovic gave up four runs, including a two-run home run, to make the score 8-7. But the Indians sealed the game by scoring three runs in the top of the eighth and won the tight game, 11-7.[56]

The next day the Indians easily defeated an All-Niigata squad, 5-0.[57] After this second game, locals persuaded Masuko to bring the team to the town of Shibata, about 20 kilometers to the east, for a doubleheader on September 22. The Suquamish arrived with great fanfare, as the small municipality had never attracted a major baseball club before. On the beautiful baseball day with soft sunlight after a rain, at the 16th Infantry Regiment Training Parade Grounds, laid out beside the ruins of Shibata Castle, the Indians beat the Aurora Club 18-3 in the four-inning opening game (the game was called after four innings because of the large margin in score), and came from behind to win over the Homon team, 3-1 in the second.[58] Since leaving Tokyo, the Suquamish had not lost a game, winning nine and tying another.

At some point in their travels through Tochigi Prefecture, they stopped at Nikko, home to the world-famous Tosho-gu shrine and Shinkyo Bridge (now a UNESCO World Heritage Site). Lawrence Webster recalled in 1982:

> We went up and toured that one day. And they had two bridges on it. This one bridge was for the commoners. I found this out later. And that's the one we went in on. ... Art Sackman and I got separated from the gang. ... And the other was kind of a private bridge for the "makato" [Mikado] or whatever was the boss in that country at that time. And you weren't supposed to use it. And we got separated ... Art and I. And when ... we come out, we seen the guys going on the other side, they had already gone out. So, this bridge that is carpeted with red linoleum [lacquer] and brass railings on it, we just started across it, shoes and all. And, boy, about the time that we hit that, there was a ki-yaying behind us. We couldn't understand what they were saying. We decided we were in trouble, and we just kept going and got out of there. But Mosco (Masuko) told us afterwards, when we come off that – on that bridge, anybody walking that bridge is only supposed to be the royalty, and they're supposed to take their shoes off. ... And they was supposed to

take them off when they come across it. And here we just come across in our shoes. I guess we were the heathens that day.[59]

As the Suquamish were first Native American ball club to tour Japan, Masuko expected the team to draw huge crowds and extensive media coverage. But neither happened. The three losses at the start of the tour continued to haunt them. During their trip to the north the Tokyo and national newspapers ignored the team entirely. As the gate receipts in these small northern cities, against high-school and town teams, were meager, the players had only received one paycheck since coming to Japan. Funds were running low. In the last week of September, they headed south to try their luck in Osaka.

Somewhere on their trip south, Masuko and his assistant Aoki disappeared, absconding with what little money the team had made. The Suquamish players were stranded in a strange city with no contacts and no money.

The squad settled in at Mikuni Ryokan in Osaka's Nipponbashi neighborhood. Luckily, the players meet a local tailor who spoke some English. According to Webster, he "helped us arrange games with different teams around Osaka and Kobe and Kyoto."[60] They tried to arrange games with the Star Club and Diamond Club, the city's top two semipro teams, but were rebuffed.[61] Instead, they scheduled a pair of games with the Honolulu Nippons, one of two teams from Hawaii touring Japan at that time, which also lacked native Japanese opponents. The Nippons … were "composed of Japanese, Portuguese, and one U.S. Marine on furlough."[62]

The Suquamish won the first game, 4-3, at the Doshisha Baseball Grounds on Wednesday, September 28. Entering the bottom of the third inning, the Hawaii team was leading 3-0, but the Suquamish scored four runs on a triple and an error. After this inning neither team scored a run.[63] On Saturday, October 1, the Indians also won the rematch, held at the Toyonaka Baseball Grounds, 9-4. In the bottom of the second, the Indians scored two runs on an error by the third baseman, a single, and a double. After this inning, the Suquamish team led the Hawaii team throughout the game. Pitcher George went nine innings, allowing five hits, and four BB/HBP, while striking out nine batters. The Hawaiian team committed eight errors, which cost them the game. The Indians had seven hits and seven BB/HBP, and struck out five times. In this game Ogi, a Japanese player, was the shortstop for the Indians.

It is unknown why and how Ogi joined the team, or who Ogi was.[64]

Just over a week later, on Saturday, October 9, at Kyoto's Okazaki Park Grounds, the Suquamish played their final game in Japan, against the Kyoto Orient Club, which was announced as an amalgamation of former players of Kyoto University, Kyoto Daiichi High School, and Doshisha. But "in fact, many of the players were alumni of Kyoto Daiichi High School, and they had been away from baseball for some time. The game was hardly worth watching."[65] The Suquamish won easily, 12-2.

Unable to schedule more games, the team faced a crisis. They had been staying at the Mikuni Ryokan for about 10 days and owed the inn about 1,200 yen. The hotel contacted the police, who came to investigate on October 12. Team captain Bill Rose explained that not only could they not pay the bill, but they also had no money for food or tickets to return to the United States.[66]

The next day, the players turned to the American consulate office in Kobe for help.[67] After a two-week delay, the team boarded the *Arabia Maru* in Kobe and left Japan on October 27. Like everything else on this tour, even the trip home was difficult as the ship was hit by a typhoon. Woody Loughrey recalled, "We started back from Kobe. … It was 23 [sic] days we were on the ocean. … We hit a storm out there. … I thought we were going down a couple of times. It was really bad … and everybody was afraid."[68] Finally, the team arrived in Seattle on November 11 at 6:30 P.M.[69]

The players were initially bitter about their experience.[70] "We had a terrible time," one of the players told the *Tairiku Nippo*, a Japanese-language newspaper in Vancouver. "I used to admire Japan, but after this trip, my expectation was reversed. People in Osaka may be said to be good in business, or crafty, … [but] our stay in Osaka was an aggravating experience. … When we were in Osaka, if they treated us like a gentleman, how thankful we would have been."[71] They contacted a lawyer about the stolen wages, but the legal action went nowhere.

In 1982, 61 years later, Lawrence Webster reminisced, "I used to cuss every once in a while, when I'd think about it. In later years, I'm glad I took the trip, whether I made any money or not."[72] Woody Loughrey agreed, "[I] wouldn't have traded that trip for ten times the amount they were going to give me. … I wouldn't give anything to miss that trip. It was really something."[73]

HARRY SAISHO AND THE 1921 SHERMAN INDIANS TOUR

In late September of 1921, as the abandoned Suquamish Indians were playing their last games in Osaka, the Sherman Indians, sponsored by Harry Saisho, arrived in Yokohama.

Saisho was born in Miyakonojo on Japan's southern island of Kyushu in 1882. He played baseball at Miyazaki High School, where he was captain of the team that won the prefectural championship in 1901. After graduation, Saisho attended Waseda University's language school before immigrating to San Francisco in 1903. Two years later, he moved to Los Angeles and joined the baseball club at the *Rafu Shimpo* newspaper, where he met Masuko.

After spending the 1906 season with Guy Green's Japanese team, Saisho returned to Los Angeles and organized the Nanka baseball club. The Nanka played other amateur teams for several years but Saisho dreamed of turning the squad into a professional barnstorming team. In 1909 he recruited former Waseda University captain Shin Hashido, renamed the club the Japanese Base Ball Association (JBBA), and made arrangements to tour the Midwest. But the plan failed after the team lost its first three games. Two years later, Saisho tried again and led the JBBA across the Midwest, playing about 130 games in five months. Playing mostly town nines, and a few independent clubs, the JBBA won just 25 of the 87 games for which results are known but in general they were well-received, and thousands of fans came out to watch them play. In September it began to rain, forcing games to be canceled. With no income but still having to pay travel expenses, the JBBA began to lose money. At the end of September, the team limped into St. Louis, broke. After two final games against the African American St. Louis Giants, the team disbanded, and the players headed home to Los Angeles.

After the 1911 season, Saisho retired from baseball, focused on farming in California's Imperial Valley, and saved his money. In 1920 he married and in December he traveled with his bride to Japan for a traditional ceremony. While in Japan, he visited with his old JBBA teammate Shin Hashido, who had recently helped organize Japan's first professional baseball club, Nihon Undo Kyokai (Nihon Athletic Association), featuring many of his former Waseda teammates. With the Nihon Undo Kyokai's backing, Saisho decided to bring a team of Native Americans to Japan.[74] He expected to be the first person to bring over a Native American squad and thought he could make his fortune. He returned to California and began organizing his tour with a team of Native Americans from the Sherman Institute.

Founded in 1892 and operated by the US government, the Sherman Institute was the first "off-reservation" boarding school for Native Americans in California. First located in Perris, the institution moved to Riverside, about 50 miles southeast of downtown Los Angeles, in 1903. The school educated children from 5 to 20 years old with the explicit goal of assimilating them into White American society. Like many government-sponsored Native American schools, the Sherman Institute encouraged the boys to play football and baseball to help instill "American values." The school soon became known for its outstanding football squad and strong baseball team. Hashido's Waseda squad, during its 1905 tour, played a team from the Institute in a hard-fought game on May 20. The Japanese came out on top, 12-7; the game made the front pages of nearly every local newspaper's sport section.[75]

Unable to use actual students enrolled at the Sherman Institute, Saisho recruited several recent graduates and other Native Americans to make the trip in September 1921. According to the *Riverside Independent Enterprise*, "Japanese agents in Los Angeles were attracted to the Indian team after a game played with the Japanese team in that city which the Indians came out winners. The Indians have been playing together for some time, it is said, and have developed some remarkable baseball talent."[76]

Saisho decided to invest most of his life savings into the tour, confident of its success. "He was a dreamer, but not a very good provider," his daughter remembered.[77] He posted $5,000, "to guarantee the traveling and living expenses of the 13 players during the ocean trip and during their tour of Japan."[78] Riverside newspapers added that Paul Hoffman, the superintendent of the Mission Agency for the Bureau of Indian Affairs, helped make the final arrangements. The players received $200 each and had all their expenses paid. The squad, dubbed the Sherman Indians, planned to play 15 games in Japan between September 25 and October 20 against "the leading Japanese universities."[79]

The team warmed up with a game against "an all-star team composed of players selected from the Los Angeles Japanese Baseball League" at White Sox Park (East Fourth and Anderson Streets) on September 4 before leaving for Japan on the 8th on board the *Mexico Maru*.[80] The Indians won, 16-11, and the proceeds from the game were used to help fund the trip.[81]

Although previous reports stated that the team would include 12 or 13 players, only 10 made the trip. Saisho stayed in California so 26-year-old Alexander James (aka Alex Jim) led the squad. James, listed as a full-blood Mission Indian from the Cabazon Reservation, had played on the Sherman Institute's baseball and football teams from 1909 to 1911.[82] Two other confirmed Sherman alumni were on the roster. Eighteen-year-old Harry Jim, probably Alexander's brother or first cousin, who was also a Mission Indian from the Cabazon Reservation, attended the Institute in 1916 and 1917, while 20-year-old Harmon Twist, from the Mohave Tribe, played right field for the school's team in 1918-19.[83] Other players were: George Bravo, 23; Victor E. Costo, 18; Cecil Cruz, 20; John Martin, 24; J.C. Oliver, 27; Thomas Ornelas, 26; and Walter G. Webb, 21, a Yuma Indian. Four years after the tour, Cecil Cruz married George Bravo's sister.[84]

The team arrived in Yokohama on September 29 and immediately things began to go wrong. According to the *Japan Advertiser*, "The Indians … were so anxious to embark that they neglected to obtain passports or other papers which would gain them admittance to Japan." Unable to enter the country, the team remained on the ship for several days as the American consulate general pleaded their case to the Japanese government.[85] After gaining permission to disembark, the team spent a week practicing at the Nihon Undo Kyokai's Shibaura Grounds in Shiba, Tokyo, before starting its tour in Osaka.[86]

The Sherman Indians were the seventh of ten American baseball clubs to tour Japan that fall. When the team arrived, five of these squads were in the country: the University of Washington, the Vancouver Asahi, the Hawaiian Nippon, and Masuko's Suquamish and Canadian teams. The Seattle Asahi would arrive the following day. The University of California had visited that spring and the Hawaiian Hilo would arrive on October 5 and the Hawaii All-Stars on October 22.

With Nihon Undo Kyokai's backing, Saisho's Sherman Indians received the media attention Masuko's Suquamish lacked. The *Osaka Mainichi* sponsored the team's games in Western Japan and covered them in print. The articles, calling the Native Americans "Black," exaggerated racial differences to build mystique and sell tickets.[87] On October 8 the newspaper previewed their first game under the headlines, "A Major Baseball Game, Black People vs. Stars, at 3 P.M. This Afternoon at Toyonaka Athletic Field – The Attack by the Black Troop, Looking Gruesome – Shiny Eyes and Extremely Strong!" It continued:

The black troop, the Sherman Indians, who arrived yesterday in Osaka, will have their first game against Star Club. Let's see how strong they are and how powerful they are as the black troop is known to be fierce. It's amazing what you can see. The coming of the Black Team. Glowing eyes. Awesome arm strength!

Sherman Indians arrived at Osaka

The train from Tokyo bound for Shimonoseki arrived at Osaka Station. The Black squad vigorously jumped out of the second-class car in the middle of the train onto the platform at 8:27 the night of October 7. They are ferocious people with hulking physiques and glittering eyes. They looked like a Daikokusama [god of wealth] from India, as they carried large bags with lots of bats and gloves. This is the first impression in Osaka of the Sherman Indians who are believed to be an unfathomably strong team. In the next moment, I [the reporter] said … "Welcome, everybody!" Captain … Alexander [James] … bared his white teeth in his pitch-black face, saying "Thank you" and grabbed my hand with his big hand [in a handshake]. His grip power was unusually strong, and I felt like my hand was shattered. [Imagine the] speed of their pitches and the power of bat swings by that strength! Imagine their looks shining pitch black on the field, and you will know the game will become terrifying.

Nihon Undo Kyokai manager Atsushi Kono speaks:

"The Sherman Indian team was recently formed with graduates of a school in Riverside, U.S. All I know of the team is the rumor that the team is strong. I guess that their fielding might be [a] shortcoming because it was hastily assembled team. One of the pitchers, the catcher and the center fielder are very good players. The captain is the oldest, and others are in the range of 17 to 20 [sic]."

The party of 15 people immediately went to Takarazuka, where they enjoyed Japan's autumn night with beautiful stars.[88]

A large crowd came out early to the Toyonaka Grounds "to watch the Black team's power. The ferociousness peculiar to the Black team also appeared in practice and it became a vigorous battle with the Star team."[89]

Although the Star was a semipro club consisting of top collegiate alumni, they had trouble with Indians starter Cecil Cruz. Cruz struck out 15 while surrendering just four hits and a walk in the tight game. Sherman's porous defense, however, undermined their ace's efforts as five errors cost the Indians the match. The Star struck first, picking up single runs in the third, fifth, and seventh innings to build a 3-0 lead. In the bottom of the seventh, Indians left fielder Walter Webb homered to put Sherman on the scoreboard. The Indians threatened in the ninth as Harry Jim led off with a single but a one-out line drive by John Martin was speared by the shortstop Kichibei Kato, who nabbed the runner off first for a game-ending double play. The fast-paced game took 90 minutes.[90]

After the game, the Nihon Undo Kyokai tried to bolster the Indians by loaning them two of their junior players. One was 19-year-old Eiichiro Yamamoto, of Shimane Commercial School who joined the Nihon Undo Kyokai after graduation. He had a pro career with the Nihon Undo Kyokai and the Takarazuka Undo Kyokai, and later played on the Tokyo Giants from 1936 to 1942. The other player loaned to the Indians was Masaru Kataoka, a catcher for the Nihon Undo Kyokai and Takarazuka Undo Kyokai. After retiring from playing, he worked as clubhouse manager for the pro Hankyu team. Several other Japanese players joined the Shermans in later games.

The next day, Sunday, October 9, the Shermans played the Diamond Club, another semipro team of former college stars. For the showdown, the Diamond engaged two of Japan's best players: pitcher Michimaro Ono and Hideo Mori. The pair had been batterymates at Keio University in 1919 and 1920. With a blazing fastball, Ono was the team's ace and eventually was elected to Japan's Hall of Fame. Mori was the team's top hitter, batting cleanup, but was also a strong pitcher. After graduating, both joined the staff of the *Osaka Mainichi Shimbun* and played on the company team, Daimai.

Intrigued by the reports of the close game against the Star, fans packed the Toyonaka ballpark for this second game. The *Osaka Mainichi Shimbun* noted, "the Black team had a strong desire get revenge for the previous day's loss."[91] Cruz once again took the mound for the Indians against Ono. With the two aces facing each other, spectators anticipated "a fierce pitchers' battle." For the first three innings, the pitchers dominated, then in the top of the fourth the Diamond scored three, highlighted by Mori's two-run single to center field. The Indians narrowed the score with two runs in the sixth before the Japanese broke the game open in the eighth as Ono led off with a home run and his teammates tacked on another three en route to a 7-3 victory.

On October 10 the Indians faced off against Daimai, the semipro team sponsored by the *Osaka Mainichi* newspaper company, at Hanshin Naruo Grounds. As it was the last game for the Shermans in the Kansai area, a large crowd came early to the ballpark to secure the best seats. Walter Webb began the game on the mound for the Indians and Michimaro Ono pitched for the second consecutive day for the Japanese.

Sherman opened the scoring with one run in the bottom of the second, but Daimai came right back the next inning as a single, three walks, and a double steal scored one run and loaded the bases with two outs for Hideo Mori. The star catcher came through with a triple to right field to put Daimai on top, 4-1. In the bottom half, the Indians narrowed the score on a two-run single by James. Martin came on in relief and held the Japanese scoreless for four innings as the Indians surged ahead, 5-4, with two runs in the sixth. But the chance of an Indian victory fell apart in the top of the eighth as Daimai scored the tying run on a walk, a groundout, and consecutive singles. Cruz came in to try to stop the rally but to no avail. Daimai pounded out five more runs to take a commanding 10-5 lead. Sherman attempted a ninth-inning comeback but Mori, in relief, held them to a single run for the 10-6 victory.[92] Soon after the game, the Shermans headed to Tokyo.

On Saturday, October 15, the Indians played another American team at the Shibaura Grounds. Frank Fukuda and his Seattle Asahi were back in Japan for their third visit. Once again the Asahi emphasized education, cultural exchange, and trans-Pacific networking during their baseball tour. The *Tokyo Nichinichi* reported, "The Asahi ... came to Japan three years ago and impressed us by their gentleman like manners besides their baseball skills. They picked ... only superior scholar-athletes from 108 members for the tour this year. The youngest member of the squad is 15 years old and the average age is approximately 20."[93]

Cruz took the mound for the Indians against the Asahi's starter Mizutani.[94] The game began well for the Shermans as Cruz stifled the Asahi for four innings and the Indians built a 2-0 lead. Then Seattle began to hit, stringing together a run in the fifth, two in the seventh, one in the eighth, and two in the ninth to take a 6-2 lead. In the bottom of the ninth, Sherman charged back, scoring three runs on four consecutive hits off reliever Nagamine. With a runner on and one out, Fukuda brought in Nakamura in relief. Nakamura bore down and retired the next two batters to save the victory.[95]

On October 17 the Shermans played Rikkyo University, one of the weaker Tokyo collegiate teams. Both James and Rikkyo starter Jiro Takenaka pitched well, holding their opponents to six hits as James struck out eight batters and Takenaka fanned seven. The Indians pushed a run across in the eighth inning to break a tie and win, 2-1.[96] At last, after several close games, Sherman had a victory in Japan. But it did not mark a turn of events.

The next day, the Indians met the Mita Club (composed of Keio alumni) at the Shibaura Grounds. James once again took the mound for Sherman. Mita hit the undoubtedly fatigued James hard, scoring seven runs in the first four innings. By the end of the afternoon, the Keio graduates had pounded out 17 hits. The Indians scored twice in the third inning and trailed 7-2 when they brought in Yamamoto to pitch in midgame. Yamamoto quelled his countrymen and Sherman tacked on another run to enter the bottom of the ninth down 7-3. At that point, the Indians "attacked with all of their might," scoring three runs and leaving the tying run on base as the game ended.[97]

On October 22 Sherman won its second game, beating the Shoyu Club, a team of Yokohama Commercial School alumni, 6-5 at Yokohama's Nakajima Grounds. To date, no details of this game have been located.

The Indians waited for over a week to play again as inclement weather canceled games and they had trouble finding opponents. As the Sherman players were no longer students and were being paid to make the trip, many considered them to be professionals. Heavily influenced by an idealized version of the "Bushido code," most Japanese believed that being paid to play sports, including baseball, was immoral.[98] Schools worried that playing the Shermans would sully their reputations.

Perhaps Hashido and the Waseda alumni who formed the Nihon Undo Kyokai stepped in, because the Indians' final game came on October 28 against Waseda University at the Shibaura Grounds. In a tight pitchers' duel, Cecil Cruz faced off against Tadashi Hotta. Once again, however, the Indians' defense ruined Cruz's superb game. In the second inning, Waseda second baseman Tokuyoshi Tominaga led off with a walk and stole second. Jujiro Nagano struck out, but Sherman catcher Thomas Ornelas dropped the ball and then threw wildly as he tried to get Nagano running to first. As the ball rolled into the outfield, Tominaga scored and Nagano reached third. After an out, Hotta grounded back to Cruz, who threw to the plate trying to catch Nagano racing home. Nagano, however, hit the brakes and tried to return to third. Ornelas threw wildly to third and Nagano scored.

In the bottom of the sixth, with two outs, John Martin was hit by a pitch and moved to second on a passed ball. Pitcher Fujio Arita then committed an error on Bravo's grounder, allowing Martin to reach third and Bravo to second. Martin then stole home to put Sherman on the board.

The Indians nearly came back with two outs in the ninth. After Kataoka was hit by a pitch, Ornelas grounded to third, but Waseda's Junichi Ishii threw wildly to first, allowing Ornelas to reach base and Kataoka to go to third. Harmon Twist came to the plate with the game on the line but grounded to second for the final out. In the 2-1 loss, Cruz had surrendered just two hits and struck out eight, but the Indians could manage only one hit off Hotta and relief pitcher Fujio Arita.[99]

Unable to find further opponents, the players packed their bags and returned to California on November 22.[100]

Japanese fans were disappointed and felt a bit betrayed that the Sherman Indians were neither as strong nor as fierce as advertised. Despite some close games, they ended with a 2-6 record. Their offense was anemic. Over the seven games with surviving box scores they hit just .203 (48-for-236). Walter Webb led the team with a .391 batting average (9-for-23), followed by Harry Jim at .259 (7-for-27). The borrowed Japanese ballplayers did not add much offense, hitting a combined .170 (9-for-53). Yamamoto, who played in six games, hit .217 (5-for-23).

Despite the lack of games and victories, the players returned happy. They had been paid to visit Japan and thoroughly enjoyed the experience. Harry Jim's hometown paper reported, "Harry reports a wonderful voyage and says the Japanese are great ball players, as well as fans. This team played nine games in Japan, winning four [sic] of them. Their manager expects to take the team over again early in the spring."[101] The exaggeration of the team's record was also repeated in articles in the *Los Angeles Times* and the Japanese-language *Nichi Bei*.[102]

Cecil Cruz told the *Nichi Bei,* "We are happy because in addition to Nihon Undo Club paying for all the costs as it had been agreed, they gave each of us $200. This trip to Japan was so wonderful that I would like to go back there again in the future." But for Harry Saisho, the trip was a financial disaster, wiping out his savings. "Saisho," recalled his friend Masaru Akahori, "would never talk about this bitter experience."[103]

Both Masuko and Saisho had miscalculated the Japanese interest in the Wild West. According to historian Yasuo Okada, most Japanese viewed the United States not as a country of open prairies and cowboys and Indians but instead as the modern country of skyscrapers and innovative technology.[104] As a result, the Japanese public had little interest in the American West. With this ambivalence, Japanese spectators were unwilling to come to the ballpark just to watch Native American teams. Instead, they demanded a strong baseball club, which neither the Suquamish nor the Sherman Indians provided. After these two financially disastrous tours, no other Native American baseball squad would get the chance to tour Japan.

SUQUAMISH INDIANS GAMES IN JAPAN

Date	Place	Opponent	Score	Winner	Loser
August 28	Tokyo	Meiji University	0-10	Watanabe	George
August 31	Tokyo	Canadian Stars	0-20	Walberg	Sackman
September 3	Tokyo	Keio University	0-16	Aoki	George
September 12	Ryugasaki	Ryugasaki High School	2-2	None	None
September 12	Ryugasaki	All- Ryugasaki	12-2	Unknown	Unknown
September 15	Mito	All-Mito	7-0	Unknown	Unknown
September 15	Mito	Mito Commercial School	10-1	Unknown	Unknown
September 17	Utsunomiya	Utsunomiya Baseball Club	19-2	George	Satsukime
September 18	Fukushima	All-Fukushima	9-1	Woolsey	Kurokochi
September 19	Niigata	Niigata Commercial Club	11-7	Lukanovic	Kobayashi
September 20	Niigata	All-Niigata	5-0	Woolsey	Uchikawa
September 22	Shibata	Aurora Club	18-3	Sackman	Unknown
September 22	Shibata	Homon Team	3-1	Unknown	Unknown
September 28	Osaka	Honolulu Nippons	4-3	Unknown	Unknown
October 1	Osaka	Honolulu Nippons	9-4	George	Unknown
October 9	Kyoto	Kyoto Orient Club	12-2	Unknown	Unknown

Note: Upon returning to Seattle, the team claimed it had a 16-3-1 record in Japan. As results for only 16 games are known, it is likely that four games remain to be located.

SHERMAN INDIANS GAMES IN JAPAN

Date	Place	Opponent	Score	Winner	Loser
October 8	Osaka	Star Club	1-3	Nakamura	Cruz
October 9	Osaka	Diamond Club	3-7	Ono	Cruz
October 10	Osaka	Daimai	6-10	Ono	Martin
October15	Tokyo	Seattle Asahi	5-6	Mizutani	Cruz
October 16	Tokyo	Rikkyo University	2-1	James	Takenaka
October 17	Tokyo	Mita Club	6-7	Shimada	James
October 22	Tokyo	Shoyu Club	6-5	Unknown	Unknown
October 28	Tokyo	Waseda University	1-2	Hotta	Cruz

NOTES

Article titles originally in Japanese have been translated into English.

1   Guy W. Green (Jeffrey P. Beck, ed.) *The Nebraska Indians and Fun and Frolic with an Indian Ball Team* (Jefferson, North Carolina: McFarland, 2010), 10.

2   "The Japanese Ball Players," *Covington* (Indiana) *Friend*, June 22, 1906: 4.

3   Masuko's given name was Takanori but he also used Tozan or Koji. While living in the United States, he shortened his last name to Masko.

4   "International Base Ball for Riverside, Apr. 17," *Riverside* (California) *Daily Press*, April 4, 1909: 10.

5   John Stevens, *The Way of Judo: A Portrait of Jigoro Kano and His Students* (Boston: Shambhaha, 2013), 105.

6   "Two U.S. Wrestlers Arrive for Matches," *Japan Advertiser*, February 27, 1921: 7.

7   "Santel and Weber in Matches Today," *Japan Advertiser*, March 5, 1921: 10.

8   "U.S. Grapplers Find Little Profit Here," *Japan Advertiser*, May 8, 1921: 4.

9   "U.S. Grapplers Find Little Profit Here."

10   "U.S. Grapplers Find Little Profit Here."

11   "U.S., Arriving and Departing Passenger and Crew Lists, 1882-1965 for Takanori Masuko," Ancestry.com; "Deep Sea Vessels," *Seattle Daily Times*, July 3, 1921: 14.

12   *Bremerton* (Washington) *Searchlight*, August 10, 1921.

13   "Two Teams to Japan," *Seattle Daily Times*, July 27, 1921: 16; "American Teams Ready for Games," *Japan Times and Mail*, August 24, 1921: 5.

14   "Two Teams to Japan"; "American Teams Arrive in Japan," *Seattle Daily Times*, September 7, 1921: 15.

15   Leonard Forsman, "100th Anniversary: Suquamish Tribal Baseball Team's Tour of Japan," Suquamish Tribe, 2021, 7. https://issuu.com/suquamish.100th%20Anniversary%20of%20the%20Suquamish%20Baseball%20Team's%20Tour%20of%20Japan.pdf.

16   "Sailed from Seattle," *Seattle Daily Times*, August 6, 1921: 9.

17   "Minor Baseball," *Seattle Daily Times*, July 25, 1921: 12.

18   Forsman, 4.

19   *Bremerton Searchlight*; "Two Teams to Japan."

20   "Two Teams to Japan."

21   "Minor Baseball" *Seattle Daily Times*, July 25, 1921: 12.

22   "Minor Baseball," *Seattle Daily Times*, July 22, 1921: 15.

23   "Two Teams to Japan."

24   "Minor Baseball," *Seattle Daily Times*, August 14, 1921: 14; "Out of Town Games," *Seattle Daily Times*, August 21, 1921: 15; "Minor Baseball," *Seattle Daily Times*, August 29, 1921: 16; "Out of Town Games," *Seattle Daily Times*, September 25, 1921: 13. Experienced Suquamish players who stayed behind included pitcher Dink Staley and catchers Bade Turnpan and Bill Kitsap. Other Suquamish players listed in summer 1921 newspaper game reports, but not on the tour of Japan, include pitchers Lewis and Moss and catchers Brown and Jorgenson.

25   Forsman, 2.

26   "Two Teams to Japan."

27   Forsman, 4.

28   "Minor Baseball," *Seattle Daily Times*, July 29, 1921: 15; "Coal Mines Take Toll From Ranks of Sports World," *Seattle Daily Times*, December 20, 1925: 29; "The Timer Has the Last Word," *Seattle Daily Times*, August 21, 1937: 8.

29   Woody Loughery, *Suquamish Tribal Oral History Project*. Interview conducted by Candi Ives Bohlman, November 14, 1982, quoted in Forsman, 2.

30   Lawrence Webster, *Suquamish Tribal Oral History Project Interview W.1.02. 1982*, quoted in Forsman, 2-3.

31   "Indian Ball Team Arrives for Series," *Japan Advertiser*, August 23, 1921: 12.

32   "Two North American Teams to Make a Splash in Our Baseball World in Early Fall," *Tokyo Nichinichi Shimbun*, August 22, 1921: 7. Masuko is not actually named in the article as making this statement but he is the most likely source.

33   "American Teams Ready Games, Indian School and 'Canuck' Players Have Workout at Yokohama," *Japan Times and Mail*, August 24, 1921: 5.

34   "Miserable Baseball Team," *Tokyo Asahi Shimbun*, August 25, 1921: 5.

35   "American Tossers Blanked Meiji," *Japan Times and Mail*, August 29, 1921: 5.

36   Webster, 4-5.

37   Webster, 5.

38   Forsman, 6.

39   "Weaker Team Beyond Imagination," *Yamato Shimbun*, August 29, 1921: 3.

40   "Indians Crushed: First Game against Meiji," *Chuo Shimbun*, August 29, 1921: 3.

41   "Lo, Poor Indians Are Waxed Again," *Japan Times and Mail*, September 1, 1921: 5.

42   "Indians Lose Again," *Japan Times and Mail*, September 5, 1921: 5; "Keio's Crushing Victory," *Jiji Shimpo*, September 3, 1921: 7.

43   Webster, 4.

44   "Canadian Ballplayer Injured," *Japan Times and Mail*, September 8, 1921: 1.

45   "A Player Gets Hurt: George of the Indian Team Collided with a Train," *Tokyo Asahi Shimbun*, September 9, 1921: 2.

46   Webster, 6.

47   In 1921 Ryugasaki High School was known as Ryugasaki Middle School but for the ease of North American readers we are referring to Japanese middle schools as high schools, since the students were between 12 and 17 years old.

48   "Indians Win," *Tokyo Asahi Shimbun*, September 13, 1921: 2.

49   "Indians Win Both," *Tokyo Nichinichi Shimbun*, September 16, 1921: 9.

50   "Utsunomiya Club vs. Indians," *Shimotsuke Shimbun*, September 18, 1921: 5; "Utsunomiya Club Eventually Beaten," *Shimotsuke Shimbun*, September 19, 1921: 3.

51   Loughery, 6.

52   "Fukushima Team Suffered a Terrible Loss, 9-1," *Fukushima Minpo*, September 19, 1921: 3.

53   "Fine Warriors Even in Defeat," *Fukushima Minpo*, September 20, 1921: 5.

54   "Fine Warriors Even in Defeat."

55   "Games Against Indian Players," *Niigata Shimbun*, September 16, 1921: 3.

56   "Spectacular Baseball Game," *Niigata Shimbun*, September 20, 1921: 5.

57   "Indians Win Big," *Niigata Shimbun*, September 21, 1921: 7.

58   "Successful Baseball Games in Shibata," *Niigata Shimbun*, October 23, 1921: 5; Michiko Maejima, "A Study of Late 19th Century Military Bases and Barracks of the Former Army of Japan," *Journal of Asian Architecture and Building Engineering*, 7:2, 155-161.

59   Webster, 6.

60   Webster, 7.

61   "Poor Indian Baseball Team Duped by a Bad Promoter," *Osaka Mainichi Shimbun*, October 14, 1921: 2.

62   "Ball Team Goes to Orient," *Portland Morning Oregonian*, September 13, 1921: 12.

63   "Indians Win," *Osaka Mainichi Shimbun*, September 29, 1921: 7.

64   "Hawaii Defeated by Indians 9-4," *Kobe Yushin Nippo*, October 2, 1921: 6.

65   "Review of Baseball Fever in Kyoto," *Kyoto Hinode Shimbun*, October 27, 1921: 3.

66   "Poor Indian Baseball Team Duped by a Bad Promoter," *Osaka Mainichi Shimbun*, October 14, 1921: 2; Dave Boling, "A Puget Sound Baseball Team That Did Make It to Japan," *Tacoma News Tribune*, March 23, 2003: C11.

67   Vince O'Keefe, "Sad Suquamish Story: Stranded in Orient," *Seattle Daily Times*, July 4, 1976: H6.

68   Loughery, 7.

69   "Along the Waterfront," *Seattle Daily Times*, November 12, 1921: 13.

70   Forsman, 7.

71   "Victoria News," *Tairiku Nippo*, November 12, 1921: 5.

72   Webster, 7.

73   Loughery, 7.

74   Masaru Akahori, *Nanka Nihonjin Yakyushi* [History *of Japanese Baseball in Southern California*] (Los Angeles: Town Crier, 1956), 2.

75   "Wiry Japs Wallop Reds," *Los Angeles Times*, May 21, 1905: III1.

76   "Sherman Indians to Play Japanese Teams in Japan," *Riverside Independent Enterprise*, September 12, 1921: 1.

77   Mataye Saisho Nishi, interview with Robert K. Fitts, June 2, 2016.

78   "Indian-Japanese Baseball Game on Tomorrow's Card," *Los Angeles Evening Express*, September 3, 1921: 2.

79   "Indians to Play Ball in Japan," *Riverside Daily Press*, September 12, 1921: 3; "Sherman Indians to Play Japanese Teams in Japan."

80   "Indian-Japanese Baseball Game on Tomorrow's Card."

81   "Sherman Indians Play Japs Today," *Los Angeles Times*, September 4, 1921: 8; "Good Fight in a Close Contest," *Rafu Shimpo*, September 6, 1921: 2.

82   "Sherman Notes," *Riverside Daily Press*, February 25, 1909: 10; "General News," *Sherman Bulletin*, March 2, 1910: 2: "Thanksgiving Football," *Sherman Bulletin*, November 30, 1910: 2; "General News," *Sherman Bulletin*, February 8, 1911: 2.

83   Yoichi Nagata, *Why Was Babe Ruth Not Able to Hit Home Runs at Koshien Stadium?* (Osaka: Toho Publishing, 2019).

84   "List of United States Citizens, S.S. 'Persia Maru' Sailing from Yokohama, Japan, November 2nd, 1921, Arriving at Port of San Francisco, Calif. U.S.A. 1921," California, U.S. Arriving Passenger and Crew Lists, 1882-1959, Ancestry.com.

85   "Indian Ball Team Must Stay on Ship," *Japan Advertiser*, September 30, 1921, 5.

86   "Indian Team Lands," *Japan Advertiser*, October 1, 1921: 10; Nagata, 38.

87   The newspapers rarely referred to the Suquamish team as "Black." In fact, the *Chuo Shimbun* commented when the team arrived at Yokohama, "They are not blacks as expected in Japan." "Arrival of Both the Indians and Canadians in Japan," *Chuo Shimbun*, August 23, 1921: 3.

88   "A Major Baseball Game, Black People vs. Stars, at 3 P.M. This Afternoon at Toyonaka Athletic Field," *Osaka Mainichi Shimbun*, October 8, 1921: 7.

89   "Star Wins After Struggle," *Osaka Mainichi Shimbun*, October 9, 1921: 11.

90   "Star Wins After Struggle."

91   "Diamond Team 7 Indian Team 3, Remarkable Batters Battle at Toyonaka," *Osaka Mainichi Shimbun*, October 10, 1921: 7.

92   "Last Struggle of the Black Team." *Osaka Mainichi Shimbun*, October 11, 1921, 11.

93   "Seattle Asahi Baseball Team Arrived Late Last Night," *Tokyo Nichinichi*, October 1, 1921.

94   The first names of the Asahi players have not been identified.

95   "Asahi 6 Blacks 5," *Yorozu Choho*, October 16, 1921: 3.

96   "Rikkyo Lost," *Yorozu Choho*, October 17, 1921: 3.

97   "Mita 7 Indians 6," *Yorozu Choho*, October 18, 1921: 3.

98   Oleg Benesch, *Inventing the Way of the Samurai* (Oxford, England: Oxford University Press, 2014), 164-67.

99   "Waseda 2 Indians 1," *Yorozu Choho*, October 29, 1921: 3.

100   "Sherman Indian Nine Returns from Orient," *Los Angeles Times*, November 23, 1921: III1.

101   "Returns from Japan," *Banning* (California) *Record*, December 1, 1921: 2.

102   "Sherman Indian Nine Returns from Orient"; Nagata, 85-86.

103   Quoted in Nagata; Akahori, 2.

104   Yasu Okada, "The Japanese Image of the American West," *Western Historical Quarterly* 19, no.2 (1988): 141-159.

105   "Indian Players Are Home After Japanese Tour," *Seattle Daily Times*, November 15, 1921: 15.

1921 VANCOUVER ASAHI'S TOUR TO JAPAN

By Satoshi Matsumiya

(translated by Yobun Shima)

The Vancouver Asahi team was formed in 1914 with players who were mostly graduates of the Vancouver Japanese Community National School. Ihachi Miyasaki (a.k.a. Matsujiro Miyasaki), who ran a transportation business, became the manager of the team, which was organized through the Shiga Prefecture network and Matsumiya stores' connections. The team played and practiced in vacant lots near the school and at Powell Grounds.[1]

In 1918, the Asahi was reorganized under the leadership of president Sotojiro Matsumiya by recruiting top players from nearby Japanese Canadian teams (such as the Yamato, Mikado, and Victoria Nippon) to form a stronger team now named the Asahi Baseball Club.[2] In July 1918 they formed the Vancouver International League with Caucasian teams and started to play league games.[3] That year, the Asahi finished second in the International League but lost the playoffs.[4] The following year, they won the International League with an overwhelming record of 11 wins and 1 loss. Although the Asahi featured a full lineup of Japanese players against White teams who were bigger and more powerful, they showed that teamwork and smart game play could win the league championship.[5] Japanese Canadian baseball fans were excited by the victory and gathered at the Powell Street Grounds to share their hopes for an Asahi tour to Japan. But team members said, "No, it's too early for that. We will have to polish our team's skills before demonstrating them to the Japanese people in our ancestral country."[6]

In 1920 the presidency of the Asahi team changed to Henry Masataro Nomura, who decided to rename

Vancouver Asahi players bound for Japan on the SS Kashima Maru *(Courtesy of the Nikkei National Museum 1997.8.9)*

the team the Asahi Athletic Club, withdraw from the International League, and join the higher-ranked Vancouver City League to improve Asahi's performance.[7] Nomura had relocated in 1917 from St. Louis to Vancouver, where he started practicing dentistry on the second floor of Royal Bank.[8] He was a passionate advocate of a theory for healthy baseball and sports but some of the players did not agree with him and they sometimes rebelled.

Asahi finished third in the City League in the 1920 season with a record of 10 wins and 14 losses.[9] At the end of the season, there was a resurgence of talk about a tour to Japan. Some Japanese Canadians enthusiastically proposed that the team should demonstrate their baseball ability in their ancestral country to help raise the spirits of the team's players. It was around this time that Yuji Uchiyama, one of the Asahi players, had returned to Vancouver after accompanying the Seattle Mikado team on their Japan tour. Uchiyama told the Asahi players about the current baseball situation in Japan. The Japanese Canadian Nisei (second-generation) players, who hoped of visiting their motherland, listened to him with shining eyes, and the team's expectations for a tour to Japan rose at once.[10] Nomura, as the leader of the team, showed great interest in the idea of a Japan tour and told many people about the plan to help gain support. Nevertheless, six players (Barry Kiyoshi Kasahara, Harry Miyasaki, Junji George Ito, Bull Oda, Tom Nichi Matoba and Sotaro Matsumiya) decided to withdraw from the Asahi team to form a new baseball club named the Vancouver Asahi Baseball Team (also known as the Tigers).[11] The two groups were not in agreement over whether to go on the Japan tour. It was also rumored that they were divided over Nomura's management policy.

Nomura's Asahi Athletic Club rejoined the City League while the new Vancouver Asahi Baseball Team (the Tigers) joined the Terminal League, which had been previously known as the International League. Therefore, the two Asahi teams played in separate leagues. At the end of the 1921 season, the Asahi Athletic Club decided to follow Nomura's plan and go on a tour to Japan.

On August 24, the day of the departure for Japan, a send-off party for the team was held at the Yang Ming Lou restaurant. Tour leader Nomura said, "We have been negotiating with Makoto [Shin] Hashido of the Japan Athletic Association for a long time. And they decided to invite us to Japan officially, so here we are today. The games will be played mainly against the Japanese university teams. And we will also visit

Hokkaido plus Kansai to foster friendship between Japan and Canada."[12]

The touring party consisted of 19 members: 12 Japanese players, four Caucasian players, and three leaders.[13] These were Henry Masataro Nomura and his wife, Lovenda; scorer Yosomatsu (Nishizaki) Horii; umpire Dr. Fletcher; pitchers Mickey Kitagawa (captain), Tokikazu Tanaka, and Tat Larson; catchers Yo Horii, and Jack Wyard; first baseman Happy Yoshioka; second basemen Joe Nimi and Yuji Uchiyama (manager); third baseman Ernie Paepke (coach); shortstop George Iga; left fielders Joe Brown and Tamotsu Miyata; center fielder Eddie Kitagawa; right fielder Ted Furumoto; and substitute Takashi Kikukawa. The four Caucasian players were added to the Japan tour team for promotional reasons and to reinforce the squad.

The players' spirits were high because the Japan trip was not only a tour of their ancestral country but was also a mission to promote friendship between Canada and Japan and to introduce British Columbian industry. The players received new uniforms, enjoyed the send-off party, and each expressed his determination to do his best. At 11:30 P.M., about 200 Japanese Canadians and Caucasians gathered at the pier to see the team off. The players lined up on the deck of the *Kashima Maru* with bouquets of flowers in their hands, donated by volunteers, and shouted "Banzai! Banzai!" The ship sailed off with a whoosh that pierced the air.[14] A series of reports about the tour were to be written by manager Yuji Uchiyama and sent to the *Tairiku Nippo* (*Continental Daily Newspaper*) in Vancouver under the title "The Baseball Tour."

The trip to Japan took two weeks. Also traveling on the *Kashima Maru* was the University of Washington baseball team, which was also touring Japan. In all, 10 teams from North America and Hawaii toured Japan that year: the University of California, Washington University, the Hawaiian Nippon, the Hawaiian Hilo, the Hawaii All-Stars, the Canadian Stars, the Suquamish Indians, the Sherman Indians, the Seattle Asahi, and the Vancouver Asahi. All of them were hoping to play with Japanese university teams. This phenomenon showed how popular Japanese baseball had become and how active baseball exchanges between Japan and the United States were.

As the voyage progressed, the Asahis played catch, ran, and played pepper on the deck during the day to prevent their bodies from getting too slow. Sometimes, their precious baseballs flew overboard into the sea.[15] In the evening they met to discuss strategy and learn the signs. There were some players, however, who could not get up from their beds owing to seasickness.

On September 9 in the evening, after the long voyage, the *Kashima Maru* at last dropped anchor at Yokohama Port.

The group stepped onto the shores in Japan. On the dock, Shin Hashido of the Japan Athletic Association, Tatsuki Nakamura, a board member of the Asahi, and Kinzaburo Fukunaga, former scorer for the Asahi, were on hand to welcome them. The team got into cars and later settled down at the Tsukuiya Ryokan Inn, where they spent their memorable first night in Japan with a sense of relief.[16]

During the voyage on the ship, the itinerary was programmed and decided by wireless telegraph exchanges. Since the first game was scheduled to be held two days later against the Tomon Club, the group transferred on September 10 to the Maruya Ryokan Inn at Shinbashi, Tokyo. That evening, they went to the Japan Athletic Association Stadium at Shibaura to practice. There, dozens of baseball fanatics had been waiting for hours to watch them play. The players were very impressed with the enthusiasm for baseball in Japan. The Asahi members spent the night not only excited but also nervous in anticipation of the game next day.

The first game of the Japan tour was played at 2:30 P.M. on September 11 against the Tomon Club at sunny Shibaura Stadium which was filled to capacity. In the second inning, Tat Larson walked the first batter. A fielder's choice plus a hit batsman loaded the bases with one out. A sacrifice bunt then put Tomon ahead 1-0. After that, Larson's screwball became excellent and it looked as though he would control the rest of the game. But in the fifth inning, Junichi Ishii and Tadao Ichioka of Tomon got hits, and in the sixth Tomon scored another run. Larson was replaced by Tokikazu Tanaka in the seventh inning. Tanaka, however, was hit hard in the ninth inning and was replaced by Mickey Kitagawa. The final score was a disappointing 12-0 loss. The next day's newspaper reported, "Asahi's hitting seemed to be a little bit weak. It was pity that they were so quiet and gentlemanly that they became nervous and stiff."[17]

Cursed by the long autumn rains, the second game, held at Shibaura Stadium on September 16 against Hoyu Club of Hosei University, was prolonged. In the second inning, Jack Wyard doubled and Joe Brown reached on an error to put runners on second and third. George Iga followed with a squeeze, scoring Wyard. Yo Horii then hit a groundball back to the pitcher, who

threw high to first base, allowing Horii to reach first safely and Brown to score. This was all the scoring as Asahi got their first win, 2-0, on the Japan tour.[18]

The third game was against the Taiyo Club, but it was rained out in the third inning. A game against Rikkyo University was held at Shibaura Stadium on September 20. Larson pitched well, but his teammates could gain only two hits and they lost the game, 3-1.[19]

Asahi then left Tokyo and moved to the Kansai area. In the Kansai newspapers, the Asahi were introduced as the most orderly and exemplary team representing the youth of Canada. Special attention was paid to the three Kitagawa brothers and the Caucasian players Joe Brown and Ernie Paepke.[20] On September 23 a game against the Kobe Diamond Club was played at Toyonaka Stadium, Osaka, in occasional light rain. The crowd was in a frenzy from the first inning as the two teams exchanged hits, but the game was rained out in the sixth inning, ending in a 4-1 victory for Asahi. The next day, September 24, the team played the Shoshin Club at Toyonaka Stadium. Mickey Kitagawa was the starting pitcher and his younger brother, Yo Horii, completed the battery.[21] The Asahi won, 4-0, thanks to the efforts of the four White players.[22]

On September 27 the Asahi moved to Wakayama to play the Wakayama High School team and lost 5-3. Later, Takashi Kikukawa wrote, "We underestimated them because we thought they were only a high school team. But they were a championship team that was excellently organized."[23] Shinjiro Iguchi, Wakayama High School's shortstop, later joined the Waseda University team and became a strong hitter. He was inducted into the Japan Baseball Hall of Fame in 1998 for his great contributions to amateur baseball.

The next day, September 28, the team returned to Toyonaka Stadium to play the Star Club. The event drew so much attention that the crowd started to fill the stadium three hours before the game began. In the first inning, the Star Club grabbed the lead on a bases-loaded walk, but in the fourth inning, the Asahi got the run back to tie it up 1-1. The Asahi scored again to make it 3-1 in the seventh inning, but in the next inning the Star Club scored two runs to tie the game at 3-3. The game went on until the 11th inning when, due to sunset, it was ruled a tie. This game was the most exciting and spectacular one during the tour.[24]

On October 1 the Asahi team traveled to Kyoto to play Doshisha University.[25] Larson started the game and Asahi won 10-7. After the game, the team left Kyoto and headed for Morioka in the Tohoku region of northern Japan. In Morioka, they played two games against the Toryo Club, winning 9-2 on October 11 with Tokikazu Tanaka as the starter, and losing 4-3 on the next day with Larson as the pitcher.

At this time, Uchiyama wrote to the *Tairiku Nippo* regarding the differences between the Asahi and other North American teams visiting Japan. He said, "We are a young team accompanied by white players. Our baseball skills might not be high enough to satisfy the Japanese fans, but our main purpose is to introduce our team on behalf of Canada. And not to make a profit.[26]

The Asahi then moved to Hokkaido and played three games against the Taiyo Club in Hakodate.[27] On October 16, with Larson on the mound, they lost 8-0 but the following day Mickey Kitagawa pitched the Asahi to a 10-4 victory. In the deciding game, on October 19, Larson shut out the Taiyo Club as the Asahi won 1-0. As the touring Canadian Stars happened to also be staying at Hakodate, the Asahi decided to play a game against them on October 20. The crowd at the Kashiwano Baseball Stadium was small and rattled because the game did not include native Japanese players. The Asahi started Ted Furumoto, who was usually an outfielder, on the mound. Furumoto gave up seven runs in the bottom of the second inning and the Asahi lost the game 10-0.[28]

Next, the Asahi went to Sapporo. There, they lost 4-1 to Hokkaido University on October 23 and in the following two days split a pair with the Kyowa Club. On October 27 they returned to Morioka and played a third game against the Toryo Club. Larson started and the Asahi won 2-0. They ended October and their time in the north by beating an amateur club, 11-9, in Sendai before returning to Tokyo.

Back in the capital, the Asahi stayed at Waseda University in Totsuka and on November 6 played the university team. The Asahi put Larson on the mound, but he had a rough start, allowing eight walks, as the team committed nine errors and lost 10-1.[29]

Before the scheduled final game of the tour, on November 7 against Keio University, Ed Kitagawa was injured and could not play. To replace him, the team recruited Tom Matoba to play. Matoba, their former teammate who had left to form the Tigers, was visiting Japan as a player for the touring Seattle Asahi, but his team had finished their tour and had disbanded. He just happened to be in the ballpark to watch the Asahi-Keio game. In the first inning, Matoba hit the first pitch for a single into center field. The second batter, George Iga, then grounded back to the mound, but the Keio pitcher threw wildly to second base, putting runners on first and third with no outs.

Consecutive groundouts scored a run and a two-out error by the second baseman allowed another run to come home. In the second inning, Joe Nimi doubled, and Iga scored a run. Paepke pitched well, and the Asahi upset Keio 3-1.[30] Before the game, the magazine *Baseball World* had predicted that Keio would win. They later reported that by beating the Japanese powerhouse, the Asahi had a good souvenir for the team to bring back home.[31]

After the game, the Caucasian Asahi players returned to Canada. Meanwhile, the Hawaii Hilo team, which was also visiting Japan, asked to play an exhibition game with Asahi on November 10. The result was a 9-5 Asahi loss.[32] Soon afterward, the Mita Club (Keio University's alumni team) asked for a chance to avenge Keio university's defeat. With only the Japanese Canadian players remaining on the Asahi team, people predicted an easy victory for Mita, but during the November 13 game, Tokikazu Tanaka pitched so well that the Asahi team won 2-0.[33] This marked the end of all the games in Japan.

The team had traveled about 2,000 miles in Japan, from Hokkaido to Kansai. When the Asahi put up good fights, they received cheers from the spectators in many places. The team finished with a record of 12 wins, eight losses, and one tie against Japanese teams. If the games with non-Japanese teams such as Canadian Stars and Hawaii Hilo are included, the record was 12 wins, 11 losses, and one tie. It was not an embarrassing result at all.

Many Japanese newspapers and fans expressed their hope that the Asahi team would visit Japan again because the players were so gentlemanly and friendly. Nomura brought with him a movie film introducing Canada and showed the film at various locations with the cooperation of the *Tokyo Nichinichi* newspaper to help promote friendship between Japan and Canada. The film was shown at the Ministry of Education's exhibit of movies and at the Minister of Education's official residence and was well received.[34]

At the end of the tour, manager Yuji Uchiyama said, "Our tour to Japan was a great success by overcoming many challenges such as the internal struggle prior to our departure from Vancouver, an unexpected large number of American teams also visiting Japan, schedule changes due to rain, plus financial problems." He went on to share his thoughts on baseball in Japan. "There were many lessons to learn from the Japanese baseball techniques which are well studied and controlled in terms of strategy. However, there is a big difference in physical strength. The speed of the batted ball is inferior to that of any Canadian baseball team. It will take some time to develop their physical strength and they will have to study it scientifically. In Japan, the strong teams are Waseda, Keio and Diamond Star. These teams [would] have the possibility to reach top positions in the City League and the Terminal League in Vancouver."[35]

On December 2, Mr. and Mrs. Henry Masataro Nomura, Joe Nimi, Takashi Kikukawa, and Yuji Uchiyama gathered at Yokohama and boarded the *Fushimi Maru* to return to Vancouver. Tokikazu Tanaka, Mickey Kitagawa, Eddie Kitagawa, Yo Horii, Yosomatsu (Nishizaki) Horii, Happy Yoshioka, and Ted Furumoto spent New Year's Day at their ancestorial hometowns and returned to Vancouver on the *Kashima Maru* on January 26.

On Sunday, February 5, after taking a break on returning from Japan, the touring team attended a party to welcome them back, which was organized by a group of young Asahi players from the junior (nontouring) team. Totaro Fujino, the junior team manager, presided over the party.[36] Each group of younger players in attendance was given new uniforms as souvenirs from the Japan tour. The gifts were presented with the hope that the next generation of Asahi players would be able to visit Japan and continue the friendship between Japan and Canada.

As the 1922 baseball season approached, there were growing voices from baseball fans for the two Asahi teams to merge and become one team. At the same time, the players of both teams began to feel that they should put aside their past feelings and unite, so they gathered at the Vancouver Japanese Community National School to discuss the issue. As a result, the two teams decided unanimously to merge and play in the Terminal League.[37] The combined team was led by Mickey Kitagawa, with Harry Miyasaki as manager,

Eddie Kitagawa as captain, and Ted Furumoto as secretary.

The Asahi took advantage of the experience gained from the Japan tour and worked hard to train the players under the direction of Harry Miyasaki. The merger was supposed to make the new Asahi stronger. However, unexpectedly, it failed to produce good results and they ended up at the bottom of the league. The Asahi's original players were getting older and beginning to show signs of decline – new blood was needed.

Four years later, in 1926, when the younger players began to develop and show their abilities, the Asahi came back far stronger than ever. The team utilized the disciplined strategy that they had experienced during their tour of Japan. They had a well-trained and strong defense, and, above all, refined sportsmanship. They were masters of small ball, using set plays, stolen bases, hit-and-runs, etc. Their specialties were double plays and coordinated plays such as the two-run squeeze. The team won the Terminal League championship that year with an overwhelming 23-3 record.[38]

From then on, Asahi's style of play featured "Brain Baseball" based on fair play. They were enthusiastically supported not only by Japanese Canadians but also by Caucasians, and continued to be a top team until the beginning of World War II, winning many championships. In 2003 the Asahi team was inducted into the Canadian Baseball Hall of Fame. From time to time, there were talks of another tour to Japan, but it never materialized.

Looking back, the 1921 trip to Japan was a turning point in Asahi's history. The knowledge and skills gained in Japan were passed on to younger players and contributed to establish Asahi's tradition.

1921 VANCOUVER ASAHI GAMES IN JAPAN

Date	Place	Opponent	Score	Pitcher	Catcher
September 11	Shibaura	Tomon Club	0-12	Larson	Horii
September 16	Shibaura	Hosei University	2-0	Larson	Horii
September 17	Shibaura	Taiyo Club	3in	Brown	Wired
September 20	Shibaura	Rikkyo University	1-3	Larson	Horii
September 23	Toyonaka	Kobe Diamond Club	4-1	Larson	Wired
September 24	Toyonaka	Shoshin Club	4-0	Kitagawa	Horii
September 27	Wakayama	Wakayama High School	3-5	Paepke	Wired
September 28	Toyonaka	Star Club	3-3	Larson	Wired
October 1	Kyoto	Doshisha University	10-7	Larson	Wired
October 11	Morioka	Toryo Club	9-2	Tanaka	Horii
October 12	Morioka	Toryo Club	3-4	Larson	Horii
October 16	Hakodate	Taiyo Club	0-8	Larson	Horii
October 17	Hakodate	Taiyo Club	10-4	Kitagawa	Horii
October 19	Hakodate	Taiyo Club	1-0	Larson	Horii
October 20	Hakodate	Canadian Stars	0-10	Furumoto	Horii
October 23	Sapporo	Hokkaido University	1-4	Kitagawa	Horii
October 24	Sapporo	Kyowa Club	0-1	Larson	Horii
October 25	Sapporo	Kyowa Club	9-1	Paepke	Horii
October 27	Morioka	Toryo Club	2-0	Larson	Horii
October 31	Sendai	Sendai Amateur Club	11-9	Larson	Horii
November 6	Totsuka	Waseda University	1-10	Paepke	Horii
November 7	Shibaura	Keio University	3-1	Paepke	Horii
November 10	Yokohama	Hilo, Hawaii	5-9	Kitagawa	Horii
November 13	Shibaura	Mita Club	2-0	Tanaka	Horii

NOTES

1   "Remembering the Asahi: Founding of the Asahi," *Continental Times*, January 9, 1973: 3.

2   "General Meeting of the Asahi, 1918; New Year Party and New Board Members," *Tairiku Nippo (Continental Daily News)*, February 4, 1918: 5.

3   "Inauguration of International League," *Tairiku Nippo*, July 19, 1918: 5.

4   "1918 Game Reports: Vancouver International Baseball League," *Western Canada Baseball*. http://www.attheplate.com/wcbl/1918_100i.html.

5   "Asahi as League Champion. Teams Ranking in International League," *Tairiku Nippo*, August 12, 1919: 3.

6   "Asahi as League Champion."

7   "General Meeting of the Asahi: Dr. Henry Masataro Nomura Selected President of the Asahi," *Tairiku Nippo*, December 15, 1919: 5.

8   "Dr. Nomura Passed the Dental Examination. Dr. Nomura Opened a Dental Clinic," *Tairiku Nippo*, September 3, 1919: 5; "Dr. Nomura's Early Life," *Tairiku Nippo*, July 16, 1923: 5.

9   "1920 Game Reports: Vancouver City League August 12," *Western Canada Baseball*. http://www.attheplate.com/wcbl/1920_100i.html.

10 "Japan Tour," *Tairiku Nippo*, August 28, 1920: 5; "Yuji Uchiyama Is Back Home," *Tairiku Nippo*, February 1, 1921: 5; "Yuji Uchiyama Reports on Seattle Mikado Japan Tour," *Tairiku Nippo*, August 29, 1921: 5.

11 "New Asahi Baseball Team (Tigers) Founded with 6 Former Asahi Players," *Tairiku Nippo*, March 9, 1921: 5.

12 Makoto Hashido was known as Shin Hashido when he was the captain of the Waseda University team that toured the West Coast of the United States in 1905. "A Send-off Party for the Asahi Athletic Club," *Tairiku Nippo*, August 25, 1921: 5.

13 "Members of the Japan Tour Team Announced," *Tairiku Nippo*, August 24, 1921: 5.

14 "Departure of the Asahi Japan Tour Team," *Tairiku Nippo*, August 26, 1921: 5.

15 "The Ocean Voyage Log: Players Aboard the Kashima Maru Bound for Japan," *Tairiku Nippo*, October 1, 1921: 5.

16 Yuji Uchiyama, "Arrival at Yokohama Port," *Tairiku Nippo*, October 14, 1921: 5.

17 Yuji Uchiyama, "Game Between the Asahi and Tomon Club," *Tairiku Nippo*, October 29, 1921: 5.

18   "Game Report: The Asahi and Hosei University," *Tairiku Nippo*, October 4, 1921: 5.

19   "Game Report: The Asahi and Rikkyo University," *Tairiku Nippo*, October 6, 1921: 5.

20   "Tour to Kansai Area," unidentified newspaper, September 21, 1921. Newspaper clippings by Eddie Kitagawa on file at the Nikkei National Museum, Burnaby, British Columbia. All citations to the Nikkei National Museum refer to these clippings.

21   Yo Horii was born Yo Kitagawa but was adopted into the Horii family.

22   "The Asahi and Diamond Club," *Osaka Jiji*, September 23, 1921. Nikkei National Museum.

23   "Takashi Kikukawa's Memoir," *Tairiku Nippo*, July 19, 1927: 5.

24   "The Asahi and Star Club," *Tairiku Nippo*, October 18, 1921: 5.

25   "Interview with Manager Uchiyama," unidentified newspaper, October 11, 1921. Nikkei National Museum.

26   "Interview with Manager Uchiyama."

27   Yuji Uchiyama, "Tour Report: Game Reports from September 11 to November 7," *Tairiku Nippo*, November 25, 1921: 2.

28   "The Asahi and Canadian Stars," unidentified newspaper, October 21, 1921. Nikkei National Museum.

29   Yuji Uchiyama, "Game Report: The Asahi and Waseda University," *Tairiku Nippo*, November 24, 1921: 5.

30   "The Asahi and Keio University," unidentified newspaper, November 7, 1921. Nikkei National Museum.

31   Review of the Asahi Japan Tour," *Baseball World*, November, 1921: 124.

32   Yuji Uchiyama, "Game Report: An Exhibition Game Between the Asahi and Hawaii Hilo," *Tairiku Nippo*, November 29, 1921: 5.

33   Yuji Uchiyama, "Game Report: The Asahi and Mita Club," *Tairiku Nippo*, November 30, 1921: 5.

34   "Film Introducing Canada Was Shown," *Tairiku Nippo*, unknown date; Nikkei National Museum.

35   Yuji Uchiyama, "Review of the Tour by Yuji Uchiyama," *Tairiku Nippo*, December 20, 1921: 5.

36   "Welcome Party for the Asahi Tour Team Back Home," *Tairiku Nippo*, February 6, 1922: 5.

37   "Merger of the Two Asahi Teams," *Tairiku Nippo*, March 28, 1922: 5.

38   "The Asahi's Victory in Terminal League in 1926," *Tairiku Nippo*, August 13, 1926: 2.

THE DIAMOND STAGE:

HERB HUNTER'S 1922 TOUR OF JAPAN

By Adam Berenbak

THE PLOT

The Polo Grounds. New York's National League champs were on the verge of beating the mighty Yankees for the second year in a row. The 1922 World Series was once again a series in one park, as each game for the past two years had found a home at Coogan's Bluff. As the triumph neared, Herbert Hunter, a former Giant attending the game, received a cablegram inviting him and the stars of the Series on a tour of Japan. Eager to capitalize on this moment, he recruited several Yanks and Giants, including the dashing George Kelly, to make the trip across the Pacific. Little did they know that they had just been swept up in an international plot to corrupt baseball, a plot not too distant from the Black Sox conspiracy that had nearly ruined faith in the great game.

Luckily for the history of the sport, this was not the truth of the 1922 tour of Japan, nor a plot in any sense other than fictional. The United Pictures Company had assembled a team of actors, both American and Japanese, as well as a loose script about an international conspiracy plot, to travel with the group of major-league all-stars, assembled by Hunter, during their trip overseas.[1] Known officially as the All-American Baseball Team but often called the Herb Hunter All-Stars, they sailed across the Pacific after the 1922 season to face college and club teams that represented the height of Japanese talent. In addition to the professional actors, the American and Japanese ballplayers portrayed themselves in the film, participating in the unique experience of acting on two stages at once – in front of the crowds that gathered in Japanese ballparks as well as future crowds in theaters. It might be said that somewhere between fact and fiction lies the truth, and while the tour did not produce the kind of melodrama filmgoers would be eager to view, the games generated their own drama and myths, straddling that line between fact and fiction in the legacy of international baseball.

VANCOUVER

The Canadian Pacific Railway train number 1 arrived in British Columbia on October 17, 1922, carrying with it the team of major leaguers set to sail for Japan and begin a tour of baseball diplomacy. On the 19th the Vancouver weather held and the touring pros, led by Herb Hunter, opened their trip with a 16-1 walloping of Ernie Paepke's local squad, providing a thrill to a crowd that had little access to major-league ball as well as a proper warm-up prior to the long boat ride to Japan.[2] During the game, George Kelly, Irish Meusel, Joe Bush, and Fred Hofmann all saw playing time. Because all four had participated in the recent World Series, this technically broke the rules against Series stars barnstorming together.[3] However, due to the pickup nature of the game, neither the press nor the players, and especially not the fans, seemed to care. The team boarded the *Empress of Canada* for Honolulu immediately after the game.[4]

Once aboard and on their way, the team received a telegram from Judge Kenesaw Mountain Landis, hired as commissioner two years prior to clean up the game wrecked by what has become known as the Black Sox Scandal. Reports had reached Landis that the barnstorming rules he guarded with such ferocity had been broken. Just the year before, he had chastised, suspended, and fined Babe Ruth for similar barnstorming infractions. He was furious, especially after only reluctantly giving Hunter permission for the tour.[5] The tourists communicated with home via Bob Brown, sponsor of the Vancouver game, to whom they messaged a wireless reply to Judge Landis's barnstorming complaint. Brown in turn sent an explanation over the wire assuring Landis that there was no intentional rule-breaking and that the entire experience fostered nothing but goodwill and economic possibilities in the Northwest.[6] What went unmentioned in the press was that the game was not on the printed schedule, and it was probably the unscheduled barnstorming that added to Landis's ire. Landis made no reply but was reported sleepless over the incident.[7] His objections to barnstorming, along with his reported racial prejudice, combined with the events of the 1922 tour to shape the relationship between US and Japanese baseball for the next decade.[8]

Tour organizer Herbert Harrison Hunter had been a professional ballplayer since 1914, and signed with John McGraw's Giants in 1915. Though he had been touted as a sure-bet prospect, Hunter was never able to fulfill those promises in New York or anywhere else in the big leagues. He had first made his way to Japan as part of the 1920 Gene Doyle tour that featured primarily Pacific Coast League players.[9] An eccentric among eccentrics, and more of an entertainer on baseball's stage, Hunter was always a dandy (to McGraw's consternation and confusion), and enjoyed

Herb Hunter on the 1922 tour of Japan

sticking out, wearing "a fresh chrysanthemum every day" and touring the nightlife of Tokyo as a celebrity.[10] During the 1920 tour, Hunter began coaching the Waseda University nine.[11] He seemed to enjoy the way the students looked up to him; he treated them to elaborate dinners and allowed them to worship him.[12]

He found work back in the States in 1921, playing the majority of the year in the South Atlantic League before an end-of-season call-up to the St. Louis Cardinals. In the fall Branch Rickey released him in support of his endeavors in Japan.[13] Though Hunter, born in Boston on Christmas Day 1895, had played in only 39 games over four seasons with the Giants, Red Sox, Cardinals, and Cubs, his major-league experience, however brief, was highly valued in Japan. In the winter of 1921 and into early 1922, Hunter returned to Japan to coach both Waseda and Keio Universities and developed a friendship with the "father of Japanese baseball," Isoo Abe.[14]

With Abe's help, a sponsorship by Mariya Sporting Goods, and the backing of the *Mainichi Shimbun* newspaper company, Hunter sought to arrange for a group of major leaguers, including Babe Ruth, to tour Japan after the end of the 1922 season.[15]

Having witnessed the unrealized potential of the 1920 Doyle tour, as well as the value in the promise of Ruth, he knew the revenue was there. And it wouldn't hurt to align himself with Ruth, the most popular player in the world, to achieve his financial and celebrity ambitions. After spending the whole winter in Japan, he sailed back in February of 1922 with a mission to build a roster, armed with a guarantee of $50,000, though it would be only to cover expenses.[16] Hunter envisioned this as the first of what would be annual tours, with him at the center, his mission to promote himself as much as to establish regular international competition with a real "world series."[17]

Although Hunter had also worked with Keio as well as other teams that would eventually form the Big Six University system, it was his relationship with the Waseda team that played the biggest role in getting the first real major-league tour of Japan under way. Waseda was eager to become the dominant team in Japan as well as the foremost ambassador of the Japanese game. Between the beginning of 1920 and the All-Stars' visit in the fall of 1922, the team had faced US competition seven times on both sides of the Pacific.[18] Instrumental in their drive were Abe, who had founded the Waseda team and had led the first-ever transcontinental tour when his team traveled the US West Coast in 1905, and Chujun Tobita, a man on a mission. Tobita had played with the Waseda nine back in 1910 when the University of Chicago had beaten them soundly, and the loss inspired the second baseman. Now the manager of Waseda, he drove the team with his famous "death training," developed to hone the skills and spirit of the young players. Success, in part, meant beating Chicago, and "[i]f the players do not try so hard as to vomit blood in practice, then they cannot hope to win games."[19]

With Waseda's support, the backing of the *Mainichi Shimbun*, a tentative agreement from both American League President Ban Johnson and Landis that goodwill tours would benefit the game (as long as its participants conducted themselves as diplomats and nobody got injured), and even the support of President Warren Harding, who noted the tour's "real diplomatic value," Hunter assembled an all-star squad for the 1922 tour.[20]

But first a roster would need to be constructed. Rogers Hornsby, Harry Heilmann, and Frank Frisch topped Hunter's list, but all of his backers in Japan were especially pining for home-run hitters Babe Ruth and George "High Pockets" Kelly. Near the height of his fame, Ruth was a draw everywhere he went, and Japanese fans reportedly clamored for a chance to see him in person – something that didn't happen for another 12 years. Ruth proved to be unattainable, and most of the others declined for various reasons – even an invitation to Art Nehf that was initially accepted fell through when John McGraw requested that he stay stateside.[21]

In the end, Hunter secured the 1921 National League home run king George Kelly and put together a team featuring members of the 1922 World Series competitors. Included with Kelly were fellow Giants Casey Stengel and Irish Meusel, along with Waite Hoyt, Fred Hofmann, and Joe Bush from the Yankees. Also on the team were future Hall of Famer Herb Pennock, Amos Strunk, Brooklyn outfielder Bert Griffith, Luke Sewell, Riggs Stevenson, and Bibb Falk. Rounding out the group was John "Doc" Lavan, Hunter's ex-teammate on the Cardinals.[22] The agreement with Landis included a clause that the players would receive no 1923 contract until they reported to spring training in good health after returning from the tour.[23] *New York Sun* sportswriter Frank O'Neill joined as an organizer as well as reporter, along with George Moriarty, who was along as much to be the eyes and ears of Landis as umpire.[24] It may have been Moriarty who had reported the barnstorming infraction, but nonetheless his role seemed to be keeping an eye on the proclivities of some of those players prone to take a drink outside the

confines of Prohibition.[25] Some of the organizers' and players' wives accompanied the team, a request made in light of the 1920 tour's unruly behavior.[26]

After arriving in Yokohama on the last day of October, the Americans checked into the Tokyo Imperial Hotel. The hotel was one of the few structures to survive the great earthquake that struck Japan in September of the following year. That disaster, known as the Great Kanto Earthquake, devastated Tokyo and led to fires and tsunamis that killed more than 100,000 people.

Japan's fortunes had fluctuated since the end of the Meiji period, a decade prior to Hunter's tour. The silk market, and the stock market along with it, had crashed in 1920, and the country's place on the world stage was precarious.[27] Tension between the United States and Japan was high as arguments were about to begin in front of the US Supreme Court regarding barring immigrants of Asian descent from becoming naturalized American citizens.[28] The importance of the diplomatic aspect of baseball tours grew as these tensions grew, and the 1922 tour proved how successful the tours could be. This diplomatic endeavor was showcased on the baseball diamond at the Shibaura Grounds in Tokyo's Minato ward.

THE GAMES

Competition finally got underway on November 4 in a game between Hunter's All-Americans and Keio University at the Shibaura Grounds. Built by Kiyoshi Oshikawa, a former Waseda player and the founder of the Nihon Athletic Association, the diamond at Shibaura was the players' home for the weeks they were in Tokyo. The team practiced there daily from 10 until noon and used the field for most of their games.[29] Keio's captain, Kazuo Takasu (who later became the first manager of the Nankai Hawks) had befriended Hunter during the previous year when Hunter was coaching the Japanese teams.[30] Keio featured shortstop Shinji Kirihara, a future team captain and Hall of Famer credited for reviving the Keio-Waseda rivalry before perishing in World War II, and Kyoichi Nitta, who shared both pitching and catching duties but faced the Americans as the ace of their squad.[31]

Umpired by George Moriarty as well as local umpire Daisuke Miyake, the game set the tone for many of the games on the tour, with the Americans shutting out Keio, 6-0. Herb Pennock took the mound for the United States and immediately gave up a leadoff double to Kirihara before settling down to allow five hits over nine innings. For Keio, Nitta gave up two triples and a wild pitch in addition to a monster home run by Bibb Falk that rolled all the way to the clubhouse on the other side of the grounds.[32] Despite getting hit hard, the visiting tourists praised Nitta and his spitball, saying he "pitched good ball."

The following day at 2 P.M., the All-Americans faced Waseda University with their ace Goro Taniguchi on the mound. Taniguchi, another future Hall of Famer, was favorably compared to White Sox pitcher Dickie Kerr by the visiting Americans, due not only to his speed but also his assortment of breaking pitches, including his "change of pace which baffled" the American hitters.[33] He scattered eight hits while his teammates scored the only run that was tallied against Hunter's team during the first six games of the tour. Shortstop Tadashi "Teddy" Kubota, whom Herb Hunter had described as the best shortstop he had ever seen, drove in the sole run in the third with a smoking liner off Bullet Joe Bush. That, however, was not enough to make up for the four runs eked out by the Americans, all on singles.[34]

Midweek practice games against Meiji along with instructional sessions with some of the Keio and Waseda squads filled up the tourists' time. They spent time in the lobby of the Imperial Hotel fielding questions from the university ballplayers on pitching methods and philosophy.[35] It's possible that an underclassman on the Meiji squad named Shunichi Amachi may have been there too, paying attention to the forkball grip of Joe Bush so he might teach it later to Shigeru Sugishita, who became known as the God of the Forkball in Japan.[36]

During the first week of the tour, Doc Lavan was not in the lineup. His absence was variously explained as being so sick that he would have to leave the tour, reeling from a weeklong case of sea sickness, or ailing from "old injuries."[37] Whatever the cause, the man they called Doc because of his medical degree from the University of Michigan, finally appeared in the Saturday game against Waseda. Also making his tour debut against Waseda was Casey Stengel, who had ridden the bench the previous weekend, possibly due to the strained muscle that had kept him sidelined during most of the World Series.[38] What wasn't reported was whether Japan's lack of prohibition laws affected any of the players, though there were vague rumors of bad behavior.[39] Herb Hunter, there primarily to organize and manage, ended up playing in nearly all of the games.

Prior to the November 11 game, Stengel, Bush, and Bert Griffith couldn't resist making their own stage. The three performed "their noted comedy act before the grandstand" to a crowd roughly half the size of the previous weekend's turnout, due primarily to a cold snap in Tokyo. Their clowning may have been the only fun the frozen fans had, as Pennock proceeded to mow down the Waseda nine, striking out 10 and allowing only two singles over the full nine innings. Waseda starter Aiichi Takeuchi, a first-year student fresh from an appearance in the 1921 Koshien high-school tournament, was driven from the mound in the fourth, though his replacement, Goro Taniguchi, did not fare much better. In all, they gave up 19 hits and 13 runs to the US team, including home runs by Riggs Stephenson, George Kelly, and a fully recuperated Doc Lavan.[40]

The next day, according to The Sporting News and other US-based media, Waite Hoyt no-hit the Keio team.[41] Yet initial reports of the game in Japan show that after giving up nothing but a sixth-inning walk, Hoyt allowed a scratch hit by second-string third baseman Shoichi Takagi in the eighth. Although the American papers saw it as an error, Takagi hit a ball over Hoyt's head in front of second base, and though Hunter dived for it he couldn't hold on. Takagi was awarded first base, as well as a hit in the box score published in the Japan Advertiser. He then stole second but was caught off the bag for a double play. Hoyt pitched a one-two-three ninth, and the 20 hits and 12 runs his teammates had compiled off Kyoichi Nitta, including another homer from Falk (who hit for the cycle), led to a comfortable American victory.

SHIBAURA TO TOSHO-GU AND BACK

Nestled in the mountains north of Tokyo is the small city of Nikko, which, in addition to scenic views and multiple onsen (hot spring spas) is the gateway to Nikko National Park and Tosho-gu Shrine. The park was well known as a destination for visiting Westerners, and the traveling ballplayers spent the next few days visiting the shrines and hot springs along with hiking before returning to the comforts of the Imperial Hotel and the thrill of the diamond stage.[42]

On November 15 at the Yokohama Municipal Park, the Americans faced off for a second time against Meiji. Up front in the stands was Theodore Roosevelt's son, Kermit, in Japan on a tour of his own, yelling "bully!" as he cheered on Tairiku Watanabe, the team's ace.[43] The All-Americans won handily, 11-0, before adjourning to the home of Ryozo Hiranuma. A Keio graduate who after World War II presided over the Japanese Olympic Committee, Hiranuma hosted a dinner and party that featured, according to the local press, "Occidental dancing." Golf as well as more social occasions followed, as they were invited to a reception at the Viscount Shibusawa's home the next day before finally having a day to rest up for the last slate of games in Tokyo.[44] Rumors of "at least one of the boys as a boor" surfaced as well.[45]

Back on the Shibaura diamond on Saturday, November 18, Joe Bush shut out the Tomon Club 12-0 with heavy run support from George Kelly's home run and Irish Meusel's triple. The Tomon Club, made up of Waseda alumni, was fortified with several current Waseda players, including Goro Taniguchi and Teddy Kubota. Tomon could only string together three hits with no runs, but one of them was walloped by Katsuo Tanaka, whom both the visiting players and press insisted on calling "Babe Ruth" Tanaka. The title was not hyperbole, as he became one of the heaviest-hitting college players of all time and ended up in the Japanese Baseball Hall of Fame. Taniguchi looked less sharp than in his previous start, giving up 20 hits against two strikeouts, but was spared an extra run when Tanaka threw out Amos Strunk at home.[46]

There were rumors in the press that the Mita Club was recruiting a ringer for its coming game against the Americans. Hideo Mori, the well-known catcher for the Diamond Club who during the previous year had teamed with Mita Club ace Michimaro Ono to form "the strongest battery in the country," was scheduled to work behind the plate for Sunday's game.[47] It was the first hint that the final contest at Shibaura would prove the most dramatic moment of the tour. Ono, who had been the ace of the Keio team only a few years before, was to be on the mound for Mita, which fielded a mix of current and former Keio players. One of those former players was Zensuke Shimada (who had played under the name Nenosuke Fukuda against the 1908 Reach All-Americans and the University of Wisconsin in 1909), regularly a catcher but playing third base due to Mori's place behind the plate.

Hoyt opened the game by striking out the first two batters but then Shimada snuck a home run just over the left-field wall, the first four-bagger hit against US pitching during the tour. It was the beginning of a poor day for the Yankee ace. Without his best stuff, Hoyt did not get much help from his fielders, who allowed Mita to score six runs in an error-filled third. But the real star was Ono, whose breaking pitches broke in all the right places, improving inning to inning with expert pitch calling by Mori. Bibb Falk, who seemed to hit everything he had seen since arriving in Tokyo, was the only American to solve the great Ono – garnering three of the six American hits. In the end, Mita outhit and outscored the US team in the 9-3 win. It was the first time a Japanese team had ever topped a visiting professional team.[48]

Yet the media had a different take on the game. The *Yomiuri Shimbun* reported that Hoyt and his teammates had intended to offer a diplomatic bone to the Mita Club in the opening innings before ultimately securing a win, but that the cold weather and bad luck allowed the game to slip away from them. The *Kokumin Shimbun* was blunter, claiming the Hunter All-Stars had purposely lost to ensure a larger attendance in future games, and that such a tactic amounted to "an insult to the Mita club."[49]

These stories made their way into the American press, which were then interpreted through a racist predisposition that considered people of Asian descent naturally inferior to Western men. As a result, the loss was then framed as intentional on the part of Hunter and company.[50] Yet George Moriarty seemed convinced the loss was the result of Hoyt's "bad arm which resulted from excess work in teaching pitching tricks to the college hurlers when the weather was none too inviting," and Ono's stellar pitching.[51] The original report in the *Japan Times* concluded Hunter's squad was simply unprepared against a superior battery that was playing its best on that day.[52] In other words, the kind of possibility one finds in any baseball game. However it was interpreted, the victory shaped the perception of international play on both sides of the Pacific for the rest of the decade.

The 1922 All-American team

That day at Shibaura proved to be high drama on the silver screen as well as the diamond. The baseball film that had begun production back in New York found its own drama that was vastly different from Ono's great performance. In the script, George Kelly did not appear in the final game – he had been kidnapped by nefarious henchmen who had offered him a bribe to throw the games against the Japanese contingent. He was said to have "free[d] himself just in time to rush to the diamond near the end of the crucial game and win the series for the American team by a timely pinch hit."[53] It was the narrative the Americans had hoped for. There is no evidence that the movie was ever released, but the drama on the actual diamond against Mita ensured that the Hunter tour would last longer in memory than any drama in a lost film.

WESTERN JAPAN

After the Mita game, the Americans left Tokyo out of Yokohama port on November 20, sent off by a gift-toting crowd of admirers wishing them a safe trip to Kobe.[54] It took several days for the party to sail around Wakayama into Osaka Bay, find a berth at Kobe port and travel inland 30 kilometers to Takarazuka, home of the renowned Takarazuka Revue. After another day of rest and relaxation, the All-Americans played their first game outside of Tokyo on November 23. They once again met the Keio nine, facing Kyoichi Nitta and his spitter for the third time. He had a tough time with the major-league hitters, giving up 14 hits, including four homers, two by Amos Strunk. Nitta wasn't helped by his defense, which committed seven errors. Herb Pennock shut down the Keio hitters and came away with a 14-0 victory.[55]

The next day at Takarazuka, Michimaro Ono faced off against Hoyt in a rematch of the much-discussed Mita loss at Shibaura a week before. This time Ono, pitching for the Daimai Club (the Osaka *Mainichi Shimbun*'s company team), did not have quite the same stuff, and gave up 20 hits to go along with 10 errors committed behind him. However, Hoyt was similarly owned by the opposition, giving up 13 hits and 5 runs.[56] The team traveled back across Osaka Bay for a game at the Naruo Grounds on the 27th, scoring 12 runs on three straight homers in the third and a run in each inning thereafter.[57] The Star Club could put only one on the board, on an RBI double by Waseda alumni Shizuo Takamatsu, in a game that did not last even an hour. Perhaps the teams were eager to get back across the bay for a 120-guest banquet held at the Oriental Hotel in Kobe.[58] The large crowd gave a standing ovation to Hunter after he was introduced by host and toastmaster D.H. Blake, an expatriate businessman and a supporter of college baseball.[59]

Hunter's tourists next made the 75-kilometer journey, following the path of the Yodo River from Osaka to Japan's old capital, Kyoto. There they played two games against assembled teams at the Okazaki Park in the shadow of the Heian Shrine. In the first game, the Americans rapped out 16 hits and were aided by eight errors by the All-Kyoto nine in a 12-3 victory.[60] On the first day of December the All-Americans hammered the Kyoto all-stars again, 18-0, as no Japanese runner reached third base.[61]

The next day the Americans were back in the Osaka Bay area for two more games at Naruo. The first game saw the Hunter All-Stars take on the best players in Western Japan, the All-Kwansai team. Herb Pennock once again pitched well in a 12-3 victory.[62] In addition to facing their nemesis Ono again, one of the pitchers the Americans faced that day was young Shinjii Hamazaki. The 5-foot-1 Hamazaki may have been one of the shortest players in the history of the game, but he was also one of the most durable. After pitching for Keio University, Kobe, and the Diamond Club, he played for the All-Japan squad in both the 1931 and 1934 US tours before taking a break from baseball until after World War II. Starting in 1947, the 45-year-old served as player-manager of the Hankyu Braves and won his final game on the mound in 1950 at age 48. He continued as manager of the Braves through 1953 and later led the Takahashi and Tombo Unions and Kokutetsu Swallows before being enshrined in the Hall of Fame in 1978.[63] He is also well known for appearing on a famous cover of *Yakyukai* magazine alongside O'Neal Pullen of the Philadelphia Royal Giants during their 1927 tour of Japan.[64] Assisting him behind the plate was Hideo Mori, the star catcher who had helped Mita upset the All-Americans on November 19.

The next day, Sunday, December 3, a combination of Diamond Club and Mita Club players formed an All-Japan team to face Joe Bush and the US contingent. It was the final time Hunter's team faced Ono, and he again lacked the magic that he had during his early victory. The tourists took it, 10-0.[65]

Before setting sail for Korea and China, Hunter's team played a few more games in Kobe. On the Monday afternoon after facing Ono, they soundly beat the Kobe Commercials, 17-5, at the Kobe Recreation Ground. The next day, December 5, Joe Bush slammed four homers in a 20-3 victory over the Kwansei Gakuin University nine.[66] Though most reports of the tour cite this as the final game, the Americans managed one more victory as they traveled westward, a 16-5 win over the Nakajima Mining team in Iizuka before sailing for Korea.

Hunter then led his crew to the Chosen Hotel in Seoul, where the team played the All-Korean team at the South Manchuria Railway grounds at Yongsan.[67] A brief stop in Shanghai left time for two quick games, a 19-3 victory over the Shanghai Club and a 16-1 win over the Hongkong Club, before the *Empress of Asia* sailed for the Philippines. As the ship left port, the players waved to the large crowd that had assembled to see them off. When they arrived in Manila the team faced off against clubs made up of expatriates and US military personnel at Fort Mills as well as against a tough team of Filipino employees of the Manila Street Railway, which resulted in a close game.[68] The steamer *President Jefferson* carried them to Japan for the New Year before cruising back across the Pacific in early 1923.[69]

HONOLULU AND HOME

Nuuanu Memorial Park lies just outside the downtown Honolulu limits. On January 23, 1923, Hunter and the touring ballplayers, along with local dignitaries and members of the Cartwright family, visited the park to lay a wreath in a ceremony honoring Alexander Joy Cartwright, at that time known as the father of baseball. The ceremony was the last diplomatic mission for the tourists.[70] Their stay in Hawaii included several games against local teams, including a doubleheader at Moiliili Park in which the All-Americans beat the Japanese Hawaiian Asahi 17-5 and the All-Chinese 16-0, and later the Braves, 12-0.[71] The final game of the tour was at Moiliili against Gusty Lozier's Wanderers on January 24, a 6-1 victory for Hunter and his team.[72] Local fans were thrilled to watch Hunter's All-Americans after feeling cheated by the visiting 1920 Doyle All-Stars, which had misrepresented the magnitude of its star power.[73] This time, the real stars had arrived. The next day, they boarded the *T.K.K. Korea Maru* for San Francisco, where they had hoped to squeeze in one more contest against a team of San Francisco police officers. However, despite an exchange with Hunter in which he praised the tourists, Judge Landis turned down the request for the game, setting the stage for more rejection to follow.[74]

The Mita loss, as well as the flaunting of his barnstorming rules in Vancouver, seem to have influenced Landis's decision to disallow further international barnstorming, preventing Hunter from continuing his mission. The Mita loss in particular fueled Landis's well-documented prejudices. "For Landis, the loss represented a desecration of the supremacy – and perhaps the integrity, if it was indeed a thrown game – of white American manhood for which the game of baseball stood," concludes historian Sayuri Guthrie-Shimizu.[75]

These views, combined with the Great Kanto Earthquake of September 1, 1923, which devastated the country's infrastructure, took countless lives, and interrupted domestic sports, played a large role in limiting international competition at the major-league level. Over the next decade there were tours by college, Japanese American, and African American teams, as well as a women's ball club, but no American or National Leagueteams went to Japan.

After the 1923 season, Hunter proposed a barnstorming tour of Canada, which featured Harry Heilmann, Rogers Hornsby, and other stars not involved in the 1923 World Series, which seemed to appease Landis. But the tour never came to fruition.[76] He also continued his travels to Japan as a coach and organizer. But his dream of annual tours of major-league competition were thwarted by Landis, and aside from a visit he arranged with Ty Cobb in 1928, it was not until 1931 that he would succeed in organizing another sanctioned major-league tour.[77] By then Herb Hunter had begun to fade into the background, a victim of his own eccentricities, which allowed Lefty O'Doul to take over as the primary baseball ambassador to Japan by finally delivering Babe Ruth in 1934. Hunter continued to straddle the worlds of entertainment and baseball just as he straddled the worlds on each side of the Pacific, organizing other international sporting endeavors and even attempting to organize a football tour to Japan, but by the end of World War II, he was no longer in the diplomacy business.[78] So, like a lost film, Hunter's 1922 tour, as well as his grand plan to be the center of the diamond stage and true baseball ambassador, would persist only in memory as an influence to future ambassadors of the game. But he cemented his place in the core group of "baseball ambassadors," along with Lefty O'Doul, Isoo Abe, and Cappy Harada – men who brought the United States and Japan closer together through the mutual love of baseball.

1922 HERB HUNTER ALL-AMERICAN GAMES IN JAPAN

Date	Place	Opponent	Score	Winner	Loser
November 4	Tokyo	Keio University	6-0	Pennock	Nitta
November 5	Tokyo	Waseda University	4-1	Bush	Tanaguchi
November 11	Tokyo	Waseda University	13-0	Pennock	Takeuchi
November 12	Tokyo	Keio University	12-0	Hoyt	Nitta
November 15	Yokohama	Meiji University	11-0	Pennock	Watanabe
November 18	Tokyo	Tomon Club	12-0	Bush	Tanaguchi
November 19	Tokyo	Mita Club	3-9	Ono	Hoyt
November 23	Takarazuka	Keio University	14-0	Pennock	Nitta
November 25	Takarazuka	Daimai Club	25-5	Hoyt	Ono
November 27	Nishinomiya	Star Club	12-1	Bush	Hitomi
November 29	Kyoto	All-Kyoto	12-3	Hoyt	Hitomi
December 1	Kyoto	All-Kyoto	18-0	Falk	Nagahama
December 2	Nishinomiya	All-Kwansai	12-3	Pennock	Ishikawa
December 3	Nishinomiya	Diamond Club	10-0	Bush	Ono
December 4	Kobe	Kobe Commercial	17-5	Kelly	Nishimura
December 5	Kobe	Kwansei Gakuin	20-3	Hoyt	Tsuji
December 6	Iizuka	Nakajima Mining	16-5	Unknown	Unknown

NOTES

1   "All-American Baseball Stars Enact Roles of Movie Actors," *Japan Advertiser*, November 19, 1922: 14.

2   "Ernie Paepke to Lead Local Nine," *Vancouver Sun*, October 18, 1922: 8; "Vancouver Ball Fans See Majors in Action," *Vancouver Province*, October 19, 1922: 21.

3   "Landis After All-Stars for Violating Rules Here," *Vancouver Province*, November 1, 1922: 28.

4   "Line-Ups for This Morning's Ball Game," *Vancouver Sun*, October 19, 1922: 8.

5   "Landis After All-Stars for Violating Rules Here"; Dan Daniel, "Touring Leaguers Must Remain Fit," *New York Herald*, October 21, 1922: 12.

6   "Landis After All-Stars for Violating Rules Here."

7   "Getting Away from Old Lines," *The Sporting News*, November 9, 1922: 4.

8   Sayuri Guthrie-Shimizu, *Transpacific Field of Dreams: How Baseball Linked the United States and Japan in Peace and War* (Chapel Hill: University of North Carolina Press, 2012), 122-23.

9   Herb Hunter profile, SABR BioProject. https://sabr.org/bioproj/person/herb-hunter/.

10 "Cards' Utility Player a Spectacular Figure in World of Baseball," *St. Louis Star and Times*, February 8, 1922: 15; Ed R. Hughes, "Baseball Invasion of the Orient Breaks Up in Big Blow-Off at Kobe, Japan," *San Francisco Chronicle*, January 28, 1921: 7; W.N. Stone, "Baseball Thrills Fans in the Orient, Writes Hunter, Former Traveler Gardener," *Arkansas Democrat* (Little Rock), January 28, 1921: 15.

11 Hughes: 13.

12 "Miller Here for Preseason Visit," *Arkansas Gazette*, February 20, 1921: 13.

13 "'Japanese Ball Players Already Approach U.S. Professionals,' Former Cardinal Says," *St. Louis Post-Dispatch*, April 17, 1922: 14.

14 "'Japanese Ball Players Already Approach U.S. Professionals,' Former Cardinal Says."

15 "Arm in Arm for Baseball," *The Sporting News*, February 16, 1922: 1.

16 Ed Frayne, "Kenworthy Makes Bitter Attack on M'Credie," *Los Angeles Record*, March 16, 1922: 11.

17 "Japan Rapidly Adopting America's National Game," *Washington Post*, May 11, 1922: 17.

18 Kazuo Sayama and Bill Staples, Jr., *Gentle Black Giants: A History of Negro Leaguers in Japan* (Fresno, California: Nisei Baseball Research Project Press, 2019), 177.

19 Robert K. Fitts, *Banzai Babe Ruth: Baseball, Espionage, & Assassination during the 1934 Tour of Japan* (Lincoln: University of Nebraska Press, 2012), 169.

20 "Japanese Want to See the Babe," *Lebanon* (Pennsylvania) *Daily News*, April 6, 1922: 9; "Conducting a Proper Tour," *The Sporting News*, June 22, 1922: 4; "Harding Says Tour of Ball Clubs Will Be of Diplomatic Value," *Shreveport Times*, October 6, 1922: 8.

21 James McLain, "Japs Pick Cardinals to Win World Series," *St. Louis Star and Times*, April 22, 1922: 11; "Japanese Admire Ruth and Kelly," *Los Angeles Record*, March 16, 1922: 11.

22 "American Star Ball Players Ready for Fray," *Japan Times & Mail*, November 1, 1922: 8.

23 "Major Leaguers on Tour in Orient Will Not Get Contracts," *Port Huron* (Michigan) *Times Herald*, October 21, 1922: 13.

24   "Tourists Leave Chicago," *New York Times*, October 16, 1922: 22; Guthrie-Shimizu, 123.

25   "Caught on the Fly," *The Sporting News*, October 19, 1922: 8.

26   "Conducting a Proper Tour;" "Baseball Tourists Start Trip Today," *New York Times*, October 14, 1922: 16.

27   Andrew Gordon, *A Modern History of Japan: From Tokugawa Times to the Present* (New York: Oxford University Press, 2014).

28   United States Congress, House Committee on Immigration and Naturalization, *Japanese Immigration, Hearings Before the Committee on Immigration and Naturalization, House of Representatives, Sixty-Sixth Congress, Second Session* (Washington: Government Printing Office, 1921).

29   Yusuke Suzumura, *The Formation of First Professional Baseball Team in Japan*, Academia, https://www.academia.edu/29232638, last accessed December 1, 2021.

30   "In Real Peace Conference: Arm in Arm for Baseball," *The Sporting News*, February 16, 1922: 1."

31   Dennis Snelling, *Lefty O'Doul: Baseball's Forgotten Ambassador* (Lincoln: University of Nebraska Press, 2017), 184.

32   "Americans Defeat Keio Team, 6 to 0, in First Game Here," *Japan Advertiser*, November 5, 1922: 8.

33   Frank F. O'Neill, "Japan Teams Prove Class on Ballfield," *Japan Times & Mail*, November 6, 1922: 1.

34   "Waseda Makes Run but Loses, 4 to 1," *Japan Advertiser*, November 7, 1922: 10.

35   "American Nine Well Pleased at Reception," *Japan Times & Mail*, November 17, 1922: 1.

36   Tyler Kepner, *K: A History of Baseball in Ten Pitches* (New York: Anchor Books, 2019), 142.

37   "Most Anything in Sports," *Baltimore Evening Sun*, November 17, 1922: 38; "Americans Sweep Japs Off Their Feet," *The Sporting News*, November 16, 1922: 1; "Waseda and Keio Games to Be Last," *Japan Advertiser*, November 10, 1922: 10.

38   "Waseda and Keio Games to Be Last."

39   Frank F. O'Neill, "American Nine Well Pleased at Reception," *Japan Times & Mail*, November 17, 1922: 1.

40   "Big Leaguers Slug Way to a 13-0 Win," *Japan Advertiser*, November 12, 1922: 8.

41   "Americans Sweep Japs Off Their Feet."

42   "Yokohama to See U.S. Stars Today," *Japan Advertiser*, November 15, 1922: 10.

43   Watanabe went on to a brief stint managing in the inaugural season of the Central League in 1950.

44   Frank F. O'Neill, "Meiji Players Lose Contest to Americans," *Japan Times & Mail*, November 16, 1922: 1.

45   O'Neill, "American Nine Well Pleased at Reception."

46   "Americans Defeat Tomon Team, 12-0," *Japan Advertiser*, November 19, 1922: 8.

47   "Americans Defeat Tomon Team, 12-0."

48   "Americans Beaten in Comedy Display," *Japan Advertiser*, November 21, 1922: 10.

49   "Tokyo Press Realizes Something Was Wrong," *Japan Advertiser*, November 21, 1922: 10.

50   "Better Call 'Em Home, Judge," *The Sporting News*, November 30, 1922: 4.

51   George Moriarty, "Moriarty Praises Players Conduct on Tour of East," *The Sporting News*, February 15, 1923: 3.

52   "Americans Beaten in Comedy Display."

53   "All-American Baseball Stars Enact Roles of Movie Actors."

54   "Players Get Send-Off," *Japan Advertiser*, December 20, 1922: 10.

55   "Americans Defeat Keio Nine, 14-0," *Japan Advertiser*, November 24, 1922: 10.

56   "Osaka Team Loses to Americans 25-5," *Japan Advertiser*, November 26, 1922: 8.

57   "All-American Team Defeats Stars Nine," *Japan Times & Mail*, November 28, 1922: 8.

58   "Kobe Americans Fete Big League Players," *Japan Advertiser*, November 28, 1928: 10.

59   "International Commercial Events," *The Trans-pacific: A Weekly Review of Far Eastern Political, Social, and Economic Developments*, Volume 7, September 1922: 77.

60   "Tourists Run Away as Usual," *Chattanooga Daily Times*, December 2, 1922: 12.

61   "America Nine Wins," *Japan Times & Mail*, December 2, 1922: 1.

62   "Two Victories End Big Leaguers' Visit," *Japan Advertiser*, December 5, 1922: 10.

63   https://baseball-museum.or.jp/hall-of-famers/hof-058/.

64   Sayama and Staples, 1.

65   "Two Victories End Big Leaguers' Visit."

66   "Americans Win Last Game by 20-3 Count," *Japan Advertiser*, December 7, 1922: 10.

67   "Americans in Seoul," *Japan Times & Mail*, December 8, 1922: 1.

68   "Touring Ball Team Wins Another Game," *Victoria* (British Columbia) *Daily Times*, December 23, 1922: 10; "Defeats Fillipino Team," *Grand Island* (Nebraska) *Daily Independent*, December 22, 1922: 3.

69   "Barnstormers Start Homeward Journey," *Richmond Times Dispatch*, December 26, 1922: 9; "Ball Players Returning," *Japan Times & Mail*, December 28, 1922: 1.

70   "Big Leaguers to be Guests Today of Ad Clubbers," *Honolulu Advertiser*, January 24, 1923: 3.

71   "Hunter's Team Wins," *Japan Times & Mail*, January 24, 1923: 8; "Major Leaguers to Play Braves at 3:30 Today," *Honolulu Star Bulletin*, January 23, 1923: 10; Doc Adams, "Coueism Shows at Local Ball Arena as Games Improve," *Honolulu Advertiser*, January 24, 1923: 4.

72   Doc Adams, "Leaguers Defeated Wanderers 6 to 1; Best Game of Four," *Honolulu Advertiser*, January 25, 1923: 4.

73   Mike Jay, "Hunter Bunch to Do Much to Wipe Away Bad Taste Left by That Last Team," *Honolulu Star-Bulletin*, January 19, 1923: 8.

74   "Herb Hunter Sends Reply to Landis," *Honolulu Star Bulletin*, January 22, 1923: 7; "Landis Puts Ban on Game Sunday," *San Francisco Examiner*, February 3, 1923: 29.

75   Guthrie-Shimizu, 123.

76   "Heilmann to Play with Herb Hunter," *Detroit Free Press*, September 3, 1923: 10.

77   Fitts, 16.

78   https://sabr.org/bioproj/person/herb-hunter/.

KENICHI ZENIMURA, "THE FATHER OF JAPANESE AMERICAN BASEBALL," AND THE 1924, 1927, AND 1937 GOODWILL TOURS

By Bill Staples Jr.

Few baseball fans know the story of early twentieth-century Nikkei (Japanese American) baseball. Despite this lack of awareness, the Nikkei impact is still visible in today's game. It's subtle, though, visible only to the well-informed. The legacy is not a retired uniform number displayed inside a major-league ballpark, but the names on the back of the uniforms. In 2022 those names are Akiyama, Darvish, Kikuchi, Maeda, Ohtani, Sawamura, and Suzuki – and in 2025, it will almost certainly include Ichiro on a plaque in the National Baseball Hall of Fame.[1]

The national pastime has unofficially become the international pastime, and this is the enduring legacy of Nikkei baseball and the work of pioneers like Kenichi Zenimura (1900-1968).[2]

During the years 1923 to 1930, no major-league team barnstormed in Japan.[3] The highest-caliber competition from the United States during this time came in the form of Nikkei and Negro League teams like Zenimura's Fresno Athletic Club (FAC) and the Philadelphia Royal Giants. During this major-league void, Nikkei and Negro Leaguers helped elevate the level of play in Japan and set the stage for the 1931 and 1934 tour of stars like Lou Gehrig and Babe Ruth, and the start of the professional Japanese Baseball League in 1936.

In 1962 Zenimura was crowned the "Dean of Nisei Baseball" by veteran *Fresno Bee* sports reporter Tom Meehan.[4] Shortly after Zeni's death in 1968, the same sentiment was echoed by *Bee* reporter Ed Orman.[5] Approximately 25 years later, baseball historian Kerry Yo Nakagawa refined that tribute for a new audience, calling Zenimura "The Father of Japanese American Baseball."[6] Nakagawa and others believe that Zeni deserves this title for his unparalleled career and collective impact as a player, manager, and global ambassador.

PREWAR GOODWILL AMBASSADOR

Between 1905 and 1940, roughly one out of four (26.5 percent) tours across the Pacific featured a Nikkei team visiting Japan.[7] When examining the tours between 1923 and 1940, Zenimura's impressive impact becomes apparent. Of the 53 tours during this period, Zenimura was involved, to some degree, with 17 (32 percent) of those efforts.[8] When he himself was not traveling, Zeni supported or influenced 14 different tours by other Nikkei teams, visiting Japanese

Kenichi Zenimura (right) with his cousin Tasumi Zenimura (left) in 1928

ballclubs, Negro League teams, and major-league all-stars.[9]

The following is an in-depth look at Zenimura's three major tours – 1924, 1927, and 1937 – in which he participated directly, allowing him to shine in his homeland of Japan.

THE 1924 TOUR

The seeds for Zenimura's 1924 tour were planted on Independence Day in 1923 when the Fresno Athletic Club battled the Seattle Asahi for the National Nikkei Baseball Championship. The Asahi had earned the respect of the baseball world by winning the majority of their games during tours to Japan between 1915 and 1923.[10] In a best-of-three series, the FAC defeated the Asahi to become the undisputed Nikkei baseball champions. With the victory, Fresno also won the right to tour Japan the following year.[11]

In preparation for the tour, the FAC scheduled games against high-caliber competition, including the Pacific Coast League Salt Lake City Bees, who conducted spring training in Fresno. In a three-game series, the FAC surprised the Bees with a 6-4 victory in game one, marking the first time a Nikkei team defeated a PCL ballclub.[12] The series also marked the presence of Frank "Lefty" O'Doul. Newly signed from San Francisco, O'Doul did not compete in the loss, but his powerful bat helped the Bees take games 2 and 3.[13]

More important than O'Doul's on-field performance was the historical significance of his involvement. The gregarious southpaw would later be enshrined in the Japanese Baseball Hall of Fame for his life's work as a celebrated ambassador of US-Japan baseball relations.[14] Most likely, this 1924 encounter marks O'Doul's first interaction with ballplayers of Japanese ancestry.

On September 2, 1924, the FAC boarded the *SS President Pierce* for Japan.[15] Six weeks later they stepped inside Koshien Stadium to play their first opponent, Daimai. The FAC recorded a shutout 5-0 victory behind the arm of Kenso "The Boy Wonder" Nushida. Fresno pitchers did not allow a run until their third game, on October 14, a 4-3 loss in a rematch with Daimai.[16]

During their 46-day stay in Japan (October 11 to November 26), the Fresno team traveled approximately 1,300 miles (about 2,100 kilometers), covering nine cities – starting in Osaka, with stops in smaller locales between Hiroshima, Tokyo, and Yokohama. They played 27 games, finishing with a 20-7 record and an overall .741 winning percentage.[17]

After watching the Fresno captain compete on the field, a reporter with the *Japan Times* wrote, "Zenimura is one of the smartest and most colorful players the writer had ever seen. He was the terror of the diamond, a man who played every position in baseball. He was tricky, shrewd and positive poison to every opponent."[18]

In Tokyo, Zeni penned his thoughts on the Japan tour experience in a letter to the *Fresno Morning Republican*, which was published on December 5. It read:

Tokyo, Japan

November 16, 1924

Mr. T.P. Spink

Sports Editor,

The Republican.

Dear Sir: –

The Fresno team is doing a [*sic*] good work in Japan and so far our record stands 18 victories and 5 lost. In today's game we played against Keio and defeated them by the score of 8 to 4. We gave the last four runs in the last of the ninth after two men gone.

In Japan it doesn't pay to win a game in a far margin. If we do then there won't be any crowd coming to the next game, saying that we are too strong for this Japan team and so on. We had many examples in Osaka.

Beat Diamonds

One day we played against the pro team of Osaka which is known as Diamonds and in our first game we defeated them by a score of 11-2. In this game quite a many fans [*sic*] came to see the outcome but on the following day with the same teams there was hardly any people in the stand[s]. For this reason, it is hard for the visiting team to play a game in Japan.

Another thing disadvantaging us is the way these Tokyo umpires calls [*sic*] on decisions against us. … I can't figure the way these umpires make a bad decision when ever the play is close. We had enough of the raw decisions in Tokyo, but what can we do in Japan!!!

Meet Champions

Tomorrow we are playing against Waseda, the
intercollegiate champions of Japan. We hope
to beat them badly and by the time this letter
reaches you, you will be able to get the result.

On the way to the States I am figuring of
stopping over to Honolulu and spend my
Christmas and New Year's there. About
five of the players are going to do the same
and eleven of the remaining players will
be in Fresno by 13th of December 1924.

As soon as the team reaches to Fresno
we would like to play a three game
series with the Fresno Tigers.

Yours truly,

K. ZENIMURA

(Captain).[19]

The Waseda contest mentioned in the letter resulted
in a 3-2 loss for Fresno. FAC lost the game, but won
the respect of the opposing manager, Chujun Tobita.
He praised the visiting team's baseball skills, saying
they were "amazing" in their demonstration of technique and power.[20]

***

Zenimura's next goodwill tour would not occur
for another 16 months (April 1927); however during
this period the FAC competed against the all-Black
semipro Los Angeles White Sox, a strong West Coast
African American club, forming a connection that
eventually made a huge impact on US-Japan baseball
relations.

On September 6, 1925, the FAC traveled to White
Sox Park in Los Angeles to play a doubleheader, the
first against the "Diamond Japs," the visiting Daimai
Club from Japan, and then an afternoon contest with
the Los Angeles White Sox, led by manager Lon
Goodwin.[21] Behind the pitching of Nushida, the FAC
defeated the White Sox, 5-4.[22]

The following year, the FAC and White Sox scheduled a rematch, a doubleheader in Fresno over the
Fourth of July weekend. The FAC won both games,
9-4 and 4-3.[23] This series created the opportunity for
Zenimura and Goodwin to discuss plans for parallel
tours of Japan the following year. On December 21,
approximately five months after their two-game series
in Fresno, the *Nippu Jiji* reported that Goodwin's Los
Angeles White Sox had received an invitation to tour

Japan from officials in Fukuoka City, one of the locations where the FAC competed during the 1924 tour.[24]

***

THE 1927 TOUR

In early 1927 the FAC announced plans for a
second tour of Asia. The schedule called for 40 games
in Japan, China, and Korea, and a stop in Honolulu on
the way home.[25] The Tokyo press reported the arrival
of Zenimura's team in April:

The Fresno Japanese baseball team augmented
by three American players reached Japan a
few days ago and will make their first public
appearance in Tokyo at the Meiji Shrine Field
Tuesday afternoon when they lineup against
the fast Meiji University nine. The visitors
had a couple of nice workouts already and are
raring to go. They are rapidly recovering from
their long trip across the Ocean and should
provide plenty of opposition against the local
teams. One of their proudest records is that
of defeating the Royal Giants who are now in
Japan and cleaning up on the Japanese nine.

The Fresno team carries with them seventeen
members including half a dozen pitchers
so they are well supplied with plenty of
reserve players in case of emergency. Hunt
and Hendsch are two of their leading hurlers
while Simons, the other American entry[,]
will carry the bulk of the catching burden.

Manager Zenimura will probably handle the
shortpatch himself and he needs no introduction to the Japanese sporting public for he
made his initial bow a few years ago when
the Fresno squad made their first trip here.[26]

The FAC received generous press coverage during
their tour. Fans were provided with detailed information to get to know the Fresno pastimers:

Ken Zenimura, manager and shortstop[,]
is the mainstay of the Fresno team. He has
steered the team for the past several years
through 4 successful seasons. Upon graduation from Mills High School in Honolulu
in 1919, where he was captain, he went over
to the mainland to join the Fresno Club and
continue his higher education. While in

Honolulu he was captain of the Asahi Ball Club. This is his second trip to Japan.

Captain Fred Yoshikawa, catcher, played for four years on the McKinley High School team in Honolulu. He captained the team through a series of games with Mills High which was headed by Manager Zenimura. He is a graduate of the Technical College of Kansas. This is his second trip to Japan.

Harvey Iwata, the left fielder, is a graduate of Fresno High, and is now making a special study of agricultural science. He was captain of the Fresno High team that won the Pacific Coast Championship in 1920. This is his second trip to Japan.

Ty Miyahara, third baseman, proud of the fact that he was received at the White House by President Coolidge last year. He made his first trip to Japan with the Honolulu Asahi team (in 1920). He also made a trip with the Fresno team in 1924. He studied at Center College, at Danville, Kentucky, where he played Center Varsity as a third baseman. At present he is a student at Columbia University.

Anthony Kunitomo, second baseman, joined the Fresno Club last year. He is attending Regis College at Denver, where he also played second baseman on the Varsity team. He has made his college team for the past three years.

Michael Nakano, first baseman, is attending college in Alameda, California. He was considered the best first baseman in the Japanese baseball league in 1926 on the coast.

John Nakagawa, centerfielder, is known in the states and here in Japan as the Japanese "Babe Ruth." He pitched and played outfield for Fresno High, finishing there in 1926. This is his second trip to Japan.

Tandy Mimura, third baseman, is still in high school, attending Dinuba High. He made the highest batting average on his high school team last season.

Ken Furubayashi, outfielder, made his first trip to Japan in 1924. He pitched on his high school team Orosi High. On his last trip to Japan he was a Fresno pitcher but is now in the outfield, owing to his heavy hitting.

Samuel Yamasaki is the team's leading batter and a third baseman, playing the same position now on the Fresno High School team. He will finish high school next year and he is the youngest member of the aggregation.

Richard Kawasaki pitched for both Los Angeles High School and a Japanese team in that city. He joined Fresno in 1926 as a member of the pitching staff.

James Hirokawa is on his second trip to Japan with Fresno, playing second base also for the Fresno State College.

Thomas Mamiya finished McKinley High School and has now joined Fresno to take up higher education in the states. He pitched for his high school and for the Asahi team and has the reputation of being the best Japanese pitcher in Hawaii.[27]

It's worth noting that the three Caucasian ringers, Eldridge Hunt, Charlie Hendsch, and Jud Simons, are not detailed in the press.

The FAC won its first five games in Japan: two games against Keio, both by the score of 6-2, featuring future Japanese Hall of Famer Shinji Hamazaki; two games against Meiji, 10-5 and 6-0, against Hall of Famer Fujio Nakazawa; and a thrilling 10-inning, 3-2 victory over Hosei University.[28]

On April 20 the FAC and Lon Goodwin's ballclub, now called the Philadelphia Royal Giants, met head-to-head in the newly constructed Meiji Jingu Stadium in Tokyo. Captain Zenimura shared his eagerness and excitement to play the upcoming game with Goodwin's club with reporters.

The Fresno players, who have defeated the invading Royal Giants in America in baseball, will have the opportunity of demonstrating their superiority over the same nine when they cross bats in their first game in Japan on Friday afternoon at the Meiji Shrine [Jingu] Field. This match ought to attract a huge attendance as both teams have shown great strength in their contests against the local nines.[29]

According to Japanese baseball historian Kyoko Yoshida, Zenimura's comments about previously defeating the Royal Giants caused quite a stir with several players, especially Biz Mackey, Rap Dixon, and Andy Cooper. They openly expressed their disappointment with the FAC, wondering why the Fresno players would lie to the media about previously beating them.[30] More than 90 years later, we now see the historical misunderstanding that unfolded between Zenimura and the Negro Leaguers.

Based on his comments to the press, it appears that Zenimura was under the impression that the Negro League team he was scheduled to play in Tokyo was the same L.A. White Sox squad he had help defeat three times prior to the 1927 tour. Zeni was not aware that the Royal Giants team that boarded the ship in April was actually taken from two different rosters: Cooper, Dixon, Frank Duncan, O'Neal Pullen, and Mackey from Goodwin's 1926-27 Royal Giants California Winter League team and select members of Goodwin's 1926 semipro L.A. White Sox.

While the misunderstanding was unfortunate, it worked in favor of the Royal Giants. Biz Mackey channeled his anger into his bat, and more than 10,000 baseball fans at Meiji Jingu Stadium saw the future Hall of Famer singlehandedly defeat Fresno, 9-1.[31] "Mackey, the star shortstop of his team, was the heaviest slugger of the day, getting three safeties on four official trips to the diamond, one being a four-ply wallop, and the other two, a three sacker and a double." He was a single shy of hitting for the cycle.[32]

His historic home run, the first ever hit at Meiji Jingu Stadium, whistled through the air and landed in the center-field bleachers.[33] The ball then rolled out of sight some hundred feet into a clump of trees.[34]

According to reports, the game was much closer than reflected by the final score. It was still anyone's ballgame after the sixth inning, with a 2-0 score, but the Royal Giants "blew the lid off" the game by scoring four runs in the seventh and then adding three more runs in the eighth. The FAC was able to get on the score board in the ninth inning thanks to a double by Jud Simons and an RBI single off future Hall of Famer Andy Cooper by pinch-hitter Sam Yamasaki.[35]

After the game it was reported that the Fresno Japanese would have a chance to "wreak their sweet revenge upon the boastful Colored nine" in a follow-up game scheduled for Friday.[36] But the game was rained out and never rescheduled. For most players on both teams, they would have to wait until they returned to the United States for a rematch when the FAC battled the "Hilldale Royal Giants" (the CWL Philadelphia Royal Giants roster playing under a slightly modified team name) in March 1928 in Fresno.[37]

After the rained-out contest, each team went its separate way to play the best semipro, industrial, and college teams in Japan, China, Korea, and Hawaii. Both squads completed their respective tours with impressive winning records. The FAC finished with a 40-8-2 record, a solid .800 winning percentage. Playing against the same competition, the Philadelphia Royal Giants finished with a 35-2-1 record, an amazing .921 winning percentage.[38]

Perhaps more important than the wins and losses was the positive cross-cultural impact made by the tours. The Japanese players and fans were enamored with the Royal Giants, and the feeling was mutual. In Japan, both the Nikkei and Negro players found sanctuary from the racism they faced back in America. In the end, both teams were recognized by their Japanese hosts as true sportsmen and gracious ambassadors for the United States during the tour.[39]

After their games near Tokyo in April and May, the FAC team barnstormed a series of games in June in Hiroshima prefecture, Shikoku island, Hokkaido, Chosen (the Japanese name for Korea), and Manchuria (northeast China).[40] In early August Zenimura and his men left Japan for an 11-game series on the Hawaiian islands. Highlights from Hawaii include

- A 4-2 victory over the All-Hawaiians, the undisputed leaders of the Hawaii league, at Honolulu Stadium, in which Zenimura stole home for the first run of the game.

- A 5-4 victory over the Honolulu Asahi. Kawasaki belted a home run, while Nakagawa closed the game to defeat future Japan Hall of Famer pitcher Bozo Wakabayashi.

- In a 10-4 victory over the Maui All-Japanese at Wailuku, Iwata went 3-for-4 with a home run, triple, single, and sacrifice. Defensively he recorded four putouts and one assist, and kept a home run from clearing the fence with his bare hand, holding the runner to a double.

After the last out of the final contest was logged on the Islands, the FAC boasted a 42-6-2 record in 50 games during their six-month tour.[41]

On September 6, Zenimura and his FAC teammates departed Honolulu and set sail for America on the passenger ship *Taiyo Maru*. Not on the return ship with the team were the three Caucasian ringers, Hunt, Hendsch, and Simons. The trio had returned home early in June, as they objected to the living conditions during the tour, wanted more money for their efforts once they saw the large crowds flocking to the games, and overall were unhappy during their time in Japan.[42]

The *Fresno Bee* announced the FAC's return home on September 8. After spending half of 1927 touring across the Pacific, many of the team members opted to stay in San Francisco for some rest and relaxation. Captain Zenimura announced "that many offers for games again in the Orient were received by the club, and another trip probably will be made next year."[43]

***

After the 1927 tour, another event involving Zenimura occurred that would greatly impact US-Japan baseball relations.

On October 29, 1927, Babe Ruth and Lou Gehrig arrived in Fresno as part of their West Coast tour. Four Japanese Americans were selected to compete with Gehrig's team: Zenimura, Iwata, Nakagawa, and Yoshikawa.[44] Ruth wowed the fans with a mammoth home run, but it was not enough to overcome a 10-run deficit. The Bustin' Babes lost 13-3 to the Larrupin' Lous.[45] After the game, Fresno-based photographer Frank Kamiyama captured a photo of Ruth and Gehrig towering over the four Nikkei players, in what would become one of the most visually striking and memorable photos in baseball history.

In addition to the game, a dinner was held at the Hotel Fresno to honor the two Yankees stars. During the event, it appears that Ruth and Zenimura discussed a tour to Asia and that the Babe asked him for assistance in arranging a tour to Japan.[46]

Several weeks after this historic encounter, Zenimura sent letters written on the back of copies of the Kamiyama photo to his Japanese contacts. They responded. "I got a call from Japan to see if I could get Ruth to go to the Island and play for a $40,000 guarantee," said Zenimura. "I contacted Ruth and he said he would go for $60,000. It was too much but a few years later he went and made a big hit."[47]

In 2017 a copy of one of Zenimura's letters sent in November 1927 was discovered by Dr. Masaki Yoshikatsu, curator of the Hankyu Culture Foundation in Osaka. Zenimura's message was buried in the archives as part of a photo collection donated by the family of Masaru Kataoka, former executive with Daimai (*Osaka Mainichi* newspaper). Kataoka was also once a member of the Nihon Undo Kyokai (Shibaura Association), Japan's first pro team, which disbanded after the 1923 Tokyo earthquake, and reorganized as the Takarazuka Athletic Club.[48] In 1921 the Nihon Undo Kyokai loaned him to the Sherman Indians team during their tour of Japan.

The Fresno Athletic Club on their 1927 Asian tour (courtesy of Bill Staples Jr. and the Nisei Baseball Research Project)

The back of the photo contained the following hand-written message from Zenimura (now known as the "Kataoka Letter"):

This picture was taken at Fresno when Babe Ruth and Gehrig of the New York Yankees visited us on October 29th. We played against them and made a wide reputation for our team.

Babe Ruth is interested to visit Japan and has asked me to try and line up things in Japan so that he may be able to come to Japan with our team. I wrote to the Meiji University asking them to what extent they can offer to have Babe Ruth in Japan. I believe that it will draw to have Babe Ruth in Japan.

I am sending this picture to you so that you may have this picture in your leading page. It's my remembrance to you. Kindly extend my best wishes to all of your players. Hoping to meet you again in Japan.

I am yours truly,
K. Zenimura

The discovery of the Kataoka Letter documenting Zenimura's efforts to negotiate a tour for Babe Ruth to Japan corroborates Zeni's 1962 *Fresno Bee* interview, and further solidifies his role as an important ambassador of US-Japanese baseball relations.

THE 1937 TOUR

Harry Kono, Alameda florist, baseball enthusiast, and close friend of Zenimura's, made a name for himself in 1936 serving as a scout for Dai Tokyo of the fledgling Japanese Baseball League, when he signed pitcher James Bonner, the first African American to play in Japan.[49]

On February 12, 1937, the *Hayward Daily Review* announced that Kono was making the final plans to take a ballclub to Japan. The team had already received financial guarantees from Tokyo managers and sailing was set for March.[50] Eight Fresno players were included in the Kono Alameda All-Star team, which departed in March on the *Chichibu Maru* from San Francisco, bound for Honolulu to begin a 42-game schedule.[51] The 20 men on the roster included: Harry Kono, manager; Ken Zenimura, business manager and coach/player (second base, catcher); Kenso Nushida, assistant coach; pitchers Shig Tokumoto, Masa Yano, Paul Allison, and Marion Alleruzo; and position

players Noboru Takagi, Wilson Ishida, Norman Riggs, Ty Shirachi, Charles Davis, Tut Iwahashi, Frank Mirikitani, Charles Hiramatsu, Kiyo Nogami, Ky Miyamoto, Al Sadamune, and Frank Yamada.[52]

With plenty of time to pass on the 18-day journey from California to Japan, Zenimura wrote the following letter, dated March 17, 1937, to *Fresno Bee* sports editor Ed Orman:

Tomorrow we will arrive in the Land of the Rising Sun – Japan. It is reported that on the same day as our arrival, Prince Chichibu is sailing for Seattle and later will pass through Canada en route to attend the coronation in England. The entire battle fleet will guard the ship on which Prince Chichibu is sailing and I can imagine that the sendoff will be a great one. We are lucky to be on hand to witness the sight from the Yokohama Bay on Chichibu Maru.

I cannot write about Japan yet so I will drop you a line to let the Fresno fans know about Honolulu. The ship was delayed in reaching the islands due to a heavy storm that lasted for two days. Instead of arriving around 8 A.M. we finally reached port at 11:30 A.M. When the ship made headway toward the pier, the famous Hawaiian Band played "California, Here I Come" and many other popular songs. The sports editors of various papers met us and placed leis of flowers around our necks, meaning Welcome to the Paradise.

After taking several pictures of the team we were all invited for a short sightseeing trip. Jimmy Hirokawa, one-time Fresno State baseball player who played with the college in 1922 and 1923, was there and arranged for five automobiles for the players to drive on the sightseeing trip. ...

We came back to the ship and dressed in baseball uniforms and rushed to the park to play against the Asahi. For four innings we played a swell game, but after Kunihisa scored by stealing home the players became excited and blew up. Our team made eight errors during six innings, The final score was 10 to 0. It was a good workout for the players. We will win most of our games in Japan. If I should fail in Tokyo, I will be taking the next ship back to the states.

Paul Allison and Marion Alleruzo both are enjoying the voyage but I expect to see them make good in Japan. Both are working out every morning and they seem to be in shape. I probably will start Alleruzo in the first game in Japan. In Honolulu I signed another pitcher, Ed Suzuki, the best Japanese pitcher in the islands. This boy no doubt will win most of the games with his speed. I made a quick decision to take the pitcher and I believe that I made a wise move.

This morning I received a wire from Manila stating they want us to play eight games there. The Warner & Barnes Company, Ltd., is trying to promote the games. I have written to them stating my terms. If they are suitable I probably will divide the team into two squads and take twelve players to Manila.

I will let you know later about this. If we do go we probably will play one game in Shanghai and another in Hong Kong in China before arriving in Manila. I will ask Paul Allison to write to you about his ideas on the voyage and if he does kindly publish it in your paper. I will write to you from Yokohama, giving you the results of the four games we play there.

Thanks for the space given us in your sports page. Please extend our best regards to all the American baseball fans in Fresno.

Sincerely yours, KEN ZENIMURA

Coach, Kono All-Stars[53]

The Kono Alameda All-Stars returned home on July 15, after notching a 41-20-1 record in Asia. Game results were not published; however, what we lack in quantitative details is made up with a wealth of qualitative information shared by Zenimura after the tour. An article published by the *Fresno Bee* in Ed Orman's *Sport Thinks* column captures Zeni's rich experiences, insight, and perspectives on baseball in Japan in 1937:

Kenny Zenimura, Fresno's leading Japanese exponent of the great American national pastime of baseball, is back home after a sojourn in his native land, and the popular little baseball man has a bag full of interesting tales about Japan.

Being sports minded, Kenny paid more attention to things athletic in the land of the rising sun, and particularly his sport – baseball. The Nipponese, believes Zenimura, have improved in baseball proficiency at least 100 percent within the last decade. It was in 1927 that Zenimura took a squad of ball players, American and Japanese, to Japan for a barnstorming trip. Baseball then was just beginning to sprout wings in that country, but today it is vastly different.

"Baseball has blossomed into THE sport in Japan now and the Japanese can play ball which compares favorably with the brand played in America," related Zenimura. "I was agreeably surprised. Ten years ago the Japanese did not know the scientific points of playing. Today they know as much as we do in this country, or just about, at the least. Where they used to be weak hitters, the Japanese now can hit them hard and far. I saw many home runs inside of parks with fences some 420 feet from the plate."

Zenny, now a West Fresno automobile dealer, noted the new generation of Japanese people is larger in stature and for that reason the young ball players get more power at the plate. Always noted as fancy and fast fielders and base runners, the Japanese now are only coming into their own as distance hitters.[54]

Although Zenimura was engaged as coach for the tour, when he reached Japan he was surprised to discover that he was "barred on the diamond on the pretense of being a professional" and it was a month before he could help out his squad. As result, the team lost many games during his absence from the field.[55]

Wasting no time in Japan, when pushed to the sidelines Zenimura was also engaged as a scout for teams playing in a professional league around Tokyo and for a Honolulu team. His international baseball contacts encouraged him to send talented California ballplayers to Hawaii and Japan.[56]

In fact, four players stayed behind to play professional baseball in Asia: Tut Iwahashi and Shiro Kawakami signed with the Dairen Gitsugyo team in Manchuria; while Kiyo Nagami and Frank "Den" Yamada joined Hankyu Shokugyo in the fledgling Japanese Professional Baseball League.[57]

***

Upon returning home from the 1937 tour, Zenimura immediately shifted focus to plans to take a team to Tokyo for an amateur baseball competition associated with the 1940 Olympic Games. He reserved more than 60 rooms in a Tokyo hotel to accommodate his travel party.[58] The Games were canceled in July 1938 due to the war between China and Japan.[59] The news was a disappointment to Zenimura, the first of many leading up to one of the darkest chapters in US history – the mass incarceration of Japanese Americans during World War II.

Just as he had done before the war, while behind barbed wire at Gila River, Arizona – one of 10 camps constructed by the US government to incarcerate approximately 120,000 people of Japanese ancestry between 1942 and 1945 – Zenimura used the game of baseball to break down barriers, bond communities, and bring joy to the lives of others. After the war, he continued to play, manage, scout, and help others co-ordinate tours to Hawaii and Japan.[60] Zeni continued to scout and connect talent with Japanese teams. His two sons, Kenshi and Kenso, were among the first Americans to play for the Hiroshima Carp, in 1953.[61] Zeni also arranged for outfielder Satoshi "Fibber" Hirayama, a California native and multisport athlete to play in Japan, where he went on to enjoy a 10-year all-star career (1955-1964) with Hiroshima. When Zenimura died in 1968, Fibber delivered his eulogy. "The reason I was able to go to Japan and have a great career was because of Mr. Zenimura's faith in me," Hirayama later remarked.[62]

***

During his lifetime, Zenimura played a major role in helping to construct "Baseball's Bridge Across the Pacific." The ballplayers who cross that bridge – in both directions – are indebted to him and other Nikkei baseball pioneers who worked tirelessly to build it. In fact, Zenimura's lifelong friend and tour counterpart in Japan, Takizo "Frank" Matsumoto, was inducted into the Japanese Baseball Hall of Fame in 2016 for similar work on that side of the Pacific.[63]

With this in mind, multiple requests have been made to officials in Cooperstown asking for Nikkei baseball and "The Father of Japanese American Baseball" to be properly honored in the National Baseball Hall of Fame with a permanent presence equal to what is currently in place for other historically marginalized ballplayers (i.e. Negro Leaguers, Latinos, and women).[64] Since the early 2000s, these requests have fallen on deaf ears.

In 2018, the Baseball Writers Association of America enthusiastically accepted Zenimura's nomination for inclusion on the highly anticipated Early Baseball Era ballot. They responded, "[B]e assured Mr. Zenimura will be given appropriate consideration."[65] Despite Zeni's meeting all the criteria for Early Baseball Era consideration and his impressive resume as a global baseball ambassador, the committee members assembled by the Hall of Fame failed to give his nomination "appropriate consideration."[66] In fact, despite the enthusiastic assurance from the BBWAA, Zenimura's nomination was not even discussed.[67]

Instead, the only aspect of Zenimura's legacy embraced by the Hall of Fame today is his handmade wooden home plate from the wartime incarceration camp at Gila River, Arizona.[68]

When the wooden object was initially included in the Hall of Fame's traveling exhibit "Baseball as America" in 2002, it was considered a "riveting" artifact that helped "tell the honest story of baseball."[69] Who knows, perhaps it still does? But maybe it also teaches us that baseball's "honest story" is still evolving.

For example, with the alarming increase in anti-Asian attitudes and hate crimes stemming from the COVID pandemic, the Hall of Fame's decision to only display an artifact created by a Japanese American incarcerated behind barbed wire now smacks of tokenism, and is indicative of the systemic racism that still exists in baseball's power structure today. Zenimura's home plate, devoid of the larger story and legacy of Nikkei baseball, has now become a symbolic reminder of the ongoing marginalization of people of Asian ancestry in the United States – and of the work that remains to achieve true diversity, equity, and inclusion in America – and in baseball.[70]

Perhaps this too is part of Kenichi Zenimura's legacy. Only time will tell.

1924 FRESNO ATHLETIC CLUB GAMES IN JAPAN

During their 27-game tour of Japan in late 1924, Zenimura's Fresno Athletic Club finished with a 20-7 record (.741 winning percentage).

Date	City	Grounds	Opponent	Score	Battery
October 11	Osaka	Koshien	Daimai	5-0	Nushida-Yoshikawa
October 12	Osaka	Koshien	Star Club	7-0	Hirano-Yoshikawa
October 14	Osaka	Koshien	Daimai	3-4	Sako-Yoshikawa
October 15	Kyoto	Neyagawa	Kyoto U Alum	0-4	Nakagawa-Kawamura
October 17	Osaka	Koshien	Diamond Club	11-2	Sako-Yoshikawa
October 18	Osaka	Koshien	Diamond Club	6-2	Tomiyama-Yoshikawa
October 21	Takarazuka	Takarazuka	Takarazuka Club	2-1	Nushida-Yoshikawa
October 23	Hiroshima	Koryo	Kenchiku	14-1	Nakagawa-Yoshikawa
October 24	Hiroshima	Koryo	Zenrin	8-2	Shimamura-Kawamura
October 24	Hiroshima	Koryo	Hiroshima Star	8-7	Hirano-Yoshikawa
October 26	Hiroshima	Koryo	Kobe-Mikage	6-5	Nakagawa-Yoshikawa
October 26	Hiroshima	Koryo	All-Hiroshima	9-7	Furubayashi-Yoshikawa
October 29	Kushu-Kokura	Kokura	Takarazuka Club	4-3	Nushida-Yoshikawa
October 31	Fukuoka	Fukuoka	Takarazuka Club	1-0	Furubayashi-Yoshikawa
November 1	Fukuoka	Fukuoka	All-Fukuoka	17-3	Sako-Yoshikawa
November 2	Kumamoto	Kumamoto	All-Kumamoto	5-1	Nakagawa-Yoshikawa
November 3	Kumamoto	Kumamoto	Kobe-Mikage	0-3	Tomiyama-Yoshikawa
November 7	Tokyo	Nakano	Hoyu Club	2-4	Sako-Yoshikawa
November 9	Tokyo	Komazawa	Meiji Univ.	3-8	Nushida-Yoshikawa
November 10	Tokyo	Ikebukuro	Rikkyo Univ.	11-8	Sako-Kawamura
November 15	Tokyo	Meguro	Keio Univ.	8-4	Nushida-Yoshikawa
November 16	Tokyo	Totsuka	Waseda Univ.	2-3	Tomiyama-Yoshikawa
November 19	Tokyo	Totsuka	Takarazuka Club	6-0	Sako-Yoshikawa
November 21	Yokohama	Yokohama	Shoyu Club	9-0	Nakagawa-Yoshikawa
November 23	Tokyo	Totsuka	Sundai Club	3-16	Sako-Yoshikawa
November 25	Yokohama	Yokohama	Toyu Club	13-2	Nushida-Yoshikawa
November 26	Yokohama	Yokohama	All-Yokohama	5-1	Furubayashi-Yoshikawa

Note: Game details for the 1927 and 1937 tours not available.

NOTES

1   "Future Eligibles, 2025," National Baseball Hall of Fame, www. baseballhall.org/hall-of-famers/future-eligibles#2025-eligibles.

2   Bill Staples Jr., *Kenichi Zenimura, Japanese American Baseball Pioneer* (Jefferson, North Carolina: McFarland, 2011), 3-7.

3   In 1928 Ty Cobb toured Japan a couple of months after his retirement with Bob Skawkey and Fred Hoffmann, but not as part of an organized team. "Ty Cobb Will Tour Japan for Baseball," *Arizona Daily Star* (Tucson), October 10, 1928: 4.

4   Tom Meehan, "Fresno's Ken Zenimura, Dean of Nisei Baseball in US, Recalls Colorful Past," *Fresno Bee,* May 20, 1962: 8-S.

5   Ed Orman, "Zenimura, Dean of the Diamond," *Fresno Bee,* August 2, 1970: 3-B.

6   Jeff Davis, "A Slice of Japanese Americana," *Fresno Bee,* May 3, 1996: D1.

7   Kazuo Sayama and Bill Staples Jr., *Gentle Black Giants: A History of Negro Leaguers in Japan* (Fresno, California: Nisei Baseball Research Project Press, 2019), 176-180.

8   "Playing and Talking about Baseball Across the Pacific," Library of Congress, www.loc.gov/item/webcast-8949, 39:40 mark.

9   "Playing and Talking about Baseball Across the Pacific."

10   "Japanese Clubs to Play Series Here for Title," *Fresno Bee*, July 3, 1923: 4.

11   "Fresno Japanese Win Championship from Seattle Club," *Fresno Bee*, July 5, 1923: 12.

12   F.H. Vore, "Japanese Win from Bees 6 to 4," *Fresno Bee*, March 10, 1924: 4.

13   W.S. Tyler, "Bees Wallop Japanese 15–2," *Fresno Bee*, March 31, 1924: 4.

14   Brian McKenna, "Lefty O'Doul," SABR BioProject, https://sabr.org/bioproj/person/lefty-odoul/.

15   Associated Press, "Fresno Japs Will Invade the Orient," *Los Angeles Times*, July 18, 1924: 11.

16   "Nippon Ball Tour of Fresno Highly Successful," *Honolulu Star-Bulletin*, December 11, 1924: 12.

17   "Nippon Ball Tour of Fresno Highly Successful."

18   Meehan.

19   "F.A.C. Team Wins in Japan," *Fresno Morning Republican*, December 5, 1924: 19.

20   Kerry Yo Nakagawa, *Through a Diamond: 100 Years of Japanese American Baseball* (San Francisco: Rudi Publishing, 2001), 18-19.

21   "Star Jap Nine to Play Series Here," *Los Angeles Times*, September 6, 1925: 1a, 8.

22   "Fresno, 5; White Sox, 4," *Los Angeles Times*, September 7, 1925: 13.

23   "Fresno All-Stars Win Again from L.A. Team, 4 to 3," *Fresno Bee*, July 6, 1926: 10.

24   "Negro Baseball Team to Japan," *Nippu Jiji*, December 21, 1926: 10.

25   "Japanese Ball Club to Invade Orient Again," *Fresno Bee*, January 4, 1927: 10.

26   "Fresno Japanese Nine to Play Meiji in 1st Game," *Japan Times*, April 5, 1927: 8.

27   "Fresno Combine Arrives to Play Local Tossers," unknown Honolulu paper, August 2, 1927, from the Harvey Iwata 1927 Tour Scrapbook, National Baseball Hall of Fame.

28   Harvey Iwata 1927 Tour Scrapbook, National Baseball Hall of Fame.

29   "Fresno Japanese Plays Basketball 1st Game April 20," *Japan Times*, April 15, 1927: 8.

30   Email correspondence with Kyoko Yoshida, 2007.

31   "Royal Giants Swamp Fresno Japanese 9-1," *Japan Times*, April 22, 1927: 8.

32   "Royal Giants Swamp Fresno Japanese 9-1."

33   "Royal Giants Swamp Fresno Japanese 9-1."

34   "Royal Giants Swamp Fresno Japanese 9-1."

35   "Royal Giants Swamp Fresno Japanese 9-1."

36   "Royal Giants Swamp Fresno Japanese 9-1."

37   Frank Irwin, "Hubbard Leads Giant Team in Busy Session," *Fresno Morning Republican*, March 19, 1928: 7.

38   Stephen Ellsesser, "Black Giants Were Treated Like Royalty," MLB.com, February 23, 2007.

39   "Royal Giants Won 26, Tied One on Their Japanese Tour," *Chicago Defender*, June 25, 1927: 9.

40   From the Harvey Iwata 1927 Tour Scrapbook, National Baseball Hall of Fame.

41   Jane Leavy, *The Big Fella: Babe Ruth and the World He Created* (New York: Harper, 2018), 400.

42   "Firemen Ready to Meet Calpets This Afternoon," *Fresno Bee*, June 12, 1927: D1.

43   "Fresno Baseball Club Back from Orient," *Fresno Bee*, September 8, 1927: 12.

44   "Plans Progress for Ruth-Gehrig Game in Fresno," *Fresno Bee*, October 18, 1927: 15.

45   Ed W. Orman, "Fans Pack Park to Watch Ruth Gehrig Perform," *Fresno Bee*, October 29, 1927: 7; Ed W. Orman, "Babe Ruth Hits Homer to Thrill Crowd of 5,000," *Fresno Bee*, October 30, 1927: 1D.

46   Kataoka letter, shared with the author by Masaki Yoshikatsu, curator of the Hankyu Culture Foundation, Osaka, Japan, 2018.

47   Meehan.

48   Kataoka letter.

49   Ralph Pearce, James Bonner Biography entry, *Gentle Black Giants: A History of Negro Leaguers in Japan*, 211-219.

50   "Local Pitcher to Make Japan Tour," *Hayward (California) Daily Review*, February 12, 1937: 3.

51   "Fresno Players Will Sail for Japan Tonight," *Fresno Bee*, March 2, 1937: 3B.

52   "Fresno Players Will Sail for Japan Tonight."

53   "Zenimura Writes About Trip of Baseball Club," *Fresno Bee*, April 6, 1937: 2-3-B.

54   Ed W. Orman, "Sport Thinks," *Fresno Bee*, August 11, 1937: 2-B.

55   Orman, "Sport Thinks."

56   Orman, "Sport Thinks."

57   Nakagawa, 65.

58   Orman, "Sport Thinks."

59   John Findling et al., *Encyclopedia of the Modern Olympic Movement* (Santa Barbara, California: Greenwood Publishing Group, 2004), 120.

60   Meehan.

61   "Zenimura Boys to Play with Japan Team," *Honolulu Advertiser*, June 14, 1953: Sec 3, 10.

62   Documentary: Diamonds in the Rough: Zeni and the Legacy of Japanese-American Baseball (Chip Taylor Communications, 2004), 22.

63   Takizo Matsumoto entry, Baseball-Reference.com, https://www.baseball-reference.com/bullpen/Takizo_Matsumoto.

64   Gregory Lamb, "Backstory: The Players in the Shadows." *Christian Science Monitor*, June 29, 2006, www.csmonitor.com/2006/0629/p20s01-alsp.html.

65   Email correspondence with BBWAA leadership, October 2018.

66   Shanthi Sepe-Chepuru, "Negro Leagues Players Up for Hall Review." MLB.com, October 23, 2021, www.mlb.com/news/hall-of-fame-considering-negro-leagues-players-for-induction.

67   Email correspondence with voting members of the Early Era Committee, December 2021.

68   Alex Coffey, "A Field of Dreams in the Arizona Desert." National Baseball Hall of Fame, https://baseballhall.org/discover/a-field-of-dreams-in-the-arizona-desert.

69   Josh Getlin, "Trade Centre Balls among Exhibit," *Edmonton (Alberta) Journal*, April 1, 2002: D2.

70   Email correspondence with Japanese American Citizens League (JACL) leadership, April 22, 2021.

71   *Asahi Sports*, No. 32-34, 1924, 1 Japan (compiled and shared by Kyoko Yoshida); and "Nippon Ball Tour of Fresno Club Highly Successful," *Honolulu Star-Bulletin*, December 11, 1924: 12.

THE SAN JOSE ASAHI'S 1925 TOUR OF JAPAN AND KOREA

By Ralph M. Pearce

The San Jose Asahi Baseball Club was one of a number of Japanese teams to organize in Northern California between 1903 and 1915. Other cities to organize early teams included San Francisco, Oakland, Alameda, and Florin. The name Asahi means Morning Sun in Japanese and was a popular team name. San Jose's first Asahi team was made up of Issei (first-generation immigrants) players and lasted only a few years. In 1918 one of the former Issei players encouraged a young Nisei (second-generation) fellow, Jiggs Yamada, to reconstitute the team with Nisei players. Jiggs, a catcher, enlisted the assistance of 15-year-old pitcher Russell Hinaga, and the two soon put a team together.

Unlike the Issei players, these young Nisei players were born in the United States and had attended English-language schools with a largely Caucasian enrollment. Because of this, both a generational and cultural gap existed between the Issei and Nisei. Through the shared love of baseball, Nisei teams like the San Jose Asahi helped bridge this divide. In the early 1920s, a sympathetic newspaper columnist in San Jose, Jack Graham, encouraged the Asahi to extend that bridge by participating in games outside the Japanese leagues. This participation drew the larger San Jose community to the Asahi Diamond in Japantown, and there Caucasians began to mingle with Japanese Americans, helping to establish familiarity and friendship.

Another bridge in the making was the growing baseball friendship between the United States and Japan. Japan's enthusiasm for the game had been spreading since its introduction in the 1870s. The tradition of international baseball exchanges began

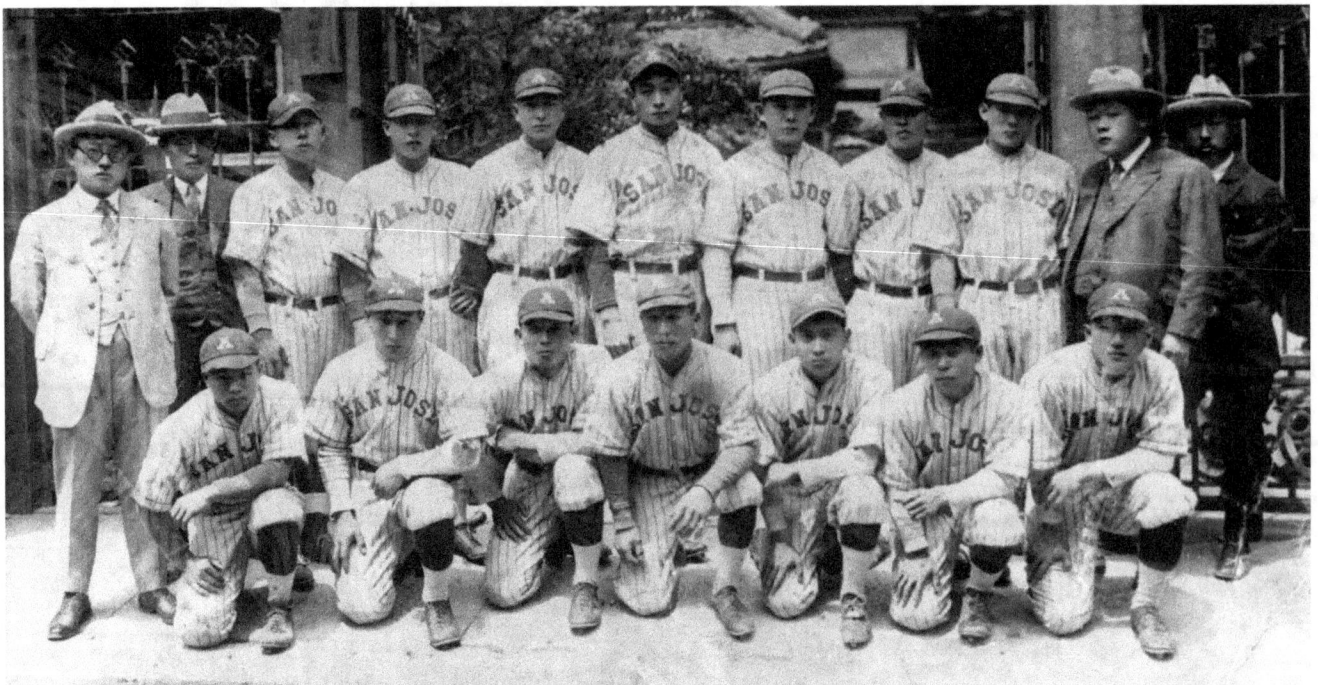

The Asahi in Osaka, Japan, during their 1925 tour. From left, back row: Kichitaro Okagaki, Nobukichi Ishikawa, Jay Nishida, Morio Sera, Harry Hashimoto, Jimmy Araki, Earl Tanbara, Mr. Takeshita, Fred Koba, and two Japanese officials. Front row: Tom Sakamoto, Sai Towata, Jimmie Yoshida, Jiggs Yamada, Frank Ito, Russell Hinaga, Ed Higashi. (Kanemoto Collection, Kifune Family Album).

with Waseda University's 1905 tour of the American West Coast and continues to this day. This friendship through the two nations' shared love of baseball helped foster cultural appreciation and understanding.

San Jose's opportunity to visit Japan came in 1925 at the invitation of Meiji University, whose baseball club had toured the United States the year before. The timing couldn't have been better for the Asahi; several of the players – Jiggs Yamada, Morio "Duke" Sera, Fred Koba, and Earl Tanbara – were anticipating retirement from the team. It was agreed that they would stay with the Asahi until their return from Japan.

It is believed that Meiji University provided some funds for tour expenses, though much of the burden was on the team and its Issei supporters. The first obstacle was the cost of transporting 17 passengers to and from Japan. Jiggs Yamada explained how this was accomplished:

> Well first, we had to get some way to go to Japan. A boat was the only thing we could get. We happened to have a boy, Earl Tanbara. … Tanbara's folks, mother and father, worked for the Dollar Steamship Company family in Piedmont. So when he graduated high school, we had his father talk to Mr. Dollar and ask him if he could do us a favor. He said, "Sure, as soon as Earl [goes] to Cal [Berkeley] and graduated, he's got to work for me at the steamship company." They were going to open up an agent in India. So he said, "Sure, if he promises to do that, I can have him going on our boat to Japan." … So that's how we got to go to Japan on a boat. People figured it was funny how we got to go to Japan … because at that time the steamship boat was expensive.[1]

A few days before departure, Asahi supporter Seijiro Horio gave $800 to Nobukichi Ishikawa, the team's treasurer. This appears to have been the primary funding source for the team's trip.

Jack Graham publicized the coming tour to Japan in a number of articles. On March 18, 1925, the day before the team departed, he wrote: "There will be a big delegation of fans in attendance and a bumper crowd of Japanese fans will be on hand to see their favorite sons in their final game in this city. The Asahi team will sail on Saturday for Japan, where they will play a series of games in the flowery kingdom. On their return, they will stop in the Hawaiian Islands, where they will play seven or more games. It will be the latter part of June before they return. The Asahi team has made many friends in this city by their gentlemanly manner in playing the national game, and whenever they stage a game here there is always sure to be a big turn-out."[2]

The next day, Graham ran a column praising the Asahi and encouraging local pride in the team as representatives of San Jose. A large photograph of the team ran at the top of the sports section, remarkable in that images of local teams rarely appeared in either American or Japanese American papers at the time. The caption read in part: "The Japanese Asahi baseball team will leave San Jose on the first leg of its journey to the land of cherry blossoms this morning, when it takes the train to San Francisco where it will stay until Saturday, when it will embark on the *President Cleveland* for Japan."[3]

The team members making the trip to Japan were pitchers Jimmy Araki and Russell Hinaga; catchers Ed Higashi and Jiggs Yamada; first baseman Harry Hashimoto; second baseman Tom Sakamoto; third baseman Morio "Duke" Sera; shortstop Fred Koba; third baseman-outfielder Sai "Cy" Towata; outfielders Frank Takeshita, Frank Ito, and Earl Tanbara; and utility players Jitney Nishida and Jimmie Yoshida. While the team was in Japan, the strong Asahi "B" team continued to play in San Jose against teams of its caliber. Asahi Diamond was also made available for use by other local teams and management of the diamond was temporarily turned over to locals Happy Luke Williams and Chet Maher.

The Asahi, along with the trip's manager, Kichitaro Okagaki, and its treasurer, Nobukichi Ishikawa, left San Francisco on March 21, 1925, and a little over two weeks later they arrived in Japan, giving them about a week to recover before their first game. When the team arrived in Japan, Earl Tanbara purchased two Mizuno baseball scorebooks. Earl kept meticulous track of each game, including dates, locations, and the names of all the players.

The Asahi played their first game on Thursday, April 9, against their hosts Meiji University. They lost 8-2 with Araki going the distance on the Meiji grounds. The Asahi played their second game on Saturday, April 11, against Waseda University. They were playing better now, though they lost in a 12-9 slugfest. Russ Hinaga and Jimmy Araki shared the pitching chores, Frank Ito got a double, Harry Hashimoto had a triple, and Cy Towata and Earl Tanbara hit home runs. Each side recorded only one error.

The Asahi played their third game two days later with a rematch against their hosts, Meiji University.

Jimmy Araki again pitched the entire game with Ed Higashi doing the catching. Araki was knocked around for a 9-4 loss, despite a batch of errors by Meiji. Next up – the very next day – was Keio University, another tough team. If the Asahi were ready for a win, it would have to wait for another day. Araki and Hinaga pitched the team to a 20-4 shellacking, the Asahi racking up seven errors along the way.

Two days later, on April 16, the Asahi faced Tokyo Imperial University. Once again Araki and Hinaga teamed up. The team was sharper that day, making only one error. Harry Hashimoto hit two doubles, chalking up a run. That was the Asahi's only run, though, to six for Tokyo and their fifth loss in five games. The Asahi played for the love of the game, but they were serious competitors and this situation was not acceptable. Jiggs Yamada explained the problem and the remedy:

> We didn't play so good because our legs were shaking and all that and the ball was different. It was a regular size American ball, but the cowhide, it slips. The pitcher couldn't play, pitch curves or anything and the players themselves couldn't throw the bases, so we couldn't play good. So finally we told the manager [Okagaki] of our team "Get us some American balls." So they sent us a one dozen box of American balls, then we started to play different. Then we started to play our regular play.[4]

Teammate Duke Sera confirmed the situation, saying that after leaving Tokyo, the manager saw to it that future Japanese teams could use their own baseballs when they were in the field, and that the Asahi players would use American balls when they were in the field.[5]

On April 18, the Asahi played yet another strong university nine. This time it was against Hosei. Jimmy Araki took to the mound for the Asahi and despite several errors, the team finally got its first win. The Asahi won 7-4 and scored all their runs in the first three innings, thanks in part to a home run by Araki himself. The team followed up a week later with a 25-5 victory over Sendai, with Hinaga pitching and Araki sharing left field with Tanbara. The Asahi suffered another loss on May 1, against Takarazuka before beginning a 13-game winning streak.

The Asahi had played their first six games in Tokyo against strong university teams before venturing north to Sendai. From Sendai, they headed south about 500 miles to Osaka. They played three games in the Osaka area and one game in nearby Kyoto. In the game against Kyoto Imperial University, Tom Sakamoto hit a dramatic "Sayonara Home Run" or walk-off home run in the 10th inning to win 3-2.

From Osaka, the team headed south to Hiroshima for two games. As they traveled the country by train, they continued to accumulate wins and, more importantly, became acquainted with the land of their parents.

One of the players, Duke Sera, had been born in Hawaii, and then raised by his uncle in Hiroshima. His uncle had sent him to Stanford University to complete his education. When the team visited Hiroshima, Duke's uncle held a reception for the team. According to Yamada, when the uncle met Duke and the team he quipped, "What the hell are you doing with this bunch here? You're supposed to be studying!"

After the final game in Hiroshima on May 12, the Asahi traveled 400 miles back to Tokyo. It was the team's original intention to return to the United States sometime in June. Whatever plans they may have had, however, were altered upon their return to Tokyo (except for Duke Sera, who had to return to his studies at Stanford). Jiggs shared the change of plans:

> In Tokyo, there's a letter to our manager that they want us to go to Korea, because the Korean government, the American Consulate and all that, were anxious to see us play against the Japanese there. It was a lot of fun there, because the American consuls and their families invited us to dinner the night before the game. In Keijo [now Seoul], the capital of Korea, they all came out to watch us play. When we played, first we had infield practice and batting practice and all that and you know we talk nothing but English. We don't talk Japanese when we're playing ball. Then this guy, this American guy says 'Oh boy, we got an American team here, we haven't got a Japanese team!'[6]

The Asahi played four games in Japanese-occupied Korea (then known as Chosen) between May 16 and May 21. The first two games were played in the capital, the third game in Taikyu (now Daegu), and the final game in Fusan (now Busan). All transportation to and from Korea had been provided for by the Asahi newspaper in Japan. The games in Korea were covered by a Japanese-language newspaper, the *Keijo Nichinichi*. They devoted the most attention to a game that they sponsored, which was played on May 17 against the All-Keijo team. The translated article reads:

"The game between San Jose and Keijo was played at the Ryuzan Railroad grounds in the middle of the afternoon of the seventeenth day, with plate umpire Marunaka and base umpires Ishihara and Suzuki. It was a very fine day. A big crowd swarmed and got excited over the unprecedented great game. Keijo, an uprising team, won the All Korea Championship last year. On this day, pitcher Takahashi performed well for Keijo and San Jose's Hinaga held Keijo batters in check with his breaking balls. The game went into extra innings. Finally, despite Keijo's good efforts, San Jose batters rallied to score five runs in the 12th and Keijo lost a close game."[7]

The article gives an inning-by-inning account of the game, summarizing as follows:

"The Keijo team was expected to push San Jose hard, if Takahashi pitched well. As Takahashi had few pitches, we expected that he would be rallied against at some point in the game and that Keijo would be beaten by four or five runs. In other words, San Jose's attack was delayed to the twelfth. That was the reason Keijo luckily fought gamely into the extra innings. But it was clear that San Jose looked stronger than Keijo. … Keijo, good at overcoming pinches, played better than it was able to. ... Keijo batters hit well the fastballs off breaking-baller Hinaga. San Jose was confident to win the game, but they should have brought in a new pitcher in the seventh. It was a costly error [by San Jose] that allowed Hioki to score in the ninth [tying the game]. Pitcher Takahashi pitched superbly, using breaking balls on the outside of the plate; however, he wasn't good with a runner on. It was an unexpectedly close contest for San Jose. It proved that Keijo played well. Keijo is expected to win another Championship this year. Keijo fans in the stands were not broadminded enough to cheer for their overseas countrymen, guests from afar. The San Jose players must have felt sad. The Keijo fans, lacking understanding and moderation, jeered at the San Jose players. Keijo fans betrayed the expectations of San

Jose's players who wanted to bring back good impressions of their land and countrymen."[8]

The Asahi arranged for their return trip to Tokyo to begin from the southern island of Kyushu. The team contained many players whose families were from either Kumamoto (on Kyushu) or Hiroshima, so the team's first stop would be Kumamoto where they beat the All-Kumamoto team 7-1. Hinaga's father had written ahead to family in Kumamoto that Russ would try to visit while in Japan. Yamada was also from Kumamoto and had written to his uncle and grandparents, whom he'd never met. Harry Hashimoto and Fred Koba were also from Kumamoto.

Jiggs Yamada told a story about arriving at one of the many stops along the way to Kumamoto. It was common for peddlers to walk along the station platform offering their wares to the passengers sitting inside the trains waiting to depart. If a passenger was interested in something, he would just open the window to make the transaction. At one stop, Jiggs and the players sitting near him could hear one of peddlers outside gradually making his way up to them calling out, "Sushi! Manju! Sushi! Manju!" When the peddler had come up even with their window, they all looked out and saw that it was Russ Hinaga! Jiggs said that this was a typical stunt for Russ, describing him as a funny, comical guy.[9]

The Asahi were well treated by the relatives in Kumamoto. They were honored at a reception and, according to Yamada, had a very good time. In fact, it was in Kumamoto that Jiggs met his future wife, Aki.[10] From there, they traveled north to Matsuyama on the island of Shikoku. After playing two games on Shikoku, they crossed back over to the main island of Honshu to return to Hiroshima.

Two more games were played in Hiroshima. The first was a no-hitter pitched by Jimmy Araki on June 6 against Koryo, presumably a high-school team, at the Kannon Grounds. Araki started the first inning by putting the opposing batters down in order, with two strikeouts and Cy Towata throwing a batter out at first. The Asahi replied with a run to finish the inning. In the second inning, Koryo's batters kept first baseman Harry Hashimoto busy with two batters thrown out and a fly out at first. The Asahi responded with another run before ending the inning with two fly outs. The third inning didn't go so smoothly for the Asahi as its defense disrupted what was otherwise a perfect game. Koryo got its first runner on base on an error by third baseman Towata. Towata threw the next batter out at first, with the runner now safe at second. The following batter hit into a fielder's choice at third. The next at-bat produced another error, this time by Fred Koba at shortstop. The error resulted in the Koryo batter making it safely to first and allowing a runner to advance to second. Araki was able to end the inning with a strikeout. The Asahi did better on offense that inning, tallying its final three runs. The rest of the game went well for San Jose, as Araki retired 18 straight batters and finished with a no-hitter. The final score was 5-0, with six strikeouts. The second game in Hiroshima was the Asahi's seventh and final loss of the tour and ended their 13-game winning streak.

From Hiroshima, the team headed south again, back to the southern island of Kyushu. There they played two games in Fukuoka to begin an 11-game winning streak. In a game on June 15 against All-Montetsu, after each team scored a run in the first inning, neither team scored for 10 more innings. Jimmy Araki went the distance for the Asahi. Finally, in the bottom of the 11th inning, Fred Koba scored on a hit by Higashi to win the game. After beating the All-Fukuoka club on June 16, the Asahi began their trek northward.

The father of one of the players owned a railroad on the northern island of Hokkaido.[11] The player made arrangements through his father for the team to play in Sapporo. On their way to Sapporo, the Asahi played two games in Osaka, then two games in Mito, about 50 miles northwest of Tokyo. Having traveled nearly the entire length of Japan from Fukuoka to Sapporo, the Asahi played two games in Sapporo on July 1 and 2. Then they went south to play two games against the Ocean Club in Hakodate. From there they left for Yokohama (just south of Tokyo) and played the final game of their tour against the Yokohama Seinen-dan on July 9. In the fourth inning of this game, Earl Tanbara hit the series' only grand slam.

After the shaky start against the Tokyo-area universities, the team had collected an impressive 26 wins and 7 losses. The Asahi scored 216 runs and allowed only 104 runs. Over half of the runs allowed came in the first five games. In their winning streak of 13 games, there were three shutouts in a row and a no-hitter. In the 11-game winning streak, there were four shutouts in a row. Jimmy Araki threw seven shutouts, one of which was his no-hitter against Koryo. Russ Hinaga also did quite well with five shutouts, one of which was a three-hitter. Eight players collected a total of 17 home runs with Earl Tanbara leading the pack with five. Catcher Ed Higashi had the highest batting average, .342. Tanbara followed at .318 with 40 more at-bats.[12]

Asahi third baseman Duke Sera observed that the Japanese infielders were cautious and that it was fairly easy to beat the throw to first; meanwhile the Japanese outfielders were faster than they were. He mentioned that the umpires in Tokyo were particularly unfair when it came to calling strikes over the corner of the plate, which hurt curveballer Russ Hinaga. The Asahi took advantage of the fact that they could understand their opponents' Japanese while only speaking English with each other.[13]

The Asahi departed Yokohama for the return voyage to the United States on July 14, and arrived home on July 29. Though this was just one of many baseball exchanges over the course of the twentieth century, the Asahis made an important contribution to an enduring friendship between two countries. It was a friendship that began on a baseball diamond, and then grew to something more; a friendship that endured even war. For the players themselves, this journey of friends to the land of their parents and forefathers left them with memories to last a lifetime.

1925 SAN JOSE ASAHI GAMES IN JAPAN AND KOREA

Date	Place	Opponent	Score	Winner	Loser
April 9	Tokyo	Meiji University	2-8	Yasuda	Araki
April 11	Tokyo	Waseda University	9-12	Fujimoto	Hinaga
April 13	Yokohama	Meiji University	4-9	Nakamura	Araki
April 14	Tokyo	Keio University	4-20	Nakahama	Hinaga
April 16	Tokyo	Tokyo Imperial University	1-6	Azuma	Hinaga
April 18	Tokyo	Hosei University	7-4	Araki	Matano
April 25	Sendai	Sendai	25-5	Hinaga	Muraoka
May 1	Takarazuka	Takarazuka	2-4	Onuki	Araki
May 5	Nishinomiya	Kobe Commercial	3-2	Araki	Kashima
May 8	Nishinomiya	Kwansei Gakuin	4-1	Araki	Imakita
May 11	Hiroshima	Tiger Club	6-0	Hinaga	Kimura
May 12	Hiroshima	All-Kure	3-0	Araki	Sakoda
May 16	Seoul, Korea	Ryuzan	5-0	Araki	Oi
May 17	Seoul, Korea	All-Keijo	9-4	Araki	Takahashi
May 19	Daegu, Korea	Taikyu	6-4	Araki	Aoyama
May 21	Busan, Korea	All-Fusan	12-1	Hinaga	Ide
May 25	Kumamoto	All-Kumamoto	7-1	Araki	Hironaga
May 30	Matsuyama	Matsuyama Commercial	10-0	Araki	Nakamura
May 31	Matsuyama	Tetsuden	1-0	Hinaga	Usui
June 6	Hiroshima	Koryo	5-0	Araki	Nawaoka
June 7	Hiroshima	All-Kure	6-8	Sakoda	Hinaga
June 15	Kitakyushu	All-Montetsu	2-1	Araki	Narimatsu
June16	Fukuoka	All-Fukuoka	9-5	Hinaga	Yasuda
June 21	Nishinomiya	Star Club	7-0	Araki	Matsumoto
June 22	Nishinomiya	Diamond Club	5-0	Hinaga	Moriguchi
June 28	Mito	All-Mito	17-1	Araki	Tachi
June 28	Mito	All-Mito	10-0	Hinaga	Uyeno
July 1	Sapporo	Wagona Club	5-0	Araki	Isazawa
July 2	Sapporo	Wagona Club	7-0	Hinaga	Isazawa
July 4	Hakodate	Ocean Club	3-0	Araki	Hashimoto
July 5	Hakodate	Ocean Club	6-3	Hinaga	Kuji
July 9	Yokohama	Yokohama Seinen-dan	11-3	Araki	Masuda

SOURCES

Ralph M. Pearce has adapted this chapter from his book, *From Asahi to Zebras* (San Jose: Japanese American Museum of San Jose, 2005).

NOTES

1   Jiggs Yamada, interview, October 23, 1993.

2   Jack Graham, "Asahi Team Will Play Portland Beavers Here Today," *San Jose Mercury Herald*, March 18, 1925: 22.

3   "Asahi Ball Team Leaves Today on Tour of Japan," *San Jose Mercury Herald*, March 19, 1925: 18.

4   Yamada, interview.

5   Theron Fox, "Nippon Manager Tells of Tour of Ball Outfit," *San Jose Evening News*, August 3, 1925: 8.

6   Yamada, interview.

7   "Peninsula Champion Defeated by Narrow Margin," *Keijo Nichinichi*, May 19, 1925: 3. Translation by Yoichi Nagata.

8   "Peninsula Champion Defeated by Narrow Margin."

9   Yamada, interview.

10 Glenn Iida, interview, May 30, 2011.

11 Jiggs Yamada was unable to remember which player.

12 Earl K. Tanbara, *San Jose Asahi Japan Tour Scorebook 1925*.

13 Jack Graham, "Japanese College Seeks Ruth for Exhibition Tour," *San Jose Mercury Herald*, June 16, 1925: 18.

RETHINKING THE PHILADELPHIA BOBBIES 1925 TOUR IN JAPAN: "EMBARRASSMENT TO THE NATION" OR "GREAT SUCCESS"?

By Kat D. Williams, Ph.D.

Crack! The ball hits the bat. Smack! That ball hits Edith Houghton's waiting glove at short who quickly throws to first to get the batter and all in a twinkling of an eye. These women play the game in a manner that would no doubt delight the heart of many a manager who ever saw them play.[1]

Writing about a baseball game between the Passaic Girls and the Lansdale Chryslermen, this unnamed reporter was shocked to see women play baseball with talent and dedication. "It was surprising to watch the brand of ball that these girls can play," he continued. "They take their baseball in a serious way and all the jeering of the 'wise guys' who stand on the sidelines and do the looking on cannot daunt them." Even the crowd's "jeers soon turn to cheers when they see the girls in real action."[2] The reporter's shock at the women's quality of play was not a new phenomenon. Rather, it echoed hundreds of other local news reports about female baseball players written in sports pages during the early 1920s. Why so shocked? Did they not read each other's work?

Perhaps it was a lack of public interest in women's baseball that kept reporters from recognizing a growing trend? But that wasn't the case. Even reports of large crowds and fervent fans did not stick in the minds of sports reporters. Approximately 1,500 fans showed up to the Lansdale, Pennsylvania, game, roughly 20 percent of the town's population. Meanwhile, in Maple Shade, New Jersey, the largest crowd of the season came to watch the "famous invading lassies," the Philadelphia Bobbies, play the local baseball club.[3] In that game, shortstop Edith Houghton had five hits, including two doubles and a home run. By this time, the late 1920s, Houghton had been widely written about. She was a standout on the Philadelphia Bobbies team that toured Japan in 1925 and was so well-known that fans in small towns clamored to see her play. There was public interest. Still, in story after story, sports reporters seemed shocked to see women playing baseball at a high level.

Were they skeptical of other reporters' assessment of good baseball? Some of the language was kind of over the top. In a *Philadelphia Inquirer* article, "The Quaker City Maids of the Diamond," Gordon Mackey hailed the play of Edith Houghton and Edith Ruth. "Both members liked to play baseball and they COULD play the game – make no mistake on that

Leona Kearns of the 1925 Philadelphia Bobbies in Japan. (Library of Congress, Prints & Photographs Division, LC-DIG-ggbain- 38869)

score." In a baseball barnstorming tour their play was legendary but, "like Alexanders in skirts or Hannibals in bloomers, they longed for other worlds to conquer after they had cleaned up most of the alleged sterner sex in duels of the diamond in 1925."[4] Houghton "could play shortstop in a way that would make Joe Boley toss his glove in the air and yell, 'bravo,'" and Ruth was "the holder of the initial sack and how she can go after those quick throws and hug that base is nobody's business." Team play was also lauded with the same exaggerated language. "What an infield. They work with the rhythm and snappiness that is characteristic of any big-league team." That over-the-top language – Hannibals in Bloomers and shouts of bravo! – made the players appear aberrant. There is almost a freak-show quality to the enthusiastic description.

Reporters' continued surprise at women's good play was most certainly related to the more common descriptions of women's baseball which emphasized the players' femininity." For decades reporters introduced female players as "neat," "attractive in their uniforms," and as "spectacles." They simply skipped over a discussion of their play and instead focused on their appearance, their "dainty hands," and how it must have been hard for them to hold the glove. They marveled at their "feminine strength" and how hard it must have been to play against "professional strength." They were used to writing about women who were, in their eyes, not very talented and unwilling to get dirty or to take the game seriously. A report about the Hollywood Bloomer girl team began, "A bevy of beauties from Hollywood, California took time out from powdering their noses and gave a picked team of the Coca Cola Greys the battle of their lives. ... The ladies put up a good game but couldn't stand up under the strain."[5] Even when their play was good and the individual talent exceptional, reporters were still likely to describe games as "an unusual tussle," played by nine "fair maidens."[6] Most women had been described in these terms for decades. Just because they donned a baseball uniform did not mean that would change.

To reporters and to many men who played, managed, or promoted baseball, there was a set of expectations, standards for play, and a distinct language used to discuss the game and its male players. There were no such expectations or standards for women. As a result, women's play was judged against that of men, making it difficult for them to be seen as talented players. So they were not. Because it was unfathomable to even think of women in actual baseball terms

– a slugger, a hurler, or aggressive on the basepaths – a whole other language emerged to describe women's baseball. Reporters sprinkled some baseball terms in among talk of their physical appearance – "The long-legged beauty on the third base bag sure can play the hot corner."[7] And because women were used to being described this way they did not resist. They just kept playing.

Women's insistence on playing and the dilemma of reporters tasked with reporting on their games ultimately combined to establish a separate set of standards and expectations for female baseball players. And over time, two separate baseball spheres, one for men and one for women. From our twenty-first-century perspective, we could claim that these gender-specific standards worked against women who sought legitimacy as baseball players. It could be argued that creating separate baseball spheres took agency or control away from women. Nothing could be further from the truth.

Existing in separate spheres was not new to women. They lived, worked, and studied under a different set of standards than men. So it was likely no surprise to them that the same would happen within the game of baseball. As they had always done, though, women never stopped pushing against the boundaries forced upon them. They learned the game, played it, and from within their baseball sphere, they defined for themselves what baseball meant. They set their own standards and, most significantly, they defined baseball success in their own terms. As it was for men, winning games, playing well, and making money were all part of women's definition of success, but that was only the beginning. Baseball was an opportunity, a new experience, and a location where women could excel in an endeavor previously off-limits to them. Playing the game provided women with a chance to see the country and ultimately the world. It allowed them to make their own money and to realize a sense of independence. To many players, success was found in the opportunities baseball afforded them and not only in the box score.

There are many examples to illustrate the ways in which women embraced their separate baseball sphere and used it to their benefit, but none is more engaging than the story of the Philadelphia Bobbies and their 1925 barnstorming tour of Japan. The Bobbies' tour provides an opportunity to show how women not only embraced their separate baseball sphere but used it to challenge traditional definitions of baseball success and to define for themselves how and where they fit into the narrative of baseball. The tour shows how one set of baseball standards were used to plan, guide, and then judge the tour, and how another set, the ones defined and accepted by the women themselves, provide a completely different interpretation. One side saw the tour as an unmitigated disaster, while the other saw it as a great success.

*

The Bobbies, named for the popular 1920s haircut "the bob," were formed in 1922 by Mary O'Gara. The team was made up of young women from around Philadelphia. Edith Houghton's friend, Edith Ruth, whose nickname was "the original Babe Ruth," was masterful on the mound. Loretta Jester-Lipski, nicknamed "Sticks," was best known for her power at the plate, while Nettie Gans was the team's left fielder. And, of course, there was "The Kid," Edith Houghton. Houghton was 10 when she joined the team and 13 when the team left for Japan. The other players were less known and likely had less playing experience, but everyone loved being on the diamond. The team played two or three games a week, sometimes against men's teams and other times taking on nearby Bloomer Girl teams. O'Gara, who was also the manager of the team, usually held out a portion of the ticket sales for herself and paid the players a rate of $5 to $10 per game. Women were making money playing and coaching baseball.

To aid in the team's growth, O'Gara hired a local booking agent, R.H. Cross, a vaudeville and amusement agency. Entertainment agencies were often the groups setting up exhibition games for women's baseball teams; this most certainly added to the circus-like atmosphere of many women's games. The firm scheduled games for the Bobbies against local clubs in the Philadelphia area and eventually in other places such as New Jersey, upstate Pennsylvania, and Pittsburgh. Due to their widespread travel and, most significantly, their outstanding play, within two years the Bobbies were one of the most popular female teams on the East Coast.

Fortunately for the Bobbies, they were reaching that peak just as a shift in public opportunities for women was also taking place. American women were going to college in greater numbers than ever before. They were working, cutting their hair, and, starting in 1920, they were voting. It was the era of a new, more independent woman and women's baseball was poised to take advantage. Coincidentally, baseball promoters were taking advantage of a worldwide growth in baseball and the simultaneous spread of capitalism.

Male professional baseball players began making trips to Japan as early as 1908. Sending American baseball teams on barnstorming tours in Asian countries became profitable for promoters as well as players. It should be no surprise then that an astute Japanese promoter, T. Shima, suggested an all-female barnstorming tour to Japan.[8]

While baseball had been played in the country since the 1870s, Shima was riding a new wave of baseball popularity in Japan. American barnstorming tours helped to spread excitement about the game throughout Japan and made stars of American baseball teams and players. Even female players such as Edith Houghton, Nettie Gans, and Edith Ruth, who had not played in Asia before, were known baseball celebrities. Japanese women were big fans of the game and made up a significant portion of the crowds who watched American barnstormers. But there were no women's baseball teams for the Bobbies to play on their tour. They would play against men.

Shima's first contact in the United States was with Eddie Ainsmith.[9] A veteran of barnstorming, Ainsmith was a longtime major-league catcher and a successful promoter, so he was known among Japanese baseball promoters. In 1920 Ainsmith traveled with Herb Hunter on a barnstorming tour of Japan. Because of his previous success in Japan, and despite his having no experience with women's baseball, he was the first person T. Shima contacted with the idea of an all-women's barnstorming tour. Ainsmith accepted the offer to organize the tour.

Unfamiliar with women's baseball but anxious to take advantage of another barnstorming tour, Ainsmith contacted R.H. Cross, the company that booked games for women's baseball teams. The company introduced Ainsmith to Mary O'Gara. When Ainsmith first approached O'Gara about the trip to Japan, she and the team jumped at the chance. They would play the game they loved, travel to a foreign country, and get paid a great deal of money in the process, a previously unheard-of opportunity for women.

The Japanese promoters, Ainsmith, and O'Gara negotiated the terms and ultimately agreed to a rate of $800 per game for the players and coaches, along with first-class transportation for the players, O'Gara, Ainsmith, and Earl Hamilton, another former major-league player. Transportation and expenses were also paid for Ainsmith's wife, Loretta, and Hamilton's wife, Edna. The women served as chaperones for the players. Unlike the male barnstormers, every female baseball team had to travel with chaperones. Even though the 1920s ushered in a modern era for women, one where they had more freedom, it was still frowned upon for women to travel alone.

With the details of the tour settled, O'Gara and the team were ready to begin the trip of a lifetime. On September 23, 1925, they boarded a train in Philadelphia headed for Seattle. The plan was to play games against men's teams along the way and to meet up with the Ainsmiths and the Hamiltons once they arrived in Seattle. Naturally they had no idea what lay ahead, but their diaries and letters home show they were ready for a level of travel and adventure most women of the time could not imagine. Excitement and opportunity embraced and motivated the players. "We are off at last!" wrote Nettie Gans, the Bobbies' left fielder, who kept a diary throughout the trip, which provides a valuable insight into the players' experiences. "Everyone in fine spirits."[10] Spangler highlighted the travel from Philadelphia to Pittsburgh; St. Paul; Great Falls and Whitefish, Montana; Spokane; and finally to Seattle, where the team met Ainsmith and Hamilton and prepared for the final leg of their trip to Japan. On October 6, 1925, Spangler wrote, "Farewell old USA-All aboard for the Orient. Bobbies came on the President Jefferson, First Class!"[11]

After long, rough days at sea, on October 19, 1925, the SS *Thomas Jefferson* docked in Yokohama, Japan. The Bobbies were excited to see the city, but apparently not nearly as excited as the city was to see them. Spangler wrote, "We awakened early, passed doctor's inspection, had about a million pictures taken then walked down the gangplank to Japanese soil!"[12] The Bobbies, the Ainsmiths, and the Hamiltons were met by a throng of media and large crowds of curious onlookers. Photographers overwhelmed the girls with requests for photos and interviews. Edith Houghton, the youngest and arguably the best of the players, was a favorite of the Japanese media, who showered her with gifts. Everyone, though, including Ainsmith and Hamilton, was treated as special guests. The welcome was lengthy but "after some time," Spangler wrote, "we rode jinrikashaws [sic] to the Maranouchoi [Marunouchi] Hotel. We were greeted at the station by boys from the University we are going to play against. Bouquets galore and banners too."[13]

The team's popularity continued throughout the early days of the tour. Even though the Bobbies were not slated to play top-rated or high-quality teams, their first few games in Tokyo drew crowds of more than 20,000 people. Some estimates were as high as 100,000.[14] At the Bobbies' first game, against Nippon

University, Tokyo's mayor, Yoshikoto Nakamura, threw out the first pitch and the crowd was standing room only. Reports of the game must have seemed unusual to the players, since the headlines did not belittle the team or comment on the strain their "feminine energy" must have suffered during the game. The *Japan Times* reported, "Several thousand fans showed up at the baseball diamond … prepared to look down from the superior height of their sex and giggle gleefully at the attempts of the girls from America to play baseball. … The crowd that came there to laugh and not to see baseball were disappointed."[15] Another headline read, "What Do the Philadelphia Bobbies Look Like? – They Look Like Good Ball Players."[16] These reports could be seen as proof against the idea of separate baseball expectations for men and women. The reality is, however, that in no other country in the world was baseball more tied to masculinity than in the United States. There was no need for Japanese baseball to exist within separate spheres. Japanese women were not traveling the world playing baseball or threatening the masculine ties to the game. The Japanese reports did likely have an impact on the Bobbies, however. Seeing themselves and their play described by the Japanese press (often in English) in terms usually reserved for male baseball players may have contributed to the women's positive view of the tour and of themselves as ballplayers.

On October 23 the Bobbies played Nippon University and lost 6-0. The next day they played Nippon Dental College and lost 2-1. On October 25 they played and lost their third game, 24-7, against the Shochiku Kamata Movie Studio. The Bobbies played their last game in Tokyo on October 25, losing by a score of 24-7. Again, the Japanese newspapers all but ignored the score and praised the players. The *Japan Times* reported on "Stick" Jester, Edith Ruth, and Flo Eakin, who, according to the *Times*, "showed a cool head when she had a man in the hot box between second and first with a man riding third. … [W]hen the man on third [made] a dash for the plate she ripped the ball into the catcher, a splendid throw which Ainsmith fumbled."[17] The Bobbies had been in Japan only 10 days at that point and their adventures were just beginning.

The Bobbies and their entourage left Tokyo on October 29 for Osaka, where they were scheduled to play another round of games. They arrived at the Dobuil Hotel on the night before Halloween, "mischief night." "We created costumes," Spangler reported in her diary, and "stood outside the hotel. No doubt the Japanese thought, 'what is going on here?' They don't celebrate mischief night I guess."[18] The Bobbies were not going to miss an opportunity to celebrate even as they prepared to play baseball the next day. On October 31 they played the Foreign Language School and despite losing the game 6-3, the Bobbies continued to experience the very best Japanese culture had to offer, including the benefit of the doubt from reporters. Because reporters tended to provide little detail about women's games, we have few specifics about the games themselves. There are very few descriptions of good plays or hits, and other than descriptions of the women or comments about their presence on the field, the only real statistics we have for the games are the final scores.

On November 1 the Bobbies won their first game, 1-0 against Osaka Dental College. The next day they played the actors from the Kansai Movie Talkers, losing 9-5, and on the 5th they lost to Osaka Mainichi Newspaper 23-16. After a day off, the Bobbies played the Nikkatsu Movie Studio on the 7th and the Kyoto Chamber of Commerce on the 8th, losing both games, 20-5 and 16-5 respectively. In the second game of a doubleheader on the 8th, they lost to Ritsumeikan University. On November 16, the day Ainsmith left to start the extended tour in Formosa, the team played the Canadian Academy and lost 34-3. The Bobbies played a high-school team and tied them, and then played two more games, losing to Iyo Railroad, 4-2, and defeating the Hiroshima Yachiyo Club, 6-0.

Like the Japanese newspapers, Spangler's diary and Leona Kearns's letters home all but ignore the team's losses. Spangler's October 25 entry only mentioned that they had a game, then recalled meeting the "Rudolph Valentino of Japan, a good looking fellow. Some of the girls went over to the Imperial Hotel to see his show."[19] Then on October 26, "We went to a party in the American Embassy, Tokyo, Japan. Each of the Bobbies received a present. Fereba got a beautiful bedspread and pillowcases – beautifully embroidered."[20] In a letter to her parents, Leona Kearns jovially wrote, "We girls are not allowed to drink the water here, so we are going to live on beer."[21] Then later, Kearns declared that "this trip has ruined me. When I get home, I will find myself pressing buttons and ordering my breakfast in bed."[22] On the surface, it seems as though they are feeding a traditional narrative about women not being serious athletes. But there was another layer to this story.

Spangler and Kearns' focus on events other than those that occurred on the diamond does not mean the team did not take the games seriously or care about the wins and losses. The players wrote a great deal about the game, their individual play and how they had learned from their coaches. "Mr. Hamilton spent a lot of time showing me how to throw a slow ball," Nellie Kearns wrote in a letter home.[23] And Spangler confessed to her diary that the team would have had a better chance to win if "we were faster on the basepaths." Then she added, "Edith, our shortstop displays her talents beautifully. So does Jenny Phillips."[24] For the women, the play on the field was important and exciting, but playing baseball was about so much more. It was about the opportunities the game afforded them, the experiences and independence they enjoyed because of baseball. "I can't believe I am in Japan. A farm girl like me," Kearns wrote to her mother.[25] As if to reinforce Leona's thoughts, Spangler wrote in her diary, "We went to a party at the American Embassy today. Can you imagine?"[26] Young women, and especially the mostly working-class women of the Bobbies, would not have been able to imagine such a trip without baseball.

But not everything was positive. There is no indication in Spangler's diary or other letters written by players that they knew the Bobbies were in financial trouble. But they were and the Japanese media was definitely aware. The first line of a *Japan Times* article from November 7, 1925, stated, "The Philadelphia Bobbies are in trouble." After remarking on the team's lack of money, the reporter offered their low-level play as a reason: "They are a little below the class of a fast Japanese Middle School team and have not been able to meet any teams with whom a game would draw a big crowd."[27] While the Bobbies and their Japanese opponents may have played below a high-school level, this article marks the first time Japanese reporters refer to them in this way.

In Spangler's November 13 entry we see the first mentions of financial difficulties. "Unlucky 13th, Mary [O'Gara] fell, not too bad. Mr. Ainsmith and Mary discussed going to Formosa with the girls. I believe it has something to do with money being paid. She didn't want us to go without her although Mr. Ainsmith and Mr. Hamilton had their wives with them. The girl he brought from Chicago went with him as did two of our girls."[28] What Spangler did not know was that the tour was losing money daily. Ticket sales were diminishing, and the Japanese government had decided to tax all future professional baseball games in order to claim a percentage of the receipts.[29] These realities dug into the tour's profits. Then, claiming that they had lost too much money, financial backers simply refused to cover any further expenses. In what was the final straw, the tour's initial backer, T. Shima, went bankrupt, and two of his promoters disappeared. Ainsmith was made aware of these issues in early November so by the 13th he was clearly seeking alternatives. Having run out of funding, he decided the best option was to push forward with the tour.

Either because he simply had no other choice or because he still believed the venture could be profitable, Ainsmith pushed to expand the tour into Korea, Formosa, and Western Japan rather than end it and return to the United States. Mary O'Gara and most of the players were against Ainsmith's plan. Having demanded return passage home and been denied by the initial tour's promoters, the players were leery and refused to play or travel any farther with Ainsmith. He did persuade three of the players, Leona Kearns, Edith Ruth, and Nellie Shank, to accompany him and his wife and (presumably) Hamilton to Korea. To fill out the team, Ainsmith recruited male Japanese players.[30]

With their promoters and investors gone, O'Gara and the remaining Bobbies were stranded in Kobe. The group's plight was widely reported in both Japanese and American newspapers. In those reports responsibility for the tour's failure was broadly assigned. The American newspapers blamed the Japanese promoters for abandoning the Bobbies and the previously complimentary Japanese papers blamed the players and their losses for the tour's financial problems.[31]

Despite the shift in reporters' coverage of the Bobbies and their obvious financial difficulties, neither Spangler's diary entries nor letters from other players mention fear or uncertainty about their predicament. There are likely multiple reasons for this. As we have seen, the women rarely wrote about negative aspects of the trip, choosing instead to focus on their adventures, Japanese culture, and food. Also, there were a number of people trying to help the Bobbies. The American Consulate tried, unsuccessfully, to secure passage for the women, and an American businessman, Henry Sanborn, who owned a small hotel in Kobe came to their rescue. Sanborn allowed them to stay at his hotel and provided them with meals while trying to raise money for their passage home. The young women no doubt felt anxious about getting back home, but they must also have felt that with so much attention being paid to their story, things would work out.

Things did work out. Due to Sanborn's diligent efforts a "Mr. N.H.N. Mody, a British-Indian, volunteered to provide funds for their passage home."[32]

It wasn't until Spangler's November 18 entry, when she wrote, "Fereba and I did sort of a Jumping Jack act up in the hall of the hotel. 'We're Going Home.' Banzai! (Hurrah in Japanese)," that we see how anxious she was about being stranded.[33] Spangler's excitement when she found out that their trip home has been funded shows her eagerness to leave, but that is the only indication that she or the team was anything other than happy to be playing baseball in Japan.

On November 18, several of the individuals who had assisted the Bobbies bade them farewell as they boarded the *Empress of Russia* to begin their trip home.[34] They spent Thanksgiving on the ship and arrived in Vancouver, British Columbia, on December 1. Five days later, most of the Philadelphia Bobbies returned home to Philadelphia. For O'Gara and the Bobbies who remained with her, their Japanese barnstorming tour was nearly over.

For the seven who set off for Korea, the hardship was to continue, however. Despite a promise to guarantee money for passage to the United States, the Korean promoters reneged on the promise when they realized that Ainsmith's team had only three girls. With no money to continue, the group was stranded in Hiroshima. As they had done when the initial tour ran out of money, Ainsmith and Hamilton solicited travel funds from other businessmen. The American consul, E.R. Dickover, even tried to help them by reporting the promoters to the police. Nothing worked. With the help of family and friends, Ainsmith was able to secure enough money for his and his wife's passage, but not for the girls. On December 27, 1925, Eddie and Loretta Ainsmith set sail for home.

Once again Henry Sanborn stepped up to care for stranded Bobbies. Before departing for home, Ainsmith took the girls back to Kobe, where Sanborn agreed to house and feed them while he and others worked to secure their passage home. At Sanborn's urging, the US State Department negotiated with the Canadian Pacific Steamship Company, which provided passage for the girls. On January 18, 1926, they left Japan aboard the *SS Empress of Asia.*[35]

Likely relieved their ordeal was almost over, the girls settled into their quarters. Just a few days into the trip, the ship experienced gale-force winds and heavy snow squalls. All passengers were stuck below deck for safety as the ship tossed back and forth. During a brief calm, Leona Kearns and Nellie Shank went to the deck, despite warnings not to do so. Early in the afternoon on January 21 a large wave crashed into the ship, washing Kearns overboard. The captain was notified immediately and turned the ship around to search for her. The search lasted about an hour but was called off due to low visibility. Leona Kearns was declared lost at sea.[36]

The tragic death of Leona Kearns brought an end to the badly funded, haphazardly planned, and irresponsibly implemented first-ever all-female barnstorming tour of Japan. Reports of Kearns' death also set off a set of dueling narratives that described the trip. As the Bobbies' losing streak grew, fan support dwindled, and Japan's media got word of their financial situation, some Japanese officials, and even State Department personnel began blaming the Bobbies for its failure. Pointing to the team's "lack of talent," American consul Dickover wrote in his 1926 report about the Bobbies' failures in Japan that it was quickly "apparent that the girls could not play a sufficiently strong game to compete with any school team in Japan."[37]

After Kearns's death, finger-pointing began between Japan and the United States, each blaming the other for the tragedy. And while the rhetoric was heated between the two countries, they did agree on one thing: The problems began with the Bobbies themselves and their bad play. Dickover declared "the trip a financial failure from the start" due to a lack of competitive play by the Bobbies.[38]

Most records and newspaper reports show that by nearly every measure used at the time, the tour was a failure. Those measures, however, were created within the male-focused baseball sphere and included a set of standards and expectations that were very different from the ones women defined for themselves. Recognizing that fact allows for a contrasting narrative to emerge, one defined by and embraced by the women. The questions we ask about the tour, its successes and failures, are very different if we shift the perspective and therefore the narrative itself.

In the letters, diaries, and interviews produced by the Bobbies, there was no talk of failure. Instead, while honestly recording their losses and at times bad play, they also lauded their success. They spoke of freedom, adventure, and opportunity. They analyzed their own play on the field. Spangler mentioned the sharp play of Nellie Shank, the successful pitching of Edith Ruth, and the masterful play of Edith Houghton at shortstop. But in no place do they identify the tour as a failure. What accounts for the drastically different accounts of the trip? We have already seen how the creation of different baseball spheres for men and women played out in newspapers, which clearly accounts for much of the negative reporting, but that is only part of the story.

Reports of the trip by journalists, State Department officials, politicians, and Japanese promoters were written by men, using male baseball standards. For them, financial success, strengthened connections between the two governments, and winning were the necessary elements for success. On those grounds the tour was a failure. Further, these officials were primed to blame the women for that failure because women ballplayers had been depicted as either incompetent or aberrant. After all, they knew all along that women couldn't play ball.

But when we shift the gaze and the definition of success a bit, we get a very different view of the tour, one influenced and informed from within a woman's baseball world. Judged by standards they could never live up to in the press and elsewhere, women did not shrink away from the game. Rather, they kept playing and found measures of success that fit their baseball reality. When the Bobbies embarked on a barnstorming tour of Japan, they did so under a set of rules and expectations already in place – a prescription for success that was tried and true for male barnstormers. It is no surprise, then, that they were held responsible for its financial failure. Those writers of history, the keepers of the game, had no other standard on which to judge. But women did. For decades, they had been navigating between the boundaries of baseball's separate spheres. And from that experience women began to develop a different way of defining, playing, and understanding baseball. Experience and opportunity were discussed alongside balls and strikes. Travel and independence influenced the game's success as much as wins and losses. They had little say in the planning of the trip or how to proceed when things got difficult. But once it was over, their perspective, their definition of success and their thoughts on what is important about the game, made their way into the narrative of baseball history.

Nettie Spangler's last diary entry was dated December 6, 1925.

PHILADELPHIA AT LAST! There were crowds of people at the gate when we got off the train. Of course, photographers were there to take pictures. I don't know how we stood still; we were so excited. There were smiles and tears and I am sure every girl on the team would agree that there is no place like home. ... I thanked the good lord for bringing us home safe and for the great time I had playing ball with the PHILADELPHIA BOBBIES in Japan.[39]

Perhaps it was naïveté or denial or simply young women experiencing the world for the first time, but whatever it was, and despite the financial hardships and the losses, the Bobbies' trip was a complete success to the young women who completed it. That too should be part of Japanese barnstorming history.

1925 PHILADELPHIA BOBBIES GAMES IN JAPAN

Date	Place	Opponent	Score
October 23	Tokyo	Nippon University	0-6
October 24	Tokyo	Nippon Dental College	1-2
October 25	Tokyo	Shochiku Kamata Movie Studio	7-24
October 31	Osaka	Foreign Language School	3-6
November 1	Osaka	Osaka Dental College	1-0
November 2	Osaka	Kansai Movie Talkers	5-9
November 5	Osaka	Osaka Mainichi	16-23
November 7	Osaka	Nikkatsu Movie Studio	5-20
November 8	Kyoto	Kyoto Chamber of Commerce	5-16
November 8	Kyoto	Ritsumeikan University	lost
November 16	Kobe	Canadian Academy	3-34
11/19-12/10*	Matsuyama	Matsuyama Commercial High School	0-0
11/19-12/10*	Matsuyama	Iyo Railroad	2-4
11/19-12/10*	Hiroshima	Hiroshima Yachiyo Club	6-0

The exact dates of these final three games, played with only three women, are unknown.

NOTES

1   "Chryslermen Beat Bloomer Girls, 10-8," unknown source, Edith Houghton player file, National Baseball Hall of Fame.

2   "Chryslermen Beat Bloomer Girls, 10-8."

3   Unknown source, Edith Houghton player file, National Baseball Hall of Fame.

4   Gordon Mackey, Unknown source, Edith Houghton player file, Hall of Fame. National Baseball Hall of Fame.

5   "Local Team Wins over Girls Nine," unknown source, Edith Houghton player file, National Baseball Hall of Fame.

6   "Local Team Wins over Girls Nine."

7   "Local Team Wins over Girls Nine."

8   Despite research in the Japanese sources, Shima's first name is unknown.

9   Barbara Gregorich, "Dropping the Pitch: Leona Kearns, Eddie Ainsmith and the Philadelphia Bobbies," *The National Pastime* 43 (2013).

10 Nettie Gans Spangler Diary, Women in Baseball (WIB): Philadelphia Bobbies subject file, National Baseball Hall of Fame.

11 Spangler Diary.

12 Spangler Diary.

13 Spangler Diary.

14 Most sources estimate the attendance at 20,000 people, but some articles cited figures as high as 50,000 and 100,000. See "Girl Ball Players Returning Broke," unknown source, Edith Houghton Hall of Fame player file; "Girl Ball Players Expect to Defeat Winsted Players," unknown source, Edith Houghton Hall of Fame player file; "Girls' Baseball Tour of Orient a Failure," *Lethbridge* (Alberta) *Herald*, December 1, 1925.

15 "Bobbies Nine Defeated in Opening Game," *Japan Times & Mail*, October 24, 1925: 8.

16 "What Do the Philadelphia Bobbies Look Like? – They Look Like Good Ball Players," *Japan Times & Mail*, October 20, 1920: 8.

17 "Bobbies Beaten Big Score in Final Game Here," *Japan Times & Mail*, October 26, 1925: 8.

18 Spangler Diary, 2.

19 Spangler Diary, 5.

20 Spangler Diary, 6.

21 Letter from Leona Kearns to her mother, quoted in Barbara Gregorich, "Dropping the Pitch," *The National Pastime* 43 (2013).

22 Letter from Leona Kearns to her mother. WIB: Philadelphia Bobbies subject file, National Baseball Hall of Fame.

23 Letter from Leona Kearns to her mother. WIB: Philadelphia Bobbies subject file, National Baseball Hall of Fame.

24   Spangler Diary, 2.

25   Letter from Leona Kearns to her mother. WIB: Philadelphia
      Bobbies subject file, National Baseball Hall of Fame.

26   Spangler Diary, 4.

27   "Deck Space for the Bobbies May Be the Outcome,"
      Japan Times & Mail, November 7, 1925: 8.

28   Spangler Diary, 8.

29   Associated Press, "Japan to Levy Tax Upon Baseball Game,"
      December 5, 1925, Edith Houghton Hall of Fame player file.

30   Barbara Gregorich, *Research Notes for Women at Play, Volume III.* (Report
      from the American Consulate, Kobe, Japan, March 11, 1926), 52-53.

31   Gregorich, *Research Notes for Women at Play,* 51.

32   Gregorich, *Research Notes for Women at Play,* 52.

33   Spangler Diary, 9.

34   Gregorich, *Research Notes for Women at Play,* 52

35   Gregorich, *Research Notes for Women at Play,* 53.

36   See "Girl Ball Players Returning Broke," unknown source, Edith
      Houghton player file, National Baseball Hall of Fame; "Girl Ball
      Players Expect to Defeat Winsted Players," unknown source,
      Edith Houghton Hall of Fame player file; "Girls' Baseball Tour
      of Orient a Failure," *Lethbridge Herald,* December 1, 1925.

37   Gregorich, *Research Notes for Women at Play,* 51.

38   Gregorich, *Research Notes for Women at Play,* 51.

39   Spangler Diary, 12.

GENTLE BLACK GIANTS: NEGRO LEAGUERS IN JAPAN, PHILADELPHIA ROYAL GIANTS TOUR, 1927

By Bill Staples Jr.

Kazuo Sayama, baseball historian, author, and member of the Japanese Baseball Hall of Fame (enshrined in 2021), states with great passion and conviction that had it not been for the tours of the Negro Leagues' all-star Philadelphia Royal Giants in 1927 and the early 1930s, a professional baseball league in Japan would not have started when it did, in 1936.

"There is no denying that the major leaguers' visits were the far bigger incitement to the birth of our professional league. We yearned for better skill in the game," said Sayama. "But if we had seen only the major leaguers, we might have been discouraged and disillusioned by our poor showing. What saved us was the tours of the Philadelphia Royal Giants, whose visits gave Japanese players confidence and hope."[1]

Sayama first learned about the Royal Giants as a member of the Society for American Baseball Research in the early 1980s. Like the fictional Ray Kinsella, who heard voices telling him to build a baseball diamond in the middle of his cornfield, Sayama was a man possessed during much of the early part of that decade, researching and documenting the history of the Royal Giants.[2]

Also fueled by the desire to honor the Black US soldiers who coached him as a boy in Yokohama during the post-World War II occupation, Sayama hit the library stacks and microfiche in the archives and traveled the world interviewing anyone with a connection to the team.[3]

In doing so he discovered that the Negro Leaguers had visited Japan just as many times as the famous All-American major leaguers during the 1920s and 1930s (three times each), yet historians on both sides of the Pacific had all but forgotten the Philadelphia Royal Giants.

"It is unfair that no words of gratitude have been spoken by the Japanese to this team," lamented Sayama.[4] He changed that by publishing his seminal work in Japan in 1985, *Kuroki Yasashiki Jaiantsu*, which details the events of their tours and the impact the team made while in Japan. Best of all, he captured firsthand accounts from many Japanese players who competed against the all-Black team, men who were so impressed and impacted by the touring players' unique blend of baseball skill and human kindness that it inspired a term of endearment from Japanese players – with gratitude and fondness in their hearts, they referred to their guests as "Gentle Black Giants."

The Philadelphia Royal Giants were indeed the first all-Black team to play in Japan, but their games did not mark the first time for Black and Japanese baseball teams to compete head-to-head on a diamond. The history of games between ballplayers of Japanese ancestry and Black teams dates to at least May 19, 1908, when the Issei (first-generation Japanese in America) Mikado's Japanese Base Ball Team from Denver played the Lexington (Missouri) Tigers. But earlier undocumented games probably took place.[5] After that contest, and long before the Royal Giants set sail for Japan in 1927, dozens of such games occurred. Of those matchups, the following are noteworthy for their ties to the Royal Giants:

- **December 4, 1915, Honolulu – Chinese Travelers vs. 25th Infantry Wreckers.** Outfielder Andy Yamashiro, the first Japanese American to sign a contract in Organized Baseball (in 1917), honed his skills competing in Hawaii as a member of the mixed-Asian Chinese Travelers (comprising Chinese, Japanese and Hawaiian players) against top-Black talent like Wilbur "Bullet" Rogan, Robert Fagen, Dobie Moore, and Oscar "Heavy" Johnson, all members of a military team known as the 25th Infantry Wreckers.[6] Fagen and Rogan later barnstormed across the Pacific as members of the Royal Giants.[7] Yamashiro managed the Hawaii Asahi ballclub that competed against the Royal Giants in 1927.

- **June 2, 1924, Washington, DC – Meiji**

Cover of the May 1927 issue of Yakyukai *depicting O'Neal Pullen and Shinji Hamazaki*

University vs. Howard University.
This game marked the first time a visiting team from Japan defeated an all-Black team. The Meiji roster included Saburo Yokozawa, a second baseman who in 1927 would compete against the Royal Giants in Japan as a member of the Daimai club.[8]

• **September 6, 1925, Los Angeles – Fresno Athletic Club vs. L.A. White Sox.**
Over 3,000 fans packed into White Sox Park to witness Kenichi Zenimura's Japanese nine defeat Lon Goodwin's ballclub, 5-4. This encounter led to a rematch a year later, setting the wheels in motion for Goodwin to take his ballclub to Japan in 1927.[9]

Plans to take a Negro League team to Japan were proposed in the early 1920s but failed to materialize. On February 21, 1921, the *Chicago Defender* wrote, "A syndicate of Japanese here representing authorities at Waseda, Tokio [sic], Yokohama and Kobe Universities in Japan, announced last week that they are eager to take an all-star baseball team made up of members of the Race to their fatherland next fall for a series of games. A large sum of money has been deposited in a local bank to defray all expenses, which guarantees the proposition is in good faith."[10]

The goals of the planned 1921 tour were ambitious. "The spokesman further stated that ... the main idea is to put baseball on a firm foundation, and to have the interest manifested in the pastime [in Japan] as in this country [United States]."[11] The stars never aligned for that Negro Leagues all-star tour of Japan to occur. That would take another five years.

As a follow-up to their thriller in 1925, Lon Goodwin and Zenimura scheduled a rematch for the L.A. White Sox and the Fresno Athletic Club (FAC), a doubleheader in Fresno over the Fourth of July weekend, 1926. Zenimura's team, bolstered by a few non-Japanese players, called themselves the Fresno All-Stars. They defeated the L.A. White Sox in both games, 9-4 and 4-3.[12]

Off the field, it was customary for Zeni to invite visiting teams to social outings the night before a game. Thus, the Fourth of July weekend created the opportunity for Zenimura and Goodwin to discuss the possibility of parallel tours of Japan in the future.

Born in Hiroshima, Japan, Zenimura had visited his motherland as a baseball ambassador a few times prior to 1926. In 1921-22 he traveled to Hiroshima, where he coached baseball at Koryo High School. In 1924 he returned with his FAC, completing a successful 46-day tour of Japan, playing 28 games and finishing with a 21-7 record.[13]

By the summer of 1926, Zeni already had plans in place for another tour of Japan for the following spring. He had learned valuable lessons during the first tour and shared them with the Fresno press. "In Japan it doesn't pay to win a game [by] a far margin. If we do then there won't be any crowd coming to the next game … One day we played against the pro team of Osaka which is known as Diamonds and in our first game we defeated them by a score of 11-2. In this game quite a many fans [sic] came to see the outcome but on the following day with the same teams there was hardly any people in the stand[s]. For this reason, it is hard for the visiting team to play a game in Japan."[14]

Months later, Goodwin received a chance to put Zenimura's advice into practice. On December 21, approximately five months after the series in Fresno, the *Nippu Jiji* reported that Goodwin's L.A. White Sox – not the Philadelphia Royal Giants – had received an invitation to tour Japan from officials in Fukuoka City, one of the locations where the FAC competed during the 1924 tour.[15]

To help plan his team's tour, Goodwin turned to Joji "George" Irie, a Japanese native who was known in Los Angeles's Little Tokyo area as an active sports and entertainment manager. The *Japanese Who's Who in California* described Irie as a man "with an impressive mien and stature of such dignity," adding that professionally he was "agile and enthusiastic, quick to weigh the interests, and daring enough to take any means to achieve his ends; his inscrutable ability defies imagination for his swiftness and vehemence."[16]

Born in 1885 in the Yamaguchi Prefecture of Japan, Irie arrived in the United States at age 20 and went east to study law at the University of Pennsylvania. He returned to California in the early 1920s and worked as a translator in sectors that served the legal needs of the Japanese immigrant community. He eventually caught the attention of Yoshiaki Yasuda, president of the Japan-US Film Exchange Company, who hired him to be the organization's secretary. In that role, he helped Yasuda oversee the world of entertainment in LA's Little Tokyo, including sumo, kembu (Japanese sword-fight theater), baseball, and gambling.[17] In 1935, several years after Irie's involvement in the Royal Giants ended, Yasuda was assassinated by the yakuza (Japanese mob). According to Professor Kyoko Yoshida, this murder, coupled with the photos of the Royal Giants posing with sumo and other figures of Japan's underworld, suggest that Irie's work might have placed himself, Goodwin, and the Royal Giants, in close proximity to the Japanese mob during the 1927 tour.[18]

Before the team departed for Japan, Irie sent officials there an advance roster of the players slated to join the tour. The names reflected on the list included all of the members of the Philadelphia Royal Giants entry in the 1926-1927 California Winter League: O'Neal Pullen, C; Frank Duncan, 1B-C; Newt Allen, 2B; Newt Joseph, 3B; Willie Wells, SS; James Raleigh "Biz" Mackey, SS, P, C; Carroll "Dink" Mothell, Utility; Norman "Turkey" Stearnes, OF; Herbert "Rap" Dixon, OF; Crush Holloway, OF; Andy Cooper, P; Bill Foster, P; George Harney, P; Wilbur "Bullet Joe" Rogan, P-OF.[19]

Of those 14 players, Goodwin could persuade only five to take him up on his offer to tour Japan – Pullen, Duncan, Mackey, Dixon, and Cooper. Goodwin had fallen out of favor with organized Negro Leagues baseball in the East, and delivered a parting shot when the team sailed off for Japan. "The National Negro and the Eastern Leagues are cutting salaries to a place where a ballplayer is not fairly paid for services rendered," Goodwin told the press.[20]

To fill out the roster, Goodwin recruited players from his semipro team, the L.A. White Sox. Thus, when the ship pulled away from Los Angeles on March 9, 1927, the revamped Philadelphia Royal Giants roster comprised O'Neal Pullen, C; Frank Duncan, 1B-C; Robert Fagen, 2B; Jesse Walker, 3B; James Raleigh "Biz" Mackey, SS, P, C; John Riddle, 3B-SS; Julius "Junior" Green, OF; Herbert "Rap" Dixon, OF; Joe Cade, OF; Andy Cooper, P; Ajay Johnson, P; Eugene Tucker, P; Alexander "Slowtime" Evans, P; Lonnie Goodwin, manager; and George Irie, promoter/interpreter.

As a result of the roster change, the team chemistry changed too. For the five members of the Philadelphia Royal Giants of the California Winter League, baseball was their full-time profession. For the others, it was a passion and an extracurricular activity outside of their day jobs. For example, Ajay Johnson was a police officer who would later become one of the first Black lieutenants in LAPD history. John Riddle attended the University of Southern California, where he also played football and earned a degree in architecture. Joe Cade was a US Navy Veteran and firefighter, who became a favorite in Hawaii to fans with military ties. The captain of the team was Mackey, whose ability to play multiple positions combined with his laid-back

demeanor and patience in teaching others made him the perfect fit as a team leader on a goodwill tour.[21]

After a rocky 5,497-mile, 20-day journey crossing the Pacific Ocean, the Royal Giants arrived in Yokohama on March 29. The team spent two days working out their sea legs and preparing to do battle against the best college, amateur, and industrial leagues teams Japan had to offer. Their first game, against the Mita Club, was scheduled for April 1.[22]

Coverage by *Yakyukai (Baseball World)* magazine revealed that the Japanese media misunderstood the ethnicity of their dark-skinned guests. "The 'Philadelphia Royal Giants' sounds like a magnificent name. This team of American Indians became very famous. ..."[23]

Setting aside the mix-up on players' racial backgrounds, *Yakyukai* detailed the events of the first game: "The stadium was jam-packed because people had heard that the black players had the reputation of being a powerful team. While the Mita Club were practicing on the field, the Royal Giants entered with big smiles and were welcomed by loud applause from the crowd. They wore off-white jerseys just like the Sundai uniform. The Royal Giants started to entertain the fans. They began light warm-ups and batting practice. They hit very well for sure. All their hits looked like line drives. They were well-built and physically much stronger than Mita's batters. During fielding practice, the shortstop, Mackey, showed off his strong arm. The speed of the ball was like a bullet. The first baseman (Duncan) also performed well with his slick glove work. Both Mackey and the first baseman shined among the infielders. However, some flaws in their fielding skills were noticeable. If the Japanese team were to stand a chance, they needed to take advantage of the Giants' weak points. ... There were two umpires, Ikeda and Oki. The game started with the Mita going to bat first. The pitchers were Takeo Nagai and Cooper."[24]

After Tokyo Mayor Hiromichi Nishikubo tossed the first ceremonial pitch, the Royal Giants proceeded to win their first game in Japan, a 2-0 victory over the Mita Club.[25]

The first Japanese player to bat against the Royal Giants was future Japanese Hall of Famer Shinji Hamazaki, who struck out against Cooper's fastball. The lefty forced the next two batters, Eiji Sugai and Nagai, to ground out. Three up, three down.[26]

The Royal Giants came out swinging, with the leadoff hitter Frank Duncan lining a single to center field. He broke for second base as Robert Fagen, the number-two hitter, successfully executed the hit-and-run by placing a groundball to the opposite side of the field, between first and second. Duncan scored the first run of the game – and of the tour.[27]

Mita threatened to score in the second, with a leadoff hit by Eiichi Nomura to right-center. Michimaro Ono then hit a slow roller back to the pitcher Cooper, who attempted to get the force out at second. The speedy Nomura beat the throw, resulting in runners on first and second. With two on and no outs, catcher O'Neal Pullen fired a bullet to second base, catching Nomura leaning too far toward third. The next batter, Kiyoshi Okada, grounded to shortstop Mackey for a 6-4-3 inning-ending double play.[28]

The first inning set the tone that defense would be the deciding factor in this game. In the bottom of the second inning, Hamazaki dazzled fans with an exciting play in the outfield. After Mackey reached first on a walk, Cade hit a long drive to the right-center gap. Hamazaki sprinted and reached out to catch the ball just before it hit the ground. The hero quickly became the goat. On the next play Hamazaki mis-played Slowtime Evans's fly ball, allowing it to roll to the fence and for Mackey to score from first.[29]

The offensive attack of both clubs was held in check from the third inning on. Mita pitcher Nagai took control of the game and limited the damage by the Royal Giants, who continued to mount rallies, but failed to convert any opportunities to score. Cooper pitched a three-hit shutout and allowed no walks.

The low-scoring game caught the attention of the Japanese fans, media, and opposing teams who were in attendance to scout the Royal Giants in preparation for future games. Observers noted that "the Royal Giants' batting was not as strong as expected … [and] left an impression of being unbalanced."[30]

Others agreed. "I saw them hit and field and noted their fine plays here and there, but somehow they lacked refined skills," wrote a *Yakyukai* reporter. "Their game strategy was limited. Their poor base running was especially noticeable. Of course, my conclusions could not be definitive after watching just one game, but this is what I observed."[31]

The game-two rematch with Mita was a high-scoring affair, with the Royal Giants winning, 10-6. In the top of the seventh inning, the game was tied, 6-6. After shutting down the Mita bats in the inning, the Royal Giants rallied, starting with Cade's single past third base. Julius Green bunted for an infield hit. With runners on first and second, John Riddle stepped to the plate and hit a line drive off pitcher Shinji Hamazaki's

glove. The ball ricocheted to right field, allowing Cade and Green to cross home plate. With the score now 8-6, Fagen singled past short, driving in Riddle. Dixon doubled to score Fagen for the 10th and final run.[32]

Overall, the second game was an impressive display of offensive skill, with three hitters having perfect 3-for-3 days at the plate. They were:

- Hamazaki – a single, two doubles, and a walk
- Dixon – two singles, a double, a sacrifice fly, and a walk
- Mackey – two singles, a triple, and two walks

In fact, Mackey's triple bounced off the center-field fence, which at the time established the record for the farthest ball ever hit at Meiji Jingu Stadium. He later topped that in other games.[33]

Several baseball magazines and newspapers wrote about the Royals Giants' skills displayed in their first two games against Mita. The *Undo Kai* magazine shared their impressions: "On the first day, I was shocked to see how strong their arms were. Every player had one. Especially shortstop Mackey's 'bullet ball.' He had a cannon for an arm, as did Duncan, the first baseman. The catcher Pullen's powerful arm was beyond our imagination! If I may be allowed to use hyperboles, I'd say that they throw a ball so hard that you cannot even see it. They could throw a ball from second to home, first to third, home to second – straight to its target on a line without a crow hop. Furthermore, they threw with amazing velocity."[34]

The editorial added, "With their strong arms, they were good defenders. Rather than being skillful and agile like dogs and rabbits, they were big and powerful like cows and horses."[35]

The *Undo Kai* magazine writers assessed their pitching staff as well. "Cooper threw on the first day, which seemed to indicate that he was the ace of the team. His performance confirmed that he did indeed have the skill of an ace. The rest of the pitching staff didn't compare to Cooper. Due to the fact that everything else was solid except for their pitching, the Giants were Chujun regarded as a mysterious team."[36]

Chujun Tobita, the former manager of Waseda University and an influential figure within Japanese college baseball, had prior experience observing Negro Leagues teams in the United States, and shared his views of the visitors in the *Asahi Sports*. Based on the two games that he attended in Tokyo, Tobita thought that not every one of the Royal Giants was an elite player.

"When I visited America last year (1926), I truly enjoyed watching the Negro League games in Indianapolis. … [T]he games were just like the major leagues. The only difference was the color of the ballplayers' skin." From the stands, Tobita observed that "only half of the players of the Royal Giants team have dark skin, while the rest appear to be mixed race. Those players of many races, whose gloves and hands are the same color, must be considered 'All-Americans.' The team is not only mixed race, they are mixed talent as well. Many of the players have the appropriate skills to be considered semipros, but not all of them can be considered elite, professional ballplayers."[37]

Tobita also possessed an understanding of the history of US race relations and shared a rare perspective from a Japanese national. "Because blacks were once slaves, the whites were perceived as superior in America. And eventually people with yellow skin were discriminated against as well. I suspect that the increasing population of the black race must be viewed as a threat to the white community. It would be especially disruptive to the white baseball community.

"It is odd that American Indians are allowed to join the major league teams, but players of African descent, who are citizens of the country, are not allowed to join. Just because of the color of their skin, they are not treated as equal human beings. They face so much discrimination back home in America – I heard the players say that if a war took place between the US and Japan, they would cheer for Japan. Life is not as simple as baseball. When they say that they would cheer for Japan, they are saying that we are a colored race, too," Tobita concluded.[38]

After the two games in Tokyo, the team boarded a train for an overnight trip to Osaka, where they were scheduled to play at Koshien Stadium against Daimai, a semipro team.

In the first game against Daimai, Junior Green pitched the Royal Giants to a 7-2 victory. After a much-needed day off for rest, the Royal Giants returned to Koshien for a rematch. Goodwin selected the multitalented Mackey to start on the mound for the Royal Giants.

The pitcher for the Japanese team was the highly respected star Michimaro Ono. He had pitched for Mita against the Royal Giants in the first game in Tokyo and held the team to just two runs. Ono was known as a fastball pitcher and in 1922 had become

a fan favorite when he defeated Herb Hunter's All-Americans, 9-3 – the first victory for a Japanese team over a major-league squad.

Then 30 years old and a bit past his prime, Ono still had something to prove against the Royal Giants. The contest became a pitchers' duel between Mackey and Ono. By the eighth inning, no Daimai batter had reached second base. The Royal Giants recorded six scattered hits and failed to produce a run … kind of.

In the top of the fourth inning a controversial play occurred. Daimai backup catcher Shigeyoshi Koshiba watched the action from the bench, and years later shared his version of the events.

"There was one out with a runner on third when the [Royal Giants] batter smashed a big hit to right field. The outfielder ran far and made a great play. The runner on third, of course, tagged up to ensure a run. The ball was thrown to the catcher from the right fielder, but it was too late. After that, the catcher threw the ball to first. The runner on first base was trying to run to second and quickly returned back to first, but he arrived late and was tagged out. It was the third out and ended the inning. That was okay, but the umpires should have counted the runner who tagged up from third. The run was made before the third out. However, the umpire mistakenly called 'no run,' thinking it was a double play."[39]

According to the official records, with one out in the fourth inning, Dixon singled and then Pullen smashed a hit to right field. With runners now on first and third, Cade hit a fly ball to right field. The speedy Dixon tagged up and scored easily. Pullen, not as fleet afoot, failed to make it back to first base in time and was tagged for the third out.

Daimai player Saburo Yokozawa remembered what happened next. "[The Royal Giants] did not argue with the umpire's call. … Initially, they showed their dissatisfaction with unhappy faces, but they quickly accepted the decision. 'If that's your call, we will agree with you.' They accepted easily, just like that. We were the ones in shock."[40]

Yokozawa recalled that "some players from the Japanese team tried to point out the erroneous call to the umpire, Tomigashi-kun, but he did not change his ruling. During this time, the Black players started to run onto the field to take their positions, saying, 'That's okay!' I could not believe what they did. I have never seen a team act like them before."[41]

Now, with the bad call behind them, the Daimai club was batting in the bottom of the ninth inning. With two outs, Yokozawa smashed a single to left field. Sugai then hit a soft fly ball to right field destined for an outfielder's glove. At that moment it appeared that the game was headed to extra innings as a 0-0 tie, but to everyone's surprise, Evans, the pitcher turned outfielder, dropped the ball and Yokozawa came home to score the winning run. Daimai defeated the Giants, 1-0. Or did they?

According to Yokozawa, the score was later corrected to a tie game, 1-1. "Even we, the ones who played against them, did not think that we actually won the game," he confessed. "To tell the truth, everybody in the media was trying to figure out which Japanese team could upset the Royal Giants. Everybody thought that we would be the ones. It might have affected the umpires' thinking. Maybe they were hoping for the first win by a Japanese team to occur as soon as possible."[42]

The Japanese hosts were impressed with the Royal Giants' display of sportsmanship. "Typically, teams from the US were arrogant," wrote Kazuo Sayama. "They were full of pride because they believed America was an advanced baseball country. The attitude of most teams was, 'Let us teach you! [I]nstead, of, 'Let us enjoy baseball together!'"[43]

It is worth noting that this was not Yokozawa's first interaction with Black ballplayers. He was a member of the championship Meiji University team in 1923, earning the right to tour Hawaii and the mainland United States in 1924. During their four-month goodwill tour, Meiji competed against semipro and college teams – including the historically Black college Howard University. "We always thought that the baseball in America was for white people, so at first we were really confused by their presence," said Yokozawa.[44]

On Wednesday, April 6, the Royal Giants played their final contest of the three-game series against Daimai at Koshien. Coming off the 1-1 tie, the Royal Giants were seeking redemption. They attacked early and scored often. They tallied four runs in the second inning and another in the third, giving them a comfortable 5-0 lead through five innings of play. In the sixth inning, the bats of the Royal Giants doubled their total run production, making it a 10-0 ballgame. Daimai brought in Ono in the seventh inning to stop the damage. The Japanese hosts would not score until the bottom of the ninth, when Nakagawa and Takasu started a late-inning rally to score two runs. Final score, a 10-2 victory for the Royal Giants.[45]

The game also marked a celebrated milestone in the world of Japanese baseball history. The fifth run scored as the result of a triple hit by Rap Dixon off Daimai pitcher Tairiku Watanabe. The fans witnessed history in the making in the third inning, as Dixon's triple was the longest hit recorded at Koshien at the time.[46]

Known as "Koshien Dai Undojo" (great public space) when it opened in August 1924, Koshien Stadium was a vast multipurpose community sports stadium used for baseball, rugby, and football (soccer). When used for baseball, the field specifications were:

- Left- and right-field foul poles – 361 feet / 110 meters
- Center field – 390 feet / 119 meters
- Left- and right-center gaps – 420 feet / 128 meters

In his record-setting blast, Dixon hit a line drive off the left-center-field fence (420 feet). The speed of the ball was such that after it hit the wall it bounced back toward the infield, allowing him to safely reach third base.

The spot where Dixon's blast hit the wall was later painted white by Koshien officials to commemorate his great hit for future generations. Unfortunately, the outfield fence of Koshien was later demolished and the white mark was erased. Over time, the name of Rap Dixon was also forgotten in Japan.

The day after Dixon's record-setting blast, the Royal Giants played their final game at Koshien, a 6-0 victory over the Kansai Daigaku (University) ballclub.[47]

April 8 marked a day off for the Royal Giants, perhaps a travel day to their next destination, Kyoto. The respite provided time for reflection for manager Goodwin, who wrote a letter to the editor of the *Asahi Sports* magazine, expressing his gratitude and positive impressions of their first week in Japan. Goodwin wrote:

Dear Japanese players and fans from the baseball field, although we had admired the Yamato race for some years, our respect for you grew immensely after being treated so well by the Japanese people.

In this tour to Japan, our biggest surprise was the quality of Japanese baseball, which is improving and becoming closer to that of a real league. Before we came here, we used to talk about Japanese baseball. We concluded that the Japanese had not reached the professional level yet. However, to our surprise, once we came here and watched the Japanese baseball teams, not only were we amazed, we realized that our prediction was way off from reality.

Even on our way to Japan, we continued to discuss the same topic, and dreamed of Japan as the ship came closer to land. We were most interested to find out what kind of baseball fields there were in Japan. We decided that the Japanese fields must be very tiny, poorly equipped, perhaps the same as Class D fields in America, or promenade-like places. However, after observing the Meiji Shrine [Jingu] Stadium with great earnestness and then seeing the gigantic Koshien Stadium, we realized we were wrong again. Especially Koshien Stadium – it was larger and more splendid than the stadiums in America. The capacity of 80,000 spectators in Koshien Stadium was beyond that of Yankee Stadium, which is proudly said to be the number one stadium in the world after having millions of dollars spent on it. In comparison to Koshien Stadium, Yankee Stadium would be dwarfed.

The difference between the two stadiums is that Yankee Stadium is privately owned by a rich club, while Koshien is used by everyone. This should be emphasized, so that Koshien Stadium stands proudly.

Throughout the games against the Japanese teams, we could not help but be amazed by the aggressive nature of their defense. We reckoned that they knew how to play inside baseball. Up to today, we lost one important game to the Daimai team, but this was a scoreless game to the end and a fantastic fight between our captain Mackey and the ace pitcher, Ono, of the Diamonds. Unfortunately, it became our first loss since we arrived in Japan. However, we truly enjoyed the game that was played by the Yamato souls. We not only admired and praised the skillful pitcher Ono, but we also thought that the Daimai Club were not any lesser than a major league team in the way they fought back with Ono as a leader in that day's game.

We believe that Japanese baseball will continue to thrive greatly in the future. However, our admiration for Japanese

baseball is due not only to the skills that were shown in the Daimai game, but also to the respectable sportsmanship that the Japanese players demonstrated.

Frankly, we think there is not any other country where we could play and enjoy games while not paying any attention to wins or losses. We especially admire the passionate baseball fans, who are well educated and watched the games with respectful manners. That left us with a great impression of Japanese baseball. The more we thought about the dilapidated American stadiums, the better and nobler the Japanese stadiums appeared. We think that the stadiums are used by all the fans, and are for the Japanese people to enjoy real sports.

We wish great success and a promising future to Japanese baseball society, and we also express thankfulness for their hospitality and kindness from the bottom of our hearts to our Japanese hosts through *Asahi Sports*.

Lon Goodwin

Manager, Philadelphia Royal Giants
April 8, 1927[48]

The Royal Giants mesmerized others wherever they went in Japan, both on and off the field. Reporter Takeshi Mizuno discussed his thoughts on the personality and style of the Royal Giants in the June 1927 issue of *Yakyukai*. Under the headline "The Gentle Baseball Players," he wrote:

Even during the game, they were relaxed. Their actions and behavior in the hotel after the game were mellow as well. The volume of the conversation among themselves was kept to a minimum. Nobody could tell if they were there or not. During the interviews after the game, they responded with humility. The gossip by the women in the rear tenement was noisier.

Mr. Irie shared these qualities. Their personalities were very calm and they were cordial. Because they lived in a white-dominated country and were not treated equally in America, the blacks related more to the Japanese American side in America, and liked the Japanese Americans. In this tour to Japan, they all enjoyed themselves, and they received a big welcome everywhere they went. They were uncomfortable at times because they were not used to this sort of positive treatment, but they had big smiles on their faces.

When they were not playing baseball they liked to shoot billiards and go for walks for enjoyment. They also adored children and played with them gleefully. When they played billiards in the hotels, which they did often, they respectfully took turns to shoot. They also went to cafes and such, without any special agenda.[49]

After getting much-needed rest and relaxation, the team zig-zagged across central Japan by train, competing against college and industrial ballclubs, and one of the earliest professional teams, the Takarazuka Club. Officially known as the Takarazuka Athletic Association, they were founded as the Shibaura Association after Kazumi Kobayashi bought the team and combined it with Hankyu Railway.

Considered by many to be the best team in Japan, the Takarazuka Club outslugged the Royal Giants 11-10 in base hits. Shut out until the ninth inning, Takarazuka fought hard and managed to score three runs to threaten the Royal Giants, but still ended up on the losing end of a close 4-3 ballgame.[50]

Goodwin and his club had a three-day break for rest and travel for their next series of games back in Tokyo, where they battled the popular Tomon Club and Sundai Club.

They headed to the bustling section of Tokyo known as Kanda-nishikicho and stayed at the Hosenkaku Hotel, a majestic, Western-style hotel located near the Shinbashi station. Despite the convenience of train travel, the team preferred automobiles and drove through the Yotsuya and Akasaka sections of the city to enjoy the cherry blossoms in full bloom.[51]

Other sites in Japan that impressed the Royal Giants' players included the Miyako Odori (a traditional spring dance festival) in Kyoto, the Azuma Odori (indoor stage show) in Tokyo, the hot spring baths in Beppu, and the performances by the geishas who "moved swiftly, all legs and elegant, swaying hands." The players praised the dancers, "Oh, beautiful! Beautiful!" The Royal Giants told their hosts that what they really wanted was to bring their friends and family to experience Japan instead of just telling them about it.[52]

The Royal Giants' game on April 16 against Tomon was played at Waseda University's Totsuka Field. Meiji Jingu Stadium was not available because the other US team touring Japan, the Japanese American Fresno Athletic Club, had booked a game there the same day against Hosei University. Both American teams were popular in Japan, so fans in Tokyo struggled to decide which game to attend.

Additionally, the Tomon Club, which consisted of Waseda players and alumni, had lost many star players, as the Waseda varsity team had left for America on a goodwill tour of their own. The Royal Giants defeated Tomon, 6-2, behind the pitching of Ajay Johnson. Photographs featured in *Asahi Sports* showed fans packed in the stands, filling all the seats from the infield to the outfield.[53]

The next day fans returned to see the same two teams do battle. Tomon fastball pitcher Shoichiro Tase carried the weight of the crowd on his shoulders. He lacked a good breaking ball, so the Royal Giants sat on his fastball all day and feasted on his pitches.

Dixon hit a home run over the left-field wall, as well as a triple. Mackey also hit a double to left-center. These two alone accounted for the bulk of the runs, while Evans and Cooper held the Tomon batters to just one run on nine scattered hits. The Royal Giants defeated Tomon, 8-1.[54]

A former Tomon player, right fielder Kimitsugu Kawai, reflected years later how the games against the Royal Giants were for many Japanese their first exposure to people of African descent. "We were all surprised that everybody was so dark. I remember that we joked around. … We thought that if we played with them, the white ball would turn black," he confessed.[55]

Kawai also recalled that even though the Royal Giants were very good players and popular in Japan, at the time of their game he had heard reports that the team was struggling to earn enough money for their return tickets home. "We felt disappointment for them when we heard about their situation."[56]

The Japanese fans had high expectations for the matchup between the Royal Giants and the Fresno Athletic Club, scheduled for April 20. It was the FAC's second tour of Japan, so they had many Japanese fans. The team was made up of talented Nikkei (Japanese American) players and three White players – Charles Hendsch, a relief pitcher; Eldridge Hunt, starting pitcher; and Jud Simons, a catcher. The FAC had yet to lose a game during their second tour.

Additionally, FAC coach Kenichi Zenimura repeatedly told the Japanese press that he was eager for a rematch against the visiting Black team, which his team had defeated several times in California.

After reading Zenimura's statements in the newspapers, newcomers to Goodwin's team did not take kindly to his comments. For many of the star players, this was their first time competing against the FAC, but for others who were members of the L.A. White Sox, they knew the truth. Perhaps Goodwin used Zenimura's case of mistaken team identity as fuel for his players? We may never know for sure. What we do know is that star additions like Mackey, Dixon, Duncan, and Cooper played angry, and it was to their advantage in the end.[57]

A sellout crowd filled Meiji Jingu Stadium to witness the battle between the two American teams. The Royal Giants relied on their ace, Andy Cooper, while Fresno sent Thomas Mamiya to the mound. The Royal Giants bats were hot early. With two outs in the first inning, Mackey smashed a triple to left-center field. Dixon hit a line drive to right field, scoring Mackey. Mamiya made the necessary adjustments and cooled off the Royal Giants' bats.

The Fresno ace lost steam in the sixth inning. Mackey belted a solo home run to deep center field. The next inning, the Royal Giants scored four more runs on a combination of singles and extra-base hits – consecutive singles by Walker, Cooper, and Fagen, followed by a sacrifice fly by Mackey and a triple by Dixon. The power continued in the eighth inning. With the bases loaded – Cade had doubled, Green walked, and Walker singled – Fagen drove in a run, and Mackey smashed a double, scoring three additional runs.

Trailing 9-0 in the bottom of the ninth inning, Fresno pinch-hitter Simon doubled off Cooper, and pinch-hitter Sam Yamasaki drove a single to right field, scoring Simon for Fresno's lone run. Goodwin's team defeated Zenimura's, 9-1.[58]

Additional observations about the game were detailed in the June 1927 issue of *Undou Kai (Athletic Society)* magazine.

These undefeated teams prepared their best lineups as if they were trying to win a championship. The Fresno team used their starting pitcher, Mamiya, and the blacks sent out a big left-handed pitcher, Cooper, but there was no competition between the two. Mamiya had a sturdy, big body for a Japanese person and threw hard, but Cooper was like a hornless bull and threw fastballs from his

shining, black, muscular arm. The velocity of their pitches was incomparable. No one from the Fresno team could hit Cooper's heavy, fast sinker. The power and speed startled Fresno. At times they could not even swing their bats. On the other side, the pitches from Mamiya added fuel to the blacks' fiery offense. They hit his slow ball and curve ball without mercy. He gave up one home run, three triples, two doubles, and a total of 17 hits. This performance was evidence that his skill was not as great as Cooper's.[59]

Offensively, every Royal Giants batter recorded a hit except Green. Hitting cleanup, Dixon had two triples and a single. Mackey was the MVP of the day, a single shy of hitting for the cycle, driving in seven of the Royal Giants' nine runs.

According to Sayama, the difference in power between the two teams was shown in this battle. Mackey's home run especially symbolized it. In fact, this home run was the first one ever hit over the fence in Meiji Jingu Stadium."[60] The ball passed over the head of the center fielder, went over the fence, and bounced on the grass of the bleacher section before disappearing outside the stadium.

The home run against Fresno was the first of three round-trippers for Mackey at Meiji Jingu. He hit one to all sections of the outfield:

- His first: April 20 off Fresno pitcher Thomas Mamiya, sixth inning, first batter, first pitch, over the center-field bleachers (417 feet / 127 meters).

- His second: April 25 off Sundai Club pitcher Tadashi Nakatsugawa, seventh inning, one runner on base, one ball and two strikes, hit to the left-field bleachers (358 feet / 109 meters).

- His third: April 28 off Saint Paul Club pitcher Shuzo Nawaoka, third inning, first batter, first pitch, hit to the right-field bleachers (358 feet / 109 meters).[61]

After a scheduled rematch against Fresno was rained out the next day, the Royal Giants players enjoyed a four-day break before their next contest, against the Sundai Club. On April 25 at Meiji Jingu Stadium, Ajay Johnson pitched a two-hit shutout, leading the team to an 8-0 victory. The offensive highlight of the day was a sixth-inning home run by Mackey into the left-field grass section.[62]

Royal Giants pitcher Johnson continued his dominance against Japanese batters with a 14-0 shutout against Rikkyo University (aka Saint Paul's University) on April 28. He allowed six hits and one walk. According to *Yakyukai*, "The game was a devastating loss. ... It was an unavoidable loss and it was expected." Rikkyo committed 10 errors, so not even the Royal Giants, who made it a practice to keep the games competitive to attract fans for future games, could have kept the score close.[63]

Some disappointed fans lingered in the stadium after the game. In their attempt to please the audience, the Royal Giants held an impromptu baseball skills demonstration – something the crowd had never seen before:

- Dixon showed off his arm by throwing one ball after another from home plate over the outfield wall and beyond the left-field grass section. Both fans and opposing players were amazed.

- Next, Mackey entertained the crowd by hitting balls to the outfield grass sections. He tossed the ball up to himself and displayed his beautiful hitting form.

- The skills demonstration concluded with Duncan and Dixon showing off their baserunning. They ran around the diamond in 14.02 seconds, amazing the Japanese fans.

Until then, teams that came to Japan usually entertained fans by acting goofy, making silly faces, or performing imitations of birds and running around mimicking bird calls. Sometimes they performed silly dances during the games. Some Japanese players and fans were annoyed by these childish acts.[64]

With 13 games completed (and a 12-0-1 record), the Royal Giants left Tokyo again for a tour that included stops in Nagoya, Hiroshima, Fukuoka, and Toyama. Details and highlights from the final six games in Japan were not published, but we know that the team went undefeated, with Cooper and Pullen doing the majority of the battery work.[65]

Except for a 17-0 defeat of Koryo Junior High School, the Royal Giants kept the scores close and the games competitive against the Japanese teams. The indelible impressions they made stuck in the memory of Yasuo Shimazu, Diamond Club shortstop, who reflected on playing against the all-Black team from the United States:

I wonder if the Royal Giants were purposefully making the game fun for the fans. Because of that, we were able to play great games. ... It was later when I started to think this way. While we were playing, we did not even think about it. We were just playing hard. At that time, one of my cousins was living in America. I heard about the caliber of the Negro Leagues from him. I might have had preconceptions about them. He told me so many times about the level of black baseball and how it was not any lower than that of the major leagues. We held our own against a team that was as good as a major league team. ... We were totally ecstatic. However, when I reflect on it now, this was not the case. The major league team came to Japan soon after and compared to them we were like a little league team. The major leaguers must have felt that we were no competition, so they were goofing around on the field. I am not sure where the game occurred, but this is what I saw.

While Lefty Grove was pitching, the left fielder, Al Simmons, lay down at his position. The shortstop, Maranville, turned his back to the batter. He sometimes put his face under his crotch and yelled, "Hey, Come on!" In 1934, Babe Ruth played defense while holding an open umbrella during a rainy game. He also played with his rubber boots on. Although they were trying to be playful for the fans, it was not fun for us. We were disappointed in ourselves for the difference in our abilities, and at the same time, we could not hold our composure to endure their foolishness. The black team, however, was not like that. They were trying to play a competitive game. They also provided fans entertainment, but they never made fun of anybody. What they did was show off their arms by making long throws, and show off their speed on the bases. As for the catcher, he threw the ball like an arrow down to second base on his knees, but during the games, he stood up and threw it down like a textbook play.

As for the black baseball team, they made their money from the spectators. They needed to do something fun in order to get as many people as possible to come watch the games. We did not think of that. We thought that we had close, competitive games because of our ability. … It was shown in their attitude, I think. They worked so hard to try to win. We were so amazed that we were competing head-to-head. They seriously made us think that we were as good as them. While they acted like they were playing hard, they were actually pretending in order to push us to play our best, which resulted in an entertaining game for the fans. … I wonder if this was what they were trying to achieve.[66]

On May 16-17, the Royal Giants played a two-game series against Kansai University in Toyama. Game one resulted in a 7-5 victory powered by the battery of Cooper and Pullen, and game two a 10-4 victory behind Johnson and Pullen. The team then boarded a ship for Korea, where they would play five more games.[67]

The team left Kobe on May 17 for the Japanese-occupied colony of Chosen, the Japanese name given to the country known today as Korea. The games were organized by the *Keijo Nippo*, the Japanese-language newspaper authorized by the government. Additionally, the newspaper promoted the tour as contests against Korea's "strongest teams" but all the opposing players and teams turned out to be Japanese – the last two being Yongsan Railway Club and the Industrial Bank. Thus, Korean athletes were excluded entirely from playing in these games, making the final five games, in essence, just an extension of the Japan tour.

On May 18, the Royal Giants defeated the Daegu All Stars, 14-2, behind a rare pitching appearance by outfielder Rap Dixon. The next day the team traveled south to Busan, where it delighted the fans with an impressive win over a local ballclub. Slowtime Evans pitched a shutout, winning 11-0.

The Royal Giants next traveled to Seoul for three games, where they received special diplomatic treatment. Two welcome banquets were held on May 20 and 21, and their parade was filmed for a newsreel. At the May 20 game, US Consul General Ransford Stevens Miller honored the Negro Leaguers with a ceremonial first pitch, perhaps marking one of the earliest times for a White American official to participate in a Negro League baseball pregame ceremony.

According to historian Kyoko Yoshida, the Royal Giants' final three games in Korea were the most political of the entire tour. Japanese government officials saw the games as a way to demonstrate Japanese political and cultural supremacy through baseball. "The American game helped shape not only the Japanese identity but also its empire," said Yoshida. For the Negro Leaguers, it was a chance to show off their power and pride in the presence of White American politicians. Thus, the Royal Giants won by wide margins in these games, including a 22-4 victory in the game witnessed by Miller.

In late May, the Royal Giants boarded the *Siberia Maru* of the Nippon Yusen Kaisha Line and sailed for Hawaii for a final 11-game series. After the 4,540-mile journey, they reached Honolulu on June 4. The next day the Royal Giants arrived at Honolulu Stadium for a game against the Asahi, the local Japanese American team. Over 8,000 fans gathered for the game, many of whom were familiar with the exceptional talent of Negro Leagues baseball. A decade earlier, many watched the likes of Bullet Rogan, Dobie Moore, and Heavy Johnson compete with the mighty 25th Infantry Wreckers while stationed at the Schofield Barracks. In fact, the Honolulu newspapers often incorrectly referred to the visiting team in 1927 as "Rogan's Giants."[68]

In the first game in Hawaii, Asahi pitcher Jimmie Moriyama struck out several of the Giants batters, but star players Cooper and Mackey led the Royal Giants to an easy 10-0 victory over the local club.

Evans shifted behind the plate to give a rest to Pullen, who enjoyed a rare afternoon in left field. In the eighth inning, Pullen made the highlight play of the day with a long, spectacular run for a fly ball. He had to leave his feet to catch the ball and in doing so executed a perfect dive – catching the ball as he hit the ground. Because of his size and speed, he slid along the green grass on his stomach for at least 10 feet, holding the ball high in his glove for all to see that he had indeed made the catch.

The press described the Royal Giants as "one of the most popular teams ever seen in action here," adding, "They are full of pep, fun, and good baseball."[69]

After a 7-3 victory over the Standard Oil club that boasted former major-league pitcher Johnnie Williams, the Royal Giants experienced their first undisputable defeat of the tour, a 3-1 loss to the All-Chinese ballclub. Dixon belted a triple in the first inning and scored on Pullen's sacrifice fly, but after that the Giants' bats went cold. Yu Chun, a side-arm pitcher for All-Chinese team, stifled the Royal Giants, striking out nine batters. Cooper had eight strikeouts, and allowed just one run in the first inning and two runs in the fourth.[70]

After the game, many fans thought that the Royal Giants threw the game. Honolulu Stadium manager J. Ashman Beaven came to their defense. "Personally I think the story about the game being thrown is nothing but a lie," he said. "The Chinese defeated the Giants fair and square and I am positive that the visiting players would not even consider being unsportsman-like or unfair in any way." Beavan offered $500 to anyone who could provide proof that the Giants threw the game. "I merely make the above offer to show to the public that these stories are nothing but lies," he said.[71]

On June 26 the Royal Giants lost its second game of the tour to the Honolulu Braves and their cur-veball artist Sam Guerrero. The Giants outslugged the Braves, eight hits to four. They were able to put runners in scoring position but failed to drive in runs. The Braves shortstop, Camacho, went 1-for-3 at the plate and scored the game's only run. In light of the fixed-game controversy, one Hawaii newspaper ran the headline: "1-0 The Royal Giants proudly lost the game!"[72]

After the game, the Royal Giants gathered for a joint team photo with the Asahi, who were waiting to play the second game of the twin bill. In the photo, manager Goodwin and star player Mackey gripped a large trophy and pennant presented to the team by the Hawaii Undokai, a Japanese sports organization.[73] Among the Asahi players was a young relief pitcher named Tadashi "Bozo" Wakabayashi, an 18-year-old who would later attend Hosei University and become the ace of the Osaka/Hanshin Tigers, and an eventual member of the Japanese Baseball Hall of Fame.

After 11 games in Hawaii, the Royal Giants sailed home on July 2, and arrived home six days later, on July 8. In total, the Philadelphia Royal Giants Goodwill Tour of 1927 lasted 121 days (March 9 to July 8) and covered 13,305 miles.[74] The well-traveled and weary team played a total of 38 games, finishing with a 35-2-1 record. They won 21 of 22 with a tie in Japan, were 5-0 in Korea, and had a 9-2 record in Hawaii.

One might think that the Royal Giants were wel-comed home with a heroes' parade. They were not. The star players of the team returned to the United States to discover that they all faced a possible five-year ban from their Negro League clubs in the East. Mackey, Cooper, Dixon, and Duncan all faced career-ending punishment for "jumping their contracts" and missing regular-season games while across the Pacific. The players appealed, and asked for forgiveness and for their suspension to be reduced. Their pleas worked.

They all received a lesser penalty of a $200 fine and a 30-day suspension.[75]

Despite the new terms of the agreement with the league, all but one of the managers put their star players back on the field almost immediately. The *Chicago Defender* observed, "Hilldale played Mackey as soon as he could get into a uniform on his return. Harrisburg did the same with Dixon and Detroit did the same with Cooper. Only one owner lived up to the agreement. He was J.L. Wilkerson of the Kansas City Monarchs [regarding Frank Duncan]."[76]

Goodwin's club received an offer to return to Hawaii the following year at the request of Kanichi Takizawa, an official with the Oahu Plantation Japanese Baseball League, and president and publisher of *Sports of Hawaii*, a Japanese monthly magazine devoted to athletics.[77]

Shortstop John Riddle also received an offer to return to Hawaii, but not for baseball. A profession-al football team in Hawaii invited him to return, and even added an incentive to put his degree from the University of Southern California to work with a po-sition in an architect's office.[78]

While manager Goodwin and other players crossed the Pacific again for games in Hawaii and Asia during the late 1920s and early 1930s, not everyone did. Pitcher Ajay Johnson returned to the Los Angeles Police Department but kept a prized ukulele in his home and strummed it with joy as he fondly reflected on his baseball experiences abroad.[79]

Between 1928 and 1931, the Royal Giants made several tours to Hawaii, where they continued to barn-storm across the Pacific and lay the foundation for future tours to Japan. Catcher O'Neal Pullen organized two tours to Hawaii, as the Cleveland Royal Giants in 1928 and as the Pullen Royal Giants in 1929. His teams played 44 games, finishing with a 29-14-1 record.

After a brief hiatus, the team returned to Hawaii in 1931 as the Philadelphia Royal Giants under the leader-ship of manager Goodwin. Goodwin's roster featured several Cuban players, including Clemente Delgado, Virginio Gamiz, Javier Perez, and Eusebio "Miguel" Gonzales. The presence of the light-skinned Gonzales is noteworthy – he played for the 1918 Boston Red Sox, thus his inclusion perhaps marks the first time for a former major leaguer to participate in a Negro League tour.[80]

These summer tours to the islands gave the new members of the Royal Giants an opportunity to build chemistry on the field, and off-field business relation-ships. During the 1931 summer Hawaii tour, Goodwin arranged for Honolulu Asahi team owner Steere Noda to join the Royal Giants for another tour to Japan in 1932. The 1932-33 tour of Asia was a success. Between July 23, 1932, and January 14, 1933, the team played 46 games in 175 days, covering a distance of 15,819 miles.[81]

Just as he had during the 1927 tour, Mackey continued to mesmerize fans and make headlines during the 1932 tour. Biz dazzled fans in Hawaii by playing all nine positions against the Honolulu Asahi. He started the game at catcher, worked his way across the infield during the next four innings, all three outfield spots in the sixth, seventh, and eight innings, and closed the game on the mound. The Royal Giants easily trimmed the Asahi, 5-1. After going undefeated in Hawaii, the team played 24 games in Japan, finishing with a 23-1 record. The most notable moment of this tour occurred in the second game in Japan, a 10-7 victory over Tomon. In the eighth inning, relief pitcher Wakahara hit Mackey with a wild pitch. Wakahara took off his cap and bowed respectfully to apologize. Mackey respectfully bowed back before taking his base.[82]

The Royal Giants returned to Japan again in December 1933, but the winter rain did not allow for any games to be played, so the team continued on to the Philippines and Hawaii. Fans in Japan missed out seeing baseball greats in action like Bullet Rogan, Chet Brewer, Dink Mothell, and Andy Cooper.[83] Still, the earlier tours of the Negro Leaguers left their mark on the people of Japan.

Historian Kaz Sayama believes, "Had the great all-stars from the major leagues suddenly arrived in Japan in 1927, our elite players might have lost their desire for baseball. It might have made them think it would be a mistake to form a professional team in Japan. They could have been discouraged from building for the future of Japanese baseball. … [T]he Black American ball club returned to Japan at the best possible time."[84]

According to Sayama, the 1931 tour of the major league All-Americans left the Japanese feeling disheartened by the results of the games. But instead of feeling helpless, they had been "immunized" with hope by the Royal Giants four years earlier. Goodwin, Mackey, Cooper, Dixon, Duncan, and the others helped the Japanese players prepare for and accept their losses with a positive attitude. "The gentleman-like black giants ... live in the hearts of the Japanese players," says Sayama.[85]

The year 2022 marked the 150th anniversary of US-Japan baseball relations (1872-2022). For decades no one talked about the Royal Giants and the important role they played in the emergence of professional baseball in Japan. That changed because of the passionate efforts of historian Kazuo Sayama, who captured the stories of the Japanese players who faced them and preserved them for future generations to appreciate. The legacy of the first Negro League team to tour Japan – the 1927 Philadelphia Royal Giants – will live on forever as well.

1927 ROYAL GIANTS TOUR SCHEDULE & GAME RESULTS[86]

Date	Place	Opponent	Score	Battery
April 1	Tokyo	Mita Club	2-0	Cooper-Pullen
April 2	Tokyo	Mita Club	10-6	Mackey-Pullen
April 3	Osaka	Diamond Club	7-2	Green-Pullen
April 5	Osaka	Diamond Club	1-1	Mackey-Pullen
April 6	Osaka	Daimai	10-2	Cooper-Pullen
April 7	Osaka	Kansai Daigaku	6-0	Green-Pullen
April 9	Kyoto	Doshiska Daigaku	2-0	Johnson-Pullen
April 10	Kyoto	Diamond Club	4-2	Johnson-Pullen
April 12	Osaka	Prebus Club	9-6	Evans-Pullen
April 13	Takarazuka	Takarazuka	4-3	Green-Pullen
April 16	Tokyo	Tomon Club	6-2	Johnson-Pullen
April 17	Tokyo	Tomon Club	9-1	Evans-Pullen
April 20	Tokyo	Fresno Club	9-1	Cooper-Pullen
April 25	Tokyo	Sundai Club	8-0	Johnson-Pullen
April 28	Tokyo	Rikkyo Daigaku	14-0	Johnson-Pullen
April 29	Nagoya	Zenshinehu	4-0	Cooper-Pullen
May 1	Dogo Iyo	Iyo Tetsudo	8-1	Cooper-Pullen
May 4	Hiroshima	Koryo Chugaku	17-1	Green-Pullen
May 7	Kokura	Kokura All-Stars	11-4	Evans-Pullen
May 8	Haka	Fukuoka All-Stars	12-4	Cooper-Pullen
May 15	Toyama	Kansai Daigaku	7-5	Johnson-Pullen
May 18	Taikyu	Taiku All-Stars	14-2	Dixon-Pullen
May 19	Fusan	Fusan	11-0	Evans-Pullen
May 20	Keijo	Shousan Bank	22-4	Evans-Pullen
May 21	Keijo	Ryuzan R.R. Club	6-0	Johnson-Pullen
May 22	Keijo	Ryuzan R.R. Club	17-0	Cooper-Pullen
June 5	Honolulu	Hawaii Asahi	10-0	Cooper-Evans
June 8	Honolulu	Standard Oil	7-3	Green-Pullen
June 11	Honolulu	All-Hawaiians	7-0	Cooper-Pullen
June 12	Honolulu	All-Chinese	1-3	Cooper-Pullen
June 15	Honolulu	Commercial League All-Stars	5-3	Johnson-Pullen
June 18	Honolulu	Elks	2-0	Evans-Pullen
June 19	Honolulu	Filipinos	11-0	Cade-Pullen
June 22	Honolulu	Luke Field Flyers	13-0	Cooper-Pullen
June 25	Honolulu	All-Chinese	5-3	Mackey-Pullen
June 26	Honolulu	Braves	0-1	Evans-Pullen
June 29	Honolulu	Braves	5-4	Cooper-Pullen

NOTES

1   Kazuo Sayama and Bill Staples Jr., *Gentle Black Giants: A History of Negro Leaguers in Japan* (Fresno, California: Nisei Baseball Research Project Press, 2019), 19.

2   Sayama and Staples, 10.

3   Sayama and Staples, dedication/front matter.

4   Sayama and Staples, 19.

5   "Tigers Gave Japs Jiu Jitsu," *Lexington* (Missouri) *Intelligencer*, May 23, 1908: 8.

6   "Travelers, All-Army and P.A.C. Teams Win," *Honolulu Star-Bulletin*, December 6, 1915: 13. Robert Fagen's name is often misspelled as Fagan.

7   The Japanese community on the island of Hawaii embraced the 25th Infantry Wreckers. Their passion for the team and its players is encapsulated in the efforts of a young Nisei ballplayer, Itaru Miyanishi, who fell in love with the game of baseball watching the all-Black Wreckers in Honolulu and later had his first name legally changed to Rogan.

8   "Defeats Japanese Nine," *Washington Evening Star*, June 3, 1924: 30.

9   "Fresno, 5; White Sox, 4," *Los Angeles Times*, September 7, 1925: 13.

10   "All-Star Baseball Club May Go to Japan," *Chicago Defender*, February 5, 1921: 6.

11   "All-Star Baseball Club May Go to Japan."

12   "Fresno All-Stars Win Again from L.A. Team, 4 to 3," *Fresno Bee*, July 6, 1926: 10.

13   Bill Staples Jr., *Kenichi Zenimura, Japanese American Baseball Pioneer* (Jefferson North Carolina: McFarland, 2011).

14   "F.A.C. Team Wins in Japan," *Fresno Morning Republican*, December 5, 1924: 19.

15   "Negro Baseball Team to Japan," *Nippu Jiji*, December. 21, 1926: 10.

16   Motomitsu Matsumoto, *Japanese Who's Who in California* (Tokyo: Bunsei Shin, 2003).

17   Kyoko Yoshida, "Appendix G: Biography of George Irie," in Sayama and Staples, *Gentle Black Giants*, 203.

18   Yoshida, "Appendix G: Biography of George Irie," 203.

19   Sayama and Staples, 161.

20   "Goodwin Flays Big League Salaries on His Departure," *Afro-American*, March 19, 1927: 14.

21   Sayama and Staples, 65.

22   Kyoko Yoshida, "Barnstorming the Empire: The 1927 Philadelphia Royal Giants Visit Colonial Korea," in Sayama and Staples, 270.

23   "Mita vs. Black People Game One," *Yakyukai*, May 1927: 110.

24   "Mita vs. Black People Game One," 110-112; Sayama and Staples, 32.

25   Yoshida, "Barnstorming the Empire: The 1927 Philadelphia Royal Giants Visit Colonial Korea," 270.

26   "Mita vs. Black People Game One," 110-112; Sayama and Staples, 33.

27   "Mita vs. Black People Game One," 110-112; Sayama and Staples, 34.

28   "Mita vs. Black People Game One," 110-112; Sayama and Staples, 34.

29   "Mita vs. Black People Game One," 110-112; Sayama and Staples, 34.

30   Sayama and Staples, 35.

31   Uncredited article in *Yakyukai*, May 1927: 108-09, quoted in Sayama and Staples, 35.

32   "Mita vs. Black Team Game Two," *Yakyukai*, May 1927: 112-114; Sayama and Staples, 36.

33   Sayama and Staples, 36.

34   Aomine [first name unknown], title unknown, *Undo Kai*, May 1927, quoted in Sayama and Staples, 39.

35   Aomine, 39.

36   Aomine quoted in Sayama and Staples, 40.

37   Suishu Tobita quoted in Sayama and Staples, 44.

38   Tobita, 44.

39   Shigeyoshi Koshiba quoted in Sayama and Staples, 49.

40   Saburo Yokozawa, interview with Kazuo Sayama, 1983, quoted in Sayama and Staples, 50.

41   Yokozawa, 50.

42   Yokozawa, 50.

43   Sayama and Staples, 49.

44   Yokozawa, 42.

45   Sayama and Staples, 54.

46   Sayama and Staples, 55.

47   "Royal Giants Won 26; Tied One on Their Japanese Tour," *Chicago Defender*, June 25, 1927: 9.

48   Lon Goodwin to *Asahi Sports*, April 8, 1927, quoted in Sayama and Staples, 53.

49   Takeshi Mizuno, "The Gentle Baseball Players," *Yakyukai*, June 1927, quoted in Sayama and Staples, 51.

50   Sayama and Staples, 61.

51   Uncredited article in *Yakyukai*, June 1927, quoted in Sayama and Staples, 72.

52   Sayama and Staples, 72.

53   Sayama and Staples, 73-74.

54   Sayama and Staples, 75.

55   Kimitsugu Kawai, interview with Kazuo Sayama, quoted in Sayama and Staples, 76.

56   Kawai.

57   Sayama and Staples, 265.

58   Sayama and Staples, 80.

59   Uncredited article in *Undou Kai*, June 1927, quoted in Sayama and Staples, 81.

60   Sayama and Staples, 83.

61   Sayama and Staples, 84.

62   Sayama and Staples, 88.

63   Uncredited article in *Yakyukai*, June 1927, quoted in Sayama and Staples, 89.

64   Yasuo Shimazu interview with Kazuo Sayama, quoted in Sayama and Staples, 64-65, 90.

65   Sayama and Staples, 248.

66   Shimazu.

67   Kyoko Yoshida, "Barnstorming the Empire: The 1927 Philadelphia Royal Giants Visit Colonial Korea," 272.

68   William Peet, "Braves Blank Rogan's Giants in Stadium
      Game 1-0," *Honolulu Advertiser,* June 27, 1927: 5.

69   Pete Doster, "Rogan's Giants Whitewash Asahis in First
      Appearance," *Honolulu Star-Bulletin,* June 6, 1927: 11.

70   Pete Doster, "Giants Defeat Standard Oil Outfit in 7-3
      Game," *Honolulu Star-Bulletin,* June 9, 1927: 10.

71   "'Faked Game' Stories Draw Hot Reply from J.A.
      Beaven," *Honolulu Star-Bulletin,* June 14, 1927: 8.

72   Sayama and Staples, 102.

73   "Stadium Shorts," *Honolulu Advertiser,* June 27, 1927: 6.

74   Sayama and Staples, 241.

75   "30 Day Suspensions for Four Players," *Afro-American,* July 9, 1927: 15.

76   "Fays Says – Mackey Jumped," *Chicago Defender,* September 24, 1927: 8.

77   "Negro All-Stars Agree to Play Here Next Year,"
      Honolulu Star-Bulletin, December 3, 1927: 8.

78   "'Pros' Ask for Jonnie Riddle," *Afro-American,* July 23, 1927: 14.

79   Arnold P. Townes (Ajay Johnson's nephew),
      phone interview September 2008.

80   Sayama and Staples, 301.

81   Sayama and Staples, 284.

82   Sayama and Staples, 121.

83   Sayama and Staples, 329.

84   Sayama and Staples, 68.

85   Sayama and Staples, 154.

86   "Royal Giants Won 26; Tied One on Their Japanese
      Tour," *Chicago Defender,* June 25, 1927: 9.

TY COBB'S LAST HURRAH: THE 1928 COBB TOUR

By Tom Hawthorn

On an offday on the road in Cleveland, Tyrus Raymond Cobb, hailed for much of his career as the greatest player the game had ever known, announced his impending retirement. It was September 17, 1928. He had last been a starter in late July when he batted second for the Philadelphia Athletics before trotting out to right field. He went 2-for-5 that day with a single and a double, scoring what would be the winning run in a 5-1 game on a passed ball. Since then, he had been used sparingly as a pinch-hitter, going 1-for-9.

The Georgia Peach was in his 24th season, a 41-year-old man who was now caught stealing more often than not. He appeared in only 95 games for Connie Mack's team. While his .323 batting average was far from disgraceful, it was still his poorest performance in two decades.

Many of his younger teammates spent the rare offday at the racetrack. Cobb invited reporters to gather in his room at the glamorous Hollenden Hotel, where he handed each of them a typewritten statement in which he announced his retirement even "while there still may remain some base hits in my bat."[1] The player spoke informally with the writers for hours, examining his career (he called Carl Weilman the toughest pitcher he faced) and expressing a desire to do nothing but enjoy his family's company for a year. The only item on his agenda was some winter hunting near his home in Augusta, Georgia.

"I am just baseball tired and want to quit," Cobb said. "I will be leaving baseball with a lot of regrets and still with a light heart. It's hard to pull away from a game to which one has given a quarter-century of his best manhood and which paved the road to lift me to a place of prominence and affluence."[2]

He had been for a time the highest-paid player in the game, earning nearly a half-million dollars in salary over the seasons, while investments in a car company later absorbed by General Motors, as well as in Coca-Cola from his home state, ensured that he faced few future privations.

The news of his pending retirement was greeted by newspapers as the passing of an era.

"He is worth more than a million dollars," noted the *Morning Call* of Allentown, Pennsylvania, "and is not worrying about his future or the price of pork chops."[3] The newspaper predicted that he might become a minority owner of a franchise in the high minors.

Cobb recorded his 4,189th hit, a double, against the Washington Senators as a pinch-hitter on September 3. He played what would be his final game in the majors eight days later, popping out to Mark Koenig at shortstop to lead off the ninth in a 5-3 loss at Yankee Stadium. He would get his final two hits in an A's uniform in Toronto in an exhibition game at Maple Leaf Stadium on September 14. Then it was on to Cleveland to sit on the bench.

For a player reputed to be ill-tempered, he was wistful about spending time with his family.

"Guess it's time to get out of the game and play with my kids before they grow up and leave me," he said in announcing his pending retirement. "And there's that trip to Europe that I promised Mrs. Cobb this year."[4]

His wife, Charlotte Marion Lombard, known as Charlie, did not get to see Europe in 1928. Three weeks after the hotel room session to announce his retirement, Cobb was traveling through Virginia on his way home to Georgia when he told friends of plans to play baseball overseas. In Japan.

The news broke nationally on October 7 when the Associated Press carried on its wires a news item based on a *Richmond Times-Dispatch* story. The report said Cobb would spend seven weeks in Asia, accompanied by former pitcher Walter Johnson, the manager of the Newark Bears of the International League.

Three days later, George A. Putnam, secretary-owner of the San Francisco Seals and a friend of Cobb's, offered further details. The player was going to give lectures on the game. He was also going to suit up and play with university teams. The tour was sponsored by the Osaka newspaper *Mainichi Shimbun* and four universities – Waseda, Meiji, Osaka, and Keio, whose own baseball team had toured the United States for six weeks earlier in the year.[5]

Cover of the January 1929 issue of Yakyukai *showing Ty Cobb with Keio players Takayoshi Okada and Saburo Miyatake*
(Coutesy of Robert Klevens, Prestige Collectibles)

The *Pittsburgh Press* had a scoop on the pending trip by several days. Sporting editor Ralph Davis, who was in New York to cover the first game of the World Series on October 4, slipped in a final paragraph at the end of his lengthy report on the Yankees' 4-1 victory over the St. Louis Cardinals. He noted that Cobb had popped into the press box at Yankee Stadium and mentioned that he was off to Japan later in the month with two players on a tour organized by Herb Hunter.[6]

Hunter, whose own major-league career as a weak-hitting infielder-outfielder lasted 39 games with four different teams, first traveled to Japan with Doyle's 1920 All-Americans and ended up coaching at several Japanese universities after the tour. In 1922, after what was his final season as a player, he led an all-star team of players, including Waite Hoyt, Herb Pennock, Casey Stengel, and George "High Pockets" Kelly, on a successful tour of Japan, Korea, China, the Philippines, and Hawaii. Hunter would go on to become a baseball ambassador, making at least 10 goodwill trips to Japan between 1920 and 1937.[7]

A month before Cobb made his announcement, Hunter got a cablegram from Japan inviting him to bring over another team of major leaguers. The assignment was going to be difficult, as active players were now banned from playing exhibition games after October 31.[8] Hunter hoped whatever disappointment the hosts might feel would be assuaged by bringing the greatest all-around player the game had seen. According to Cobb biographer Charles C. Alexander, Hunter offered Cobb $15,000 for his services.[9]

Also joining the tour were Bob Shawkey, a savvy right-hander who had gone 195-150 over 15 seasons as a starter in the majors, mostly with the Yankees. When they released him after the 1927 season, Shawkey held team records for wins, shutouts, strikeouts, and innings pitched.[10] He was a pitching coach and starter with the Montreal Royals in 1928, going 9-9.

His catcher was former Yankees teammate Fred Hofmann, a 34-year-old journeyman who when once asked how he batted (right, left, or switch), responded, "Poor."[11] He was nicknamed "Bootnose" for an obvious facial feature. Hofmann hit .226 for the Boston Red Sox in 1928 in what proved to be his final major-league campaign, though he continued playing in the minors until age 43.

Joining the three players was Ernest Cosmos "Ernie" Quigley, a stocky umpire born in the Canadian province of New Brunswick. Quigley lettered at the University of Kansas as a football player and hurdler in track and field for the Jayhawks. A limited minor-league career gave way to coaching football and officiating in three sports. By the time he retired, he estimated he had worked 400 college football games, 1,400 college basketball games (as well as the 1936 US Olympic qualifying tournament), and more than 3,000 major-league games. He officiated three Rose Bowl games and six World Series, the most notable being the one remembered as the 1919 Black Sox series.[12]

Tagging along were Seals owner Putnam and travel agent Frank Ploof of Tacoma, Washington, described as a sponsor of the trip. The latter, who stood nearly 6-feet tall though weighing just 150 pounds, posed for a photograph in a baseball uniform with the three players.[13]

After traveling across the continent to Seattle, Cobb met with Japanese consul Suemasa Okamoto and his wife. He also led his tour mates, bolstered by local players, in defeating an amateur team from West Seattle by 12-5. Cobb went 4-for-6.

The baseball tourists boarded the steamship *SS President Jefferson* of the American-Oriental Mail Line in Seattle on October 20, the ship departing at 11 A.M. Cobb was accompanied by his wife and three youngest children, Herschel, Beverly, and James. Quigley and Hunter were also joined by their families. Although some newspapers were still reporting that Johnson was on the tour, the old pitcher had backed out after signing days earlier to manage the Washington Senators.

The steamship's other passengers included businessmen from railroad and automobile companies, as well as a handful of globe-trotting tourists, among them a Kansas City doctor and the former mayor of Keokuk, Iowa.[14] Traveling in steerage were many former crew members from China who had just lost their jobs to Americans as part of the awarding of a contract to carry the mails. More than half of the 123 Chinese crew were to be replaced.[15]

The steamship sailed north through Puget Sound and across the Strait of Juan de Fuca before pulling into the Rithet Piers at Victoria, British Columbia.

As cargo and mail were loaded, Cobb took advantage of the layover to do a quick tour of the provincial capital. A large crowd of fans surrounded him. They were uncertain whether this was indeed the famous baseballer until "one youngster hollered out, 'Hello, Mr. Cobb,'" reported the *Victoria Daily Times*. "The famous baseballer looked at the boy for a few seconds and then said with a smiling face, 'Hello, Sonny, and how are you?'"[16]

After arriving in Yokohama, the trio of ballplayers conducted clinics with translators, while Quigley demonstrated umpiring techniques. The players donned university team uniforms and played a series of games with teams from the Tokyo Big Six League.

"Cobb couldn't control his zest to win, even in those games," Hunter later told *The Sporting News*. "Wearing the uniform of a Japanese college, he wanted to win as badly as when he was with the Tigers. And pity the young Japanese player who didn't understand him and threw to the wrong base!"[17]

As many as 4,000 students attended a clinic conducted at Waseda University, staying on the field until it was so dark they could no longer see the ball. Quigley's evening officiating classes attracted as many as 400, including officers of the imperial army. The ump found all his students to be attentive, though he felt they never mastered the balk rule.[18]

The 12 games in which the American players took part were well attended with crowds as large as 22,000 reported. Tickets were the equivalent of 50 cents, or about $7.50 in today's money. Cobb played first base with Shawkey on the mound and Quigley behind the plate calling balls and strikes. (Hofmann did not play, so as to observe the major-league rule about taking part in exhibitions after October 31.) Cobb also did brief stints in the outfield and on the mound. One report on his return noted that he had surrendered just one run in 18 innings.[19]

Whenever Cobb appeared in public, he was mobbed by dozens of Japanese children, who trailed after him.

The visitors were feted with elaborate banquets heavy on rice and dried fish.

Cobb was one of 12,631 foreigners to visit Japan in 1928 and one of only 3,240 American tourists. Earlier in the year, a baseball team from the University of Illinois team had also toured the country.

While on their way home, Hunter sent a telegram to the *Honolulu Star-Bulletin* seeking to organize two games in Hawaii. As it turned out, football games were scheduled for the dates the Cobb party sought and Honolulu Stadium manager J. Ashman Beaven did not want to remove the football grandstands to make way for exhibition baseball.[20]

Despite the snub, the party was greeted warmly. "To the touring baseball players we extend ALOHA," wrote William Peet, sports editor of the *Honolulu Advertiser*.[21] A fleet of Dodge Victory cars met the boat. The players were given a tour of the city's sites before being feted at a banquet at the year-old Royal Hawaiian, a seaside luxury hotel built on Waikiki

Beach. The guest list included the governor and the mayor.[22]

Days after leaving Hawaii, the *President Jefferson* docked in San Francisco during a squall at daybreak on December 12, 1928. The 150 cabin passengers included Cobb, who on his arrival assured newsmen he was permanently retired as a player, except perhaps for the occasional exhibition. He insisted he planned on taking a year off.

"Do you know that out of my 24 years in professional baseball I have had less than 10 years with my family?" he said. "From now on I hope to be with the wife and children all the time. I'm going to travel and the family will travel with me, no mistake."[23]

Cobb picked up a smattering of Japanese on the trip. On his return, a fan spotted him and asked, "It's you, is it, Mr. Cobb?" Cobb responded automatically, "*Sou desu hai, arigato*." ("So it is. Yes. Thank you.")[24]

"I had a wonderful trip," Cobb said. "I enjoyed every minute of it and they showed me a wonderful time there."[25]

He offered his thoughts on the future of the sport in Japan. "What Japan needs is professional baseball. There is a lot of school and college baseball there, but after the players leave school they do not keep up baseball. A professional league there would make baseball the most popular thing in Japan."[26]

Cobb marveled at the Japanese players' fielding and speed, while noting that they were better hitters than had been described. Cobb's opinion was shared by the others. "Japan has a great baseball future, and someday is going to be heard from in diamond annals," Hunter said after returning from his visit. "We enjoyed our stay immensely – courteously treated all the time and the Japanese in turn seemed to enjoy us."[27]

Shawkey thought his hosts not good hitters,[28] though he too was impressed by their fielding and throwing. "I loved it in Japan," he recalled decades later, "and it was amazing how keen these people were on baseball."[29] Quigley disagreed with Shawkey's assessment as to hitting prowess.

"Don't let anyone tell you that the Japanese cannot hit a curved ball or throw one," he said. "I found the Japanese intensely interested in baseball. Although the game is played by college students and high school students almost exclusively, nearly everyone in Japan that we came in contact with was baseball mad."[30]

Cobb's 1928 visit would be overshadowed by more substantial tours before and after (in 1922, 1931, and 1934). A handful of souvenirs have been sold by auction in recent years, including the January 1929 edition of *Yakyukai* (*Baseball World*) magazine featuring Cobb on the cover in a Daimai uniform flanked by Takayoshi Okada and Saburo Miyatake of Keio University. The magazine sold for $345 in 2021, though much of the spine cover was missing.[31] In 2019 Leland's sold a copy for $637.20.[32] In 2006 Robert Edward Auctions sold an autographed photograph of Cobb in a Tokyo uniform for $3,190,[33] while two years later another autographed photo featuring Cobb in a Daimai uniform sold for $1,528.[34] Yet another signed photograph showing Cobb seated in a dugout with three men was sold by Shafran Collectibles for $1,750.[35]

The tour ended in some acrimony. Cobb felt he had been cheated of money by Hunter, baseball writer Fred Lieb wrote in his 1977 memoir, *Baseball as I Have Known It*.[36]

After two months on the road, Cobb at last arrived home on December 18, 1928, his 42nd birthday. "Little did I think when I started playing baseball 24 years ago in Georgia," he said, "that I would play my last game in Japan."[37]

SOURCES

In addition to the sources cited in the Notes, the author consulted:

Fitts, Robert K. *Banzai Babe Ruth: Baseball, Espionage, and Assassination During the 1934 Tour of Japan* (Lincoln: University of Nebraska Press, 2012).

Leerhsen, Charles. *Ty Cobb: A Terrible Beauty* (New York: Simon and Schuster, 2015).

Nowlin, Bill. "Herb Hunter" SABR BioProject, SABR.org. https://sabr.org/bioproj/person/herb-hunter/.

NOTES

1   James C. Isaminger, "Ty Cobb to Retire This Fall After 24 Years of Service," *Philadelphia Inquirer*, September 18, 1928: 24.

2   "Ty Cobb Will Quit at End of Season," *New York Times*, September 18, 1928: 24.

3   "Connie Mack Asks Waivers on Three Veterans, Ty Cobb, Bush and Speaker," *Allentown* (Pennsylvania) *Morning Call*, November 3, 1928: 20.

4   "Ty Cobb Will Quit at End of Season."

5   "Cobb to Lecture to Japan Teams," *Miami Herald*, October 12, 1928: 8.

6   Ralph Davis, "Yankees' Victory Changes Sentiment," *Pittsburgh Press*, October 5, 1928: 54.

7   Jimmie Thompson, "The Crow's Nest," *The State* (Columbia, South Carolina), July 7, 1943; 9. Articles in the *Japan Times* verify that Hunter was in the country in 1920, 1921, 1922, 1928, early 1931, late 1931, 1932, 1933, 1934, and 1935.

8   National Baseball Hall of Fame, "At Home on the Road." Accessed January 27, 2022. https://baseballhall.org/discover-more/history/barnstorming-tours.

9   Charles C. Alexander, *Ty Cobb* (New York: Oxford University Press, 1984), 237.

10   Stephen V. Rice, "Bob Shawkey," SABR BioProject, https://sabr.org/bioproj/person/bob-shawkey/.

11   Bill Nowlin and Rory Costello, "Fred Hofmann." SABR BioProject, https://sabr.org/bioproj/person/fred-hofmann/.

12   Larry R. Gerlach, "Ernie Quigley: An Official for All Seasons," *Kansas History: A Journal of the Central Plains* 33 (Winter 2010-2011): 218-39.

13   "Ty and Others Go to Japan to Treat Natives," *The Sporting News*, November 15, 1928: 7.

14   "Jefferson Will Take Heavy List to Orient Ports," *Victoria* (British Columbia) *Daily Times*, October 19, 1928: 10.

15   "Replacing Chinese," *Tacoma* (Washington) *Daily Ledger*, October 19, 1928: 10.

16   "Ty Cobb Pays Visit to City," *Victoria Daily Times*, October 22, 1928: 8.

17   Fred Lieb, "Fred Lieb and Herbert Hunter Will Carry Gospel of Major League Baseball to Japan in 1931; First Oriental Diamond Missionary Tour in Nine Years," *The Sporting News*, January 1, 1931: 3.

18   "Cobb and Putnam Home After Tour of Orient," *Sacramento Bee*, December 13, 1928: 27.

19   Abe Kemp, "Give Me a Line" (column), *San Francisco Examiner*, December 14, 1928: 33.

20   "No Game Here," *Honolulu Star-Bulletin*, November 16, 1928: 14.

21   William Peet, "Sport Flashes," *Honolulu Advertiser*, December 6, 1928: 11.

22   "Royal Welcome Is Planned for Our Famous Visitors," *Honolulu Advertiser*, December 6, 1928: 10.

23   Ed A. Charlton, "President Jefferson's Pilot Guides Big Liner Safely Through Squall in Record Breaking Docking Here," *San Francisco Examiner*, December 13, 1928: 31.

24   Russell J. Newland, "Home from Orient, Cobb Says He Has Scored His Last Run," *Atlanta Constitution*, December 13, 1928: 16.

25   Pete Doster, "Georgia Peach Played Last Baseball Games During Japanese Tour," *Honolulu Star Bulletin*, December 6, 1928: 14.

26   Doster.

27   "'Herb' Hunter Back, Sees Great Baseball Future for Nipponese," *Red Bank* (New Jersey) *Daily Standard*, January 4, 1929: 1.

28   "Japs Can't Hit the Ball," *Syracuse Herald*, January 25, 1929: 49.

29   Bill Reddy, "Keeping Posted," *Syracuse Post Standard*, February 15, 1971: 15.

30   Frank Roche, "Baseball and Not Jiu Jitsu Is Most Popular Sport Now in Japan, Noted Umpire Says," *Los Angeles Times*, December 17, 1928: 13.

31   https://prestigecollectiblesauction.com/bids/bid-place?itemid=5498. Date accessed: February 26, 2022.

32   https://auction.lelands.com/bids/bidplace?itemid=96124. Date accessed: February 26, 2022.

33   https://robertedwardauctions.com/auction/2006/spring/647/1928-cobb-signed-japanese-barnstorming-photo-psa/ Date accessed: February 26, 2022.

34   https://robertedwardauctions.com/auction/2008/spring/842/1928-cobb-signed-japan-tour-photo/ Date accessed: February 26, 2022.

35   http://www.shafrancollectibles.com/shop/new-items/ty-cobb-1928-signed-daimai-japan-tour-photo/ Date accessed: February 26, 2022.

36   Fred Lieb, *Baseball as I Have Known It* (New York: Coward, McCann and Geohegan, 1977), 198.

37   Doster.

HERB HUNTER'S DREAM TOUR: 1931 – A RABBIT, TWO LEFTYS, AND AN IRON HORSE VISIT A DANGEROUS JAPAN

By Dennis Snelling

It was a tour initially framed by the dreams of retired fringe major-league outfielder Herb Hunter, the continuing quest of a Japanese newspaper publisher to bring Babe Ruth to Japan before he retired as a player, and the metastasizing of Japanese militarism.

The tour ended with the best baseball team to visit Japan up to that time—including seven future Hall of Famers—winning all 17 games they played in the country, Japan's political landscape in violent disarray, Babe Ruth still not having visited the country, and the beginning of the end of Herb Hunter's global baseball aspirations.

By 1931, Hunter was considered "Baseball's Ambassador to Japan." He had first crossed the Pacific

1931 All-Americans in front of the Oriental Hotel in Kobe (National Baseball Library, Cooperstown)

Ocean 11 years earlier with a group of minor-league and marginal major-league players. During that trip, Hunter partnered with pitcher Charlie Robertson to earn money on the side, coaching the Waseda University baseball team.[1]

Hunter developed an affinity for the country—and the potential it offered him to make his mark on the baseball world—returning in 1921 to coach the baseball teams of both Waseda and Keio universities, wearing a chrysanthemum in his lapel each day.[2] The *San Francisco Chronicle* reacted to this news by derisively challenging its readers to visualize the ex-San Francisco Seals outfielder coaching baseball to anyone, since Hunter's reputation was that of the proverbial million-dollar athlete with a ten-cent head. He was physically gifted, but legendary for his on-field blunders.[3]

He once executed an outstanding running catch with the bases loaded and one out in the ninth, only to absent-mindedly exit for the clubhouse, oblivious to the fact that the ball was still in play.[4] On another occasion, with two out and the bases loaded, he decided to showboat on an easy fly, making a one-handed swipe at the ball, which he dropped. Three runs scored.[5]

It was said that Hunter had once nearly spiked himself dodging a line drive. "He played that ball like a camel," the account went. "He was not hurt but he had a narrow escape. A lot of runs scored while Herbie was untangling himself."[6]

Even when Hunter's efforts won a game, it sometimes resulted from a bonehead move. He stole home in a game against Portland on a 3-and-0 count and two runners on base. He was called safe, his run the eventual game-winner despite the fact that he never touched home plate, not to mention that during the play the shocked hitter had backed into the catcher, which should have been ruled interference. Al C. Joy of the hometown *San Francisco Examiner* wrote,

"Just why he stole home at that particular moment nobody seems to know. And just why Umpire Casey did not call him out for several reasons nobody seems to know."[7]

Despite his shortcomings, Hunter's connections to Japanese universities enabled him to organize a troupe of major leaguers to Japan in 1922, and make several subsequent visits, including in 1928, when he enlisted Ty Cobb, Bob Shawkey, and Fred Hofmann. Hunter was now ready to bring another team of major-league all-stars to the Orient in 1931.

But he was not to be wholly in charge of the effort. Commissioner Kenesaw Mountain Landis, mindful of the international implications of such an event, and noting Hunter's checkered success with past ventures—especially when it came to handling money—permitted the tour to proceed only under the supervision of veteran sportswriter Fred Lieb.[8]

Hunter acquiesced—he had no choice—and once the tour was approved by major-league owners in mid-January, he prepared to finalize arrangements with Japan's largest newspaper, *Mainichi Shimbun*.[9]

Catching wind of Hunter's intentions, Matsutaro Shoriki, publisher of the rival *Yomiuri Shimbun*, intercepted him, ultimately persuading the American to award his newspaper exclusive sponsorship of the tour's Tokyo segment. When *Mainichi Shimbun* backed out of sponsoring games in other parts of the country, Shoriki stepped in despite the added, and significant, financial burden, gambling that the event would put his publication on the map.[10]

Arrangements complete, Hunter returned to his home in Red Bank, New Jersey, where he managed a semipro team headquartered on his diamond, Hunter's Field, while Fred Lieb pursued ballplayers for the trip.[11]

A 14-man roster was ultimately secured, including four 1931 World Series participants: Al Simmons, Mickey Cochrane, Lefty Grove, and Frankie Frisch.[12] To Shoriki's disappointment there would be no Babe Ruth—who claimed barnstorming and movie commitments—but Ruth's teammate and co-American League home run champion Lou Gehrig would be there. So would Willie Kamm, Rabbit Maranville, Muddy Ruel, George Kelly, Lefty O'Doul, Larry French, and Tom Oliver. Boston Braves pitcher Bruce Cunningham, a right-hander who had won only three of 15 decisions in 1931, and outfielder Ralph Shinners, who was just completing his career in the International League, rounded out the roster.

Fred Lieb had thought the All-Stars unbeatable—although they did not start out that way.

The team initially gathered in California in early October for a series of games in the Bay Area, and lost four of five against lineups composed almost entirely of Pacific Coast League players.[13] The third game, against the San Francisco Seals, proved the most embarrassing. Lefty Grove, who arrived after the first two games along with the other World Series participants, took the mound and was battered for six runs in the first inning. The All-Stars began pointing fingers, with Grove loudly complaining about not having enough time to warm up. The left-hander settled down, shutting out San Francisco from the second inning through the fifth and striking out seven. But the All-Stars lost, 7-4, while collecting only four hits.[14]

Stateside exhibitions complete, the All-Stars boarded the luxury liner *Tatsuta Maru* for Japan; ship captain Shunji Ito, a talented golfer, accommodated the Americans by converting his deck-side course into a batting cage.[15] On the way, there was a quick stop in Honolulu to play another tune-up game against locals.

During the brief sojourn in Hawaii, the team slaughtered a group of local semipros, 10-0, before 12,000 fans—many of them arriving from other islands.[16] The famously dour Grove displayed uncharacteristic enthusiasm afterward, declaring himself enamored with Hawaii and musing, "…wonder what my chances are of buying a small place here, I can use this old sunshine in January and February."[17]

While the All-Stars cavorted in paradise, events in Asia were unfolding at a dramatic and dangerous pace. A month before the players' departure for Japan, a renegade faction of the military, seeking war with China, destroyed a section of the South Manchuria Railway and blamed it on the Chinese. This contrivance provided the pretext for Japan to invade Manchuria; the Japanese government was caught off-guard by its own armed forces, but did nothing of consequence to curtail the action, and was widely condemned in the court of world opinion. As a result, the country the American ballplayers entered was far more dangerous and unstable than they appreciated.

Thousands of enthusiastic Japanese baseball fans were on hand when the *Tatsuta Maru* docked following its two-week passage. After the mayors of Yokohama and Tokyo made brief presentations, the players boarded a special train bound for the capitol. There, the party was met by limousines waiting to convey them through the streets of downtown Tokyo.

Fred Lieb described the journey "a continual ovation." Special flags combining the emblems of the American and Japanese national banners were provided to those lining the route. Fans jammed the streets, pressing in on the motorcade as shouts of "banzai" and "welcome" rained down from office windows. Some of the more enthusiastic jumped onto limousine running boards to shake the hand of Rabbit Maranville or Lefty Grove—repeatedly shouting "Thirty-One!" at the latter in recognition of his total wins for Philadelphia that year.[18]

The Americans were flabbergasted. "I will remember this reception to my dying day," remarked Lou Gehrig. "I do not know of anything in my entire career that has touched me as much as this welcome." Frankie Frisch added, "It made me feel like a great military hero or a man who had flown across the Pacific."[19]

Other than George Kelly, who had been a member of Hunter's 1922 All-Stars, none of the players had previously visited Japan. The world was more compartmentalized than today, and the visitors were surprised and astonished by the modernity of Tokyo, on course to becoming one of the world's major cities. At the same time, there were obvious differences in food, language, and customs—it was both fascinating and disorienting.

Because Japan lacked professional baseball, the Americans would challenge college teams from the Tokyo Big Six University League—the highest level of baseball in the country—as well as all-star teams of alumni from those colleges and a few industry-sponsored squads.

Despite massive unemployment in Japan due to the collapse of the silk industry, 65,000 attended the opening contest; the ceremonial first pitch was thrown by Japanese Education Minister Tanaka, decked out in formal dress, including a top hat. The starting pitcher for Rikkyo University, Takeshi Tsuji, pitched well, allowing only four hits and four runs, all unearned, in six innings. Three of the unearned runs were due to missed fly balls by the Japanese right fielder, who did not wear sunglasses—according to Fred Lieb, it was considered cowardly to use them.

Al Simmons complimented Tsuji afterward for his deceptive sidearm delivery and impressive control, but the first game was an easy, 7-0, win for the All-Stars behind Bruce Cunningham, who allowed only two hits.[20]

The second game nearly resulted in a shocking Japanese victory. Masao Date, pitching for Waseda University, impressed Lieb, who afterward said that the Americans felt he would be a major league prospect if he were in the States. Date calmly escaped a first-inning bases-loaded jam by fooling Frankie Frisch on a full-count curveball, taken for strike three.[21]

The game was tied, 1-1, until the seventh, when Larry French surrendered a bases-loaded two-run double that gave Waseda a 3-1 lead. French, the possessor of an explosive temper, was removed from the game and furiously hurled his glove in disgust upon reaching the bench, cursing and screaming, "I've traveled nine thousand miles to be knocked out of the box by a bunch of Japanese college players!"[22]

Things did not get better. With only three pitchers along for the tour, others were utilized as emergency hurlers, including Lou Gehrig, who relieved French and allowed two more runs to score on a wild pitch and an out, stretching Waseda's lead to four runs.[23]

Lieb, whom Landis had made responsible for the comportment of the players, watched in horror as French began hurling racial epithets from the bench. He attempted to shush the pitcher, pointing to Viscount Taketane Sohma, sitting at the end of the bench. Sohma, director of general offices at the Imperial Palace, had been educated in America and understood every word. To Lieb's relief, he diplomatically chose not react to French's tirade, which continued despite Lieb's entreaties.[24]

The Americans ultimately stormed back to win, 8-5, saving French the embarrassment of losing, as Masao Date tired while Lefty Grove, who replaced Gehrig, struck out six straight batters on 19 pitches to end the game. Lieb later revealed that the All-Stars were arguing among themselves on the bench until Date walked the bases loaded and Lefty O'Doul promptly cleared them with a double to key a seven-run eighth inning.[25]

Grove took command of the third game, against Meiji University, although the Americans were finding it difficult to score at will against Japanese pitchers, putting the lie to the predictions of Japanese naval officers aboard the *Tatsuta Maru* that they would score at least 20 runs every game. Meiji University kept the game close; starting pitcher Kakusaburo Onitsuka retired the first eight American batters he faced, and another pitcher, Yutaka Yasogawa, took care of Al Simmons and Willie Kamm on pop ups with the bases loaded later in the game. Meanwhile, Lefty Grove struck out 11 in six innings of shutout ball and the All-Stars won, 4-0.

The seventh game was a lopsided, 11-0, win over the same All-Stars behind Grove, who was so dominant that the outfielders sat down in the outfield during the ninth inning—an unfortunate flashback to showboating that plagued the 1922 tour. Grove allowed only three singles.[26]

Despite the losses, the Japanese appetite for baseball seemed insatiable. Lou Gehrig noted that at every ballpark, thousands of those lacking a ticket remained outside, patiently waiting until after the game to catch a glimpse of the Americans. "The enthusiasm for baseball among the Japanese just about borders on the fanatical," he explained. "At times it would take hours for our cars to take us from the park to the hotel."[27] Fred Lieb recounted seeing scores of locals occupying vacant lots before breakfast, playing baseball while wearing traditional wooden sandals.[28]

The American contingent traveled to Sendai, a city of 200,000 in the north of Japan nicknamed "The City of Trees."[29] The players were greeted at the train station at 7:00 A.M. by 10,000 people, virtually all of them frantically waving American flags, and then led to a waiting room equipped with 20 specially-upholstered chairs. There, three men in formal dress provided an official welcome to the city.[30]

The game in Sendai drew 15,000; Fred Lieb was told it was the largest crowd to ever gather in the city. While the players were taken by automobile to the ballpark, located atop a hill five miles from town, nearly half of those attending made their way on foot. There was a streetcar line, although the tracks ended some two miles from the ballpark. Despite the obstacles, fans were on hand three hours before game time, eager to soak in the experience.[31]

During the contest, easily won by the Americans, 13-2, Mickey Cochrane hit a home run that caromed off a flag-pole and struck a Japanese fan in the face. The injured man was escorted across the diamond to a restroom in the clubhouse, where he was treated for injuries to his mouth and sent on his way with 20 yen (the equivalent of about $10). A few minutes later, a doctor and nurse, thinking the man still in the bleachers, brought the game to a halt by tearing across the playing field, frantically looking for the injured party before receiving assurances that he had been safely removed.[32]

Between games, the players went sightseeing, played golf, and were treated as celebrities at official receptions and a seemingly endless string of parties. Rabbit Maranville celebrated his 40th birthday at the home of Taketane Sohma. A gong was struck 40 times to mark each year since the Rabbit's birth, and the shortstop received a pair of ivory pigeons, a cake with a chocolate rabbit perched atop it, and a brand-new baseball glove signed by Japanese dignitaries and members of the All-Star team.

"Let somebody try to get that glove away from me," declared Maranville. "I intend to have that glove shellacked as soon as I get home so that the signatures do not fade. Then I'll see that it stays in the House of Maranville."[33]

The Rabbit, whose physical dimensions were similar to those of the Japanese against whom he played, became a crowd favorite, especially when catching pop flies in his vest pocket, or in his lap while sitting on the infield. Japanese players attempted to imitate him, and fans doubled over with laughter as baseballs ricocheted off heads.[34] Despite his deserved reputation for light hitting, Maranville even got into the act offensively, hitting two home runs in a one-sided victory against a team representing the Yawata Iron Works.[35]

At one point the Americans were hosted by Japanese Prime Minister Reijiro Wakatsuki. Unfortunately, when Wakatsuki was summoned from his office on urgent business, several of the players and their wives began filling their pockets with mementoes, including cigars, pens, and even small vases.[36] Wakatsuki proved far beyond gracious in ignoring the obvious affront.

While all seemed relaxed and festive on the surface, the Americans remained blissfully unaware of the danger lurking in the country they were visiting. The same day the All-Stars defeated Keio University, a mass meeting was held in Tokyo to condemn the League of Nations for *its* condemnation of the Japanese invasion of Manchuria. In defiance, Japan sent additional troops to assist in a tense standoff outside Tahsing, which they had occupied.[37]

Meanwhile, the All-Star roster, numbering only 14 to begin with, was depleted during the middle of the tour, with both Lou Gehrig and Lefty O'Doul sidelined by injury.

Gehrig was hit by a pitch, suffering painful bone bruises to several fingers. During the tour's seventh game, O'Doul suffered broken ribs in a collision with Japanese infielder Osamu Mihara.

O'Doul's injury resulted from an incident ignited by name-calling on the part of the All-Stars. Upset by Gehrig's injury, the Americans began insulting the Japanese, who for the most part took it in stride, with the exception of Mihara, who began returning the insults.

O'Doul declared that he would teach Mihara a lesson, and bunted to the right side of the infield in his next at bat. As planned, Mihara fielded the ball and rushed over to tag O'Doul. But Mihara recognized O'Doul's intentions and was ready, meeting the American full force and sending him to the ground, clutching his ribs. O'Doul was out for the final 10 games. Worse, he was unable to golf.[38]

After being sidelined, O'Doul instructed Japanese players and visited with old friend Sotaro Suzuki, whom he had met in New York in 1928, when Suzuki was working in the States for a silk firm and O'Doul was playing for the Giants. Suzuki, now employed by Matsutaro Shoriki at his newspaper, especially enjoyed sitting in the hotel lobby in Yokohama with its spectacular views of the harbor, talking baseball

1931 All-American Tour Program

with O'Doul and the other American stars.[39] And with time on his hands, O'Doul made an effort to educate himself about Japan and its culture.

Despite his abbreviated performance, Lefty O'Doul boasted the highest batting average on the tour at .615, including five doubles and two triples. Frankie Frisch was second at .404.[40] Al Simmons led the team with five home runs. As a team the All-Stars batted .346, scoring 149 runs while allowing only 30.

Bruce Cunningham and Larry French pitched well, but Lefty Grove was especially dominating; he did not allow an earned run during the entire trip and struck out 55 batters in 38 innings. In Yokohama, he emptied the outfield prior to the last out, and then instructed Maranville and Frisch to turn their backs to the plate before striking out the final hitter on three pitches to end the game.[41]

After their 17th contest, against Yokohama Commercial High School, the Americans sailed back to the States.

Herb Hunter and Fred Lieb insisted that the Japanese would eventually match the Americans in caliber of play, with Lieb declaring their outfield defense already major-league quality.[42] "Outfielders on the teams the All-Stars played could go back just as far, come in as fast and cover just as much ground as any outfielder in either major league," he said.[43] Mickey Cochrane added, "…to get a ball over their head, you practically have to hit it out of the park, for they crash into the fences as though they were made of rubber."[44]

In addition to Masao Date, another pitcher who impressed the Americans was a diminutive left-hander from Keio University, Seizo Ueno. He tossed a complete game in a tough, 2-0 loss, allowing only six hits and one earned run; Bruce Cunningham defeated him with a one-hitter. Ueno pitched three innings of hitless relief in another game.[45]

When the players landed in San Francisco, Mickey Cochrane reported, "I didn't know a country could be so baseball-crazy as Japan is. I know I signed so many shoes I could not count them; papers, hats, shirts, gloves, in fact, everything they could find. It was a wonderful trip, but, believe me, your skyline this morning was the prettiest sight I have seen since we left."[46]

Catcher Muddy Ruel—a practicing attorney in the off-season and the first ballplayer ever admitted to practice before the United States Supreme Court—felt the game was held back by the lack of a middle class in Japan and thought it a shame that the country lacked professional baseball. As an example, he pointed to a player he had befriended, third baseman Shigeru Mizuhara. "I asked Muzi [sic] what he was going to do after he finished college," said Ruel, "and he informed me that he was delighted to be able to say he had lined up a job as a driver of a street car. Imagine that—and he is the best third baseman in Japan."[47]

Al Simmons was puzzled that the Japanese were excellent on defense, but impotent with the bat. "The Japanese lads," said Simmons, "of course, are physically small compared to us, but that fact should not prevent them from being good hitters. For we have many fine hitters among the small men in the big leagues."[48]

Herb Hunter praised the Japanese, noted no obvious tensions about Manchuria, and announced that when conditions improved, he would start an eight-team Japanese major league, backed with $6,000,000 from Japanese businessmen.[49]

But conditions did not improve, either for Hunter or for US-Japan relations. Prime Minister Wakatsuki's government resigned while the Americans were returning home, in large part due to its inability to control the Japanese military. That task fell to his successor, Tsuyoshi Inukai, who had publicly supported the invasion of Manchuria. In January 1932, three Japanese soldiers pulled American consul Culver Chamberlain from his automobile and punched him in the face several times, bringing rebuke from the United States government and demand for apologies and arrests.[50] Four days later a Korean activist made an attempt on the life of Emperor Hirohito, at which point Inukai and

his government offered its resignation, but Hirohito refused to accept it.[51]

Four months later, Inukai was assassinated inside his residence by 11 junior officers.[52]

Herb Hunter returned to Red Bank, New Jersey, basking in what he considered his greatest success, much to the chagrin of Matsutaro Shoriki. The Japanese newspaper publisher was angry that—despite gate receipts that had far exceeded expectations—Hunter intended to hold on to all of the extra money, leaving Shoriki in debt even as he had taken on sponsorship of the entire tour. Hunter, who for some reason ended up handling tour funds despite an order from Landis not to, reluctantly surrendered a slightly larger cut, but Shoriki still suffered a significant financial loss underwriting an obviously a successful venture.[53] He would not forget this.

Hunter returned to Japan in 1932 on a coaching tour with Lefty O'Doul, Ted Lyons, and Moe Berg, but he did not lead any more all-star teams to the country or have anything to do with establishing professional baseball there, largely due to the same weaknesses of which Landis had been wary, and that Matsutaro Shoriki had experienced to his own detriment. In the summer of 1934, Hunter took a team from Harvard University to Japan. But four months later, when the most important major-league tour of them all was staged, Herb Hunter was left out in the cold in favor of an effort spearheaded by Lefty O'Doul that featured, finally, the long-awaited appearance of Babe Ruth in Japan.

1931 ALL-AMERICAN GAMES IN JAPAN

Date	Place	Opponent	Score	Winner	Loser
November 7	Tokyo	Rikkyo University	7-0	Cunningham	Tsuji
November 8	Tokyo	Waseda University	8-5	Grove	Fukuda
November 9	Tokyo	Meiji University	4-0	Grove	Onizuka
November 10	Sendai	All-Meiji	13-2	Cunningham	Nakamura
November 12	Maebashi	All-Japan	14-1	French	Tsuji
November 14	Tokyo	All-Japan	6-3	Cunningham	Miyake
November 15	Tokyo	All-Japan	11-0	Grove	Watanabe
November 17	Matsumoto	All-Japan	15-0	French	Tase
November 18	Tokyo	Keio University	2-0	Cunningham	Ueno
November 19	Shizuoka	Hosei University	8-1	Grove	Wakabayashi
November 21	Nagoya	All-Keio	5-1	French	Ueno
November 22	Osaka	All-Waseda	10-0	Cunningham	Date
November 23	Osaka	All-Keio	8-0	Grove	Ueno
November 24	Shimonoseki	Yawata Iron Works	17-8	French	Ohka
November 26	Osaka	Kansai University	7-2	Cunningham	Honda
November 29	Yokohama	All-Yokohama	3-2	French	Ryu
November 30	Yokohama	Yokohama Commercial	11-5	Grove	Araki

1931 ALL-AMERICAN TOUR BATTING AND PITCHING STATISTICS[54]

All-American Batting Statistics	BA	G	AB	R	H	2B	3B	HR	RBI	SO	BB	SB
Maranville	.230	17	74	16	17	3	0	2	8	5	9	2
Simmons	.394	17	66	23	26	5	1	5	21	0	6	1
Oliver	.364	17	66	14	24	4	3	1	11	2	7	3
Kamm	.369	17	65	18	24	6	1	1	18	2	6	3
Frisch	.404	13	47	12	19	3	0	0	12	2	11	0
Kelly	.298	14	47	10	14	1	0	2	10	2	6	1
Ruel	.333	12	45	11	15	2	1	0	8	0	6	2
Shinners	.357	11	42	7	15	4	1	3	9	2	1	4
Cochrane	.395	11	38	11	15	3	0	3	9	0	8	3
O'Doul	.615	7	26	13	16	5	2	0	7	0	4	0
French	.318	7	22	1	7	1	0	0	4	2	3	0
Cunningham	.273	8	22	5	6	1	0	1	2	4	4	0
Gehrig	.313	5	16	6	5	2	0	0	6	1	4	1
Grove	.125	8	16	2	2	0	0	1	4	2	2	0

All-American Pitching Statistics	ERA	G	W	L	IP	H	HR	SO	BB	R	ER
Cunningham	0.90	6	6	0	50	22	0	19	8	5	5
French	2.57	7	5	0	49	43	1	19	12	16	14
Grove	0.00	8	6	0	38	15	0	55	8	1	0
Maranville	0.00	2	0	0	5	3	0	1	2	2	0
Frisch	9.84	2	0	0	3.2	2	0	2	5	4	4
Kelly	0.00	1	0	0	3	1	0	1	0	0	0
Kamm	6.00	1	0	0	3	5	1	0	2	2	2
Gehrig	0.00	1	0	0	1	0	0	0	1	0	0
Shinners	0.00	1	0	0	.1	0	0	0	1	0	0
Simmons	-	1	0	0	0	0	0	0	1	0	0
Oliver	-	1	0	0	0	1	0	0	0	0	0

NOTES

1 "Haoles Team to Hold First Big Meeting Tuesday," *Honolulu Advertiser*, February 5, 1921: Section 2, 4.

2 "Herb Hunter Is Not Worrying," *San Francisco Chronicle*, February 6, 1922: 14; "Japan's Ball Fans Look to Cards to Win," *Honolulu Advertiser*, May 17, 1922: 4.

3 Ed R. Hughes, "Baseball Invasion of the Orient Breaks Up in Big Blow-Off at Kobe, Japan," *San Francisco Chronicle*, January 28, 1921: 7.

4 "Herb Hunter in S.F. from Japan," *San Francisco Examiner*, February 27, 1931: 21, 22. This is the most famous of the stories about Herb Hunter and was repeated innumerable times in various incarnations over the years.

5 Ed R. Hughes, "First No-Hit Game of Year Defeats Seals," *San Francisco Chronicle*, July 26, 1919: 8.

6 Ed R. Hughes, "Los Angeles Takes Seaton to Help Staff," *San Francisco Chronicle*, March 24, 1918: 10.

7 Al C. Joy, "Herb Hunter Steals Home in Seventh and Wins Game for Seals," *San Francisco Examiner*, October 11, 1917: 21.

8 Fred Lieb, *Baseball as I Have Known It* (New York: Coward, McCann & Geoghegan, Inc., 1977), 198.

9 Robert K Fitts, *Banzai Babe Ruth* (Lincoln: University of Nebraska Press, 2012), 16; William Peet, "Hunter Banking on The Bambino," *Honolulu Advertiser*, February 20, 1931: 10.

10 Fitts, 18.

11 "Herb Hunter to Manage R.B. Towers the Coming Season," *Red Bank* (New Jersey) *Standard*, March 13, 1931: 7.

12 A rule was adopted that allowed only three of the four World Series players to appear in the same game. Frederick G. Lieb, "More Baseball Now Being Played by Japanese Youths Than by Youngsters of the United States, Asserts Fred Lieb," *The Sporting News*, January 7, 1932: 7.

13 "Brubaker Clan Beats Gehrigs," *Oakland Tribune*, October 12, 1931: 19, 20; Ed R. Hughes, "Seals Defeat Major League Stars, 5-3," *San Francisco Chronicle*, October 13, 1931: 21, 23; "Major League Stars Defeat Seals, 13-6," *San Francisco Chronicle*, October 15, 1931: 25; "Major League Stars Lose to Home Team; Grove Pitches," *Sacramento Bee*, October 15, 1931.

14 "Seals Bombard Lefty Grove to Beat Big Leaguers, 7-4," *San Francisco Chronicle*, October 14, 1931: 27.

15 Bob Roberts, "Pilot Fees to Be Cut; Oaks Home from L.A." *San Francisco Chronicle*, October 15, 1931: 16.

16 Don Watson, "Record Crowd Sees Major Leaguers Win, 10-0," *Honolulu Star-Bulletin*, October 21, 1931: 11.

17 William Peet, "Grove Likes Hawaii and May Live Here," *Honolulu Advertiser*, October 22, 1931: 10.

18 Frederick G. Lieb, "Japs Greet Touring Major League Stars," *The Sporting News*, December 3, 1931: 7.

19 Lieb, "Japs Greet Touring Major League Stars."

20 "Tokio Nines Play Well," *Japanese American News*, December 2, 1931: 8.

21 Frederick G. Lieb, "Touring the Orient," *The Sporting News*, December 10, 1931: 4.

22 William Peet, "Sport Flashes," *Honolulu Advertiser*, December 14, 1931: 10.

23 Frederick G. Lieb, "More Baseball Now Being Played by Japanese Youths Than by Youngsters of the United States, Asserts Fred Lieb."

24 Lieb, *Baseball as I Have Known It*, 203; "Touring the Orient," *The Sporting News*, December 24, 1931: 4.

25 Peet, "Sport Flashes;" Abe Kemp, "Major Stars Return from Japanese Trip," *San Francisco Examiner*, December 19, 1931: 18; Lieb, "More Baseball Now Being Played by Japanese Youths Than by Youngsters of the United States, Asserts Fred Lieb."

26 "Major Leaguers Score Sixth Win," *Nippu Jiji*, November 16, 1931: 3.

27 "Baseball in Japan Amazes Lou Gehrig," *Boston Globe*. December 23, 1931: 11.

28 Peet, "Sport Flashes."

29 In 2011, Sendai was struck by an earthquake and tsunami that destroyed the Fukushima Daiichi nuclear plant.

30 Lieb, "Touring the Orient," *The Sporting News*, December 17, 1931: 4.

31 Lieb, "Touring the Orient," *The Sporting News*, December 17, 1931: 4; Dennis Snelling, *Lefty O'Doul: Baseball's Forgotten Ambassador* (Lincoln: University of Nebraska Press, 2017), 95.

32 Lieb, "Touring the Orient," *The Sporting News*, December 17, 1931: 4.

33 Frederick G. Lieb, "Touring the Orient," *The Sporting News*, December 24, 1931: 4.

34 "Interest in Japan Amazing to Gehrig," *New York Times*, December 23, 1931.

35   Lieb, "More Baseball Now Being Played by Japanese Youths Than by Youngsters of the United States, Asserts Fred Lieb."

36   Lieb, *Baseball as I Have Known It*, 204; *The Sporting News*, January 7, 1932: 7.

37   International News Service, "Compromise on Manchurian Row May Be Offered," *Nippu Jiji*, November 14, 1931: 1.

38   Lieb, *Baseball as I Have Known It*, 205.

39   Letter, Sotaro Suzuki to Lefty O'Doul, February 5, 1932.

40   Frederick G. Lieb, "O'Doul Best with Bat on Japanese Tour," *The Sporting News*, January 14, 1932: 7; Pfc. Howard Bryan, "The Babe in Japan," *Pacific Stars & Stripes*, April 25, 1948: 9.

41   Abe Kemp, "Major Stars Return from Japanese Trip," *San Francisco Examiner*, December 19, 1931: 18.

42   Don Watson, "Solem Strong on Condition," *Honolulu Star Bulletin*, December 14, 1931: 10.

43   Peet, "Sport Flashes."

44   Kemp.

45   Lieb, "More Baseball Now Being Played by Japanese Youths Than by Youngsters of the United States, Asserts Fred Lieb."

46   Kemp.

47   James M. Gould, "Baseball Now Japan's National Game, Says 'Muddy' Ruel, Back from Tour," *St. Louis Post-Dispatch*, December 29, 1931:

4B. Mizuhara, who was eventually inducted into the Japanese Baseball Hall of Fame, was held as a prisoner during and after World War II by the Russians until Cappy Harada secured his release, which was celebrated during an emotional pre-game ceremony at which Mizuhara declared, "I, Mizuhara, have finally come home." (See Sayuri Guthrie-Shimizu, *Transpacific Field of Dreams*, Chapel Hill, North Carolina: University of North Carolina Press, 2012, 249.)

48   "Tokio Nines Play Well," *Japanese American News*, December 2, 1931: 8.

49   Sidney Wain, "Hunter, Back at Fair Haven, Tells of Baseball Experiences in Japan," *Long Branch* (New Jersey) *Daily Record*, December 30, 1931: 8. Hunter had earlier written to his brother in Melrose, Massachusetts that he planned to remain behind to start a professional league in Japan in 1932. ("Crowds Watching U.S. Team Play," *Boston Globe*, December 18, 1931: 32.)

50   Constantine Brown, "Stimson Prepares to Act in Attack on U.S. Consul," *Washington Evening Star*, January 4, 1932: 1

51   Associated Press, "Hirohito Escapes Injury in Bomb Attack in Tokio," *Washington Evening Star*, January 8, 1932: 1.

52   Hugh Byas, "Army to Stop Agitation," *New York Times*, May 16, 1932: 1. Fortunately, film star Charlie Chaplin, a guest of Inukai, was away from the residence at the time of the attack, attending a sumo match.

53   Fitts, 21.

54   Yoshikazu Matsubayashi, *Baseball Game History: Japan vs, U.S.A.* (Tokyo: Baseball Magazine, 2004), 85.

MURDER, ESPIONAGE, AND BASEBALL: THE 1934 ALL-AMERICAN TOUR OF JAPAN[1]

By Robert K. Fitts

Katsusuke Nagasaki's breath billowed as he loitered outside the Yomiuri newspaper's Tokyo offices. The morning of February 22, 1935 was chilly. But that was good; nobody would look twice at his bulky overcoat. Matsutaro Shoriki, the owner of the *Yomiuri Shimbun*, was late. Nagasaki strolled up and down the block, trying to remain inconspicuous.

Finally, at 8:40 A.M. a black sedan cruised down the street. Nagasaki halted in front of a bulletin board by the building's entrance. He studied the announcements as a short, balding man with thick-framed glasses emerged from the car. As Shoriki began to climb the stairs into the building, Nagasaki strode forward, pulling a short samurai sword from beneath his coat. The blade flashed through the air, striking Shoriki's head. The bloodied newspaper owner stumbled forward, as Nagasaki fled.[2]

Later that day, Nagasaki walked into a local police station and gave a detailed confession. The primary reason for the assassination attempt: Shoriki had defiled the memory of the Meiji Emperor by allowing Babe Ruth and his team of American all-stars to play in the stadium named in honor of the ruler.

Three months earlier, nearly a half-million Japanese had lined the streets of Tokyo to welcome the ballplayers to Japan. The players' motorcade was led by Ruth in an open limousine. At 39, he had grown rotund, and just weeks before had agreed to part ways with

The 1934 All-Americans outside Nagoya Castle (Yoko Suzuki Collection)

the New York Yankees. But to the Japanese, he still represented the pinnacle of the baseball world. Sharing the car was his former teammate Lou Gehrig. The rest of the All-American baseball team, distributed three or four per car, followed: manager Connie Mack, Jimmie Foxx, Earl Averill, Charlie Gehringer, Lefty Gomez, Lefty O'Doul, and a gaggle of lesser-known stars.

Only one player didn't seem to belong – a journeyman catcher with a .238 career batting average named Moe Berg. Although he was not an All-Star caliber player, his off-the-field skills would explain his inclusion on the team. Berg was a Princeton University and Columbia Law School graduate who had already visited Japan in 1932. He was multilingual, causing a teammate to joke that Berg could speak a dozen languages but couldn't hit in any of them. Berg would eventually become an operative for the Office of Strategic Services (OSS), the forerunner of the CIA, and many believe that the 1934 trip to Japan was his first mission as a spy.

The pressing crowd reduced the broad streets to narrow paths just wide enough for the limousines to pass. Confetti and streamers fluttered down from multistoried office buildings, as thousands waved Japanese and American flags and cheered wildly. "Banzai! Banzai, Babe Ruth!" echoed through the neighborhood. Reveling in the attention, the Bambino plucked flags from the crowd and stood in the back of the car waving a Japanese flag in his left hand and an American in his right. Finally, the crowd couldn't contain itself and rushed into the street to be closer to the Babe. Traffic stood still for hours as Ruth shook hands with the multitude.[3]

Ruth and his teammates stayed in Japan for a month, playing 18 games in 12 cities. But there was more at stake than sport: Japan and the United States were slipping toward war as the two nations vied for control over China and naval supremacy in the Pacific. Politically Japan was in turmoil. From the 1880s through 1920s, Japan had enjoyed a form of democracy. This period saw great strides in modernization, a flourishing of the arts, and close ties to the United States. Yet, as Japan's power grew, so did its nationalism. A growing minority of Japanese citizens felt that the country should take its place among the world powers by expanding its military and colonizing its neighbors. Ultranationalist societies began assassinating liberal politicians and members of the free press. By the early 1930s, the civilian government could no longer control elements of the military. In 1931 nationalistic officers engineered the invasion of

Manchuria and twice plotted to overthrow the government. War between the United States and Japan seemed inevitable.

Politicians on both sides of the Pacific hoped that the goodwill generated by the tour and the two nations' shared love of baseball could help heal their growing political differences. Many observers, therefore, considered the all-stars' joyous reception significant. An article in the *New York Times*, for example, said, "The Babe's big bulk today blotted out such unimportant things as international squabbles over oil and navies."[4] Connie Mack added that the tour was "one of the greatest peace measures in the history of nations."[5]

Yet, not all Japanese wished the nations reunited. At the Imperial Japanese Army Academy, just two miles northwest of the parade, a group known as the Young Officers was planning a bloody coup d'etat, an upheaval that would jeopardize the tour's success and put the players' lives at risk. In another section of Tokyo, Nagasaki and his ultranationalist War Gods Society met at their dojo. Their actions would tarnish the tour with bloodshed.

The 1934 tour began not as a diplomatic mission but as a publicity stunt to attract readers to the *Yomiuri Shimbun*. Matsutaro Shoriki had purchased the financially troubled newspaper in 1924 and quickly turned it into Tokyo's third-largest daily by increasing its entertainment sections.[6]

In 1931 Shoriki decided to bolster sports coverage by sponsoring a team of American all-stars to play in Japan. The team, which included Lou Gehrig, Lefty Grove, and five other future Hall of Famers, won each of the 17 games against Japanese university and amateur teams, and the newspaper's circulation soared. But Shoriki wasn't satisfied. The major-league team had lacked the greatest drawing card in baseball – Babe Ruth.

Shoriki immediately began organizing a second tour. Working closely with Sotaro Suzuki, a sportswriter who had lived in New York for nearly a decade, and National League batting champion Lefty O'Doul, Shoriki lined up the powerful 1934 squad. Most of the players' wives accompanied their husbands on the trip, and the Ruths brought along their 18-year-old daughter, Julia. The tourists boarded the luxury liner *Empress of Japan* in Vancouver, British Columbia, on October 20 and, after a stop in Honolulu, arrived in Yokohama on November 2.

Although American teachers had introduced baseball in 1872, Japan didn't have a professional league. To challenge the Americans, Shoriki brought together

Japan's best amateur players to form the All-Nippon team. The team included 11 future members of the Japanese Baseball Hall of Fame and numerous colorful personalities.

Two players, in particular, stood out. The first was hard to miss: 18-year-old Victor Starffin was the blond-haired, blue-eyed, 6-foot-3 son of a Russian military officer who had served Czar Nicholas II. During the Russian Revolution, the Starffins escaped by traveling in a freight train packed with typhoid patients, and later by hiding from the Red Army in a truck carrying corpses. After years on the run, the family settled in Japan. Young Victor fell in love with baseball and soon became a regional star. He hoped to play college ball, but in 1933 his father was convicted of killing a young Russian woman who worked in his teashop. The Yomiuri newspaper promised to use its influence to help Victor's father if the young man would forsake college and play for the All-Nippon team.[7]

The All-Nippon squad also included a young American who hoped to become the first ethnic Japanese to make the major leagues. Jimmy Horio was born in Hawaii and left for California to follow his dreams at the age of 20. He played semipro for several years without breaking into Organized Baseball. Hearing that Shoriki was creating a team to challenge the visiting major leaguers, Horio traveled to Tokyo to try out. He hoped a stellar performance against the All-Americans would lead to a major-league contract. As a switch-hitter with power, Horio made the All-Nippon team easily and hit cleanup, but would fail to impress the Americans.[8]

Over the next four weeks, the All-Americans and All-Nippon traveled together throughout Japan, visiting the northern island of Hokkaido; the industrial cities of Yokohama, Nagoya, and Osaka; the ancient capital of Kyoto; Kokura on the southern island of Kyushu; and, of course, Tokyo.

The tour began with two games at Tokyo's Meiji Jingu Stadium. Prior to the games, fans camped out overnight to secure the best general-admission seats. They followed the Babe's every move. A reporter stated, "The fans went crazy each time Ruth did anything – smiled, sneezed, or dropped a ball."[9] One old man brought a pair of high-powered binoculars, amusing himself and neighboring fans by focusing on the Bambino's famous broad nose, making his nostrils fill the lens.[10] Another fan, who worked in a textile factory designing kimono and undergarment patterns, had a novel plan. He would sit as close as possible to the field and study the Bambino's face. He would

memorize every feature, every wrinkle. Then he would return to the factory and create a pattern of the Babe's face for a new line of Babe Ruth underwear. He was certain he would become rich.[11]

The Babe relished the attention and transformed into a comedian. During batting practice, he purposely missed some pitches – twisting himself around like a pretzel before falling over. Later, he began a game of shadow ball – hitting an imaginary grounder to Rabbit McNair at shortstop, who fielded it convincingly and started a double play, timed with perfect realism. The opening game itself was less interesting than Ruth's antics. It pitted the All-Americans against the Tokyo Club, a team of recently graduated players from the Tokyo area, not the All-Nippon squad. It took just a few minutes for the fans, and players, to realize the difference in skill level between the two teams – the ball even sounded louder when coming off the American bats. The Americans seemed to score at will, pilling up 17 runs to Tokyo's 1. To the crowd's disappointment, none of the Americans hit a home run. Afterward, the Babe apologized for not going deep, telling reporters, "I was a little tired today, but tomorrow I will do my best to hit a home run."[12]

The next day, November 4, the All-Americans played their first game against All-Nippon. It was the first time in history that true all-star teams representing the two countries clashed. Prior to the 1930s, visiting American professional teams were a mishmash of stars, journeymen, and minor-league players, and while the 1931 American club was a legitimate all-star team, it played only Japanese collegiate and company squads. The All-Nippon lineup featured six future Hall of Famers – Naotaka Makino, Hisanori Karita, Osamu Mihara, Minoru Yamashita, Jiro Kuji, and pitcher Masao Date. Although Date pitched "courageously," and limited the All-Americans to five runs, the game's outcome seemed inevitable.[13] Jimmie Foxx, Lou Gehrig, and Earl Averill homered, with Averill going out twice. On the other side of the scorecard, American pitcher Joe Cascarella dominated the Japanese, giving up just three hits and walking only two.

Next, the All-Americans traveled north. As they boarded a ferry to cross the straits to reach Hokkaido, officials handed each traveler a small map with three coastal areas circled in red. Large cursive writing proclaimed, "Photographing, sketching, surveying, recording, flying over the fortified zone, without the authorization of the commanding officer of this fortress are strictly prohibited by order." The handout was not an empty threat. Japan was paranoid about espionage, and officials even inspected Ruth during the trip to make sure that he wasn't taking photographs. But neither the proscription nor the officials stopped Moe Berg. Defying the warning, Berg whipped out his camera and filmed the area.[14]

The teams played two games in the northern provinces, enduring bone-chilling winds and frosted fields. Once again, the Americans won comfortably. On November 8 in Hakodate, the All-Americans took control of the game minutes after the first pitch as Averill hit a two-out, first-inning grand slam. Meanwhile, Lefty Gomez dazzled the fans and opponents with both his speed and control. Up 5-1, manager Ruth brought in third baseman Jimmie Foxx to close out the game. The burly third baseman preserved the victory by allowing just one run in the final three innings. The following day in Sendai, Ruth went deep twice and Gehrig, Foxx, and Bing Miller each hit one out in a 7-0 American victory.

As the teams returned to Tokyo, two dozen army officers met at an isolated restaurant. Their purpose – to overthrow the Japanese government.

The Great Depression had hit rural Japan particularly hard, leading to widespread starvation. At the same time, large trading companies, known as *zaibatsu*, flourished due to the unstable markets and rampant inflation. The conspirators, led by Captain Koji Muranaka, belonged to the loosely organized Young Officers movement. The Young Officers felt that Japan's government had betrayed its citizens by putting the interests of big business before the welfare of the populace. The group advocated the violent overthrow of civilian rule, the declaration of martial law, and the Emperor taking direct control of the government. The divine Emperor, they believed, would end rural poverty by redistributing wealth and would lead Japan to world prominence by conquering Asia.[15]

On November 27 Japan's parliament would meet in a special session. Once the politicians gathered, the Young Officers and their troops planned to attack the Diet Building, slaughter the civilian government, and seize power. Other sympathetic troops would battle loyalist regiments in the streets of Tokyo. No mention was made of Babe Ruth and the ballplayers, but as the Imperial Hotel faced the Emperor's palace and was just a few blocks from the Diet Building, Muranaka's plan put the Americans in the line of fire.[16]

Meanwhile, the ballclubs stayed in the Tokyo area for 10 days, playing six games, attending banquets, and visiting the local tourist spots. The games were one-sided. The All-Americans won all six comfortably, scoring 60 runs while surrendering 12. The highlight came on November 10 at Meiji Jingu Stadium when Lefty Gomez, the man who claimed to have invented a rotating goldfish bowl to allow tired fish to rest, struck out 18 batters and pitched seven no-hit innings before surrendering two singles during a 10-0 American romp. A week later, on the 17th, All-Nippon grabbed their first lead of the tour by scoring three runs in the second inning. But tiny Shinji Hamazaki, the 5-foot-1 former star hurler from Keio University, could not contain the American lineup. Gehrig homered to lead off the third inning and Foxx followed with the longest home run in the history of Meiji Jingu Stadium. The ball landed three-quarters up the high left-field bleachers, bounced once, and careened out of the stadium into the empty lot below. The All-Americans tacked on 13 additional runs off poor Hamazaki, who was left on the mound to suffer for the entire game. During the romp, Foxx played all nine positions and the portly Ruth even took a turn at shortstop.[17]

Throughout the tour, players and fans noted the differences between American and Japanese baseball. The two teams played and approached the game differently. Just as modern American baseball reflects its roots as a nineteenth-century urban game popularized during a time of industrialization, rapid economic growth, and mass immigration, the Japanese game, known as *yakyu*, reflects its origins in the cultural turmoil of the early Meiji period.

In the late 1880s, Japan struggled to establish its national identity. During the previous two decades it had transformed from a medieval society into a modern country with radically new political, economic, educational, and even social institutions. Many Japanese feared that the country was losing its native culture and abandoning time-honored traditions and values in favor of shallow materialism and frivolous Western fads. These concerns led to the philosophy of *wakon yosai* (meaning Japanese spirit, Western technology), the concept that Japan could import Western technology, institutions, and even ideas, but would imbue them with Japanese spirit. This philosophy may be illustrated best in baseball.

Although American teachers introduced baseball in the early 1870s, the distinctive approach that would characterize Japanese baseball for over 100 years developed in the early 1890s at Japan's elite First Higher School, often called Ichiko. Following the concept of *wakon yosai*, the Ichiko players approached baseball as a martial art. "Sports came from the West," a team member later explained. "In Ichiko baseball, we were playing sports but we were also putting the spirit of Japan into it. ... Yakyu is a way to express the samurai spirit."[18]

Ichiko's brand of baseball, known as Spirit Baseball, emphasized unquestioning loyalty to the team as well as long hours of grueling practice to improve the players' skills and mental endurance. Proponents of Spirit Baseball argued that a strong spirit could overcome physical shortcomings and lead to victory on the field. Thus, practices were designed to not only hone skills but also to develop mental fortitude through long, difficult drills that pushed players to their limits.[19] Spirit Baseball offered hope to the All-Nippon team. Infielder Tokio Tominaga told reporters, "Many fans think that the small Japanese can never compete with the larger Americans, but I disagree. The Japanese are equal to the Americans in strength of spirit."[20]

On November 20 a 17-year-old Japanese pitcher's spirit was nearly strong enough to conquer the All-Americans. Aided by the midday sun in the batters' eyes, Eiji Sawamura pitched the game of his life in the small town of Shizuoka at the foot of Mt. Fuji. He recorded 11 straight outs, including consecutive strikeouts of Gehringer, Ruth, Gehrig, and Foxx, before the Bambino broke up his no-hitter. The shutout continued until Gehrig homered in the seventh to give the Americans a 1-0 victory.[21]

The next morning, as the Japanese unfurled their newspapers and read the headlines, Sawamura became a national hero. Although the Japanese had not won, they showed that they were capable of conquering their opponents. The game would become a symbol of Japan's struggles against the West. Many Japanese felt that with enough fighting spirit and practice, their countrymen could surpass the major leaguers, just as they believed their military would surpass the Western powers. As years passed, the importance of the game grew and Sawamura's stature increased as he became a symbol of Imperial Japan. Today, Japan's annual

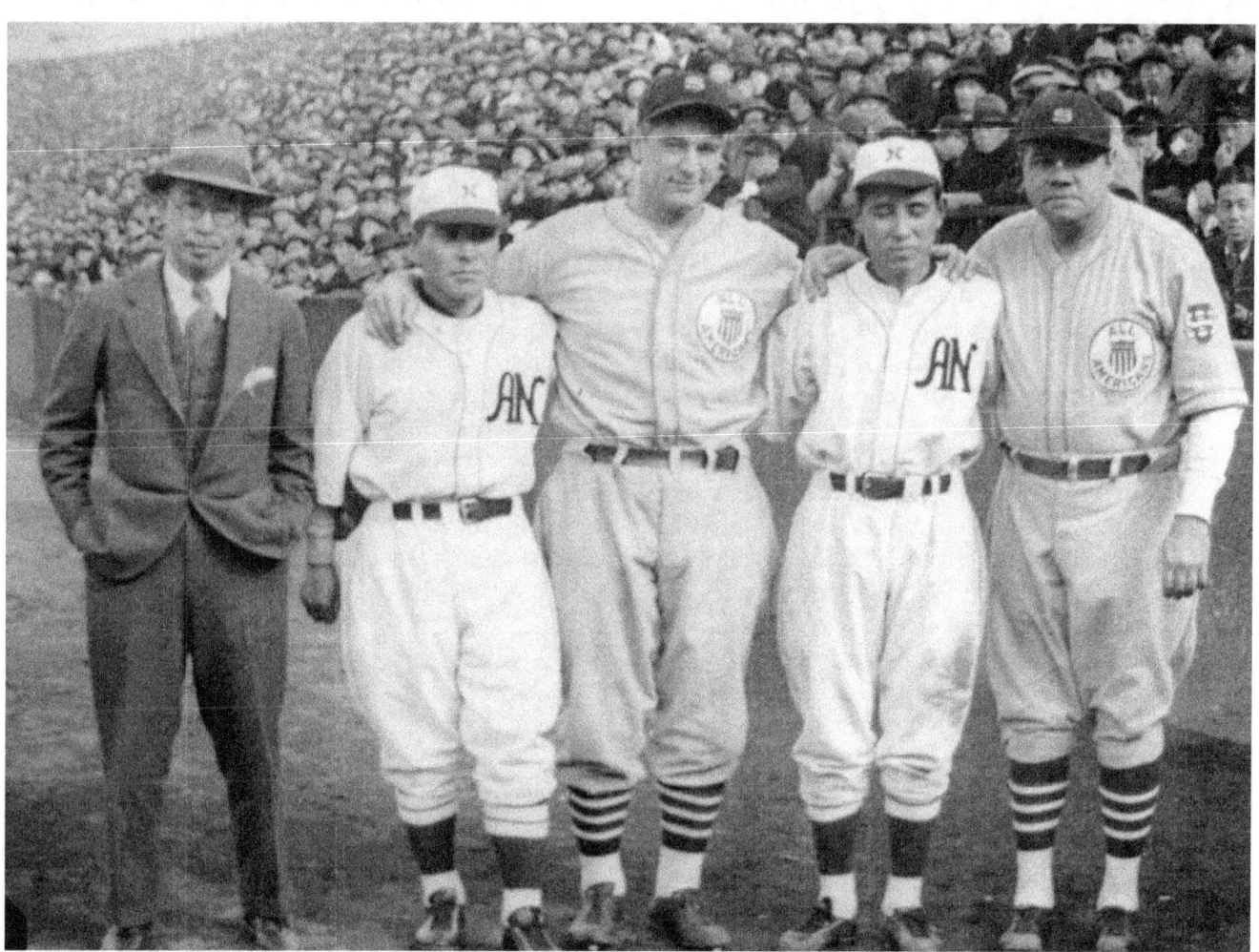

Sotaro Suzuki, unidentified All-Nippon player, Lou Gehrig, Hisanori Karita, and Babe Ruth (Yoko Suzuki Collection)

award for the best pitcher is called the Sawamura Award.

By November 20, Captain Koji Muranaka's plans to seize control of Japan were almost ready. The special session of parliament was due to convene in seven days. Knowing that previous coup attempts had been betrayed from the inside, Muranaka had kept his group of assassins small. But Muranaka had not scrutinized his followers closely enough. Suspicious of Muranaka, the commander of the military academy had instructed a cadet to infiltrate the group and expose their plans.[22]

The same day as Eiji Sawamura pitched his masterpiece, the Kempeitai, Japan's dreaded military police, arrested Muranaka and his conspirators. News of the plot remained hidden until the Tokyo War Crimes Tribunal in 1946. Only a handful of men knew that bloodshed, revolt, and maybe even civil war, had nearly disrupted the All-American baseball tour.

Sawamura's pitching masterpiece gave the All-Nippon confidence as the two teams embarked on an eight-day, six-game junket in southern Japan. Their thousand-mile journey included stops in Nagoya, Osaka, Kokura, and Kyoto.

At Nagoya, the Japanese once again nearly upset the Americans, entering the bottom of the eighth with a 5-3 lead. Japanese starter Masao Date was visibly tired, but manager Daisuke Miyake elected to leave him in as the All-Americans scored three runs to take a 6-5 lead. Perhaps to give the All-Nippon a chance to win, the All-Americans brought in Jimmie Foxx to pitch the ninth. With one out, Isamu Fuma tripled into the right-center alley to put the tying run just 90 feet away. Osamu Mihara, Waseda's former star second baseman, was due up next. Mihara had just one hit and five strikeouts in 14 at-bats against the Americans, so Miyake decided to bring in the 5-foot-1 pitcher Shinji Hamazaki to pinch-hit. Hamazaki was not inept with the bat. When not pitching for Keio University, he played the outfield and had hit .308 during the 1927 Big Six season. But still, it seems a strange choice. The All-Americans brought the infield in to defend against the squeeze and also prevent Fuma from scoring on a groundball. Hamazaki swung away and struck out. Mamoru Sugitaya, a solid outfielder with seven hits against the major leaguers, popped out to second to end the game. Both Lou Gehrig and the *Japan Times* criticized Miyake's managerial decisions. Each felt that the Japanese might have won the game had Miyake brought in Sawamura in the eighth inning or had tried a squeeze play to score Fuma in the ninth.[23] After the two close games, the All-Americans increased their focus and won the remaining six games easily with a combined score of 80-17.[24]

The November 26 game in Kokura provided one of the most enduring images of the tour. Driving rain had made the condition of the field laughable. Ankle-deep mud covered the dirt infield and pond-like puddles dotted the outfield. Normally, the game would have been canceled, but between 20,000 and 30,000 fans had squeezed into the tiny stadium to watch the American stars. Despite the rain, they had begun to arrive early in the morning, filling the seats hours before game time. The outfield contained no bleachers, just a grassy slope where spectators huddled together. The rains had flooded the area and 11,000 squatted or knelt with water up to their hips. Among the dedicated, wet fans sat a man with an ancient samurai sword. He had walked 80 miles to attend the game and announced that he would present the sword as a token of friendship to the first American to hit a home run.[25]

The game itself was a joke. Ruth, Gehrig, Averill, and Rabbit McNair played in rubber boots and Ruth – borrowing an umbrella from a fan – huddled under it while playing first base. The score remained 0-0 for the first three innings before the Americans started to hit. Three runs came across in the fourth and Averill won the sword by hitting a long fly into the soggy fans sitting beyond right field. An inning later with the bases loaded, Ruth stepped to the plate and dug in with his big rubber boots. The crowd laughed and began chanting, "Home Run! Home run!" According to Osamu Mihara, after the count went to 3-and-0, Ruth stepped out of the batter's box and gestured to the fans that he would hit a home run. Shinji Hamazaki threw the next pitch down the middle and the Sultan of Swat connected with a mighty swing. The ball rose in a majestic arc and sailed over the right-field seating area and into the mist beyond. Initially stunned by the blast, the wet and happy fans erupted with a "tremendous ovation" for the Bambino.[26] The All-Americans ended with 11 hits and eight runs, but the *Osaka Mainichi* noted that "they can hit almost at will" and would have hit many more "had they cared to run out every hit."[27] On the mound, Cascarella dominated the Japanese hitters with "baffling hooks and drops" as he scattered seven hits and gave up a single run for the 8-1 victory.[28]

Throughout the tour, Moe Berg left the group to explore on his own. Wherever he went, he took numerous pictures.

On November 29 Berg informed Connie Mack that he felt unwell and would miss the afternoon's game.

Immediately after the team left for the Omiya ballpark, Berg dressed in a black kimono, combed his hair in a Japanese style, and put on geta (traditional wooden sandals). It was just above freezing outside, so he probably slipped on an Inverness overcoat, concealed his 16-millimeter movie camera beneath it, and quietly left the hotel. He headed southeast through Ginza to St. Luke's International Hospital, a tall structure with panoramic views of Tokyo.[29]

Pretending to visit the American ambassador's daughter, Berg took the elevator to the top floor and climbed the spiraling staircase to the top of St. Luke's 50-meter-tall tower. There, he pulled out his movie camera and panned the skyline, holding the camera still on a group of factories to the west and again on the waterfront. To cap off the footage, he focused on Mt. Fuji, just visible on the southwestern horizon.

During World War II, Berg became a spy for the OSS. He was even sent on a mission to assassinate Werner Heisenberg, the leading German physicist, if he had evidence that Heisenberg was close to creating an atomic weapon. Many believe that the trip to Japan was Berg's first mission as a spy.[30] But in truth, there is no evidence to support this claim other than Berg's bizarre behavior.[31] Personally, I believe that the 1934 Japan trip was a pivotal point in Berg's espionage career. Not because it was his first mission, but because it sowed the seeds for his future career as a spy. It was while shooting clandestine pictures in Asia for the thrill that Berg realized his true calling.

By staying in Tokyo, Berg missed an opportunity to beef up his paltry .111 batting average. The ballpark at Omiya was small, holding just 8,000 spectators, with short outfield fences. The All-Americans wasted little time as they crashed home run after home run. By the end of the first, they were up 10-0. The barrage continued and with the Japanese down 23-5 in the bottom of the eighth, Miyake brought in 18-year-old Victor Starffin for his first, and only, appearance in the series. The young Russian was wild at first, walking Lou Gehrig and later Earl Averill, but both his fastball and curve were working well, and he struck out Jimmie Foxx between the two walks and induced Bing Miller to ground into a double play to end the inning. In all, the All-Americans hit 10 home runs — three by Gehringer, two apiece by Ruth and pitcher Earl Whitehill, and one each by Foxx, Gehrig, and catcher Frank Hayes.

The All-Americans played their last game on Japanese soil in Utsunomiya, a small city 60 miles north of Tokyo, on December 1. In recognition of his untiring efforts throughout the tour, Ruth named Sotaro Suzuki as the game's manager. Suzuki was apprehensive as national hero Eiji Sawamura would start for All-Nippon. If the young hurler pitched well and the Americans relaxed and lost, people would blame him. The day was cold, so Suzuki set up a charcoal burner in the dugout for warmth. His apprehension grew as fans passed the Americans sake bottles and the ballplayers, who had adapted well to Japanese drinking customs, heated the liquor over the burner. Despite the alcohol, and a dropped fly ball by an inebriated Earl Averill, Suzuki had little to worry about. The Americans pounded out nine runs in the first four innings and the All-Americans went home 14-5 winners.[32]

On December 2 thousands of flag-waving fans crowded into Tokyo's Ueno Station to say adieu. "Goodbye, Goodbye!" they shouted as Ruth sniffled and yelled "Sayonara, Sayonara! Banzai Japan!" Averill wept openly while Gehrig yelled, "See you again soon!" As the train readied for departure, the crowd quieted to hear Ruth's final speech, "I don't know how to show my appreciation, but if I have a chance I will come back," he concluded.[33] The train took the players to Kobe, where they boarded the *Empress of Canada*. They stopped briefly in Shanghai for a game against local all-stars, before finishing the tour with three games in Manila.

The success of the 1934 tour surprised American observers. Connie Mack found the Japanese "crazy about the great national game of America."[34] Capitalizing on the tour's success, Shoriki kept the All-Nippon team intact and organized the professional Japanese Baseball League. Shoriki's squad, renamed the Tokyo Yomiuri Giants, barnstormed in North America in 1935 and 1936, and went on to dominate the Japanese league for decades.

As the All-Americans left Japan, Americans and moderate Japanese proclaimed the goodwill tour a diplomatic success. Prince Iyesato Tokugawa, a direct descendant of the shogun who had united Japan in 1603, stated, "Between two great peoples able really to understand and enjoy baseball there are no national differences which cannot be solved in a spirit of sportsmanship."[35]

According to *The Sporting News*, Connie Mack summed up the consensus when he said that the trip did "more for better understanding between Japanese and Americans than all the diplomatic exchanges ever accomplished."[36] Furthermore, Mack assured listeners "that there would be no war between the United States and Japan."[37]

The Sporting News added, "[W]e believe that the recent trip to the Orient of baseball's finest has served to delay, if not prevent, any possible conflict. We like to believe that countries having such a common interest in a great sport would rather fight it out on the diamond than on the battle field."[38]

It did not take long, however, for that feeling to vanish.

Several weeks after the ballplayers departed on the *Empress of Canada,* Japan pulled out of the Washington Naval Treaty, which had limited the size of the major powers' navies. Two months later, Katsusuke Nagasaki attacked Shoriki. Details of Captain Koji Muranaka's failed coup were not made public, but a military tribunal held in March 1935 let the rebels off with a six-month suspension from active duty.

A year later, on February 26, 1936, Muranaka joined 23 other Young Officers in a violent rebellion that assassinated several high-ranking government officials and narrowly missed the prime minister. Rival military units crushed the rebels and arrested their leaders. Nineteen, including Muranaka, were executed. Despite the coup's failure, the events led to a series of civilian governments more sympathetic to the military's nationalist agenda.[39] In July 1937 Japan invaded China. Whatever hope there had been for reconciliation between the United States and Japan vanished. Ultimately, the two countries' love for baseball could not overcome Japan's desire for regional dominance.

During the war, the military seized control of professional baseball. The fascists outlawed English baseball terms and redesigned uniforms to imitate military styles. Many members of the All-Nippon team served in the military and several, including Eiji Sawamura, lost their lives. Instead of chanting "Banzai Babe Ruth," Japanese infantry screamed "To hell with Babe Ruth!" as they charged to their deaths in the jungles of the South Pacific.[40]

Yet, the goodwill tour was not a complete failure. Several of the friendships cemented during the 1934 visit survived the war and helped reconcile the two nations. Lefty O'Doul, who remained close to both Shoriki and Sotaro Suzuki, traveled to Japan at his own expense in 1946 to renew the friendships and help restart Japanese baseball. Three years later, O'Doul organized the first of several baseball tours held during the Allied occupation. Once again, baseball was used as a diplomatic tool to help bring the nations closer together, but this time with lasting success.[41]

1934 ALL-AMERICAN GAMES IN JAPAN

Date	Place	Opponent	Score	Winner	Loser
November 3	Tokyo	Tokyo	17-1	Whitehill	Takahashi
November 4	Tokyo	All-Nippon	5-1	Cascarella	Date
November 8	Hakodate	All-Nippon	5-2	Gomez	Aoshiba
November 9	Sendai	All-Nippon	7-0	Whitehill	Takeda
November 10	Tokyo	All-Nippon	10-0	Gomez	Sawamura
November 11	Tokyo	Ruth vs. Miller	13-2	Brown	Cascarella
November 13	Toyama	All-Nippon	14-0	Whitehill	Mizuhara
November 17	Tokyo	All-Nippon	15-6	Brown	Hamazaki
November 18	Yokohama	All-Nippon	21-4	Gomez	Aoshiba
November 20	Shizuoka	All-Nippon	1-0	Whitehill	Sawamura
November 22	Nagoya	All-Nippon	6-5	Cascarella	Date
November 23	Nagoya	All-Nippon	6-2	Gomez	Takeda
November 24	Osaka	All-Nippon	5-3	Whitehill	Date
November 25	Osaka	Miller vs. Ruth	5-1	Brown	Aoshiba
November 26	Kokura	All-Nippon	8-1	Cascarella	Hamazaki
November 28	Kyoto	All-Nippon	14-1	Gomez	Sawamura
November 29	Omiya	All-Nippon	23-5	Whitehill	Takeda
December 1	Utsunomiya	All-Nippon	14-5	Brown	Sawamura

1934 ALL-AMERICAN TOUR BATTING AND PITCHING STATISTICS

All-American Batting Statistics	BA	G	AB	R	H	2B	3B	HR	RBI	SO	BB	SB
Eric McNair	.354	18	82	22	29	9	0	0	11	5	5	1
Charlie Gehringer	.288	18	80	24	23	3	1	4	21	1	13	1
Babe Ruth	.408	18	76	27	31	3	0	13	33	7	13	1
Earl Averill	.378	18	74	23	28	4	0	8	29	7	15	1
Bing Miller	.375	18	72	18	27	5	0	4	18	2	7	0
Lou Gehrig	.310	18	71	25	22	5	1	6	18	4	13	2
Jimmie Foxx	.286	17	63	19	18	2	0	7	14	15	11	1
Frank Hayes	.226	14	53	12	12	2	0	1	8	10	10	1
Harold Warstler	.267	12	30	6	8	0	0	1	2	8	6	1
Earl Whitehill	.458	9	24	9	11	1	0	3	11	6	2	0
Moe Berg	.111	6	18	4	2	1	0	0	3	1	1	0
Lefty Gomez	.412	6	17	3	7	1	0	0	2	2	3	0
Joe Cascarella	.200	6	15	1	3	0	0	0	0	3	0	0
Clint Brown	.250	5	12	0	3	0	0	0	1	3	0	0

NICHIBEI YAKYU: US TOURS OF JAPAN

All-Nippon Batting Statistics	BA	G	AB	R	H	2B	3B	HR	RBI	SO	BB	SB
Hisanori Karita	.276	16	58	6	16	3	0	0	2	1	5	3
Kumeyasu Yajima	.295	14	44	4	13	2	1	0	2	8	4	1
Jimmy Horio	.195	15	41	4	8	0	0	1	1	6	4	0
Osamu Mihara	.158	11	38	4	6	1	0	0	2	8	2	5
Mamoru Sugitaya	.222	12	36	2	8	2	0	0	3	3	1	0
Saburo Shintomi	.167	13	36	6	6	1	1	1	5	3	4	0
Haruyasu Nakajima	.222	12	36	2	8	2	0	0	3	3	1	0
Isamu Fuma	.294	11	34	2	10	1	3	0	5	9	3	0
Fujio Nagasawa	.226	11	31	1	7	0	0	0	2	1	5	3
Toshiharu Inokawa	.348	11	23	3	8	1	0	1	1	1	0	0
Shigeru Mizuhara	.095	10	21	2	2	1	0	0	3	3	1	0
Minoru Yamashita	.158	7	19	3	3	1	0	0	1	2	0	0
Jiro Kuji	.056	7	18	0	1	0	0	0	0	1	1	0
Tokio Tominaga	.333	4	12	1	4	0	0	0	1	2	1	0
Kenichi Aoshiba	.167	6	12	1	2	0	0	0	0	2	2	0
Shinji Hamasaki	.273	9	11	0	3	1	0	0	0	2	0	0
Eichiro Yamamoto	.100	7	10	1	1	0	1	0	1	2	0	0
Motonobu Makino	.000	4	10	0	0	0	0	0	0	3	2	0
Masao Date	.444	5	9	0	4	1	1	0	0	2	1	0
Nobuo Kura	.182	4	8	1	1	0	0	0	0	1	0	0
Tokue Ihara	.429	4	7	0	3	0	0	0	0	2	0	0
Eiji Sawamura	.000	5	7	0	0	0	0	0	0	5	2	0
Kaichi Takeda	.000	3	7	1	0	0	0	0	0	2	1	0
Nobuaki Nidegawa	.000	3	7	0	0	0	0	0	0	2	0	0
Takenosuke Murai	.333	3	6	2	0	0	0	0	0	1	0	0
Hisashi Asakura	.400	2	5	0	2	0	0	0	1	2	0	0
Eibin Ri	.200	6	5	1	0	0	0	0	0	2	1	0
Yukio Eguchi	.000	1	2	0	0	0	0	0	0	2	1	0
Victor Starffin	.000	1	0	0	0	0	0	0	0	0	0	0

All-American Pitching Statistics	ERA	G	W	L	IP	H	HR	SO	BB	R	ER
Earl Whitehill	1.41	6	6	0	51	32	1	30	10	9	8
Lefty Gomez	1.47	6	5	0	43	29	1	34	21	8	7
Joe Cascarella	4.62	5	3	1	39	49	4	26	8	21	20
Clint Brown	2.73	5	4	0	33	18	0	7	9	12	10
Jimmie Foxx	1.50	3	0	0	6	6	0	5	1	2	1

All-Nippon Pitching Statistics	ERA	G	W	L	IP	H	HR	SO	BB	R	ER
Kenichi Aoshiba	7.83	6	0	3	33.1	49	8	17	25	39	29
Eiji Sawamura	7.85	6	0	4	28.2	33	8	25	25	34	25
Shinji Hamasaki	9.23	7	0	2	26.1	33	9	10	14	37	27
Kaichi Takeda	13.73	3	0	3	19.2	41	13	5	11	32	30
Masao Date	7.00	3	0	3	18	27	4	6	11	16	14
Shigeru Mizuhara	30.00	1	0	1	3	8	2	2	3	10	7
Victor Starffin	0.00	1	0	0	1	0	0	1	2	0	0

NOTES

1   Adapted from Robert K. Fitts, "Murder, Espionage, and Baseball: The 1934 All-American Tour of Japan," *NINE: A Journal of Baseball History and Culture* Volume 21, No. 1 (Fall 2012): 1-11, by permission of the University of Nebraska Press.

2   Details from Nagasaki's attack on Shoriki are drawn from Shinichi Sano, *Kyo-kaiden: A Century of Matsutaro Shoriki and His Kagemushas* [in Japanese] (Tokyo: Bungei Shunju, 1994); Associated Press, "'Patriot' Stabs Noted Publisher in Tokyo for Sponsoring Babe Ruth's Tour in Japan," *New York Times*, February 22, 1935: 1; "President of Yomiuri Attacked and Injured," *Osaka Mainichi*, February 23, 1935: 2; "Slashed by Sword, Yomiuri President Victim of Attack," *Japan Times*, February 23, 1935: 1-2; *Yomiuri Shimbun*, February 23, 1935: 1. Shoriki survived the attack and after 50 days in a hospital returned to work.

3   Stuart Bell, "Japan Belongs to Babe," *Cleveland Press*, November 23, 1934: 44; "Babe Ruth Comes with Strong U.S. Baseball Team," *Japan Times*, November 2, 1934: 1-2.

4   Associated Press, "Tokyo Gives Ruth Royal Welcome," *New York Times*, November 3, 1934: 9.

5   "Mack Hails Ruth as Peace Promoter," *New York Times*, January 6, 1935: s7.

6   Edward Uhlan and Dana L. Thomas, *Shoriki: Miracle Man of Japan* (New York: Exposition Press, 1957).

7   Natasha Starffin, *Glory and Dream on a White Ball: My Father V. Starffin* [in Japanese] (Tokyo: Baseball Magazine, 1979); John Berry, *The Gaijin Pitcher: The Life and Times of Victor Starffin* (LaVergne, Tennessee: CreateSpace, 2010).

8   Yoichi Nagata, *Jimmy Horio and U.S./Japan Baseball: A Social History of Baseball* [in Japanese] (Osaka: Toho Shuppan, 1994).

9   Naoki Fujio, "1934 Tour," *Yakyukai* 25, no. 3 (1935): 184.

10 Fujio.

11 "Baseball Battle U.S.-Japan Madness!" *Yomiuri Shimbun*, November 5, 1934: 3.

12 "Baseball Battle U.S.-Japan Madness!"

13 Associated Press, "U.S. Stars Hit 4 Home Runs in Japan; Idolized Ruth Fails," *Washington Post*, November 6, 1934: 17.

14 John Quinn, 1934 Tour Scrapbook, private collection.

15 This simplified summary of the Young Officers' position is based on Delmer Brown, *Nationalism in Japan* (Berkeley: University of California Press, 1955); Ben-Ami Shillony, *Revolt in Japan* (Princeton: Princeton University Press, 1973); and Christopher W.A. Szpilman, "Kita Ikki and the Politics of Coercion," *Modern Asian Studies* 36, no. 2 (May 2002): 467-90.

16 Details of Muranaka's plans are based on accounts written after World War II. For a discussion of the 1934 plan see H.G. Schenck, *The Brocade Banner: The Story of Japanese Nationalism* (Washington: General HQ Far East Command Military Intelligence Section, 1946), 67-68; Shillony, 45-46; Royal Jules Wald, *The Young Officers Movement in Japan, ca. 1925-1937: Ideology and Actions* (Ann Arbor: University Microfilms, 1949), 168-69.

17 "Americans Rout All-Japan Nine; Ruth Hits Homers," *Japan Times*, November 18, 1934: 1.

18 Quoted from the introduction of *Yakyu Bushi Fukisoku Dai Ichi Koto Gakko Koyukai* (Tokyo, 1903), translated by Robert Whiting and reprinted in Whiting, *The Samurai Way of Baseball* (New York: Warner Books, 2005), 6.

19 Robert Whiting, "The Samurai Way of Baseball and the National Character Debate," *The Asian-Pacific Journal: Japan Focus* (September 2006).

20 Tokio Tominaga "Interview," *Yakyukai* 25, no. 1 (1935): 138.

21 "Americans Beat All-Japan Nine By 1-0 Score," *Japan Times*, November 21, 1934: 5; "Sawamura Permits Americans 1 Run," *Osaka Mainichi*, November 21, 1934: 3; Sotaro Suzuki, *Sawamura Eiji: The Eternal Great Pitcher* [in Japanese] (Tokyo: Kobunsha, 1982), 75-77; Eiji Sawamura, "Interview," *Yakyukai* 25, no. 1 (1935): 160-61; "Big Pitcher Battle," *Yomiuri Shimbun*, November 20, 1934: 5.

22 Details of how the plot was discovered are fragmentary and sometimes contradictory. See Wald, 168-69; Shillony, 45-46; and Schenck, 67-68.

23 Suzuki, *Sawamura*, 93-94.

24 Suzuki, *Sawamura*, 93-94.

25 John Quinn, "American League Stars Tour Far East," Spalding Official Base Ball Guide 1935 (Chicago: A.G. Spalding 1935), 264-65; Sotaro Suzuki, *Unofficial History of Japanese Professional Baseball* [in Japanese] (Tokyo: Baseball Magazine, 1976).

26 Osamu Mihara, *My Baseball Life* [in Japanese] (Tokyo: Toashuppan, 1947).

27 "Ruth, Averill Knock Home Runs at Kokura," *Osaka Mainichi*, November 28, 1934.

28 "Ruth Hits Homer With 3 Men On," *Japan Times*, November 28, 1934: 5.

29 The description of Berg's visit to St. Luke's is taken from Nicholas Dawidoff, *The Catcher Was a Spy* (New York: Vintage Books, 1995), 94-95.

30 Louis Kaufman, Barbara Fitzgerald, and Tom Sewell, *Moe Berg: Athlete, Scholar, Spy* (Boston: Little Brown, 1974).

31 Dawidoff; Robert K. Fitts, *Banzai Babe Ruth* (Lincoln: University of Nebraska Press, 2012).

32 Suzuki, *Unofficial History*, 258.

33   "U.S.-Japan Baseball Games Are Over," *Yomiuri Shimbun*, December 2, 1934: 5.

34   Connie Mack, *My 66 Years in the Big Leagues* (Philadelphia: Universal House, 1950), 58.

35   "America-Japan Society Honors Baseball Players," *Japan Times*, November 16, 1934: 2; Associated Press, "Calls Baseball Bond Between U.S.[,] Japan," *New York Times*, November 16, 1934: 29; "Baseball Stressed as Trans-Pacific Tie," *Japan Advertiser*, November 16, 1934.

36   "Tourists Prove Benefits of Jaunts," *The Sporting News*, January 17, 1935: 4.

37   "Scribes Honor Mack, Dizzy Dean, Maranville," *The Sporting News*, February 7, 1935: 1.

38   "Stifling Good-Will Tours," *The Sporting News*, January 3, 1935: 4.

39   Shillony, 147-48.

40   Associated Press, "'To Hell with Babe Ruth, Yell Charging Japanese," *New York Times*, March 3, 1944: 2.

41   William N. Dahlberg, "A Tool for Diplomacy: Baseball in Occupied Japan 1945-1952" (paper presented at SABR 40, Atlanta, August 6, 2010); John Gripentrog, "The Transnational Pastime: Baseball and American Perceptions of Japan in the 1930s," *Diplomatic History* 34, no. 2 (2010): 247-73.

THE 1935 WHEATIES ALL-AMERICANS: A BOXFUL OF GLOBAL AMBITION

By Keith Robbins

"Last year in the Guide it was the pleasure of the editor to call attention to the fact that the Japanese had so thoroughly grasped Base Ball that they were bent on some day playing an American team for the international championship."[1] So proclaimed John Foster in the 1913 *Spalding's Guide*. That anticipated "some day" finally arrived in November of 1935; that "American team" was the Wheaties All-Americans. The nascent beginnings of the hoped-for "international championship" series participants were the Wheaties All-Americans and Tokyo's best amateur teams.

The 1935 Wheaties All-Americans were not just a team, but part of a multi-year effort to create a global sports organization. The team was the brainchild of Leslie "Les" Mann, a former major-league player who became a college coach and leading organizer and promoter of amateur baseball. Mann wanted to make baseball an Olympic sport and to create organized international competition. But first the European-based Olympic Committee had to be convinced that the American national pastime would be appropriate for their global games.

Given the complex requirements established by the International Olympic Committee, it took Mann five years to create the new necessary domestic and international amateur baseball organizations to push his plan forward. By 1935 he had the pieces in place to stage an amateur baseball exhibition in Tokyo "to encourage Japan to form an amateur organization ... for participation in [an] Olympic Baseball championship,"

1935 Wheaties All-Americans

and to show Olympic officials that baseball was a viable and legitimate international sport.[2] The 1935 Wheaties All-Americans were trailblazers on a global goodwill baseball mission – to bring baseball to the Olympic Games.

THE GREAT FINANCIAL CHALLENGE

Initially, Mann had promises of financial support from the major leagues, and the A.G. Spalding & Bros. firm. As the Great Depression wore on and corporate profits declined, that support waned.[3] Needing more financial resources for the expensive transpacific journey, Mann went looking outside the traditional sports funding sources, and found General Mills. Thus, the team was dramatically introduced to the American public by Wheaties Cereal on the *Jack Armstrong, All American Boy* radio show. This amateur ballclub was known as the 1935 Wheaties All-Americans.

UNEASE WITH COMMERCIAL SPONSORSHIP NAME

The Minneapolis cereal producer subsidized the trip for $12,000, and the "Wheaties" name was prominently displayed on the left sleeve of the players' uniform.[4] Yet the name "Wheaties" is not listed in many sources describing the team. The Japanese Olympic committee objected to the name as a symbol of the commercial corruption of amateur sport.[5] The *Japan Advertiser* and the *Japan Times & Mail*, for example, did not use the Wheaties name when referring to the team, yet the *Honolulu Advertiser* called it by its Wheaties moniker.[6]

SELECTING THE TEAM

With his trademark bravado, Les Mann announced that the final player selections were taken from a baseball talent pool of 500,000 to 1 million American youths.[7] To narrow the pool, Mann and General Mills created a contest. Consumers could nominate an amateur player by writing his name on a Wheaties box top and mailing it to Mann. Players with the most box-top votes would be given a tryout. Some 1,000 players were nominated out of the countless thousands of Wheaties breakfast cereal box tops submitted. This list was narrowed down to a final 100, who were then reviewed by trusted scouts and a selection committee.[8] Other players were added to the list through

recommendations of top collegiate and amateur coaches.[9] Forty players were then selected to the first and second teams and announced in newspapers in the fall of 1935. The final candidates for the Japan trip were announced nationally in late September. This was the first nationally selected amateur baseball All-American team.[10]

THE 1935 WHEATIES ALL-AMERICANS

The final team included 16 ballplayers: pitchers George Adams (Colorado State University), Lou Briganti (Textile High School, Manhattan), George Simons (University of Pennsylvania), Hayes Pierce (Tennessee Industrial School, Nashville), and Fred Heringer (Stanford University); catchers Ty Wagner (Duke University) and Dirk Offringa (Ridgefield High School, Wyckoff, New Jersey); infielders Bob Chiado (Illinois Wesleyan College), Leslie McNeece (Fort Lauderdale High School), Alex Metti (Fisher Foods, Cleveland), Frank Scalzi (University of Alabama), Ted Wiklund (Kansas City), and Ralph Goldsmith (Illinois Wesleyan); outfielders Jeff Heath (Garfield High School, Seattle), Ron Hibbard (Western Michigan Teachers College), and Emmett "Tex" Fore (University of Texas).[11] The manager was Max Carey and the coaches Les Mann and Herb Hunter.

The players were selected not only for their ability but also for their character to act as ambassadors during a nearly three-month-long trip to a foreign land. The team also reflected Mann's habits of clean living and notable positive behaviors. Carey, an old-school veteran player, gruffly lamented, "Only two of them smoke, and none of 'em drink. What kind of a ball team is this?"[12]

Briganti, McNeece, and Offringa were teenagers, and all but McNeece had graduated from high school. Metti, Pierce, Simons, and Wiklund were well-established amateur or semipro ballplayers. Wiklund's semipro career was unique; he attended Missouri Teachers College at Warrensburg and was the starting guard for their basketball team, but the college had no baseball team. His baseball fame was generated at the local sandlot Ban Johnson Amateur League of Kansas City, where he was the league MVP. Heringer and Wagner had graduated from college that spring and kept their amateur status active. Scalzi returned to Tuscaloosa to finish his college career as a three-year starter and Alabama's team captain, and led the club to three consecutive SEC baseball titles. Scalzi's immortality in Alabama sports history was cemented: He was football Coach Bear Bryant's college roommate. Wagner was the captain of coach Colby Jack Coombs' winning Duke baseball team. Adams, Chiado, Goldsmith, Fore, and Hibbard were underclassmen ballplayers. Hibbard also had played for the Battle Creek (Michigan) Postum team against the 1935 barnstorming Dai Nippon Baseball Club. Like Babe Ruth, he too was struck out by the Japanese great Eiji Sawamura.[13] Hibbard was the only player who had faced Japanese opposition before the trip.

The All-Americans boarded the NYK line's passenger ship *Taiyo Maru* on October 17 in San Francisco, with a scheduled arrival at Yokohama on November 3. The joyous troupe posed for syndicated newspaper photos in their grand quasi-Olympic apparel.[14] The ballplayers wore white buck shoes, white dress pants, white shirts, red neckties, red sweater-vests, and resplendent and elegant dark blue baseball sweaters. The embossed logo was Art Deco-inspired, with giant USA letters and an eagle emblem atop a red and white shield. Adding to the ensemble, all the players wore the now-traditional USA signature Olympic beret. Honoring their bat sponsor, many were holding their Louisville Sluggers high.[15]

JAPANESE TOURISTS

Once in Japan, the ballplayers were given the special tourist treatment and were well feted. Staying at the historic Imperial Hotel, they attended private receptions at the Pan-Pacific Club, the US Embassy, and the Japanese government's Education Department. Iesato Tokugawa, a member of the Japanese royal family and chairman of the 1940 Japanese Olympic Committee, sponsored a banquet for the American baseball tourists.[16] Bob Chiado and his Illinois collegiate teammate, Ralph Goldsmith, were overwhelmed by the authentic Japanese cuisine experience. Writing back to his hometown newspaper, Chiado remarked:

> They say that [the sukiyaki's] aroma is a great appetizer for it is said to be a mixture of all those best kitchen smells which excite the salivary glands and thus make the mouth water but neither Ralph nor I could eat it. …
> [A]bout all we could do was to eat the rice, and the dessert, which was persimmons. …
> The main feature of the suki yaki dinner is a large fish, done up artistically. At this time, we were using chop sticks and sitting on the floor. After this came some raw fish,

and some more fish, and "Goldie" and I were happy when the party was over.[17]

In typical first-time tourist behavior, the more sushi the mid-westerners saw and were offered, the more they became homesick. The lumbering first baseman and football player lamented, "I will still stick to those big T-bone steaks."[18]

Chiado overcame his fear of raw fish to enjoy and admire Japanese architecture, the scenic mountainous landscape, and the island nation's unique cultural and historic sites. The team traveled north to the Kinugawa Onsen and spent the night in Nikko. "We lived native for the night here, all sleeping on the floor, in keeping with an old Japanese custom" on traditional tatami mats, Chiado noted with a tourist's pride of accomplishment. The team visited the famous Dawn Gate, the Sacred Stable, and the famous vermillion-lacquered bridge at the Futarasan-jinja shrine. Then the team hiked through the snow to the mountain peaks. Overwhelmed with the scenic views of the numerous majestic waterfalls, Chiado wrote back home glowingly, "The Nikko Shrine is probably the most beautiful sight in Japan, if not the world."[19]

Some of the baseball tourists carried with them letters of introduction to selected Japanese officials and industry leaders. New Jersey's Dirk Offringa carried a letter of introduction from the governor of New Jersey to certain dignitaries in Tokyo. The letter allowed Offringa to create a collection of souvenirs that made him a popular presenter when he returned to New Jersey.[20]

Back in Tokyo, the intrepid Midwestern tourist/reporter Chiado found city life modern and familiar. Chiado noted the abundance of both taxicabs and bicycles, including specialized department-store delivery bicycles darting throughout the Japanese metropolis. He noted how expensive individual automobile ownership was due to high gas prices and taxes and that Tokyo streets were overflowing with thousands of taxis. Chiado reported on up-to-date Tokyo, which had "all the modern devices and equipment of any of our leading cities and compares favorably with Chicago."[21]

Being college athletes, they were keenly observant of their opponents. The Japanese college experience was six years, not the United States' traditional four years. Unlike the small-town, coed Illinois Wesleyan where he played, Chiado noted that all the opponents came from male-only urban universities with student bodies of 10,000-plus. Being a starter on the baseball team as an underclassman, Chiado was taken aback by the Japanese seniority system. He remarked, "[E]ven if a freshman was a stronger player in Japan, than a four-year man, he would not play because of seniority." Chiado noted with some envy that Japanese baseball players received preferential and exceptional collegiate athletic treatment, "The college teams all have special houses to live in and are not scattered about campus … as are our boys."[22]

Witnessing how the game was played in Japan with an air of respectful honor, Chiado wrote, "They are a jump ahead of us certainly as to sportsmanship."[23] Ever respectful of the experience, Chiado concluded that the Japanese baseball tourist experience was both "a marvelous trip" and educational, commenting, "We have learned a great deal."[24]

HIGHLY SKILLED EXHIBITIONS

By 1935, Tokyo's Big Six Collegiate Baseball League teams had played many American college teams and beaten them handily. In March of 1935, the Harvard nine's lack of performance was described as "[t]he least said … the better. … [T]hey underestimated the strength of the Japanese collegians."[25] In August, Yale's varsity nine faced the same fate. The Elis' baseball coach, former big-leaguer Smoky Joe Wood, remarked pensively, "I know exactly what the Japanese college teams can do. … [T]hey are mighty tough. … [I]f we are lucky enough to win half our games, I shall consider the trip a success."[26] Yale was not lucky, going 4-6-1.[27]

Beating the Big Six teams and capturing the favor of a smart, rabid Japanese baseball fan would be challenging, a Ruthian task. Chiado remarked that manager Mann and coaches Carey and Hunter stressed the serious nature of the trip and noted that the 1935 Wheaties All-Americans "were not out for a joyride."[28] Much was at stake, as the Wheaties All-Americans vs. Japanese Big Six Series would determine the unofficial amateur champion of the baseball world. Moreover, a successful tour would help persuade the Japanese authorities to join the 1936 Olympic baseball exhibition game in Berlin and to establish future tournaments, fulfilling Les Mann's Olympic baseball ambitions.

DIFFERENT BASEBALL APPROACHES

The series presented a test of different baseball philosophies. Japanese teams were noted for playing a "small ball" offensive game, while the American approach focused more on power hitting. Japanese

batters were noted for their keen understanding of the strike zone, being aware of game situations, employing bunts, and hitting behind the runners as needed. Hayes Pierce noted that his fellow pitchers were pressured when runners got on, since "the first thing they think of when they get on base is to steal."[29] But Max Carey, had who led the National League in stolen bases in 10 seasons, was not impressed, stating in US papers that the Japanese players were not as fast as perceived.[30]

BASEBALL AS METAPHOR

Japanese national pride in achieving parity with the United States on both the baseball diamond and high seas was a driving force in 1935. In his articles, Chiado observed, "When a Japanese boy plays against an American, he has his country at heart, and wins for his country."[31] In November, as the Wheaties All-Americans played the Big Six colleges on the Meiji Jingu diamond, British, American, and Japanese diplomats were preparing their governments' positions on naval strength for the 1935 London Naval Conference.[32] The British and American position called for a weaker Japanese naval ship ratio of 10:10:7, while the Japanese position sought parity and no quotas. Chiado concluded: "Every time a Japanese nine beats an American team, the natives feel that it is just like winning a war."[33]

THE BALLGAMES

The All-Americans had five days to regain their legs from three weeks at sea, practice, and do some sightseeing before their first game. They wound up playing just eight games, after some scheduled games were rained out. All the games were played during the day, which allowed time for banquets and sightseeing and helped avoid the November cold.

MEIJI UNIVERSITY GAME

With great anticipation, the series began on November 8 against Meiji University in front of 5,000 spectators, the largest crowd of the tour. Morris Hughes from the US Embassy threw out the first pitch.[34] Before the game the Americans posed for a team photo with Japanese baseball officials Matsutaro Naoki, Takeji Nakano, and Takizo Matsumato.[35] Meiji was a solid team in 1935, finishing third in the Big Six, but was in disarray after their manager of 12 years had resigned a week earlier, to the shock of many. The Meiji starting nine, however, was not dismayed, and was "sent afield with the intention to win."[36] Pitcher Akira Noguchi, a future professional all-star, set the tone for this team. Summoning all the *yamato damashi* for the auspicious moment, he was in control of the game from the first pitch.[37]

Then in midgame, volcanic ash started to fall, having been wafted from the erupting Mt. Asama, some 90 miles north of Tokyo. This could be the first instance in recorded baseball history of a volcano delay. To the surprise of the US ballplayers, they were facing a new Japanese adversary, *Kononhanaskuya-hime*, the mythical Japanese volcano goddess. The afternoon sky turned into twilight shades of blue, gray, and white, creating a sense of foreboding mystery and obscuring the flight of the ball.

While the spectators kept their seats and just covered their heads with newspapers, the ballplayers picked ash out of their hair, eyes, gloves and warm-up sweaters and out from their low shirt collars. Bob Chiado remarked, "It was a hair-raising experience for us but none of us were hurt. ... [I]t did not bother the Japanese athletes in the least. ... It resembled a slight drizzle, only it wasn't wet."[38] Starter Hayes Pierce was unnerved. The Associated Press concluded, "The volcano contributed to Pierce's ineffectiveness and his retirement in the sixth inning."[39] As the eruption subsided and the ash lessened, the Americans found themselves down five runs. A plucky American ninth-inning rally impressed local sportswriters, one of whom noted that the team "has plenty of pep."[40] Yet it was not enough, as the Wheaties All-Americans lost, 5-4. The *Honolulu Star-Bulletin* observed that the volcanic eruption and ash gave "the United States ... an excellent alibi for losing their first game."[41]

RIKKYO NINE TRIUMPHS

The next day, November 9, Japan's collegiate baseball talent was in full evidence in the form of Rikkyo University. A freshman with an American nickname, Lefty Koyama, dominated from the first pitch, allowing only three hits in seven innings. He was relieved by right-hander Yoshio Shioda, who allowed two hits in finishing the game. "Rikkyo virtually played the visitors off their feet in the first inning with some clever bunting and put three runs across," a sportswriter commented.[42] Future Japanese Baseball Hall of Famer Masaru Kageura was walked twice, the first

instance with the bases loaded. In his only official at-bat, he smacked a long triple.

Both American pitchers – righty George Simons and lefty George Adams – had trouble adjusting to the Japanese style of play as they walked eight batters, gave up nine hits, and topped off their wildness with a wild pitch and a passed ball. The Americans fielded poorly as well, committing four errors. Their only bright spot was turning three double plays, which kept the score in single digits. The Wheaties boys eked out one last-inning run to keep from being shut out. Game two was a convincing Rikkyo 7-1 victory.[43]

YOKOHAMA SCHOOL SHELLACKED

On November 10, the US team traveled to nearby Yokohama and played the Yokohama Higher Commercial School baseball team, an elite prep school and a non-Big Six University opponent. To make the game "more competitive," recent New York Textile High School graduate Lou Briganti was selected to start. In his only appearance in Japan, the schoolboy pitched a complete-game shutout aided by five double plays. At the plate, it was the collegians leading the hit parade with Ron Hibbard's home run, Skeeter Scalzi's triple, and Ted Wiklund's two doubles. The Yokohama youngsters were handily beaten, 9-0.[44]

RESERVED HOSPITALITY OF WASEDA

The fourth game, played on November 11, saw the intrepid Americans play the powerful Waseda collegians. Only 1,500 fans came to the cavernous Meiji Jingu ballpark. When Waseda played Yale five times in August, they used five different lineups. The range of scores reflected these changes: Yale lost 8-5 then won 7-0, tied 8-8, then lost 14-0 and 9-3.[45] That dynamic lineup trend continued with the Wheaties All-Americans game, with Waseda starting many of their reserve players. The *Japan Times and Mail* put a positive spin on the Waseda lineup, calling it "the team's full strength for the coming spring season."[46] Waseda's top players from the fall were not in the starting lineup.

Fred Heringer dominated from the first inning. In response, in the middle innings the Waseda coach replaced his starters with the pennant-winning Big Six regulars. Yet the switch was too little, too late. Heringer stayed hot and pitched a shutout, giving up just five hits. Batterymate Ty Wagner kept the runners in check by throwing out two baserunners attempting to steal second. A Waseda player was thrown out at third attempting to leg out a triple.[47] Adding to his fielding success, Wagner went 3-for-5 with a double and triple. The game was not close; it was a convincing Wheaties victory, 7-0.[48]

In a noble gesture of sportsmanship and hospitality, the Waseda ballclub presented each American with a special goodwill gift, an elegant Japanese bronze trophy of three crossed bats in a tripod position placed over home plate. Each trophy was engraved with the player's name and position in English with the phrase: "From Waseda University to All-American Amateur Baseball Team 1935." The *Harrisburg Evening News,* Ty Wagner's hometown paper, described it as "a beautiful trophy."[49]

After their first games, a clear image emerged: the US amateurs neither captured the interest of the Japanese baseball fan nor earned the media's respect. The Japanese baseball fans ignored these contests – under 10,000 fans were listed as attending all the games, and the *Japan Times and Mail* reported that many Japanese sportswriters were sorely disappointed with the Americans' performance.[50] The Big Six Collegiate teams had some very good ballplayers and these teams' collective talent, intensity, and teamwork resulted in Japanese victories. Both the Meiji and Rikkyo teams fielded players who would go on to become future professional stars and even Japanese Baseball Hall of Famers. The American college amateurs were outmatched if not out-nerved. So convincing were the victories that Japanese American baseball reporter Leslie Nakashima noted, "Japanese clubs … can really play good ball afield."[51]

As the US players acclimated to the esprit of Japanese baseball, the next four games were more competitive. Three of the four games were very close – with the potential winning runs on base as the final out of the game was recorded.

HOSEI VARSITY HUSTLES

On November 12, the Americans faced Hosei University in front of just 500 fans. Hosei had finished with only one victory in the 1935 Big Six fall league, but they turned out to be a formidable opponent. Kazuto Tsuruoka, later the winningest manager in Japanese professional baseball history and a Japanese Baseball Hall of Famer, batted third and played third base. The *Japan Advertiser* described the contest as "a hard fought game in

which the lead changed hands four times" and "the most exciting game the Americans had played so far." The Japanese hero was Shinichi Nakamura, who hit a two-run triple that gave Hosei the lead in the second inning. A walk to Tsuruoka started the game-winning rally. For the All-Americans, Les McNeece definitely ate his Wheaties that morning and started the scoring off with a first-inning solo home run. In their desperate ninth-inning rally, pinch-hitting pitcher Fred Heringer kept the last inning going with a base hit, but when the dust settled, the American tying run was stranded at third and Hosei clung to victory, 5-4.[52]

THE RAILWAY TEAM DERAILED

On November 14 the All-Americans tackled the Railway Bureau team, Totetsu. A few days earlier, the semipro railroaders had beaten the professional Tokyo Giants, winning 9-4 on 16 hits.[53] Heringer again started and was nearly unhittable for the first seven innings, giving up just one hit and striking out six. No Totetsu player made it past second base while the Wheaties batters scored six runs, aided by triples by Scalzi and Heath.

In the eighth inning, the All-Americans' fielding sagged, enabling their opponent to score two unearned runs. Heringer remained on the mound to start the bottom of the ninth. With national pride on the line, the Railway Bureau baseballers staged a spirited rally. In a magical small-ball fashion, they did not hit the ball out of the infield but almost pulled out the victory.

The excitement started with two walks. An attempted fielder's choice combined with a subsequent error at second base allowed a run to score. Then came the first out as Heringer picked off the runner at first base while the other runner remained at third – a high-risk play that caught the overzealous Japanese baserunner off guard. But Heringer then hit a batter, who stole second base, and walked another, to load the bases.

Heringer, still on the mound, reared back and claimed a strikeout victim for the second out. The eighth batter of the inning came to the plate. Heringer responded by issuing his fourth walk of the inning, forcing in the second run. The bases were still loaded. With the score now 6-4 and two outs, the runners were ready to sprint on any contact or wild pitch. The situation was perilous. Heringer was out of gas. Mann, who had written the baseball textbook used at Springfield College's Theory of Baseball course, finally realized the gravity of the situation.[54] The *Japan Times and Mail* wrote, "Coach Mann elected to take no chance and sent Adams, a southpaw to replace Heringer on the mound."[55]

At the plate was right fielder Ito, the Railway's Bureau third-place hitter. Adams, feeling the pressure of the moment, skipped his second delivery in the dirt. As the live ball bounced up the third-base line, Dirk Offringa, the team's backup catcher, pounced on it, making a great save. First baseman Ted Wiklund and pitcher Lefty Adams sprinted home to guard the plate and kept the Totetsu runner, Fujimatsu, at third base. With the three American players at the plate, and in front of the umpire, Offringa handed the ball to Wiklund the first baseman, not pitcher Adams. Adams then went back to the mound. The *Japan Advertiser* reported the next series of events:

> As Adams went into a windup Hoshino moved off the sack, ready to dash for second. The moment he left the bag Wiklund produced the ball and touched him for the final out. … Only Mr. Nomoto, base umpire, noticed the play and the spectators as well as the local players were taken completely by surprise.[56]

In a stunned silence, the game was over. The *Japan Times and Mail* observed the obvious: "Everyone seemed dumbfounded."[57]

On Friday, December 13, Offringa's hometown newspaper proudly proclaimed, "Dirk Fooled the Japs." The newspaper writer with a great deal of hometown swagger boasted that "the Oriental players still have a lot to learn about the sport. … [I]t took Dirk Offringa, former Ridgewood High catching star[,] to teach them an old, old trick."[58]

In looking at the game description, some 80 years later, having an American umpire would have helped the Japanese. As Adams began his windup without the ball, a balk should have been declared for the pitcher "[m]aking any motion to pitch while standing in his position without having the ball in his possession."[59]

John Foster, the *Spalding's Guide* editor, commented, "Note section 7 carefully. … No pitcher will foolishly try a 'hidden ball' trick when there is runner on third who may score the winning run by a balk being declared."[60] What clean-playing, rule-knowing Coach Mann or even hard-nosed Max Carey said in the clubhouse after the game is unknown. The Japanese response was not and was printed in the Japanese sports magazine *Undonenkan* by former Waseda manager turned sports journalist Suishu Tobita, who wrote a scathing description of the series.[61]

KEIO NINE TAMED

Two days later, on November 16, in a nearly empty Meiji Jingu stadium, the All-Americans played a tight game against Keio University. Keio finished fourth in the Big Six League that fall and in August had crushed Yale, 10-0.[62] The All-Americans were outhit 10 to 5, yet pitcher Hayes Pierce was in control when it counted, striking out six and walking only one. He was in danger in the third and fourth innings but survived to continue on. Nine Keio batters were stranded on base. Keio hurler Tamotsu Kusumoto was also effective, striking out seven and walking four. The difference came down to timely power hitting by future major-league All-Star Jeff Heath, who walloped a titanic home run and knocked a triple, to plate three runs. The American lead was stretched with two more runs, scored small-ball style by a walk, a bunt hit, two errors, and a fly ball. With no volcanic siren's call to unnerve him, Pierce was steady and rose to the occasion. The *Japan Advertiser* informed its readers that "Keio made a desperate effort to tie the score in the last inning, but in vain, due to Pierce's tight pitching."[63] Thus, the All-Americans prevailed, 5-4.[64]

TOKYO CLUB CITY CHAMPS CONQUERED

The final game of the tour against the Tokyo Club on November 20 was not close. In August, before their fall season started, Yale had beaten them 7-0; in November, at the conclusion of their fall season, the All-Americans finished them off, 6-0.[65] The battery of Heringer and Wagner were the game's heroes again. Heringer gave up six hits, struck out four, and walked only two in his second shutout. Wagner hit a three-run home run. With his throwing reputation from earlier games, no Tokyo runner attempted a stolen base, nor got past second base.[66] In 1939, when Les Mann created the International Amateur Baseball Federation Hall of Fame, Ty Wagner was the 1935 team honoree for his efforts.[67]

On November 22 the All-Americans left Japan on the regularly scheduled NYK Line passenger *Tayo Maru* for the three-week Pacific crossing. Unlike many other tourist teams, the Wheaties All-Americans played no games during their Honolulu stop. Upon landing back home, the team disbanded.

POST-SERIES REVIEW

On the field, the games were mostly competitive and tightly contested. The styles of play – Japanese small ball vs. American power hitting – yielded the same number of runs scored at 21. The hit totals were similar: The Big Six collegians knocked out 38 while the Americans had 41.[68] (The walk totals were not recorded in the box scores but the American pitchers were noted for their wildness.) The difference in home run totals was noticeable. No Japanese ballplayer hit a home run against the American pitchers, while four Wheaties All-Americans hit home runs: Jeff Heath, Ty Wagner, Ron Hibbard, and Les McNeece. Speedster Skeeter Scalzi found Japanese pitchers similar to the SEC hurlers and led the team in triples with three. By winning five of the eight games, the Wheaties All-Americans were crowned by the *Jack Armstrong* radio show as the amateur baseball champions of the world.[69]

On both sides of the Pacific, Organized Baseball looked inward. Japan focused on creating a professional league. The US major leagues declined to financially support the Olympic baseball movement and also banned further foreign barnstorming trips. Les Mann and Max Carey dissolved their baseball partnership and went their separate ways. By New Year's Day 1936, the Wheaties All-American baseball team was a proverbial Depression-era baseball orphan, shunned by its organizing committee, by opponents, and by Organized Baseball. The entire venture had become so unpalatable for General Mills that Wheaties cereal executives concluded: "The contest not only failed to bring in the anticipated returns, but it proved most embarrassing."[70]

On the Olympic baseball front, the news was sober and serious. Japan would not send a team to play in the 1936 Berlin Olympics baseball demonstration game.[71] The acrimonious debate within the US Olympic Committee and the Amateur Athletic Union community on the question of attending the 1936 Berlin Summer Games led to an irreversible split between those organizations.[72] Mann's amateur baseball organizations lost many amateur and collegiate baseball contacts. The proposed 1937 amateur Japan-USA World Series did not occur. By 1938, Japan withdrew its sponsorship of the 1940 Tokyo Olympic Summer games, which as it turned out were not held because of World War II.[73] It would be another 80-plus years before teams from the USA and Japan would play for an Olympic Gold Medal in Tokyo.[74]

Rebuffed by its baseball competitors, unsupported by its financial patron, and jilted by its amateur allies, the 1935 Wheaties All-Americans devolved into a cliché, a Depression-era baseball orphan. With their ambitious Olympic mission unfinished and unfulfilled, this ballclub faded into obscurity.

1935 WHEATIES ALL-AMERICAN GAMES IN JAPAN

Date	Place	Opponent	Score	Winner	Loser
November 8	Tokyo	Meiji University	4-5	Noguchi	Pierce
November 9	Tokyo	Rikkyo University	1-7	Koyama	Simons
November 10	Yokohama	Yokohama Commercial	9-0	Briganti	Matsumoto
November 11	Tokyo	Waseda University	7-0	Heringer	Endo
November 12	Tokyo	Hosei University	4-5	Uzawa	Pierce
November 14	Tokyo	Totetsu	6-4	Heringer	Minami
November 16	Tokyo	Keio University	5-4	Pierce	Kusumoto
November 20	Tokyo	Tokyo Club	6-0	Heringer	Kikutani

NOTES

1   John B. Foster, "Editorial Comment," *Spalding's Official Base Ball Guide*, No. 37 (March 1913): 7.

2   Red McQueen, "Hoomalimali," *Honolulu Advertiser*, December 2, 1935: 10. His column calls the team the Wheaties.

3   Harold Seymour, *Baseball: The Peoples' Game* (New York: Oxford University Press, 1990), 287.

4   McQueen.

5   Sayuri Guthrie-Shimizu, *Transpacific Field of Dreams* (Chapel Hill: UNC Press, 2012), 169.

6   Leslie Nakashima, "US Amateur Baseball Champs to Play Here," *Japan Times and Mail*, September 6, 1935: 5; "Keio Nine Nosed Out by Americans, 5-4," *Japan Advertiser*, November 17, 1935: 8; McQueen.

7   "Amateur Baseball Has Revival in US," *Japan Advertiser*, November 2, 1935: 2.

8   Associated Press, "Can You Imagine This! Not a Tar Heel on List," *Raleigh* (North Carolina) *News and Observer*, September 29,1935: 8; "McNeece Given Recognition Among 1,000 Seeking Berths," *Miami News*, September 8, 1935: 9.

9   "Amateurs to Invade Japan," *The Sporting News*, October 15, 1935: 2; United Press, "40 Amateurs Chosen for Tour of Orient," *Indianapolis Times*, September 23, 1935: 15.

10   The American Baseball Coaches Association did not start picking its "All-American" teams until 1949. https://www.abca.org/ABCA/Who_We_Are/About_the_ABCA/ABCA/Who_We_Are/About_the_ABCA.aspx?hkey=c64bedc6-95dd-40ca-a406-d81571bf2d6e.

11   United Press, "Name US Stars for Japanese Tour," *Pittsburgh Press*, September 24, 1935: 27. Joe Copp was listed in on board the *Taiyo Maru* but did not make the trip: "Amateur Ball Team Starts Japan Jaunt," *Honolulu Advertiser*, October 18, 1935: 12; Les Mann, *Baseball Around the World: History and Development of the USA Baseball Congress* (Springfield, Massachusetts: International Amateur Baseball Federation, 1941), 13.

12   Lewis Lapham, "On the Gangplank," *San Francisco Examiner*, December 8, 1935: 70.

13   "Japanese 'Schoolboy' Allows but Two Hits," *Battle Creek* (Michigan) *Enquirer*, June 11, 1935: 9. Hibbard did get one of the two hits off Sawamura. The game was an 0-0 tie that lasted 12 innings.

14   United Press, "Amateur Team Goes to Japan," *Minneapolis Star*, October 17, 1935: 17.

15   World Wide Photo, "All-Americans Sail for Japan," *Minneapolis Star Tribune*, November 3, 1935: 88.

16   Mann, *Baseball Around the World*, 14. Old Embassy information is https://americancenterjapan.com/aboutusa/usj/4737/.

17   Robert Chiado, "All-Americans Are Glad to Get Away from Suki Yaki Dinner," *Bloomington* (Illinois) *Pantagraph*, December 9, 1935: 10.

18   Chiado, "All-Americans Are Glad to Get Away from Suki Yaki Dinner."

19   Robert Chiado, "All Americans Find Nikko Shrine One of Most Interesting Spots," *Bloomington Pantagraph*, December 10, 1935: 15.

20   "Offringa in School Talk," *Ridgewood* (New Jersey) *Sunday News*, March 8, 1936: 21.

21   Robert Chiado, "Mt Asama Erupts but Fails to Dim or Disturb Players on Jap Nine," *Bloomington Pantagraph*, December 4, 1935: 10.

22   Robert Chiado, "Psychology, Strategy Important in Japs Winning Games from U.S.," *Bloomington Pantagraph*, December 12, 1935: 16.

23   Chiado, "Mt Asama Erupts but Fails to Dim or Disturb Players on Jap Nine."

24   Chiado, "Mt Asama Erupts but Fails to Dim or Disturb Players on Jap Nine"; Robert Chiado, "Noise Is Real Test of Good Food in Japan, Writes Robert Chiado," *Bloomington Pantagraph*, December 11, 1935: 12.

25   William Peet, "Sport Flashes," *Honolulu Advertiser*, February 23, 1935: 8.

26   William Peet, "Sport Flashes, Yale's Coach Hands Out Inside Stuff," *Honolulu Advertiser*, July 24, 1935: 14.

27   Associated Press, "Yale Baseball Team Wins in Japan, 7-3," *St. Louis Post Dispatch*, September 9, 1935: 15.

28   Robert Chiado, "This All-American Outing in Japan Is Serious Business, Chiado Writes," *Bloomington Pantagraph*, October 20, 1935: 12.

29   "Japs' Speed Is Main Topic of Local Hurler," *Nashville Tennessean*, December 11, 1935: 12.

30   Art Routzong, "Along Sports Trail with Art Routzong," *Dayton* (Ohio) *Herald*, December 17, 1935: 19.

31   Chiado, "Psychology, Strategy Important in Japs Winning Games from US."

32   "US Will Ask Big Nations to Limit Navies," *Biloxi* (Mississippi) *Herald*, December 6, 1935: 1.

33   Robert Chiado, "Psychology, Strategy Important in Japs Winning Games from US."

34   "Meiji Team Defeats Americans, 5 to 4," *Japan Advertiser*, November 8, 1935: 8.

35   Mann, *Baseball Around the World*, 13.

36   Leslie Nakashima, "US Amateur Nine Drops First Game to Meiji, 5-4," *Japan Times and Mail*, November 9, 1935: 8.

37   Robert Whiting, *You Gotta Have Wa: When Two Cultures Collide on the Baseball Diamond* (New York: Macmillan, 1989), 41. The term means Japanese fighting spirit.

38   Chiado, "Mt Asama Erupts but Fails to Dim or Disturb Players on Jap Nine."

39   Associated Press, "Volcanic Ash Hits Players," *Salt Lake Telegram*, November 7, 1935: 19.

40   Nakashima, "US Amateur Nine Drops First Game to Meiji, 5-4."

41   Associated Press, "Shower of Ashes Fails to Check Japan Ball Game," *Honolulu Star-Bulletin*, November 7, 1935: 16.

42   Leslie Nakashima, "Rikkyo Defeats US Amateurs, 7-1, Who Fail to Hit," *Japan Times and Mail*, November 10, 1935: 8.

43   "Rikkyo Nine Beats US Amateurs, 7-1," *Japan Advertiser*, November 9, 1935: 8.

44   "US Amateur Nine Defeats Yokohama Commercials, 9-0," *Japan Times and Mail*, November 11, 1935: 1.

45   "Waseda Defeats Yale by 8 To 5," *Japan Times and Mail*, August 19, 1935: 1; "Yale Loses in Kwansai," *Japan Advertiser*, September 9, 1935: 8; "Yale Blanks Waseda," *Hartford Courant*, August 19, 1935: 9; "Yale in Tie Game; Loses to Meiji," *Berkshire Eagle*, (Pittsfield, Massachusetts), August 26, 1935: 13.

46   Leslie Nakashima, "Waseda Bows to US Amateur Nine by 7 to 0," *Japan Times and Mail*, November 12, 1935: 8.

47   "Americans Blank Waseda Nine, 7-0," *Japan Advertiser*: 4.

48   Nakashima, "Waseda Bows to US Amateur Nine By 7 to 0."

49   "Tour Ended by Amateur Nine," *Harrisburg* (Pennsylvania) *Evening News*, December 19, 1935: 19.

50   Nakashima, "Rikkyo Defeats US Amateurs, 7-1 Who Fail to Hit."

51   Nakashima, "Rikkyo Defeats US Amateurs, 7-1 Who Fail to Hit."

52   "Hosei Nine Shades Americans, 5-4," *Japan Advertiser*, November 13, 1935: 8.

53   "Giants Win and Lose," *Japan Advertiser*, November 11, 1935: 8. A few days later the Giants got even, defeating the Totetsu, 2-0. "Giants Beat Railway Nine," *Japan Advertiser*, November 16, 1935: 8.

54   HS DeGroat, "Baseball Theory Notes," 1935. It was a coaching course offered to freshmen and sophomores at Springfield College. Courtesy Springfield College Archives.

55   "US Amateurs Top Totetsu Nine, 6-4 for Second Win," *Japan Times and Mail*, November 16, 1935: 5.

56   "Americans Defeat Rail Bureau Team," *Tokyo Advertiser* November 15, 1935: 8.

57   "US Amateurs Top Totetsu Nine, 6-4."

58   "Dirk Fooled the Japs," *Ridgewood* (New Jersey) *Herald*, December 13, 1935: 22.

59   John B. Foster, editor, *Official Base Ball Rules, 1936* (New York: American Sports Publishing Company, 1936), 21-22. Printed as a supplement to the *Spalding's Official Base Ball Guide of 1936.*

60   Foster, 21-22.

61   Guthrie-Shimizu, 273.

62   "Keio Nine Crushes Yale Invaders, 10-0," *Japan Advertiser*, August 21, 1935: 8.

63   "Keio Nine Nosed Out by Americans, 5-4," *Japan Advertiser,* November 17, 1935: 8.

64   "US Amateur Nine Defeats Keio, 5-4 for Third Win," *Japan Times and Mail,* November 18, 1935: 1.

65   United Press, "Yale Beats Tokyo Baseball Nine," *Visalia* (California) *Times Delta,* August 23, 1935: 8.

66   "US Amateur Nine Beats Tokyo Club 6-0 in Farewell," *Japan Times and Mail*, November 22, 1935: 8.

67   Leslie Mann, *USA Baseball Congress 1940* (Springfield, Massachusetts: USA Baseball Congress, 1940), 20.

68   *Japan Advertiser* and *Japan Times and Mail* published all the box scores from November 1935.

69   Dinty Dennis, "Out of Dinty's Dugout," *Miami Herald,* December 5, 1935: 15; Kent Owen, "Along Radio Lane," *Racine* (Wisconsin) *Journal Times*, November 30, 1935: 10.

70   Email to author from Katie Gamache, Consumer Relations Analyst-Archives, General Mills, July 2, 2021.

71   (No headline), *St. Louis Globe-Democrat*, December 2, 1935: 23.

72   International News Service, "McPherson Favors US Withdrawal," *Bloomington Pantagraph,* December 2, 1935: 8; Illinois Wesleyan University President Harry W. McPherson favored boycotting the 1936 Summer Olympics, possibly making Wesleyan baseball players Chiado and Goldsmith ineligible for the 1936 Olympic Baseball Team.

73   Organizing Committee of the XIIth Olympiad Tokyo, *Report of the Organizing Committee on Its Work for the XIIth Olympic Games of 1940 in Tokyo Until the Relinquishment* (Tokyo: Issihki Printing Co: 1940), 121. Officially it was announced on July 16, 1938.

74   "Tokyo 2020 Baseball/Softball Baseball Results," Olympics. com. Accessed December 14, 2021. https://olympics.com/en/ olympic-games/tokyo-2020/results/baseball-softball.

THE GREATEST PIECE OF DIPLOMACY EVER: THE 1949 TOUR OF LEFTY O'DOUL AND THE SAN FRANCISCO SEALS

By Dennis Snelling

There are moments, sometimes fleeting, often accidental, when sport transcends mere athletic competition. These moments are not judged by wins or losses, nor by runs scored or surrendered. The baseball tour of Japan undertaken by Lefty O'Doul and his San Francisco Seals in October 1949 serves as a prime example—an event that changed the course of history.

At the tour's conclusion, General Douglas MacArthur, Supreme Commander of the Allied Powers in Japan, declared, "This trip is the greatest piece of diplomacy ever. All the diplomats put together would not have been able to do this."[1]

In a letter supporting a campaign aimed at Lefty O'Doul gaining membership in the National Baseball Hall of Fame at Cooperstown, MacArthur's successor, General Matthew Ridgway, wrote, "Words cannot describe Lefty's wonderful contributions, through baseball, to the postwar rebuilding effort."[2]

In September 1945, a month after Japan's surrender, reporter Harry Brundidge landed in the country and was barraged with queries about O'Doul. Lefty's old friend Sotaro Suzuki, who first met O'Doul in New York in 1928 and was instrumental in organizing the 1934 tour featuring Babe Ruth, wanted Lefty to know he was okay. Emperor Hirohito's brother inquired about the San Francisco ballplayer. Prince Fumimaro Konoe, the former prime minister of Japan, told Brundidge that O'Doul should have been a diplomat.[3]

If the 1934 tour was a watershed moment in the history of baseball between the United States and Japan, then 1949 served as a bookend, providing a yardstick for the Japanese after they had been shut off from the rest of the baseball world for 13 years. And, while he is not enshrined in Cooperstown, the 1949 tour is a major reason that Lefty O'Doul *is* in the Japanese Baseball Hall of Fame.

Immediately after the end of the war, Douglas MacArthur was tasked with maintaining order in an occupied Japan, while at the same time maintaining the morale of its citizens. Communists were gaining a foothold, taking advantage of everyday Japanese life that was harsh, plagued with shortages of food, housing, and other basic necessities. Ruins and rubble pockmarked the country's major cities, and families were disrupted by severe illness and death. Orphans hustled on the streets to survive, bullied, abused, and used; most of them homeless because existing orphanages could accommodate—at best—one-tenth of the need. Those who did make it into orphanages were sometimes stripped of their clothing in winter to prevent their escape.[4]

MacArthur saw sports as a means to boost the spirit of the Japanese, and assigned General William Marquat and his aide-de-camp, a California-born Japanese American named Tsuneo "Cappy" Harada, to rebuild athletic facilities around the country. University and professional baseball soon flourished, and in 1948 the amateur game was boosted through an affiliation with the National Baseball Congress, which served as an umbrella organization for semi-pro baseball in the United States and was expanding its reach to other countries. Within two years a Japanese team, All-Kanebo, was hosting a team from Fort Wayne, Indiana, in a well-received "Inter-Hemisphere Series," won by Fort Wayne in five games.

While local baseball remained extremely popular, it was not enough to arrest the decline in morale, leading MacArthur to grill his aides about the deteriorating situation. The story goes that Cappy Harada proposed an American baseball tour, recalling the one that had brought Babe Ruth to Japan 15 years earlier. He further suggested minor-league manager and two-time National League batting champion Lefty O'Doul, widely considered the most popular living American player by the Japanese, as the man to lead such a mission.

San Francisco Seals 1949 Tour of Japan Program with Lefty O'Doul

MacArthur reportedly replied, "What are you waiting for?"[5]

O'Doul had spent three years pushing for just such a tour and was indeed interested. In March 1949 General Marquat announced that he was deciding between two proposals, one involving O'Doul and his PCL San Francisco Seals, and the other Bob Feller and his All-Stars.[6]

O'Doul enthusiastically made his pitch, declaring, "I think we can contribute something to postwar Japan." While his plan involved minor-league players versus Feller's big leaguers, the veteran manager held an advantage due to his popularity and willingness to play for expenses only. He lobbied Marquat to choose his proposition over Feller's, arguing, "A well-trained team which has been playing together all season doubtless could demonstrate much more than a group of all-stars who had been on different teams all season."[7]

Marquat agreed, and in July 1949, Seals general manager Charlie Graham Jr. arrived in Japan to finalize what was hoped to be a 22-game tour beginning in mid-October.

Graham was quoted as saying that General MacArthur told him, "The arrival of the Seals in Japan would be one of the biggest things that has happened to the country since the war." Graham said that the General added, "It takes athletic competition to put away the hatred of war and it would be a great event for Japan politically, economically, and every other way."[8]

Lefty O'Doul had visited Japan more than a half-dozen times by 1949, highlighted by trips while still an active player in 1931 and 1934, the latter of which led to an opportunity for him to play a role in establishing the first successful Japanese professional team, the Tokyo Giants. He had even helped that team stage two tours of the United States, in 1935 and 1936.

Now, 15 seasons into managing the San Francisco Seals, O'Doul was on a plane in October 1949 bound for Japan. There was some disappointment that for financial reasons the schedule had been pared to 10 games, but O'Doul couldn't help experiencing an emotional mix of excitement and anxiety, reflecting the gravity of the moment.

Even so, he and his players were unprepared for the reception that awaited. The motorcade, led from Shimbashi Station by the Metropolitan Police band, was greeted by, according to some accounts, nearly one million people lining a route that stretched five miles. By all accounts, it was the largest gathering in Japan since the end of the war.

The players were astounded by the reception. "It got the boys off on the right foot," crowed an enthusiastic Seals owner Paul Fagan. Charlie Graham Jr. sputtered, "I couldn't believe it. Never have we seen such a demonstration anywhere."[9] Infielder Dario Lodigiani exclaimed, "You would have thought we were kings."[10]

As the 22-vehicle caravan wound through the streets of downtown Tokyo, the players were nearly obscured by a five-color flurry of confetti flung from office windows while they attempted to navigate a sea of humanity pinching the thoroughfare, fans close enough for the players to shake hands, and even sign a few autograph books.[11] O'Doul shouted above the din, "This is the greatest ever!"[12]

It was at this point O'Doul realized that when he greeted those along the route with a triumphant "banzai," it was not returned.

"I noticed how sad the Japanese people were," recalled O'Doul during an interview nearly 20 years later. "When we were there in '31 and '34, people were waving Japanese and American flags and shouting 'banzai, banzai.' This time, no banzais. I was yelling 'Banzai', but the Japanese just looked at me."[13]

O'Doul asked Cappy Harada, "How come they don't yell banzai?" Harada replied, "That's the reason you're here, Lefty. To build up the morale so that they will yell 'banzai' again."[14]

The players spent their second day in Japan as a guest of Douglas MacArthur, highlighted by a luncheon served at the general's home. MacArthur made a few remarks acknowledging the undertaking, and reminded the athletes of the importance he placed on the tour.[15] He then turned to O'Doul and, noting his dozen-year absence from the country and the esteem in which he was held by Japanese baseball fans, told the Seals manager, "You've finally come home."[16]

In public, players were treated as celebrities, provided special badges with their names printed in both English and Japanese so they would be recognized wherever they went. According to Seals outfielder Reno Cheso, every team member was assigned a car and driver, standing at the ready 24 hours a day.[17]

The Americans were quickly exposed to the Japanese mania for baseball. There were more than two dozen magazines devoted to the sport in Tokyo alone, and the game was played everywhere, all the time. "It was nothing to see Japanese kids playing ball on the streets and in vacant lots as early as six o'clock in the morning," noted Dario Lodigiani—without revealing whether he was witnessing this as he was rising for the day, or as he was crawling back to his hotel following a raucous night.[18]

And then there were the autograph seekers—none of the Seals had ever seen anything like it, O'Doul included. Bellboys served as lookouts, and when the players returned to their hotel they confronted a gauntlet of fans in the lobby, each with baseballs and autograph books at the ready.

"I remember the hordes of people who used to line up seeking Babe Ruth's autograph when the Babe was at the height of his career," said O'Doul. "But that was a bit more than a puddle of beseeching humanity compared to the ocean we encountered on every street corner, store, and hotel lobby in Kobe and Tokyo."[19]

Many were repeat customers, looping back multiple times to obtain a signature on a ball or a program. Seals owner Paul Fagan was approached by one such man for three straight mornings. When he appeared for a fourth day in a row, Fagan asked him why he wanted another autograph from him. The man cheerfully replied, "All I need is four of your signatures and I can swap them for one of O'Doul's!"[20]

The evening after lunch with MacArthur, O'Doul quashed a potential rumble at the Tokyo Sports Center, during a rally held in the team's honor. People had lined up for nine hours in anticipation of gaining admittance; while 15,000 successfully obtained a coveted seat, 2,000 more remained outside, frustrated when the doors were locked.[21]

Made aware of the situation, which threatened to turn ugly, O'Doul rushed outside and apologized for not being able to admit the unlucky fans. He then told them, "I think speaking to you personally will no doubt serve to promote goodwill and friendship." The crowd peacefully dispersed.[22]

The day before the first game, following a two-hour workout that included his taking a few swings, O'Doul made it clear that the Seals would respect their opponents. "In order to show our gratitude," he said, "we intend to fight to the best of our ability and win the first goodwill game with the Giants with our best members."[23]

The manager of the Tokyo Yomiuri Giants, Osamu Mihara—who had broken O'Doul's ribs in a collision at first base during the 1931 tour—also vowed to use his best lineup, with one exception; his starting pitcher would be Tokuji Kawasaki, arguably the team's third-best hurler. Mihara gambled that Kawasaki's unusual breaking pitches would surprise the Americans.[24] Since

this would be the only meeting between the Seals and the team O'Doul had helped launch, Mihara's choice disappointed many Japanese commentators, who had wanted to measure how their best professional team matched up against O'Doul's squad.[25]

Fifty-five thousand fans jammed Korakuen Stadium for the tour's first contest—the largest crowd ever to attend a game there. The stands were packed three hours before the first pitch despite a steady drizzle that had threatened cancellation.

O'Doul addressed the fans before the game began, and the crowd roared its approval when he began his speech with a single word—a word he knew they would appreciate. The word was, "Tadaima," translated in English as "I am home."[26]

He presented a dozen American bats to each manager of the Japanese professional teams, and received thanks from the Japanese chairman of the event, Frank Matsumoto. Cappy Harada then introduced the Seals players to the crowd, and Mrs. Douglas MacArthur threw the ceremonial first ball to Seals pitcher Con Dempsey.[27]

Controversy would not absent itself from this event. The Japanese were surprised—and thrilled—when the national anthems of both nations were played and their flags flew together, the first such instance since the war. In contrast to the deep emotional response of the crowd, some in the American military contingent were angered by the display.

Cappy Harada then ignited a firestorm by saluting both flags, a gesture that did not go unnoticed by the crowd. That salute, coming from a Japanese American no less, further infuriated some of Harada's fellow American officers, who wanted him punished immediately. Complaints reached General MacArthur, who quashed the objections by revealing that he not only approved, but had asked Harada to do it, and Harada continued to do so for the remainder of the tour.[28] O'Doul was pleased by the raising of the flags, and reflected on the emotion of that day. "I looked at the Japanese players and fans," he remembered nearly two decades later. "Tears. [Their eyes] were wet with tears. Later, somebody told me my eyes weren't too dry either."[29]

The Seals easily won the opener, 13-4, even though San Francisco starter Con Dempsey was less than sharp, having been idle for three weeks. The 52-year-old O'Doul, energized by his return to Japan, grabbed a bat in the eighth and grounded out as a pinch-hitter. Pittsburgh Pirates left-hander Bill Werle, a former Seal added to the roster because several of the current Seals could not make the trip, relieved Dempsey and hit two batters in the fifth, but settled down and struck out the side the next inning. Werle closed the game with a one-two-three ninth, a pair of strikeouts and a slow roller to the mound.[30] Werle's opposite, Kawasaki—chosen because Osamu Mihara thought he would prove more effective against the Seals lineup—failed to make it out of the first inning. Afterward, Kawasaki blamed his underwhelming performance on the American horsehide baseballs that were used, complaining that they were more slippery than the cowhide baseball normally employed by the Japanese.[31]

Retired pitcher Yushi Uchimura thought the defeat a positive. "The Japanese by playing by themselves will become swell-headed in their own small world and never improve," he explained. "In order to help Japanese baseball improve, it is best to play from time to time with American teams and learn their best points one after another."[32]

O'Doul criticized Mihara for not starting his ace pitcher, Hideo Fujimoto (who went on to win 200 games in Japan with a career earned run average of 1.90), before quickly softening his critique by offering, "Of course such a question is up to the manager and I have no right to say anything."[33]

Among those attending the second game were 1,400 orphans, including more than 200 from the Roman Catholic-operated Salesian School, whose students were easily recognizable in their dark navy caps, adorned with a large, yellow "S" on the front. The school's band alternated musical numbers with the Air Force Band.[34] The game itself, with the Seals taking on the Far East Air Force, was no contest, a 12-0 win for San Francisco behind Al Lien.[35]

Despite the lopsided result, there was significance to the day. A Japanese commentator for *Asahi Shimbun* noticed that American soldiers were relocated from choice seats to make room for the orphans, and stated that had it been up to the Japanese, these orphans—if invited at all—would have been placed in the far reaches of the ballpark. The editorial concluded, "The Japanese should not forget this humanism together with the art of ball playing."[36]

Before the third game, a rare night contest against a Japanese All-Star team, O'Doul was photographed shaking hands with Crown Prince Akihito, who was attending his first game, and four decades later would succeed his father as Japan's emperor.[37]

Due in part to sub-standard lighting, the Seals failed to score until the seventh inning. Victor Starffin, who had pitched for the original Tokyo Giants at Seals

Stadium during that team's barnstorming tour of the United States 14 years earlier, took the mound against San Francisco. The son of Russian refugees and therefore not a Japanese citizen, Starffin had become one of the country's greatest pitchers, leading Japanese baseball with 27 wins in 1949. He tossed four shutout innings before leaving due to tightness in his elbow.[38] Left-hander Hiroshi Nakao added two more scoreless frames before the Seals touched him for a pair of un-earned runs in the seventh.

The Japanese never came close to crossing the plate. Cliff Melton allowed only one hit and struck out six in five innings, and then Milo Candini, who had won 15 games for the Oakland Oaks in 1949 after appearing in three contests for the Washington Senators, struck out nine in four innings of relief as the Seals won, 4-0, before a crowd of 60,000 at Stateside Park.

Despite O'Doul's unceasingly rosy outlook—he was determined not to let any negative incidents gain traction—there were sporadic examples of unsportsmanlike outbursts from Japanese fans. For instance, at the end of this game, a frustrating loss for the Japanese, it was said that several local fans hurled empty Coca-Cola bottles in the direction of Seals players as they exited the diamond.[39] Some players, especially those who had fought in the Pacific during the war, were concerned about their reception by the average Japanese on the street. But other than a few stares and disapproving glances here and there, they were greeted warmly. Any animosity remained below the surface.

On October 19 the Seals took on another cadre of Americans, an Army-Navy All-Star team, scoring six runs in the top of the first inning to put the game away before it even began. Rain that fell throughout the

Tokuji Kawasaki of the Yomiuri Giants and Con Dempsey of the Seals

contest limited the crowd to roughly 10,000 hardy souls, as San Francisco played its final game before departing Tokyo for five exhibitions in Osaka and Nagoya, after which they would return to Japan's capital for the final game on October 29, against a Japanese All-Star team.[40]

On October 20 O'Doul announced an 11th contest to be played on October 30, vs. an all-star team of Japanese university players. It would be "Kids Day," with everyone under age 15 admitted free of charge—the same as annual events O'Doul had held in San Francisco. The idea was hatched during the initial motorcade, when O'Doul witnessed hordes of children, clamoring for a glimpse of the American ballplayers.

"Thousands of kids lined the route, waving flags and shouting at the players as they went by," he explained. "I realized that for most of these youngsters it would be their only opportunity to see the team, and yet they seemed happy and contented. I determined then and there to make it possible for those youngsters to see a game."

"These kids are the future diplomats, businessmen, politicians, industrial leaders, bankers and teachers of Japan. I wanted to stage a contest that would be *their* game."[41]

On October 21, 55,000 fans gathered at Nishinomiya Stadium, near Osaka, to see the Seals play the All-West Japanese All-Stars. It was a surprisingly competitive game, with the Japanese tying the contest in the fifth inning. Bill Werle ultimately came away with a complete game, 3-1, victory in a pitchers' duel with young submariner Shisho Takesue, who had pitched the clincher a year earlier in Japan's National Baseball Congress tournament championship game.[42]

The Seals made two errors, one of which resulted in the only run of the game for the All-Stars, while the Japanese turned three double plays and committed only one miscue, when Takesue attempted to pick off Dario Lodigiani at second after a stolen base and threw the ball into center field, allowing Lodigiani to score.[43]

The Japanese noted the strategy, approach, and attitude of the Americans. Retired pitcher Kyoichi Nitta spoke at length with Seals coach Joe Sprinz. Nitta explained, "Among the many things I learned, I was most impressed to find out that each of his players think of baseball as a serious business, play only with the team in mind, and constantly behave like sportsmen." Nitta also observed that O'Doul was always teaching, even during games. "I can well understand,"

he concluded, "that they are being polished each moment and improving with each play."[44]

American reporters questioned O'Doul about the Japanese willingness to see their players lose. O'Doul explained that the Japanese wanted to see how they measured up against the best. "That's their psychology," he said. "If they [could defeat the Americans every time], nobody would go to another game. What's the use of seeing something inferior?"[45]

A paid crowd of 85,762, plus another 15,000 admitted via passes, greeted the San Francisco Seals on October 23 at Koshien Stadium, the largest ballpark in Japan, to see them take on the best the Japanese had to offer, the All-Japan All-Star team.[46] All-Japan tallied first, in the third inning, thanks to Takeshi Doigaki's double off Milo Candini, followed by a sacrifice and a successful squeeze play.

The Seals tied the score in the sixth off Hideo Fujimoto, and the All-Stars nearly answered in the bottom of the frame, putting two runners on base with no one out. But Cliff Melton retired the next three batters to end the threat. The game remained tied, 1-1, into the ninth, when the Seals loaded the bases with no one out against Fujimoto, who later admitted, "I was not afraid from the beginning of the Seals hitters. I mixed sliders and shoots about half and half, but when it came to the ninth inning, I began to feel tired."[47]

All-Japan brought in Hiroshi Nakao to relieve Fujimoto, but he promptly threw four straight balls to Jackie Tobin to force in the lead run. Nakao settled down, striking out Jim Moran, and All-Japan then executed a sparkling double play—Jim Westlake grounded back to Nakao, who threw to catcher Doigaki at home plate for an out. Doigaki then fired to first to nip Westlake to end the inning. It was outstanding defensive execution, but proved too little, too late. Melton struck out the side in the bottom of the ninth to clinch a 2-1 win.[48]

O'Doul praised the Japanese after the game: "The reason why the Seals could not hit in the pinches was because Fujimoto threw killers when the game was in danger. I have no criticism of such a fine game." Sprinz thought that the Japanese batters should have been more aggressive against Melton in the ninth, but also praised the All-Japan team: "This is the best game since we came to Japan."[49]

Tetsuharu Kawakami, widely considered Japan's best hitter despite struggling against the Seals, sought out O'Doul after the game for advice. The two discussed batting grips and stances, and O'Doul encouraged the Japanese star, telling him to continue as he had been, while adding one criticism. "Incidentally, Kawakami," said O'Doul, "you show what you expect from the pitcher too much in your stance and expression. As a result, the pitcher fools you."[50]

The Seals finally lost on October 26, in Nagoya, but not to Japanese ballplayers. Rather they were bested, 4-2, in 11 innings by the same Far East Air Force All-Stars they had crushed by a 12-0 score in the second game of the tour.[51]

San Francisco quickly rebounded, defeating the All-Japan team in a game played despite torrential rain courtesy of Typhoon Patricia. O'Doul coached at third base, holding a Japanese umbrella while perched atop an improvised platform consisting of cinder blocks.

For a while it appeared that the Japanese might capture their first win—All-Japan led, 4-1, at the end of the fifth inning, the only Seals tally coming on Brooks Holder's home run in the fourth. Despite miserable conditions—with groundballs into the outfield coming to a dead stop in puddles—no one wanted a rainout called with the Japanese in the lead. So everyone soldiered on.

In the sixth inning, 20-year-old Reno Cheso took his turn at bat while wearing a jacket to ward off the rain—until O'Doul called time and ordered him remove it. Relieved of the extraneous gear, Cheso promptly hit a grand slam off Takehiko Bessho, completely turning the game around. The Seals eventually won, 13-4.[52]

"We had advertised that we'd play rain or shine," said O'Doul. "So we figured if [the fans] could sit in the rain, we certainly could play in it."[53] He told a *Yomiuri Shimbun* reporter, "I have never seen in all my life such enthusiastic fans." He then joked, "However, I must say that it's natural for Seals to win in water."[54]

Cheso was treated as a hero. When he attempted to buy a camera the next day at a local shop, his money was refused. The shopkeepers insisted making it a gift.[55]

Now it was back to Tokyo to finish the tour.

On October 29, before an overflow crowd of between 60,000 and 70,000 in Tokyo, including Mrs. Douglas MacArthur and her 11-year-old son, Arthur, the Seals narrowly escaped defeat in their toughest battle against the Japanese.

Before the game, O'Doul and each of the Seals were presented *happi*—ceremonial Japanese coats. O'Doul's had his name embroidered on the front, and he posed with a child while wearing it, along with a Japanese towel wrapped about his head.[56]

Cliff Melton started for the Seals against Victor Starffin, with San Francisco managing only a single by Brooks Holder in seven innings. The game remained scoreless into the ninth. San Francisco finally took a 1-0 lead on outfielder Dick Steinhauer's home run off Shisho Takesue.[57] Steinhauer, who had struck out in his previous two at bats, admitted afterward, "I was expecting a curve…but it came in higher than I expected. …It was pure accident that I hit the home run."[58]

The Japanese attempted to tie things up in the bottom of the ninth. Pinch-hitter Kazuto Yamamoto singled and went to second on a ground ball by Shigeru Chiba. But Milo Candini struck out Takeshi Doigaki and Fumio Fujimura to end the game.[59]

O'Doul was impressed, declaring, "When I left San Francisco for Japan this time, I did not think, to tell you the honest truth, that Japanese baseball had improved to this extent."[60]

Fifty thousand children, chosen by lot because the demand for the free tickets was 10 times that, were on hand at Korakuen Stadium on October 30 for "Lefty O'Doul Day." When O'Doul, Del Young, and Dario Lodigiani appeared on the field at 10:30 that morning to conduct an impromptu clinic for several of the university ballplayers, the children on hand rushed forward in a quest to obtain O'Doul's autograph. In their enthusiasm, they accidentally dislodged a protective screen, sending several of them spilling onto the playing field. No one was hurt, but the children worried that "Uncle" O'Doul might be angry with them. Relieved after being assured he was not, they cheerfully returned to their seats to await the start of the ceremonies.[61]

O'Doul opened the festivities by proclaiming, "I am really glad to have such a large crowd of children. I am fifty-two years old but to show how glad I am, I will pitch at the beginning of the game." He then told them, "In order to become a great man, you should study hard. In the same way if you want to become a good ball player you must study hard by obeying the instruction of your teachers."[62]

As a treat, children were allowed to purchase Coca-Cola for half-price—normally the drink was unavailable to Japanese citizens, but special permission had been granted to sell it to everyone at the ballparks during the Seals tour. Families slipped yen to their children for extras to be brought home. Free programs were distributed, and Seals players batted 1,000 soft sponge baseballs into a sea of excited youngsters, whose reaction to a ball falling near them was characterized as resembling "the scramble of a horde of ants for a lump of sugar." A group of 500 deaf children invited by O'Doul gesticulated wildly during the ceremony; after the game they presented him an ornate flower basket of their own creation.[63]

As promised, O'Doul began the game on the mound, and managed to shut out the Japanese Collegiate All-Stars for the first two innings. But he weakened in the third, allowing three hits, throwing a wild pitch, and surrendering two runs before departing with the score tied, 2-2. The Seals eventually won, 4-2, in 13 innings, besting university pitcher Junzo Sekine, who went the distance and later forged a long career in Japan as a two-way player, pitching and playing the outfield.[64] Afterward, O'Doul posed with sumo star Kanematsu Maedayama, and tirelessly signed autograph after autograph. As *Asahi Shimbun* put it, "This was the best day ever for young baseball fans."[65]

Many agreed it had been not only a success for the children there that day, but also a success in the effort to mend relations between the two countries. The vice-chairman of the Tokyo Metropolitan Board of Education wrote to O'Doul about the impact of the event, telling him, "This splendid program contributed much to [implant] sportsmanship and international comity in the minds of Japanese boys all over the country."[66]

Festivities complete, O'Doul retreated to the clubhouse and addressed reporters, repeating his earlier statements that the Japanese had improved greatly in the past 15 years, and singling out three players he felt could be successful in America—Takeshi Doigaki, Tetsuharu Kawakami, and Kaoru Betto.[67]

After changing out of his uniform, O'Doul had one more important task—about which he was most enthusiastic. Along with Paul Fagan and Charlie Graham Jr., O'Doul was driven to the National Athletic Meet for an audience with Emperor Hirohito. The Emperor shook hands and told them, "I am heartily pleased that you are trying to promote goodwill and friendship between the United States and Japan through baseball games."[68]

According to American accounts, the emperor then turned to O'Doul. "It is a great honor to meet the greatest manager in baseball. I am very happy to meet you and I certainly am appreciative and proud of the good work the Seals have done on the tour and very happy it has been successful. It is by means of sports that our countries can be brought closer together. I am glad I can thank you personally for it."

"I've waited a long time for this day," replied O'Doul.[69] Later noting that he had lost 100 games for the first time in his managerial career during the 1949 season, O'Doul quipped, "It's a good thing he didn't know I finished in seventh place last season."[70]

General MacArthur was thrilled with the tour, and congratulated O'Doul and his players, proclaiming, "Eighty million people heard about you, five million saw you and five hundred thousand watched you play."[71] By the end of the tour when Lefty O'Doul yelled "banzai," the Japanese answered back in kind. Communists, previously visible on street corners, had vanished.[72]

Japanese Hall of Famer Masao Date, who had played against the Americans in 1931 and 1934, recognized the impact the 1949 tour had on the Japanese people. "When [the war] was over," wrote Date some 40 years later, "we were [destitute]. We had hard times in daily life, even in getting food. So we spent day after day without hopes or dreams. In this hardship situation Lefty O'Doul [returned.] What he did was, through baseball, encourage Japanese people to work for recovery. Especially, he cheered up our children … who were to carry this country in the future."[73]

The trip yielded a profit of $97,000, nearly all of it designated for the building of a youth baseball field and donations to various health organizations and orphanages.[74]

O'Doul noted the great welcome the team had received, and told reporters, "When we first arrived at the Haneda Airport I felt that all the Japanese were our good friends. And the longer we associate with them, the wider they open their heart's door to us."[75] O'Doul added that he wanted to bring an American ballplayer the next year to work with Japanese youth baseball players—that wish would result in Joe DiMaggio's first trip to Japan, in October 1950.[76]

The Japanese were anxious to hear a final assessment of their play from O'Doul. He complimented their defense, calling it near-major-league caliber, but explained that their pitchers threw too much, risking shoulder injuries. He urged them not to worry about having smaller statures than their American counterparts, pointing to the example of Paul Waner, who became a star despite his small physique.

O'Doul stressed that sportsmanship was the most honorable way to play, and advised the Japanese to create a farm system, noting that by the time a player reaches the American major leagues he has already refined his skills, unlike in Japan.[77]

Former pitching star Kyoichi Nitta insisted that the 1949 tour was a milestone event that would accelerate the development of quality baseball in Japan. To make his point, he invoked the Japanese adage, "Frogs in a well do not know of the wide ocean." Acknowledging that several of the contests were close, Nitta implored the Japanese not to be fooled into thinking they rivaled the Americans in talent. Reminding fans that the Seals were a minor-league team, he wrote, "We should learn from the admirable and the superior technique based on fundamentals of the Seals and start all over again. Japanese baseball clubs should realize that they are little frogs in a well that have been allowed to catch a glimpse of the wide ocean."[78]

O'Doul and several of the players remained in Japan for a week after the tour ended, finally departing on November 6. General William Marquat, who would call the tour "a goodwill effort seldom equaled and certainly never exceeded in the history of international sports relationships," was on hand to say goodbye at the airport.[79] A large crowd assembled, a band played *Auld Lang Syne*, and the players were "besieged with flowers."[80]

One by one, the players disappeared into the aircraft, shouting, "Sayonara, Sayonara!" and waving handkerchiefs—echoing O'Doul's famous tradition of swinging his bandanna to rally the home crowd during games. Finally, only O'Doul remained outside. He turned and addressed those who had assembled. "I'm very happy that our tour was a great success," he said. "I shall never forget the rest of my life the kind welcome shown to us during our stay. I would like to come again next year.

"To the children of Japan, I'd like to say, 'Take good care of yourselves,' and to the professional ballplayers of Japan, I'd like to leave the message, 'Practice alone will perfect your techniques.' Once again then, Sayonara."[81]

1949 SAN FRANCISCO SEALS GAMES IN JAPAN

Date	Place	Opponent	Score	Winner	Loser
October 15	Tokyo	Yomiuri Giants	13-4	Werle	Kawasaki
October 16	Tokyo	Far East Air Force	12-0	Lien	Price
October 17	Tokyo	Kanto All-Stars	4-0	Candini	Nakao
October 19	Tokyo	Army-Navy All-Stars	9-2	Drilling	Lewe
October 21	Nishinomiya	Kansai All-Stars	3-1	Werle	Takesue
October 22	Osaka	Army-Navy All-Stars	16-0	MacDonald	Isom
October 23	Osaka	All-Japan	2-1	Melton	Fujimoto
October 26	Nagoya	Far East Air Force	2-4	Price	Lien
October 27	Nagoya	All-Japan	13-4	Werle	Bessho
October 29	Tokyo	All-Japan	1-0	Candini	Tempo
October 30	Tokyo	College All-Stars	4-2	Lien	Sekine

1949 SAN FRANCISCO SEALS TOUR BATTING AND PITCHING STATISTICS[82]

Seals Batting Statistics	BA	G	AB	R	H	2B	3B	HR	RBI	SO	BB	SB
Dario Lodigiani	.269	11	52	11	14	3	2	1	9	1	4	1
Brooks Holder	.378	11	45	11	17	3	1	1	6	2	11	0
Jim Westlake	.200	11	45	6	9	1	0	1	6	8	9	1
Richard Steinhauer	.343	8	35	8	12	2	0	1	6	6	3	1
Dick Lajeskie	.412	8	34	5	14	2	4	1	9	5	5	1
Jackie Tobin	.353	8	34	7	12	3	0	0	2	3	7	0
Reno Cheso	.241	9	29	7	7	2	1	1	9	3	8	1
Strick Shofner	.462	8	26	8	12	2	2	0	4	3	9	0
Roy Jarvis	.333	7	24	3	8	3	1	0	6	1	3	1
Jimmy Moran	.304	7	23	4	7	2	0	0	2	3	2	0
Gene Brocker	.316	5	19	4	6	1	0	0	5	2	1	0
Ray Orteig	.273	5	11	1	3	1	0	0	1	0	2	0
Dick Briskey	.333	3	9	2	3	0	1	0	2	1	1	0
Bill Werle	.111	3	9	0	1	0	0	0	0	1	2	0
Con Dempsey	.000	3	6	0	0	0	0	0	0	1	0	0
Bill MacDonald	.400	3	5	0	2	1	0	0	2	1	1	0
Cliff Melton	.000	3	5	0	0	0	0	0	0	1	0	0
Al Lien	.000	3	5	1	0	0	0	0	0	3	2	0
Milo Candini	.250	3	4	1	1	0	0	0	0	0	0	0
Lefty O'Doul	.000	2	3	0	0	0	0	0	0	0	0	0
Dick Drilling	.000	1	3	0	0	0	0	0	0	2	0	0
Joe Sprinz	.500	1	2	0	1	0	0	0	0	0	0	0

Seals Pitching Statistics	ERA	G	W	L	IP	H	HR	SO	BB	R	ER
Bill Werle	1.96	3	3	0	23	19	0	15	2	6	5
Bill MacDonald	0.00	3	1	0	16	10	0	16	5	0	0
Al Lien	1.13	3	2	1	16	6	1	20	2	2	2
Cliff Melton	0.00	3	1	0	15	4	0	15	1	0	0
Con Dempsey	2.57	3	0	0	14	14	0	9	5	5	4
Milo Candini	0.75	3	2	0	12	4	0	18	1	1	1
Dick Drilling	0.00	1	1	0	5	5	0	3	2	2	0
Lefty O'Doul	6.00	1	0	0	3	3	0	0	1	2	2

Japanese Batting Statistics	BA	G	AB	R	H	2B	3B	HR	RBI	SO	BB	SB
Takeshi Doigaki	.235	4	17	1	4	1	1	0	2	1	0	0
Fumio Fujimura	.250	4	16	1	4	1	0	0	2	1	0	0
Shigeru Chiba	.176	5	14	1	1	0	0	0	0	5	2	0
Tetsuharu Kawakami	.071	5	14	1	1	0	0	0	1	5	0	0
Noboru Aota	.000	5	13	0	0	0	0	0	0	3	0	0
Kaoru Betto	.231	4	13	0	3	1	0	0	0	3	0	0
Kikuji Hirayama	.111	4	9	0	1	0	0	0	0	1	0	0
Katsumi Shiraishi	.125	4	8	0	1	0	0	0	1	2	1	0
Makoto Kozuru	.000	3	8	0	0	0	0	0	0	4	1	0
Hiroshi Oshita	.000	4	6	0	0	0	0	0	0	4	0	0
Michio Nishizawa	.333	3	6	0	2	0	0	0	0	1	0	0
Kiyoshi Sugiura	.167	3	6	1	1	0	0	0	0	3	0	0

Japanese Pitching Statistics are unavailable

NOTES

1   United Press International, "Giants' Visit to Japan Lauded Before Congress," *Pacific Stars & Stripes*, October 18, 1960: 19. MacArthur was also quoted as saying that O'Doul had done, "more to establish friendly relations with that country than 100 diplomats." Walter Addiego, "O'Doul Off for Australia to Direct Japanese Tour," *The Sporting News*, November 17, 1954: 21.

2   Undated letter, Matthew B. Ridgway to the members of the Baseball Hall of Fame Veterans Committee, Lefty O'Doul Clip File, National Baseball Hall of Fame and Museum.

3   Harry T. Brundidge, "O'Doul 'Greatest American' to Japanese," *The Sporting News*, March 12, 1958: 13-14; Dennis Snelling, *Lefty O'Doul: Baseball's Forgotten Ambassador* (Lincoln: University of Nebraska Press, 2017), 2.

4   "Editorial," *Asahi Shimbun*, October 18, 1949.

5   Robert K. Fitts, *Remembering Japanese Baseball: An Oral History of the Game* (Carbondale: Southern Illinois University Press, 2005), 3.

6   Howard Handleman, "Hopes Still Alive for Nippon Tour," *Pacific Stars & Stripes*, March 18, 1949: 3.

7   Russell Brines, "Occupation Heads Ponder Proposed Japan Ball Tour," *Pacific Stars & Stripes*, May 27, 1949: 3.

8   Jim McGee, "Seals Will Make Exhibition Tour of Japanese Cities in October," *The Sporting News*, August 3, 1949: 15.

9   Sgt. Howard Milner, "Japan Welcomes Seals with Great Reception," *Pacific Stars & Stripes*, October 13, 1949: 3.

10 Prescott Sullivan, "The Low Down," *San Francisco Examiner*, November 8, 1949: 25.

11 "The Seals Arrive in Tokyo," *Asahi Shimbun*, October 13, 1949.

12 "Lefty O'Doul and Seals Get Rousing Greeting in Japan," *The Sporting News*, October 19, 1949, 23.

13 Kent Nixon, "I'd Rather Be in Japan Hall of Fame," *Pacific Stars & Stripes*, February 20, 1968: 22. Roughly translated, "banzai" means "long live." It can also mean "ten thousand years."

14 Fitts, 4.

15 Jim McGee, "Seals' Trip Gave Jolt to Communism in Japan," *The Sporting News*, November 16, 1949: 4.

16 "Seals Honored by Gen MacArthur," *Yomiuri Shimbun*, October 14, 1949; Associated Press, "MacArthur Lunches with Seals Players," *Pacific Stars & Stripes*, October 14, 1949: 3.

17 Author interview, Reno Cheso, November 11, 2010; Snelling, 162.

18 Prescott Sullivan, "The Low Down," *San Francisco Examiner*, November 8, 1949: 25.

19 Bob Stevens, "Scraps of Paper Replace Old American Zeenut Photo Game," *San Francisco Chronicle*, November 20, 1949: 6H.

20 Stevens.

21 Sgt. Howard Milner, "Huge Rally Honors Seals," *Pacific Stars & Stripes*, October 14, 1949.

22 "O'Doul Pacifies Angry Crowds," *Yomiuri Shimbun*, October 14, 1949; "Sports Center Overpacked With Crowds to Welcome Seals," *Mainichi Shimbun*, October 14, 1949.

23 "Will Score Big Victory, Mgr. O'Doul Pledges," *Asahi Shimbun*, October 15, 1949.

24 "Will Score Big Victory, Mgr. O'Doul Pledges."

25 "Two Ace Giant Players Comment on Seals," *Asahi Shimbun*, October 16, 1949.

26 Sayuri Guthrie-Shimizu. *Transpacific Field of Dreams* (Chapel Hill: University of North Carolina Press, 2012), 217.

27 "Seals Cop First 13-4," *Nippon Times*, October 16, 1949: 1, 3.

28 Fitts, 4; John Holway, *Lefty & The Geisha*. http:baseballguru.com, baseballguru.com/jholway/analysisjholway32.html.

29 Nixon.

30 "Seals Cop First 13-4," *Nippon Times*, October 16, 1949: 1, 3.

31 "The Seals View the Giants," *Mainichi Shimbun*, October 16, 1949.

32 "On Seeing the Seals Play Their First Game," *Asahi Shimbun*, October 16, 1949. Sukeyuki (AKA Yushi) Uchimura was a Doctor of Medicine at Tokyo University and a proponent of teaching Japanese the American style of play.

33 "I Would Have Started Out with Fujimoto," *Asahi Shimbun*, October 16, 1949.

34 "War Orphans Invited to Seals Game," *Asahi Shimbun*, October 17, 1949.

35   Sgt. Howard Milner, "Seals Easy Winners Over FEAF, Giants," *Pacific Stars & Stripes*, October 17, 1949; "Frolicking Seals Blank FEAF Team in 12-0 Walkover," *Nippon Times*, October 17, 1949: 1.

36   "Editorial," *Asahi Shimbun*, October 18, 1949.

37   Leslie Nakashima, "Seals Beat All-Stars," *Nippon Times*, October 18, 1949: 1.

38   Starffin was the first Japanese pitcher to win 300 games, and still holds a number of Japanese pitching records, including wins in a season, 42, most consecutive 30-win seasons, three, (both records shared with Kazuhisa Inao), and most career shutouts, 83.

39   Bunshiro Suzuki, "U.S.-Japanese Baseball and Japanese Spectators," *Yomiuri Shimbun*, October 29, 1949.

40   United Press, "Seals Easy Victory Over G.I. All-Stars," *Pacific Stars & Stripes*, October 20, 1949: 3.

41   "Seals, University All-Stars to Play for Children Only," *Pacific Stars & Stripes*, October 21, 1949; "Special Free Ball Game for Children," *Yomiuri Shimbun*, October 21, 1949.

42   Five hundred teams in 20 districts participated, with the 20 champions participating in the tournament finals. Takesue, pitching for Fukuoka, defeated Beppu, 8-1, on a four-hitter to win the Senior Division before a crowd of 30,000. There was also a junior division, with 1,300 teams, that culminated in a championship game played before 60,000. *National Baseball Congress Official Baseball Annual, 1949*, 290-294.

43   "Oh So Happy—Seals Win Again From Japanese," *San Francisco Chronicle*, October 22, 1949: 1H; "Seals Trim Kansai Stars in Hard-Fought Game, 3-1," *Nippon Times*, October 22, 1949: 1; Snelling, 184.

44   Kyoichi Nitta, "We Learn from the Seals," *Yomiuri Shimbun*, October 19, 1949; Snelling, 185.

45   Interview of O'Doul by Lawrence Ritter, August 29, 1963.

46   *Spink Official Baseball Guide - 1950*, 131.

47   "All-Japan Loses Close Game Despite Fine Fielding," *Yomiuri Shimbun*, October 24, 1949.

48   Sgt. J.D. Greshan, "Seals Easily Tops Over GI All-Stars," *Pacific Stars & Stripes*, October 24, 1949; "All-Japan Loses Close Game Despite Fine Fielding," *Yomiuri Shimbun*, October 24, 1949; "Seals Take Ball Thriller From Japan All-Stars 2-1," *Nippon Times*, October 24, 1949: 1.

49   "Fielding Is Big League Caliber Says O'Doul," *Yomiuri Shimbun*, October 24, 1949.

50   "Don't Take Your Eyes From the Ball Advises O'Doul," *Yomiuri Shimbun*, October 24, 1949.

51   "FEAF Beats Seals in 11 Inning Game," *Pacific Stars & Stripes*, October 27, 1949. The Seals lost on a two-run walk-off home run by Albert Dickerson off Al Lien. Earl Price, who had pitched in the Florida International League, was the winning pitcher for the Air Force team.

52   "All-Japan Again Loses to Seals," *Yomiuri Shimbun*, October 28, 1949; author interview of Reno Cheso, November 11, 2010.

53   United Press, "Cheso Connects in Big Seals Win," *Pacific Stars & Stripes*, October 28, 1949: 3; "O'Doul, Home From Japan, Praises Native Ballplayers," *The Sporting News*, November 30, 1949: 16.

54   "O'Doul Expresses Thanks to Japanese Fans," *Yomiuri Shimbun*, October 28, 1949.

55   Author interview of Reno Cheso, November 11, 2010; United Press, "Cheso Connects in Big Seals Win," *Pacific Stars & Stripes*, October 28, 1949: 3; "200,000 See Frisco Seals in Four Contests in Orient," *The Sporting News*, November 2, 1949: 17.

56   "Sayonara Game," *Asahi Shimbun*, October 30, 1949.

57   "Seals Win With Homer in the Last Inning," *Mainichi Shimbun*, October 30, 1949; "Final Game Between Seals and All-Japan," *Yomiuri Shimbun*, October 30, 1949.

58   "'Accidental Hit' Says Modest Steinhauer," *Yomiuri Shimbun*, October 30, 1949. Kazuto Yamamoto was known as Kazuto Tsuruoka after 1958, the name by which he was inducted into the Japanese Baseball Hall of Fame in 1965.

59   "Seals Win with Homer in the Last Inning."

60   "U.S.-Japanese Baseball and Japanese Spectators," *Yomiuri Shimbun*, October 30, 1949.

61   "50,000 Boy Fans Give Rousing Ovations on O'Doul's Day," *Yomiuri Shimbun*, October 31, 1949.

62   "50,000 Boy Fans Give Rousing Ovations on O'Doul's Day."

63   "50,000 Tots See Seals in Action," Nippon Times, October 31, 1949; "Children's Paradise," Asahi Shimbun, October 31, 1949; "50,000 Boy Fans Give Rousing Ovations on O'Doul's Day"; Guthrie-Shimizu, 219.

64   "50,000 Tots See Seals in Action"; International News Service, "Back Pat Given by Lefty O'Doul," *Pacific Stars & Stripes*, October 31, 1949; Jimmy McGee, "Jap Emperor Hails O'Doul as 'Greatest Pilot,'" *The Sporting News*, November 9, 1949: 14.

65   Shimizu Kon, "Children's Paradise," *Asahi Shimbun*, October 31, 1949.

66   Joe Wilmot, "It All Adds Up to 'O'Douro, We Love You,'" *San Francisco Chronicle*, February 6, 1950: 1H.

67   International News Service, "Back Pat Given by Lefty O'Doul."

68   "Emperor Shakes Hands with O'Doul, Fagan and Graham," *Yomiuri Shimbun*, October 31, 1949. Some wire services reported the meeting as having taken place at the Imperial Palace, but *Yomiuri Shimbun* reported that the meeting was pre-arranged to occur at the athletic meet.

69   Associated Press, "Mikado Meets Lefty O'Doul," *Chicago Tribune*, October 31, 1949: Part 4, 1.

70   McGee, "Jap Emperor Hails O'Doul as 'Greatest Pilot.'"

71   Jim McGee, "Seals' Trip Gave Jolt to Communism in China," *The Sporting News*, November 16, 1949: 4.

72   McGee, "Seals' Trip Gave Jolt to Communism in China."

73   Masao Date letter, December 11, 1991, Lefty O'Doul clip file, National Baseball Hall of Fame and Museum.

74   "Profit From Seals Trip, $97,000, to Go to Charity," *The Sporting News*, March 8, 1950: 28.

75   Takata, "Listening to Mr. Fan and Mr. O'Doul," *Mainichi Shimbun*, November 1, 1949.

76   O'Doul would also invite five future Japanese Hall of Famers to spring training with the San Francisco Seals in 1951 and followed that during the post-season by organizing a team of major-league all-stars, plus a couple of PCL players, for the first tour of major leaguers to Japan since 1934.

77   "Sayonara Game," *Asahi Shimbun*, October 30, 1949.

78   "50,000 Boy Fans Give Rousing Ovations on O'Doul's Day"; Snelling, 257.

79   Prescott Sullivan, "The Low Down," *San Francisco Examiner*, December 3, 1949: 15.

80   "Sayonara, O'Doul-San," *Yomiuri Shimbun*, November 7, 1949.

81   "Sayonara! O'Doul-San."

82   Listed Japanese players have a minimum of 5 at-bats. Yoshikazu Matsubayashi, *Baseball Game History: Japan vs, U.S.A.* (Tokyo: Baseball Magazine, 2004), 87; Nippon Professional Baseball Records, https://www.2689web.com/nb.html.

JOE DIMAGGIO'S LAST HURRAH: THE 1951 LEFTY O'DOUL ALL-STAR TOUR

By Robert K. Fitts

In 1951 American troops still occupied Japan, but their mission had shifted. Rather than seeing the country as a former enemy to be subjugated, Japan was now viewed as an ally in the fight against communism. As the war in Korea raged, Japan became a strategic center for United Nations troops, providing a supply base, command center, and behind-the-lines support that included hospitals. It became vital to US policy that democracy flourish in Japan and that ties between the two nations remain strong.

Since the end of World War II, US forces had consciously used the shared love of baseball to help bind the two nations together. To this end, Maj. Gen. William F. Marquat, the occupation forces' Chief of Economic and Scientific Section, had restarted Japanese professional and amateur baseball immediately after the war. He also worked closely with Frank "Lefty" O'Doul to organize baseball exchanges. O'Doul made three trips to Japan between 1946 and 1950, bringing over the San Francisco Seals in 1949 and Joe DiMaggio in 1950. In August 1951, O'Doul announced that after the season he would return to Japan for the fourth time; this time taking an all-star team of major leaguers and Pacific Coast League stars on a goodwill tour to bolster ties between the two countries.

Sponsored by the Yomiuri newspaper, and organized by Sotaro Suzuki, the team was to play 16 games during a four-week trip starting in mid-October. The roster included American League batting champ Ferris Fain, Bobby Shantz, and Joe Tipton of the Athletics; Joe DiMaggio, Billy Martin, and Eddie Lopat of the Yankees; Dom DiMaggio and Mel Parnell of the Red Sox; Pirates Bill Werle and George Strickland; and PCL standouts Ed Cereghino, Al Lyons, Ray Perry, Dino Restelli, Lou Stringer, Chuck Stevens, and Tony "Nini" Tornay. To accommodate the All-Stars' schedule, Japanese baseball Commissioner Seita (also known as Morita) Fukui canceled the final games of the Nippon Professional Baseball League so that the Japan Series could be concluded before the all-stars arrived.[1]

As the all-star squad was about to depart, Joe DiMaggio made a stunning announcement. He was considering hanging up his spikes. In a meeting in New York, Yankees President Dan Topping supposedly told his star, "You are going to Japan. ... You will have a lot of time for thought. So, think it over, and when you get back to New York, call me up and we will go over this matter again."[2]

O'Doul's team gathered in San Francisco on October 15 and the next day boarded a Boeing 307 Stratoliner for the long flight to Hawaii. After an hour's delay before takeoff, the plane finally departed. Thirty minutes later, an engine began to sputter and then died. "Boy, was I scared," recalled Bobby Shantz. "It's no fun to have a motor conk out and see nothing below you but Pacific Ocean!" The Stratoliner returned safely to San Francisco and after three hours of repairs tried again. As the plane neared Hawaii, O'Doul told his players to change into their uniforms. The team was scheduled to play a 7:30 P.M. game in Honolulu and although they would be late, Lefty planned to keep the engagement.[3]

Once they touched down at 9:45 P.M., a police escort whisked the ballplayers to Honolulu Stadium, where 15,000 fans were still waiting for the visitors to arrive. By 10:30 they were playing ball. The exhausted All-Stars put in a poor performance against the local semipros. The Hawaiians scored six off Shantz and Lopat as starting pitcher Don Ferrarese (who had played minor-league ball and eventually had an eight-year major-league career) held the visitors to a single run in four innings before the All-Stars erupted for five in the fifth inning to tie the score. Reliever Ed Correa, however, stymied the All-Stars for the remainder of the contest, striking out eight, as the Hawaiians pushed across two more runs to win 8-6. To the great disappointment of the crowd, Joe DiMaggio did not start and only appeared as a pinch-hitter in the eighth inning –Correa fanned him on three pitches.[4] One irate fan later wrote to the *Honolulu Star-Bulletin*:

Do you honestly think that the way you let 15,000 people down the other night is true sportsmanship? Folks came piling into the Honolulu stadium at 7:00 PM and waited for six hours. … They came in droves, young and old. Old women carrying babies, dads with their kids, who should have been in bed in order to be ready for school the next day. And for what? ... they all came for the one purpose of seeing one man in action, Joe DiMaggio. All through the game an old grandmother sat holding her grandson, who kept asking, 'Where's DiMaggio, Gramma, where's DiMaggio? And when he finally did appear for an instant in the 8th, I looked over at them, and they were still waiting there, sound asleep! Yep, Lefty, you sure let us down.[5]

After the game ended at 12:55 A.M., the All-Stars trudged back to the airport and boarded a flight to Tokyo.[6]

General Marquat met the team when it arrived at Haneda Airport at 4:30 P.M. After a brief press conference, Marquat ushered the players into 15 convertibles for a parade through downtown Tokyo.

As dark fell, nearly a million fans lined the streets of Tokyo to welcome the team. "I never saw so many people in my life," recalled Shantz.[7] "Baseball-worshipping Japanese fans choked midtown Tokyo traffic for an hour and rocked the city with screams of 'Banzai DiMaggio!' … in a tumultuous welcome," the United Press reported.[8] "Magnesium flares flashed through the sky as the motorcade inched through the mob. DiMaggio and O'Doul were in the lead convertible, just behind a Military Police jeep that used its hood to push back the mob to clear a path. 'Banzai DiMaggio! Banzai O'Doul!' the mob shouted. Scraps of paper rained from the windows of office buildings."[9]

From left to right: Takehiko Bessho, Eddie Lopat, Joe DiMaggio, and Tetsuharu Kawakami

Yets Higa, a Honolulu businessman who accompanied the team to Japan, said, "The cars finally slowed down to almost a snail's pace as thousands of Japanese baseball fans walked right up to the cars to touch the celebrities from America. The crowd intensified its enthusiasm as an American band played Stars and Stripes [Forever]. The whole thing was so fantastic that I couldn't believe my eyes. Never in my life have I seen such a tremendous welcome given to any team."[10] The "surging crowds gave the ball players one of the greatest receptions ever accorded any visitors to Japan," added the *Nippon Times*.[11]

The next afternoon, Thursday, October 18, 5,000 spectators showed up at Meiji Jingu Stadium (renamed Stateside Park by the occupation forces) to watch the visiting ballplayers practice. O'Doul and DiMaggio remained the center of attention. "When O'Doul walks off or on the field, going to his car, walking to the locker room or any other time he appears in public, people seemed to spring right out of the ground. Baseball fans of all ages press in on him and beg for an autograph or just mill around, trying to catch a glimpse of 'Refty.' Joe DiMaggio is the same way. … It becomes almost impossible for him to move from one place to another for the people who want him to sign cards, baseballs, scraps of paper, old notebook covers or anything they happen to have handy."[12]

That evening more than 3,000 fans jammed the Nippon Gekijo, Asia's largest movie theatre, to see the ballplayers. Thousands more waited outside after being turned away from the sold-out event. During the brief ceremony, Sotaro Suzuki introduced the players as each stepped forward and bowed to the audience. After the introductions, O'Doul spoke: "The long war with cannons and machine-guns is ended. Let's promote Japanese-American friendship by means of balls and gloves. There is no sport like baseball to promote friendship between two countries. *Oyasuminasai* [goodnight]."[13]

On October 19, after 10,000 fans came to watch them practice, the ballplayers met with Gen. Matthew B. Ridgway, commander of the United Nations forces in Korea and the Supreme Commander of the Allied Powers in Japan. The general told the team that he was "very happy the major leaguers had come to Japan and felt sure their visit would promote good relations between the United States and Japan." Ridgway also asked if the squad could travel to Korea to entertain the troops.[14]

The gates of Korakuen Stadium opened at 8 A.M. the following day to accommodate the expected throng for the opening game against the Yomiuri Giants. The players themselves arrived for practice at 11:40. By 1:30, 50,000 fans packed the stands as baseball comedian Johnny Price began his show. Often known as Jackie, Price had been a longtime semipro and minor-league player (with 13 major-league at-bats for the Cleveland Indians in 1946), who had turned to comedy. During the 1940s and '50s, he performed at minor- and major-league parks across the United States. His act included accurately pitching two baseballs at the same time, blindfolded pitching, bunting between his legs, catching pop flies down his pants, and both playing catch and batting while hanging upside down by his ankles from a swing set. His signature act featured shooting baseballs hundreds of feet in the air with an air-powered "bazooka" and then catching them from a moving jeep.[15] The Japanese fans adored the show, having never seen anything like it in their serious games.

At 1:45, an announcer introduced the two teams and numerous dignitaries as they lined up on the field. Just as the pregame ceremonies and long-winded speeches seemed endless, General Marquat yelled, "Let's get on with the ball game!" and a few minutes later the teams took the field.[16]

The Yomiuri Giants had just completed one of their most successful seasons, running away with the Central League pennant by 18 games and then topping the Nankai Hawks in the Japan Series, four games to one. Their star-studded roster included seven future members of the Japanese Baseball Hall of Fame. Nevertheless, "manager Shigeru Mizuhara readily admitted that his championship team didn't have a chance, but he promised his ball players will be hustling all the way to put up a good fight."[17]

It did not take long for the All-Stars to grab the lead. After starter Takehiko Bessho retired leadoff batter Dom DiMaggio on a fly to right field, Billy Martin beat out a grounder to the shortstop. Ferris Fain then stroked a line-drive single into center field, sending Martin to third. Joe DiMaggio stepped to the plate and on a 2-2 count, "answering the fervent pleas of the fans" slammed a sharp single by the third baseman to score Martin. But a nifty double play turned by second baseman Shigeru Chiba ended the inning.[18]

Leading off the bottom of the first for Yomiuri was Lefty O'Doul's protégé Wally Yonamine. Yonamine was the first American star to play in the Japanese leagues after World War II. Frustrated by not reaching the inaugural Japan Series in 1950, Yomiuri executives wanted to import an American player to strengthen their lineup and teach the latest baseball techniques.

They reasoned that hiring a Caucasian player so soon after the end of the war would lead to difficulties, so instead they searched for the best available Japanese American player. They soon settled on Hawaiian-born Yonamine, who had not only just finished a stellar year with the Salt Lake City Bees of the Pioneer League but had also become the first man of Japanese descent to play professional football when he joined the San Francisco 49ers in 1947. In his first season with Yomiuri, Yonamine became an instant star, batting .354 with 26 stolen bases. He went on to have a 12-year Hall of Fame career in Japan.

Yonamine battled starter Mel Parnell before drawing a walk. With a one-out single by Noboru Aota, the Giants threatened to even the score, but Parnell got out of the jam and proceeded to shut down Yomiuri for the next five innings. In the meantime, Bessho retired the next 10 All-Stars and the fifth inning began with the score still 1-0. Two errors, a walk, and a single in the fifth, however, increased the All-Stars' lead to 4-0. The Americans tacked on another three runs and Bill Werle came on in relief of Parnell, holding Yomiuri scoreless for the 7-0 victory.[19]

After the game it began to rain. The precipitation slackened to a continuous drizzle by game time the following afternoon, October 20, when the All-Stars tackled the Mainichi Orions, winner of the inaugural Japan Series in 1950. The 1951 squad, however, was not as strong, finishing in third place in the Pacific League, 22½ games behind the Nankai Hawks.

The event began with the usual pregame ceremonies. Penny Ridgway, the general's wife, threw out the first pitch and Johnny Price entertained the 50,000 damp spectators with his antics. Not all went as planned, however, as Price failed to clear his "bazooka" and was struck in the elbow with a baseball. He was rushed to the Tokyo Army Hospital, where X-rays showed no significant damage.[20]

Once the game started, the muddy field caused grounders to "roll erratically" and players had difficulty "getting out of the muck around the batter's box." The conditions may have helped American starter Bobby Shantz. "The Orions could do absolutely nothing with him. Despite the rain, [his] control was fine, and he was very seldom behind the hitters." On the other hand, the All-Stars feasted on Orions starter Takeshi Nomura and reliever Toshihide Yamane, scoring 11 times on 20 hits with home runs by the

DiMaggio brothers and Shantz. Eddie Lopat came on for the visitors to close out the easy 11-0 victory.[21]

After spending October 22 shopping in Tokyo, where "hundreds of people surrounded and trailed after the … athletes as they peered into stores," the All-Stars and Yomiuri Giants traveled by train to Sendai in northern Japan to play on the 25th.[22] Thirty thousand fans, including 5,000 GIs from California's 40th Division, packed the ballpark. In a symbolic gesture to emphasize unity between the two nations, the 40th Division's band played both national anthems as the flags were raised prior to the game. Then the spectators witnessed an exciting game.

Although the Americans went out to a 2-0 lead in the second inning, the Japanese tied the score in the fifth as left fielder Hiroyoshi Komatsubara tripled in Yuko Minamimura and then scored as Yasuo Kusunoki executed a perfect squeeze bunt – causing the fans to jump "to their feet, waving red paper fans in great excitement." The All-Stars moved back on top in the next frame as Joe DiMaggio doubled and Dino Restelli slammed a pitch into the left-field stands. In the seventh, Komatsubara tripled again and scored on an infield out to cut the American lead to 4-3. In the eighth, however, Billy Martin homered and Restelli singled in Chuck Stevens to seal a 6-3 victory.[23]

The All-Stars returned to Tokyo the next day and were Marquat's dinner guests that evening at the Washington Heights Club, where they spent most of the time autographing menus and baseballs.[24] The following day, October 27, the All-Stars and Giants met again, this time in the city of Utsunomiya, 60 miles north of Tokyo. Although Yomiuri scored in the first inning to hold a lead for the first time in the tour, the All-Stars answered quickly with three runs in the top of the second and went on to win 11-4.

After rain postponed a scheduled game in Tokyo, the Americans traveled to Toyama to play a squad of Central League all-stars. The city's mayor personally greeted each player as the All-Stars left the railroad station through a "specifically constructed arch of welcome."[25] The team then paraded through town in open cars as thousands of fans cheered their arrival. The 30,000 spectators who packed the small stadium were disappointed to learn that Joe DiMaggio would not be in the lineup as he had slipped and fallen in his hotel bathroom, injuring his back. The game began as a pitchers' duel. Mel Parnell pitched masterfully, shutting out the Japanese for eight innings on four hits. The Central League team started 18-year-old Masaichi Kaneda. In his second year of pro ball, the slim southpaw had showed promise, winning 22 games (but losing 21) and striking out 233 batters (but walking 190) in 350 innings. Kaneda matured into one of Japan's greatest pitchers – the only hurler to win 400 games. Kaneda pitched well, holding the Americans to two runs and four hits in five innings before the lanky, bespectacled Shigeru Sugishita took over. O'Doul's All-Stars entered the ninth inning with just a 3-0 lead before both teams' bats came alive with the Americans plating three more and a two-run homer by Michio Nishizawa spoiling Parnell's shutout.[26]

As the All-Stars departed for a three-game stint in Osaka, Eddie Lopat, troubled by a sore arm, left the team and headed back to the United States. The Osaka games began on November 2 against the Pacific League champion Nankai Hawks, led by wily player-manager Kazuto Yamamoto (also known as Kazuto Tsuruoka). As a player, Yamamoto had just won his third MVP award and as a manager would lead the Hawks to 11 pennants in 23 years at their helm. He became the manager responsible for sending Masanori Murakami to the United States in 1964.

The game at Namba Stadium had sold out but heavy rain before the game discouraged spectators and just 10,000 showed up to the ballpark. Those who stayed home missed a great game. Yamamoto decided to challenge the Americans with a series of pitchers rather than just rely on his ace. Haruyasu Eto and Nobuo Nakatani shut out the visitors for five innings before Ferris Fain hit "a towering home run into the right-field stands" off Takeo Hattori in the sixth inning to give his side a 1-0 lead.[27] After the home run, Hattori and Susumu Yuki continued to shut out the Americans. Meanwhile Bill Werle (who managed Masanori Murakami when he came to the States in 1964) held down the Hawks, scattering nine hits in a complete-game shutout.[28]

The next day's game at famed Koshien Stadium against a combined Yomiuri Giants and Hanshin Tigers team could not have been more different. The All-Stars pounded all five Japanese pitchers for 13 runs on 19 hits including six home runs. With a 13-2 lead, O'Doul turned the mound over to Kenny Lehman of the US Army's 40th Division. Lehman had pitched for the Hollywood Stars in 1950 and went on to pitch for Brooklyn, Baltimore, and the Philadelphia Phillies in the majors. Lehman "retired the side without trouble."[29]

On Sunday, November 4, the American All-Stars began a four-game set against the All-Japan squad. Although the All-Japan roster contained numerous future members of the Japanese Baseball Hall of Fame, some complained that player selection was not based on actual performance and that a number of the past season's top players had been omitted. Commissioner Seita Fukui "however, pointed out that the games to be played with the American major leaguers are wholly of a goodwill character and cautioned against placing too much emphasis on the strength of the Japanese representatives."[30]

Fifty thousand fans packed Koshien Stadium to watch the two nations' all-stars battle. The Americans scored quickly as Joe DiMaggio lashed a two-out double in the top of the first off Takehiko Bessho to drive in two. The Japanese retaliated with two runs off Mel Parnell in the fourth, momentarily knotting the game before Chuck Stevens doubled home Ferris Fain in the top of the fifth to put the Americans back in the lead. In the bottom of the sixth, Kenny Lehman took the mound again and pitched four scoreless innings to save the 4-2 victory. After the game, reporters peppered Joe DiMaggio with questions about his retirement, but the Yankee Clipper restated that he was still undecided about his future in baseball.[31]

The All-Stars headed back east the next day, stopping in Shizuoka to play the All-Japan squad on November 6 and Nagoya on the seventh to meet the Dragons. Neither team challenged the Americans as the All-Stars beat All-Japan 6-1 and the Dragons 11-1.[32] O'Doul's team had now won every contest, outscoring their opponents 76-15.

The All-Stars' perfect record ended the next day in Nishinomiya.

Thirty thousand fans crowded into the ballpark to watch the Pacific League All-Stars, managed by Kazuto Yamamoto, challenge the Americans. Bobby Shantz took the mound for the All-Stars and held the Japanese to just three hits in seven innings. Unfortunately for Shantz, two of the three hits were sharp RBI singles by Mainichi Orions outfielder Kaoru Betto, which put the Pacific Leaguers up 2-0.

Having nearly upset O'Doul's squad earlier in the week, Yamamoto once again threw a succession of fresh pitchers at the Americans. Nankai ace Haruyasu Eto started and was followed by Yasuo Yonekawa of the Tokyu Flyers, Nobuo Nakatani of the Hawks, Tokuji Kawasaki of the Nishitetsu Lions, Giichi Hayashi of the Daiei Stars, and Susumu Yuki of the Hawks. The hurlers held the Americans scoreless, and Joe DiMaggio hitless, until the eighth inning, when a bunt hit, an error, a triple, and a wild pitch allowed the All-Stars to tie the game.

The two teams entered the 11th inning knotted, 2-2. With one out, Betto struck again, smoking another single. He then stole second base to put the winning run in scoring position. Right-handed relief pitcher Ed Cereghino bore down and stuck out future Hall of Famer Tokuji Iida. Yamamoto then sent Takuji Kochi to pinch-hit for Shosei Go. With the game in jeopardy, O'Doul walked to the mound and brought in his ace, lefty Mel Parnell, who fanned Kochi to get out of the jam. After 2 hours and 54 minutes of baseball, dusk had fallen. All agreed that the game would end in a tie.[33]

Two days later, on Saturday, November 10, the Central League All-Stars adopted Yamamoto's strategy against the Americans. On a crisp, misty day at Meiji Jingu Stadium, 54,000 fans watched four of Japan's top pitchers – 1951 Rookie of the Year Kiyoshi Matsuda, Takehiko Bessho, Masaichi Kaneda, and Shigeru Sugishita – hold O'Doul's squad scoreless for seven innings. Meanwhile, GI Kenny Lehman limited the Japanese to just two hits in the first six innings but surrendered an unearned run.

With his team down 1-0 in the top of the eighth, Joe DiMaggio stepped into the batter's box. The 6-foot-tall Sugishita stood on the mound, peering down at his catcher through his thick, round glasses. Although the lanky hurler always looked a bit comical in his baggy flannel uniform, he could pitch. He would win three Sawamura Awards for the season's best pitcher and finish his career with a 2.23 ERA. "When DiMaggio came up," Sugishita later told reporters, "I felt tremendous pressure. … I was half inclined to walk him."[34] The Yankee Clipper fouled off a pitch and then connected with his long graceful swing, slamming "a towering fly into the stands in left field" to tie the game.[35]

In the top of the ninth, the Americans surged ahead as relief pitcher Al Lyons walked, Dom DiMaggio tripled, and Billy Martin hit a fly ball scoring Dom to put the Americans on top, 3-1. After a walk to Fain and a groundout by Stevens, the inning came to an end with Joe DiMaggio grounding to third. It proved to be DiMaggio's last professional at-bat as he announced after the game that he needed to return to the United States for unspecified "business reasons." A month later, DiMaggio retired.[36]

On Sunday, as Joe DiMaggio waited for his flight at Haneda Airport, his team faced the All-Japan squad at Jingu. After two close games, the All-Stars' bats unleashed against starter Masaichi Kaneda and four relievers. The Americans pounded out 21 hits and 12 runs as Mel Parnell blanked the Japanese on four hits.[37]

After a couple of days off, O'Doul's All-Stars once again faced off against Kazuto Yamamoto's Pacific League All-Stars. Seventeen-year-old Ed Cereghino took the mound for the Americans, and the Pacifics began with Susumu Yuki. The Japanese took the lead in the second inning, as Tokuji Iida tripled down the right-field line and after an out, Kazuo Horii walked. With runners on first and third, Hawks shortstop Chusuke Kizuka surprised the Americans with a perfect squeeze bunt and Iida streaked home for the first run. Next Yuki, the pitcher, walloped a double to left, scoring Horii to put his team up 2-0.

A single by Ferris Fain followed by a Chuck Stevens triple put the Americans on the board in the top of the third, but the Pacifics retaliated in the bottom of the inning as Kaoru Betto walked and Iida doubled him in. Down 3-1, O'Doul brought in Bobby Shantz to start the fourth inning. Shantz dominated the Pacifics, allowing just three hits and no runs for the remainder of the game, but it was too late as Yuki, Takeshi Nomura, Yasuo Yonekawa, and Giichi Hayashi shut down the Americans' offense to preserve the 3-1 victory.[38]

A surprised reporter for the *Nippon Times* wrote, "The upset victory was not only the first loss of the American All-Stars in 14 starts but was also the first time 'Lefty' has played for or managed a losing team here." Even the *New York Times* covered the upset, incorrectly stating, "An American professional baseball team was beaten by a Japanese club today for the first time in history."[39] According to *The Sporting News*, "The victory produced a national sensation in Japan."[40]

On the heels of the defeat, the All-Stars had a four-day hiatus as comedian Johnny Price, Dom DiMaggio, Mel Parnell, Billy Martin, Ferris Fain, and George Strickland headed off to Korea to visit American troops. The players were flown by a US Army plane to the Kumsong front – an active war zone. There they visited "the front-line infantry companies [to] talk baseball to the combat weary fighters."[41]

On Saturday, November 17, the All-Stars returned to action at Korakuen Stadium against the All-Japan squad. Although the Pacific League All-Stars had given the Americans trouble, the supposedly more talented All-Japan team had not played well, losing their previous three games, 4-2, 6-1, and 12-0. This final matchup was no exception, as O'Doul's squad pounded All-Japan 14-5.[42]

The All-Stars' tour ended on Monday, November 19, with a charity game against the Yomiuri Giants at Meiji Jingu Stadium. For what was heralded as "O'Doul Day," Lefty invited 30,000 Japanese schoolchildren as well as United Nations soldiers from the Army hospitals in Tokyo to be his guests at the ballpark. After the game, O'Doul donated 100,000 yen (worth $2,777 at the time) to Hinode Gakuen, a private school for the mentally challenged in Tokyo.[43]

The children were treated to a cracking good game. Yomiuri went out to a quick lead, scoring four in the bottom of the first off Mel Parnell. The All-Stars chipped away, tallying two in the third, one in the fifth, and two in the seventh to enter the bottom of the ninth on top 5-4.

Dusk had fallen as reliever Bobby Shantz faced Hiroyoshi Komatsubara with two outs and Mitsuo Uno on first. Komatsubara hit a high pop fly to shallow left. Shortstop George Strickland went out and left fielder Dino Restelli charged in, but neither could see the ball in the darkened sky. It fell for a double as Uno raced around the bases to score the tying run. After the inning, all agreed that it was too dark to continue, and the game ended in a 5-5 draw. A perfect finish for a charity event.[44]

The next day the All-Stars boarded a 10:05 P.M. flight back to the United States. As they departed, the players gushed about the Japanese hospitality.[45] "I found the Japanese to be wonderful hosts," exclaimed Bobby Shantz. "They wouldn't let us do a thing. After a game they would come to our rooms and get the uniforms and have them cleaned. Almost anything we wanted was served on a silver platter. I never met such friendly people. They are great cooks too. ... I can sincerely say I thoroughly enjoyed the trip. I'd love to go back to Japan for another tour."[46]

O'Doul praised the Japanese players. "Don't underestimate Japanese baseball. It is developing in rapid strides and right now is capable of competing in Class A or lower leagues in the United States. ... We had a pretty well balanced aggregation of American players on this trip – a club that could make United States teams in every league step lively. In every game the Japanese played fine baseball and did not appear to be outclassed by any means. I am really amazed at the progress made in baseball technique in the three years since I first came to Japan in the postwar period. The Japanese have some good long-ball hitters such as Tetsuharu Kawakami, Michio Nishizawa and Kaoru Betto. They always have been top fielders and the pitching has improved a lot since the early days. Yamamoto and Mizuhara are top strategists as managers."[47]

Although the 1951 tour did not have the diplomatic impact of the 1934 All-American or 1949 Seals tours, newspapers in both the United States and Japan agreed that the visit helped solidify goodwill between the two nations. A *New York Times* editorial proclaimed, "News that a half a million Japanese turned out in Tokyo to shout 'banzai' for Joe DiMaggio and Lefty O'Doul is the sort of thing that keeps up our hope for some eventual international understanding. ... What we are all trying to find is those means of communication that can jump across language and culture-pattern barriers. Sport is one of those means ... We don't expect the world to be transformed on the playing fields, but every little bit helps. When the Japanese shout their 'banzais,' in this case they are helping to shout in a better world."[48]

NICHIBEI YAKYU: US TOURS OF JAPAN

1951 ALL-STARS GAMES IN JAPAN

Date	Place	Opponent	Score	Winner	Loser
October 20	Tokyo	Yomiuri Giants	7-0	Parnell	Bessho
October 21	Tokyo	Mainichi Orions	11-0	Shantz	Nomura
October 25	Sendai	Yomiuri Giants	6-3	Werle	Matsuda
October 27	Utsunomiya	Yomiuri Giants	11-4	Shantz	Fujimoto
October 31	Toyama	Central League All-Stars	6-2	Parnell	Kaneda
November 2	Osaka	Nankai Hawks	1-0	Werle	Hattori
November 3	Osaka	Giants & Tigers	13-2	Shantz	Fujimura
November 4	Osaka	All-Japan	4-2	Parnell	Bessho
November 6	Shizuoka	All-Japan	6-1	Lyons	Hayashi
November 7	Nagoya	Nagoya Dragons	11-1	Werle	Sugishita
November 8	Nishinomiya	Pacific League All-Stars	2-2	None	None
November 10	Tokyo	Central League All-Stars	3-2	Lyons	Sugishita
November 11	Tokyo	All-Japan	12-0	Parnell	Kaneda
November 13	Okayama	Pacific League All-Stars	1-3	Yuki	Cereghino
November 17	Tokyo	All-Japan	14-5	Lehman	Yonekawa
November 19	Tokyo	Yomiuri Giants	5-5	None	None

1951 LEFTY O'DOUL ALL-STARS TOUR BATTING AND PITCHING STATISTICS[49]

American Batting Statistics	BA	G	AB	R	H	2B	3B	HR	RBI	SO	BB	SB
Billy Martin	.329	16	79	15	26	6	1	3	7	1	2	1
Dom DiMaggio	.319	16	72	16	23	4	1	3	14	13	10	2
George Strickland	.221	16	68	7	15	2	2	1	7	6	4	0
Lou Stringer	.254	16	63	12	16	2	1	3	14	11	8	2
Ferris Fain	.417	16	60	14	25	4	1	3	14	2	15	2
Dino Restelli	.358	16	53	11	19	3	0	3	11	5	6	0
Chuck Stevens	.404	13	52	11	21	5	4	2	13	5	4	0
Joe Tipton	.263	14	38	8	10	1	0	2	4	6	6	0
Joe DiMaggio	.296	9	27	3	8	2	0	2	6	2	5	0
Bobby Shantz	.471	6	17	4	8	2	0	1	5	0	0	0
Al Lyons	.353	10	17	5	6	1	0	1	6	2	4	1
Tony Tornay	.294	7	17	2	5	1	0	0	0	1	0	0
Mel Parnell	.143	7	14	3	2	0	0	1	1	1	2	0
Bill Werle	.154	5	13	1	2	0	0	0	2	2	0	0
Ray Perry	.200	7	10	1	2	0	0	1	1	4	1	0
Kenny Lehman	.000	4	6	0	0	0	0	0	0	1	0	0
Ed Cereghino	.000	4	2	0	0	0	0	0	0	2	0	0
Eddie Lopat	1	1	1	0	1	0	0	0	0	0	0	0

American Pitching Statistics	ERA	G	W	L	IP	H	HR	SO	BB	R	ER
Mel Parnell	2.25	7	4	0	35.1	25	1	25	15	9	9
Bobby Shantz	1.54	6	3	0	35	27	0	22	7	9	6
Bill Werle	1.33	5	3	0	27	24	0	10	7	5	4
Al Lyons	0.50	4	2	0	18	12	1	9	4	2	1
Kenny Lehman	1.69	4	1	0	16	12	0	11	6	4	3
Ed Cereghino	2.45	4	0	1	10.2	7	0	9	7	3	3
Eddie Lopat	0.00	1	0	0	3	2	0	0	2	0	0

Japanese Batting Statistics	BA	G	AB	R	H	2B	3B	HR	RBI	SO	BB	SB
Tetsuharu Kawakami	.216	11	37	2	8	1	0	0	3	3	1	0
Shigeru Chiba	.290	11	31	2	9	1	0	0	1	3	1	0
Noboru Aota	.333	11	27	3	9	2	0	0	1	6	2	0
Kaoru Betto	.308	7	26	3	8	1	0	1	3	5	4	1
Yoshiyuki Iwamoto	.125	6	24	2	3	3	0	0	0	1	1	0
Fumio Fujimoto	.304	7	23	3	7	2	0	0	0	1	3	0
Yuko Minamimura	.211	6	19	2	4	0	0	0	3	1	0	1
Takeshi Doigaki	.222	7	18	0	4	0	0	0	0	0	5	0
Saburo Hirai	.294	7	17	1	5	1	0	0	1	3	1	1
Mitsuo Uno	.118	7	17	3	2	1	0	0	0	5	5	1
Tokuji Iida	.250	6	16	1	4	2	1	0	2	3	0	0
Chusuke Kizuka	.067	7	15	1	1	0	0	0	1	5	0	0
Yasuo Kusunoki	.067	9	15	0	1	0	0	0	1	7	2	0
Hiroyoshi Komatsubara	.286	7	14	3	4	1	2	0	3	2	2	0
Kazuo Kageyama	.167	6	12	0	2	1	0	0	0	0	4	0
Kazuto Yamamoto	.500	5	10	0	5	1	0	0	2	1	1	1
Michio Nishizawa	.375	3	8	1	3	1	0	1	2	1	2	0
Kazuo Hori	.250	3	8	0	2	0	0	0	0	1	1	0
Hiroshi Oshita	.143	4	7	0	1	0	0	0	0	1	0	0

NICHIBEI YAKYU: US TOURS OF JAPAN

Japanese Pitching Statistics	ERA	G	W	L	IP	H	HR	SO	BB	R	ER
Takehiko Bessho	5.32	5	0	2	21.2	23	2	9	9	15	13
Shigeru Sugishita	6.30	5	0	2	20	26	4	14	8	15	14
Takumi Otomo	5.25	4	0	0	12	19	0	6	4	11	7
Masaichi Kaneda	4.09	6	0	2	11	10	1	4	11	8	5
Kiyoshi Matsuda	5.73	4	0	1	10.1	13	3	2	5	10	7
Tadashi Eto	3.60	4	0	0	9.2	9	1	2	5	4	4
Yasuo Yonekawa	6.75	5	0	1	8	9	3	5	3	6	6
Takeo Hattori	9.00	4	0	1	7.1	16	1	5	3	8	8
Takeshi Nomura	11.25	2	0	1	7.1	16	3	1	4	10	10
Susumu Yuki	1.29	3	1	0	7	6	0	5	4	1	1
Hideo Fujimoto	7.71	2	0	1	7	11	2	2	3	8	6

NOTES

1. Both the Yomiuri Giants and the Nankai Hawks had already clinched their pennants. "Caught on the Fly," *The Sporting News*, October 10, 1951: 27.

2. Dan Daniel, "DiMag, Topping Shadow Box on Clipper's 100 Grand Pay," *The Sporting News*, October 24, 1951: 4.

3. Bobby Shantz, *The Story of Bobby Shantz* (Philadelphia: J.B. Lippincott, 1953): 127; Jim McGee, "O'Doul Stars Have Rough Time in Air and at Honolulu," *The Sporting News*, October 24, 1951: 2.

4. Jim McGee; Carl Machado, "15,000 See O'Doul Stars Bow to Locals, 8-6," *Honolulu Star-Bulletin*, October 16, 1951: 18.

5. K.B., "Wanted to See, DiMag – Disappointed," *Honolulu-Star Bulletin*, October 20, 1951: 4.

6. Machado.

7. Shantz, 130.

8. United Press, "Million Screaming Fans in Tokyo Jam Traffic to Acclaim DiMaggio," *New York Times*, October 18, 1951: 35.

9. United Press, "Million Screaming Fans in Tokyo Jam Traffic to Acclaim DiMaggio."

10. Red McQueen, "Hoomalimali," *Honolulu Advertiser*, October 27, 1951: 10.

11. "Tumultuous Welcome Given U.S. Ballplayers," *Nippon Times*, October 18, 1951: 1.

12. Sgt. Clarkson Crume, "Chotto Matte," *Pacific Stars and Stripes*, October 19, 1951: 13.

13. United Press, "O'Doul Stars Are Cheered in Theater," *Honolulu Advertiser*, October 19, 1951: 12.

14. United Press, "Touring All Stars Get Assist from Ridgeway," *New York Daily News*, October 20, 1951: 119.

15. Andrew Sharp, "Jackie Price," SABR BioProject, https://sabr.org/bioproj/person/jackie-price/.

16. Fred N. Miike, *Baseball Mad Japan* (Tokyo: Privately published, 1955), 40.

17. "U.S. Major League Ball Team to Make Japan Debut Today," *Nippon Times*, October 20, 1951: 1.

18. Sgt. Clarkson Crume, "All Stars Halt Giants, 7-0," *Pacific Stars and Stripes*, October 21, 1951: 16.

19. Crume, "All Stars Halt Giants, 7-0": 15.

20. Shantz, 131.

21. Sgt. Clarkson Crume, "All-Stars Blank Mainichi," *Pacific Stars and Stripes*, October 22, 1951: 16.

22. United Press, "Jap Crowds Gape at Major Leaguers," *Brooklyn Daily Eagle*, October 22, 1951: 15; Leslie Nakashima, "Bosox Stars Happy Boudreau Now Pilot," *Pacific Stars and Stripes*, October 24, 1951: 15.

23. Leslie Nakashima, "Big Leaguers Beat Nippon Giants, 6 to 3," *Honolulu Star-Bulletin*, October 25, 1951: 8; N. Sakata, "O'Doul's All-Stars Continue March of Victory in Japan," *The Sporting News*, November 7, 1951: 17.

24. "Members of the 20-Man All American Baseball Squad," *Nippon Times*, October 27, 1951: 3.

25. United Press, "Big League Stars Triumph in Japan," *New York Times*, November 1, 1951: 39.

26. "American All-Stars Defeat Central Leaguers 6 to 2," *Nippon Times*, November 1, 1951: 2.

27. "Fain's Homer Beats Hawks in Osaka Tilt," *Japan Times*, November 3, 1951, 2.

28. United Press, "Stars Nip Hawks on Fain's Homer," *Pacific Stars and Stripes*, November 3, 1951: 15.

29. United Press, "Stars on Hit Spree," *Pacific Stars and Stripes*, November 4, 1951: 15.

30. "All-Japan Ball Players Named to Play Against U.S. Team," *Nippon Times*, October 17, 1951: 2.

31. Associated Press, "'Clipper' Comments on Retirement Plans," *Pacific Stars and Stripes*, November 5, 1951: 16.

32. United Press, "Al Lyons Hurls, Hits in 'All-Stars' Victory Against Japan Pros," *Pacific Stars and Stripes*, November 7, 1951: 15; "U.S. Major Leaguers Trounce All-Japan, 6-1, in Shizuoka," *Nippon Times*, November 7, 1951: 2; United Press, "All-Stars Batter Dragons," *Pacific Stars and Stripes*, November 8, 1951: 15; "U.S. All-Stars Win 10th Game as Werle Whips Dragons 11-1," *Nippon Times*, November 8, 1951: 2.

33. "Japanese Tie Americans in 11-Inning Osaka Contest," *Pacific Stars and Stripes*, November 9, 1951: 15; "Inspired All-Pacific Nine Holds Visitors to 2-2 Tie," *Nippon Times*, November 9, 1951: 2.

34   Kyushi Yamato, "Zoku Nichibei Yakyu Haikenki," *Baseball Magazine* 9, no. 1 (1952): 81.

35   Sgt. Clarkson Crume, "DiMaggio Brothers Pace U.S. Triumph Over Central Stars," *Pacific Stars and Stripes*, November 11, 1951: 14.

36   Crume, "DiMaggio Brothers Pace U.S. Triumph Over Central Stars;" "American Ball Team Edges Central League All-Stars, 3-2," *Nippon Times*, November 11, 1951: 2; N. Sakata, "All Star Jap Pros Hand U.S. Team First Loss on Trip," *The Sporting News*, November 21, 1951: 17.

37   United Press, "U.S. Nine Blanks Japanese, 12-0, With 21-Hit Assault at Tokyo," *New York Times*, November 12, 1951: 37; Sgt. Clarkson Crume, "All-Stars Whip All-Japan," *Pacific Stars and Stripes*, November 12, 1951: 15.

38   United Press, "Pacific League Team Whips All-Stars, 3-1," *Pacific Stars and Stripes*, November 14, 1951: 15.

39   "Japan Nine Finally Scores 1st Win Over U.S. All-Stars," *Nippon Times*, November 14, 1951: 1; United Press, "U.S. in First Loss to Japanese Team," *New York Times*, November 14, 1951: 55. The Mita Club beat the All-Americans, 9-3, on November 19, 1922.

40   N. Sakata, "All Star Jap Pros Hand U.S. Team First Loss on Trip," *The Sporting News*, November 21, 1951: 17.

41   Sgt. Jim Gilbert, "DiMaggio, Parnell Reach Front Lines," *Pacific Stars and Stripes*, November 15, 1951: 16.

42   United Press, "All-Stars Take 13th On Home Run Spree," *Pacific Stars and Stripes*, November 18, 1951: 15.

43   "O'Doul Day to Be Feted Mon. at All-Stars' Farewell Game," *Nippon Times*, November 17, 1951: 2; "O'Doul Gives 100,000 Yen to Hinode Gakuen Here," *Nippon Times*, November 20, 1951: 2.

44   "Giants Tie All-Stars, 5-5 In Sayonara Ball Game," *Nippon Times*, November 20, 1951: 2; Leslie Nakashima, "U.S. Stars End Trip in Tie with Yomiuri; 30,000 Kids Watch," *Pacific Stars and Stripes*, November 20, 1951: 14.

45   United Press, "American All-Stars Head for Honolulu; O'Doul Lauds Foes," *Pacific Stars and Stripes*, November 21, 1951: 15.

46   Shantz, 132, 135.

47   Ema Mori, "Japanese Game Is Making Rapid Strides, Says Lefty," *The Sporting News*, November 28, 1951: 18.

48   Editorial, "Baseball Fans in Tokyo," *New York Times*, October 19, 1951, 26; "Welcome All-Stars," *Nippon Times*, October 19, 1951: 6.

49   Yoshikazu Matsubayashi, *Baseball Game History: Japan vs, U.S.A.* (Tokyo: Baseball Magazine, 2004), 88; Nippon Professional Baseball Records, https://www.2689web.com/nb.html.

THE COLD WAR, A RED SCARE, AND THE NEW YORK GIANTS' HISTORIC TOUR OF JAPAN IN 1953

By Steven K. Wisensale

On the morning of June 29, 1953, readers of the *Globe Gazette* in Mason City, Iowa, were greeted by a headline on page 13: "New York Giants Invited to Tour Japan This Fall."[1]

The Associated Press in Tokyo reported that Shoji Yasuda, president of the *Yomiuri Shimbun*, had formally invited Horace Stoneham, owner of the New York Giants, to bring his team to Japan for a goodwill tour after the season. The tour was to commemorate the 100th anniversary of Commodore Matthew Perry's arrival in Japan in 1853, when he forced the isolated nation's ports to open to the world.[2]

An excited Stoneham quickly sought and was given approval for the trip from the US State Department, the Defense Department, and the US Embassy in Tokyo. The tour was also endorsed by Baseball Commissioner Ford Frick. However, two hurdles remained for Stoneham: He needed his fellow owners to suspend the rule that prohibited more than three members of a major-league team from playing in postseason exhibition games.[3] And at least 15 Giants on the major-league roster had to vote yes for the tour.

With respect to the first hurdle, previous postseason tours had consisted primarily of major-league all-stars, not complete teams. The 1953 Giants, however, became trailblazers as the first squad to tour Japan as a complete major-league team.[4] The second rule was a requirement set forth by the Japanese sponsors of the

Freddie Fitzsimmons of the New York Giants gives a pitching clinic for the All-Japan team (©Courtesy of the San Francisco Giants)

tour. They wanted their Japanese players to compete against top-quality major leaguers.

WAIVER IS GRANTED

The waiver Stoneham sought was granted by team owners on July 12 when they gathered in Cincinnati for the All-Star Game "We will now proceed with our plans for the goodwill tour," said an upbeat Stoneham.[5]

Another person who was extremely happy with the owners' decision to support the Giants' tour of Japan was Tsuneo "Cappy" Harada. Harada was a US Army officer serving with the American occupation force in postwar Japan and an adviser to the Yomiuri Giants. One of his tasks was to restore morale among the Japanese people through sports, particularly baseball. It was Harada who suggested to General Douglas MacArthur that the San Francisco Seals be invited to Japan for a goodwill tour in 1949.[6] Working closely with Lefty O'Doul, Harada coordinated the tour, which MacArthur later declared was "the greatest piece of diplomacy ever," adding, "all the diplomats put together would not have been able to do this."[7] O'Doul would play a central role in 1953 by assisting Harada in coordinating the Giants' tour.[8]

After the owners granted approval, Harada flew to Honolulu, where he met with city officials and baseball executives to share the news that Hawaii would host two exhibition games during the team's layover on their journey to Japan.

At a press conference on July 18 in Honolulu, Harada explained why the Giants were chosen for the tour: They were the oldest team in major-league baseball, and they had Black players. A Honolulu sportswriter observed: "The presence of colored stars on the team will help show the people of Japan democracy at work and point out to them that all the people in the United States are treated equally."[9]

Harada's statement was not exactly accurate. First, while the Giants were one of the oldest professional teams, they were not the oldest. Five other teams preceded them: the Braves, Cubs, Cardinals, Pirates, and Reds. And Harada's statements regarding racial diversity and "equality for all" were misleading. By the end of the 1953 season only eight of the 16 major-league clubs were integrated. Jim Crow laws were firmly in place in at least 17 states and the Supreme Court's decision in *Brown v. Board of Education*, which ended segregated schooling, was a year away. However, Harada was correct in emphasizing the visual impact an integrated baseball team on the field could have

on fans, and society as a whole, as Jackie Robinson taught America in 1947.[10]

The Giants also were selected because of Harada's close relationship with Lefty O'Doul and O'Doul's strong connection to Horace Stoneham, which began in 1928 when Lefty played for the Giants. At one point Stoneham even considered hiring O'Doul as his manager.[11] Harada, who was bilingual, lived in Santa Maria, California, where, in the spring of 1953, he arranged for the Yomiuri Giants to hold their spring-training camp. Working closely together, Harada and O'Doul (with Stoneham's approval) scheduled an exhibition game in Santa Maria between the New York Giants and their Tokyo namesake. O'Doul introduced Harada to Stoneham, and the seeds for the Japan tour were planted.[12]

A CLUBHOUSE VOTE

The one remaining hurdle was a positive vote by at least 15 Giants. Prior to voting, they were told that the tour would take place from mid-October to mid-November. They would play two games in Hawaii on their way to Japan, 14 games in Japan, and a few games in Okinawa, the Philippines, and Guam before returning home. They understood that all expenses would be covered by the Japanese, and they should expect to make about $3,000, depending on paid attendance at the games. On July 25, when the Giants lost, 7-5, to the Cincinnati Reds on a Saturday afternoon before 8,454 fans at the Polo Grounds, the team voted 18 to 7 to go to Japan.

Two players who voted yes were Sal Maglie and Hoyt Wilhelm. Several weeks later Maglie backed out, citing his ailing back, which needed to heal during the offseason. Ronnie Samford, an infielder and the only minor leaguer to make the trip, replaced Maglie. Hoyt Wilhelm faced a dilemma: His wife was pregnant. But his brother was serving in Korea. He chose to make the trip when he learned he could visit his brother during the tour.

Only two players' wives opted to make the trip and at least one dropped out prior to departure.[13] One obvious absentee was the Giants' sensational center fielder who was the Rookie of the Year in 1951: Willie Mays. Serving in an Army transport unit in Virginia, he would not be discharged until after the tour ended, but in time for Opening Day in 1954.[14]

Players who voted no provided a variety of reasons for their decisions. Alvin Dark and Whitey Lockman cited business commitments made before the invitation arrived; Rubén Gómez was committed to playing another season of winter ball in his native Puerto Rico; Bobby Thomson's wife was pregnant; Larry Jansen preferred to stay home with his large family in Oregon; and Dave Koslo wanted to rest his aging arm. Tookie Gilbert also voted no but offered no reason for his decision.[15]

Nonplayers in the traveling party included owner Stoneham and his son, Peter; manager Leo Durocher and his wife, Hollywood actress Laraine Day; Commissioner Frick and his wife; Mr. and Mrs. Lefty O'Doul; equipment manager Eddie Logan; publicist Billy Goodrich; team secretary Eddie Brannick and his wife; and coach Fred Fitzsimmons and his wife.[16] Also making the trip was National League umpire Larry Goetz, who was appointed by National League President Warren Giles and Commissioner Frick.[17]

The traveling party's itinerary was straightforward. Most members left New York on October 8 and, after meeting the rest of the group in San Francisco, flew to Hawaii on October 9 and played two exhibition games. They left Honolulu on October 12 and arrived in Tokyo on October 14. After completing their 14-game schedule against Japanese teams, they left Tokyo on November 10 for Okinawa, the Philippines, and Guam before returning to the United States.[18]

Another team of major leaguers was touring Japan at the same time. Eddie Lopat's All-Stars, including future Hall of Famers Yogi Berra, Enos Slaughter, Eddie Mathews, Nellie Fox, Robin Roberts, and Bob Lemon, and recent World Series hero Billy Martin, were sponsored by the *Mainichi* newspaper, one of *Yomiuri Shimbun's* major competitors. Lopat's team won 11 of 12 games and earned more money than the New York Giants.[19]

THE TOUR IN HISTORICAL CONTEXT

When Dwight D. Eisenhower assumed the US presidency on January 20, 1953, he inherited a Cold War abroad that was intertwined with the nation's second Red Scare at home.[20] The Soviet Union engulfed Eastern Europe with what Winston Churchill referred to as an iron curtain; and China, which witnessed a Communist revolution in 1949, became a major threat in Asia. On June 25, 1950, nearly 100,000 North Korean troops invaded US-backed South Korea, commencing the Korean War, which lasted until 1953.

The invasion had a major impact on Japan-US relations. In particular, the United States had to reevaluate how to address the rise of communism in Asia as well as quell the growing opposition to US military bases in Japan. On September 8, 1951, representatives of both countries met in San Francisco to sign the Treaty of Peace that officially ended World War II and the seven-year Allied occupation of Japan, which would take effect in the spring of 1952. Japan would be a sovereign nation again, but the United States would still maintain military bases there for security reasons that would benefit both countries. In short, "it was during the Korean War that US-Japan relations changed dramatically from occupation status to one of a security partnership in Asia," opined an American journalist.[21] And such an arrangement needed to be nurtured by soft-power diplomacy in the form of educational exchanges, visits by entertainers, and tours by major-league baseball clubs. In 1953 the New York Giants served as exemplars of soft power under the new partnership between the United States and Japan.[22]

A CELEBRATORY ARRIVAL AND A SUCCESSFUL TOUR

The Giants easily won their two games in Hawaii. The first was a 7-2 win against a team of service all-stars, and the second was a 10-1 victory over the Rural Red Sox, the Hawaii League champions in 1953. Also present in Honolulu was Cappy Harada, who talked of his dream of seeing a "real World Series" between the US and Japanese champions, while emphasizing that the quality of Japanese baseball was getting closer to the level of play of American teams. He noted that the Yomiuri Giants and the New York Giants had split two games during spring training. "We beat the Americans in California and they beat us in Arizona," he said. Then, almost in the form of a warning to the traveling party that was about to depart for Japan, Harada reminded reporters that Yomiuri was a powerhouse, having led its league by 16 games.[23]

When the Pan American Stratocruiser carrying the Giants landed at Tokyo's Haneda International Airport at 1:00 P.M. on October 14, it was swarmed by Japanese officials, reporters, photographers, and fans. Consequently, the traveling party could not move off the tarmac for more than an hour before boarding cars for a motorcade that wound its way through Tokyo streets lined with thousands of cheering fans waving flags, hoping to get a glimpse of the American ballplayers.[24]

That evening in the lobby of the Imperial Hotel, Leo Durocher boldly stated that he expected his Giants to win every game on the tour. He also expected a home-run barrage by his club because the Japanese ballparks were so small. "We shouldn't drop a game to any of these teams while we're over here," he boasted. Perhaps realizing that his comment was not the most diplomatic way to open the tour, Durocher quickly put a positive spin on his view of the Yomiuri Giants in particular. "They are the best-looking Japanese ball team I've seen," he said. "They showed a great deal of improvement during their spring workouts in the States."[25] Yomiuri would win their third straight Japanese championship two days later.

Over the next two days, the visiting Giants attended a large welcoming luncheon, participated in a motorcade parade through Tokyo, and held workouts at Korakuen Stadium. "Giants Drill, Leo's Antics Delight Fans" read a headline in *Pacific Stars and Stripes* on October 16, the day before the series opened.[26] Each day Durocher and several of his players conducted a one-hour clinic on the "fundamentals of American baseball." A photo captured the Giants demonstrating a rundown play between third base and home.[27]

Before the Giants' arrival, the US Armed Forces newspaper *Stars and Stripes* published a two-page spread profiling the players on both teams.[28] For the Japanese people, a *Fan's Guide* was distributed widely. Gracing the cover was a color photograph of Leo Durocher with his arm around Yomiuri Giants manager Shigeru Mizuhara, a World War II veteran who had spent five years in a Soviet prison. Inside the guide were ads linked to baseball and numerous photos and profiles of players from both the New York Giants and Eddie Lopat's All-Stars. Near the back of the guide, however, was an error: a photo of Mickey Mantle. Mantle had backed out of the trip with Eddie Lopat to undergo knee surgery in Missouri.[29]

THE GAMES

The team's 14-game schedule was broken down into five games with the Yomiuri Giants, five games against the Central League All-Stars, two games with the All-Japan All-Stars, and single contests with the Chunichi Dragons and the Hanshin Tigers. The first three games were played in Tokyo's Korakuen Stadium, which held 45,000 fans.

The ceremonies before the first game were lavish. There were speeches and an exchange of gifts. The mayor of Tokyo gave Durocher a key to the city and a gift for his wife. Durocher returned the favor by giving a New York Giants banner to the mayor. At one point

Ford Frick stepped before the microphone to share a letter from President Eisenhower: "Dear Mr. Frick: I was delighted to hear that through your good offices the plan for the Japanese tour of the New York Giants has been successfully completed. For myself, I enthusiastically support this kind of sporting and human relationship between the people of Japan and the U.S. The United States of America seeks the friendship of all, the enmity of none – for in real friendship there is strength and only through strength can come the peace and freedom which mean happiness and well-being for the world." Japanese Premier Shigeru Yoshida welcomed the New York Giants to Japan and said of the visit: "I hope it will be significant not only for the Japanese baseball world but for goodwill and a better understanding between both peoples." Shortly after the exchange of gifts and greetings, a helicopter hovered above the ballpark and dropped the game ball by a small parachute onto the infield.[30]

Whatever dreams Cappy Harada harbored about a "real World Series" were certainly smashed temporarily as he watched Durocher's Giants crush his Yomiuri Giants, 11-1, before a capacity crowd. The Giants hammered out 12 hits, including home runs by outfielders Dusty Rhodes and Monte Irvin. Starting pitcher Al Worthington, who went five scoreless innings, and reliever Hoyt Wilhelm, who pitched the final four innings, held Yomiuri to one run on seven hits. In a losing cause, 36-year-old third baseman Mitsuo Uno collected a pair of hits against New York's pitchers.[31]

Games two and three of the tour were also played in Korakuen Stadium, again before capacity crowds. In game two against the Central League All-Stars, the Giants won, but not as convincingly as the day before. The Japanese squad led 3-0 after the first two innings, but the New Yorkers scored two runs in the third before Hank Thompson tripled in the fifth to tie the game. Don Mueller's home run in the ninth inning finished off the All-Stars, 5-3. After the game, Durocher praised Japan's pitching and particularly the performance of 20-year-old Masaichi Kaneda of the Kokutetsu Swallows. "I wish we had that guy," said Durocher. "As a matter of fact, I think he could make any Class A club in the States."[32] The reference to A-level baseball and on rare occasions to Double-A baseball was as high as assessments went by Americans on the tour. Neither Durocher nor Frick ever labeled Japanese baseball in general, or any one player in particular, above the US Double-A level.

Game three was another low-scoring contest against the Japanese All-Stars. Solo home runs by center fielder Dusty Rhodes and shortstop Daryl Spencer led the offense. Seven solid innings of pitching by Jim Hearn and effective relief by Hoyt Wilhelm in the final two innings gave the Giants their third win in a row, a 4-1 victory.[33] In their first three games in Tokyo, the Giants drew 128,000 fans, more than 42,000 per game.

As the Giants moved into more rural regions of the country, attendance declined and so did news coverage. Games four and five were played before smaller crowds in Sapporo and Sendai, both in northern Japan. In game four, the New York Giants once again demolished the Yomiuri Giants, 8-1, thanks to Al Worthington's one-hit pitching for seven innings. Durocher's offense was highlighted by a triple from Monte Irvin.[34] In game five in Sendai, the Giants broke open a 4-4 tie in the seventh inning to defeat a combined Yomiuri-Kokutetsu squad, 10-4. Don Mueller had four hits and Monte Irvin had three to lead the assault. Masaichi Kaneda, the young pitcher Durocher wished he had, gave up 15 hits.

The Giants continued their winning ways in games six through nine. In game six they defeated Yomiuri, 4-1, in Shizuoka for the third time in as many games, this time beating their ace pitcher Takehiko Bessho.[35] Traveling on to Nagoya on October 24, the Giants defeated the Chunichi Dragons, 9-6, but had to overcome an early 6-0 deficit.[36] On October 26 the pitching performance of the tour was turned in by Marv Grissom in Okayama against the Pacific League All-Stars. Pitching a complete game, he surrendered only three hits in the 4-0 shutout, while striking out 15. At one point he struck out six in a row.[37] Two days later in Hiroshima, the Giants got another outstanding pitching performance, this time from Jim Hearn, as they squeaked by with a 3-2 win over the Central League All-Stars.[38]

The highlight of the tour for Japanese fans came on October 31 when a crowd of 30,000 at Tokyo's Korakuen Stadium saw their Giants finally defeat the Americans, 2-1. The stars of the game were Takumi Otomo, who gave up one run on seven hits, and shortstop Saburo Hirai, who hit a go-ahead home run off Hoyt Wilhelm in the eighth inning. The victory was only the fourth by a Japanese team against an American major-league team since 1920. This game was also unique in another respect. Lefty O'Doul sat in the Tokyo dugout advising manager Mizuhara on how to pitch to New York's hitters. In short, O'Doul may have been Japan's first bench coach, as he constantly reminded Otomo to pitch the Americans high

in the zone rather than low, where they preferred their pitches.[39]

Perhaps embarrassed by their first defeat, Durocher's team unleashed a 23-hit attack that produced a 16-5 win over the Central League All-Stars in Tokyo in the 11th game of the tour. Leading the assault was Dusty Rhodes, who drilled three home runs into the right-field seats. Hank Thompson, Al Corwin, Sam Calderone, and Monte Irvin also hit homers in the rout.[40] After traveling to Hamamatsu for game 12, where they played the Central League All-Stars to a 4-4 tie in a game called because of darkness after nine innings, the tour paused for a side trip to Korea between November 3 and 5.[41] Leo Durocher, coach Fred Fitzsimmons, umpire Larry Goetz, and seven players visited American troops on several military bases. The players were Dusty Rhodes, Sam Calderone, Bill Rigney, Monte Irvin, Bobby Hofman, Don Mueller, and Hoyt Wilhelm, who had a chance to visit his brother on the front lines.[42]

If the New Yorkers wanted to make a definitive statement about the superiority of American baseball over Japanese ball, they did so in the last two games of the tour, outscoring their opponents 19-0. In game 13 in Osaka on November 6, the Giants scored 12 runs on 14 hits to support another brilliant pitching job by Marv Grissom, who shut out Osaka on six hits. Ronnie Samford, Hank Thompson, and Monte Irvin hit home runs to lead the attack.[43] And in the final game of the tour, a similar picture was painted. In a convincing 7-0 win over the Japanese All-Stars, Al Worthington tossed a three-hitter, and was backed by a 15-hit attack led by Monte Irvin, Dusty Rhodes, and Bobby Hofman, who all produced extra-base hits. In an award ceremony after the game, Marv Grissom and Don Mueller were each given 30,000 yen (about $84 in 1953 dollars) for the best pitcher and hitter on the tour. Mueller hit .388 followed by Monte Irvin at .364. Dusty Rhodes led the team in home runs with six, less than half of Babe Ruth's output of 13 homers in during the 1934 tour.[44]

A TRANSACTION LOST IN TRANSLATION?

The second game in Osaka was almost forfeited and the diplomatic mission tarnished when six of the Giants players, claiming they had heard their final pay for the tour would be $331 and not $3,000, threatened to boycott the game. Still in street clothes, the six Giants – Jim Hearn, Al Worthington, Hoyt Wilhelm, Al Corwin, Sam Calderone, and Daryl Spencer – played cards in the clubhouse while their teammates were in uniform. According to the original agreement, the players were to get a 60 percent cut of the ticket sales for the last two games of the tour. However, when they learned that only 5,000 of the 24,000 fans in the stands in game one in Osaka actually paid for a ticket, and that only 12,800 fans of 35,000 fans in the stands for the second game bought tickets, the six players revolted.

Only after Durocher huddled with officials from *Yomiuri Shimbun* and the players were assured they would be paid $1,000, did they suit up and go on the field. Some players had passed up lucrative offseason job opportunities to make the trip. Monte Irvin, for example, earned $7,000 every winter as a luncheon and dinner speaker for a beer distributor.[45] To make matters worse, perhaps, the Giants learned later that each of Eddie Lopat's All-Stars earned $4,000 for their trip – and did so without any "lost in translation" type of episodes.[46] It was as late as November 25 that

confusion over the final payout continued when an anonymous Giants player disclosed that in the end each player got only about $660, not the $1,000 that was reported.[47]

With the Osaka incident behind them, the team left Japan with a record of 12 wins, one loss, and a tie. They continued on to Okinawa, the Philippines, and Guam where they played exhibition games against US service teams, winning two of three, before returning home. Little did they realize during their return flight that the team that finished 35 games out of first place in 1953 would be World Series champions a year later. Whether or not the tour was a team bonding experience for Durocher and his players is open to question, but the thought deserves some consideration.

A DREAM DEFERRED FOR CAPPY HARADA

In news coverage throughout the tour, Durocher, Stoneham, and Frick occasionally flirted with Cappy

Opening ceremonies for the New York Giants in Osaka (©Courtesy of the San Francisco Giants)

Harada's concept of a "real World Series" between American and Japanese winners, but quickly directed their attention toward the play of individual Japanese players, rather than discuss a complete Nippon team being on par with US major-league teams. The Americans' view that the quality of Nippon baseball in 1953 fell somewhere between A and Double-A level was probably accurate. After all, the Americans dominated the Japanese throughout the tour. They defeated the league champion Yomiuri Giants four out of five times and also beat two sets of all-star teams as well as the Chunichi Dragons and the Hanshin Tigers rather handily in most cases. They outscored their Japanese opponents 102-45 and outhit them 173-94, while holding the Japanese hitters to a .195 batting average.[48] Even more sobering for Harada and Nippon baseball was that seven of New York's top stars did not even make the trip. Whatever parity existed between the Americans and the Japanese, it was in their defensive play: The New York Giants committed 18 errors, while the Japanese teams had 11 errors combined. On several occasions Frick praised the sound fundamentals exhibited by the Japanese during the tour.[49]

However, despite the disappointing outcome for Japan, at least three Japanese players captured the attention of the New York club during the tour. One was Masaichi Kaneda of the Kokutetsu Swallows, who pitched effectively against the New Yorkers in game two, earning praise from Durocher.[50] Also of interest was Saburo Hirai, the Yomiuri shortstop, who hit .382 in 34 at-bats with four doubles and a home run. *Pacific Stars and Stripes* described him as "a player whose glove work was almost unbelievable. He is a solid right-handed hitter, a long-ball man, a terror on the bases and one of the top figures in Japanese baseball."[51]

But most impressive perhaps was Takumi Otomo of the Yomiuri Giants, winner of the 1953 Sawamura Award as the best pitcher in Japanese baseball. Otomo had a 27-6 won-lost record, 173 strikeouts, and a 1.86 ERA in 281⅓ innings in 1953.[52] It was Otomo who held the New York club to one run in the only win recorded by a Japanese team during the tour. In 25 innings he struck out 15 hitters and produced an impressive 2.88 ERA, which was about 3.5 runs below the composite ERA of Japanese pitchers who faced Durocher's club. An attempt by Stoneham to sign him to a contract failed as Yomiuri's asking price of $10,000 plus three American ballplayers was much too high for Stoneham. Little did the Giants owner realize that he

would have to wait 11 years before having another opportunity to sign a Japanese player.[53]

A fourth player who was clearly on the Giants' radar screen during the tour was Yomiuri's Wally Yonamine. The Hawaii native, who is referred to as "the man who changed Japanese baseball," was the first American to play professional ball in Japan after the war, arriving in 1951. He had a stellar career, collecting three batting titles and an MVP award. He was honored by the emperor and inducted into the Japanese Baseball Hall of Fame. However, whatever interest the Giants may have had in Yonamine in 1953 probably vanished quickly, as they watched the Yomiuri center fielder go 0-for-22 at the plate in five games.[54]

Clearly, Cappy Harada's dream of a "real World Series" was not realistic in 1953, nor is it much more feasible today. Other than the flirtation with such a fantasy every four years in the form of the World Baseball Classic that Japan has captured twice (as of 2022) since its inception in 2006, a "real World Series" is not yet visible on the horizon. At least for now, the Japanese baseball hierarchy will have to be satisfied with the individual performances of players like Masanori Murakami, Hideo Nomo, Hideki Matsui, Ichiro Suzuki, and Shohei Ohtani in the United States as a proxy for some measure of baseball equivalency between the two nations. More importantly, however, the 1953 tour served as a good example of "soft power diplomacy" at a crucial point in the diplomatic history of Japan-US relations. It was the early years of the Cold War and at the height of the Red Scare when the Giants journeyed to Japan. It was less than a year after America's role as an occupying force ended and a new partnership of cooperation between the two countries began. What the New York Giants did in Japan in 1953 mattered.

EPILOGUE

The day after the Giants departed Haneda International Airport, Vice President Richard Nixon arrived in Tokyo to deliver a speech before the American-Japan Society. He emphasized the importance of US-Japan relations in the postwar period, especially after the Communist takeover of China. He reminded his audience that if Japan fell under Communist domination, so would all of Asia. Therefore, he argued, although disarmament was an important goal, Japan needed to increase its forces and forge closer ties with South Korea in order to defend Southeast Asia. The domino theory that would dominate American foreign policy for decades was operative, and major US involvement in Vietnam was only a decade away.[55]

On February 7, 1954, less than three months after Nixon's speech in Tokyo, there appeared on the front page of the Sunday *New York Times* sports section a photograph of Commissioner Frick and Giants owner Stoneham presenting President Dwight D. Eisenhower a gift from the Japanese people in appreciation of the Giants' goodwill tour. Accompanying the photo was a story that described the gift as a 110-pound [*sic*] Samurai battle protector in the form of "a suit of metal and cloth armor worn in Japan during the Shogun dynasty more than 700 years ago [that] was given to President Eisenhower today on behalf of the baseball fans of Japan." The photo caption explained that the presentation was made on behalf of Matsutaro Shoriki, owner of the *Yomiuri Shimbun* and regarded as the "father" of professional baseball in Japan.[56]

The bases had been circled, and at least one of many diplomatic missions had been completed, but many more tours would follow, as two nations, once at war, grew closer together. What appeared as a small, obscure story on page 13 of the *Globe Democrat* in Mason City, Iowa, on June 29, 1953, grew into a story of much more significance, earning a place on the front page of the *New York Times* sports section seven months later. Perhaps Yogi Berra could best summarize the importance of the Giants tour in 1953 with his own concise words of wisdom: "Little things are big," said Yogi.

1953 NEW YORK GIANTS GAMES IN JAPAN

Date	Place	Opponent	Score	Winner	Loser
October 17	Tokyo	Yomiuri Giants	11-1	Worthington	Iratani
October 18	Tokyo	Central League All-Stars	5-3	Grissom	Kaneda
October 19	Tokyo	All-Japan	4-1	Hearn	Yuki
October 21	Sapporo	Yomiuri Giants	8-1	Worthington	Otomo
October 22	Sendai	Giants & Swallows	10-4	Grissom	Kaneda
October 24	Shizuoka	Yomiuri Giants	4-1	Hearn	Bessho
October 25	Nagoya	Chunichi Dragons	9-6	Wilhelm	Sugishita
October 27	Okayama	Pacific League All-Stars	4-0	Grissom	Yonekawa
October 29	Hiroshima	Central League All-Stars	3-2	Hearn	Hasegawa
October 31	Tokyo	Yomiuri Giants	1-2	Otomo	Wilhelm
November 1	Tokyo	Central League All-Stars	16-5	Grissom	Bessho
November 3	Hamamatsu	Central League All-Stars	4-4	None	None
November 7	Osaka	Hanshin Tigers	12-0	Grissom	Kajioka
November 8	Osaka	Central League All-Stars	7-0	Worthington	Otomo

1953 NEW YORK GIANTS TOUR BATTING AND PITCHING STATISTICS[57]

Giants Batting Statistics	BA	G	AB	R	H	2B	3B	HR	RBI	SO	BB	SB
Don Mueller	.388	14	67	17	26	3	2	3	11	3	1	0
Dusty Rhodes	.323	14	62	12	20	0	1	6	16	7	3	0
Hank Thompson	.295	14	61	11	18	0	3	3	17	5	4	1
Daryl Spencer	.250	14	56	9	14	4	0	1	6	4	4	1
Monte Irvin	.364	14	55	11	20	1	2	3	13	1	4	0
Ron Samford	.243	11	37	12	9	3	0	1	4	4	4	0
Wes Westrum	.265	11	34	5	9	4	0	0	2	3	5	0
Sam Calderone	.421	6	19	4	8	0	0	1	3	1	0	0
Bill Rigney	.313	5	16	3	5	1	0	0	2	4	1	0
Marv Grissom	.063	5	16	1	1	0	0	0	3	3	1	0
Davey Williams	.286	8	14	3	4	2	0	0	2	3	5	1
Jim Hearn	.333	4	9	0	3	1	0	0	1	3	1	0
Al Worthington	.286	5	7	0	2	1	0	0	0	1	2	0
Bobby Hofman	.281	14	5	8	16	3	0	1	11	4	7	1
Hoyt Wilhelm	.400	5	5	1	2	0	0	0	1	0	0	0
Al Corwin	.250	5	4	1	1	0	0	1	1	1	0	0

Giants Pitching Statistics	ERA	G	W	L	IP	H	HR	SO	BB	R	ER
Marv Grissom	1.85	5	5	0	39	26	3	39	6	8	8
Al Worthington	1.61	5	3	0	28	18	0	7	18	6	5
Jim Hearn	1.07	4	3	0	25.1	21	0	16	3	4	3
Hoyt Wilhelm	3.00	5	1	1	18	10	2	9	6	6	6
Al Corwin	2.31	2	0	0	11.2	8	1	7	3	4	3
Monty Kennedy	6.00	2	0	0	3	3	0	3	2	2	2

Japanese Batting Statistics	BA	G	AB	R	H	2B	3B	HR	RBI	SO	BB	SB
Saburo Hirai	.382	10	34	6	13	4	0	1	2	6	4	1
Michio Nishizawa	.192	7	26	0	5	3	0	0	3	9	0	0
Fumio Fujimura	.227	7	22	2	5	1	0	2	5	5	2	0
Wally Yonamine	.000	6	22	2	0	0	0	0	0	3	2	1
Tetsuharu Kawakami	.048	9	21	0	1	0	0	0	1	1	1	0
Satoshi Sugiyama	.250	7	20	2	5	0	0	2	3	5	0	0
Kazuo Higasa	.150	8	20	0	3	1	0	0	1	1	1	0
Kenshi (Harvey) Zenimura	.471	5	17	3	8	0	0	0	0	1	1	0
Jun Hirota	.188	9	16	0	3	0	0	0	1	1	2	0
Shigeru Chiba	.125	6	16	0	2	0	0	0	1	1	2	0
Takao Sato	.455	4	11	3	5	1	1	1	2	1	1	0
Mitsuo Uno	.273	5	11	2	3	0	0	0	0	0	3	0
Yuko Minamimura	.091	4	11	0	1	0	0	0	1	0	1	0
Akira Noguchi	.400	5	10	1	4	0	0	0	0	0	2	0
Shinsuke (Larry) Yoji	.200	6	10	1	2	0	0	0	0	1	0	0
Makoto Kozuru	.100	4	10	1	1	0	0	0	0	2	3	0
Takashi Iwamoto	.125	5	8	1	0	0	0	0	0	0	3	0
Masayasu Kaneda	.250	3	8	0	2	0	0	0	0	4	0	0
Chusuke Kizuka	.000	2	8	0	0	0	0	0	0	2	0	0
Futoshi Nakanishi	.250	2	8	0	2	0	0	0	0	1	0	1
Yoshio Yoshida	.000	2	6	0	0	0	0	0	0	0	1	0
Bunji (Dick) Kashiwaeda	.200	3	5	0	1	0	0	0	0	1	2	0

Japanese Pitching Statistics	ERA	G	W	L	IP	H	HR	SO	BB	R	ER
Takumi Otomo	2.88	6	1	2	25	21	0	15	6	8	8
Masaichi Kaneda	9.78	4	0	2	19.1	30	2	10	13	21	21
Takehiko Bessho	6.59	3	0	2	13.2	19	6	6	3	12	10
Ryohei Hasegawa	3.46	3	0	1	13	18	3	5	5	8	5
Shigeru Sugishita	9.00	2	0	1	8	9	1	2	7	9	8
Tokuji Kawasaki	1.29	2	0	0	7	7	1	0	1	1	1
Masanori Iratani	4.50	2	0	1	6	3	2	1	2	3	3
Masatoshi Gondo	10.50	2	0	0	6	12	0	5	3	7	7
Susumu Yuki	6.00	2	0	1	3	4	1	1	2	3	2
Yasuo Yonekawa	6.00	1	0	1	3	2	1	0	1	2	2
Tadayoshi Kajioka	22.50	2	0	1	2	5	0	0	1	5	5

NOTES

1   "New York Giants Invited to Tour Japan This Fall," *Mason City* (Iowa) *Globe Gazette,* June 29, 1953: 13.

2   For more information on this topic refer to Columbia University's *Asia for Educators* website at Commodore Perry and Japan (1853-1854), http://afe.easia.columbia.edu/tps/1750_jp.htm#perry.

3   Restrictions on barnstorming tours can be traced back to 1921-1922 under Commissioner Kenesaw Mountain Landis.

4   The New York Giants under John McGraw and the Chicago White Sox under Charles Comiskey toured Japan together in 1913 but the rosters were heavily supplemented with players from other teams.

5   "Cleveland Awarded 1954 All-Star Game; N.Y. Giants' Tour of Japan Okayed," *Allentown* (Pennsylvania) *Morning Call,* July 13, 1953: 12.

6   Robert K. Fitts, *Remembering Japanese Baseball: An Oral History of the Game* (Carbondale: Southern Illinois University Press, 2005), 3.

7   Dennis Snelling, *Lefty O'Doul: Baseball's Forgotten Ambassador* (Lincoln: University of Nebraska Press, 2017), 243.

8   Snelling, 236.

9   Andrew Mitsukado, "Giants Receive Japan Bid to Play 12-Game Series," *Honolulu Advertiser,* July 19, 1953: 20.

10 In the fall of 1953 Jackie Robinson's integrated barnstorming team was banned from taking the field in Birmingham, Alabama, by Commissioner of Public Safety Eugene "Bull" Connor, who was notorious for using police dogs and firehoses against civil-rights demonstrators.

11 Snelling, 39; Fitts, *Remembering Japanese Baseball,* 1-10.

12 Steven Treder, *Forty Years a Giant: The Life of Horace Stoneham* (Lincoln: University of Nebraska Press, 2021), 167.

13 "18 Giants to Make Trip to Japan, Philippines," *New York Herald Tribune,* July 26, 1953: B 2.

14 The Giants repeatedly sought an early discharge for Mays but failed, even after his mother died giving birth to her 11th child. See Treder, 170.

15 Arch Murray, "Giants in Japan, Trip Hailed as Aid in International Affairs," *The Sporting News,* October 14, 1953: 19.

16 *New York Herald Tribune,* July 26, 1953: B 2.

17 "Giles Picks Goetz for Japan Tour," *Cincinnati Enquirer,* September 3, 1953: 18. Goetz got upset early on when he heard fans shouting "goetsu, goetsu," thinking they were saying something derogatory about him. He relaxed when he learned the fans were simply saying "get two, get two" as in a double play.

18 "Giants' Itinerary," *The Sporting News,* October 14, 1953: 19.

19 "Martin Arrives Home, Praises Japan Junket," *Pacific Stars and Stripes,* November 13, 1953: 21. During a post-tour interview in Oakland, Martin stated that each of the Eddie Lopat All-Stars made about $4,000.

20 In 1953 Senator Joseph McCarthy (R-Wisconsin) in 143 days of hearings questioned more than 600 witnesses in an effort to identify and expel communists in government and other institutions. The Cincinnati Reds became the Redlegs for six years to avoid being confused with the "Russian Reds."

21 Olivia B. Waxman, "How the US and Japan Became Allies Even After Hiroshima and Nagasaki," *Time,* August 6, 2018: 23.

22 Harvard professor Joseph Nye coined the term "soft power" in 1990. Soft power is defined as a collaborative act that lies in the ability to attract and persuade another person or country to do something that benefits both. Hard power is the use of military or economic might to coerce person or country to do something.

23 Carl Machado, "Lefty O'Doul Says PCL in Best Shape in History," *Honolulu Star Bulletin,* October 10, 1953: 6.

24 "New York Club Arrives in Japan," *Tampa Tribune,* October 15, 1953: 2-B.

25 Sgt. Mike Hickey, "Durocher Sees Clean Sweep in Games with Tokyo Giants," *Pacific Stars and Stripes,* October 15, 1953: 14.

26 Sgt. Mike Hickey, "Giants Drill, Leo's Antics Delight Fans," *Pacific Stars and Stripes,* October 16, 1953: 14.

27 Cpl. Pete Johnstone (photographer), "Clinical Diagnosis," *Pacific Stars and Stripes,* October 19, 1953: 14.

28 Sgt. Mike Hickey, "Giants vs. Giants," *Pacific Stars and Stripes,* October 3, 1953: 6-7.

29 "Mantle's Bad Knee Ready for Surgery," *Pacific Stars and Stripes,* November 3, 1953: 18.

30 Associated Press, Tokyo, *Pacific Stars and Stripes,* October 18, 1953: 13; N. Sakata, "Capacity Crowds Watch Giants in First Four Japanese Games," *The Sporting News,* October 24, 1953: 17.

31 "New York Overpowers Tokyo Giants 11-1," *Pacific Stars and Stripes,* October 18, 1953: 13.

32 Sgt. Mike Hickey, "New York Edges All-Stars 5-3," *Pacific Stars and Stripes,* October 19, 1953: 13.

33 Associated Press, "41,000 See Giants Take Third in a Row on Japanese Tour," *St. Louis Globe Democrat,* October 20, 1953: 16.

34 Associated Press, "More Than 25,000 See Giants Win Fourth in a Row," *Honolulu Advertiser,* October 22, 1953: 11.

35 Associated Press, "Giants Top Tokyo for Sixth Straight," *Scrantonian Tribune* (Scranton, Pennsylvania), October 25, 1953: 44.

36 Associated Press, "Giants Win," *Arizona Daily Star* (Tucson), October 26, 1953: 10.

37 "Marv Grissom Fans 15 as New York Giants Win to Maintain Clean Slate," *Pacific Stars and Stripes,* October 28, 1953: 13.

38 Associated Press, "Giants, Lopat's Stars Win Again," *Nashville Banner,* October 29, 1953: 41.

39 Associated Press, "O'Doul Helps Beat Giants," *San Francisco Examiner,* November 1, 1953: 47.

40 United Press, "Giants Shellac Japanese," *Pacific Stars and Stripes,* November 1, 1953: 14.

41 Cpl. Perry Smith, "Darkness Stops NY," *Pacific Stars and Stripes,* November 4, 1953: 14.

42 "New York Giants Group to Make Korean Junket," *Pacific Stars and Stripes,* October 31, 1953: 18.

43 Cpl. Perry Smith, "Grissom Blanks Osaka as Giants Rap 3 Homers," *Pacific Stars and Stripes,* November 8, 1953: 13.

44 "Durochermen Draw Well During Baseball Junket," *Pacific Stars and Stripes,* November 3, 1953: 15.

45 Cpl. Perry Smith, "Giants Net $331 Each, Expected $3,000." *Pacific Stars and Stripes,* November 10, 1953: 13. The $331 amount was merely a rumor that was later disproved.

46 "Martin Arrives Home, Praises Japan Junket," *Pacific Stars and Stripes,* November 13, 1953: 21.

47 Larry Jackson, "Giants Earned Only $660 Each on Tour," *The Sporting News,* November 25, 1953: 18.

48   Robert K. Fitts, *Wally Yonamine: The Man Who Changed Japanese Baseball* (Lincoln: University of Nebraska Press, 2008), 159.

49   *Asahi Shimbun*, October 18 – November 19, 1953. Thank you to Michael Westbay of Japan Ball.com for translating and compiling the box scores.

50   Sgt. Mike Hickey, "New York Edges All-Stars, 5-3," *Pacific Stars and Stripes,* October 19, 1953: 13.

51   Harry Grayson, "Maybe Durocher Can Find His Kind of Giants on One of the Hustling Japanese Clubs," *Elmira* (New York) *Advertiser,* October 28, 1953: 13.

52   Daniel E. Johnson, *Japanese Baseball: A Statistical Handbook* (Jefferson, North Carolina: McFarland, 1999).

53   Fitts, *Wally Yonamine,* 159.

54   Fitts, *Wally Yonamine*, 159. Also see Robert K. Fitts, *Mashi: The Unfilled Dreams of Masanori Murakami, The First Japanese Major Leaguer* (Lincoln: University of Nebraska Press, 2014), 39.

55   Jonathan Movroydis, "Vice-President Nixon on the Future of US-Japan Relations," Richard M. Nixon Presidential Library, October 1, 2018. Nixon's entire speech can be accessed at Vice President Nixon on the Future of U.S.-Japan Relations, nixonfoundation.org. https://www.nixon-foundation.org/2018/10/vice-president-nixon-future-u-s-japan-relations/.

56   Associated Press, "Japan's Fans Send Gift to Eisenhower," *New York Times*, February 7, 1954: C1.

57   Listed Japanese players have a minimum of 5 at-bats, 5 innings pitched, or a decision. Yoshikazu Matsubayashi, *Baseball Game History: Japan vs, U.S.A.* (Tokyo: Baseball Magazine, 2004), 90; Nippon Professional Baseball Records, https://www.2689web.com/nb.html.

THE 1953 EDDIE LOPAT ALL-STARS' TOUR OF JAPAN

By C. Paul Rogers III

Eddie Lopat was a fine, soft-tossing southpaw during a 12-year baseball career with the Chicago White Sox and most famously the New York Yankees. Called the Junkman because of his assortment of off-speed pitches, Lopat was also something of a baseball entrepreneur. He not only ran a winter baseball school in Florida, but, after barnstorming in Japan with Lefty O'Doul's All-Stars following the 1951 major-league season, was very receptive to Frank Scott's plan to put together a star-studded assemblage of major leaguers to again tour Japan after the 1953 season. Scott, a former traveling secretary of the Yankees who had since become a promoter, proposed calling the team the Eddie Lopat All-Stars.[1] By 1953, after O'Doul's 1949 breakthrough overseas trip to Japan with his San Francisco Seals of the Pacific Coast League, postseason tours to the Land of the Rising Sun had become more common.[2] In fact, in 1953 the New York Giants also barnstormed in Japan at the same time as did Lopat's team. For the Lopat tour, Scott secured the Mainichi Newspapers, owners of the Mainichi Orions of Japan's Pacific League, as the official tour sponsor.[3]

Lopat and Scott spent much of the 1953 regular season recruiting players for the tour, including a somewhat reluctant Yogi Berra. Unbeknownst to Yogi, he was already a legend among Japanese baseball fans. At the All-Star Game in Cincinnati, a Japanese sportswriter who was helping Lopat and Scott with their recruiting was aware of Berra's reputation as a chowhound and told Yogi about the exotic foods he would be able to consume in Japan. Yogi was skeptical, however, and wondered if bread was available in Japan. When the writer and Lopat both assured Yogi

1953 Eddie Lopat All-Stars

that Japan did indeed have bread, he signed on for the tour.[4]

Under the prevailing major-league rules, barnstorming "all-star teams" were limited to three players from any one team.[5] With that constraint, a stellar lineup of major leaguers signed on for the tour including, in addition to Berra, future Hall of Famers Mickey Mantle, Robin Roberts, Eddie Mathews, Bob Lemon, Nellie Fox, and Enos Slaughter. All-Star-caliber players like Eddie Robinson, Curt Simmons, Mike Garcia, Harvey Kuenn (the 1953 American League Rookie of the Year), Jackie Jensen, and Hank Sauer committed as well, as did Gus Niarhos, who was added to serve as a second catcher behind Berra.[6] Whether a slight exaggeration or not, they were billed as "the greatest array of major league stars ever to visit Japan."[7]

Lopat and his Yankees teammates Mantle and Berra were fresh off a tense six-game World Series win over the Brooklyn Dodgers in which all had played pivotal roles. Lopat had won Game Two thanks to a two-run eighth-inning homer by Mantle, while Berra had batted .429 for the Series. A casualty to the tour because of the long season and World Series, however, was the 21-year-old Mantle, who, after battling injuries to both knees during the year, needed surgery and was a late scratch.[8] Lopat quickly added Yankees teammate Billy Martin, who had hit .500 with 12 hits and eight runs batted in in the Series to win the Baseball Writers' MVP Award.[9]

The Lopat All-Stars were to first play four exhibition games in Colorado and began gathering at the famous Broadmoor Hotel in Colorado Springs on October 6. Baseball had a no-fraternizing rule then and many of the players looked forward to getting to know ballplayers from other teams and from the other league. The Phillies' Robin Roberts, who was known for his great control on the mound, remembered spotting fellow hurler Bob Lemon of the Cleveland Indians in the bar at the Broadmoor and going over to introduce himself. Lemon asked Roberts what he wanted to drink and Roberts said, "I'll have a 7-Up."

Lemon didn't say anything but pulled out a pack of cigarettes and offered Roberts one. Roberts said, "No, thanks, I don't smoke."

Lemon chuckled and said, "No wonder you don't walk anyone."[10]

The Lopat team's opposition in Colorado was a squad of major leaguers put together by White Sox manager Paul Richards and highlighted by pitchers Billy Pierce and Mel Parnell, infielders Pete Runnels

and Randy Jackson, and outfielders Dave Philley and Dale Mitchell.[11]

The big-league sluggers quickly took to the rarefied Colorado air as the teams combined for nine home runs in the first contest, a 13-8 victory for the Lopat All-Stars over the Richards group on October 8 in Pueblo. The 21-year-old Mathews, coming off a gargantuan 47-homer, 135-RBI season with the Braves, slugged two circuit shots (including one that traveled 500 feet), as did the Cubs' 36-year-old Hank Sauer, the Cardinals' 37-year-old Enos Slaughter, and, for the Richards team, Detroit catcher Matt Batts. Two days later, the Lopats blasted the Richards team 18-7 in Colorado Springs before the four-game series shifted to Bears Stadium in Denver for the final two contests. The results were the same, however, as the Lopat team won in the Mile-High City 8-4 and 14-8, the latter before a record crowd of 13,852, as four-time American League All-Star Eddie Robinson of the Philadelphia A's and Mathews both homered off Billy Pierce and drove in four runs apiece.

Mathews went 7-for-8 in the two Denver contests and posted Little League-like numbers for the whole Colorado series, driving in 17 runs in the four games, while the veteran Slaughter had 12 hits, including two homers, two triples, and three doubles.[12]

The Lopat All-Stars then flew to Honolulu for more exhibition games after a brief stopover in San Francisco. On October 12 and 13 they played a pair of games in Honolulu against a local team called the Rural Red Sox and it did not take long for disaster to strike. In the first inning of the first game before a jammed-in crowd of 10,500, Mike Garcia of the Indians was struck in the ankle by a line drive after delivering a pitch. Garcia, who had won 20, 22, and 18 games the previous three seasons, was unable to push off from the mound after the injury and had to leave the game.[13] Although Garcia stayed with the team for most of the tour, he was able to pitch only sparingly in Japan.[14]

Despite the loss of Garcia, the major leaguers clobbered the locals 10-2 and 15-0. After the second game, first baseman Robinson, who had homered in the rout, was stricken with a kidney-stone attack and was briefly hospitalized.[15] He quickly recovered and resumed the tour for the All-Stars, who had brought along only 11 position players.

On October 14 the Lopat squad flew to Kauai, where they pounded out 22 hits and defeated the Kauai All-Stars, 12-3, on a makeshift diamond fashioned from a football field. World Series MVP Martin was honored before the game and given a number of gifts, including an aloha shirt and a calabash bowl. He celebrated by smashing a long home run in his first time at bat and later adding a double and a single.[16] The homer sailed through goalposts situated beyond left field, leading Robin Roberts to quip that it should have counted for three runs.[17]

The big leaguers next flew to Hilo on the Big Island, where on October 17, 5,000 saw them defeat a local all-star team, 8-3, in a game benefiting the local Little League. But much more serious opposition awaited them back in Honolulu in the form of a three-game series against the Roy Campanella All-Stars, a team of African American major leaguers headed by Campanella, the reigning National League MVP, and including stellar players like Larry Doby, Don Newcombe, Billy Bruton, Joe Black, Junior Gilliam, George Crowe, Harry "Suitcase" Simpson, Bob Boyd, Dave Hoskins, Connie Johnson, and Jim Pendleton.[18]

The Lopats won the first game, 7-1, on the afternoon of October 18 over an obviously weary Campanella team that had flown in from Atlanta the previous day, with a plane change in Los Angeles. Jackie Jensen, then with the Washington Senators, was the hitting star with two home runs, while the Phillies' Curt Simmons allowed only a single run in eight innings of mound work. By the next night, Campy's squad was in much better shape and defeated the Lopat team 4-3 in 10 innings behind Joe Black.[19]

Roberts pitched the first nine innings for the Lopats with Yogi Berra behind the plate. In one at-bat, Campanella hit a towering foul ball behind the plate. Campy actually knocked the glove off Yogi's hand on the follow-through of his swing. Berra looked down at his glove on the ground and then went back and caught the foul ball barehanded.

Roberts picked up Yogi's glove and handed it to him, asking him if he was okay. Yogi said, "That friggin' ball hurt like hell."

Over the years Roberts wondered if he had somehow made that story up, since he never again saw a bat knock the glove off a catcher's hand. Over 30 years later, he saw Berra at an Old-Timers game in Wrigley Field in Chicago and asked him about it. Yogi said, "That friggin' ball hurt like hell," the exact thing he had said in 1953.[20]

On October 20 Campanella's squad won the rubber game, 7-1, behind the three-hit pitching of Don Newcombe. Nellie Fox displayed rare power by homering for the Lopats' only run, while George Crowe hit two homers and Junior Gilliam one for the Campanellas.[21]

The Lopat team stayed at the famous Royal Hawaiian Hotel on Waikiki Beach and had such a great time in Hawaii that many didn't want to leave. Many of the players had brought their wives[22] but some like Eddie Mathews, Billy Martin, and Eddie Robinson were single and so enjoyed the Honolulu nightlife. Not surprisingly given his before and after history, Martin got into a dispute with a guard at a performance of hula dancers attended by the entire team and sucker-punched him.[23] Fortunately for Martin, no charges appear to have been brought.

The Lopat squad did have a schedule to keep and flew on a Pan American Stratocruiser to Tokyo's Haneda Airport, arriving at 1:05 P.M. on October 22. They could scarcely have anticipated the frenzied reception they received. Although the New York Giants had been in the country for a week and had played five games, thousands of Japanese greeted the plane. After being officially greeted by executives from the trip sponsor, Mainichi, and receiving gifts from beautiful young Japanese women, the ballplayers climbed into convertibles, one player per car, to travel to the Nikkatsu Hotel, which would be their headquarters.[24] The trip, which would normally take about 30 minutes, took almost three hours because of the throngs of fans lining the route and pressing against the cars as Japanese mounted and foot police were overwhelmed.[25] Eddie Mathews likened it to the pope in a motorcade without police or security while it reminded Robin Roberts of a ticker-tape parade in New York City.[26]

That evening the Americans were guests at a gigantic pep rally in their honor at the Nichigeki Theater, where Hawaiian-born Japanese crooner Katsuhiko Haida introduced each player.[27] American Ambassador John M. Allison also hosted a reception at the US Embassy for both the Lopats and the New York Giants, who had just returned to Tokyo from Sendai.[28]

The Lopat squad's first game was the following afternoon, October 23, against the Mainichi Orions in Korakuen Stadium before 27,000. The Orions, who had finished fifth out of seven teams in Japan's Pacific League, had the honor of playing the initial game due to its ownership by the Mainichi newspapers.[29] Jackie Jensen won a home-run-hitting contest before the game by smacking six out of the yard, followed by Futoshi Nakanishi of the Nishitetsu Lions with three and then Berra, Mathews, and Hank Sauer with two each. Bobby Brown, stationed in Tokyo as a US

Army doctor, was seen visiting in the dugout with his Yankee teammates Lopat, Berra, and Martin before the contest.[30]

The US and Japanese Army bands played after the home-run-hitting contest, followed by helicopters dropping bouquets of flowers to both managers. Another helicopter hovered low over the field and dropped the first ball but stirred up so much dust from the all-dirt infield that the start of the game was delayed.[31]

The game finally began with Curt Simmons on the mound for the Americans against southpaw Atsushi Aramaki. The visitors plated a run in the top of the second on a single by Sauer, a double by Robinson, and an error, but the Orions immediately rallied for three runs in the bottom half on three bunt singles and Kazuhiro Yamauchi's double. The Orions led 4-1 heading into the top of the ninth but the Lopats staged a thrilling rally to tie the score behind a walk to Mathews, a two-run homer by Sauer, and Robinson's game-tying circuit clout.[32]

Garcia, who had relieved Simmons in the seventh inning, was still pitching in the 10th but after allowing a single, reaggravated the leg injury suffered in Hawaii. He was forced to leave the game with the count of 1 and 1 against the Orions' Charlie Hood, who was a minor-league player in the Phillies organization.[33] (Hood was in the military stationed in Japan and had played 25 games for Mainichi during the season.) When Garcia had to depart, Lopat asked for volunteers to pitch. Roberts, sitting in the dugout, said he would and went out to the mound to warm up.

During the game Roberts had told Bob Lemon next to him that he was familiar with Hood from Phillies spring training and that he was a really good low-ball hitter. Then, on his first pitch, Roberts threw Hood a low fastball which he ripped down the right-field line for a game-winning double. Lemon ribbed Roberts for the rest of the trip about his throwing a low fastball to a low-fastball hitter.[34] In one of baseball's little coincidences, Roberts and Lemon would both be elected to the Hall of Fame on the same day in 1976, 23 years later.

The Lopat squad's loss in the opener was only the third ever suffered by an American team of major leaguers in a postseason tour of Japan.[35] The All-Stars were certainly embarrassed by losing to a mediocre team and afterward Roberts told the Japanese press, "Look, it's a goodwill trip and so this was some of our goodwill. You won the first game, but you won't win anymore."[36]

It turned out Roberts was right. The major leaguers turned the tables quickly the next day, October 24, against an All-Pacific League team, 13-7. Before the game, the press brought over the starting pitcher for the Japanese, Tokuji Kawasaki, for some photos with Roberts, who was starting for the Americans. Kawasaki could understand some English, so Roberts asked him, "How many games did you win this year?"

Kawasaki said, "Twenty-four. One more than you, huh?"[37]

Of course, he was correct, Roberts had won "only" 23 games for the Phillies in 1953.[38] But Roberts quickly got even as his team pounded out 17 hits, of which seven were home runs, including three by Sauer and two by Berra. Little Nellie Fox hit one as did Roberts himself as he coasted to the victory.[39] It was more of the same the next day against the same opponent. The Lopats won 10-3 as Sauer hit another one out of the park, as did Mathews, Jensen, and Lemon before a record 40,000 fans.[40]

The teams headed north to Sendai for a rematch the next day, October 26, before a near-capacity crowd of 25,000. Curt Simmons took the slab for the Americans and through five innings the game remained a scoreless tie. In the sixth, Slaughter's triple led to the game's first run. The Lopat squad then plated two more in the seventh to extend the lead to 3-0 on an error, singles by Kuenn and Slaughter, a walk, and a sacrifice fly. That was the final tally as Simmons scattered five hits in tossing a complete-game shutout.[41]

The teams traveled south to Fukuoka for the fifth game of the tour on October 28 and drew a sellout crowd of about 30,000. Behind the pitching of Bob Lemon, the Americans breezed to a 9-4 win.[42] Although the foul lines of the ballpark were only 300 feet, only Sauer managed a home run, and he hit two, one in the first inning and one in the ninth, to give him seven in the five games played in Japan.[43] Sauer had won the National League MVP Award in 1952 playing for the Chicago Cubs, with 37 homers and 121 runs batted in before battling injuries in 1953 that limited him to 19 round-trippers.[44]

Sauer belted two more homers two days later in Shimonoseki, making nine in six games, as the Americans had 13 hits in a 6-2 win over the Pacific All-Stars. Mathews broke out of a slump with a home run, double, and single, while Berra slugged the fourth home run of the day for the Lopat squad. On the mound, Roberts coasted through the game and used his fastball sparingly, according to one report. The Japanese were not used to the arm strength of the Americans, whether from the mound or the field, and for the third game in a row had a man thrown out at home plate, in this case by Slaughter from center field.[45]

The Americans moved to Osaka next for three games in the area and visited three Army hospitals before their first matchup against the Nankai Hawks, champions of the Pacific League. The Hawks, however, seemed overawed by their opposition, committing five errors and for the most part flailing at Lopat's off-speed assortment from the mound. The final score was 15-1 as Kuenn and Jensen smacked home runs and Mathews had four hits and four RBIs.[46]

The most excitement occurred in bottom of the fifth inning with the score 10-0. Yogi Berra vociferously objected to consecutive pitch calls by umpire Johnny Stevens and got himself ejected.[47] The Japanese fans seemed stunned, "as though witnessing a terrible tragedy."[48] But since Stevens was part of the Lopat travel party, some wondered whether it was "a bit of pre-arranged buffoonery." In any event, Berra took to the press box after his ouster and continued to heckle Stevens, to the entertainment of the Japanese press corps.[49] At least backup catcher Gus Niarhos got to catch a few innings.

The venue then shifted to Nishinomiya Stadium, halfway between Osaka and Kobe, for an October 31 contest against the Hankyu Braves, who had finished second in the Pacific League, four games behind the Hawks. Before 30,000 partisan fans, the Braves put up a much sterner fight and took a 3-2 lead into the seventh. It was the first time the Americans had trailed since the opening game. But after a single by Curt Simmons and a walk to Kuenn, Enos Slaughter blasted a three-run homer, his second of the day, to forge a 5-3 lead. In the eighth, Berra's double, Jensen's single, and a double by Billy Martin closed out the 7-3 victory as Simmons went all the way on the mound.[50]

In spite of the string of defeats, Japanese enthusiasm for the tour did not wane. The next day the Lopat squad faced the Pacific League All-Stars in the same venue before an overflow crowd of 50,000. The result was all too similar for the home squad, an 8-2 defeat as the Americans cracked four home runs among their 13 hits. Mathews hit two over the fence while Jensen and Sauer each hit one. Lemon, relying primarily on his curveball, allowed only two hits and a run in six innings of work.[51]

Eighteen-year-old Sadao Nishimura, who had been loaned to the Lopats by the Nishitetsu Lions of Fukuoka a few days earlier to compensate for Garcia's general unavailability,[52] pitched the final three innings for the visitors, allowing only a single run.[53] Lopat and Berra were so enthralled with Nishimura that they hoped to interest the Yankees in signing him.[54] Roberts took a particular interest in working with Nishimura and it may have paid off as the 19-year-old went 22-5 with a 1.77 ERA for the Lions in 1954.[55]

Another young Japanese pitcher impressed the Americans during the tour. Lefty Masaichi Kaneda was only 20 years old but had just completed his fourth season for the Kokutetsu Swallows of the Central League.[56] He displayed a major-league-caliber fastball and a sharp-breaking curveball.[57] In two appearances spanning eight innings, however, the Lopat squad touched him for five runs. Kaneda, despite pitching most of his 20-year career for the habitually weak Swallows, went on to win 400 games and become Japan's "God of pitching."[58]

Nagoya was the next stop for the Lopat crew, where the opposition was the Central League All-Stars for the only time on the tour. The Central Leaguers had given the New York Giants some tough games on their tour, but on this day, they surrendered seven runs in the second inning and by the fifth trailed 9-0 before rallying for six late runs to make the final score 9-6. Homers by Kuenn, Sauer, and Berra knocked in six of the runs. The 26-year-old Jensen, who hadn't pitched since his college days at the University of California, threw seven innings and allowed only three runs.[59]

Back to Tokyo for the final two games of the Japanese portion of the tour, the Lopats finished with a flourish, defeating the Pacific All-Stars, 10-0 and then All-Japan, 16-2. Robinson, Mathews, and Berra swatted home runs in the first game while in the finale the Americans smashed a hard-to-believe nine home runs.[60] Sauer's 12th homer in 12 games traveled an estimated 500 feet and sailed completely out of Korakuen Stadium.[61] For that feat, Sauer was awarded a motorcycle at home plate. Sauer's blast disappointed Lopat, who had negotiated with the sponsor that he would get the motorcycle if no one actually hit a ball that carried out of the ballpark.[62] Whether Sauer managed to get it back to the States remains an open question.

After winning 11 of 12 in Japan and playing 12 games in 13 days, the Lopat All-Stars were not done yet. They still had two games to play in Okinawa and two in Manila before heading home. At the first stop, at the Camp Kue baseball diamond in Okinawa, the Lopats defeated the Okinawa All-Stars, a team of Army and Air Force personnel, 14-1 and 6-0, behind Roberts and Jensen.[63]

The team's flight to Manila after the game was delayed 17 hours when a truck clipped a wing of their plane while it was sitting on the tarmac.[64] The Lopats arrived at Manila's Rizal Memorial Field an hour late, but still had no difficulty defeating the Canlubang Sugar Barons, the champions of the Manila Bay League, 17-0, behind Roberts's three-hitter.[65]

The opposition for the tour finale on November 8 was much tougher, as the Mainichi Orions, the only team to defeat the Lopat squad in Japan, had flown into Manila to start their own mini-tour. The Lopats eked out a narrow 1-0 win before 11,000 cheering fans, with the only run scoring in the seventh on a single by Kuenn that drove in Martin from second.[66] The weather was so oppressively hot and humid that Lemon, pitching a shutout, was unable to continue after five innings and was replaced by Lopat.[67]

With the final victory, the Lopat All-Stars finished with an overall 24-3 record, with two of the losses coming to the Campanella All-Stars in Hawaii.[68] After

the loss in their first game in Japan, the Americans reeled off 15 straight victories to finish the tour.

The long trip home for the exhausted All-Stars was not without incident. Their Pan American Clipper developed an oil leak, which resulted in a four-hour unscheduled delay in Guam for repairs, causing the team to miss their connection in Honolulu.[69]

The delays undoubtedly bothered Jackie Jensen, whose fear of flying eventually led to his early retirement from baseball.[70] On the flight home, he used a sleeping mask and managed to fall sound asleep. Billy Martin, who had earlier been Jensen's teammate with the Yankees and the Oakland Oaks, grabbed an oxygen mask and a captain's cap and shook Jensen awake, yelling, "Put on your Mae West, we're going down! We're going down!"[71]

Gallows humor aside, the Lopat tour was by any measure a great success. It drew 365,000 fans for the 12 games while the Giants tour drew 338,000 as the Japanese had a seemingly unquenchable thirst for major-league baseball.[72] Mathews, Berra, and Sauer were

Eddie Lopat All-Stars vs. Mainichi Orions, October 23, 1953

1953 Eddie Lopat All-Stars Welcoming Parade

particular favorites because of their penchant for the long ball.[73] The Japanese fans also loved little Nellie Fox because of his "booming infield chatter."[74]

The Americans were lavished with gifts at every turn and, combined with their own shopping, had to send most of their belongings home by ship.[75] In turn, the major leaguers appear to have been amiable guests, signing endless autographs, even for the many fans who invaded their dugout. They also little complained about their arduous schedule in which they often arose at 5 A.M. to travel to their next destination to play a game that same day. In the more remote locales, their accommodations were less than luxurious[76] and the playing fields were sometimes made of volcanic ash, which tended to stick to their spikes.[77]

The Japanese loved home runs and the Americans accommodated them, smashing 42 in the 12 games.[78] Sauer's 12 round-trippers are still the second-most home runs hit by a player during a trip to Japan. (Babe Ruth holds the Japanese tour record with 13 home runs in 18 games.) Mathews and Berra each popped six balls out of the park in Japan. The Americans soon got used to the Japanese infielders bowing to them as they circled the bases after a home run.[79] In Tokyo, at least, home-run hitters were greeted at home plate by young girls with boxes of candy, which the major leaguers donated to Japanese orphanages.[80]

The Lopat team hit .325 for the tour, led by Fox's .435 and Sauer's .423, Slaughter's .393, and Berra's .386.[81] The pitchers had a $5 sweepstakes for the top-hitting moundsman, which Bob Lemon won handily by going 3-for-7.[82] In contrast, the Japanese collectively batted .238 and poled only three home runs. Twenty-year-old future Japan Baseball Hall of Famer Futoshi Nakanishi of the Nishitetsu Lions batted .313 in 32 at-bats to lead the hosts. Nakanishi had led the Pacific League with 36 circuit clouts and had just missed the Triple Crown. Although he did not homer against the Americans, he did raise eyebrows by defeating Mathews in a pregame home-run-hitting contest in Tokyo, 6 to 5.[83]

Overall, the contrast in playing styles was dramatic, with the Americans' swing-from-the-heels approach and the Japanese playing small ball and bunting at any time, even when several runs down. According to Curt Simmons, Japanese players were motivated by being paid 10,000 yen for every run they scored against the foreign visitors.[84] Even the Japanese press acknowledged that Japanese baseball players had a long way to go to match the strength and skill of the major leaguers.[85] But there was room for hope for an eventual World Series between Japan and the United States, fueled by several close games against both the Lopat All-Stars and New York Giants.[86]

The Lopat All-Stars arrived back in San Francisco on November 12, nearly five weeks after they had gathered in Colorado for the start of the tour. In the interim they had traveled almost 30,000 miles. Each pocketed $4,000 for the trip and all regarded it as one of the best times of their lives.[87] The players especially enjoyed the royal treatment from the Japanese fans and, as an added bonus, they made friendships and connections among themselves that endured.[88] The trip was lauded by the US State Department as a huge diplomatic success.[89] Army officials agreed, telling Lopat that the two postseason tours that year had created more goodwill in Japan than the Army had been able to stir up in five years.[90]

ACKNOWLEDGMENT

The author thanks Greg Ivy, Skipper Steele, Frank Jackson, and Rob Fitts for their ready help with the research of this article.

1953 EDDIE LOPAT ALL-STARS GAMES IN JAPAN

Date	Place	Opponent	Score	Winner	Loser
October 23	Tokyo	Mainichi Orions	4-5	Aramaki	Garcia
October 24	Tokyo	Pacific League All-Stars	13-7	Roberts	Kawasaki
October 25	Tokyo	Pacific League All-Stars	10-3	Lopat	Aramaki
October 26	Sendai	Pacific League All-Stars	3-0	Simmons	Abe
October 28	Fukuoka	Pacific League All-Stars	9-4	Lemon	Kawasaki
October 29	Shimonoseki	Pacific League All-Stars	6-2	Roberts	Hayashi
October 30	Osaka	Nankai Hawks	15-1	Lopat	Nakahara
October 31	Nishinomiya	Hankyu Braves	7-3	Simmons	Shibata
November 1	Nishinomiya	Pacific League All-Stars	8-2	Lemon	Yuki
November 2	Nagoya	Central League All-Stars	9-6	Jensen	Sugishita
November 3	Tokyo	Pacific League All-Stars	10-0	Roberts	Aramaki
November 4	Tokyo	All-Japan	16-2	Lopat	Kaneda

1953 EDDIE LOPAT ALL-STARS TOUR BATTING AND PITCHING STATISTICS[91]

American Batting Statistics	BA	G	AB	R	H	2B	3B	HR	RBI	SO	BB	SB
Enos Slaughter	.393	12	56	17	22	8	2	4	12	1	4	3
Eddie Mathews	.340	12	53	14	18	2	0	6	16	5	8	3
Hank Sauer	.423	12	52	17	22	4	0	12	27	5	7	1
Harvey Kuenn	.308	12	52	13	16	2	0	4	8	0	2	1
Eddie Robinson	.196	12	51	7	10	2	0	3	7	4	4	0
Jackie Jensen	.333	12	48	10	16	6	0	4	14	5	4	3
Yogi Berra	.386	12	44	11	17	2	1	6	9	1	3	0
Billy Martin	.219	11	32	4	7	2	1	0	2	1	1	4
Nellie Fox	.435	6	23	5	10	1	0	1	2	0	2	0
Robin Roberts	.091	4	11	1	1	0	0	1	1	1	0	0
Curt Simmons	.300	4	10	1	3	0	0	0	0	2	0	0
Gus Niarhos	.222	8	9	2	2	0	1	0	3	2	2	0
Eddie Lopat	.250	3	8	3	2	0	0	0	1	0	2	0
Bob Lemon	.429	6	7	5	3	1	0	1	2	0	3	1
Mike Garcia	.000	2	2	0	0	0	0	0	0	0	0	0
Sadao Nishimura	.000	2	1	0	0	0	0	0	0	1	0	0

American Pitching Statistics	ERA	G	W	L	IP	H	HR	SO	BB	R	ER
Curt Simmons	3.12	4	2	0	26	27	0	15	6	10	9
Bob Lemon	1.64	5	2	0	22	14	0	13	8	8	4
Robin Roberts	2.45	4	3	0	22	22	1	16	4	7	6
Eddie Lopat	1.35	3	3	0	20	12	2	8	4	4	3
Jackie Jensen	3.86	1	1	0	7	10	0	2	3	3	3
Sadao Nishimura	1.50	2	0	0	6	2	0	6	4	1	1
Mike Garcia	2.08	2	0	1	4.1	8	0	0	3	2	1

Japanese Batting Statistics	BA	G	AB	R	H	2B	3B	HR	RBI	SO	BB	SB
Futoshi Nakanishi	.313	8	32	5	10	3	0	0	3	3	1	0
Chusuke Kizuka	.241	9	29	5	7	0	0	1	1	1	0	0
Isami Okomoto	.125	8	24	2	3	0	0	1	1	3	2	0
Tokuji Iida	.217	9	23	0	5	0	0	0	3	3	2	0
Kazuo Horii	.273	7	22	1	6	0	1	0	3	1	3	0
Hiroshi Oshita	.286	8	21	0	6	2	0	0	2	6	2	0
Takuzo Miyake	.188	9	16	1	3	1	0	0	0	4	3	0
Shosei Go	.333	5	15	1	5	0	0	0	1	1	0	1
Itsuro Hondo	.083	7	12	0	1	0	0	0	0	1	0	0
Michio Nishizawa	.333	2	9	1	3	1	0	0	1	0	0	0
Satoshi Sugiyama	.500	2	8	2	4	1	0	1	2	3	1	0
Kazuo Kageyama	.000	6	7	1	0	0	0	0	1	0	4	0
Junji Nakatani	.167	3	6	0	1	1	0	0	1	0	0	0
Yasuhiro Fukami	.000	4	6	0	0	0	0	0	0	3	3	0
Takeshi Doigaki	.167	3	6	0	1	0	0	0	0	1	0	0
Kazuhiro Yamauchi	.600	2	5	1	3	2	0	0	0	0	1	0
Yoshio Yoshida	.600	1	5	1	3	0	0	0	0	0	0	0
Akira Noguchi	.400	1	5	1	2	1	0	0	0	0	0	0
Katsuki Tokura	.200	5	5	2	1	0	0	0	0	1	1	0
Jun Matsui	.000	4	5	0	0	0	0	0	0	1	0	0

Japanese Pitching Statistics	ERA	G	W	L	IP	H	HR	SO	BB	R	ER
Atsushi Aramaki	4.74	5	1	2	19	15	6	2	6	12	10
Tokuji Kawasaki	17.10	5	0	2	10	19	9	1	6	19	19
Giichi Hayashi	8.00	3	0	1	9	17	5	4	1	11	8
Masaichi Kaneda	5.63	2	0	1	8	8	3	1	5	5	5
Susumu Yuki	8.53	4	0	1	6.1	8	3	1	1	6	6
Hachiro Abe	4.50	2	0	1	6	7	1	3	2	3	3
Yasuo Yonekawa	3.60	2	0	0	5	6	1	1	2	2	2
Junzo Sekine	10.80	2	0	0	5	10	3	3	0	6	6
Eiji Shibata	10.80	2	0	1	5	8	2	2	2	6	6
Toshio Takamatsu	0.00	1	0	0	4	4	0	0	0	0	0
Hisafumi Kawamura	4.50	2	0	0	4	3	1	1	2	2	2
Hiroshi Nakahara	9.00	1	0	1	3	3	0	3	2	4	3
Shigeru Sugishita	33.75	1	0	1	1.1	6	1	0	1	5	5

NOTES

1 Eddie Robinson with C. Paul Rogers III, *Lucky Me: My 65 Years in Baseball* (Dallas: SMU Press, 2011), 100; Eddie Mathews and Bob Buege, *Eddie Mathews and the National Pastime* (Milwaukee: Douglas American Sports Publications, 1994), 92.

2 Douglas MacArthur, Supreme Commander of the Allied Powers in Japan, declared at the end of the Seals tour that "[t]his trip is the greatest piece of diplomacy ever. All the diplomats put together would not have been able to do this." "O'Doul Off for Australia to Direct Japanese Tour," *The Sporting News,* November 17, 1954: 21.

3 Dan Daniel, "Lopat to Lead Major Stars to Japan," *The Sporting News,* June 3, 1953: 1.

4 Yogi Berra with Dave Kaplan, *Ten Rings: My Championship Seasons* (New York: Harper Collins Publishers, 2003), 131; Allen Barra, *Yogi Berra: Eternal Yankee* (New York: W.W. Norton & Co., 2009), 182.

5 "Giants' Fall Trip to Japan Okayed; 15 Players to Go," *The Sporting News*, July 22, 1953: 7.

6 Future Hall of Famers Warren Spahn, Red Schoendienst, and Pee Wee Reese also initially committed to the tour, as did Bobby Shantz. All, however, ended up withdrawing, mostly because of injury issues. Daniel; "Giants' Fall Trip to Japan Okayed," 7; Mathews and Buege, 93.

7 Robin Roberts with C. Paul Rogers III, *My Life in Baseball* (Chicago: Triumph Books, 2003), 122; Mathews and Buege, 92-93.

8 "Sports in Brief," *Los Angeles Times,* October 1, 1953: 32; Jane Leavy, *The Last Boy: Mickey Mantle and the End of America's Childhood* (New York: Harper Collins, 2010), 103-111; David Falkner, *The Last Hero: The Life of Mickey Mantle* (New York: Simon & Schuster, 1995), 108.

9 "Two Expeditions to Japan Leave on Successive Days," *The Sporting* News, October 14, 1953: 19. With Mantle's withdrawal, Lopat could add another Yankee without violating the rule against having more than three players from one team on the tour.

10 Roberts with Rogers, 122.

11 Philley and Eddie Robinson, who was the first baseman for Lopat's All-Stars, were then teammates with the Philadelphia Athletics and were both from Paris, Texas, a town of about 15,000 people in Northeast Texas. Paris also produced football's Raymond Berry and Gene Stallings.

12 "Lopat's All-Stars Win Four Before 31,241 in Colorado, *The Sporting News,* October 21, 1953: 15.

13 "Garcia Injures Leg in Hawaiian Game," *The Sporting News,* October 21, 1953: 15, 18.

14 Hal Lebovitz, "Report by Garcia After Japan – His Injury Is a Bruise," *The Sporting News,* November 18, 1953: 17.

15 "Garcia Injures Leg in Hawaiian Game," 18.

16 Red McQueen, "22,800 See Majors' All-Stars in Hawaii," *The Sporting News,* October 28, 1953: 17-18.

17 Roberts with Rogers, 123. It actually did account for three runs since two men were on base. McQueen: 18.

18 Newcombe was in the Army but was able to pitch due to a 28-day furlough. McQueen: 17.

19 "Campanella Team Wins – Defeats Lopat's Squad, 4-3, in Tenth Inning at Honolulu," *New York Times,* October 21, 1953: 39; McQueen: 17.

20 Roberts with Rogers, 122-23.

21 McQueen: 17.

22 Carmen Berra, Joanne Fox, Jane Lemon, Libby Lopat, Mary Roberts, Dot Simmons, Ruth Slaughter, and Zoe Ann Olsen, the Olympic diving champion who was married to Jackie Jensen, all accompanied their husbands to Hawaii. "Yanks' Billy Martin Mobbed on His Arrival in Honolulu," *The Sporting News*, October 21, 1953: 15; Mathews and Buege, 93. However only Mary Roberts and Dot Simmons accompanied their husbands to Japan as well. Pfc. Jack Squires, "Chotto Motte – All-Star Notes," *Pacific Stars and Stripes,* November 6, 1953: 12.

23 Mathews and Buege, 93-4.

24 Sgt. Mike Hickey, "Japanese Fete Lopat All-Stars with Gala Reception, Parade," *Pacific Stars and Stripes,* October 23, 1953: 15.

25 "Big Crowds Greet Lopat's All-Stars at Contests in Japan," *The Sporting News,* November 4, 1953: 17.

26 Mathews and Buege, 96; Roberts and Rogers, 123.

27 "Big Crowds Greet Lopat's All-Stars at Contests in Japan."

28 Hickey, "Japanese Fete Lopat All-Stars with Gala Reception, Parade."

29 The Orions had won 56 and lost 62, with two ties in 1953, finishing 14½ games out of first place. Daniel E. Johnson, *Japanese Baseball: A Statistical Handbook* (Jefferson, North Carolina: McFarland & Company, 1999), 71.

30 "Big Crowds Greet Lopat's All-Stars at Contests in Japan." Carlo DeVito, *Yogi: The Life & Times of an American Original* (Chicago: Triumph Books, 2008), 157.

31 Mathews and Buege, 96.

32 Sauer won a $325 Nikon camera for hitting the first home run by an American on the tour. "Big Crowds Greet Lopat's All-Stars at Contests in Japan."

33 "Big Crowds Greet Lopat's All-Stars at Contests in Japan."

34 Roberts with Rogers, 123-24.

35 Sgt. Mike Hickey, "Mainichi Orions Surprise All-Stars, 5 to 4," *Pacific Stars and Stripes,* October 24, 1953: 15. The Herb Hunter team lost in 1922, the DiMaggio All-Stars in 1951, and then this one. The Negro League Royal Giants also lost a game in 1932,

36 Roberts with Rogers, 124.

37 Roberts with Rogers, 124.

38 Moreover, Kawasaki's 24 wins were in a 120-game regular season, as opposed to the major leagues' 154-game year.

39 Sgt. Mike Hickey, "All-Star HRs Down Japanese, 13-7," *Pacific Stars and Stripes,* October 25, 1953: 14; "Big Crowds Greet Lopat's All-Stars at Contests in Japan."

40 The Americans led just 4-2 before erupting for five runs in the sixth. Sgt. Mike Hickey, "Big Sixth Inning Humbles Pacific Leaguers, 10-3," *Pacific Stars and Stripes,* October 26, 1953: 14.

41 Pfc. Jack Squire, "Lopat Stars Win, 3-0, at Sendai," *Pacific Stars and Stripes,* October 27, 1953: 14.

42 "Lopat Team Scores, 9-4," *New York Times,* October 29, 1953: 45.

43 Pfc. Jack Squire, "Sauer Belts Two More HRs as Lopats Win," *Pacific Stars and Stripes*, October 29, 1953: 14.

44 Sauer rebounded in 1954 and slugged 41 home runs and drove in 103 runs for the Cubs.

45 Pfc. Jack Squire, "Four Circuit Blows Top Pacific All-Stars, 6 to 2," *Pacific Stars and Stripes,* October 30, 1953: 15.

46 Pfc. Jack Squire, "Ed Lopat's All-Stars Bang Out 15 to 1 Win," *Pacific Stars and Stripes,* October 31, 1953: 15.

47 DeVito, 158.

48 Lebovitz.

49 Squire, "Ed Lopat's All-Stars Bang Out 15 to 1 Win." According to *The Sporting News*, however, Berra had had previous run-ins with Stevens, who was an American League umpire. "Berra Raised Only Rhubarb on Lopat's Tour of Japan," *The Sporting News*, November 11, 1953: 15.

50 Pfc. Jack Squire, "Slaughter Paces All-Stars in 7 to 3 Victory," *Pacific Stars and Stripes*, November 1, 1953: 14.

51 Pfc. Jack Squire, "Four Circuit Clouts Highlight Stars' Win," *Pacific Stars and Stripes*, November 2, 1953: 15.

52 "Japanese Pitcher Joins Lopat's Stars," *Pacific Stars and Stripes*, October 29, 1953: 14.

53 Garcia, who had pitched little since his injury in Hawaii, returned home on November 1 due to the reported serious illness of his mother-in-law. "Barnstorming Season Winds Up with Games in Far East, Mexico," *The Sporting News*, November 18, 1953: 18; Squire, "Four Circuit Clouts Highlight Stars' Win."

54 Dan Daniel, "Lopat and Berra Plug Pair of Jap Pitchers to Yankees," *The Sporting News*, November 25, 1953: 16. Apparently nothing came of Lopat's recommendation to the Yankees. Nishimura had a relatively brief but very successful career in Japan for the Nishitetsu Lions, winning 82 games with a .636 won-loss percentage and a lifetime 2.44 earned-run average.

55 This according to John Holway, who served in Korea but was in Japan in time to witness the two 1953 postseason tours. http://baseballguru.com/jholway/analysisjholway36.html.

56 Kaneda had won 23 of the 45 victories for the last-place Swallows, his third straight 20-win season.

57 A number of major-league teams, including the Yankees and the New York Giants, were reportedly interested in signing Kaneda. Dan Daniel, 16; Robert Obojski, *The Rise of Japanese Baseball Power* (Radnor, Pennsylvania: Chilton Book Company, 1975), 52-53.

58 Robert Whiting, *The Chrysanthemum and the Bat* (New York: Dodd, Mead & Company, 1977), 109. In 1989, 36 years later after 1953, Kaneda happened to meet Robin Roberts at the Don Drysdale Celebrity Golf Tournament in Palm Springs, California. Through an interpreter, Roberts learned that Kaneda considered Roberts "his teacher" because he had copied Roberts' drop and drive delivery after seeing him pitch in Japan in 1953, even though Roberts was a right-hander. Kaneda was then manager of the Lotte Orions and invited Roberts and his wife, Mary, to attend the Orions' spring training in Japan in 1990. While there, the Robertses saw a tape of Kaneda's pitching motion, leading Mary Roberts to say to her husband, "My goodness, he looks like a left-handed you." Roberts with Rogers, 124-25.

59 Pfc. Jack Squire, "Lopats Triumph as Jensen Hurls," *Pacific Stars and Stripes*, November 3, 1953: 15.

60 Sgt. Mike Hickey, "Lopat Romp, 10-0," *Pacific Stars and Stripes*, November 4, 1953: 15.

61 "Lopat Stars Tab 11-1 Mark in Nippon," *The Sporting News*, November 11, 1953: 15; Sgt. Mike Hickey, "Lopats Go Homer-Happy," *Pacific Stars and Stripes*, November 5, 1953: 15.

62 Daniel, "Lopat and Berra Plug Pair of Jap Pitchers to Yankees."

63 "Lopat Stars Belt Okinawa Troops," *Pacific Stars and Stripes*," November 6, 1953: 15; "Jensen Hurls Stars to 6-0 Victory Over Okinawa Club," *Pacific Stars and Stripes*," November 7, 1953: 15.

64 Daniel, "Lopat and Berra Plug Pair of Jap Pitchers to Yankees."

65 "All-Stars Trounce Filipinos, 17-0, Behind Roberts," *Pacific Stars and Stripes*, November 8, 1953: 14.

66 United Press, "Lopatmen Clip Orions in Finale," *Pacific Stars and Stripes*, November 9, 1953: 14.

67 Enos Slaughter with Kevin Reid, *Country Hardball: The Autobiography of Enos "Country" Slaughter* (Greensboro, North Carolina: Tudor Publishers, 1991), 152.

68 That includes the four pre-tour games in Colorado against major-league opposition.

69 Slaughter with Reid, 152.

70 Many believe that Jensen's fear of flying began on the Lopat All-Stars tour. Mark Armour, "Jackie Jensen," https://sabr.org/bioproj/person/jackie-jensen/; George I. Martin, *The Golden Boy: A Biography of Jackie Jensen* (Portsmouth, New Hampshire: Peter E. Randall Publisher, 2000), 88.

71 Robinson with Rogers, 101; Roberts with Rogers, 126. The Mae West was an inflatable life preserver used by the military in World War II. When inflated, it made the wearer appear to have large breasts like the big-bosomed actress Mae West, hence the name.

72 "Giants and Lopat Stars Attract 703,000 at 24 Games in Japan," *The Sporting News*, November 11, 1953: 15.

73 "Martin Arrives Home, Praises Japan Junket," *Pacific Stars and Stripes*, November 12, 1953: 15.

74 Pfc. Jack Squires, "Chotto Motte – All-Star Notes," *Pacific Stars and Stripes*, November 6, 1953: 12.

75 Slaughter with Reid, 152.

76 Squires, "Chotto Motte – All-Star Notes."

77 Slaughter with Reid, 151.

78 In contrast, the Japanese hit three home runs against the Lopats.

79 According to Eddie Mathews, the Japanese did not cheer but clapped three times when something good happened. Mathews and Buege, 97.

80 Hickey, "Lopats Go Homer-Happy."

81 Eddie Robinson struggled the most among position players, hitting .196 with three home runs. Robinson always viewed the junkballing Lopat as the toughest pitcher he faced in the big leagues, and it is probable he had the same difficulty adjusting to the Japanese pitchers' assortment of off-speed deliveries. Robinson with Rogers, 154.

82 Daniel, "Lopat and Berra Plug Pair of Jap Pitchers to Yankees." Of course, Lemon had broken into the big leagues as an outfielder-third baseman.

83 Obojski, 51.

84 "Runs Mean Yen, Japs Bunt at Any Time, Curt Reports," *The Sporting News*, November 25, 1953: 16.

85 A. Satoru Ikeda, "Time at Bat," *Nippon Times*, October 28, 1953: 5.

86 Gayle Talbot (Associated Press), "Japan in World Series? It's Less Dreamlike Now," *Nippon Times*, November 23, 1953: 65.

87 "Martin Arrives Home, Praises Japan Junket"; Daniel, "Lopat and Berra Plug Pair of Jap Pitchers to Yankees"; Mathews and Buege, 98.

88 For example, in 1966 Eddie Lopat was the general manager of the Kansas City Athletics and hired Eddie Robinson as his assistant GM. Later, in 1972 when Robinson was general manager of the Atlanta Braves, he hired Eddie Mathews to manage the Braves. He also fired Mathews in 1974. Robinson with Rogers, 154, 170, 174-75.

89 "State Department Lauds Teams' Tour," *Nippon Times*, November 23, 1953: 5.

90 Daniel, "Lopat and Berra Plug Pair of Jap Pitchers to Yankees."

91 Listed Japanese players have a minimum of 5 at-bats, 3 innings pitched, or a decision. Yoshikazu Matsubayashi, *Baseball Game History: Japan vs. U.S.A.* (Tokyo: Baseball Magazine, 2004), 89; Nippon Professional Baseball Records, https://www.2689web.com/nb.html.

GOOD OPTICS: THE 1955 YANKEES TOUR

By Roberta J. Newman

On Thursday, October 20, 1955, the New York Yankees and their entourage landed at Tokyo's Haneda Airport to begin a three-week, 16-game goodwill tour of Japan. There, they were mobbed by kimono-clad young women bearing bouquets, an eager press corps, and a thousand devoted fans.[1] The result was chaos, as children, autograph seekers, journalists, businessmen, and advertisers of all stripes besieged the Yankees party.[2] But the airport crowd was tiny compared with the throng lining the streets of Tokyo. An estimated 100,000 turned out to shower the motorcade – 23 vehicles carrying the players and coaching staff, team co-owner Del Webb, general manager George Weiss, Commissioner Ford Frick, and accompanying wives – with confetti and ticker tape.[3] They were also showered with rain from Typhoon Opal, but the weather, which caused significant damage and loss of life

elsewhere in Japan, did little to dampen the crowd's enthusiasm.[4]

The Yankees were not the only American visitors to arrive in Japan on that day. Former New York Governor and failed presidential candidate Thomas E. Dewey also landed in Tokyo on the Japanese leg of his world tour, with the stated aim of learning about Japan's recent economic advances.[5] In reality, Dewey's aim was to spread pro-American Cold War propaganda to a new democracy still finding its political direction, a nation he called "one of the keystones to any sound system of freedom."[6] Dewey stayed but four days, his visit garnering little coverage in the English-language press. In contrast, the Yankees remained in the spotlight and on the pages of newspapers for the entirety of their visit. If influence can be measured by column inches, the Yankees' impact on Japanese

The Yankees arrive in Japan October 20, 1955

attitudes toward America far outweighed that of the political power broker.

Ten years before the Yankees arrived, Japan was thoroughly beaten, exhausted from fighting the "Emperor's holy war." Of the early postwar period, historian John W. Dower writes:

> Virtually all that would take place in the several years that followed unfolded against this background of crushing defeat. Despair took root and flourished in such a milieu; so did cynicism and opportunism – as well as marvelous expressions of resilience, creativity, and idealism of a sort possible only among people who have seen an old world destroyed and are being forced to imagine a new one.[7]

For the Japan that greeted the Yankees, this new world had just begun to become a reality. The year 1955 – *Showa 30* or the 30th year of Emperor Hirohito's reign by the Japanese dating system – marked the beginning of what would be called the Japanese Miracle, a period of unprecedented economic growth that lasted more than three decades.[8] Ironically, war was the engine that drove the Japanese Miracle – the Cold War. In 1945, Japanese industry was crippled – almost one-third of its capacity had been demolished.[9] With staggering unemployment rates among an educated labor force, combined with the country's advantageous geographic location near Korea, China, and the USSR, Japan became an ideal place to establish new war-related industries and revive old ones.[10] In a very real sense, Japanese manufacturers played an active part of what President Dwight D. Eisenhower would come to call the "military-industrial complex" in his 1961 farewell speech. Nevertheless, in 1955, relations between the United States and Japan were occasionally tense, the United States fearing that Japan, like India, would take a neutral position in the power struggle between it and the Soviet Union. It did not. Instead, it became one of the United States's strongest allies.[11] But the strength of that alliance was still wobbly as the two nations negotiated an ultimately successful trade deal, one that would see Japan's entry into the General Agreement on Tariffs and Trade (GATT) and become a player in the global economy.[12]

Though clearly not as delicate as treaty talks with international implications, negotiations to bring the Yankees to Japan were handled with care. In a very broad sense, these negotiations were a microcosm of the larger, far more complicated economic and political talks. In June, during the broadcast of a "good will talk" for the Voice of America, Yankees manager Casey Stengel, who had toured Japan in 1922 as part of an all-star outfit, let it slip that he might be returning. An anonymous source within the Yankees intimated that the team had, in fact, been discussing the possibility of a tour, as had several other clubs.[13] Although there may have been other teams under consideration, it had to be the Yankees. As *New York World Telegram and Sun* sports columnist and *Sporting News* contributor Dan Daniel observed, "Information from U.S. Army sources says that baseball enthusiasm over there (in Japan) and rooting support for the pennant effort of the Yankees have achieved unprecedented heights."[14] Daniel, who covered the New York team, became the primary source of information regarding tour negotiations, though he did not cover the tour itself. But he was not the only sportswriter to weigh in. Writing in the *Nippon Times*, F.N. Mike concurred, noting, "The Yankees is a magic name here, where every household not only follows baseball doings in Japan, but also that in America. The Yankees, of all others epitomizes big-time baseball in the States, just as Babe Ruth, who helped to build up its name and who led the great 1934 All-Americans to Japan, represented baseball in America individually."[15] And not only were the Yankees the most recognizable and most popular American team in Japan, but their very brand meant "American baseball" and, by extension, America, to the Japanese, in the most positive sense.

Before the Yankees front office would consent to the visit, it required assurance that both governments were on board. More importantly, even after they were invited to tour by sponsor *Mainichi Shimbun*, the second largest newspaper in Japan, the organization would not begin to plan a tour without a formal invitation from the Japanese. The Japanese government laid down certain conditions, most specifically, that the visiting team would not be compensated. According to Daniel, "the proposition offers no financial gain to the club. Nor would any of the players receive anything beyond an all-expense trip for themselves and their wives."[16] In fact, it was absolutely essential that the team agree to forgo any type of payment. Writing in *Pacific Stars and Stripes*, columnist Lee Kavetski observed, "Each Yankee player is likely to be asked to sign an acceptance of non profit conditions before making the trip." Kavetski continued, "It is recalled an amount of unpleasantness developed from the Giants' 1953 tour. Upon completion of the tour, some of Leo Durocher's players complained that they had been misled and jobbed about financial remuneration. There was absolutely no basis for the complaint. And the beef unjustly placed Japanese hosts in a bad light."[17] This was hardly goodwill. Indeed, it was a public-relations disaster that extended into the realm of foreign relations. Kavetski noted, "As Joe DiMaggio, who has been to Japan twice, said to New York sports writer Dan Daniel, 'Stengel's players can perform a great service to baseball and to international friendship if they sign up for the trip even though there is no prospect for personal financial gain.'"[18]

Why did the bad behavior of a few American baseball players border on an international incident? On April 28, 1952, the San Francisco Peace Treaty, signed by 49 nations, including the United States and Japan, officially ended World War II. It also ended the Allied Occupation. As such, the Giants were guests in a newly sovereign nation trying to find its way and to establish its identity on a global stage. Tour sponsor *Yomiuri Shimbun*, Japan's largest newspaper, promised to pay each player 60 percent of the gate of their final two games in Osaka in return for their participation. Unfortunately, the resulting figure was smaller than the players expected. Only 5,000 of the 24,000 who attended the first of those games actually bought tickets. As a result, each player was to be paid $331, in addition to "walking around money." While this was no small amount – it translates to approximately $3,550 in 2021 dollars – it was nowhere near the $3,000 they believed they would net. Writing in *Pacific Stars and Stripes*, Cpl. Perry Smith noted, "The individual players did not appreciate the 'giving away of the remaining 19,000 tickets and six team members refused to dress for the final contest." Although they were eventually persuaded to take the field, they were not happy. This represented a significant cut in revenue for players accustomed to making good money during the offseason.[19]

Although the players thought they had a legitimate beef, their complaints did not play well in the press. To demand more was a public insult. Conditions in Japan had certainly improved by 1953, when the Giants toured, but they were far from ideal. Poverty and unemployment were still an issue, as was Japan's huge national debt. That representatives of a wealthy nation demanded payment from the representatives of a newly emerging nation looked especially bad. That the players themselves were no doubt viewed as wealthy by individual Japanese could not have helped, either. It was essential that the Yankees not make the same mistake, treating their hosts as inferior and not worthy of due respect.

In 1955, US-Japanese relations were still a work in progress. While arrangements for the tour were being discussed, Japanese Deputy Prime Minister Mamoru Shigemitsu visited the United States for talks with Secretary of State John Foster Dulles. At a press conference, Shigemitsu, who simultaneously served as Japan's foreign minister, "emphasized the desire of his government for a more independent partnership with the United States." For Japan to make what Shigemitsu called "a fresh start," he said, "we must talk things over frankly with the United States and see that the two governments understand each other."[20] Of course, Shigemitsu's conference with Dulles had nothing directly to do with the goodwill baseball tour. But as he suggested, conditions laid down by a government seeking recognition of its independence had to be given their due. And given the timing, it would have been terrible optics were the insult to be repeated.

Ultimately, the Yankee players agreed and the tour was organized, but not before another major wrinkle had to be ironed out. Once *Mainichi Shimbun* offered its sponsorship, its chief competitor, *Yomiuri Shimbun*, countered with an offer to another team. Commissioner Frick was not having any of it. He responded negatively, announcing that simultaneous Japanese tours by two major-league clubs was out of the question – it would be one or none. Following their own delicate negotiation, competitors *Mainichi* and *Yomiuri* came to their own agreement. The two papers would sponsor tours by American clubs in alternating years.[21]

On August 23 George Weiss announced that the visit would proceed. Beginning with five games in Hawaii and ending with several more in Okinawa and Manila, the Yankees would leave New York shortly after the World Series on October 8 and planned to return on November 18. Included in the group of 64 travelers were many of the players' wives, though some planned to stay behind in Hawaii. Among these wives were those of Andy Carey, Eddie Robinson, and Johnny Kucks, all of whom were on their honeymoons.[22]

The schedule, which included games in Tokyo, Osaka, Kyushu, Sendai, Sapporo, Nagoya, and Hiroshima, was announced on September 24. Tickets, which went on sale on October 1 for the Tokyo games to be played at Korakuen Stadium, ranged in price from 1,200 yen (approximately $3.33) for special reserved seats, to 300 yen (approximately 83 cents) for bleacher seating. Games at other stadiums would top out at 1,000 yen (approximately $2.77).[23] According to Japan's National Tax Agency, in 1955 private sector

Cover of the 1955 Yankees tour program featuring Mickey Mantle

workers earned an average annual salary of 185,000 yen (approximately $513). This was a great improvement from the poverty of the early postwar years. Indeed, it was approaching twice the annual salary that private sector workers earned in 1950.[24] But even a ticket to the bleachers would have been a considerable reach for the average worker. As a result, it is safe to assume that the live spectatorship for the Yankees games would have consisted primarily of well-off Japanese as well as American servicemen. Other Japanese fans had to make do with newspaper coverage, radio and, in many cases, television.[25] Realistically speaking, television receivers were extremely expensive, making individual ownership rare – in 1953, for example, even the least expensive receivers cost more than a year's wages for the average Japanese consumer.[26] But this didn't mean that television was only for the wealthy. As in the United States, sets were placed strategically in front of retail establishments in order to draw customers. Far more common, however, was the institution of *gaito terebi*, plaza televisions, sets situated in accessible public spaces, which gave rise to the practice of communal viewing.[27] This would have enabled many Japanese fans to watch the games.

A Japanese poster promoting the series announced, "Unprecedented – the marvelous terrific team of our time – Champion of the Baseball World – New York Yankees – coming! Sixteen games in the whole country."[28] While not entirely accurate – the Yankees went on to lose the World Series to the Brooklyn Dodgers in seven games after the poster was printed – it did not matter to Japanese fans. Given the public response to the team's arrival in Tokyo, the Yankees were, in fact, the "marvelous terrific team" of 1955.

That the series had a purpose beyond "goodwill" was publicly stated by Vice President Nixon, speaking on behalf of President Eisenhower, on October 12. Eisenhower had, in fact, been involved with the planning, according to Del Webb. Prior to arranging the tour, Webb had discussed its potential benefits with the president, Secretary Dulles, and General Douglas MacArthur, former commander of the Allied powers in Japan. "I asked the president last summer if he thought a trip by the Yankees might help bring the American and Japanese people closer to each other," said Webb. "He said it would."[29] So it was no surprise that Nixon made a statement, addressing Commissioner Frick, expressing the president's best wishes. Nixon wrote, "Appearances in Japan by an American major league baseball team will contribute a great deal to increased

mutual understanding between the people of the United States and the people of Japan, and thus to the cause of a just and lasting peace, which demands the continued friendship and cooperation of the nations of the Free World."[30] It was up to the Yankees, Nixon implied, to help cement the US-Japanese alliance, assuring that Japan would come down on the side of "freedom" rather than neutrality in the ongoing struggle against the unfree Soviet bloc. Of course, the vice president's statement was a clear example of the inflated rhetoric of Cold War propaganda. But the message was unavoidable. Public relations played an essential role in geopolitics, and this tour was, above all else, an exercise in public relations.

Having fared well on their Hawaiian stop, winning all five games against a mixture of local teams and armed forces all-stars, and having survived their mobbing at the airport, the Yankees began their hectic schedule. The sodden but jubilant welcome was followed by a series of events, receptions, and press conferences. The next day, the team worked out while Stengel, who would serve as the face of the club, and Weiss attended a luncheon at the Foreign Correspondents' Club. Lest it be thought that the tour consisted only of propaganda, the proceedings included their fair share of frivolous fun, which was also covered in the press. At the club, Stengel was presented with a gift – a large box, labeled "For Ol' Case." According to the *Nippon Times*, "Stengel stood patiently by while bearers deposited the box at his feet. Then, lo and behold, a pretty girl in a kimono crashed through the wrapping pounding her fist into a baseball glove in the best tradition of the game."[31] Sensing an opportunity to get in on the act, Weiss "went through the motions of putting the girl's name to a contract." In what might, in twenty-first-century terms, be considered in very bad taste, Weiss asked her how much she wanted. But under the circumstances, Weiss's actions were just part of the fun. Nevertheless, Stengel took a moment to emphasize the true nature of the tour. The Yankees were in Japan "on a serious mission of good will."[32]

It would be nice to say that the first game, held on Saturday, October 22, went off without a hitch. But rarely does this happen when there are so many moving parts. This time, Opal did more than just soak a parade. The typhoon caused a postponement of Game Five of the Japanese championship series between the Nankai Hawks and the Yomiuri Giants, which was scheduled to be played at Korakuen Stadium on Friday. As a result, the Yankees contest had to be moved to the evening to accommodate both games. A smaller crowd than expected – 35,000, about 5,000 shy of a capacity crowd – turned out to see the Yankees make quick work of the Mainichi Orions, beating the Japanese team 10-2.[33] After Kaoru Hatoyama, the wife of the prime minister, threw out the first pitch – the very first wife of a head of state to do so at a major-league game, exhibition or otherwise – fans and dignitaries were treated to a 10-hit barrage by the Yankees, including two home runs and a triple by rookie catcher Elston Howard. The Orions countered with seven hits, but committed a costly first-inning error in their loss. The crowd, which included Thomas E. Dewey and his wife, was not disappointed.[34]

Baseball, however, never completely supplanted diplomacy, as Prime Minister Hatoyama greeted the Yankees, Frick, and their entourage at a reception. Among the many photo ops, one stood out. Hatoyama, having been presented with a Yankees hat by Stengel, became the first Japanese prime minister to wear a baseball cap.[35]

The Yankees were once again victorious in the second game at Korakuen Stadium, this time defeating All-Tokyo (a team composed of Pacific and Central all-stars) 11-6 in front of a capacity crowd. A ninth-inning grand slam by first baseman Eddie Robinson off the Japanese Central League's Rookie of the Year, Kazunori Nishimura, sealed the victory. This time, the Japanese players' bats were not quiet. All-Tokyo managed seven hits against Bob Turley and Bob Grim. Only Mickey Mantle underperformed. Fans, perhaps unreasonably, expected big things out of the injured Mantle, who had played only part time in the World Series, a few weeks earlier. Mantle struck out three times in the second game, after whiffing once during a pinch-hitting appearance in the first game.[36]

With the third game in Tokyo postponed until later in the trip, the Yankees moved on to Sendai, 304 kilometers to the north on Japan's east coast. As in Tokyo, they were mobbed. Greeted by another throng, their motorcade tied up traffic for two hours en route from their hotel to Miyagi Stadium, where once again they went head-to-head with All-Tokyo.[37] Ending New York's winning streak, the Tokyo squad played to a 1-1 tie, despite the fact that they had but one hit. But the Yankees also committed an error, allowing All-Tokyo to score its run.[38] From Sendai, both teams flew to Sapporo, located on Hokkaido, the northernmost main island, where they played for an overflow crowd of 30,000. Returning to form, Mantle finally got going,

hitting two doubles to the delight of the spectators, in the Yankees' 11-0 rout of the all-stars.[39]

Another huge crowd, complete with its own ticker-tape parade and its own storm, greeted the Yankees in Osaka, in the southwestern part of the main island. There the American club took on the Nankai Hawks. Like the Yankees, the Hawks had been unable to win a championship, having fallen to Yomiuri Giants in the 1955 Japan Series. Japan's second-best team fell to America's as well, losing in a 7-0 shutout. The crowd was unusually sparse for this contest, for reasons beyond the control of both teams. Once again, rain interfered. Only 15,000 fans came out to see the game.[40]

There was no such paucity of spectators for the second game in the Osaka area, where 30,000 turned up at Nishinomiya Stadium on October 29 to see the All-Osaka nine lose 6-1 as the Yankees amassed 16 hits. Bob Cerv, substituting for Mantle, thrilled the crowd with a "tremendous 430-foor homer." Once again Turley and Grim performed masterfully against the best players in the region.[41]

The next day Cerv homered again and collected all four of the Yankees' RBIs against the Pacific League All-Stars. Cerv went on to double in the eighth, once again scoring Martin with the final run. The All-Stars scored as well – once in the seventh inning and once in the eighth – but it was not enough to put the Japanese team over the top.[42] Had the Yankees done nothing more than entertain Japanese baseball fans in Osaka, it most likely would have been sufficient to garner goodwill and burnish America's reputation in the eyes of the Japanese. But they were teachers as well as performers. The Yankees held a clinic for more than 200 participants. Coach Bill Dickey worked with the local players on catching techniques, while Jim Turner tutored them on pitching. Gus Mauch, the Yankee trainer, held his own clinic as well.[43] According to Tokyo journalist N. Sakata, who had recently traveled to the United States to cover an international tournament and the World Series, the Yankees' primary role was to provide instruction to their Japanese opponents. Writing in *The Sporting News*, Sakata observed, "(The Yankees') way of sliding is something we have to learn. Some of the Yankee players tell me that the Japanese way of defending bases is very dangerous to themselves. The Japanese players are not accustomed to the American way of base-sliding."[44]

Next on the itinerary, the Yankees flew to Nagoya to play the Chunichi Dragons, before returning to Osaka. A crowd of 33,000 came out to see the New Yorkers face Dragons ace Shigeru Sugishita. The Yankees touched up Sugishita for seven runs, including another home run by Robinson and doubles by Kucks and Yogi Berra, while the Dragons managed just three hits and no runs off Kucks and Tom Sturdivant.[45] Conspicuously absent was the underperforming Mantle. Injury was not the cause. The Yankees erstwhile slugger left Japan early to attend to his ill wife, Merlyn, who was expected to give birth imminently.[46] Despite Mantle's anemic performance in part-time play, Japanese fans were disappointed. They had been holding out hope that he would break out of his slump and that they would be there to witness it.[47]

November 3, a Japanese holiday celebrating the birthday of the Meiji Emperor (1852-1912), who both modernized and militarized the country, was another banner day for the Yankees. Drawing one of the largest crowds in Japanese baseball at the time, the Yankees and All-Japan played in front of 70,000, paying an average of 720 yen each, at Koshien Stadium. Once again, the Yankees emerged victorious, defeating their opponents by a score of 7-3, behind a home run from Billy Martin, who may have made the crowd forget Mantle's absence.[48]

But the real victor here was US-Japanese relations. In Osaka the Yankees made a move that, as Red McQueen, writing in *The Sporting News,* observed, "solidified the importance of their visit as good-will ambassadors of the United States and Organized Ball." Before he, too, left Japan, Weiss spoke enthusiastically about the quality of Japanese baseball, appointing Henry Tadashi "Bozo" Wakabayashi, coach of the Tombow Unions of Japan's Pacific League, an official Yankees scout. Said Weiss, "As the one who inaugurated the Yankee scouting and baseball school system, I have long wanted to institute an exchange between the Japanese pro circuits and the leagues in America. We would be interested in players who stood out and we would be very happy if we found one. However, we would not sign a Japanese player merely for publicity."[49] It is possible that Weiss was being honest. Still, it would take more than four decades for the Yankees to sign their first Japanese player, Hideki Irabu, in 1997. A genuine desire to sign a Japanese player does not seem to have been the real aim of Wakabayashi's appointment. It was, in fact, publicity, but not for the Yankees. In a sense, it represented a public recognition of the emerging status of Japanese baseball in international sports, and, by extension, a representation of Japan's independence and the type of new understanding between the American and Japanese people. While it may not have been specifically what Deputy Prime Minister and Foreign Minister Shigemitsu had in mind, it signaled the type of respect that Shigemitsu expected would be extended to Japan by the United States.

From Osaka, the Yankees once again boarded a plane, this time for Fukuoka, on the southernmost of the major Japanese islands, Kyushu, to play the Nishitetsu Lions. In the eyes of an unnamed sportswriter for the *Nippon Times*, the Yankees "annihilated" the Lions, 14-1. Perhaps this was not the best language to use, given Fukuoka's proximity to Nagasaki, but the lede on the sports page of an English-language Japanese newspaper was not noteworthy enough to cause a stir. Once again, Robinson homered – this time a grand slam. So did Hank Bauer, Andy Carey, Bob Cerv, and pitcher Don Larsen, who hit .146 during the regular season. The Lions managed five hits. A single by outfielder Hiroshi Oshita drove in Akinobu Kono for the team's only run.[50] Then it was on to Shimonoseki, at the very tip of the main island, not far from Fukuoka. Once again, the Americans poured it on, touching up the Pacific-Central All-Stars pitching for 19 hits and 12 runs. All-Stars shortstop Yasumitsu Toyoda managed a two-run homer off Turley in the third inning for the Pacific-Central team's only runs.[51]

The tour's last stop before returning to Tokyo for the final series of games was Hiroshima, where the Yankees defeated the Central All-Stars, 6-2. This time the New York squad had to come from behind to defeat its opponents, who jumped out to an early 2-0 lead.[52] Perhaps not surprisingly, the game, not the city's history, was the emphasis of this visit. By 1955 Hiroshima had rebounded. The city played a significant role in the Japanese Miracle, becoming a center for weapon manufacturing and procurements during the Korean War.[53] Nevertheless, concerns about the long-term effects of radioactive fallout remained.

While the Yankees were in Japan, a small group from Hiroshima were visiting New York, but for different reasons. An item in the *Nippon Times* about a member of the Yankees traveling party tells a story not included on the sports page. Toshio Ota, a transplanted Hiroshima resident living in New York, accompanied the team on its trip. Ota reported to the newspaper about the welfare of the Hiroshima Maidens.[54] A group of 25 girls and young women – *hibakusha*, survivors of the atomic bombs – who had been badly disfigured in the attack, were taken to New York under the auspices of the American Friends Service Committee and several other organizations, with the help of *Saturday Review* editor Norman Cousins, to undergo reconstructive plastic surgery. Both the patients and physicians came to be seen as symbols of developing understanding and goodwill between the United States and Japan, as did the Yankees on their tour, though in a far more important fashion. Moreover, the Maidens' treatment cast a public spotlight on the devastation of nuclear warfare.[55]

On November 10 the Yankees returned to Tokyo for four games, three that had been previously scheduled and the rescheduled contest against the Yomiuri Giants. Once again facing the Central League All-Stars, the Yankees continued their streak against Japan's best, winning 6-1. And once again they came from behind, this time after Yoshio Yoshida tripled, scoring on a fielder's choice. In fact, the Yankees were held hitless over the first three innings by pitcher Kazunori Nishimura but broke out in the fourth with four runs.[56] The streak continued the next day, as the Yankees rode roughshod over the Japanese champions, shutting out the Giants 11-0. As in the previous game, the Yankees were held scoreless, though not hitless, until the fourth inning. Then the tide turned. They scored three in the fourth and eight in the sixth. Despite a triple by Morimichi Iwashita and doubles by Takashi Iwamoto and Andy Miyamoto, a Hawaiian member of the Giants squad, the Tokyo effort turned into an exercise in futility.[57]

Korakuen Stadium also hosted the final two games of the tour, as the Yankees played the Pacific League All-Stars and the Japan All-Stars. Neither the first game against the Pacific team nor the two that preceded it drew huge crowds, but attendance was still substantial. Some 20,000 turned out to see the Yankees shut out their Japanese opponents yet again, this time by 10-0, outhitting the All-Stars 12 to 4.[58] Not surprisingly, the final game, played on November 13, drew quite well. According to the *Nippon Times*, 35,000 cheering fans joined the Yankees, "saying say-onara." Surprisingly, unlike 14 out of the previous 15 contests, the Tokyo outfit outhit the Yankees, 8 to 7. Yogi Berra homered twice in the Yankees' 9-3 win. But as was true for the other 15 games, the spectators had not come to see the Japanese win, but rather, to see the American celebrities do what they did best.[59]

Still, there were doubts that the Yankees had given the games their all. After the final contest, Tokuro Konishi, a former professional manager, announced to his radio audience that the Yankees had played only to 70 to 80 percent of their ability, so as not to make the local players look too bad. A bemused Stengel replied, "Our players gave their best to win and I'm proud of the fine impression they made." American League umpire John Stevens, who worked the whole series, concurred. "We had a wonderful trip," noted Stengel. "The fans treated us swell."[60]

After a final day packing and shopping in Tokyo, the Yankees departed for Okinawa, then a United States protectorate, and the Philippines. Unlike the 1953 Giants tour, the Yankees' goodwill trip was an unmitigated success. Indeed, even the *New York Times*, which had paid it scant attention, declared it so.[61] Red McQueen, writing in the *Honolulu Advertiser*, agreed. "This morale, patriotic and goodwill stuff can be stretched a bit too far, but in the case of the recent visit of the New York Yankees and their present tour of Japan and the Philippines, it is one of the most diplomatic excursions in the history of sports," opined McQueen. "Except for the explicit purpose of spreading goodwill between the respective nations, it is doubtful that a venture of this nature could ever have materialized."[62] Whether or not the tour had a direct effect on US-Japanese relations, it provided great optics. It was a public-relations coup. While the relationship between the two nations, one already a global superpower, the other on its way to becoming a major player in the world economy, would take a few more years to form into a solid alliance, Japan finally came down firmly on the side of the United States in the Cold War. The Yankees' goodwill tour provided a vision of what cooperation between the two countries might look like. By respecting Japan's newfound sovereignty and serving as exemplary guests – even Martin, Ford, and Mantle, while he was there, seem to have behaved themselves – the New York Yankees and major-league baseball as a whole participated in what might be called their own Japanese miracle.

1955 NEW YORK YANKEES GAMES IN JAPAN

Date	Place	Opponent	Score	Winner	Loser
October 22	Tokyo	Mainichi Orions	10-2	Bryne	Aramaki
October 23	Tokyo	All-Tokyo	11-6	Turley	Kaneda
October 25	Sendai	All-Tokyo	1-1	None	None
October 26	Sapporo	All-Tokyo	11-0	Kucks	Kajimoto
October 28	Osaka	Nankai Hawks	7-0	Byrne	Maruko
October 29	Nishinomiya	All-Osaka	6-1	Turley	Abe
October 30	Nishinomiya	Pacific League All-Stars	4-2	Ford	Yonekawa
November 1	Nagoya	Chunichi Dragons	7-0	Kucks	Sugishita
November 3	Osaka	All-Japan	7-3	Bryne	Kaneda
November 5	Fukuoka	Nishitetsu Lions	14-1	Larsen	Otsu
November 6	Shimonoseki	Pacific & Central All-Stars	12-2	Turley	Hasegawa
November 8	Hiroshima	Central League All-Stars	6-2	Ford	Nishimura
November 10	Tokyo	Central League All-Stars	6-1	Bryne	Nishimura
November 11	Tokyo	Yomiuri Giants	11-0	Larsen	Otomo
November 12	Tokyo	Pacific League All-Stars	10-0	Turley	Kajimoto
November 13	Tokyo	All-Japan	9-3	Konstanty	Otomo

1955 NEW YORK YANKEES TOUR BATTING AND PITCHING STATISTICS[63]

Yankees Batting Statistics	BA	G	AB	R	H	2B	3B	HR	RBI	SO	BB	SB
Billy Martin	.300	16	70	12	21	3	0	2	8	4	7	3
Andy Carey	.228	15	57	10	13	1	0	7	21	9	8	1
Elston Howard	.411	16	56	9	23	1	2	3	13	2	4	1
Bob Cerv	.400	16	55	20	22	6	0	5	20	1	7	0
Yogi Berra	.380	16	50	12	19	3	1	2	11	1	6	0
Hank Bauer	.327	14	49	13	16	1	0	3	8	2	7	3
Gil McDougald	.265	14	49	17	13	2	1	1	8	5	6	5
Bill Skowron	.281	14	32	13	9	0	0	1	7	2	3	1
Irv Noren	.367	11	30	8	11	3	1	1	5	3	5	2
Eddie Robinson	.240	12	25	5	6	0	0	4	12	2	5	0
Jerry Coleman	.238	13	21	1	5	0	0	0	2	5	4	0
Mickey Mantle	.333	7	15	3	5	3	0	0	2	4	2	1
Frank Leja	.385	9	13	0	5	0	0	0	0	4	0	0
Charlie Silvera	.250	9	12	2	3	0	0	0	1	3	1	0
Tommy Byrne	.091	6	11	2	1	0	0	1	2	5	1	0
Bob Turley	.250	4	8	1	2	0	0	0	0	2	0	0
Don Larsen	.429	4	7	3	3	1	0	1	2	0	1	0
Johnny Kucks	.333	3	6	1	2	0	0	0	0	0	0	0
Whitey Ford	.167	4	6	0	1	0	0	0	0	1	1	0
Bob Grim	.167	5	6	0	1	0	0	0	0	1	0	0
Tom Morgan	.000	4	4	0	0	0	0	0	0	4	0	0
Jim Konstanty	.333	4	3	0	1	0	0	0	1	1	0	0
Tom Sturdivant	.500	4	2	0	1	0	0	0	1	0	0	0

Yankees Pitching Statistics	ERA	G	W	L	IP	H	HR	SO	BB	R	ER
Bob Turley	1.17	4	4	0	23	11	2	20	15	3	3
Whitey Ford	2.25	4	1	0	20	8	0	8	12	5	5
Tommy Byrne	1.42	4	4	0	19	13	1	9	8	3	3
Bob Grim	2.50	5	2	0	18	15	1	15	3	6	5
Johnny Kucks	0.00	3	2	0	16	8	0	8	0	0	0
Don Larsen	1.76	4	2	0	15.1	10	0	12	3	3	3
Tom Morgan	0.00	4	0	0	13	9	0	6	3	1	0
Tom Sturdivant	0.00	4	0	0	12	7	0	10	4	0	0
Jim Konstanty	1.13	4	0	0	8	6	0	4	1	1	1
Bob Wiesler	27.00	1	0	0	.2	2	0	0	3	2	2

Japanese Batting Statistics	BA	G	AB	R	H	2B	3B	HR	RBI	SO	BB	SB
Kazuhiro Yamauchi	.379	8	29	6	11	2	1	2	4	2	3	2
Yoshio Yoshida	.208	8	24	1	5	2	1	0	2	2	2	0
Yukihiko Machida	.136	7	22	1	3	0	0	1	1	4	1	0
Futoshi Nakanishi	.222	6	18	1	4	1	0	0	1	4	5	0
Kihachi Enomoto	.111	8	18	1	2	0	0	0	1	6	6	0
Charlie Luis	.111	8	18	1	2	0	0	0	1	1	5	1
Takao Sato	.353	5	17	2	6	2	0	0	0	4	3	0
Satoru Sugiyama	.333	5	17	2	6	2	0	0	0	3	0	0
Yasumitsu Toyoda	.118	6	17	2	2	0	0	1	2	1	1	0
Isami Okamoto	.143	6	14	1	2	1	0	0	0	2	3	0
Hiroshi Oshita	.308	4	13	0	4	2	0	0	2	2	1	0
Makoto Kozuru	.091	5	11	0	1	0	0	0	0	3	0	0
Kohei Sugiyama	.200	4	10	0	2	1	0	0	0	2	0	0
Tokuji Iida	.000	5	10	0	0	0	0	0	0	4	0	0
Hiroyuki Watanabe	.444	5	9	0	4	0	0	0	4	0	2	0
Michio Nishizawa	.000	3	9	0	0	0	0	0	0	4	0	0
Jiro Kanayama	.125	3	8	0	1	0	0	0	0	1	0	1
Bunjiro Sakamoto	.125	4	8	0	1	0	0	0	0	2	0	0
Fibber Hirayama	.167	2	6	2	1	0	0	0	0	0	1	0
Tetsuharu Kawakami	.167	4	6	0	1	0	0	0	0	0	2	0
Tokuzo Harada	.000	4	6	1	0	0	0	0	0	2	0	0
Chico Barbon	.200	2	5	0	1	0	0	0	0	1	1	0

Japanese Pitching Statistics	ERA	G	W	L	IP	H	HR	SO	BB	R	ER
Masaichi Kaneda	6.75	6	0	2	16	20	4	11	8	12	12
Kazunori Nishimura	10.80	7	0	2	13.1	16	4	10	9	16	16
Ryohei Hasegawa	6.92	5	0	1	13	18	4	3	8	10	10
Takumi Otomo	3.72	3	0	2	9.2	8	1	4	4	4	4
Yasuo Yonekawa	5.19	4	0	1	8.2	9	1	3	3	7	5
Atsushi Aramaki	3.38	3	0	1	8	7	2	6	1	8	3
Takao Kajimoto	9.95	3	0	2	6.1	8	2	1	4	7	7
Sadaaki Nishimura	12.79	3	0	0	6.1	11	2	1	3	10	9
Isao Wada	6.00	2	0	0	6	5	0	2	2	4	4
Shigeru Sugishita	7.50	2	0	1	6	7	1	4	3	6	5
Taisei Nakamura	3.18	2	0	0	5.2	5	1	1	4	2	2
Hisafumi Kawamura	6.35	3	0	0	5.2	10	2	4	3	4	4
Takashi Nakagawa	6.75	2	0	0	4	4	0	0	3	4	3
Giichi Hayashi	6.75	2	0	0	4	7	1	0	0	4	3
Hachiro Abe	15.00	1	0	1	3	8	1	0	1	5	5
Hiroshi Maruko	13.50	1	0	1	2	4	1	2	1	3	3
Mamoru Otsu	0.00	1	0	1	1	2	1	0	1	4	0

NOTES

1   "Mobbed at the Airport," *Nippon Times*, October 21, 1955: 1.

2   Bob Bowie, "Thousands Greet Yankees in Tokyo," *Pacific Stars and Stripes*, October 21, 1955.

3   "Royal Welcome Greets the Yankees," *Nippon Times*, October 21, 1955: 1.

4   "5 Killed, 22 Injured as Opal Hits Kinki," *Nippon Times*, October 21, 1955: 1.

5   "Dewey to Inspect Japan's 'Strides'," *Nippon Times*, October 21, 1955: 1.

6   "Dewey to Inspect Japan's 'Strides'."

7   John W. Dower, *Embracing Defeat: Japan in the Wake of World War II* (New York: W.W. Norton, 1999), 44.

8   "Japanese Miracle," *Farlex Financial Dictionary*, 2009, accessed November 27, 2021, https://financial-dictionary.thefreedictionary.com/Japanese+Miracle.

9   Aaron Forsberg, *America and the Japanese Miracle: The Cold War Context of Japan's Postwar Economic Revival, 1950-1960* (Chapel Hill: University of North Carolina Press, 2000), 17.

10   Forsberg, 27.

11   Forsberg, 42.

12   "Japan and the WTO," World Trade Organization, accessed November 27, 2021, https://www.wto.org/english/thewto_e/countries_e/japan_e.htm.

13   "Yankees May Visit Japan This Autumn," *Pacific Stars and Stripes*, June 3, 1955: 24.

14   "Bombers 'Quite Certain' to Play Here This Fall," *Nippon Times*, August 1, 1955: 4.

15   F.N. Mike, "Times at Bat," *Nippon Times*, July 23, 1955: 5.

16   "U.S., Japan Reported Backing Post-Season Tour by the Yankees," *Pacific Stars and Stripes*, June 18, 1955: 24.

17   Lee Kavetski, "Chotto Matte, Tourists," *Pacific Stars and Stripes*, August 3, 1955: 22.

18   Kavetski.

19   Cpl. Perry Smith, "Giants Net $331 Each, Expected $3,000," *Pacific Stars and Stripes*, November 10, 1953: 14.

20   "Shigemitsu Says Japan Must Move Toward Complete Independence," *Washington Post and Times Herald*, August 27, 1955: 1.

21   Dan Daniel, "Plans Shaping Up for Yankee Team to Play in Japan," *The Sporting News*, August 3, 1955: 1-2.

22   Robert W. Bowie, "Tokyo Sets Welcome for Yankees," *Pacific Stars and Stripes*, October 21, 1955: 26.

23   "Visiting Yanks to Open Against Mainichi Club," *Nippon Times*, September 24, 1955, 8. The exchange rate, as established by the Bretton Woods system, was set at a fixed rate of 360 yen per dollar between 1947 and 1971. "Timeline: Milestones in the yen's history, *Reuters*, accessed December 3, 2021, https://www.reuters.com/article/us-yen/timeline-milestones-in-the-yens-history-idUSTRE49Q1AN20081027.

24   *Statistical Survey of Actual Status for Salary in the Private Sector*, National Tax Agency in "Changes in Wage-Workers Salaries in Japan, 1950-2013," accessed December 4, 2021, https://nbakki.hatenablog.com/entry/Changes_Wage-Workers_Salary_1950-2013.

25   "Radio and TV Highlights," *Nippon Times*, October 22, 1955: 4.

26   Jayson Makoto Chun, *A Nation of a Hundred Million Idiots? A Social History of Japanese Television, 1953-1973* (New York: Routledge, 2006), 55.

27   Chun, 61.

28   "'World Champions' – It Says Here," *The Sporting News*, October 12, 1955: 18.

29 "Webb Sees Japanese in Majors Soon," *Nippon Times*, November 10, 1955: 5.

30 "Nixon Extends Yanks Best Wishes on Trip,"
Nippon Times, October 13, 1955: 5.

31 David M. Jampel, "Casey Finds Shortstop at Press Club
Lunch," *Nippon Times*, October 22, 1955: 5.

32 Jampel.

33 Red McQueen, "Yankee Crowds Total 135,000 for First Four
Games in Japan," *The Sporting News*, November 2, 1955: 7.

34 "Yanks Cop Debut," *Nippon Times*, October 23, 1955: 1, 2.

35 "Yanks Cop Debut."

36 "Yanks Batter Stars, 11-6," *Nippon Times*, October 24, 1955: 3.

37 "Sendai Pours Out to Greet Yankee Team," *Pacific
Stars and Stripes*, October 26, 1955: 24.

38 "Tokyo All-Star Nine Ties Yankees 1-1, Break Stengelmen's 7-Game
Streak," *Pacific Stars and Stripes*, October 26, 1955: 24.

39 "Yanks Hand Japan Nine 11-0 Setback," *Nippon Times*, October 27, 1955: 5.

40 "Yanks Blank Hawks," *Nippon Times*, October 29, 1955: 9.

41 "Bombers Beat All-Osaka," *Nippon Times*, October 30, 1955: 5.

42 "Yanks Beat All-Pacific, 4-2," *Nippon Times*, October 31, 1955,
5; Red McQueen, "Yankees Name Scout to Cover Japanese
Loops," *The Sporting News*, November 9, 1955: 9.

43 "200 Attend First Yankee Clinic," *Pacific Stars
and Stripes*, October 30, 1955: 24.

44 "'Yankees Trying to Teach Us,' Says Japanese Scribe,"
The Sporting News, November 9, 1955: 9.

45 "Yanks Blank Dragons, 7-0," *Nippon Times*, November 2, 1955: 5.

46 "Mickey Mantle Leaving for U.S.," *Nippon Times*, November 1, 1955: 5.

47 Red McQueen, "Yankees Name Scout to Cover Japanese
Loops," *The Sporting News*, November 9, 1955: 9.

48 McQueen, "Yankees Name Scout to Cover Japanese Loops."

49 McQueen, "Yankees Name Scout to Cover Japanese Loops."

50 "Yankees Blast Lions, 14-1," *Nippon Times*, November 6, 1955: 5.

51 "Yanks Slam Stars, 12-2," *Nippon Times*, November 7, 1955: 5.

52 "Yankees Win Again, 6-2," *Nippon Times*, November 9, 1955: 5.

53 "II Period of High Economic Growth," *Hiroshima for
Global Peace*, accessed December 5, 2021, https://hiroshi-
maforpeace.com/en/fukkoheiwakenkyu/vol1/1-36/.

54 "With Yankees," *Nippon Times*, October 25, 1955: 3.

55 Aron D. Wahrman, "Caring for the Hiroshima Maidens," *Bulletin of
the American College of Surgeons*, accessed December 5, 2021, https://
bulletin.facs.org/2020/03/caring-for-the-hiroshima-maidens/.

56 "Yanks Beat Central Stars, 6-1," *Nippon Times*, November 11, 1955: 8.

57 "Yanks Wallop Giants," *Nippon Times*, November 12, 1955: 5.

58 "Yankees Rout Pacific Stars," *Nippon Times*, November 13, 1955: 10.

59 Yanks Trip Stars, 9-3," *Nippon Times*, November 14, 1955: 5.

60 "Stengel Disclaims Yanks Held Back," *Nippon Times*, November 14, 1955: 5.

61 "Yankees' Tour Successful, New York Times Comments,"
Pacific Stars and Stripes, November 18, 1955: 24.

62 Red McQueen, "Yankee Tour Truly a Patriotic Gesture,"
The Sporting News, October 26, 1955: 15.

63 Listed Japanese players have a minimum of five at-bats, three innings
pitched, or a decision. Yoshikazu Matsubayashi, *Baseball Game
History: Japan vs, U.S.A.* (Tokyo: Baseball Magazine, 2004), 92; Nippon
Professional Baseball Records, https://www.2689web.com/nb.html.

THE BUMS IN THE LAND OF THE RISING SUN: HOW THE 1956 DODGERS' TOUR OF JAPAN MARKED THE END OF A DYNASTY

By Robert K. Fitts

The Brooklyn Dodgers straggled into Idlewild Airport in Jamaica, Queens, on the morning of October 11, 1956. It had been a long, grueling season, ending the day before with a 9-0 shellacking by the Yankees in the seventh game of the World Series. Now, less than 18 hours later, the Dodgers were leaving for a four-week goodwill tour of Japan.

The subdued party of 60 consisted of club officials, players, family members, and an umpire. Although participation was voluntary, most of the team's top players had decided to take advantage of the $3,000 bonus that came with the all-expenses-paid trip.[1] Noticeably absent were Sandy Koufax, who was sharpening his game in Puerto Rico; Sandy Amoros,

Fred Kipp, Gil Hodges, Wally Yonamine, Vin Scully, Roy Campanella and Don Demeter at the October 18 reception at Chinzanso, Tokyo

who was playing in Cuba; and World War II vet Carl Furillo who proclaimed, "I want no part of it. I've seen Japan once and there's nothing there I want to see again."[2]

As they readied to board the private flight to Los Angeles, Don Newcombe and his wife were missing. The Dodgers ace had won 27 games during the season and would win both the National League Most Valuable Player and Cy Young Awards. But he had failed spectacularly in the World Series, getting knocked out in the second inning of Game Two, and in the fourth inning of Game Seven. When asked about the up-coming trip after the Game Seven loss, Newcombe snapped, "Nuts to the trip to Japan!" "There'll be trouble if he's not on that plane!" countered Dodgers General Manager Buzzie Bavasi.[3]

Just after 11 A.M. the big pitcher arrived at the airport without wife or luggage. "The Tiger is here!" he announced as he boarded. He had spent the morning at the Brooklyn Courthouse to answer a summons on an assault charge for punching a parking attendant who had made a wisecrack about his Game Two performance. The plane left on time and after a stop in Los Angeles arrived in Honolulu at 5:30 P.M. on October 12.[4]

The Dodgers spent five days in Hawaii, attending banquets, sightseeing, sunbathing on Waikiki Beach, and playing three games against local semipro teams. As expected, Brooklyn won the first two contests comfortably, beating the Maui All-Stars, 6-0, behind 20-year-old Don Drysdale's seven perfect innings on October 13 and the Hawaii Milwaukee All-Stars, 19-0, the next day. On the 15th, Don Newcombe took the mound against the Hawaii Red Sox. Spectators serenaded him with boos and jeers as the Red Sox scored three times in the second inning and chased him from the game in the fourth. "I can't believe that I am still the target for abuse after getting 5,000 miles away from Brooklyn. I never want to come back here again! I didn't want to make this trip in the first place," he complained after Brooklyn pulled out a 7-3 win in the 10th inning. "This abuse thing has me worried," he added. "I am afraid the emotional effect might continue to grow and become a detriment to my future career."[5] After a day of sightseeing, the Dodgers left for Japan on a 10 P.M. overnight flight.

The plane touched down at Tokyo's Haneda Airport at 3:25 P.M. the following day, five hours behind schedule after mechanical trouble forced a seemingly endless stopover on Wake Island. A light rain fell from the gray sky. The weary players trudged off the plane and down the metal stairs to the tarmac where they were greeted by the first group of dignitaries and reporters. "Man, we're beat," Jackie Robinson complained as he left the plane. "We are all very tired," Duke Snider added, "but we're glad to be here. If we have a chance to shower and clean up, we'll feel much better."[6]

Japanese dignitaries and 40 kimono-clad actresses, bearing bouquets of flowers, welcomed the Dodgers as a crowd of fans waved from the airport's spectator ramp. During a brief press conference, team owner Walter O'Malley proclaimed that "his players would play their best ... and hoped that the visit would contribute to Japanese-American friendship." "We hope to give the Japanese fans some thrills," said Robinson.[7]

Despite the delay and relentless drizzle, thousands of flag-waving fans lined the 12-mile route from Haneda Airport to downtown Tokyo. Although many of the players longed for a shower, a warm meal, and a soft bed, they would not see their hotel for hours. After a brief stop at the Yomiuri newspaper's headquarters, the team went straight to a reception at the famous Chinzanso restaurant. As they arrived, the hosts presented each visitor with a *happi* coat made to resemble a Dodgers warmup jacket and a *hachimaki* (traditional headband). Dressed in their new garb, the Dodgers mingled with baseball officials, diplomats, and Japanese ballplayers for several hours. Exhausted, the Dodgers finally checked into the Imperial Hotel around 9 P.M. Some of the younger players, however, went back out, attending "a giddy round of parties" before staggering back to the hotel in the wee hours of the morning.[8]

Weary from the trip and the late night, the players struggled to get out of bed the next morning for the opening game against the Yomiuri Giants at Korakuen Stadium. Ceremonies began at 1 P.M. with the two teams parading onto the field in parallel lines behind a pair of young women clad in fashionable business suits. Each woman held a large sign topped with balloons, bearing the team's name in Japanese. As the Giants marched on the field, some of the Dodgers gaped in surprise. "We went over there with typical American misconceptions," Vin Scully later wrote. "We expected the local teams to be stocked with little yellow, bucktooth men wearing thick eyeglasses. When they first walked onto the field in Tokyo, I heard one of our players yell, 'Hey fellas, we've been mousetrapped!' One of the first ballplayers out of the dugout was a pitcher who was six feet four. ... They averaged five feet ten or so, and they were all built like athletes."[9]

Like the Dodgers, the Yomiuri Giants had just finished an exhausting season topped with a defeat in the Japan Series two days earlier. The *Japan Times* noted, "The Giants, battered and worn in their losing bid for the Japan championship …, are regarded as a pushover for the Bums. The Brooklyn club is expected to win their opener by a margin of over ten runs."[10] But that is not what happened.

The Giants jumped out to a quick 3-0 lead off Don Drysdale. At 6-feet-5 he towered over most of his Japanese opponents and expected to dominate them with his overpowering side-arm fastball. But as Scully noted, "Another misconception we had was that our big pitchers would be able to blow them down with fastballs. We were dead wrong. They murdered fastball pitching. Our guys would rear back and fire one through here and invariably the ball would come back even harder than it was thrown. They hit bullets."[11]

Brooklyn battled back to take a 4-3 lead in the fourth on five hits, including homers by Robinson and Gil Hodges. But that would be all for Brooklyn as relief pitcher Takumi Otomo, who had beaten the New York Giants in 1953, stifled the Dodgers for 5 2/3 innings. Homers by Kazuhiko Sakazaki and Tetsuharu Kawakami in the eighth gave Yomiuri a 5-4 upset victory. "The fans," wrote Leslie Nakashima of the *Honolulu Advertiser*, "could hardly believe the Dodgers had been beaten."[12] Otomo had struck out 10 in his second win over a major-league team.

Since the major-league tours began in 1908, the game was just the fifth victory by a Japanese team against 124 loses.[13] After the loss, manager Walt Alston made no excuses, "They just beat us. They hit and we didn't." Duke Snider had a particularly bad day, striking out three times and being caught off base for an out. "We're pretty tired," he explained. "But that's no excuse. We're all in good physical shape and should have won. A good night's sleep tonight and we'll roll." "We'll snap out of it," predicted Robinson. Pee Wee Reese agreed: "We don't expect to lose any more. But," he added, "we didn't expect to lose this one either."[14]

As predicted, the Dodgers bounced back the next day. Masaichi Kaneda, recognized by most experts as Japan's all-time greatest pitcher, began the game for the Central League All-Stars by loading the bases on two walks and a single before being removed from the game with a sore elbow. Roy Campanella greeted relief pitcher Noboru Akiyama with a towering drive

into the last row of the left-field bleachers to put the Dodgers up, 4-0. Campy added another home run in the third inning to pace Brooklyn to an easy 7-1 victory as Clem Labine pitched a four-hit complete game.[15]

On Sunday, October 21, approximately 45,000 fans packed Korakuen Stadium to watch Don Newcombe face the All-Japan team – a conglomeration of the top Japanese professionals. Newcombe's outing lasted just 17 pitches. He began by walking Hawaiian Wally Yonamine, then surrendered a home run and three consecutive singles before Alston took the ball.[16] The former ace "stormed from the hill" and stumbled into the clubhouse "like a sleepwalker … jerkily, almost aimlessly. He wore the frozen expression of a kid who's just seen his puppy run over. Wonder, shock, disbelief, hurt. Pinch me, I'm dreaming. … Slowly he picked up his shower shoes, detoured a sportswriter to get to his jacket. Then out the back door, back to the hotel."[17]

After the eventual 6-1 loss, manager Walter Alston noted, "Newk wasn't right again today. ... He's not throwing natural."[18] Reese explained, "He's still got it (the World Series) on his mind. It's getting to be a terrible thing. Not only does he feel he's letting himself down, he feels he's letting the club down. … Don doesn't say much, but it's building up and building up inside him. It could run him out of baseball."[19]

Unfortunately, Reese's assessment was prophetic. The next day, Newcombe announced that he had injured his elbow in the final game of the regular season. It hurt to throw curveballs. He had kept the injury to himself, hoping that rest would cure the ailment. Although his arm may have healed, Newcombe never fully recovered from the psychological injury of the blown 1956 World Series. He had begun drinking heavily in the early 1950s and his alcohol abuse intensified after the loss. After a mediocre 1957 season, he was traded to Cincinnati in 1958 and would be out of the major leagues after the 1960 season. He played his final season with the Chunichi Dragons of Japan in 1962 – coached by Wally Yonamine, who had begun the onslaught on that fateful day in Tokyo.

With the loss, the Dodgers became the first professional American club to lose two games on a Japanese tour. Criticism came from both sides of Pacific. "The touring Flatbushers once again were disemboweled by a band of local samurai," wrote Bob Bowie of the *Japan Times*.[20] "The Dodgers are known for their fighting spirit," noted radio quiz-show host Ko Fujiwara, "but they have shown little spirit in the games here

Roy Campanella, Jackie Robinson, and Duke Snider signing autographs for Japanese fans. Cappy Harada is in the dugout.

thus far."[21] The Associated Press reported that "most Japanese fans have been disappointed in the caliber of ball played so far by the Brooklyns," but Yoshio Yuasa, the former manager of the Mainichi Orions, offered the harshest criticisms.[22] "I can sympathize that the Dodgers are in bad condition from fatigue after a hectic pennant race, the World Series and travel to Japan and that they are in a terrific slump, but they are even weaker than was rumored at bat against low, outside pitches and we are very disappointed to say the least. ... It would not be an overstatement to say that we no longer have anything to learn from the Dodgers."[23]

The US media picked up these criticisms, reprinting the stories in large and small newspapers across the country. "Japanese Baseball Expert Hints Brooks Are Bums," screamed a headline in the *New York Daily News* on October 23.[24] Three days later, a *Daily News* headline noted, "Bums 'Too Dignified,' Say Japanese Hosts." The accompanying article explained that some

Japanese experts believed that the Dodgers were "too quiet and dignified on the playing field ... and ... were acting like they were all trying to win good conduct medals" rather than playing hard-nosed baseball.[25]

After a day of rest, the Dodgers flew to Sapporo in northern Japan for a rematch against the Yomiuri Giants. Before the game, Walter O'Malley addressed the team. Starting pitcher Carl Erskine recalled, "Mr. O'Malley was very upset. He thought it was a scar on the name of the Dodgers to have gone to Japan and lost two games."[26] "He was embarrassed. He held a team meeting and read the riot act. He said, 'I know this is a goodwill tour and I want you to be gentlemen. Sign autographs and be cordial. However, when you put on that Dodger uniform, I want you to remember Pearl Harbor!'"[27]

Erskine was near perfect, giving up three hits and a walk but never allowing a runner to reach second base as he faced just 27 batters. But the Dodgers continued to struggle at the plate, failing to score until Duke

Snider led off the ninth inning with a 380-foot homer over the right-center-field wall to give Brooklyn a 1-0 victory.[28]

Despite the win, many Japanese were not pleased with the Dodgers' performance. An Associated Press article noted that Tokuro Konishi, a broadcaster and former manager, "and other experts agreed that most Japanese fans have been disappointed in the caliber of ball played so far by the Brooklyns. ... Konishi said he believed the two losses could be chalked up to the fatigue from the grueling National League pennant race and seven game World Series."[29] "The Dodgers' 'old men' are tired," noted Bob Bowie of the *Pacific Stars and Stripes*. "Pee Wee Reese and Jackie Robinson and Gil Hodges and Duke Snider and Roy Campanella are so weary it's an effort for them to put one foot before another. It's been a long season and they are anxious to get back home and relax before heading for spring training in February."[30]

Indeed, the "Boys of Summer" were aging. The core of the team had been together nearly a decade. The starting lineup averaged 32 years old with Robinson and Reese both at 37. Their weariness showed on the playing field. After four games, the team was hitting just .227 against Japanese pitching. Both management and fans knew it was time to change, and the team had plenty of young talent. At the top of the list were power hitters Don Demeter, who hit 41 home runs in 1956 for the Texas League Fort Worth Cats, and his teammate, first baseman Jim Gentile, who hit 40. Outfielder Gino Cimoli had ridden Brooklyn's bench in 1956 and was now ready for a more substantial role. Smooth-fielding Bob Lillis from the Triple-A affiliate in St. Paul seemed to be the heir of Pee Wee Reese at shortstop while his teammate Bert Hamric would fight for a role in team's crowded outfield. On the mound, knuckleballer Fred Kipp had just won 20 games for the Montreal Royals and looked ready to join Brooklyn's rotation. The tour of Japan was an ideal chance try out these players. As the tour progressed, Alston moved more prospects into the starting lineup.

In the fifth game, held in Sendai, Alston gave Kipp the start and backed him up with Gentile at first, Demeter in center and Cimoli in left. For seven innings Kipp baffled the All-Kanto All-Stars, a squad drawn from the Tokyo-area teams, with his knuckleball – a pitch rarely used in the Japanese leagues, while the hurler's fellow rookies racked up five hits during an easy 8-0 win.[31]

Don Drysdale started game six in Mita, a small city about 60 miles northeast of Tokyo. For seven innings

the promising young pitcher dominated the Japanese. Then, the Japanese erupted for three runs in the bottom of the eighth inning, breaking a streak of 29 straight shutout innings by Dodger pitching. With the scored tied, 3-3, after nine innings, the Dodgers requested that they end the game so that the team could catch their scheduled train back to Tokyo.[32] Although it was not a win, an Associated Press writer called the result "a moral victory for Japanese baseball."[33] After six contests, the National League champions were 3-2-1 – the worst record of any visiting American professional squad.

Despite the Dodgers' poor start, the Japanese fans adored the team packed with household names. About 150,000 spectators attended the first five games while hundreds of thousands more, if not millions, watched the games on television or listened to them on the radio.[34] "There is widespread interest in the Dodgers and their style of play," an Associated Press article noted. All of the sports dailies and many of the mainstream newspapers covered each game in detail – often including exclusive interviews and pictorial spreads of the players. Many dailies ran "sequence shots of various Dodgers in action."[35]

Although the Dodgers were winning over the Japanese fans, their opponents on the diamond were unimpressed. Ace pitcher Masaichi Kaneda noted, "The pitchers this time were not as good as [on the previous major-league tours]. ... On the bench, I was looking forward to hitting. I had never had that feeling before."[36] Shortstop Yasumitsu Toyoda agreed: "Even their fastballs didn't look fast enough."[37] Kazuhiro Yamauchi, the star outfielder for the Mainichi Orions who hit .313 in 48 at-bats during the tour, complained that the Dodgers lacked hustle. "The Yankees [during the 1955 tour] would always try for an extra base on a hit, while some Dodger runners stopped dead."[38] Yamauchi also noted that the Dodgers had trouble with low, outside pitches. "All our pitches have been aiming for the outside corner." Yomiuri right-hander Takehiko Bessho added, "Most of them were not good at hitting curveballs. ... I wasn't [even] scared of Campanella. He looked huge, but only he could hit in one spot ... the high inside corner. ... If an umpire called [a low outside pitch] a strike, he complained. He was just desperate."[39]

During a November 11 round-table interview moderated by Masanori Ochi, several Japanese players bristled when asked about a training session run by Dodgers coach Al Campanis. Campanis was actively promoting his book, *The Dodgers' Way to Play*

Baseball, which had been translated into Japanese. "We attended it, but we already knew 'how to throw a slider,'" Tetsuharu Kawakami snidely told Ochi. "They only told us what we already knew. I think we practice small tactics more than they do." "Al Campanis only talked about general things," Takehiko Bessho added, "and nothing was new."[40]

Oblivious to the Japanese players' feelings, after the tour Campanis told Dan Daniels of *The Sporting News*, "For the good of Japanese ball, it would be well to send several American coaching staffs there for the purpose of staging clinics rather than having a different team visit each year. Of course, that wouldn't be the sort of spectacle the fans would want, but it would be more helpful to the progress of Japanese ball. We held one clinic while we were over there, and I never had a more attentive audience. They want to learn our methods and a few clinics would help them tremendously."[41]

Underwhelmed by the Dodgers, some of the Japanese players began to jeer their opponents. The Dodgers were undoubtedly unaware as the "rudeness" consisted mainly of addressing the visitors by their first names – an offensive act in Japan, especially in the mid-1950s. The players confessed during the November 11 round table interview:

Yasumitsu Toyoda: (Looking at Kaneda,) Remember you jeered at him [Newcombe] in Mito, something like 'Come on, Don!' He was offended by that.

Masaichi Kaneda: We became good at jeering. Our pronunciation became better.

Takehiko Bessho: You [Kaneda] were best at it. You called the first baseman [Gino] Cimoli, 'Gino, Gino,' and he turned and smiled at you. When the game is over, you were like 'Goodbye Gino.'

Masaichi Kaneda: 'Come on, Don' was a good one!

Masanori Ochi: Did you jeer at the other major leaguers like the Yankees?

Masaichi Kaneda: No, we just did it this year.

Takehiko Bessho: That was because we were winning.

Masaichi Kaneda: Alright, I will say 'Hey Don!' to his face. If he gets angry, I will hide quickly![42]

Undoubtedly sensing the players' distain, Fujio Nakazawa, a commentator and future member of the Japan Baseball Hall of Fame, cautioned his countrymen. "The two victories over the Dodgers should be no reason for jubilation among the players here. They should by no means become conceited. Japanese ballplayers have much to learn from the Dodgers, who have not complained about their busy schedule which started the day after their arrival. The Dodger players are always cheerful and play hard. A defeat does not discourage them."[43]

Perhaps sparked by the ongoing criticism, perhaps finally rested, the Dodgers began winning in late October as the rookies led the way. On October 27 in Kofu, Gentile hit two home runs and Demeter and Cimoli each hit one during a 12-1 romp over an all-star squad of players drawn from the Tokyo-area professional teams. The next day, Gentile went 5-for-5 with another home run as the Dodgers beat All-Japan, 6-3, in Utsunomiya.[44] On October 31 Kipp pitched two-hit ball and Gentile and Demeter each homered to pace Brooklyn to a 4-2 win over All-Japan. During these games the players began showing a little fighting spirit. Somehow, they learned the Japanese word "mekura," meaning "blind," and began shouting it at the umpire after questionable calls.[45]

"Some of those ballparks were small, [holding] 20,000 or 25,000," Carl Erskine remembers. "There were acres of bicycles in the parking lots. After the games were over, the men were all lined up along the ditch by the side of the road relieving themselves. I guess they had a couple of beers. So, it was a little unusual leaving the ballpark and passing rows and rows of men. That was a strange sight!"[46]

On the evening of October 31, the team arrived in Hiroshima and checked into the Hotel New Hiroshima, an ultra-modern structure near the Peace Park and ballpark. Local officials warned the players not to leave the hotel unescorted at night as gang-related crime made the area unsafe for tourists. The following morning the team visited the Peace Park and posed with their hats in their hands in front of the Memorial Cenotaph, the saddle-shaped concrete arch that bears the name of each person killed in the atomic bomb blast.

In a solemn ceremony before the start of the 2 P.M. game, the Dodgers presented city officials with a bronze plaque reading: "We dedicate this visit in memory of those baseball fans and others who died by atomic action on Aug. 6, 1945. May their souls rest in

Walter O'Malley, Walt Alston, and Yomiuri Giants manager Shigeru Mizuhara

peace and with God's help and man's resolution peace will prevail forever, amen."[47]

The emotion from the morning boiled over during the game against the Kansai All-Stars. In the bottom of the third inning with the Japanese already up 1-0 and one out and a runner on second, future Hall of Fame umpire Jocko Conlon called Kohei Sugiyama safe at first on what looked to be a groundout. Incensed, Jackie Robinson walked over to first to protest the call. "Everybody knew Jocko had missed the play because he was in back of the plate and couldn't see clearly," Robinson explained.[48] Conlon, of course, did not reverse his decision so Robinson persisted, eventually arguing "so loud and so long" that Conlon tossed him from the game. "I never told him how to play ball," Conlon said after the game, "and he, or anybody else, can't tell me how to run a ball game."[49]

Kansai padded its lead to 4-1 before Brooklyn tied the game in the sixth on Roy Campanella's three-run homer. The Dodgers went ahead in the seventh in a bizarre inning. After recording an out, reliever Yukio Shimabara walked Jim Gilliam, who stole second base and then moved to third on a passed ball. Shimabara then walked both Reese and Snider. With the bases loaded, Campanella fouled out to the catcher. Gilliam decided to take matters into his own hands. With two outs and the bases still jammed, he stole home to give the Dodgers the 5-4 lead. Rattled, Shimabara then made a mistake to Jim Gentile, who pounded the ball into the stands for a three-run homer. Brooklyn tacked on another two in the ninth for a 10-6 victory.[50]

After the Dodgers won 14-0 on November 2, the Japanese squads rebounded. On the 3rd the Dodgers and the All-Japan team entered the eighth inning knotted 7-7 before Brooklyn erupted for another seven to win 14-7. The following day, Japanese aces Takehiko Bessho and Masaichi Kaneda held the Dodgers to just one run for eight innings as the hosts entered the ninth leading 2-1. The Dodgers rallied in the ninth as Snider led off with a 480-foot home run to tie the game. Two outs later with the bases loaded, Robinson tried to steal the lead with a surprise two-out squeeze play. But Jackie missed the bunt and Demeter was tagged out on his way to the plate. In the bottom of the inning, Tetsuharu Kawakami, the hero of the opening game, came through again with a bases-loaded single to win the game.[51]

On the 7th the Dodgers squeaked out a 3-2 win over the All-Japan squad in Nagoya. Gil Hodges, however, stole the headlines. Alston started the normally staid first baseman in left field and to keep himself amused Hodges "pantomimed the action after almost every play for five innings. He mimicked the pitcher and the ball's flight through the air, the catcher and the umpire. When a Dodger errored, Hodges glowered and pointed his finger. He made his legs quiver, shook his fist, stamped on the ground, swung his arms, frowned and smiled in the fleeting instant between pitches." The fans loved it, cheering him so loudly as he left the game in the eighth inning that "[y]ou'd have thought it was Babe Ruth leaving."[52]

Vin Scully recalled how Hodges's antics eased a tense moment. "During a game before an overflow crowd, one of our players was called out on strikes and, in a childish display of petulance, dropped his bat on the plate, took off his helmet and hurled it to the ground with such force that it bounced up on top of the Dodger dugout. The crowd was shocked. The Japanese had never seen an umpire held up to such humiliation and it was an embarrassing moment for us in the Brooklyn party. Gil saved the day. While the crowd still sat in stunned silence, Gil suddenly appeared, jumped up on the dugout roof and approached the helmet as if it was a dangerous snake. He circled it warily, made a couple of tentative stabs at it, and quickly pounced on it, tossed it back on the field and then it did a swan dive off the top of the dugout. The fans beat their palms and shouted until they were hoarse."[53]

The Dodgers and All-Japan met again the next day at Shizuoka, a small town at the foot of Mt. Fuji, where 22 years earlier the All-Nippon behind 17-year-old Eiji Sawamura nearly beat Babe Ruth's All-Americans. Once again the Japanese team thrilled the fans of Shizuoka as pinch-hitter Kohei Sugiyama of the All-Japan squad broke a 2-2 tie in the bottom of the ninth with a walk-off single.[54] With their fourth loss, criticism of the Dodgers' performance continued. An International News Service article headlined, "Fans Debate Reasons for Dodger Losses" asked, "Are Japanese baseball teams improving, major leaguers

getting careless or the Brooklyn Dodgers just getting old?"[55]

On November 9 the Dodgers returned to Tokyo for a rematch with their hosts the Yomiuri Giants. Once again, the game was tight. Home runs by Jim Gentile and Herb Olson as well as an inside-the-park homer by Giants catcher Shigeru Fujio left the score tied up after nine innings. Jim Gilliam led off the top of the 11th with a single and two outs later stood on second base as Jackie Robinson strode to the plate. Yomiuri manager Shigeru Mizuhara called for an intentional walk but Giants ace Takehiko Bessho refused. After some discussion, Mizuhara allowed Bessho to challenge Robinson. Jackie jumped on the first pitch, pounding it foul "far over the left-field stands." On the next offering, he "drove a hot grounder through the pitcher's box," bringing Gilliam home to win the game.[56]

The win seemed to energize both the Dodgers and Robinson. They won the next two games easily, 8-2 and 10-2, as Jackie went 2-for-5 with two runs and two RBIs. After the game in Tokyo on November 12, the Dodgers flew to the southern city of Fukuoka to make up a game that had been rained out on October 30.

Fittingly, the final meeting of the 19-game series was tight. Nineteen-year-old phenom Kazuhisa Inao and Kipp dueled for eight innings, each surrendering one run. The score remained tied as Duke Snider led off the top of the ninth with a groundball to first, which the usually sure-handed Tokuji Iida muffed, allowing Snider to advance to third base. Robinson strode to the plate – unknowingly for the last time in his professional career – and grounded a single between third and short to score Snider and give the Dodgers the lead. After two outs and a walk, Don Demeter singled and Robinson crossed home plate for the final time. Immediately after the 3-1 victory, the Dodgers flew back to Tokyo and after a day of rest, returned to the United States.

Brooklyn's tour of Japan marked the end of an era. Robinson retired soon after returning to the United States. The team's troubles on the diamond continued in 1957 as they finished in a distant third place. It was time to rebuild. The games in Japan allowed many of the younger players to display their skills. Jim Gentile, for example, led the team with a .471 batting average, 8 home runs, and 19 RBIs, while Fred Kipp won three games and posted a 1.26 ERA in 43 innings.

Although Alston and others claimed that fatigue had led to the Dodgers' poor showing on the diamond, they also conceded that the greatly improved Japanese had put up stiff competition. National League President Warren Giles, who accompanied the Dodgers to Japan, noted, "[T]he quality of baseball in that country is improving steadily and the day may come when the ablest players of Japan will compete on even terms with the best the United States has to offer."[57] Walter O'Malley concurred, telling reporters that the Japanese clubs would be nearly even with US ballclubs in the not-too-distant future. "Their pitchers have uncanny accuracy. They rarely walk anyone. In fielding, particularly in the infield, the Japanese teams are really excellent. Some Japanese players could play on teams in contention in pennant races here, or at least on the better minor league clubs."[58]

When asked if any of the Japanese players were ready for the majors, Al Campanis responded:

There's one fellow who must have been really good in his prime. He's 38 years old now [actually 36] and they tell me he hasn't hit under .300 for 18 straight years [actually eight]. I would have liked to [have] got a crack at him a few years back. His name is Kawakami. ... High in my book were three others. A shortstop named Toyoda … was the best hitter in his league. His arm might have been a little short, but he had everything else. Then there was a catcher, Fujio, in his first year of pro ball. Never saw anyone with a better arm. Man, he had a rifle. Good receiver, too, and a fair hitter. But the number one prospect in my judgment was a pitcher named Sho Horiuchi, a 21-year-old right hander with the Yomiuri Giants.[59]

The following spring, the Dodgers invited Fujio and Horiuchi along with their manager Shigeru Mizuhara, to spring training at Dodgertown to help them mature as players. The invitation began a long friendship between the two clubs. The Giants would be the Dodgers' guests at Vero Beach in 1961, 1967, 1971, and 1975 and the two clubs would maintain close relations for over 65 years.

1956 BROOKLYN DODGERS GAMES IN JAPAN

Date	Place	Opponent	Score	Winner	Loser
October 19	Tokyo	Yomiuri	4-5	Otomo	Bessent
October 20	Tokyo	All-Central	7-1	Labine	Kaneda
October 21	Tokyo	All-Japan	1-6	Miura	Newcombe
October 23	Sapporo	Yomiuri	1-0	Erskine	Bessho
October 24	Sendai	All-Kanto	8-0	Kipp	Miyaji
October 26	Mito	All-Kanto	3-3	None	None
October 27	Kofu	Al-Kanto	12-1	Craig	Oishi
October 28	Utsunomiya	All-Japan	6-3	Labine	Shimabara
October 31	Shimonoseki	All-Japan	4-0	Kipp	Kajimoto
November 1	Hiroshima	Kansai All-Stars	10-6	Roebuck	Osaki
November 2	Osaka	Giants-Hawks	14-0	Craig	Horiuchi
November 3	Osaka	All-Japan	14-7	Labine	Osaki
November 4	Osaka	All-Japan	2-3	Kaneda	Labine
November 7	Nagoya	All-Japan	3-2	Craig	Oyane
November 8	Shizuoka	All-Japan	2-3	Kajimoto	Kipp
November 9	Tokyo	Yomiuri	5-4	Roebuck	Bessho
November 10	Tokyo	All-Japan	8-2	Erskine	Oyane
November 12	Tokyo	All-Japan	10-2	Craig	Kaneda
November 13	Fukuoka	All-Japan	3-1	Kipp	Inao

1956 BROOKLYN DODGERS TOUR BATTING AND PITCHING STATISTICS[60]

Dodgers Batting Statistics	BA	G	AB	R	H	2B	3B	HR	RBI	SO	BB	SB
Don Demeter	.329	19	76	12	25	2	2	5	12	14	4	2
Jim Gilliam	.317	17	63	9	20	2	0	2	8	4	8	5
Duke Snider	.345	19	58	17	20	2	0	6	11	13	4	2
Gil Hodges	.333	18	57	15	19	1	0	6	12	8	5	0
Roy Campanella	.268	17	56	10	15	2	0	4	14	6	2	0
Jim Gentile	.471	16	51	14	24	4	0	8	19	14	7	0
Pee Wee Reese	.260	19	50	9	13	3	0	2	6	3	5	2
Jackie Robinson	.327	18	49	10	16	3	0	2	9	4	6	0
Gino Cimoli	.250	18	40	5	10	2	3	1	5	8	4	0
Bob Lillis	.091	15	33	1	3	1	0	0	0	2	2	1
Randy Jackson	.208	12	24	5	5	1	0	1	3	4	3	0
Bert Hamric	.136	14	22	3	3	0	0	0	1	7	1	0
Don Zimmer	.091	9	22	1	2	0	0	1	1	7	1	0
Herb Olson	.278	11	18	5	5	0	0	2	5	3	2	0
Fred Kipp	.333	7	15	1	5	2	0	0	1	3	0	0
Roger Craig	.250	5	12	0	3	0	0	0	2	7	1	0
Clem Labine	.000	5	8	0	0	0	0	0	0	3	1	0
Ed Roebuck	.147	7	6	0	1	1	0	0	0	2	0	0
Don Drysdale	.000	3	6	0	0	0	0	0	0	5	0	0
Bob Aspromonte	.250	4	4	0	1	0	0	0	0	0	0	0
Carl Erskine	.000	3	4	0	0	0	0	0	0	0	0	0
Ralph Branca	.000	3	3	0	0	0	0	0	0	1	0	0
Don Bessent	.000	5	3	0	0	0	0	0	0	1	0	0
Don Newcombe	.000	4	3	0	0	0	0	0	0	1	0	0
Dixie Howell	.000	3	1	0	0	0	0	0	0	1	1	0

Dodgers Pitching Statistics	ERA	G	W	L	IP	H	HR	SO	BB	R	ER
Fred Kipp	1.26	7	3	1	43	25	1	26	13	6	6
Roger Craig	0.56	5	5	0	32	22	4	25	11	4	2
Ed Roebuck	2.14	7	2	0	21	16	0	11	5	9	9
Clem Labine	2.66	5	2	1	20.1	18	1	11	7	6	6
Don Drysdale	4.50	3	0	0	17.1	16	3	10	10	10	9
Carl Erskine	0.64	2	2	0	14	7	0	13	5	2	1
Ralph Branca	2.45	3	0	0	11	9	1	7	6	3	3
Don Bessent	4.09	5	0	1	11	12	4	12	3	5	5
Don Newcombe	-	1	0	1	0	4	0	0	1	4	4

VOLUME I: 1907-1958

Japanese Batting Statistics	BA	G	AB	R	H	2B	3B	HR	RBI	SO	BB	SB
Kazuhiro Yamauchi	.313	13	48	4	15	4	0	0	5	4	4	0
Yasumitsu Toyoda	.200	12	40	7	8	3	0	1	4	11	4	1
Tetsuharu Kawakami	.378	16	37	5	14	3	0	2	4	5	7	0
Futoshi Nakanishi	.286	10	35	6	10	0	0	2	5	7	4	0
Shigeru Fujio	.250	17	32	2	8	1	0	1	2	8	3	0
Andy Miyamoto	.133	16	30	3	4	2	0	1	4	8	6	1
Tatsuto Hirooka	.103	12	29	0	3	1	0	0	0	5	1	0
Masao Morishita	.179	11	28	4	5	1	0	0	3	3	3	1
Kenjiro Tamiya	.222	9	27	3	6	2	0	0	0	9	4	0
Kohei Sugiyama	.346	10	26	1	9	0	0	1	5	4	2	0
Yoshio Yoshida	.176	9	17	0	3	0	1	0	0	0	0	0
Takashi Iwamoto	.176	11	17	2	3	0	0	0	1	2	2	0
Kazuhiko Sakazaki	.313	6	16	2	5	2	0	1	1	4	2	0
Michio Nishizawa	.250	6	12	1	3	0	0	0	0	2	1	0
Jun Hakota	.167	4	12	0	2	1	0	0	0	3	2	0
Shinya Sasaki	.000	10	12	1	0	0	0	0	0	0	0	0
Wally Yonamine	.364	4	11	2	4	0	0	0	0	2	2	0
Tokuji Iida	.091	5	11	0	1	0	0	0	0	1	2	1
Kihachi Enomoto	.100	9	10	1	1	0	0	0	2	1	1	0
Katsuya Nomura	.000	5	10	0	0	0	0	0	0	2	1	0
Hirofumi Naito	.222	4	9	0	2	0	0	0	0	1	1	1
Noboru Aota	.111	9	9	0	1	0	0	0	0	2	2	0
Keishi Totoki	.143	5	7	0	1	1	0	0	1	3	0	0
Masataka Tsuchiya	.333	4	6	0	2	0	0	0	0	2	0	0
Minoru Kakurai	.167	4	6	0	1	0	0	0	0	1	1	0
Satoshi Sugiyama	.400	2	5	1	2	0	0	1	2	1	0	0
Isami Okamoto	.250	2	4	1	1	0	0	1	3	2	0	0
Akiteru Kono	1000	1	1	1	1	0	0	1	3	2	0	0

NICHIBEI YAKYU: US TOURS OF JAPAN

Japanese Pitching Statistics	ERA	G	W	L	IP	H	HR	SO	BB	R	ER
Kazuhisa Inao	2.31	6	0	1	23.1	21	4	8	3	7	6
Takumi Otomo	4.43	6	1	0	20.1	21	6	26	3	12	10
Takehiko Bessho	3.00	6	0	2	18	12	4	13	5	6	6
Sho Horiuchi	6.61	5	0	1	16.1	20	6	11	5	14	12
Takao Kajimoto	3.21	6	1	1	14	6	2	9	4	5	5
Noboru Akiyama	4.63	5	0	0	11.2	12	4	15	2	6	6
Masayoshi Miura	2.61	5	1	0	10.1	13	1	5	4	5	3
Masaichi Kaneda	13.06	7	1	2	10.1	16	5	10	8	15	15
Mitsuo Osaki	5.40	5	0	1	10	10	2	5	4	7	6
Yoshitomo Miyaji	8.22	3	0	1	7.2	8	1	4	6	8	7
Yukio Shimabara	9.95	3	0	2	6.1	9	2	4	6	8	7
Yasushi Kodama	1.93	1	0	0	4.1	4	0	5	0	2	1
Hiroomi Oyane	17.18	2	0	2	3.2	8	1	1	3	7	7
Atsushi Aramaki	2.70	3	0	0	3.1	7	0	0	0	4	1
Takumi Nomo	5.40	1	0	0	3.1	5	1	1	2	2	2
Ryohei Hasegawa	0.00	1	0	0	3	1	0	2	0	0	0
Fumio Takechi	0.00	1	0	0	2	3	0	1	1	2	0
Yoshio Tazawa	9.00	1	0	0	2	4	1	0	1	2	2
Masahiko Oishi	10.80	1	0	1	1.2	5	0	0	0	2	2
Tetsuya Yoneda	27.00	1	0	0	1	5	0	0	0	3	3

NOTES

1 "All Dodgers' O'Malley Gets Is Ride," *New York Daily News*, October 13, 1956: 36.

2 "Dodgers Invited to Tour Japan in Fall; Most Favor Trip, but Furillo Votes No," *New York Times*, May 2, 1956: S36.

3 Ed Wilks, Newcombe 'Gets Lost' After Humiliation," *Monroe* (Louisiana) *News-Star*, October 11, 1956: 12.

4 United Press, "Dodgers Arrive at 5:30 P.M. Today," *Honolulu Advertiser*, October 12, 1956: 14; Carl Lundquist, "Flatbushers Full of Frolic as They Leave For Japan," *The Sporting News*, October 17, 1956: 13.

5 Tom Hopkins, "Sportraitures," *Honolulu Star-Bulletin*, October 18, 1956: 38; Red McQueen, "Dodgers Outdraw Yankees," *Honolulu Advertiser*, October 16, 1956: 14.

6 Associated Press, "Bums Arrive in Tokyo," *Passaic* (New Jersey) *Herald-News*, October 18, 1956: 46.

7 United Press, "Japanese Fans Defy Rain to Hail Dodgers," *New York Daily News*, October 19, 1956: 155.

8 Vin Scully, "The Dodgers in Japan," *Sport*, April 1957: 92; Bob Bowie, "Actresses, Flowers, Cheers Welcome Tourists to Tokyo," *The Sporting News*, October 24, 1956: 9.

9 Scully.

10 "Bums Open Game with Giants Today," *Japan Times*, October 19, 1956: 5.

11 Scully.

12 Leslie Nakashima, "Dodgers Beaten 5-4 by Yomiuri Giants in Japan," *Honolulu Advertiser* October 20, 1956: 14.

13 Other victories came in 1922, 1951, 1953 against the Eddie Lopat All-Stars, and 1953 against the New York Giants. The Royal Giants' tours are excluded from these figures as not all of their results are known.

14 Mel Derrick, "Alston Explains: 'They Hit, and We Didn't,'" *Pacific Stars and Stripes*, October 20, 1956: 23.

15 Bob Bowie, "Dodgers Belt Central Loop Stars 7-1," *Pacific Stars and Stripes*, October 21, 1956: 24.

16 Mel Derrick, "Newcombe a Study in Dejection After Loss," *Pacific Stars and Stripes*, October 22, 1956: 24.

17 Bob Bowie, "All-Stars Rout Brooks 6-1," *Pacific Stars and Stripes*, October 22, 1956: 24; Derrick, "Newcombe a Study," 24.

18 Derrick.

19 Derrick.

20 Bowie, "All-Stars Rout Brooks 6-1."

21 United Press, "Dodgers' Good Behavior Mystifies Japanese Fan," *Honolulu Advertiser*, October 26, 1956: 14.

22 Associated Press, "Japanese Can Learn from Bums," *Hawaii Tribune-Herald* (Hilo, Hawaii), October 23, 1956: 7.

23 United Press, "Banzais Changed to Brickbats for Dodgers on Japanese Tour," *New York Times*, October 23, 1956: 42.

24 United Press, "Japanese Baseball Expert Hints Brooks Are Bums," *New York Daily News*, October 23, 1956: 124.

25   United Press, "Bums 'Too Dignified,' Say Japanese Hosts," *New York Daily News*, October 26, 1956: 125.

26   Carl Erskine, telephone interview with author, February 10, 2020.

27   Carl Erskine, *Tales from the Dodger Dugout* (Champaign, Illinois: Sports Publishing, 2000), 65.

28   United Press, "Brooks Nip Giants 1-0 on Snider's Home Run," *Pacific Stars and Stripes*, October 24, 1956: 24.

29   Associated Press, "Japanese Can Learn from Bums," *Hawaii Tribune-Herald*, October 23, 1956: 7.

30   Bob Bowie, "Newk's Tribulations," *Pacific Stars and Stripes*, October 24, 1956: 22.

31   "Brooks Whitewash All-Kanto Nine, 8-0," *Japan Times*, October 25, 1956: 8.

32   Associated Press, "Kanto All-Stars Tie Dodgers 3-3," *Pacific Stars and Stripes*, October 27, 1956: 24.

33   Associated Press, "Kanto All-Stars Tie Dodgers 3-3."

34   Bob Bowie, "Gates Spin as Bums Battle for Wins in Japan," *Sporting News*, October 31, 1956: 7.

35   Associated Press, "Japanese Can Learn from Bums."

36   "A Round Table Talk," *Baseball Magazine*, 11, no. 12 (December 1956): 76-83.

37   "A Round Table Talk."

38   Associated Press, "Yankees Showed More Hustle Than Dodgers," *Honolulu Star Bulletin*, November 14, 1956: 44.

39   "A Round Table Talk."

40   "A Round Table Talk."

41   Dan Daniel, "Over the Fence," *The Sporting News*, November 28, 1956: 12.

42   "A Round Table Talk."

43   United Press, "Japanese Warned against 'Conceit,'" *Pacific Stars and Stripes*, October 28, 1956: 20.

44   Although English-language sources list Gentile going 4 for 4, official Japanese sources have him at 5 for 5.

45   Associated Press, "Japan's Pitchers Surprise Brooks," *Pacific Stars and Stripes*, October 30, 1956: 19.

46   Erskine, telephone interview.

47   Associated Press, "Dodgers to Dedicate Game to Bomb Victims," *Pacific Stars and Stripes*, October 29, 1956: 24.

48   "Dodgers vs. Kansai All Stars at Hiroshima Stadium, Hiroshima – November 1, 1956," walteromalley.com. https://www.walteromalley.com/en/dodger-history/international-relations/1956-Summary_November-1-1956. Retrieved October 25, 2020.

49   "Jackie Drops Verbal Bomb at Hiroshima – Gets Thumb," *The Sporting News*, November 14, 1956: 4.

50   *Hochi Sports*, November 2, 1956: 2; "Dodgers vs. Kansai," United Press, "Dodgers Top Kansai, 10-6; Robby Chased," *New York Daily News*, November 2, 1956: 175.

51   Associated Press, "Bums Win 14-7 Before 60,000," *Honolulu Star-Bulletin*, November 3, 1956: 11; Associated Press, "Labine of Dodgers Loses in Japan, 3-2," *New York Times*, November 5, 1956: 44.

52   Associated Press, "Hodges Delights Fans with Baseball Performance," *Pacific Stars and Stripes*, November 8, 1956: 22.

53   Scully.

54   United Press, "Dodgers Downed by Japanese, 3-2," *New York Times*, November 9, 1956: 37.

55   International News Service, "Fans Debate Reasons for Dodger Losses," *Pacific Stars and Stripes*, November 8, 1956: 19.

56   United Press, "Dodgers Edge Tokyo Giants 5-4," *Pacific Stars and Stripes*, November 10, 1956: 24.

57   Tom Swope, "'Japanese Players Gaining Major Status Fast' – Giles," *The Sporting News*, November 21, 1956: 2.

58   United Press, "O'Malley Praises Japanese Baseball," *Pacific Stars and Stripes*, November 30, 1956: 24.

59   Daniel.

60   Yoshikazu Matsubayashi, *Baseball Game History: Japan vs, U.S.A.* (Tokyo: Baseball Magazine, 2004), 92; Nippon Professional Baseball Records, https://www.2689web.com/nb.html; "Dodgers Individual Batting Results," *Baseball Magazine*, 11, no. 12 (December 1956): 64.

CROSSROADS: THE 1958 ST. LOUIS CARDINALS TOUR OF JAPAN

By Adam Berenbak

Game Seven of the 1958 Japan Series featured a winner-take-all finish to a classic contest between two storied franchises.

In the bottom of the ninth, with a six-run lead, 21-year-old Kazuhisa Inao stared down at Shigeo Nagashima, ready to wrap up one the most famous pitching feats in Japan Series history. He had earned the win in the previous three games for the Nishitetsu Lions and was prepared to win his fourth in a row, and with it the championship. With such a comfortable lead, Inao had little to worry about, even though he faced Nagashima, the star rookie of the Yomiuri Giants. The Rookie of the Year hit a high fly ball deep into Korakuen Stadium that the Lions center fielder couldn't make a play on. Nagashima displayed his blazing speed and sailed around the bases for an inside-the-park home run. Inao then finished off the remaining Giants and took the crown.

Though Nagashima's home run had little effect on the outcome of the game, the matchup represented the best of baseball in Japan and the future of the sport. At the same moment, roughly 680 miles (1,100 kilometers) away in Seoul, the St. Louis Cardinals were playing a Korean all-star team in preparation for a 16-game tour against Japan's best. A few days later, they would face an all-star team built around Nagashima and Inao, assembled by tour sponsor *Mainichi Shimbun* and tour organizer Yetsuo Higa, to showcase the young talent that would be the future of Japanese baseball.[1]

THE TOUR STARTS

To quote Jim Brosnan, who was splitting duties by pitching for the Cardinals and covering the tour for the *St. Louis Post Dispatch*, "From one of the longest runways in the world, San Francisco, we took off on the longest trip of this or any other year. By sunrise on the tenth we gained four hours changing time zones and explaining to the stomach wha' hoppen [*sic*] in

our 28-hour day."[2] The tour began in earnest the next day in front of a mere 3,000 fans at the Maui County Fairgrounds in Kahului, on the island of Maui. They faced a team that featured Bob Turley, Lew Burdette, and Eddie Mathews bolstering a collection of local ballplayers that Higa put together.[3]

Two years before, Commissioner Ford Frick had helped arrange for the two major Japanese papers, *Yomiuri Shimbun* and *Mainichi Shimbun*, to host US tours, after each paper had tried to host teams in 1955. The solution was to alternate responsibility every other year, beginning with the 1956 Dodgers tour.[4] Yomiuri had hosted first and it was no surprise that the Giants had played a big role. This time Higa, a Nisei businessman representing Mainichi, had arranged the tour to be unlike previous tours, pitting a Japanese all-star team against the Cardinals.[5]

Although formidable, St. Louis was a team in transition. The Cardinals in 1958 had finished fifth in the National League. The only real highlights of the season were Stan Musial's 3,000th hit and the debut of Curt Flood, who eventually helped the team to three pennants. Most of the team's regulars made the trip, including Musial, Don Blasingame, Ken Boyer, Vinegar Bend Mizell, Wally Moon, Hal Smith, and Gene Green.[6] However, last-minute substitutions, even after the vaccination shots had been administered, gave rise to a team that much more resembled the 1959 Cardinals. Gene Freese, Billy Muffett, and Hobie Landrith had already received their shots and clearances when they received trade notices just days before the team left. The 1958 coaching staff was set to go, too, but they were let go at the end of the season, two weeks after manager Fred Hutchinson received his pink slip.[7]

Instead, newly minted Cardinals Alex Grammas, Bob Blaylock, and Ernie Broglio, along with brand-new manager Solly Hemus, made the trip. The pitching corps included Sam Jones, Mizell, Larry Jackson, and newcomers Blaylock and Broglio, the latter a

November 26, 1958 cover of Shukan Baseball *depicting Stan Musial and Shigeo Nagashima*

promising rookie who was later (infamously) traded for Lou Brock.[8] After tours by the San Francisco Seals in 1949 and all-star teams in 1951 and 1953, Japan had been visited by all three teams from New York. It was not shocking that the Cardinals were the third choice for 1958, behind the AL and NL pennant winners. Higa had made his play, but when major stars on both the Yanks and Braves decided against making the trip overseas, Higa was forced to reassess and offer the tour to St. Louis. His relationship with Cardinals, and the involvement of J.G. Taylor Spink, drove the decision, as well as an ability to exploit Musial's stardom against an all-star team designed to showcase Japan's youth.[9]

Also along on the tour was Cardinals broadcaster Joe Garagiola. He was at the mike to broadcast a select number of games aired via tape-delay over KMOX Radio in St. Louis. *The Sporting News* claimed it was the first time a domestic radio station had broadcast baseball from overseas.[10]

After the Kahului game, which the Cardinals took, 4-1, on Larry Jackson's strong arm and his third-inning home run off Burdette, the two teams met twice in Honolulu.[11] The Cardinals won the first game in a 9-1 rout, collecting six runs in five innings off Bob Turley, fresh off his historic Game Seven World Series win. St. Louis tacked on three more runs off Len Kasparovitch. The sole run for the Hawaiian All-Stars came when Ken Kimura drove in Wally Dupont, who had reached third when his base hit skipped past center fielder Bobby Gene Smith and rolled to the fence.[12] In the final game, St. Louis edged the Hawaiian All-Stars, 5-4. Mathews tied the game, 4-4, with a home run off Broglio in the fourth, but two consecutive Hawaiian errors in the fifth allowed the Cardinals to regain the lead. The true star of the game was former Dartmouth pitcher Jimmy Doole, a schoolteacher who held the Cardinals to one hit during the final three innings.[13] Strong seasonal rain forced the cancellation of a game in Guam, but otherwise the Cardinals soundly defeated the opposition in games at Manila and the Air Force Base in Kadena, Okinawa, before boarding the plane to Japan.[14]

JAPAN

The touring group arrived in Tokyo on October 20 to a 1,500-person welcome party at Tokyo International Airport. In 13 open-topped cars, the team then paraded through streets packed with fans before arriving at the Imperial Hotel.[15] They caught Game Six of the Japan Series and then set out on a two-day trip to South Korea to play before 25,000 fans in Seoul, including President Syngman Rhee.[16] After they returned to Japan, there was a workout in Tokyo attended by nearly as many fans, before the real contests against the Japan All-Stars began on October 24 in a sold-out Korakuen Stadium, where the 1,200-yen seats were going for 10,000 yen on the side.[17]

The Cardinals faced a formidable foe. The *Mainichi* newspaper distributed a supplement to advertise the tour that listed a Japanese roster that averaged just 24 years old – a whole generation of players coming into their own. Nankai Hawks ace Matsuo Minagawa was described as "specializing in terrific shoots," an ode to his side-arm screwball, which, along with his slider, baffled hitters into the late 1960s. He was one of the 23 future Japanese Hall of Famers on the squad, joining several players not born in Japan, like the Cuban Roberto "Chico" Barbon and Bill Nishida, a Nisei born in Hawaii. But it was Shigeo Nagashima who was the real sensation of Nippon Professional Baseball and would be "the most watched player in the coming series against the Cardinals."[18] He was already a "national hero," even before joining the Giants due to his turning Rikkyo University into champions. Nagashima signed the largest contract for a rookie in Japanese history (to that date) and came through with a spectacular performance, leading the Central League in home runs and winning the Rookie of the Year Award.[19] As the series got under way, Nagashima was praised by both Japanese and touring Cardinals as being a "major-league third baseman."[20] Besides Nagashima, the young All-Stars included Futoshi Nakanishi, Tatsuro Hirooka, and Katsuya Nomura, as well as aces Inao, Tadashi Sugiura, Takao Kajimoto, Motoshi Fujita, and 20-year-old Tetsuya Yoneda.[21] Added to that core was one of the best pitchers in the history of the game, Japan's only 400-game winner, Masaichi Kaneda, who was already well known to US fans as the man who had struck out Mickey Mantle three times in the second game of the Yankees' 1955 tour.[22] These players formed the core of Japanese baseball for the next decade as the sport moved into its own, with Nagashima at its center, epitomizing both youth and progress.

With the stadium full and the cameras broadcasting across Japan, the tour was underway. The Cardinals took the game, 5-2, but the star of the day was Nagashima, who hit a home run in a game that saw no homers from the Americans. Stan Musial went hitless. The two All-Star runs came on home runs by

Nagashima and Chunichi Dragons sure-hitting second baseman Noboru Inoue. Mizell got the win thanks to Don Blasingame, who notched three hits off Tetsuya Yoneda and Masaaki Koyama.[23]

The next day's game featured a start by Kazuhisa Inao, who did not pitch in the first game, possibly because he needed rest after his recent performance in the Japan Series. Inao, in his third full season, had attained a superhuman veneer after capturing all four of the Lions' wins in the Japan Series. The press referred to him as the "Iron Man" and "Superman."[24] The sellout crowd, including Foreign Minister Aiichiro Fujiyama, who threw out the first pitch, appeared thin due to a steady rain that eventually led to the game's premature end.[25] Nonetheless, countless fans cheered on the All-Star team from home on television.

The rain started falling in the second inning, which saw Inao, along with Nishita and future Hall of Famer Takao Kajimoto, give up 13 hits over six innings to lose 8-2. The Cardinals broke out in the fourth, knocking in four runs, all off Inao, who gave up seven hits. Larry Jackson pitched six innings, giving up four hits – though one was a 390-foot homer off Nakanishi's bat.[26] The driving rain eventually forced the umpires to call the game at the end of six innings.[27]

About 185 miles (300 kilometers) away in Sendai on October 27, the All-Stars won their first game, as Kazuhisa Inao showed off his ironman stuff. Coming back on only two days' rest, Inao pitched three innings in a relief to grab the win after southpaw Atsushi Aramaki had allowed the Cardinals to knot the game, 2-2, in the top of the seventh. In the bottom of the seventh, the Japanese surged ahead on "three walks, a wild pitch, a sacrifice bunt and two costly errors for four runs" to win, 6-3.[28]

The tour then moved to Sapporo, where on October 28, before 30,000 fans, the Cardinals won 9-1. Blaylock pitched a brilliant seven-inning stretch, giving up only an inside-the-park homer to Nagashima along with one other hit.[29] Two days later, the Cardinals won another behind Bobby Smith's two doubles, a single, and a homer, just barely missing the cycle. However, Smith didn't leave the stadium without claiming one – he was awarded a motorcycle as MVP of the game, and then proceeded to drive around the infield as the crowd cheered him on.[30] The Cardinals won again, 7-2, in Nagoya before another game scheduled for November 1 in Osaka was rained out. On November 2 the Cardinals faced Aramaki in Nishinomiya. Aramaki held the Americans to one run in five innings before being removed for a pinch-hitter.

Inao came in but the Cardinals scored three in the seventh and won handily 6-1.[31]

According to *The Sporting News*, the "Cardinals were in formal dress more than baseball flannels" as they moved from party to party, highlighted by an audience with Prime Minister Nobusuke Kishi and Ambassador Douglas MacArthur II (the general's nephew).[32]

The tour's largest crowd showed up at Koshien Stadium on November 3.[33] Each August, Koshien is home to the National High School Championship, which, along with the spring invitational, showcases the future of Japanese baseball. The 1957 tournament had featured a legendary performance by Sadaharu Oh, and the August 1958 tournament had seen the first team from Okinawa to participate – a great step forward in the relationship between the occupied island and mainland Japan.[34] Before the game, a home run contest was held. Shigeo Nagashima paced the All-Stars with seven home runs, matched only by Musial. In the end, the All-Stars eked out a 15-14 victory, though the crowd cheered each and every dinger, proving the old adage "you can't boo a home run."[35] Before roughly 50,000 energized fans at Koshien, Masaaki Koyama pitched brilliantly over eight innings holding the Cardinals to two runs. Ken Boyer proved to be the heavy hitter, tying the game in the ninth with a home run and then winning it in the 10th by driving in Blasingame.[36]

Sitting in the crowd that day was Haruki Murakami. The future award-winning writer recalled:

> When I was nine, in the fall, the St. Louis Cardinals played a goodwill game against an All-Star Japanese team. The great Stan Musial was at his peak then, and he faced two top Japanese pitchers, Kazuhisa Inao and Tadashi Sugiura, in an amazing showdown. My father and I went to Koshien Stadium to see the game. We were in the infield seats along first base, near the front. Before the game began, the Cardinals' players made a circuit of the whole stadium, tossing signed soft rubber tennis balls to the crowd. People leapt to their feet, shouting, vying to grab the balls. But I just sat in my seat, vacantly watching all of this happen. I figured that a little kid like me had no chance of getting one of those signed balls. The next instant, however, I suddenly found one of them in my

lap. By total chance, it just happened to land there. Plop – like some divine revelation.

"Good for you," my father told me. He sounded half shocked, half admiring. Come to think of it, when I became a novelist at age thirty, he said almost the same thing to me. Half shock, half admiration. That was probably the greatest, most memorable thing that happened to me when I was a boy. Maybe the most blessed event I ever experienced. Could it be that my love for baseball stadiums sprang from this incident? I took that treasured white ball back home, of course, but that's all I remember about it. What ever happened to that ball? Where could it have possibly gone?[37]

The second game in Osaka saw half the crowd but provided twice the thrill as the Japanese All-Stars punished the Cardinals for their second win of the series. Futoshi Nakanishi, whom the Cardinals nicknamed "Big Buffalo," hit a grand slam after Blaylock loaded the bases in the fourth inning, and added a two-run double in the sixth off Brosnan, driving in six of the All-Stars' nine runs. "Too much Buffalo," quipped Cardinals manager Solly Hemus after the game.[38] Tadashi Sugiura allowed two runs over nine innings to earn the victory.[39]

The home-run derby wasn't the only exhibition that *Mainichi* had planned for the tour's stop in Osaka. At their broadcast studio, the paper arranged for four members of each team, including Nakanishi and Brosnan, to participate in a singing contest live on-air.[40] Joe Garagiola taped the contest for future broadcast and referred to it as "the highlight of the whole tour."[41] Brosnan noted that the real entertainment was the lack of musical talent among professional ballplayers, and there was a general sense of teasing and self-deprecation.[42]

While the broadcast ended up a fun goodwill gesture, in the vein of so many vaudeville appearances by pro ballplayers dating back nearly a century, an undercurrent of racial insensitivity by poking fun at cross-cultural differences persisted in other aspects of the tour. The American press often contained racially insensitive terms, images, and innuendos. The *St. Louis Post-Dispatch* mocked stereotypical Japanese English with the headline "So-Sorry Cards Make Sad Sam at Home in Japan, Boot Game."[43] *The Sporting News* ran cartoons featuring buck-toothed and squinty-eyed Japanese fans – a style now called yellowface that was commonly used in American propaganda

during World War II.[44] Even Garagiola at times expressed a giddy fondness for poking fun at cultural differences, such as insensitive quips about how bowing was just a way for businessmen to check the size of your bankroll.[45]

National League Secretary-Treasurer Fred Fleig proclaimed that the Japanese All-Stars were the equivalent of Triple-A players and that they lacked "quick judgment and alertness for unexpected situations."[46] He praised Koshien Stadium as ranking with Yankee Stadium and Municipal Stadium. His comments reflected the patronizing and racially insensitive viewpoints of many in the US traveling party and press in postwar Japan. These evolving racial and national identities exemplify both countries at a crossroads, as the prejudices of the Second World War era evolved into the coming challenges of the 1960s. Though toned down from the racist rhetoric of previous times, it was still problematic. This in turn was juxtaposed with the team's solemn visit to Hiroshima.

On November 6 the teams went to Hiroshima and were greeted by Mayor Tadao Watanabe and a flower-throwing crowd in front of the Hotel New Hiroshima. Before the game, Musial and Hemus held a baseball clinic at the American Cultural Center for 250 Japanese players and fans.[47] Before 20,000 excited fans, Atsushi Aramaki faced Ernie Broglio, who pitched a complete game despite two first-inning wild pitches that led to a run. The Cardinals hit Aramaki hard, going ahead 6-1 in the top of the sixth inning. Once again it was the rookie Nagashima who provided the punch for the All-Stars. After Kenjiro Tamiya reached base in the bottom of the ninth, Nagashima patiently waited for his pitch before hitting a 3-and-2 meatball over the left-field stands. However, it wasn't enough, and the All-Stars fell, 6-3.[48]

Earlier in the day, the American visitors had visited the Memorial Monument for Hiroshima and placed floral bouquets at the base of the arch. Then the club physician, Dr. L.C. Middleman, trainer Bob Bauman, coach Johnny Keane, and players Don Blasingame and Alex Grammas visited the 72 patients at the Hiroshima Atomic-Bomb Survivors Hospital signing autographs and offering kind words.[49] Solly Hemus kept a video diary of the trip to Hiroshima, but his camera was stolen from the dugout during pregame ceremonies. Before he returned home, local fan Tsutomu Hayashi presented Hemus with a gift of over 150 feet of footage taken in Hiroshima, "in the interest of better US-Japan relations."[50]

The next day an earthquake hit while the team was waiting for a train to Fukuoka, but the players did not feel the tremors. At Heiwadai Stadium on November 8, Bishop Seiemon Fukahori of the Fukuoka Catholic Church, presented the Cardinals with a silk pennant embroidered with the team's logo. This was a thank-you from leprosy patients at the Biwasaki Leprosarium, who were expressing their gratitude for Christmas gifts the Cardinals sent to the hospital in 1941.[51] Attendance up to this point was 338,000 in addition to the millions who tuned in at home.[52] Stan Musial had knocked out 12 hits for a .324 average – however, he had yet to smack a home run. (Some of the Cardinals players complained that the Japanese balls used during the tour were dead.)[53] Meanwhile Nagashima had three, in addition to his seven from the home-run contest. Fukuoka fans came out to Heiwadai Stadium 30,000 strong on November 8, cheering Cardinals starter Phil Paine, who had pitched for the Nishitetsu Lions for a few games in 1953 while he served with the US Fifth Infantry Division stationed at Camp Drake in Fukuoka. The crowd saw him pitch out of a jam in the first by striking out Nakanishi, and then witnessed Musial finally slam his first home run, as the Cardinals won 5-1.[54]

After a 7-1 St. Louis victory in Shimonoseki, Broglio then nearly no-hit the All-Stars the next game, played three days later in Shizuoka. Supported by home runs from Wally Moon and Gene Green and 15 hits off Sugiura, Zenjiro Tadokoro, and Hiroomi Oyane, Broglio held the All-Stars hitless for 6⅔ innings. With two outs in the seventh, Kenjiro Tamiya eked out a single for Japan's only hit of the afternoon. Sam Jones finished it off with two hitless innings to hand the All-Stars their only shutout of the tour.[55]

HOME

The last game before heading back to Tokyo was played in Mito on November 13. Masayuki Dobashi started for All-Japan but was relieved in the fifth by Bill Nishita, the Nisei who had played on and off in Japan since joining Yomiuri in 1952. Nishita pitched in the International League, the American Association, and the Pacific Coast League, as well as in the Central and Pacific Leagues in Japan, and with UC Berkeley – a true journeyman. The Cardinals won 5-1, thanks to Blasingame, who repeated his four-hit day from November 9, and also Gene Green, who homered twice.[56] Green's good fortune continued into the trip home and December, when he married St. Louis model

Mari-Frances Rosenthal, a match *The Sporting News* dubbed a "wedding of blond and blond."[57]

It was back to Tokyo on the next to last day of the tour, in front of 20,000 shivering fans at Korakuen Stadium. Though they were treated to a 400-foot, two-run homer off the bat of Nakanishi, the Cardinals eventually walked away with the game, 9-2, as they racked up 16 hits. Blasingame nearly hit for the cycle: After hitting a single and triple, he homered to deep center off Tetsuya Yoneda.[58]

November 16 marked the final day of the tour. A doubleheader at Korakuen Stadium attracted 80,000 fans. In the morning Takashi Suzuki faced off against Sam Jones. A pair of solo home runs by Green highlighted the 8-2 victory for the Cardinals.[59] In the second game Japan was up 2-0 in the sixth when Boyer homered off Inao to cut the lead in half. The Cardinals took the lead in the seventh behind Lee Tate's two-run double and another Boyer RBI.[60] This brought the tour to a close with 14 wins for the Cardinals against only two wins for the Japan All-Stars, bucking the prediction by "Japanese baseball experts" that the Cardinals would match the 1956 Dodgers and lose four or five games.[61] Yet each game was a display of the young talent in the Japanese game, and an affirmation that the Japanese were becoming strong enough to complete with talent from the major leagues. Nagashima lived up to the hype and was awarded the trophy as MVP of the Japanese team, which was donated by J.G. Taylor Spink.[62] In the eyes of many Giants fans, Nagashima would be the heart of a Yomiuri team that announced during the tour that it would no longer sign foreign players, stating, "Japanese baseball should be played by Japanese players."[63]

Stan Musial hung on for a few more seasons, but it was a new generation of players who would take St. Louis to heights in the 1960s. And despite Yomiuri's announcement that it would no longer recruit foreign players, other teams leapt at the chance. During the trip, three Cardinals pitchers – Phil Paine, Bill Wight, and Jim Brosnan – were even offered contracts to pitch in Japan during the 1959 season.[64] All three declined, though only Brosnan was still officially a Cardinal after Wight was released and Paine demoted in the middle of the tour.[65] Don Blasingame's performance over the course of the tour cemented his visage in the minds of Japanese fans, and was the start of a long-lasting relationship between him and Japan.[66] He would spend a decade and a half playing, coaching, and managing in Japan after a long major-league career.

Though the Cardinals seemed to represent the end of an era, the young talent represented in the Japanese All-Star team signaled a new beginning. The 1958 tour was at the crossroads of postwar bridge-building, straddling the end of the American occupation with the 1960s and beyond. Wally Yonamine made way for Sadaharu Oh, who joined the Giants in 1959, creating the "Oh-Nagashima Cannon" that drove the golden era of baseball in Japan. Sugiura, another rookie in 1958, won both Pacific League MVP and Japan Series MVP honors in 1959 on his way to a Hall of Fame career.

And though Inao would not win another MVP after his back-to-back awards in 1957 and 1958, he won 30 games in 1959 and continued to dominate batters in Japan for the next decade. The tours of Japan that followed continued to strengthen the relationship between the two countries and their baseball leagues. When Ichiro is inducted into Cooperstown, he will have players like Nagashima and Blasingame in his baseball DNA, as well as the strong bonds engendered by 1958's new direction.[67]

1958 ST. LOUIS CARDINALS GAMES IN JAPAN

Date	Place	Opponent	Score	Winner	Loser
October 24	Tokyo	All-Japan	5-2	Mizell	Koyama
October 25	Tokyo	All-Japan	6-2	Jackson	Inao
October 27	Sendai	All-Japan	3-6	Inao	Jones
October 28	Sapporo	All-Japan	9-1	Blaylock	Yoneda
October 30	Nagoya	All-Japan	7-2	Jackson	Oyane
November 2	Nishinomiya	All-Japan	6-1	Broglio	Inao
November 3	Osaka	All-Japan	6-3	Mizell	Nishida
November 4	Osaka	All-Japan	2-9	Sugiura	Blaylock
November 6	Hiroshima	All-Japan	6-3	Broglio	Aramaki
November 8	Fukuoka	All-Japan	5-1	Jones	Inao
November 9	Shimonoseki	All-Japan	7-1	Jackson	Akiyama
November 12	Shizuoka	All-Japan	8-0	Broglio	Sugiura
November 13	Mito	All-Japan	5-1	Blaylock	Dobashi
November 15	Tokyo	All-Japan	9-2	Mizell	Kajimoto
November 16	Tokyo	All-Japan	8-2	Jones	Suzuki
November 16	Tokyo	All-Japan	4-2	Broglio	Sugiura

1958 ST. LOUIS CARDINALS TOUR BATTING AND PITCHING STATISTICS[68]

Cardinals Batting Statistics	BA	G	AB	R	H	2B	3B	HR	RBI	SO	BB	SB
Ken Boyer	.364	16	66	16	24	5	0	2	11	2	3	5
Don Blasingame	.385	16	65	15	25	5	1	1	12	3	9	6
Wally Moon	.277	16	65	9	18	4	0	2	9	8	4	0
Bobby Smith	.313	16	64	7	20	5	0	1	7	4	0	1
Joe Cunningham	.349	16	63	12	22	5	1	3	19	1	8	1
Stan Musial	.309	16	55	11	17	5	1	2	11	3	9	0
Gene Green	.231	15	52	9	12	2	0	5	11	1	2	0
Lee Tate	.156	14	32	4	5	1	0	0	3	3	0	0
Ruben Amaro	.192	14	26	1	5	0	0	0	4	5	2	0
Alex Grammas	.350	8	20	5	7	3	1	0	3	1	1	3
Hal Smith	.313	12	16	2	5	0	1	0	3	0	1	0
Larry Jackson	.273	5	11	3	1	1	0	0	2	0	0	0
Ernie Broglio	.273	5	11	3	3	0	0	0	0	1	1	0
Gary Blaylock	.125	4	8	2	1	0	0	0	0	3	1	0
Solly Hemus	.000	16	7	0	3	0	0	0	0	2	0	0
Sam Jones	.000	5	6	0	0	0	0	0	0	1	0	0
Vinegar Bend Mizell	.200	8	5	1	1	0	0	0	0	3	0	0
Phil Paine	.333	2	3	1	1	0	0	0	1	2	0	0
Jim Brosnan	.000	5	3	0	0	0	0	0	0	2	0	0

Cardinals Pitching Statistics	ERA	G	W	L	IP	H	HR	SO	BB	R	ER
Larry Jackson	1.82	5	3	0	29.2	17	2	17	3	8	6
Ernie Broglio	1.59	5	4	0	28.1	13	1	30	11	5	5
Gary Blaylock	2.08	5	2	1	26	15	2	12	6	7	6
Sam Jones	0.47	5	2	1	19	12	0	13	13	7	1
Vinegar Bend Mizell	1.76	4	3	0	15.1	13	2	15	10	3	3
Jim Brosnan	4.26	6	0	0	12.2	12	2	7	1	7	6
Phil Paine	1.13	2	0	0	8	4	1	4	2	1	1
Bill Wight	0.00	1	0	0	1	0	0	1	0	0	0

NICHIBEI YAKYU: US TOURS OF JAPAN

Japanese Batting Statistics	BA	G	AB	R	H	2B	3B	HR	RBI	SO	BB	SB
Shigeo Nagashima	.283	15	46	11	13	3	0	2	3	3	6	2
Kazuhiro Yamauchi	.190	15	42	7	8	3	0	1	1	6	6	1
Futoshi Nakanishi	.211	15	38	5	8	2	0	3	11	8	4	0
Tatsuto Hirooka	.259	10	27	3	7	2	0	1	2	5	1	0
Shigeru Fujio	.250	12	24	0	6	2	0	0	1	6	1	0
Kenjiro Tamiya	.250	10	24	3	6	1	0	0	2	7	1	0
Noboru Inoue	.045	11	22	1	1	0	0	1	1	5	2	0
Takao Katsuragi	.136	12	22	1	3	3	0	0	2	4	2	0
Katsuya Nomura	.053	14	19	2	1	0	0	1	1	4	2	0
Jack Ladra	.278	8	18	0	5	4	0	0	2	2	2	0
Yasumitsu Toyoda	.278	6	18	0	5	0	0	0	0	2	3	0
Kihachi Enomoto	.000	9	16	0	0	0	0	0	0	3	1	0
Wally Yonamine	.083	9	12	0	1	0	0	0	0	2	1	0
Toru Mori	.250	3	12	0	3	0	0	0	0	2	0	1
Yoshio Yoshida	.182	4	11	0	2	0	0	0	0	2	1	0
Yoshinori Hirose	.222	4	9	0	2	0	0	0	0	0	0	0
Seiji Sekiguchi	.111	7	9	0	1	1	0	0	0	0	0	0
Kiyoshi Doi	.000	6	6	0	0	0	0	0	0	0	0	0
Isami Okamoto	.200	2	5	1	1	0	0	1	2	0	2	0
Hiromu Fujii	.200	2	5	0	1	1	0	0	0	3	0	0

Japanese Pitching Statistics	ERA	G	W	L	IP	H	HR	SO	BB	R	ER
Tadashi Sugiura	4.18	7	1	2	23.2	25	2	10	3	11	11
Atsushi Aramaki	3.32	5	0	1	19	20	1	4	5	9	7
Kazuhisa Inao	6.62	5	1	3	17.2	21	2	5	4	14	13
Masaaki Koyama	4.50	2	0	1	14	13	1	5	1	7	7
Tetsuya Yoneda	5.14	6	0	1	14	14	1	7	7	8	8
Masayuki Dobashi	6.30	3	0	1	10	10	3	1	1	7	7
Bill Nishida	6.14	3	0	1	7.1	7	1	0	4	5	5
Takao Kajimoto	7.11	3	0	1	6.1	12	0	4	4	6	5
Hiroomi Oyane	5.79	2	0	1	4.2	6	2	0	1	3	3
Motoshi Fujita	6.75	3	0	0	4	3	0	2	0	3	3
Noboru Akiyama	9.00	2	0	1	4	7	1	1	1	4	4
Takashi Suzuki	13.50	2	0	1	4	12	1	3	1	7	6
Masaichi Kaneda	2.70	1	0	0	3.1	3	0	0	3	1	1
Hisafumi Kawamura	0.00	1	0	0	2	1	0	0	0	0	0
Ryohei Hasegawa	4.50	1	0	0	2	2	0	0	0	1	1
Yukio Shimabara	9.00	1	0	0	2	5	0	0	1	2	2
Terukatsu Tashiro	13.50	1	0	0	2	4	1	2	1	4	3
Shoichi Ono	0.00	1	0	0	1	0	0	0	1	0	0
Takayuki Hata	18.00	1	0	0	1	2	0	1	1	2	2
Sho Horiuchi	-	1	0	0	0	2	0	0	2	4	1

NOTES

1   Oscar Kahan, "Spink Trophy to Go to Japanese Player Selected by Cards," *The Sporting News*, October 1, 1958: 30.

2   Jim Brosnan, "'Eastward Ho!' With Brosnan, Or, Getting Way Up with the Birds," *St. Louis Post-Dispatch*, October 13, 1958: 4C.

3   Kahan, "Spink Trophy to go to Japanese Player Selected by Cards."

4   "Frick Suggests Nipponese Copy U.S. Organized Ball," *The Sporting News*, November 9, 1955: 9.

5   "Cardinals Get Japan Trip," *Washington Post and Times Herald*, July 31, 1958: C1.

6   Oscar Kahan, "'Cardinals Going to Japan to Win,' Devine's Promise," *The Sporting News*, October 15, 1958: 5.

7   "Two More Who Took Shots Kayoed on Bird List for Trip," *The Sporting News*, October 15, 1958: 5.

8   Kahan, "'Cardinals Going to Japan to Win,' Devine's Promise."

9   Harry Mitauer, "Cards Getting Set for Trip to Japan," *St. Louis Globe-Democrat*, July 30, 1958: 15.

10 Oscar Kahan, "Radio First – KMOX to Carry Games on Tour," *The Sporting News*, October 15, 1958: 5.

11 Red McQueen, "Cardinals Pound Burdette and Turley Before Small Crowds in Hawaii Game," *The Sporting News*, October 22, 1958: 7.

12 Kenny Haina, "Cards Shell Turley for 9-1 Victory," *Honolulu Advertiser*, October 13, 1958: 8.

13 Monte Ito, "Cards Edge Hawaii All-Stars, 5-4," *Honolulu Advertiser*, October 14, 1958: 9.

14 McQueen, "Cardinals Pound Burdette and Turley Before Small Crowds in Hawaii Game."

15 "Cardinals Will Be Contenders, Hemus Informs Japanese," *St. Louis Post-Dispatch*, October 20, 1958: 4C.

16 Lee Kavetski, "Redbirds Cop Six in Row Prior to 'Invasion' of Japan," *The Sporting News*, October 29, 1958: 10.

17 Associated Press, "20,000 Watch Cards Work Out in Tokyo, Solly Suspects Spies," *St. Louis Post-Dispatch*, October 23, 1958, 1E; "Japanese Scalpers Ask $27 for Seats Priced at $3.34," *The Sporting News*, October 22, 1958: 7.

18 "Japanese Baseball's Finest," *Mainichi – Supplement*, October 1958: 21.

19 Robert K. Fitts, *Wally Yonamine: The Man Who Changed Japanese Baseball* (Lincoln: University of Nebraska Press, 2012), 226.

20 Lee Kavetski, "Bonus Baby Nagashima in Lead for Spink Trophy as Japan's MVP," *The Sporting News*, November 12, 1958: 5.

21 "Japanese Baseball's Finest."

22 Fitts, *Wally Yonamine*, 96.

23 "Birds Win; 2 Homers by Japan," *St. Louis Post-Dispatch*, October 24, 1958: 5C.

24 "20,000 Watch Cards Work Out in Tokyo, Solly Suspects Spies," *St. Louis Post-Dispatch*, October 23, 1958, 6E.

25 Lee Kavetski, "Japanese Pitching Curbs Cardinals Homers: Musial Has Bad Day, Then Three Safe Blows in Game," *The Sporting News*, November 5, 1958: 9.

26 United Press International, "Musial Gets 3 Hits as Cards Win, 8-2," *St. Louis Post-Dispatch*, October 26, 1958: 2E.

27 "Cards Top Stars in Tokyo," *New York Times*, October 26, 1958: S10.

28 United Press International, "So-Sorry Cards Make Sad Sam at Home in Japan, Boot Game," *St. Louis Post-Dispatch*, October 27, 1958: 5C; "Japanese Deal Cards 6-3 Defeat in Sendai," *Pacific Stars and Stripes*, October 28, 1958: 24.

29 "Cardinals Get the Long Ball and Big Inning in 9-1 Win," *St. Louis Post-Dispatch*, October 28, 1958: 4B.

30 Kavetski, "Japanese Pitching Curbs Cardinals' Homers: Musial Has Bad Day, Then Three Safe Blows in Game," 10.

31 Lee Kavetski, "Cards' Japan Tour Real Good-Will Jaunt," *The Sporting News*, November 12, 1958: 5.

32 Lee Kavetski, "It's Party, Party After Party for Redbirds in Japan," *The Sporting News*, November 5, 1958: 9.

33 Kavetski, "Cards' Japan Tour Real Good-Will Jaunt."

34 Sadaharu Oh and David Falkner, *Sadaharu Oh: A Zen Way of Baseball* (New York: Times Books, 1984), 46; Satoshi Shimizu, "The Significance of Koshien in Postwar Okinawa: A Representation of Okinawa," *International Journal of the History of Sport*, Volume 29, Issue 17, November 2012.

35 "Musial, Nagashima Hit 7 as Cards Lose Homer Contest," *The Sporting News*, November 12, 1958: 5.

36 "Boyer Most Honorable Batter as Cards Beat Japanese in 10th," *St. Louis Post Dispatch*, November 3, 1958: 5B.

37 "The Yakult Swallows Poetry Collection," in Haruki Murakami, *First Person Singular* (New York: Alfred A. Knopf, 2020), 214-15.

38 "Nakanishi Ruined Us – Hemus," *Pacific Stars and Stripes*, November 5, 1958: 24.

39 "Grand Slam Homer Hit Off Blaylock as Cards Lose, 9-2," *St. Louis Post Dispatch*, November 4, 1958: 4B.

40 Jim Brosnan, "East Meets West in Harmony; Cards a Vaudeville Hit," *St. Louis Post-Dispatch*, November 7, 1958: 6C.

41 Brosnan, "East Meets West in Harmony; Cards a Vaudeville Hit."

42 Brosnan, "East Meets West in Harmony; Cards a Vaudeville Hit."

43 "So-Sorry Cards Make Sad Sam at Home in Japan, Boot Game."

44 "Having Swell Time, Wish You Were Here," *The Sporting News*, November 12, 1958: 5; "Japan Hails Cards as 'Most Spirited' Team," *The Sporting News*, November 19, 1958: 5.

45 Jim Brosnan, "Cardinals Wowed 'em in Japan," *St. Louis Post Dispatch*, November 30, 1958: 1G.

46 "'Japanese Are Good, but Need Experience in Minors' – Fleig," *The Sporting News*, November 12, 1958: 10.

47 Lee Kavetski, "Hiroshima Visit Touching Highlight of Redbird Trip," *The Sporting News*, November 19, 1958: 6.

48 "Cards Kayo 17-Game Winner in Hiroshima Victory," *St. Louis Post-Dispatch*, November 6, 1958: 6E.

49 Kavetski, "Hiroshima Visit Touching Highlight of Redbird Trip."

50 Lee Kavetski, "Redbirds Attract 430,000 in Rolling to 14-2 record," *The Sporting News*, November 26, 1958: 8.

51 Kavetski, "Hiroshima Visit Touching Highlight of Redbird Trip."

52 Lee Kavetski, "All-Out Hustle Displayed by Redbirds Makes Big Hit with Nipponese Crowds," *The Sporting News*, November 19, 1958: 5.

53 Kavetski, "Japanese Pitching Curbs Cardinals Homers."

54 United Press International, "Birds Win; Musial, Paine Star," *St. Louis Post-Dispatch*, November 9, 1958: 6G.

55 Associated Press, "Cardinals Clobber Japan Stars 8-0 With Fifteen Hits," *Japan Times*, November 13, 1958: 5; Kavetski, "All-Out Hustle Displayed by Redbirds Makes Big Hit with Nipponese Crowds."

56 "Moon and Green Hit Homers in 5-1 Cardinal Victory," *St. Louis Post-Dispatch*, November 13, 1958: 1E.

57 Oscar Kahan, "Brosnan Big Chief of Cards' Fireman Brigade – 1.67 ERA," *The Sporting News*, November 19, 1958: 8.

58 "Birds Get 16 Hits, Win, 9-2," *St. Louis Post-Dispatch*, November 15, 1958: 6A.

59 "Cardinals Have Fun, Hits, 8-2," *St. Louis Post Dispatch*, November 16, 1958: 2F.

60 Kavetski, "Redbirds Attract 430,000 in Rolling to 14-2 record."

61 Lee Kavetski, "Cards to Face 50 of Japan's Best on Jaunt," *The Sporting News*, October 15, 1958: 5.

62 Lee Kavetski, "Cardinals Vote Nagashima Top Nippon Player," *The Sporting News*, November 26, 1958: 7.

63 "Yomiuri Giants Won't Sign Foreign Players, Prexy Says," *The Sporting News*, November 19, 1958: 6.

64 Peter Golenbock, *The Spirit of St. Louis: A History of the St. Louis Cardinals and Browns* (New York: Harper Entertainment, 2000), 428.

65 Tom Hopkins, "Sportraitures," *Honolulu Star-Bulletin*, October 27, 1958: 22.

66 Robert K. Fitts, *Remember Japanese Baseball: An Oral History of the Game* (Carbondale: Southern Illinois University Press, 2005), 109.

67 Ichiro will be on the Hall of Fame ballot for the first time in December 2024.

68 Listed Japanese players have a minimum of 5 at-bats. Yoshikazu Matsubayashi, *Baseball Game History: Japan vs. U.S.A.* (Tokyo: Baseball Magazine, 2004), 93; Nippon Professional Baseball Records, https://www.2689web.com/nb.html.

TOURS OF JAPAN: VOLUME I AUTHOR BIOS

Adam Berenbak is an archivist with the National Archives Center for Legislative Archives in Washington, DC. He has been a member of SABR for over a decade and his research focuses on the history of baseball in Japan. He has published articles on Japanese baseball in the SABR *Baseball Research Journal* and on the blog *Our Game*, curated an exhibition with the Japanese Embassy's Cultural Center in DC, and contributed to a number of articles and books. He has also published several essays on other baseball topics in the *Baseball Research Journal*, *Prologue*, and *Zisk*, and he curated an exhibition on tobacco cards in conjunction with the Museum of Durham History and the Durham Bulls Athletic Park. Besides this book, his work was featured in a SABR book on Jackie Robinson.

Stephen D. Boren, MD, attended the University of Illinois for two years and then received his MD degree four years later from the University of Illinois College of Medicine. After an internship at the University of Illinois Hospital, he was drafted into the US Army and was stationed in the north part of south Korea where the real M*A*S*H had been. He subsequently did his emergency medicine residency at Milwaukee County Hospital. He later earned his MBA from Northwestern University. He has published articles in numerous SABR publications. He believes that he is the only person to be published in the *Wall Street Journal*, the *New England Journal of Medicine*, and *Baseball Digest* all in the same year. His mother wrote her Master of Arts dissertation at the University of Chicago in 1936 entitled "Athletics as a Factor In Japanese International and Domestic Relations." He has been board-certified in emergency medicine five times. He and his wife, Louise, as well as his well-known golden retriever Charlie, now reside in Aiken, South Carolina.

Mark Brunke was five days past his 10th birthday when the Seattle Mariners made their debut. He became a lifelong fan when they scored two days later. Mark is a college human resources administrator, painter, poet, musician, and filmmaker from Seattle, Washington. He is the chapter secretary for Pacific Northwest SABR, belongs to SABR's Origins of Baseball Committee, and is a contributor to Protoball.org. His writing has appeared in *The Edinburgh Companion to Twentieth-Century British and American War Literature* from the Edinburgh University Press, *Distant Replay! Washington's Jewish Sports Heroes* from 4Culture, and *Overcoming Adversity: Baseball's Tony Conigliaro Award* from SABR. He presented his research on the origins of baseball in the Pacific Northwest at the 2015 Frederick Ivor-Campbell 19th Century Base Ball Conference at the Baseball Hall of Fame. He once hit six consecutive batters in coach pitch little league, two of whom he fathered in the current millennium.

Carter Cromwell is a former sportswriter for daily newspapers and a corporate public-relations professional. He works with an independent-league baseball team and contributes baseball-related articles to various websites. When not doing that, he has a passion for world travel, photography, and rescue dogs.

James E. Elfers is the author of the Larry Ritter Award-winning book *The Tour to End All Tours: The Story of Major League Baseball's 1913-1914 World Tour* (University of Nebraska Press, 2003), a chapter of which was excerpted for this volume. This book was also a Seymour Award nominee and runner-up for the Casey Award for best baseball book of the year. Elfers is retired from the University of Delaware, where he spent 35 years at the Morris Library, mostly as a cataloger. A lifelong Phillies fan, he has seen lots of bad baseball with occasional flashes of brilliance. He currently resides in Pennsylvania's Lehigh Valley with Patti, the love of his life and a fellow writer. A Brit, she reminds him regularly that baseball is basically rounders. Elfers keeps his library skills up to snuff by working part time in his local community library. He can be reached at jeelfers@netscape.net.

Robert K. Fitts is the author of numerous articles and seven books on Japanese baseball and Japanese baseball cards. Fitts is the founder of SABR's Asian Baseball Committee and a recipient of the society's 2013 Seymour Medal for Best Baseball Book of 2012; the 2019 McFarland-SABR Baseball Research Award; the 2012 Doug Pappas Award for best oral research presentation at the annual convention; and the 2006 and 2021 SABR Research Awards. He has twice been a finalist for the Casey Award and has received two silver medals at the Independent Publisher Book Awards. While living in Tokyo in 1993-94, Fitts began collecting Japanese baseball cards and now runs Robs

Japanese Cards LLC. Information on Rob's work is available at RobFitts.com.

James Forr dragged his non-baseball-fan wife to a Hiroshima Carp game on their honeymoon. Despite this, they remain married. His book *Pie Traynor: A Baseball Biography,* co-authored with David Proctor, was a nominee for the 2010 CASEY Award. James is also a winner of the McFarland-SABR Baseball Research Award and has presented at the Frederick Ivor-Campbell 19th Century Base Ball Conference and the Jerry Malloy Negro League Conference.

Christopher Frey is a writer, director, and producer at Cross Media International, a production company based in San Francisco and Tokyo that he co-founded in 2003. While earning degrees in Asian studies and diplomacy and world affairs with a minor in Japanese from Occidental College in Los Angeles and the International Program at Waseda University in Tokyo, he was awarded a Richter International Fellowship for research conducted in Hong Kong and Southern China, as well as an Anderson Fellowship for research conducted at the Hoover Institution at Stanford University. In 1988 Chris attended his first professional baseball game in Japan as the Hiroshima Toyo Carp hosted the Yakult Swallows, then 20 years later was at Tokyo Dome to see his hometown Oakland Athletics take on the Boston Red Sox in the 2008 edition of the MLB Japan Opening Series.

John Harney is an associate professor of history at Centre College in Danville, Kentucky. He is the author of *Empire of Infields: Baseball in Taiwan and Cultural Identity, 1895-1968.* He received a doctorate in modern Chinese and East Asian history from the University of Texas at Austin. John is a Texas Rangers fan and is still bitter about the 2011 World Series.

Tom Hawthorn is a Canadian author who has written for newspapers and magazines for more than four decades. He is currently a speechwriter for the premier of British Columbia.

Len Levin is a longtime newspaper editor in New England, now retired. He lives in Providence with his wife, Linda, and an overachieving orange cat. He now (Len, not the cat) is the grammarian for the Rhode Island Supreme Court and edits its decisions. He also copyedits many SABR books, including this one. He is just down the interstate from Fenway Park, where he has spent many happy hours (and a few not so happy).

Satoshi Matsumiya was born in Kaideima-cho, Hikone City, Shiga Prefecture, Japan. He graduated from the Osaka Institute of Technology, Department of Industrial Management, and joined Naiki Kinzoku Seisakusyo Company. In July 1985 he joined Matsumiya Chemical Co., Ltd. and worked as the Hikone plant manager. Inspired by the Japanese movie *Vancouver Asahi,* in 2014 he started researching the footsteps of his grandfather Sotojiro Matsumiya, who had emigrated to Canada. In March 2017 he published a Japanese book *Matsumiya Stores and the Vancouver Asahi – Footsteps of Japanese Canadian Immigrants,* which won the 20th Self-Publishing Culture Award. In 2019 he headed a committee to host the Shin-Asahi baseball team in Hikone and published the booklet *The Shin Asahi Team's Tour to Japan.* His latest E-book is *When There Was a Japanese Baseball Club in Vancouver – My Grandfather Sotojiro Matsumiya and the Era of Canadian Immigration.*

Yoichi Nagata, a 41-year SABR member, has published books on Japanese-American outfielder Jimmy Horio, the 1935 Tokyo Giants' tour of North America, baseball at the World War II Japanese American camps in Arkansas, and others. He is still working on a history of baseball in Hawaii. When he worked at a sushi restaurant in Philadelphia in the early 1980s, Steve Carlton was a regular customer. Since then, he has been a fan of Lefty and the Phillies. He is also a fan of the now defunct Nishitetsu Lions of Fukuoka, Japan, the team he grew up with.

Roberta J. Newman is a clinical professor of liberal studies at New York University. Her work focuses on the many intersections between baseball and popular culture. She is co-author of *Black Baseball, Black Business: Race Enterprise and the Fate of the Segregated Dollar* (2014), and author of *Here's the Pitch: the Amazing, True, New, and Improved Story of Baseball and Advertising* (2019), as well as numerous articles on these and other topics. Currently, she is at work on a project dealing with Japanese baseball, manga, and cultural identities.

Joe Niese is a member of the Society for American Baseball Research and the Professional Football Researchers Association. To date, he has written four sports biographies: *Burleigh Grimes: Baseball's Last Legal Spitballer* (McFarland), *Handy Andy: The Andy Pafko Story* (Chippewa River Press), *Gus Dorais: Gridiron Innovator, All-American and Hall of Fame Coach* (McFarland), and *Zack Wheat: The Life of the Brooklyn Dodgers Hall of Famer* (McFarland). In 2015, *Handy Andy* won a bronze prize in Foreword Review's Book of the Year Award (Sports). That same year Joe received the Wisconsin Baseball Coaches Association State Media Award. *Zack Wheat* won SABR's 2021 Ron Gabriel Award and was on the shortlist of finalists for their Larry Ritter Award. Joe lives in Chippewa Falls, Wisconsin, with his wife and three children, where he works as library director of the Chippewa Falls Public Library.

Bill Nowlin, always looking for an excuse to travel, has seen the Red Sox play in Japan, England, an exhibition game in the Dominican Republic, and even in Canada. For the visit to Tokyo, he sat in on a meeting of SABR's Tokyo Chapter. A Boston native, he was born into Red Sox fandom; his father sold hot dogs at Fenway Park for a couple of years as a teenager. Now retired after 50 years with Rounder Records, Bill has written a bunch of books on Boston baseball and ballplayers, and helped edit a good number of books on other teams and other players.

Ralph Pearce is a local history author who shares a passion for Japanese baseball history. His first book, *From Asahi to Zebras: Japanese American Baseball in San Jose, California,* was published in 2005. His second book, *San Jose Japantown: A Journey,* co-authored with Curt Fukuda, was published in 2014 by the Japanese American Museum of San Jose. In 2019 he contributed a biographical sketch to the book *Gentle Black Giants: A History of Negro Leaguers in Japan* by Kazoo Sayama and Bill Staples Jr. Ralph currently works in the Dr. Martin Luther King Jr. Library's California Room, the San Jose Public Library's state and local history collection.

Carl Riechers retired from United Parcel Service in 2012 after 35 years of service. With more free time, he became a SABR member that same year. Born and raised in the suburbs of St. Louis, he became a big fan of the Cardinals. He and his wife, Janet, have three children and he is the proud grandpa of two.

Keith Spalding Robbins has spent nearly five years studying and working in the Far East in the design profession. Since returning to the United States and joining SABR, his efforts have been focused on research and periodical publications of lesser-known aspects of international baseball, with a focus on tours to Japan and Berlin. Previous published articles can be found in the Cooperstown Symposium and the Journal *NINE*. He presented at the IWBC/SABR conference in Rockford, Illinois, in 2020, and at SABR 50 at Baltimore. His specific interests include the international exhibitions of global baseball goodwill by Les Mann in the late 1930s. Mr. Robbins is a member of the Spalding family.

Paul Rogers is the co-author or co-editor of several baseball books including *The Whiz Kids and the 1950 Pennant Race* (Temple University Press, 1996) with boyhood hero Robin Roberts, and *Lucky Me: My 65 Years in Baseball* (SMU Press, 2011) with Eddie Robinson. Paul is president of the Ernie Banks-Bobby Bragan DFW Chapter of SABR and a frequent contributor to the SABR BioProject, but his real job is as a law professor at the SMU Dedman School of Law, where he served as dean for nine years. He has also served as SMU's faculty athletic representative for 35 years and counting.

Allan H. "Bud" Selig was the ninth commissioner of baseball, a position he held for 22 years, and is a member of the National Baseball Hall of Fame. In his current role as commissioner emeritus, Selig advises the commissioner and contributes to many special projects. Prior to his work as the commissioner, Selig served as the chairman of Major League Baseball's Executive Council. Selig's memoir, *For the Good of the Game*, was published by HarperCollins in July 2019. Selig has been recognized for his great work in baseball and philanthropy. His many awards include the Jackie Robinson Foundation's Lifetime Achievement Award, the Taylor Hooton Foundation's inaugural Taylor Award, the Green Sports Alliance's Environmental Leadership Award, B'nai B'rith International's Distinguished Humanitarian Award; the Boys & Girls Clubs of America's Chairman's Award, the New York Baseball Writers' William J. Slocum/Jack Lang Award, and the St. Louis Baseball Writers' "Red Award." The National Baseball Hall of Fame and Museum unveiled the Allan H. "Bud" Selig Center for the Archives of Major League Baseball Commissioners, a permanent research space within the halls of Cooperstown, dedicated in his honor. In October 2014, he was inducted into the Broadcasting & Cable Hall of Fame. Bud attended the University of Wisconsin-Madison and has been honored by having numerous scholarships named after him. He taught at Marquette University's Law School and currently teaches at Arizona State University and the University of Wisconsin- Madison. He and his wife, Sue, have three daughters, five grandchildren, and one great-grandson.

Yobun Shima was born and raised in Kyoto, Japan, and later worked for an international shipping company in Tokyo. His family members were living in Vancouver from around 1907 until the 1930s, when they returned to Japan (except for one of his uncles who remained in Canada). After retiring, Shima started to research the Vancouver Asahi when he discovered that his uncle Shoichi Shima was one of the team's original players. The Asahi was inducted into the Canadian Baseball Hall of Fame in 2003 and the BC Sports Hall of Fame in 2005. Yobun continues to track down unclaimed medalists of the team in cooperation with the BC Sports Hall of Fame, families of Asahi players, and other interested parties.

Dennis Snelling is a three-time Casey Award finalist for Best Baseball Book of the Year, including for *The Greatest Minor League: A History of the Pacific Coast League*, and *Lefty O'Doul: Baseball's Forgotten Ambassador*, which was runner-up for the award in 2017. He was a 2015 Seymour Medal finalist for *Johnny Evers: A Baseball Life*. Snelling is an active member of the Dusty Baker and Lefty O'Doul SABR chapters in Northern California. He lives in Rocklin, California.

Bill Staples Jr. of Chandler, Arizona, a SABR member since 2006, has a passion for researching and telling the untold stories of the "international pastime." His areas of expertise include Japanese-American and Negro Leagues baseball history as a context for exploring the themes of civil rights, cross-cultural relations, and globalization. He is a board member of the Nisei Baseball Research Project and the Japanese American Citizens League-Arizona Chapter, chairman of the SABR Asian Baseball Committee, and research contributor to the Negro Leagues Baseball Museum. Staples is the author of *Kenichi Zenimura, Japanese American Baseball Pioneer* (McFarland, 2011), and co-authored *Gentle Black Giants: A History of Negro Leaguers in Japan* (NBRP Press, 2019) with Japanese baseball historian Kazuo Sayama. He has contributed to numerous articles and news stories for global media including MLB.com, *Sports Illustrated*, NPR, the *Japan Times*, Kyodo News, TV Asahi, and NHK. His other SABR publications include articles in *Baltimore Baseball* (2021), *One-Hit Wonders* (2021), and *No-Hitters* (2017). He received the SABR Baseball Research Award in 2012 for the Zenimura biography and in 2020 for the article "Early Baseball Encounters in the West: The Yeddo Royal Japanese Troupe Play Ball in America, 1872." Learn more at zenimura.com.

Dr. Yusuke Suzumura, born in 1976, received a doctoral degree from Hosei University (Tokyo) in 2008, and is an associate professor of Meijo University (Nagoya), a visiting researcher of both the Hosei University Research Center for International Japanese Studies and the Hosei University Research Center for Edo-Tokyo Studies. He published the newest book *Relationship between Religion of Philosophy and Society in Kiyozawa Manshi* from Hosei University Press in February 2022. His majors are comparative philosophy, history of politics, and cross-cultural studies, and in recent years he has appeared on TV, radio, and internet media as a commentator. He is also a specialist in baseball history and has published three books since 2005. He serves as the president of the Forum for Researchers of Baseball Culture, co-executive director and an Editorial Board Member of the Japan Society for Intercultural Studies, and a member of the Society for American Baseball Research.

Steven K. Wisensale, PhD., is professor emeritus of public policy at the University of Connecticut, where he taught a very popular course for many years: "Baseball and Society: Politics, Economics, Race and Gender." In 2017 he traveled to Japan as a Fulbright Scholar where he designed and taught another course, "Baseball Diplomacy in Japan-US Relations," at two universities. His most recent SABR publications include "The Black Knight: A Political Portrait of Jackie Robinson" (a chapter in *Jackie: Perspectives on 42)* and "In Search of Babe Ruth's Statue in a Japanese Zoo" (*Baseball Research Journal*, spring 2021). He is also a regular attendee and an occasional presenter at the Cooperstown Symposium on Baseball and American Culture. An avid Orioles fan, Steve resides in Essex, Connecticut, with his wife Nan and their two dogs, Song and Blue Moon, who can run down deep fly balls consistently for very low wages and without pulling a hamstring.

Acknowledgment: Steve would like to thank Michael Westbay of Japan Ball in Yokohama for his patience and cooperative spirit in translating several important documents during his research for this chapter.

Kat Williams is a professor of women's sport history at Marshall University, president of the International Women's Baseball Center, author of several articles about women's sport including "Sport a Useful Category of Analysis," and two books, *The All-American Girls After the AAGPBL* and *Isabel Lefty Alvarez: The Improbable Life of a Cuban American Baseball Star.* Through teaching, scholarship, and advocacy Kat is dedicated to the preservation of women's sport history, and to helping girls become independent, confident leaders.

SABR Books on the Negro Leagues and Black Baseball

From Rube to Robinson: SABR's Best Articles on Black Baseball

From Rube to Robinson brings together the best Negro League baseball scholarship that the Society of American Baseball Research (SABR) has ever produced, culled from its journals, Biography Project, and award-winning essays. The book includes a star-studded list of scholars and historians, from the late Jerry Malloy and Jules Tygiel, to award winners Larry Lester, Geri Strecker, and Jeremy Beer, and a host of other talented writers. The essays cover topics ranging over nearly a century, from 1866 and the earliest known Black baseball championship, to 1962 and the end of the Negro American League.

Edited by John Graf; Associate Editors Duke Goldman and Larry Lester
$24.95 paperback (ISBN 978-1-970159-41-7)
$9.99 ebook (ISBN 978-1-970159-40-0)
8.5"X11", 220 pages

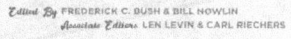

Pride of Smoketown: The 1935 Pittsburgh Crawfords

The 1935 Pittsburgh Crawfords team, one of the dominant teams in Negro League history, is often compared to the legendary 1927 "Murderer's Row" New York Yankees. The squad from "Smoketown"—a nickname that the *Pittsburgh Courier* often applied to the metropolis better-known as "Steel City"—boasted four Hall-of-Fame players in outfielder James "Cool Papa" Bell, first baseman/manager Oscar Charleston, catcher Josh Gibson, and third baseman William "Judy" Johnson. This volume contains exhaustively-researched articles about the players, front office personnel, Greenlee Field, and the exciting games and history of the team that were written and edited by 25 SABR members. The inclusion of historical photos about every subject in the book helps to shine a spotlight on the 1935 Pittsburgh Crawfords, who truly were the Pride of Smoketown.

Edited by Frederick C. Bush and Bill Nowlin
$29.95 paperback (ISBN 978-1-970159-25-7)
$9.99 ebook (ISBN 978-1-970159-24-0)
8.5"X11", 340 pages, over 60 photos

The Newark Eagles Take Flight: The Story of the 1946 Negro League Champions

The Newark Eagles won only one Negro National League pennant during the franchise's 15-year tenure in the Garden State, but the 1946 squad that ran away with the NNL and then triumphed over the Kansas City Monarchs in a seven-game World Series was a team for the ages. The returning WWII veterans composed a veritable "Who's Who in the Negro Leagues" and included Leon Day, Larry Doby, Monte Irvin, and Max Manning, as well as numerous role players. Four of the Eagles' stars—Day, Doby, Irvin, and player/manager Raleigh "Biz" Mackey, as well as co-owner Effa Manley—have been enshrined in the National Baseball Hall of Fame in Cooperstown. In addition to biographies of the players, co-owners, and P.A. announcer, there are also articles about Newark's Ruppert Stadium, Leon Day's Opening Day no-hitter, a sensational midseason game, the season's two East-West All-Star Games, and the 1946 Negro League World Series between the Eagles and the renowned Kansas City Monarchs.

Edited by Frederick C. Bush and Bill Nowlin
$24.95 paperback (ISBN 978-1-970159-07-3)
$9.99 ebook (ISBN 978-1-970159-06-6)
8.5"X11", 228 pages, over 60 photos

Bittersweet Goodbye: The Black Barons, The Grays, and the 1948 Negro League World Series

This book was inspired by the last Negro League World Series ever played and presents biographies of the players on the two contending teams in 1948—the Birmingham Black Barons and the Homestead Grays—as well as the managers, the owners, and articles on the ballparks the teams called home. Also included are articles that recap the season's two East-West All-Star Games, the Negro National League and Negro American League playoff series, and the World Series itself. Additional context is provided in essays about the effects of baseball's integration on the Negro Leagues, the exodus of Negro League players to Canada, and the signing away of top Negro League players, specifically Willie Mays. Many of the players' lives and careers have been presented to a much greater extent than previously possible.

Edited by Frederick C. Bush and Bill Nowlin
$21.95 paperback (ISBN 978-1-943816-55-2)
$9.99 ebook (ISBN 978-1-943816-54-5)
8.5"X11", 442 pages, over 100 photos and images

Friends of SABR

You can become a Friend of SABR by giving as little as $10 per month or by making a one-time gift of $1,000 or more. When you do so, you will be inducted into a community of passionate baseball fans dedicated to supporting SABR's work.

Friends of SABR receive the following benefits:
- ✓ Annual Friends of SABR Commemorative Lapel Pin
- ✓ Recognition in This Week in SABR, SABR.org, and the SABR Annual Report
- ✓ Access to the SABR Annual Convention VIP donor event
- ✓ Invitations to exclusive Friends of SABR events

SABR On-Deck Circle - $10/month, $30/month, $50/month
Get in the SABR On-Deck Circle, and help SABR become the essential community for the world of baseball. Your support will build capacity around all things SABR, including publications, website content, podcast development, and community growth.

A monthly gift is deducted from your bank account or charged to a credit card until you tell us to stop. No more email, mail, or phone reminders.

  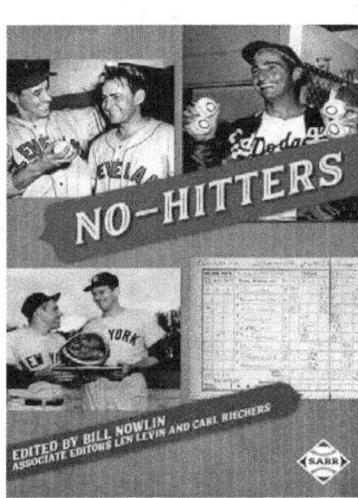

Join the SABR On-Deck Circle

Payment Info: _____Visa _____Mastercard

Name on Card: _____

Card #: _____

Exp. Date: _____ Security Code: _____

Signature: _____

- ○ $10/month
- ○ $30/month
- ○ $50/month
- ○ Other amount _____

Go to sabr.org/donate to make your gift online

Society for American Baseball Research

Cronkite School at ASU
555 N. Central Ave. #416, Phoenix, AZ 85004
602.496.1460 (phone)
SABR.org

Become a SABR member today!

If you're interested in baseball — writing about it, reading about it, talking about it — there's a place for you in the Society for American Baseball Research.

SABR memberships are available on annual, multi-year, or monthly subscription basis. Annual and monthly subscription memberships auto-renew for your convenience. Young Professional memberships are for ages 30 and under. Senior memberships are for ages 65 and older. Student memberships are available to currently enrolled middle/high school or full-time college/university students. Monthly subscription members receive SABR publications electronically and are eligible for SABR event discounts after 12 months.

Here's a list of some of the key benefits you'll receive as a SABR member:

- Receive two editions (spring and fall) of the *Baseball Research Journal*, our flagship publication
- Receive expanded e-book edition of *The National Pastime,* our annual convention journal
- 8-10 new e-books published by the SABR Digital Library, all FREE to members
- "This Week in SABR" e-newsletter, sent to members every Friday
- Join dozens of research committees, from Statistical Analysis to Women in Baseball.
- Join one of 70+ regional chapters in the U.S., Canada, Latin America, and abroad
- Participate in online discussion groups
- Ask and answer baseball research questions on the SABR-L e-mail listserv
- Complete archives of *The Sporting News* dating back to 1886 and other research resources
- Promote your research in "This Week in SABR"
- Diamond Dollars Case Competition
- Yoseloff Scholarships

- Discounts on SABR national conferences, including the SABR National Convention, the SABR Analytics Conference, Jerry Malloy Negro League Conference, Frederick Ivor-Campbell 19th Century Conference, and the Arizona Fall League Experience
- Publish your research in peer-reviewed SABR journals
- Collaborate with SABR researchers and experts
- Contribute to Baseball Biography Project or the SABR Games Project
- List your new book in the SABR Bookshelf
- Lead a SABR research committee or chapter
- Networking opportunities at SABR Analytics Conference
- Meet baseball authors and historians at SABR events and chapter meetings
- 50% discounts on paperback versions of SABR e-books
- Discounts with other partners in the baseball community
- SABR research awards

We hope you'll join the most passionate international community of baseball fans at SABR! Check us out online at SABR.org/join.

- - - ✂ -

SABR MEMBERSHIP FORM

	Standard	Senior	Young Pro.	Student
Annual:	❑ $65	❑ $45	❑ $45	❑ $25
3 Year:	❑ $175	❑ $129	❑ $129	
5 Year:	❑ $249			
Monthly:	❑ $6.95	❑ $4.95	❑ $4.95	

(International members wishing to be mailed the Baseball Research Journal should add $10/yr for Canada/Mexico or $19/yr for overseas locations.)

Participate in Our Donor Program!

Support the preservation of baseball research. Designate your gift toward:
❑ General Fund ❑ Endowment Fund ❑ Research Resources ❑_____
❑ I want to maximize the impact of my gift; do not send any donor premiums
❑ I would like this gift to remain anonymous.

Note: Any donation not designated will be placed in the General Fund.
SABR is a 501 (c) (3) not-for-profit organization & donations are tax-deductible to the extent allowed by law.

Name _____

E-mail* _____

Address _____

City _____ ST_____ ZIP_____

Phone _____ Birthday _____

* Your e-mail address on file ensures you will receive the most recent SABR news.

Dues $_____

Donation $_____

Amount Enclosed $_____

Do you work for a matching grant corporation? Call (602) 496-1460 for details.

If you wish to pay by credit card, please contact the SABR office at (602) 496-1460 or sign up securely online at SABR.org/join. We accept Visa, Mastercard & Discover.

Do you wish to receive the *Baseball Research Journal* electronically? ❑ Yes   ❑ No
Our e-books are available in PDF, Kindle, or EPUB (iBooks, iPad, Nook) formats.

Mail to: SABR, Cronkite School at ASU, 555 N. Central Ave. #416, Phoenix, AZ 85004

10/19